MANAGING INVESTMENTS

GEOFFREY A. HIRT
STANLEY B. BLOCK

McGraw-Hill
New York Chicago San Francisco Lisbon London Madrid Mexico City Milan New Delhi San Juan Seoul Singapore Sydney Toronto

The McGraw-Hill Companies

To our wives, Linda and Cathy,
for their patience, support, and encouragement.

Portions of this book have been previously published in *Fundamentals of Investment Management*, seventh edition, © 2003 by The McGraw-Hill Companies, Inc.

1 2 3 4 5 6 7 8 9 0 DOC/DOC 3 2 1 0 9 8 7 6 5 4

ISBN 0-07-141364-2

McGraw-Hill books are available at special quantity discounts to use as premiums and sales promotions, or for use in corporate training programs. For more information, please write to the Director of Special Sales, Professional Publishing, McGraw-Hill, Two Penn Plaza, New York, NY 10121-2298. Or contact your local bookstore.

This book is printed on acid-free paper.

Contents

Preface v
Acknowledgments vii

Chapter 1 The Investment Setting 1
Chapter 2 Mutual Funds 19
Chapter 3 Organization of Security Markets 47
Chapter 4 Participating in the Market 77
Chapter 5 Economic Activity 97
Chapter 6 Industry Analysis 121
Chapter 7 Valuation of the Individual Firm 141
Chapter 8 Financial Statement Analysis 167
Chapter 9 Technical Analysis and Market Efficiency 199
Chapter 10 Special Situations and Market Anomalies 223
Chapter 11 Bond and Fixed-Income Fundamentals 241
Chapter 12 Principles of Bond Valuation and Investment 271
Chapter 13 Duration and Reinvestment Concepts 291
Chapter 14 Convertible Securities and Warrants 309
Chapter 15 International Securities Markets 331
Chapter 16 Investments in Real Assets 359

Index 381

Preface

Many books on investments provide strategies on how to become a millionaire overnight through margin trading, options, and so on. Others are more academic in nature and perhaps more realistic, but the material is beyond the range of the typical reader. This book fills an important gap in the middle. The latest strategies for making and keeping money are written at a level the professional advisor or investor can appreciate and understand. Where highly sophisticated concepts are involved, they are boiled down for easy consumption. The book does not attempt to make you an instant millionaire, but rather an informed investor who consistently makes intelligent decisions because you understand the concepts behind valuation and security analysis.

There are more investment choices today than ever before. Prior to accepting or rejecting an alternative, you need a clear understanding of each option, and that is exactly what this book brings to you. Over 90 million U.S. investors now invest through mutual funds. Because of the importance of this topic, it is covered in the second chapter of the book. Recently, there has been much discussion about questionable practices on the part of mutual funds, such as favorable treatment for a small segment of their clientele, overtrading their portfolio, and charging excessive fees. *Managing Investments* covers the mutual fund industry in sufficient depth to allow you to avoid the role of victim and to reap the benefits of choosing a mutual fund that is right for you. Topics such as performance evaluation, fees charged, and types of funds are given special attention.

For those who wish to go it alone and make their own stock and bond selections, this book provides the tools to do this appropriately. Not only will you be able to enhance your skills in analyzing an individual firm, but you will be better able to assess the firm's larger industry and changing economic conditions. Through a discussion of valuation techniques, we put the reader in a position to make sound investment decisions, rather than being dependent on a midday call from a broker or a superficial story in a magazine.

Throughout the text, we stress the importance of asset allocation between stocks, bonds, real assets (real estate, collectibles, and so on), and cash and provide the necessary menu of material for the reader to make appropriate asset allocation decisions. You will understand why stocks and bonds have often moved in the opposite direction in the current decade and how you can maximize the performances of your portfolio through a better understanding of the variables that push stock and bond prices up or down. Without this knowledge, you are subject to the danger of being a "last mover" investor, meaning that by the time information gets to you, it has already had its impact and is about to reverse its course.

Your menu for asset allocation also covers the entire world. If stocks or bonds are down in the United States, you have the option of going to Europe, Asia, Latin America, or elsewhere. Once again, this can be a dangerous direction in which to go if you do not understand the dynamics, but this book will make sure that you are well informed about exchange rate exposure, market volatility, trading obstacles, and other considerations. The option of going through global mutual funds rather than direct investment is also considered. The book also provides material on the performances of emerging markets versus markets in industrialized nations.

Also on the menu are investments in real assets such as real estate, collectibles, gold and silver, and so on. In the current decade of low inflation, these assets have limited appeal. However, inflation has a way of rearing its ugly head when we least expect it, and the book provides a good reference source to use when such an event occurs.

The Internet has changed the financial landscape and methods of investing more than any other factor in the last 20 years. Throughout the text, we include Internet-related information and methods of analysis. High technology has also influenced the performance of the financial markets by creating increased volatility. The boom of the nineties, the bust of the early 2000s, and the recovery of the mid-2000s have been driven to some extent by high technology stocks (Cisco, Intel, Microsoft, Oracle, and others). Only by using sound analysis of companies and their financial statements can the investor hope to end up in the right position on the "technology investment curve." *Managing Investments* provides the necessary analytical skills throughout the text to evaluate not only high-tech stocks, but all stocks.

Investing can be a fun and rewarding process if it is based on sound fundamentals. We hope to give you the tools to make your goals come true through intelligent investing.

Acknowledgments

We are grateful to the following individuals for their thoughtful reviews and suggestions:

Richard Gritta, *University of Portland;* Arthur C. Gudikunst, *Bryant College;* Mahmoud Haddad, *University of Tennessee-Martin;* Domingo Joaquin, *Michigan State University;* Thomas M. Krueger, *University of Wisconsin-La Crosse;* David Lawrence, *Drake University;* Kyle Mattson, *Weber State University;* Cheryl McGaughey, *Angelo State University;* Majed Muhtaseb, *California State Polytechnic University-Pomona;* Jamal Munshie, *Sonoma College;* Winford Naylor, *Santa Barbara City College;* Linda Ravelle, *Moravian College;* Arnold Redman, *University of Tennessee-Martin;* George Troughton, *California State University-Chico;* Glen Wood, *California State University-Bakersfield.*

For their prior reviews and helpful comments, we are grateful to Carol J. Billingham, *Central Michigan University;* Gerald A. Blum, *University of Nevada-Reno;* Keith E. Boles, *University of Colorado-Colorado Springs;* Paul Bolster, *Northeastern University;* Jerry D. Boswell, *College of Financial Planning;* Joe B. Copeland, *University of North Alabama;* Marcia M. Cornett, *Southern Illinois University;* Betty Driver, *Murray State University;* Adrian C. Edwards, *Western Michigan University;* Jane H. Finley, *University of South Alabama;* Adam Gehr, *DePaul University;* Paul Grier, *SUNY-Binghamton;* David Heskel, *Bloomsburg University;* James Khule, *California State University-Sacramento;* Sheri Kole, *Copeland Companies;* Carl Luft, *DePaul University;* John D. Markese, *American Association of Individual Investors;* Majed R. Muhtaseb, *California State Polytechnic University-Pomona;* Harold Mulherin, *Clemson University;* Roger R. Palmer, *College of St. Thomas;* John W. Peavy III, *Southern Methodist University;* Richard Ponarul, *California State University;* Dave Rand, *Northwest Technical College;* Linda L. Richardson, *University of Southern Maine;* Tom S. Sale, *Louisiana Tech University;* Art Schwartz, *University of South Florida;* Joseph F. Singer, *University of Missouri-Kansas City;* Ira Smolowitz, *Siena College;* Don Taylor, *University of Wisconsin-Platteville;* Frank

N. Tiernan, *Drake University;* Allan J. Twark, *Kent State University;* Howard E. Van Auken, *Iowa State University;* and Bismarck Williams, *Roosevelt University.*

Omar Benkato, *Ball State University;* Lynn Brown, *Jacksonville State University;* James P. D'Mello, *Western Michigan University;* David Haraway, *University of New Hampshire;* Gay B. Hatfield, *University of Mississippi;* Joel R. Jankowski, *The University of Tampa;* Amir Jassim, *California State University, Fresno;* Peppi Kenny, *Western Illinois University;* David Louton, *Bryant College;* Spuma Rao, *University of Southwestern Louisiana.*

Grace C. Allen, *Western Carolina University;* Laurence E. Blose, *University of North Carolina-Charlotte;* John A. Cole, *Florida A&M University;* Don R. Cox, *Appalachian State University;* John Dunkelberg, *Wake Forest University;* Marcus Ingram, *Clark-Atlanta University;* Joe B. Lipscomb, *Texas Christian University;* Mike Miller, *DePaul University;* Carl C. Nielsen, *Wichita State University;* Raj A. Padmaraj, *Bowling Green State University;* and Maneesh Sharma, *Northeast Louisiana University.*

We are grateful for the support and encouragement provided by Jim Tyree of Mesirow Financial and by DePaul University and Texas Christian University. Geoffrey Hirt would like to acknowledge the support received for this project from the DePaul University Research Council.

Chapter 1

The Investment Setting

Despite the stock market bubble of the 1990s, when the market is analyzed over various long-term time periods, the results benefit from the upward rising long-term of stock prices. Between 1982 and 2001 the Dow Jones Industrial Average, the most-watched stock market indictor in the world, gained 950 percent (a gain of approximately 12 percent per year). If we take a shorter time period from the beginning of August 1994 to the beginning of August 2003, the Dow Jones Industrial Average gained approximately 10.5 percent per year, which is not so bad considering the three-year bear market that began in March–April of 2000. But not all was smooth sailing. For example, there was the great panic on Monday, October 19, 1987, in which the Dow Jones Industrial Average declined 22.6 percent in *one day.* By contrast, the largest previous single-day decline was the fabled stock market crash of 1929 when the market went down slightly over 12 percent on Black Monday of that year.

In the one-day crash of 1987, Eastman Kodak declined 26 dollars, Westinghouse Electric 20½ dollars, and Du Pont 18½ dollars. All of these firms eventually recovered.

Perhaps the most interesting example in the last decade is IBM. The stock price of this renowned computer manufacturer reached a high of 175⅞ per share in 1987. At the time, security analysts thought that "Big Blue" could go up forever with its dominance in the traditional mainframe computer market and its emergence as the leader in the rapidly growing personal computer market. Such was not to be. With the conversion of most computer applications from mainframes to microcomputers and the cloning of IBM products by its competitors, IBM rapidly lost market share and began to actually lose money in the early 1990s. This was in stark contrast to the $6 billion per year annual profits it had averaged for the prior decade. By mid-1993, the stock had fallen to 40⅝. Many investors threw up their hands in disgust and bailed out. But by the winter of 2002, the firm was once again consistently showing a profit after massive layoffs of employees and restructuring of operations, and the stock price was *up* to the equivalent of $220 (the actual stock price was $110, but there was a two-for-one stock split during this time period).

Common stocks are not the only volatile investment. In the past two decades, silver has gone from $5 an ounce to $50 and back again to $5. Gold has moved from $35 an ounce to $875 and back to $350 in 2003. The same can be said of investments in oil, real estate, and a number of other items. Commercial real estate lost more than 30 percent of its value in the late 1980s and then recovered. Other examples are constantly occurring both on the upside and downside as fortunes are made and lost.

How does one develop an investment strategy in such an environment? Suggestions come from all directions. The investor is told how to benefit from the coming monetary disaster as well as how to grow rich in a new era of prosperity. The intent of this text is to help the investor sort out the various investments that are available and to develop analytical skills that suggest what securities and assets might be most appropriate for a given portfolio.

We shall define an investment as the commitment of current funds in anticipation of receiving a larger future flow of funds. The investor hopes to be compensated for forgoing immediate consumption, for the effects of inflation, and for taking a risk.

Investing may be both exciting and challenging. First-time investors who pore over the financial statements of a firm and then make a dollar commitment to purchase a few shares of stock often have a feeling of euphoria as they charge out in the morning to secure the daily newspaper and read the market quotes or go to the Internet for the same purpose. Even professional analysts may take pleasure in leaving their Wall Street offices to evaluate an emerging high-technology firm in Austin or Palo Alto. Likewise, the buyer of a rare painting, late 18th-century U.S. coin, or invaluable baseball card may find a sense of excitement in attempting to outsmart the market. Even the purchaser of a bond or money market instrument must do proper analysis to ensure that anticipated objectives are being met. Let us examine the different types of investments.

FORMS OF INVESTMENT

In the text, we break down investment alternatives between financial and real assets. A financial asset represents a financial claim on an asset that is usually documented by some form of legal representation. An example would be a share of stock or a bond. A real asset represents an actual tangible asset that may be seen, felt, held, or collected. An example would be real estate or gold. Table 1-1 lists the various forms of financial and real assets.

As indicated in the left column of Table 1-1, financial assets may be broken down into five categories. Direct equity claims represent ownership interests and include common stock as well as other instruments that can be used to purchase common stock, such as warrants and options. Warrants and options allow the holder to buy a stipulated number of shares in the future at a given price. Warrants usually convert to one share and are long term, whereas options are generally based on 100 share units and are short term in nature.

Indirect equity can be acquired through placing funds in investment companies (such as a mutual fund). The investment company pools the resources of many investors and reinvests them in common stock (or other investments). The

TABLE 1–1 Overview of Investment Alternatives

Financial Assets	Real Assets
1. Equity claims—direct Common stock Warrants Options 2. Equity claims—indirect Investment company shares (mutual funds) Pension funds Whole life insurance Retirement accounts 3. Creditor claims Savings account Money market funds Commercial paper Treasury bills, notes, bonds Municipal notes, bonds Corporate bonds (straight and convertible to common stock) 4. Preferred stock (straight and convertible to common stock) 5. Commodity futures	1. Real estate Office buildings Apartments Shopping centers Personal residences 2. Precious metals Gold Silver 3. Precious gems Diamonds Rubies Sapphires 4. Collectibles Art Antiques Stamps Coins Rare books 5. Other Cattle Oil Common metals

individual enjoys the advantages of diversification and professional management (though not necessarily higher returns).

Financial assets may also take the form of creditor claims as represented by debt instruments offered by financial institutions, industrial corporations, or the government. The rate of return is often initially fixed, though the actual return may vary with changing market conditions. Other forms of financial assets are preferred stock, which is a hybrid form of security combining some of the elements of equity ownership and creditor claims, and commodity futures, which represent a contract to buy or sell a commodity in the future at a given price. Commodities may include wheat, corn, copper, or even such financial instruments as Treasury bonds or foreign exchange.

As shown in the right column of Table 1-1, there are also numerous categories of real assets. The most widely recognized investment in this category is *real estate,* either commercial property or one's own residence. For greater risk, *precious metals* or *precious gems* can be considered, and for those seeking psychic pleasure as well as monetary gain, *collectibles* are an investment outlet. Finally, the *other* (*all-inclusive*) category includes cattle, oil, and other items that stretch as far as the imagination will go.

Throughout the text, each form of financial and real asset is considered. What assets the investor ultimately selects will depend on investment objectives as well as the economic outlook. For example, the investor who believes inflation will be relatively strong may prefer real assets that have a replacement value reflecting increasing prices. In a more moderate inflationary environment, stocks and bonds are preferred. The latter has certainly been the case in the last 15 years.

THE SETTING OF INVESTMENT OBJECTIVES

The setting of investment objectives may be as important as the selection of the investment. In actuality, they tend to go together. A number of key areas should be considered.

Risk and Safety of Principal

The first factor investors must consider is the amount of risk they are prepared to assume. In a relatively efficient and informed capital market environment, risk tends to be closely correlated with return. Most of the literature of finance would suggest that those who consistently demonstrate high returns of perhaps 20 percent or more are greater-than-normal risk takers. While some clever investors are able to prosper on their wits alone, most high returns may be perceived as compensation for risk.

And there is not only the risk of losing invested capital directly (a dry hole perhaps) but also the danger of a loss in purchasing power. At 6 percent inflation (compounded annually), a stock that is held for four years without a gain in value would represent a 26 percent loss in purchasing power.

Investors who wish to assume low risks will probably confine a large portion of their portfolio to short-term debt instruments in which the party responsible for payment is the government or a major bank or corporation. Some conservative investors may choose to invest in a money market fund in which the funds of numerous investors are pooled and reinvested in high-yielding, short-term instruments. More aggressive investors may look toward longer-term debt instruments and common stock. Real assets, such as gold, silver, or valued art, might also be included in an aggressive portfolio.

It is not only the inherent risk in an asset that must be considered but also the extent to which that risk is being diversified away in a portfolio. Although an investment in gold might be considered risky, such might not be fully the case if it is combined into a portfolio of common stocks. Gold thrives on bad news, while common stocks generally do well in a positive economic environment. An oil embargo or foreign war may drive down the value of stocks while gold is advancing, and vice versa.

The age and economic circumstances of an investor are important variables in determining an appropriate level of risk. Young, upwardly mobile people are generally in a better position to absorb risk than are elderly couples on a fixed income. Nevertheless, each of us, regardless of our plight in life, has different risk-taking desires. Because of an unwillingness to assume risk, a surgeon earning $300,000 a year may be more averse to accepting a $2,000 loss on a stock than an aging taxicab driver.

One cruel lesson of investing is that conservative investments do not always end up being what you thought they were when you bought them. This was true of IBM as described at the beginning of the chapter. This has also been true of many other firms. Classic examples can be found in the drug industry where leading firms such as Merck and Pfizer, who have reputations for developing outstanding products for the cure of cardiovascular and other diseases, saw their stock values fall by 30 percent when a strong movement for health care regulation and cost containment began in the mid-1990s. Much crueler lessons were provided to dot-com investors in the late 1990s as "can't miss" first-mover $100 stocks became $2 disasters. The same could be said for investors in the energy company Enron, which shrank from $90 to 50¢ in 2001. Even short-term risk-averse investors in U.S. Treasury bills saw their income stream decline from 12 percent to 2 percent over a decade as interest rates plummeted. This declining cash flow can be a shock to your system if you are living on interest income.

Current Income versus Capital Appreciation

A second consideration in setting investment objectives is a decision on the desire for current income versus capital appreciation. Although this decision is closely tied to an evaluation of risk, it is separate.

In purchasing stocks, the investor with a need for current income may opt for high-yielding, mature firms in such industries as public utilities, machine tools, or apparel. Those searching for price gains may look toward smaller, emerging firms in high technology, energy, or electronics. The latter firms may pay no cash dividend, but the investor hopes for an increase in value to provide the desired return.

The investor needs to understand there is generally a trade-off between growth and income. Finding both in one type of investment is unlikely. If you go for the high-yielding utilities, you can expect slow growth in earnings and stock price. If you opt for high growth such as a biotechnology firm, you can expect no cash flow from the dividend.

Capital appreciation is an important factor in protecting a portfolio against inflation. While inflation was very tame from the mid-1980s through the late 1990s and then fell further during the recession beginning in March 2001, low inflation is not always the case. In 1979 and 1980 the U.S. economy suffered from inflation rates of 11.4 percent and 13.4 percent. Long-term inflation rates have trended at between 3 and 4 percent; an investor needs to consider this impact over long periods of time and especially into retirement. For example, if inflation averages 4 percent, something that cost $10,000 in 2004 will cost $14,800 in 2014 and $21,911 in 2024. Inflation becomes an important consideration when choosing between current income and capital appreciation.

Liquidity Considerations

Liquidity is measured by the ability of the investor to convert an investment into cash within a relatively short time at its fair market value or with a minimum capital loss on the transaction.

Most financial assets provide a high degree of liquidity. Stocks and bonds can generally be sold within a matter of minutes at a price reasonably close to the last traded value. Such may not be the case for real estate. Almost everyone has seen a house or piece of commercial real estate sit on the market for weeks, months, or years.

Liquidity can also be measured indirectly by the transaction costs or commissions involved in the transfer of ownership. Financial assets generally trade on a relatively low commission basis (perhaps 1 or 2 percent), whereas many real assets have transaction costs that run from 5 percent to 25 percent or more.

In many cases, the lack of immediate liquidity can be justified if there are unusual opportunities for gain. An investment in real estate or precious gems may provide sufficient return to more than compensate for the added transaction costs. Of course, a bad investment will be all the more difficult to unload.

Investors must carefully assess their own situation to determine the need for liquidity. If you are investing funds to be used for the next house payment or the coming semester's tuition, then immediate liquidity will be essential, and financial assets will be preferred. If funds can be tied up for long periods, bargain-buying opportunities of an unusual nature can also be evaluated.

Short-Term versus Long-Term Orientation

In setting investment objectives, you must decide whether you will assume a short-term or long-term orientation in managing the funds and evaluating performance. You do not always have a choice. People who manage funds for others may be put under tremendous pressure to show a given level of performance in the short run. Those applying pressure may be a concerned relative or a large pension fund that has placed funds with a bank trust department. Even though you are convinced your latest investment will double in the next three years, the fact that it is currently down 15 percent may provide discomfort to those around you.

Market strategies may also be short term or long term in scope. Those who attempt to engage in short-term market tactics are termed *traders.* They may buy a stock at 15 and hope to liquidate if it goes to 20. To help reach decisions, short-term traders often use technical analysis, which is based on evaluating market indicator series and charting. Those who take a longer-term perspective try to identify fundamentally sound companies for a buy-and-hold approach. A long-term investor does not necessarily anticipate being able to buy right at the bottom or sell at the exact peak.

Research has shown it is difficult to beat the market on a risk-adjusted basis. Given that the short-term trader encounters more commissions than the long-term investor because of more active trading, short-term trading as a rule is not a strategy endorsed by the authors.

Tax Factors

Investors in high tax brackets have different investment objectives than those in lower brackets or tax-exempt charities, foundations, or similar organizations. An investor in a high tax bracket may prefer municipal bonds (interest is not taxable), real estate (with its depreciation and interest write-off), or investments that provide tax credits or tax shelters.

The Taxpayer Relief Act of 1997 increased the impact of tax considerations on investments. This is especially true for capital gains, which represent the increase in value of an asset from the time of purchase to the time it is sold. Prior to the act, the maximum tax rate on long-term capital gains was 28 percent. You had to hold the asset for at least a year to qualify for this preferential treatment. Dividends, short-term capital gains, and other forms of income were taxed at a maximum rate of 39.6 percent.

The 1997 tax act lowered the maximum capital gains tax rate to 20 percent for assets held at least one year. The maximum rates apply to higher income investors, but investors in lower tax brackets were treated to proportionate capital gains tax relief as well.

The net effect of the tax laws is to put more emphasis on trying to generate income in the form of capital gains rather than dividends for tax-sensitive investors. Dividend income was given no tax relief in the 1997 tax act.

The Tax Act of 2001 further modified tax considerations by phasing down the 39.6 percent maximum tax to 35 percent by 2006. However, the capital gains tax rate was unchanged. With the miniscule tax relief given to dividend income (a reduction of only 4.6 percent over six years), capital gains are still strongly favored by high-income investors.

Ease of Management

Another consideration in establishing an investment program is ease of management. The investor must determine the amount of time and effort that can be devoted to an investment portfolio and act accordingly. In the stock market, this may determine whether you want to be a daily trader or assume a longer-term perspective. In real estate, it may mean the difference between personally owning and managing a handful of rental houses or going in with 10 other investors to form a limited partnership in which a general partner takes full management responsibility and the limited partners merely put up the capital.

Of course, a minimum amount of time must be committed to any investment program. Even when investment advisers or general partners are in charge, their activities must be monitored and evaluated.

In managing a personal portfolio, the investor should consider opportunity costs. If a lawyer can work for $200 per hour or manage his financial portfolio, a fair question would be, "How much extra return can I get from managing my portfolio, or can I add more value to my portfolio by working and investing more money?" Unless the lawyer is an excellent investor, it is probable that more money can be made by working.

Assume an investor can add a 2 percent extra return to his portfolio but it takes five hours per week (260 hours per year) to do so. If his opportunity cost is $40 per hour, he would have to add more than $10,400 ($40 × 260 hours) to his portfolio to make personal management attractive. If we assume a 2 percent excess return can be gained over the professional manager, the investor would need a portfolio of $520,000 before personal management would make sense under these assumptions. This example may explain why many high-income individuals choose to have professionals manage their assets.

Decisions such as these may also depend on your trade-off between work and leisure. An investor may truly find it satisfying and intellectually stimulating to manage a portfolio and may receive psychic income from mastering the nuances of investing. However, if you would rather ski, play tennis, or enjoy some other leisure activity, the choice of professional management may make more sense than a do-it-yourself approach.

Retirement and Estate Planning Considerations

Even the relatively young must begin to consider the effect of their investment decisions on their retirement and the estates they will someday pass along to their "potential families." Those who wish to remain single will still be called on to advise others as to the appropriateness of a given investment strategy for their family needs.

Most good retirement questions should not be asked at "retirement" but 40 or 45 years before because that's the period with the greatest impact. One of the first questions a person is often asked after taking a job on graduation is whether he or she wishes to set up an IRA. An IRA allows a qualifying taxpayer to deduct an allowable amount from taxable income and invest the funds at a brokerage house, mutual fund, bank, or other financial institution. The funds are normally placed in common stocks or other securities or in interest-bearing instruments, such as a certificate of deposit. The income earned on the funds is allowed to grow tax-free until withdrawn at retirement. As an example, if a person places $2,000 a year in an IRA for 45 consecutive years and the funds earn 10 percent over that time, $1,437,810 will have been accumulated.

The Tax Act of 2001 offers even greater potential for wealth accumulation with the maximum deduction for an IRA being phased up from $2,000 in 2001 to $5,000 in 2008.

Additionally, the Tax Act of 2001 removed the estate tax over a period of years. If someone dies between 2004 and 2005, his or her estate is exempt from taxes as long as it is under $1.5 million. Between 2006 and 2007 the amount rises to \$2.0 million; between 2008 and 2009 it rises to \$3.5 million; and after 2010 the estate tax is eliminated. The unfortunate thing about the Tax Act of 2001 is that on January 1, 2011, the act is totally rescinded and reverts back to the original law in existence in 2001. This makes planning extremely difficult because you can't depend on the rules staying the same. That has always been a feature of American politics and taxes.

MEASURES OF RISK AND RETURN

Now that you have some basic familiarity with the different forms of investments and the setting of investment goals, we are ready to look at concepts of measuring the return from an investment and the associated risk. The return you receive from any investment (stocks, bonds, real estate) has two primary components: capital gains or losses and current income. The rate of return from an investment can be measured as:

$$\text{Rate of return} = \frac{(\text{Ending value} - \text{Beginning value}) + \text{Income}}{\text{Beginning value}} \qquad (1\text{-}1)$$

Thus, if a share of stock goes from \$20 to \$22 in one year and also pays a dollar in dividends during the year, the total return is 15 percent. Using Formula 1-1:

$$\frac{(\$22 - \$20) + \$1}{\$20} = \frac{\$2 + \$1}{\$20} = \frac{\$3}{\$20} = 15\%$$

Where the formula is being specifically applied to stocks, it is written as:

$$\text{Rate of return} = \frac{(P_1 - P_0) + D_1}{P_0} \qquad (1\text{-}2)$$

where:

P_1 = Price at the end of the period
P_0 = Price at the beginning of the period
D_1 = Dividend income

Risk

The risk for an investment is related to the uncertainty associated with the outcomes from an investment. For example, an investment that has an absolutely certain return of 10 percent is said to be riskless. Another investment that has a likely or expected return of 12 percent, but also has the possibility of minus 10 percent in hard economic times and plus 30 percent under optimum circum-

FIGURE 1–1 Examples of Risk

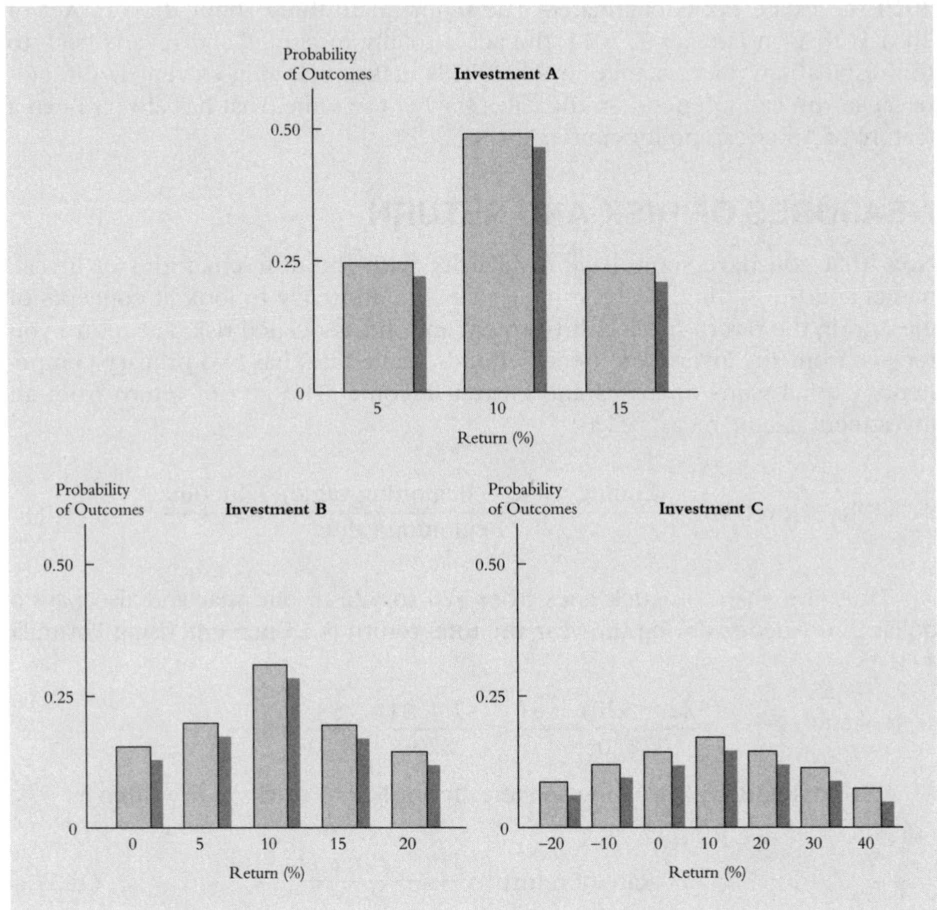

stances, is said to be risky. An example of three investments with progressively greater risk is presented in Figure 1-1. Based on our definition of risk, investment C is clearly the riskiest because of the large uncertainty (wide dispersion) of possible outcomes.

In the study of investments, you will soon observe that the desired or required rate of return for a given investment is generally related to the risk associated with that investment. Because most investors do not like risk, they will require a higher rate of return for a more risky investment. That is not to say that investors are unwilling to take risks—they simply wish to be compensated for taking the risk. For this reason, an investment in common stocks (which inevitably carries some amount of risk) may require an anticipated return 6 or 7 percent higher than a certificate of deposit in a commercial bank. This 6 or 7 percent represents a risk premium. You never know whether you will get the returns you anticipate, but at least your initial requirements will be higher to justify the risk you are taking.

ACTUAL CONSIDERATION OF REQUIRED RETURNS

Let's consider how return requirements are determined in the financial markets. Although the following discussion starts out on a theoretical "what if" basis, you will eventually see empirical evidence that different types of investments do provide different types of returns. Basically, three components make up the required return from an investment:

1. The real rate of return.
2. The anticipated inflation factor.
3. The risk premium.

Real Rate of Return

The real rate of return is the return investors require for allowing others to use their money for a given time period. This is the return investors demand for passing up immediate consumption and allowing others to use their savings until the funds are returned. Because the term *real* is employed, this means it is a value determined before inflation is included in the calculation. The real rate of return is also determined before considering any specific risk for the investment.

Historically, the real rate of return in the U.S. economy has been from 2 to 3 percent. During much of the 1980s and early 1990s, it was somewhat higher (4 to 6 percent), but in the last decade the real rate of return came back to its normal level of 2 to 3 percent, which is probably a reasonable long-term expectation.

Because an investor is concerned with using a real rate of return as a component of a required rate of return, the past is not always a good predictor for any one year's real rate of return. The problem comes from being able to measure the real rate of return only after the fact by subtracting inflation from the nominal interest rate. Unfortunately, expectations and occurrence do not always match. The real rate of return is highly variable (for seven years in the 1970s and early 1980s, it was even negative). One of the problems investors face in determining required rates of return is the forecasting errors involving interest rates and inflation. These forecasting errors are more pronounced in short-run returns than in long-run returns. Let us continue with our example and bring inflation into the discussion.

Anticipated Inflation Factor

The anticipated inflation factor must be added to the real rate of return. For example, if there is a 2 percent real-rate-of-return requirement and the anticipated rate of inflation is 3 percent, we combine the two to arrive at an approximate 5 percent required return factor. Combining the real rate of return and inflationary considerations gives us the required return on an investment before explicitly considering risk. For this reason, it is called the risk-free required rate of return or, simply, risk-free rate (R_F).

We can define the risk-free rate as:

$$\text{Risk-free rate} = (1 + \text{Real rate})(1 + \text{Expected rate of inflation}) - 1 \quad (1\text{-}3)$$

Plugging in numerical values, we would show:

$$\text{Risk-free rate} = (1.02)(1.03) - 1 = 1.0506 - 1 = 0.0506 \text{ or } 5.06\%$$

The answer is approximately 5 percent. You can simply add the real rate of return (2 percent) to the anticipated inflation rate (3 percent) to get a 5 percent answer or go through the more theoretically correct process of Formula 1-3 to arrive at 5.06 percent. Either approach is frequently used.

The risk-free rate (R_F) of approximately 5 percent applies to any investment as the minimum required rate of return to provide a 2 percent *real return* after inflation. Of course, if the investor actually receives a lower return, the real rate of return may be quite low or negative. For example, if the investor receives a 2 percent return in a 4 percent inflationary environment, there is a negative real return of 2 percent. The investor will have 2 percent less purchasing power than before he started. He would have been better off to spend the money *now* rather than save at a 2 percent rate in a 4 percent inflationary economy. In effect, he is *paying* the borrower to use his money. Of course, real rates of return and inflationary expectations change from time to time, so the risk-free required rate (R_F) also changes.

We now have examined the two components that make up the minimum risk-free rate of return that apply to investments (stocks, bonds, real estate, etc.). We now consider the third component, the risk premium. The relationship is depicted in Figure 1-2.

Risk Premium

The risk premium will be different for each investment. For example, for a federally insured certificate of deposit at a bank or for a U.S. Treasury bill, the risk premium approaches zero. All the return to the investor will be at the risk-free rate of return (the real rate of return plus inflationary expectations). For common stock, the investor's required return may carry a 6 or 7 percent risk premium in addition to the risk-free rate of return. If the risk-free rate were 5 percent, the investor might have an overall required return of 11 to 12 percent on common stock.

+ Real rate	2%
+ Anticipated inflation	3%
= Risk-free rate	5%
+ Risk premium	6% or 7%
= Required rate of return	11% to 12%

FIGURE 1–2 The Components of Required Rate of Return

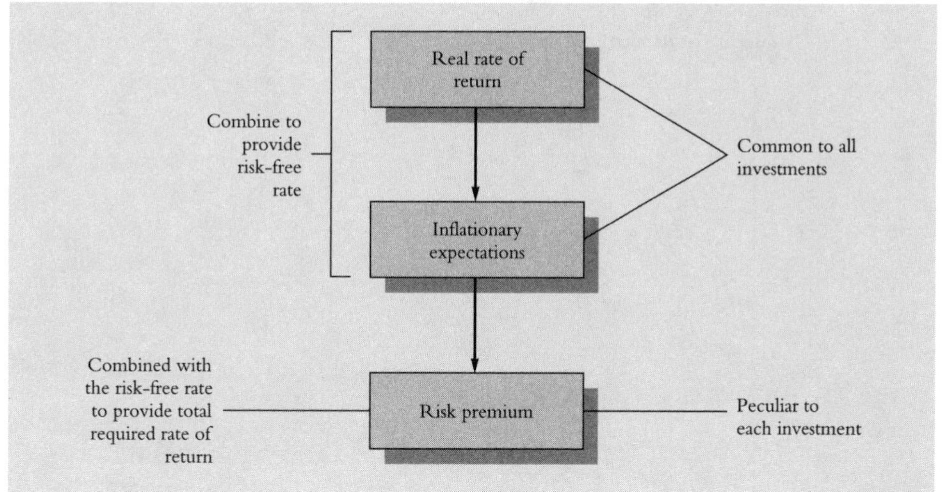

Corporate bonds fall somewhere between short-term government obligations (virtually no risk) and common stock in terms of risk. Thus, the risk premium may be 3 to 4 percent. Like the real rate of return and the inflation rate, the risk premium is not a constant but may change from time to time. If investors are very fearful about the economic outlook, the risk premium may be 8 to 10 percent as it was for junk bonds in 1990 and 1991.

The normal relationship between selected investments and their rates of return is depicted in Figure 1-3.

A number of empirical studies tend to support the risk-return relationships shown in Figure 1-3 over a long period. Perhaps the most widely cited is the Ibbotson and Associates data presented in Figure 1-4, which covers data from 1926 to 2003. Note that the high-to-low return scale is in line with expectations based on risk. Of particular interest is the geometric mean column. This is simply the compound annual rate of return. The arithmetic mean is an average of yearly rates of return and has less meaning. Risk is measured by the standard deviation, which appears to the right of each security type. This distribution of returns indicates which security has the biggest risk. Figure 1-4 shows in practice what we discussed in theory earlier in the chapter; higher returns are normally associated with higher risk.

Because the Ibbotson study in Figure 1-4 covered 78 years (including a decade of depression), the rates of return may be somewhat lower than those currently available. This is particularly true for the bonds and Treasury bills. Table 1-2, from the *Stocks, Bonds, Bills and Inflation 2004 Yearbook,* shows returns for nine different periods.

The returns just discussed primarily apply to financial assets (stocks, bonds, and so forth). Salomon Smith Barney Inc., an investment banking firm, tracks the

FIGURE 1–3 Risk-Return Characteristics

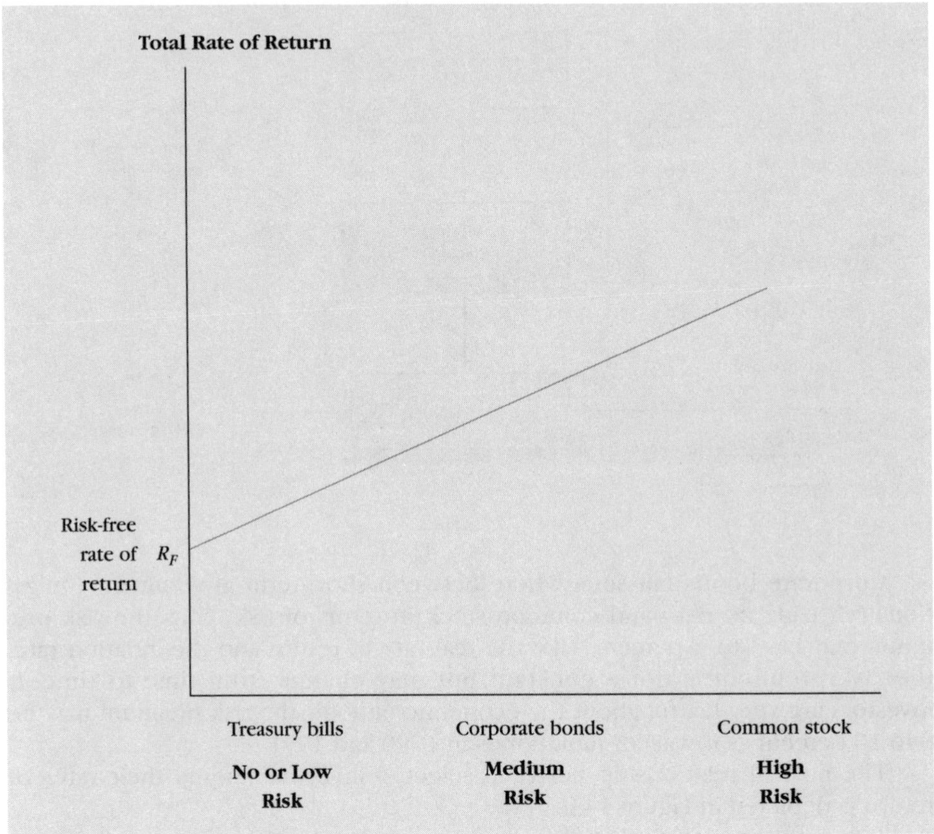

TABLE 1–2 Compound Annual Rates of Return by Decade (in Percent)

	1920s[a]	1930s	1940s	1950s	1960s	1970s	1980s	1990s	2000s[b]	1994–2003
Large company	19.2	−0.1	9.2	19.4	7.8	5.9	17.5	18.2	−5.3	11.1
Small company	−4.5	1.4	20.7	16.9	15.5	11.5	15.8	15.1	13.3	14.8
Long-term corporate	5.2	6.9	2.7	1.0	1.7	6.2	13.0	8.4	11.2	8.0
Long-term government	5.0	4.9	3.2	−0.1	1.4	5.5	12.6	8.8	10.8	8.0
Intermediate-term government	4.2	4.6	1.8	1.3	3.5	7.0	11.9	7.2	8.8	6.4
Treasury bills	3.7	0.6	0.4	1.9	3.9	6.3	8.9	4.9	3.1	4.2
Inflation	−1.1	−2.0	5.4	2.2	2.5	7.4	5.1	2.9	2.3	2.4

a Based on the period 1926–1929.

b Based on the period 2000–2003.

Source: *Stocks, Bonds, Bills and Inflation 2004 Yearbook* (Chicago: R. G. Ibbotson & Associates, Inc., 2004), p. 19.

FIGURE 1–4 Basic Series: Summary Statistics of Annual Total Returns from 1926–2003

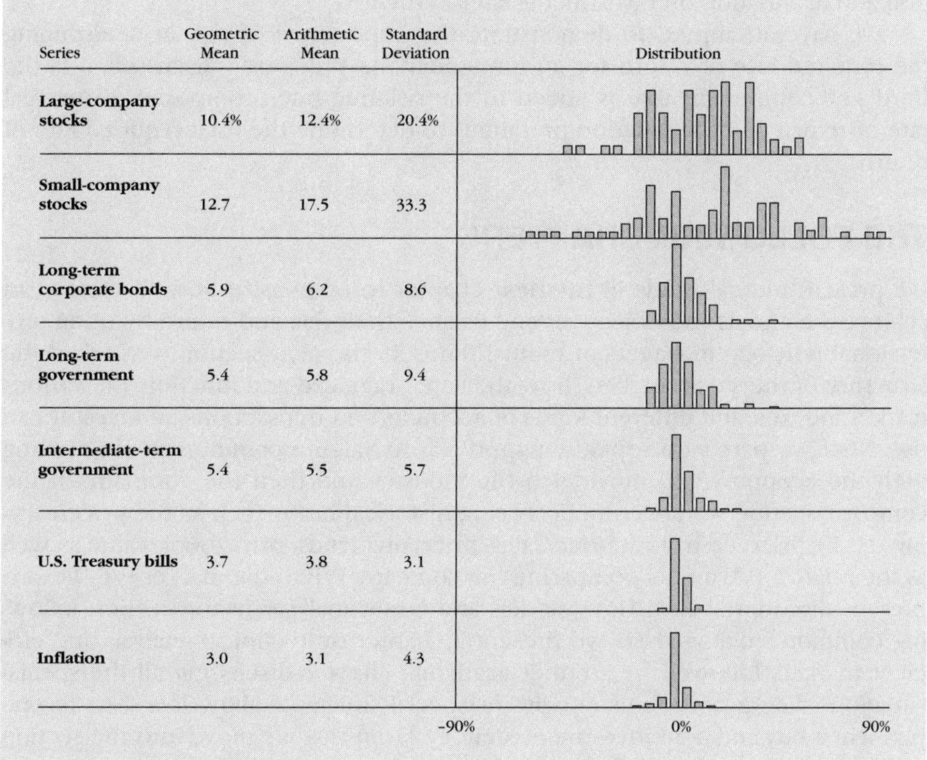

Series	Geometric Mean	Arithmetic Mean	Standard Deviation	Distribution
Large-company stocks	10.4%	12.4%	20.4%	
Small-company stocks	12.7	17.5	33.3	
Long-term corporate bonds	5.9	6.2	8.6	
Long-term government	5.4	5.8	9.4	
Intermediate-term government	5.4	5.5	5.7	
U.S. Treasury bills	3.7	3.8	3.1	
Inflation	3.0	3.1	4.3	

Source: *Stocks, Bonds, Bills and Inflation 2004 Yearbook* (Chicago: R. G. Ibbotson & Associates, Inc., 2004), p. 33.

performance of real assets as well as financial assets. Over long periods of time, common stocks generally tend to perform at approximately the same level as real assets such as real estate, coins, stamps, and so forth, with each tending to show a different type of performance in a different economic environment.[1] Real assets tend to do best in inflationary environments, while moderate inflation favors financial assets. In 1991, the best long-term performers in the Salomon study were Old Master paintings, Chinese ceramics, gold, diamonds, and stamps. After 10 years of moderate inflation, stocks and bonds had risen to the top in 2001. No doubt the pattern will shift back and forth many times in the

1. Examples of other longer-term studies on comparative returns between real and financial assets are: Roger G. Ibbotson and Carol F. Fall, "The United States Wealth Portfolio," *The Journal of Portfolio Management,* Fall 1982, pp. 82–92; Roger G. Ibbotson and Lawrence B. Siegel, "The World Market Wealth Portfolio," *The Journal of Portfolio Management,* Winter 1983, pp. 5–17; and Alexander A. Robichek, Richard A. Cohn, and John J. Pringle, "Returns on Alternative Media and Implications for Portfolio Construction," *Journal of Business,* July 1972, pp. 427–43. (While Ibbotson and Siegel showed superior returns for metals between 1960 and 1980, metals have greatly underperformed other assets in the 1980s and 1990s.)

future, although in the euphoric stock market environment of the last decade many would question this statement. More will be said about the impact of inflation and disinflation on investments later in the text.

We have attempted to demonstrate the importance of risk in determining the required rate of return for an investment. As previously discussed, it is the third key component that is added to the risk-free rate (composed of the real rate of return and the inflation premium) to determine the total required rate of return.

THE FOLLOWING CHAPTERS

We present mutual funds in the next chapter to emphasize how investors can achieve their goals and objectives and balance their risk and return by using professional portfolio managers of mutual funds. In the next section we look at the structure of the stock markets, how they are organized and function, the various market indexes, and different kinds of accounts and transactions an investor can use. Next we present a top-down approach to valuing common stocks starting with the economy and moving to the industry and then the company. In the company section we cover models using historical ratios such as the price/earnings (P/E), price/cash flow, price/sales, price/dividends, price/book value as well as the relative P/E model comparing the company P/E to the market P/E. We also present discounted cash flow models and ratios analysis. In the section following common stock analysis we present a chapter on technical analysis and efficient markets followed by a rather academic chapter discussing all the special situations where portfolio strategies or special situations allow investors to outperform a buy-and-hold investment strategy. From this we move into the section on bond analysis, in which we discuss bond contracts and the various bond types that exist as well as how to value bonds. We then look at convertible bonds as a security that has the benefits of both bonds and stocks. This is followed by a presentation of international investing as a way of reducing portfolio risk. Finally we present real assets and real estate analysis and we go through the basics of owning real estate and analyzing the cash flow from real estate investments.

Internet Resources

Website Address	Comments
www.aaii.com	A nonprofit website educating do-it-yourself investors
www.nasdaq.com	Provides information about Nasdaq stocks and market
www.nyse.com	Provides information about New York Stock Exchange, listings, and regulations
www.nareit.com	Provides information and data about real estate investment trusts
www.quicken.com	Provides understandable coverage of financial planning and investing
www.morningstar.com	Contains evaluations of and information about stocks and mutual funds
www.bondmarkets.com	Provides information about corporate and government bonds
www.amex.com	Provides information about stocks, options, and exchange trade funds on the American Stock Exchange
www.business.com	Provides a searchable database for links to sites by industry
www.investmentclubs.com	Provides information and education for investment club members
www.investopedia.com	Provides a general education site about stocks and investing
web.utk.edu/~jwachowi/part2.html	Site created by finance professor with links to information resources
www.investorwords.com	Provides links to finance sites and glossary of finance terminology
www.moneyadvisor.com	Provides insurance-based financial calculators and links to financial institutions
www.dfin.com	Provides job search links, loan calculators, financial links, and educational links
www.reuters.com	Contains business and financial market news for United States and other countries
www.instinet.com	Four largest electronic communication networks (ECNs)
www.tradearca.com	
www.redibook.com	
www.isld.com	
www.bloomberg.com/products/trdbk.html	Additional five ECNs
www.ebrut.com	
www.nextrade.org	
www.attain.com	
www.marketxt.com	

Chapter 2

Mutual Funds

In the introductory chapter we presented an overview of the goals and objectives that investors should consider in contructing an investment portfolio and also discussed the risk return trade-offs that must be made. Mutual funds are investment portfolios that allow many investors to accomplish their goals by creating a diversified portfolio of various asset classes managed by professionals. In this chapter we demonstrate how mutual funds can allow investors to tailor their own personalized investment strategy.

Mutual funds have become a very important part of investing. According to the Investment Company Institute (www.ici.org), in the year 2002, mutual funds were owned by 54.2 million U.S. households, an increase from 23.4 million households in 1990. Figure 2-1 shows both the number and percentage of U.S. households owning mutual funds between 1980 and 2002. Another fact is that in 1990 U.S.-based mutual fund assets were slightly less than $1 trillion but had grown to $6.8 trillion in June, 2003.

Because many investors use mutual funds as an investment vehicle for retirement, they are long-term investors and not likely to abandon mutual funds in down markets. However, they may change their asset allocation between stocks, bonds, and international and short-term securities. At year-end 2000, mutual funds accounted for $2.5 trillion of U.S. retirement assets, or 20 percent of the $12.3 trillion earmarked for retirement. The other $9.8 trillion was held in accounts at insurance companies, brokerage firms, banks, and pension funds.

The concept of a mutual fund is best understood by an example. Suppose you and your friends are too busy to develop the expertise needed to manage your own assets. One of your neighbors, however, has had years of hands-on experience as a trustee of his company's pension fund. You and your friends decide to pool your money and have this experienced investor act as your investment advisor. He will be compensated by receiving a small percentage of the average amount of assets under his management during the forthcoming year.

By common agreement, the pooled money is to be invested in the common stock of large, stable companies with the objective of capital appreciation and moderate dividend income; funds not so invested are to be placed in short-term T-bills to earn interest. Group members collectively contribute $100,000 and

FIGURE 2–1 U.S. Households Owning Mutual Funds, 1980–2001

	1980	1982	1984	1986	1988	1990	1992	1994	1996	1998	2000	2002
Percent of U.S. Households	5.7%	11.0%	11.9%	20.0%	24.4%	25.0%	27.0%	30.7%	37.2%	44.0%	49.0%	49.6%
Millions of U.S. Households	4.6	9.0	10.2	17.3	22.2	23.4	25.8	30.2	36.8	44.4	51.7	54.2

Source: *Fact Book 2003*, Investment Company Institute, p. 42.

decide to issue shares in the fund at a rate of one share for each $10 contributed—a total of 10,000 shares. Since you put in $10,000, you receive 1,000 shares of the fund—or 10 percent of the fund's shares. Over the next few weeks, your investment advisor uses $90,000 to purchase common stock in a number of companies representing several different industries and puts $10,000 in T-bills. The portfolio looks like this:

Companies grouped by different industries to get some diversification:

Industries	Companies
Automobiles	General Motors
Banking	Citigroup
Chemicals	Du Pont
Computers	Dell
Financial services	Merrill Lynch
Oil	Exxon-Mobil
Pharmaceuticals	Eli Lilly
Semiconductors	Texas Instruments
Telecommunications	SBC
Treasury bills: $10,000	

Since you own 10 percent of this portfolio, you are entitled to 10 percent of all income paid out to shareholders and 10 percent of all realized capital gains or losses.

The initial value of the portfolio is $100,000, or $10 per share. Assume your investment manager picked some winning stocks, and the portfolio rises to $115,000. Now each share is worth $11.50.

Your group of investors has many characteristics of a mutual fund: ownership interest represented by shares, professional management, stated investment objectives, and a diversified portfolio of assets. A multibillion dollar mutual fund would operate with many of the same concepts and principles—only the magnitude of the operation would be thousands of times larger.

ADVANTAGES AND DISADVANTAGES OF MUTUAL FUNDS

Mutual funds offer an efficient way to diversify your investments. For many small investors, diversification may be difficult to achieve. The normal trading unit for listed stocks—the "round lot"—is 100 shares. If proper diversification required a portfolio of at least 10 different stocks, the investor should purchase 100 shares of each of them. If each stock had a market value of $30, the cost would be (excluding commission) $30,000 ($30 × 100 × 10). That's a big bite for most individuals just to get started.

With a mutual fund, you are also buying the expertise of the fund management. In many cases, fund managers have a long history of investment experience and may be specialists in certain areas such as international securities, gold stocks, or municipal bonds. By entrusting your funds to capable hands, you are freeing your time for other pursuits. This may be particularly important to people such as doctors or lawyers who may be capable of earning $200 to $300 an hour in their normal practice but are novices in the market.

As will be demonstrated throughout the chapter, you can choose from a multitude of funds to satisfy your investment objectives. Thus, another advantage of mutual funds is that they can be used to buy not only stocks but also U.S. government bonds, corporate bonds, municipal securities, and so on. Also, they represent an efficient way to invest in foreign securities. With many of these advantages in mind, it is not surprising that mutual funds have enjoyed enormous growth in the last decade.

Having stated some of the advantages of mutual funds, let's look at the drawbacks. First, mutual funds, on average, do not outperform the market. That is to say, over long periods, they do no better than the Standard & Poor's 500 Stock Index, the Dow Jones Industrial Average, and so on. Nevertheless, they provide an efficient means for diversifying your portfolio. Also, a minority of funds have had exceptional returns over time (many of these have had exposure to international investments).

Some mutual funds can be expensive to purchase. However, this factor should not overly concern you because a high commission can often be avoided. As you read further into the chapter, you will become very proficient at identifying the absence or presence of a commission and whether it is justified.

An investor in mutual funds must also be sensitive to the excessive claims sometimes made by mutual fund salespeople. Often, potential returns to the investor are emphasized without detailing the offsetting risks. The fact that a fund made 20 to 25 percent last year in no way ensures such a return in the future. Although the Securities and Exchange Commission has begun clamping down on false or overly enthusiastic advertising practices by members of the industry, the buyer still needs to be cautious. We will also help develop your skills in measuring actual performance as we progress through the chapter.

A final potential drawback to mutual funds is actually a reverse view of an advantage. With more than 8,100 mutual funds from which to choose, an investor has as much of a problem in selecting a mutual fund as a stock. For example, there are approximately 2,900 stocks on the New York Stock Exchange, considerably less than the number of mutual funds in existence. Nevertheless, if you sharpen your goals and objectives, you will be able to focus on a handful of funds that truly meet your needs.

Having discussed the general nature of mutual funds and some of the potential advantages and disadvantages, we now examine the actual mechanics. In the remainder of this chapter, we shall discuss closed-end versus open-end funds, load versus no-load funds, fund objectives, considerations in selecting a fund, and measuring the return on a fund. There is also a brief description of unit investment trusts (UITs) at the end of the chapter. UITs have some attributes similar to mutual funds.

CLOSED-END VERSUS OPEN-END FUNDS

There are basically two types of investment funds, the closed-end fund and the open-end fund. We shall briefly discuss the closed-end fund and then move on to the much more important type of arrangement, the open-end fund.

Actually, these terms refer to the manner in which shares are distributed and redeemed. A closed-end fund has a fixed number of shares, and purchasers and sellers of shares must trade with each other. You cannot buy the shares directly from the fund (except at the inception of the fund) because of the limitation on shares outstanding. Furthermore, the fund does not stand ready to buy the shares back from you.

As we shall eventually see, an open-end fund represents exactly the opposite concept. The open-end fund stands ready at all times to sell you new shares or buy back your old shares. Having made this distinction, let's stay with the closed-end fund for now. The shares of closed-end funds trade on security exchanges or over-the-counter just as any other stock might; but when you look for their prices in *The Wall Street Journal,* you will find closed-end funds listed under a separate heading as illustrated in Table 2-1. This makes them more easily identifiable, but you still buy and sell them through a broker and pay a commission. We have highlighted Royce Value Trust Fund, a closed-end fund specializing in equities.

One of the most important considerations in purchasing a closed-end fund is whether it is trading at a discount or premium from net asset value. First, let's look at the formula for net asset value.

TABLE 2–1 Closed-End Funds

	STOCK (SYM)	DIV	LAST	NET CHG
	ROC TwnFd **ROC**		3.75	-0.03
	REITFnd **RIT** n	1.31	14.87	-0.11
	RoyceValTr **RVT**	1.40e	14.75	-0.03
	RoyceValTr pf	1.95	26.45	-0.05
	RoyceValTr pfA	1.83	25.70	-0.03
	SalomonWld **SBG**	.88a	11.05	0.12
	SlEmergMktFlt **EFL**	1.10	12.50	0.07
	SlEmergMkt II **EDF**	1.65	15.51	0.05
▲	SlEmergMktInco **EMD**	1.65	16.55	-0.85
	SalomonSBF **SBF**	.11e	10.22	-0.06
	SlGlblIncFd **GDF**	1.42	13.52	0.02
	SalomonHIF **HIF**	.96	10.89	-0.09
	SalomonHIF II **HIX**	1.38	11.67	0.10
	SlMuniPrtnrs **MNP**	.84	13.94	0.06
	SlMuniPrtnrsII **MPT**	.82	13.65	-0.05
	SlmnWldInco **SBW**	1.42a	15.21	-0.04
	♣ScddrGlblFd **LBF**	.60m	7.35	-0.09
	♣ScudderHigh **KHI**	.64	6.58	0.01
	♣ScudderGvt **KGT**	.36	7.11	-0.01
	♣ScudderMulti **KMM**	.74	8.85	0.14
▲	♣ScudderMuni **KTF**	.78	12.30	-0.01
	♣ScddrNwAsia **SAF**		8.37	-0.05
	♣ScudderStratIn **KST**	1.08	12.33	0.13
	♣ScudderStrat **KSM**	.87	12.50	0.04
	♣SeligQual **SQF**	.79	13.34	-0.04
	♣SeligSel **SEL**	.69	11.25	0.01
	SrHighInc **ARK**	.63e	5.75	-0.03
	♣SingaporeFd **SGF**	.01e	5.16	-0.03
	♣SMALLCapFd **MGC**	.12e	8.65	-0.05
	SourceCap **SOR**	3.50	48.75	-0.02
	SourceCap pf	2.40	31.70	0.20
	SoAfricaFd **SOA**	.28e	11.84	-0.16
	SpainFd **SNF**	.66e	7.79	-0.01
	StrtGlblInc **SGL**	1.24e	14.56	-0.27
	♣SwissHelvFd **SWZ**	.68e	10.28	-0.11
	♣TCW Fd **CVT**	.24m	4.89	0.08
	TCW/DW 03 **TMT**	.51e	10.67	0.01
	TaiwanFd **TWN**		8.65	-0.01
▲	TemplChinaFd **TCH**	.20e	12.45	0.09
▲	TempltnDrgn **TDF**	.19e	10.37	0.13
	TemplMktFd **EMF**	.15e	10.25	0.35
	TemplIncoFd **TEI**	1.00m	12.44	0.07
	TemplGlob **GIM**	.48	8.45	0.02
	TempltnRusEEur fd **TRF**	.39e	26.38	-0.01
	ThaiFd **TTF**	.05e	4.70	-0.06
	TransamInco **TAI**	1.56	24.90	0.07
	♣TriContl **TY**	.21e	14.43	-0.09

Source: Republished with permission of Dow Jones & Company, Inc., from *The Wall Street Journal*, May 30, 2003, p. C4; permission conveyed through Copyright Clearance Center, Inc.

$$\text{Net asset value (NAV)} = \frac{\text{Total value of securities} - \text{Liabilities}}{\text{Shares outstanding}} \qquad (2\text{-}1)$$

The net asset value (NAV) is equal to the current value of the securities owned by the fund minus any liabilities divided by the number of shares outstanding. For example, assume a fund has securities worth $140 million, liabilities of $5 million, and 10 million shares outstanding. The NAV is $13.50:

$$\text{NAV} = \frac{\$140\text{ million} - \$5\text{ million}}{10\text{ million shares}} = \frac{\$135\text{ million}}{10\text{ million}} = \$13.50$$

The NAV is computed at the end of each day for a fund.

Intuitively, one would expect a closed-end fund to sell at its net asset value, but that is not the case. Many funds trade at a 10 to 20 percent discount from NAV because they have a poor record of prior performance, are heavily invested in an unpopular industry, or are thinly traded (illiquid). A few trade at a premium because of the known quality of their management, the nature of their investments, or the fact they have holdings in nonpublicly traded securities that are believed to be undervalued on their books. This has normally been the case over the last decade. Some researchers even use the fact that closed-end funds do not sell for what they are worth (in terms of their holdings) as evidence that the market is something less than truly efficient in valuing securities.

Exchange-Traded Funds

A new wrinkle in closed-end mutual funds is the concept of exchange-traded funds (ETFs). These are investment company shares that trade on stock exchanges. The market determines the price of ETFs, and investors buy and sell them through brokers just like common stock. Exchange-traded funds began in 1993 and, according to the Investment Company Institute, numbered 92 ETFs by September 2001. Of these, 66 were domestic and 26 were international ETFs, and together all had a total value of $64.4 billion. This is a small percentage of total mutual fund assets but one that is expected to grow rapidly in future years.

Exchange-traded funds are essentially index-based mutual funds that imitate a market index such as the Standard & Poor's 500 Index. Of the 66 domestic ETFs, 33 used broad-based market indexes and the other 33 used industry indexes. The advantage of ETFs is that they allow the investor to buy "the market" or "an industry" just like a common stock.

In Table 2-2, we present a listing of exchange-traded funds from *The Wall Street Journal*. Most of these are listed on the American Stock Exchange. In addition to major market indexes, many of the exchange-traded funds are country specific funds. For example, on the AMEX you can see iShares for France, Germany, Japan, Hong Kong, Italy, and many more countries. Most of these are based on Morgan Stanley Capital International indexes. You can look up any of these exchange-traded funds on the AMEX website (www.amex.com) and dig down to the fees and several-page description. These funds can be bought just like common stock.

TABLE 2–2

EXCHANGE-TRADED PORTFOLIOS

Thursday, May 29, 2003
Includes Exchange-Traded Funds and HOLDRs

AMEX

	YTD % CHG	52 WEEKS HI	52 WEEKS LO	STOCK (SYM)	DIV	YLD %	VOL 100s	CLOSE	NET CHG
	4.7	100.66	72.03	Diamond **DIA**	2.00e	2.3	86138	87.40	-0.60
	2.3	85.95	58.70	PharmaHLDRs **PPH**	1.54e	2.0	5386	75.80	-0.78
	11.4	95.82	63.21	RetailHLDRs **RTH**	.54e	.7	6399	77.76	-0.58
	38.9	3.53	1.27	B2BHLDRs **BHH**		...	1205	2.75	0.04
	38.6	120.70	65.40	BiotchHLDRs **BBH**	1.92e	1.6	13883	117.20	-2.16
	21.5	11.20	5.53	BrdBndHLDRs **BDH**	.05e	.5	802	9.17	0.25
	13.3	55.48	35.96	Europe01HLDRs **EKH**	.93e	2.0	37	47.35	0.44
▲	19.3	31.10	18.85	IntArch Hldrs **IAH**	.15e	.5	134	30.76	-0.07
▲	49.9	37.43	17.88	IntrntHLDRs **HHH**	.10e	.3	2022	37.18	0.13
	36.8	3.45	1.13	IntInfr Hldrs **IIH**	.07e	2.0	1488	3.31	0.02
	6.9	53.89	38.21	Mkt2000HLDRs **MKH**	.93e	1.9	70	47.95	0.01
	5.4	121.10	87.32	RegBk Hldrs **RKH**	3.30e	3.0	626	108.30	-0.86
	8.9	71.99	44.70	OilSvcHLDRs **OIH**	.44e	.7	15378	62.39	-1.05
	33.3	39.73	17.32	SemiCon Hldrs **SMH**	.06e	.2	86537	29.53	0.78
	15.2	31.82	20.08	SftwreHLDRs **SWH**	.59e	1.9	1102	31.08	-0.05
	-2.6	34.30	20.68	TelecomHLDRs **TTH**	1.11e	4.2	814	26.17	-0.06
	12.5	88.21	49.90	UtilHLDRs **UTH**	2.86e	4.0	3311	72.15	-1.50
	6.5	42.70	27.31	WirlsHLDRs **WMH**	.49e	1.3	384	37.34	0.40
	8.5	48.13	34.25	iShrDJUSEn **IYE**	.70e	1.6	269	42.75	-0.58
	1.3	41.99	28.90	iShDJUSBM **IYM**	.66e	1.9	153	34.89	-0.14
	11.6	55.29	37.18	iShDJUSCCy **IYC**	.06e	.1	121	46.74	0.03
	5.0	48.54	36.61	iShrDJUSCNC **IYK**	.60e	1.4	186	42.70	-0.20
	11.2	93.80	64.85	iShrDJUSFin **IYG**	1.42e	1.6	208	87.14	-0.51
	6.8	56.56	39.75	iShrDJUSHlth **IYH**	.38e	.7	679	51.85	-0.45
	5.2	46.29	31.74	iShrDJUSInd **IYJ**	.38e	1.0	273	39.38	-0.25
	6.9	87.53	69.45	iShrDJUSRE **IYR**	4.88e	5.9	1369	82.64	-1.61
	9.0	50.41	35.50	iShrDJUSTot **IYY**	.61e	1.4	369	44.72	-0.12
	11.5	63.50	38.57	iShrDJUSUtil **IDU**	2.07e	3.9	1435	53.40	-0.76
	9.8	81.62	57.95	iShrDJUSFI **IYF**	1.28e	1.7	145	74.90	-0.45
	3.0	22.96	13.80	iShrDJUSTc **IYZ**	.31e	1.6	1158	19.64	-0.04
	18.4	42.75	24.75	iShrDJTch **IYW**		...	715	38.49	0.48
	8.2	99.29	67.67	iShrSP400V **IJJ**	1.16e	1.3	642	86.57	-0.08
	8.3	72.54	50.41	iShrRu3000V **IWW**	1.21e	1.9	125	63.95	-0.34
	10.8	55.52	35.96	iShrMSEMU **EZU**	.45e	.9	81	48.19	0.29
	12.2	142.63	96.15	iShrRu2000V **IWN**	2.25e	1.8	1299	125.10	0.20
	9.4	36.25	26	iShrRu3000G **IWZ**	.22e	.7	72	31.98	-0.12
	9.7	59.38	39.52	iShrSPEu350 **IEV**	1.06e	2.0	555	52.08	0.06
	7.6	78.15	55.75	iShrSP600G **IJT**	.17e	.2	398	70.02	-0.08
	7.0	95.39	62.50	iShrSP600V **IJS**	.70e	.9	344	77.85	0.49
	18.1	10.88	8.40	iShrMSAusy **EWA**	.27e	2.5	271	10.72	0.07
	26.6	11.18	7.04	iShrMSAus **EWO**	.10e	1.0	356	10.90	0.06
	11.3	12.05	7.36	iShrMSBlg **EWK**	.11e	1.0	907	10.99	0.11
	32.6	12.50	5.35	iShrMSBra **EWZ**	.11e	1.0	7949	10.58	0.21
▲	21.0	11.45	8	iShrMSCan **EWC**	.03e	.3	377	11.42	0.18
▲	14.1	113.76	99.70	iShrsMSCIEmrgMkt **EEM**		...	341	113.75	0.15
	8.2	18.98	12.01	iShrMSFra **EWQ**	.18e	1.1	416	16.02	0.14
	14.8	15.06	8.07	iShrMSGer **EWG**	.12e	1.1	1104	11.30	0.10
▲	19.8	17.40	12.44	iShrMSIta **EWI**	.38e	2.2	111	17.49	0.32
	-2.9	9.12	6.19	iShrMSJpn **EWJ**		...	21406	6.75	0.03
	-0.1	24.13	14.70	iShrMSSK **EWY**		...	1047	18.34	0.01
	5.8	6.07	4.82	iShrMSMay **EWM**	.09e	1.8	2190	5.31	-0.01
	12.8	16.85	11.08	iShrMSMex **EWW**	.52e	3.7	10409	14.04	-0.05
	-1.1	18.09	9.55	iShrMSNth **EWN**	.25e	1.9	26	13.07	-0.04
	8.4	5.60	3.05	iShrMSSng **EWS**	.08e	1.7	218	4.63	0.08
▲	22.8	21.74	14.71	iShrMSEsp **EWP**	.16e	.7	71	21.74	0.10
	6.8	14.14	9.11	iShrMSSwi **EWL**	.03e	.2	530	11.87	-0.02
	8.1	14.62	10.16	iShrMSUK **EWU**	.28e	2.2	2096	13.13	0.12
	11.7	59.95	48.36	iSHRS MSCI Pac **EPP**	.88e	1.6	282	56.51	-0.39
	1.1	40.39	35.93	iShrMSSoAfr **EZA**		...	10	39.51	0.24
	22.0	12.29	7.42	iShrMSSwe **EWD**	.12e	1.1	22	11.65	0.05
	8.2	101	71.10	iShrs GldSach **IGE**	1.43e	1.6	25	88.06	-0.73
	45.6	20.61	8.71	iShrsGSNetwkng **IGN**		...	2607	19.79	0.35
	29.1	61.40	25.85	iShrGSSmcdtor **IGW**		...	232	44.76	1.34
▲	22.0	30.89	19.15	iShrGSSftwr **IGV**		...	368	30.71	...
	20.3	40.24	22.71	iShrGSchsTch **IGM**		...	147	36.15	0.53
	5.3	115.80	101	iShrGSInvst **LQD**	4.34e	3.8	1343	115.50	0.83
▲	0.5	82.71	81	iShrsLeh1-3 **SHY**	1.12e	1.4	574	82.71	0.03
	7.0	96.21	81.32	iShrsLeh20+ **TLT**	3.44e	3.6	5083	94.78	0.82
	3.7	89.50	81.70	iShrsLeh7-10 **IEF**	2.89e	3.2	978	89.36	0.47
	7.1	123.95	85.63	iShrsMSCI EAFE **EFA**	1.88e	1.8	1981	106.05	0.50
	1.1	9.73	6.55	iShrMSHK **EWH**	.14e	1.9	6824	7.51	-0.08
	1.7	11.35	6.61	iShrMSTaiwn **EWT**		...	4971	8.29	0.08
	34.3	68.30	39.65	iShrsNasBioTch **IBB**		...	3604	66.27	-0.60
	8.6	57.32	40.89	iShrRu1000 **IWB**	.72e	1.4	1016	50.72	-0.33
	7.7	56.46	39	iShrRu1000V **IWD**	1.01e	2.0	1519	49.39	-0.54
	15.9	52.85	33.50	iShrRu2000G **IWO**	.19e	.4	2582	46.20	0.23
	15.2	65.42	44.17	iShrRuMidGrth **IWP**	.08e	.1	377	59.54	0.24
	11.5	59.57	41.46	iShrRuMid **IWR**	.60e	1.1	406	54.24	-0.01
	10.1	83.72	58.43	iShrRuMidVlu **IWS**	1.33e	1.8	163	75.44	-0.44
	10.2	45.16	32.43	iShrRu1000G **IWF**	.30e	.7	1284	40.06	-0.02
	8.7	60.46	42.70	iShrRu3000 **IWV**	.89e	1.7	946	53.23	-0.24
	14.1	98.24	64.60	iShrRu2000 **IWM**	1.04e	1.2	19214	86.49	0.55
	-3.5	81.70	54.26	iShrs S&P/Tpx **ITF**	.70p	...	2	59.84	0.69
	7.8	106.72	73.94	iShrsSP400 **IJH**	.75e	.8	351	92.80	-0.31
	7.6	54.34	40.02	iShrsSP500G **IVW**	.51e	1.1	1252	48.34	-0.01
	8.8	53.77	35.91	iShrSP500V **IVE**	.84e	1.8	884	46.80	-0.36
	7.6	53.65	41.65	iShrsSPGbl GE **IXC**	.91e	1.9	14	49.19	-0.27
	6.9	46.60	34.25	iShrsSPHlthcr **IXJ**	.25e	.6	2	43.17	-0.13
	8.6	40.64	29.01	iShrsSPGblTele **IXP**	.64e	1.6	834	39.90	...
	15.9	44.70	26.75	iShrsSPGbl IT **IXN**		...	5	39.90	0.51
	10.8	53.99	36.51	iShrsSPGbl Fn **IXG**	.57e	1.2	10	47.50	-0.50
	7.5	113.66	80.21	iShrSP400G **IJK**	.27e	.3	203	98.30	-0.03
	8.1	108.50	77.05	iShrsSP500 **IVV**	1.52e	1.6	7842	95.49	-0.25
	7.7	122.40	84	iShrsSP600 **IJR**	.67e	.6	918	105	0.39
	17.2	48.81	30.61	iShrs Tr 40 **ILF**	.92e	2.1	70	42.90	0.28
	7.6	92.20	73.85	iShrsCohen&St **ICF**	4.96e	5.7	1637	87.78	-2.35
	20.3	31.04	19.76	Nasdaq 100 **QQQ**		...	964233	29.31	0.12
▲	7.3	121.60	113.21	PwrShsDynOTC **XTFQ**		...	2	122.92	1.42
▲	6.1	114.30	107.25	PwrShsDynMkt **XTFM**		...	2	114.55	0.52
	8.1	108.56	77.07	SPDR **SPY**	1.52e	1.6	501445	95.42	-0.25
	13.3	29.38	20.65	SPDR ConsDiscr **XLY**	.17e	.6	1895	26.18	-0.03
	-0.5	25.06	17.82	SPDR ConStpl **XLP**	.41e	2.1	4745	19.85	-0.10
	7.8	27.60	19.38	SPDR Engy **XLE**	.51e	2.1	3893	24.08	-0.23
	9.4	26.69	18.52	SPDR Fncl **XLF**	.45e	1.9	11162	24.07	-0.26
	4.9	29.97	21.65	SPDR Hlthcare **XLV**	.26e	.9	814	27.86	-0.23
	4.3	25.70	17.75	SPDR Indu **XLI**	.33e	1.5	3411	21.48	-0.24
	2.6	23.95	16.53	SPDR Materials **XLB**	.46e	2.3	1835	20.35	-0.17
	12.9	18.90	11.40	SPDR Tch **XLK**	.04e	.2	7300	16.71	0.04
	13.8	26.95	14.90	SPDR Utils **XLU**	.89e	4.1	16339	21.79	-0.33
	8.2	97.90	67.85	SP400 Spdrs **MDY**	.77e	.9	9345	85.10	0.12
	6.4	60.41	43.47	sTrackDJGlTltn **DGT**	.97e	1.8	33	53.20	-0.30
	9.7	45.55	32.40	sTrackDJLCapG **ELG**	1.42e	3.5	45	40.08	-0.05
	6.7	121.70	87.55	sTrackDJLCapV **ELV**	2.22e	2.1	22	107.84	-0.87
	14.3	60.70	36.94	sTrackDJSCapG **DSG**		...	242	51.38	-0.19
	9.8	142.24	103.10	sTrackDJSCapV **DSV**	4.72e	3.6	388	130.75	-0.55
	7.6	77.91	56.20	sTrackFort500 **FFF**	1.01e	1.5	366	68.15	-0.57
▲	28.6	25.82	15.77	sTrackFort e50 **FEF**		...	122	25.91	0.37
	26.2	39.63	22.40	sTrackMSHTch35 **MTK**		...	12	36.17	0.23
▲	37.3	10.32	5.08	sTrackMSInt **MII**		...	239	10.35	0.12
	6.8	133.25	104	sTrackWlshREIT **RWR**	6.31e	5.1	208	124.21	-2.80
	12.0	60.85	43.10	♣VangdVipersExt **VXF**	.55e	1.0	19	55.58	-0.09
	8.8	101.21	72	♣VangdVipersTot	1.25e	1.4	1732	89.93	-0.15

NASDAQ

	YTD % CHG	52 WEEKS HI	52 WEEKS LO	STOCK (SYM)	DIV	YLD %	VOL 100s	CLOSE	NET CHG
	0.0	51	42.25	BldrsAsia50 **ADRA**	.02p	...	z8249	47	0.78
	5.9	54.90	43.98	BldrsEmg50 **ADRE**	.08p	...	2	54	1.85
	10.1	50.75	36.25	BldrsEur100 **ADRU**	.33p	...	5	48.99	1.59

NYSE

	YTD % CHG	52 WEEKS HI	52 WEEKS LO	STOCK (SYM)	DIV	YLD %	VOL 100s	CLOSE	NET CHG
▲	10.1	27.75	20.25	♣FrescoDJSEuro50 **FEZ**	.03p	...	1957	27.59	0.02
▲	12.5	27.60	21.15	♣FrescoDJS50 **FEU**	.20p	...	5	27.90	0.45
	6.4	54.05	39	iShrSP100Gbl **IOO**	.55e	1.2	489	47.15	-0.21

CBOE

	YTD % CHG	52 WEEKS HI	52 WEEKS LO	STOCK (SYM)	DIV	YLD %	VOL 100s	CLOSE	NET CHG
	7.9	53.90	38.70	iShrsSP100 **OEF**		...	646	47.97	-0.25

Source: Republished with permission of Dow Jones & Company, Inc., from *The Wall Street Journal*, May 30, 2003, p. C10; permission conveyed through Copyright Clearance Center, Inc.

INVESTING IN OPEN-END FUNDS

As previously indicated, an open-end fund stands ready at all times to sell new shares or buy back old shares from investors at net asset value. More than 95 percent of the investment funds in the United States are open-ended. Actually, the term *mutual fund* applies specifically to *open-end* investment companies, although closed-end funds are sometimes loosely labeled as mutual funds as well. We shall be careful to make the distinction where appropriate.

Transactions with open-end funds are made at the net asset value as described in Formula 2-1 (though there may be an added commission). If the fund has 100 million shares outstanding at an NAV of $10 per share ($1 billion) and sells 20 million more shares at $10 per share, the new funds ($200 million) are redeployed in investments worth $200 million, and the NAV remains unchanged. The only factor that changes the NAV is the up and down movement of the securities in the fund's portfolio. The primary distinctions between closed-end and open-end funds are presented in Table 2-3. All of our subsequent discussion will be about open-end (mutual) funds. These include such established names as Fidelity, Dreyfus, Vanguard, IDS, T. Rowe Price, and Templeton.

Load versus No-Load Funds

Some funds have established selling agreements with stockbrokers, financial planners, insurance agents, and others licensed to sell securities. These selling agents receive a commission for selling the funds. The funds are termed load funds because there is a commission associated with the purchase of the fund shares. The commission may run to 7.25 percent or higher.

Several stock funds are referred to as low-load funds because their sales charges are 2 to 3 percent instead of 7.25 percent. A number of funds also have a back-end load provision. While there may or may not be a front-end load in buying such a fund, there is an exit fee in selling a fund with a back-end load provision. The fee may be 2 to 3 percent of the selling price, but typically declines with the passage of time.

TABLE 2–3 Distinction between Closed-End and Open-End Funds

	Method of Purchase	Number of Shares Outstanding	Shares Traded at Net Asset Value
Closed-end fund	Stock exchange or over-the-counter	Fixed	No—there may be a discount or premium from NAV; there will be a commission
Open-end fund	Direct from fund or fund salesperson	Fluctuates	Yes—but there may be a commission

No-Load Funds

No-load funds do not charge commissions and are sold directly by the investment company through advertisements, prospectuses, and 800-number telephone orders.[1] As of 2000, no-load funds made up about 40 percent of all mutual fund assets and accounted for 50 percent of new sales. Some wonder how no-load funds justify their existence since they charge no front-end commission to purchase their shares. The answer is because of the fee they charge to manage the assets in the fund. This management fee plus expenses normally average 0.75 to 1.25 percent. On a billion dollar fund, this represents approximately $10 million a year and can be more than adequate to compensate the fund managers. It should also be pointed out that load funds also have similar management fees.

The question then becomes, why pay the load (commission)? Studies indicate there is no significant statistical difference in the investment performance of load and no-load funds. Consequently, most astute investors shop around for a no-load fund to fit their needs rather than pay a commission. This statement is not intended to dismiss the possibility that apprehensive or uncomfortable investors may benefit from the consultation and advice of a competent mutual fund salesperson or financial advisor, and thus receive a commensurate service from paying the commission. Also, some specialized funds may exist only in the form of load funds. However, whenever possible, investors are better off using the commission toward the purchase of new shares rather than the payment of a sales fee.

If you invest $1,000 in a load mutual fund and pay a 7.25 percent commission, only 92.75 percent will go toward purchasing your shares. A $1,000 investment will immediately translate into a holding of $927.50. This means the fund must go up by $72.50 or 7.82 percent, just for you to break even:

$$\frac{\$72.50}{\$927.50} = 7.82\%$$

It used to be simple to figure out which funds charged a load and which ones were no-load funds. You could look in *The Wall Street Journal* or *Barron's* to find both the price and the NAV. If the price and the NAV were equal, there was no load (commission) and if the price was higher than the NAV, there was a load and the percentage could be calculated.

Let's assume that the net asset value of the Hirt Block Fund is $13.32 and the offer price is $13.98. This means the fund has a net asset value of $13.32 per share but is offered to the public for $13.98. The difference between $13.32 and $13.98 of $0.66 represents the commission:

$13.98	Offer price
13.32	NAV (net asset value)
$ 0.66	Commission

1. Some of these funds may have a small back-end load that declines to zero with the passage of time.

In this case, the commission represents 4.72 percent of the offer price ($0.66/ $13.98 = 4.72%).[2] You will buy a fund valued at $13.32 for $13.98 because of the sales charge.

In an effort to save space, *The Wall Street Journal* has reduced the amount of information on mutual fund quotations to those found in Table 2-4 (starting under the letter **A** in the first column). This trimmed-down version shows the net asset value (NAV), the net change (NET CHG), the year-to-date return (YTD % RET), and the three-year return (3-yr % RET).

Now perhaps the best way to determine whether a mutual fund is load or no-load is to consult the *Morningstar Mutual Fund Survey* if you are only interested in no-load or low-load funds, or consult the annual publication of the American Association of Individual Investors, "Individual Investor's Guide to Low-Load Mutual Funds."

Figure 2-2 illustrates the one-page analysis on the T. Rowe Price European Stock Fund from the *Morningstar Mutual Fund Survey.* This has become the information source of choice for mutual fund investors who want to track their holdings on a quarterly basis. Morningstar ranks each mutual fund in its universe on a one-star to five-star rating system. T. Rowe Price European Stock Fund is ranked four stars in the box toward the top of the page with an above-average return and a below-average risk. As you look at the top line on the page, you will also see its ticker symbol and that it does not carry a load. The data in the table are self-explanatory but notice that the table includes annual returns, tax analysis, risk analysis, country exposure, major company holdings, and more.

There are other good sources of information, and *Forbes* publishes an annual mutual fund review every August. While this is only a one-year publication, it is very helpful for investors looking for mutual funds or evaluating their funds. While *Forbes* has reduced the scope of its coverage in its magazine, the full listing of its mutual funds is available on its website at www.forbes.com/fundsurvey. *Forbes* ranks mutual funds in up and down markets much like a professor, with an A for great performance and F for failing performance. Additionally it provides five-year returns, asset size, annual expenses per $100, the minimum initial investment, and a few other items.

If you see a fund that interests you after reviewing either the *Morningstar Mutual Fund Survey* or the *Forbes* website, you can request a prospectus. If the fund is a load fund, you can request the prospectus from your broker; if it is a no-load fund you can contact the fund directly through its 800 telephone number or website address.

DIFFERING OBJECTIVES AND THE DIVERSITY OF MUTUAL FUNDS

Recognizing that different investors have different objectives and sensitivities to risk, the mutual fund industry offers a large group of funds from which to choose.

2. It also represents 4.95 percent of the net asset value ($0.66/$13.32).

TABLE 2–4 Mutual Fund Quotations

MUTUAL FUNDS

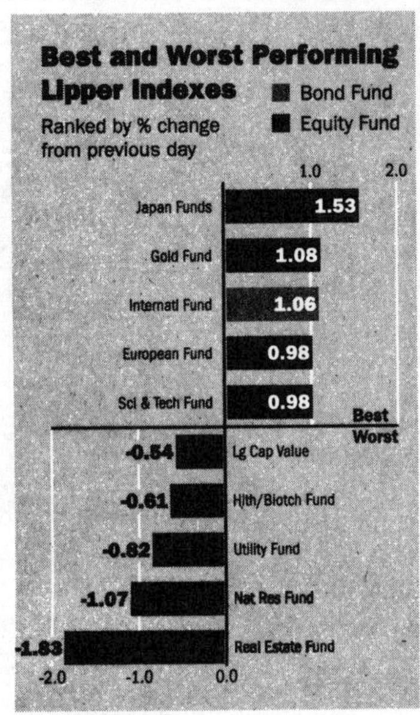

Explanatory Notes

Mutual-funds listings for Nasdaq-published share classes with net assets of at least $100 million each. **NAV** is net asset value. Percentage performance figures are total returns, assuming reinvestment of all distributions and after subtracting annual expenses. Figures don't reflect sales charges ("loads") or redemption fees. **NET CHG** is change in NAV from previous trading day. **YTD%RET** is year-to-date return. **3-YR%RET** is trailing three-year return annualized.

e-Ex-distribution. **f**-Previous day's quotation. **g**-Footnotes x and s apply. **j**-Footnotes e and s apply. **k**-Recalculated by Lipper, using updated data. **p**-Distribution costs apply, 12b-1. **r**-Redemption charge may apply. **s**-Stock split or dividend. **t**-Footnotes p and r apply. **v**-Footnotes x and e apply. **x**-Ex-dividend. **z**-Footnote x, e and s apply. **NA**-Not available due to incomplete price, performance or cost data. **NE**-Not released by Lipper; data under review. **NN**-Fund not tracked. **NS**-Fund didn't exist at start of period.

Source: Lipper

Thursday, May 29, 2003

A

FUND	NAV	NET CHG	YTD %RET	3-YR %RET
AAL Mutual A				
Balance p	11.04	-0.02	6.9	-0.8
Bond p	10.49	0.03	5.2	10.2
CGrowth p	26.20	-0.12	8.0	-9.0
EqInc p	10.61	-0.07	7.0	-6.4
HiYBdA	6.31	0.03	13.9	4.1
Intl p	7.05	0.07	3.8	-17.1
MidCap p	11.35	-0.04	7.7	-3.4
MuniBd	11.78	0.02	4.2	9.7
SmCap	12.33	0.05	8.6	1.5
AAL Mutual Inst				
Balance	11.04	-0.01	7.2	-0.3
AARP Invst				
Balanced	15.54	...	7.6	NS
CapGr	35.46	-0.08	10.1	-15.6
GNMA	15.37	...	1.0	8.4
GroInc	17.31	-0.08	8.5	NS
Income	13.13	0.04	4.5	NS
MgdMuni	9.50	...	3.5	NS
ShtTmBd	10.70	0.01	1.9	NS
ABN AMRO Funds				
BalancedN p	10.31	-0.01	4.0	-2.2

FUND	NAV	NET CHG	YTD %RET	3-YR %RET
GlGr p	13.31	0.07	7.2	-17.8
GlHltCr p	22.53	0.02	4.5	6.4
GlInc p	9.18	0.06	10.4	7.6
GlScTech p	5.51	0.04	18.0	-37.7
HYld p	4.06	...	14.1	-6.5
Inco p	6.82	0.03	8.7	6.0
IntGov p	9.55	0.02	2.1	8.7
IntlGrow p	13.43	0.10	5.1	-14.0
LimM p	10.52	0.01	0.9	6.1
LrgCpGr t	7.82	0.01	10.8	-18.7
MdCpCEq p	22.84	0.04	7.8	1.5
Muni p	8.33	0.01	4.2	8.0
Oppl p	11.00	...	8.2	-6.4
PremEqty p	8.11	-0.02	8.0	-15.1
RealEst p	16.04	-0.37	9.6	14.9
SelEqty p	12.87	-0.03	7.5	-17.9
SmCpEq p	9.13	0.03	10.9	NS
SmCpGr p	20.45	0.02	10.7	-11.6
Summit I p	8.02	-0.02	11.4	-20.7
TF Int p	11.92	0.01	3.6	8.6
Weing p	10.26	0.01	11.0	-24.2
AIM Funds B				
Agrsv t	7.33	-0.03	4.0	-15.9
Bal t	21.89	...	5.8	-7.8
BasicVal t	23.03	-0.11	10.1	-1.3

FUND	NAV	NET CHG	YTD %RET	3-YR %RET
Bal t	21.92	...	5.8	-7.8
BasicVal t	23.02	-0.11	10.1	-1.3
BlChp t	9.36	-0.01	8.8	-16.4
Chart t	9.90	-0.01	6.6	-14.1
Const t	17.05	...	8.0	-16.1
IntGov t	9.54	0.02	1.8	7.9
MdCpCEq t	20.88	0.03	7.6	0.8
PremEqty t	7.60	-0.03	7.5	-15.8
ShortTerm t	10.12	...	1.7	NS
AMF Funds				
AdjMtg	9.95	...	0.8	5.0
IntMtg	9.78	0.01	1.3	7.6
ShtUSGv	10.81	...	1.5	6.5
UltraShrt p	9.97	...	0.9	NS
USGvMtg	10.83	0.02	2.2	8.3
ARK Funds				
Balanced	12.15	0.02	10.2	-5.0
BlChpEql	13.42	-0.06	8.9	-14.9
Income	10.73	0.03	4.2	10.0
IntmFixl	10.68	0.03	4.3	9.8
MDTxFree	10.60	0.01	3.7	8.9
PATxFBd	10.67	0.01	4.2	9.3
ValEq	7.83	-0.02	7.1	-9.1
AXA Rosenberg				
US SmCp	10.14	0.03	8.2	9.3
USSmCpInv t	10.03	0.04	8.1	9.0
Accessor Fd				
Mortg	13.01	0.01	1.3	9.0
SmMidCp	16.21	...	11.0	-7.6
Activa				
IntmdBd	10.93	0.03	4.4	10.3
Value p	5.99	-0.03	7.7	-2.1
Advance Capital I				
Balanc p	16.97	...	8.8	3.2
Bond p	10.30	0.05	7.8	11.4
RetInc p	10.24	0.04	7.9	11.2
AegisValueFd	13.68	0.09	8.1	21.9
Alger American O				
Balanced	12.32	0.02	9.1	-2.2
Growth	27.95	-0.01	13.5	-14.9
LevAll	24.31	-0.04	16.6	-16.4
MidCpGr	14.61	0.05	17.3	-6.2
SmCap	13.52	0.02	10.7	-19.8
Alger Funds A				
CapApr	6.85	-0.02	16.7	-18.5
LgCapGrth	7.88	...	13.5	-14.9
MidCpGr	6.25	0.02	16.6	-6.6
Alger Funds B				
Balncd p	16.72	0.02	9.7	-5.1
CapApr t	6.49	-0.01	16.5	-19.1
LgCapGrth t	7.42	...	13.3	-15.6
MidCpGr t	5.87	0.03	16.2	-7.3
Alger Funds Inst				
CapApprl	9.83	-0.02	16.5	-17.3
MidCpGrl	12.29	0.04	17.2	-5.1
AllianceBernstein				
IntDurInstl	15.97	0.05	4.5	NS
AllianceBernstein A				
AmerGovtIncA p	7.76	0.07	13.8	12.3
BalanA p	14.41	-0.03	10.0	2.6
CorpBdA p	12.10	0.06	12.1	10.4
EmgMktDebtA p	7.89	0.06	24.9	20.4
GrIncA p	2.88	-0.02	11.2	-5.0
GrowthA p	24.25	-0.10	11.4	-18.8
HiYldA p	5.83	0.02	11.7	-0.4
IntDivMuA p	14.50	0.01	3.1	NS
MidCapGrA p	4.19	0.03	27.4	-11.5
MMSA p	5.89	0.01	2.1	5.5
MuAZ A p	10.92	0.01	2.9	8.1
MuCA A p	11.09	0.02	3.8	8.0
MuFL A p	10.44	0.01	4.1	9.3
MuInsCA A p	14.78	0.05	4.7	9.8
MuInsNatlA p	10.28	0.01	4.4	9.0
MuNY A p	9.99	0.01	3.8	8.0
NtlMuA p	10.12	0.01	3.8	7.1
PremGrA p	14.87	-0.04	8.2	-22.1
QuasarA p	15.55	0.10	12.3	-10.0
SmCapValA p	11.93	-0.05	10.5	NS
TechA p	43.96	0.33	14.6	-27.5
USGovtA	7.59	0.03	3.8	9.5
WldPrivA p	8.25	0.14	9.4	-9.0
AllianceBernstein Ad				
GrIncAdv	2.89	-0.02	11.2	-4.8
HiYldAdv	5.83	0.01	11.8	0.0
IntValAdv	10.81	0.15	12.5	NS
PremGrAdv	15.24	-0.04	8.4	-21.8
QualBndAdv	10.89	0.03	4.1	NS
SmCpValAdv	11.95	-0.05	10.5	NS
USGovtAdv	7.60	0.03	3.7	NS
ValueAdv t	9.71	-0.05	8.0	NS
AllianceBernstein B				

FUND	NAV	NET CHG	YTD %RET	3-YR %RET
AmerGovtIncB t	7.77	0.08	13.6	11.5
BalanB t	13.74	-0.03	9.6	1.8
CorpBdB t	12.09	0.06	11.7	9.6
DisValB p	11.82	-0.03	18.6	2.1
GlStrInB t	8.80	0.04	11.0	5.1
GrIncB t	2.84	-0.01	11.1	-5.7
GrowthB t	17.11	-0.06	11.2	-19.4
HiYldB t	5.83	0.02	11.4	-1.1
HlthCareB t	9.63	-0.06	7.6	-4.1
MuCA B t	11.09	0.02	3.5	7.2
MuFL B t	10.45	0.01	3.8	8.5
MuNJ B t	10.09	0.01	4.2	6.7
MuNY B t	9.98	0.01	3.5	7.2
NtlMuB t	10.11	0.01	3.5	6.4
PremGrB t	13.64	-0.04	7.9	-22.6
QualBndB p	10.89	0.04	3.7	8.9
QuasarB t	13.32	0.08	11.8	-10.8
SmCapValB t	11.88	-0.05	10.0	NS
TechB t	40.36	0.31	14.3	-28.0
USGovtB	7.59	0.03	3.5	8.7
UtilInc t	11.84	-0.10	7.6	-7.8
ValueB t	9.62	-0.06	7.5	NS
AllianceBernstein C				
AmerGovtIncC t	7.79	0.07	13.6	11.5
BalanC t	13.79	-0.03	9.6	1.8
CorpBdC t	12.10	0.06	11.8	9.6
GrIncC t	2.84	-0.02	10.7	-5.7
GrowthC t	17.13	-0.07	11.1	-19.4
MuCA C t	11.09	0.02	3.5	7.2
PremGrC t	13.67	-0.04	8.0	-22.6
TechC t	40.36	0.30	14.3	-28.0
USGovtC	7.60	0.03	3.5	8.7
AllianceBernstein I				
QuasInstll	6.03	0.04	12.7	-4.8
ReEInvl	8.55	-0.20	9.4	11.0
Am Skandia Adv Fds A				
MarCpGrA p	11.15	-0.05	10.6	-9.2
TotRtBdA p	11.12	0.03	4.7	10.0
Am Skandia Adv Fds B				
FHiYdBB t	6.96	0.01	9.9	2.2
GoSachCGB	8.85	0.03	8.5	-23.4
MarCpGrB p	10.89	-0.05	10.3	-9.7
TotRtBdB p	11.01	0.03	4.6	9.3
Am Skandia Adv Fds C				
MarCpGrC p	10.88	-0.05	10.3	-9.6
TotRtBdC p	11.01	0.03	4.6	9.4
Amer AAdvant AMR				
BalAmr	11.62	-0.03	7.8	5.4
IntBdAmr	10.59	0.03	4.2	10.4
IntlAmr	13.19	0.15	9.9	-5.8
LgCapAmr	13.60	-0.08	9.5	1.8
ShBdAmr	9.48	...	2.2	7.2
SmCapAmr	13.03	0.02	13.1	19.8
Amer AAdvant Inst				
IntlInst	13.13	0.14	9.8	-6.0
S&PInst	12.93	-0.05	8.5	-10.6
Amer AAdvant Plan				
IntlPlan	13.04	0.14	9.9	-6.2
American Century Adv				
EqInc p	6.97	-0.02	7.4	10.7
IncGro p	23.45	-0.13	8.4	-8.5
IntlGr p	6.63	0.09	4.1	-15.8
SmCpVal p	7.40	0.01	9.4	17.2
StrMod p	5.60	...	7.2	-1.6
Ultra p	22.86	-0.03	8.8	-13.2
Value p	6.40	-0.02	7.8	7.6
American Century Inv				
♣Balanced	14.00	-0.01	7.8	-1.8
CaHYMu	10.11	0.01	4.5	9.8
♣CaIntTF	11.80	0.03	3.3	8.4
♣CaLgTF	12.12	0.02	4.7	10.1
♣CaLtdTF	10.93	0.02	2.0	6.3
DivBnd	10.69	0.04	4.1	NS
♣EqGro	16.58	-0.06	9.4	-9.7
♣EqInc	6.98	-0.01	7.6	11.0
Gift	12.22	0.02	3.2	-20.6
♣GinnieMae	10.78	...	0.8	8.3
♣Gl Grwth	5.43	0.03	7.7	-12.5
♣GlGold r	8.74	0.06	-4.3	28.3
♣GovtBd	11.35	0.02	2.7	10.2
♣Grwth	15.56	0.02	7.9	-16.5
♣Heritage	9.33	0.01	2.5	-8.7
♣IncGro	23.49	-0.13	8.5	-8.2
♣InfAdjBd	11.17	0.08	6.7	12.3
♣IntDisc r	9.93	0.10	11.4	-10.7
♣IntlBnd	13.80	0.16	13.7	12.8
Intl Gr	6.65	0.10	4.2	-15.6
LgComVal	4.90	-0.03	7.9	3.3
♣LifeSci	3.76	-0.01	7.1	NS
NewOpp r	4.14	...	1.7	-20.9

Continued on Page C14

Source: Republished with permission of Dow Jones & Company, Inc., from *The Wall Street Journal,* May 30, 2003, p.C13; permission conveyed through Copyright Clearance Center, Inc.

FIGURE 2–2 T. Rowe Price European Stock Fund One-Page Analysis

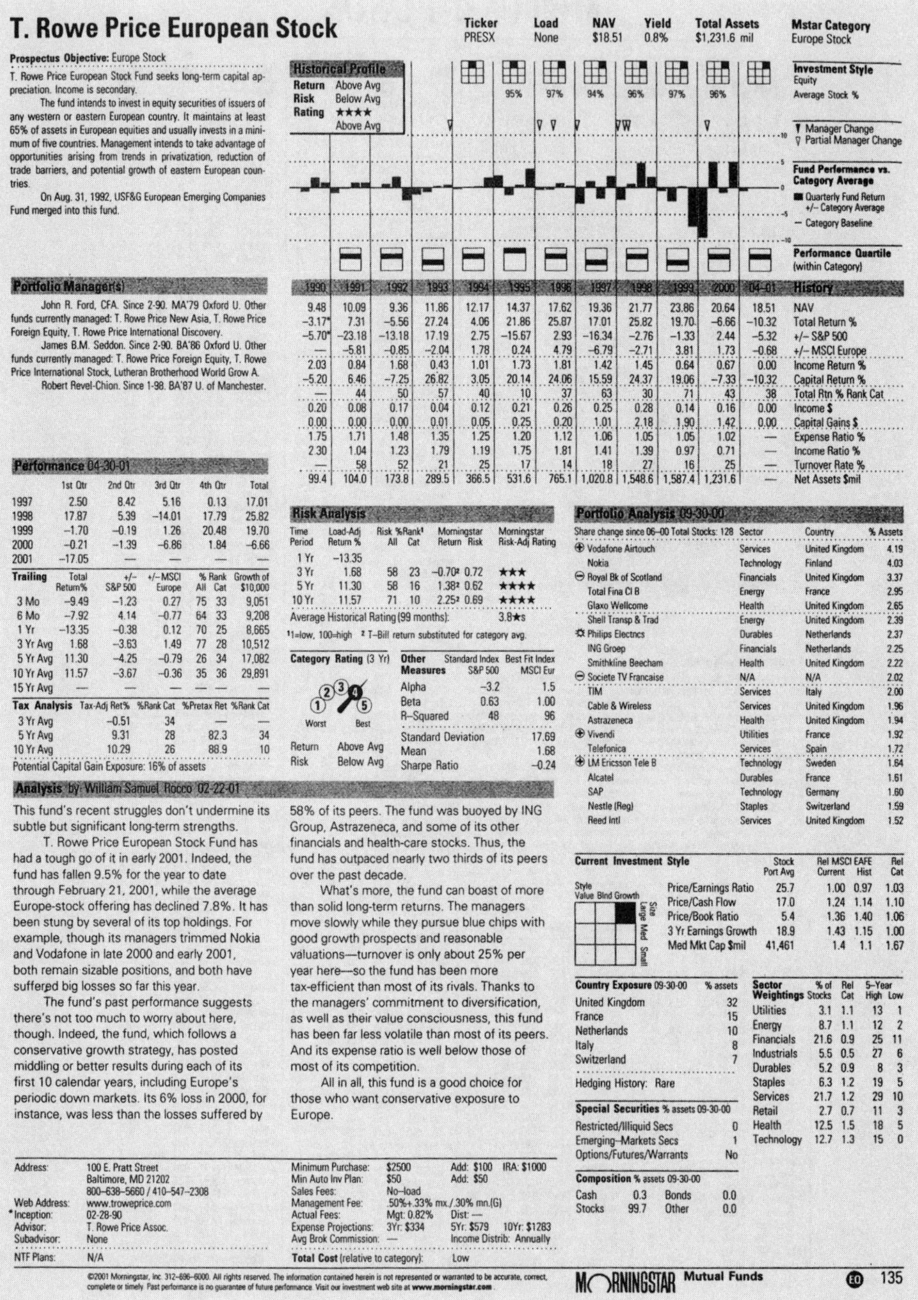

T. Rowe Price European Stock

Ticker	Load	NAV	Yield	Total Assets	Mstar Category
PRESX	None	$18.51	0.8%	$1,231.6 mil	Europe Stock

Prospectus Objective: Europe Stock

T. Rowe Price European Stock Fund seeks long-term capital appreciation. Income is secondary.

The fund intends to invest in equity securities of issuers of any western or eastern European country. It maintains at least 65% of assets in European equities and usually invests in a minimum of five countries. Management intends to take advantage of opportunities arising from trends in privatization, reduction of trade barriers, and potential growth of eastern European countries.

On Aug. 31, 1992, USF&G European Emerging Companies Fund merged into this fund.

Historical Profile
Return: Above Avg
Risk: Below Avg
Rating: ★★★★ Above Avg

Portfolio Manager(s)

John R. Ford, CFA. Since 2-90. MA'79 Oxford U. Other funds currently managed: T. Rowe Price New Asia, T. Rowe Price Foreign Equity, T. Rowe Price International Discovery.

James B.M. Seddon. Since 2-90. BA'86 Oxford U. Other funds currently managed: T. Rowe Price Foreign Equity, T. Rowe Price International Stock, Lutheran Brotherhood World Grow A.

Robert Revel-Chion. Since 1-98. BA'87 U. of Manchester.

1990	1991	1992	1993	1994	1995	1996	1997	1998	1999	2000	04-01	History
9.48	10.09	9.36	11.86	12.17	14.37	17.62	19.36	21.77	23.86	20.64	18.51	NAV
–3.17*	7.31	–5.56	27.24	4.06	21.86	25.87	17.01	25.82	19.70	–6.66	–10.32	Total Return %
–5.70*	–23.18	–13.18	17.19	2.75	–15.67	2.93	–16.34	–2.76	–1.33	2.44	–5.32	+/– S&P 500
—	–5.81	–0.85	–2.04	1.78	0.24	4.79	–6.79	–2.71	3.81	1.73	–0.68	+/– MSCI Europe
2.03	0.84	1.68	0.43	1.01	1.73	1.81	1.42	1.45	0.64	0.67	0.00	Income Return %
–5.20	6.46	–7.25	26.82	3.05	20.14	24.06	15.59	24.37	19.06	–7.33	–10.32	Capital Return %
—	44	50	57	40	10	37	63	30	71	43	38	Total Rtn % Rank Cat
0.20	0.08	0.17	0.04	0.12	0.21	0.26	0.25	0.28	0.14	0.16	0.00	Income $
0.00	0.00	0.00	0.01	0.05	0.25	0.20	1.01	2.18	1.90	1.42	0.00	Capital Gains $
1.75	1.71	1.48	1.35	1.25	1.20	1.12	1.06	1.05	1.05	1.02	—	Expense Ratio %
2.30	1.04	1.23	1.79	1.19	1.75	1.81	1.41	1.39	0.97	0.71	—	Income Ratio %
—	58	52	21	25	17	14	18	27	16	25	—	Turnover Rate %
99.4	104.0	173.8	289.5	366.5	531.6	765.1	1,020.8	1,548.6	1,587.4	1,231.6	—	Net Assets $mil

Performance 04-30-01

	1st Qtr	2nd Qtr	3rd Qtr	4th Qtr	Total
1997	2.50	8.42	5.16	0.13	17.01
1998	17.87	5.39	–14.01	17.79	25.82
1999	–1.70	–0.19	1.26	20.48	19.70
2000	–0.21	–1.39	–6.86	1.84	–6.66
2001	–17.05	—	—	—	—

Trailing	Total Return%	+/– S&P 500	+/– MSCI Europe	% Rank All	% Rank Cat	Growth of $10,000
3 Mo	–9.49	–1.23	0.27	75	33	9,051
6 Mo	–7.92	4.14	–0.77	64	33	9,208
1 Yr	–13.35	–0.38	0.12	70	25	8,665
3 Yr Avg	1.68	–3.63	1.49	77	28	10,512
5 Yr Avg	11.30	–4.25	–0.79	26	34	17,082
10 Yr Avg	11.57	–3.67	–0.36	35	36	29,891
15 Yr Avg	—	—	—	—	—	—

Tax Analysis	Tax-Adj Ret%	%Rank Cat	%Pretax Ret	%Rank Cat
3 Yr Avg	–0.51	34	—	—
5 Yr Avg	9.31	28	82.3	34
10 Yr Avg	10.29	26	88.9	10

Potential Capital Gain Exposure: 16% of assets

Risk Analysis

Time Period	Load-Adj Return %	Risk %Rank[1] All	Risk %Rank[1] Cat	Morningstar Return	Morningstar Risk	Morningstar Risk-Adj Rating
1 Yr	–13.35					
3 Yr	1.68	58	23	–0.70[2]	0.72	★★★
5 Yr	11.30	58	16	1.38[2]	0.62	★★★★
10 Yr	11.57	71	10	2.25[2]	0.69	★★★★

Average Historical Rating (99 months): 3.8★s

[1] 1=low, 100=high [2] T-Bill return substituted for category avg.

Category Rating (3 Yr)

Return: Above Avg
Risk: Below Avg

Other Measures	Standard Index S&P 500	Best Fit Index MSCI Eur
Alpha	–3.2	1.5
Beta	0.63	1.00
R-Squared	48	96
Standard Deviation		17.69
Mean		1.68
Sharpe Ratio		–0.24

Portfolio Analysis 09-30-00

Share change since 06-00 Total Stocks: 128	Sector	Country	% Assets
⊕ Vodafone Airtouch	Services	United Kingdom	4.19
Nokia	Technology	Finland	4.03
⊖ Royal Bk of Scotland	Financials	United Kingdom	3.37
Total Fina Cl B	Energy	France	2.95
Glaxo Wellcome	Health	United Kingdom	2.65
Shell Transp & Trad	Energy	United Kingdom	2.39
☼ Philips Electncs	Durables	Netherlands	2.37
ING Groep	Financials	Netherlands	2.25
Smithkline Beecham	Health	United Kingdom	2.22
⊖ Societe TV Francaise	N/A	N/A	2.02
TIM	Services	Italy	2.00
Cable & Wireless	Services	United Kingdom	1.96
Astrazeneca	Health	United Kingdom	1.94
⊕ Vivendi	Utilities	France	1.92
Telefonica	Services	Spain	1.72
⊕ LM Ericsson Tele B	Technology	Sweden	1.64
Alcatel	Durables	France	1.61
SAP	Technology	Germany	1.60
Nestle (Reg)	Staples	Switzerland	1.59
Reed Intl	Services	United Kingdom	1.52

Current Investment Style

	Stock Port Avg	Rel MSCI EAFE Current	Rel MSCI EAFE Hist	Rel Cat
Price/Earnings Ratio	25.7	1.00	0.97	1.03
Price/Cash Flow	17.0	1.24	1.14	1.10
Price/Book Ratio	5.4	1.36	1.40	1.06
3 Yr Earnings Growth	18.9	1.43	1.15	1.00
Med Mkt Cap $mil	41,461	1.4	1.1	1.67

Country Exposure 09-30-00	% assets
United Kingdom	32
France	15
Netherlands	10
Italy	8
Switzerland	7

Hedging History: Rare

Special Securities % assets 09-30-00	
Restricted/Illiquid Secs	0
Emerging-Markets Secs	1
Options/Futures/Warrants	No

Composition % assets 09-30-00			
Cash	0.3	Bonds	0.0
Stocks	99.7	Other	0.0

Sector Weightings	% of Stocks	Rel Cat	5-Year High	5-Year Low
Utilities	3.1	1.1	13	1
Energy	8.7	1.1	12	2
Financials	21.6	0.9	25	11
Industrials	5.5	0.5	27	6
Durables	5.2	0.9	8	3
Staples	6.3	1.2	19	5
Services	21.7	1.2	29	10
Retail	2.7	0.7	11	3
Health	12.5	1.5	18	5
Technology	12.7	1.3	15	0

Analysis by William Samuel Rocco 02-22-01

This fund's recent struggles don't undermine its subtle but significant long-term strengths.

T. Rowe Price European Stock Fund has had a tough go of it in early 2001. Indeed, the fund has fallen 9.5% for the year to date through February 21, 2001, while the average Europe-stock offering has declined 7.8%. It has been stung by several of its top holdings. For example, though its managers trimmed Nokia and Vodafone in late 2000 and early 2001, both remain sizable positions, and both have suffered big losses so far this year.

The fund's past performance suggests there's not too much to worry about here, though. Indeed, the fund, which follows a conservative growth strategy, has posted middling or better results during each of its first 10 calendar years, including Europe's periodic down markets. Its 6% loss in 2000, for instance, was less than the losses suffered by 58% of its peers. The fund was buoyed by ING Group, Astrazeneca, and some of its other financials and health-care stocks. Thus, the fund has outpaced nearly two thirds of its peers over the past decade.

What's more, the fund can boast of more than solid long-term returns. The managers move slowly while they pursue blue chips with good growth prospects and reasonable valuations—turnover is only about 25% per year here—so the fund has been more tax-efficient than most of its rivals. Thanks to the managers' commitment to diversification, as well as their value consciousness, this fund has been far less volatile than most of its peers. And its expense ratio is well below those of most of its competition.

All in all, this fund is a good choice for those who want conservative exposure to Europe.

Address:	100 E. Pratt Street, Baltimore, MD 21202, 800-638-5660 / 410-547-2308	Minimum Purchase:	$2500	Add: $100 IRA: $1000
Web Address:	www.troweprice.com	Min Auto Inv Plan:	$50	Add: $50
*Inception:	02-28-90	Sales Fees:	No-load	
Advisor:	T. Rowe Price Assoc.	Management Fee:	.50%+.33% mx./.30% mn.(G)	
Subadvisor:	None	Actual Fees:	Mgt: 0.82%	Dist: —
		Expense Projections:	3Yr: $334	5Yr: $579 10Yr: $1283
		Avg Brok Commission:	—	Income Distrib: Annually
NTF Plans:	N/A	Total Cost (relative to category):	Low	

MORNINGSTAR Mutual Funds EO 135

Source: Reprinted by permission of Morningstar, Inc.

In 2001, there were more than 8,100 mutual funds, each unique in terms of stated objectives, investment policies, and current portfolio. To make some sense out of this much variety, funds can be classified in terms of their stated objectives.

Money Market Funds Money market funds have had strong growth in the last two decades. (*Forbes* Mutual Fund Survey provides a helpful list of funds.) Money market mutual funds invest in short-term securities, such as U.S. Treasury bills and Eurodollar deposits, commercial paper, jumbo bank certificates of deposit (CDs), and repurchase agreements.

Money market funds are no-load, and most require minimum deposits of $500 to $1,000. Most have check-writing privileges, but usually the checks must be written for at least $250 to $500.

Because the maturities of assets held in money market portfolios generally range from 20 to 50 days, the yields of these funds closely track short-term market interest rates. Money market funds give small investors an opportunity to invest in securities that were once out of reach.

Growth Funds The pursuit of capital appreciation is the emphasis with growth funds. This class of funds includes those called aggressive growth funds and those concentrating on more stable and predictable growth. Both types invest primarily in common stock. Aggressive funds concentrate on speculative issues, emerging small companies, and "hot" sectors of the economy and frequently use financial leverage to magnify returns. Regular growth funds generally invest in common stocks of more stable firms. They are less inclined to stay fully invested in stocks during periods of market decline, seldom use aggressive techniques such as leverage, and tend to be long term in orientation.

The best way to determine the type of growth fund is to carefully examine the fund's prospectus and current portfolio.

Growth with Income Growth with income funds pay steady dividends. Their stocks are attractive to investors interested in capital growth potential with a base of dividend or interest income. Funds that invest in such stocks are less volatile and risky than growth funds investing in small companies paying low or no dividends.

Balanced Funds Balanced funds combine investments in common stock and bonds and often preferred stock. They try to provide income plus some capital appreciation. Funds that invest in convertible securities are also considered balanced since the convertible security is a hybrid fixed-income security with the opportunity for appreciation if the underlying common stock rises.

Index Funds Index funds are mutual funds that replicate a market index as closely as possible. It was pointed out earlier that exchange-traded closed-end funds were index funds that traded on exchanges just like common stock. Conversely, index funds are open-end and may be purchased directly from the fund sponsor. There are many indexes, including stock market indexes and bond market indexes as well as foreign and global indexes. If an investor truly believes that the market is efficient and that it is hard to outperform the market, he or she will try to reduce transaction costs and attempt to imitate the market. Index funds arose because of the efficient market hypothesis (presented in Chapter 9). Quite a bit of academic research indicates that it is difficult to outperform a market index unless you have superior information. Most investors do not have superior information and so index funds make sense.

Table 2-5 presents the Vanguard Idx: 500 Idx index fund, which is the largest fund at $59.7 billion as of May 26, 2003. This fund replicates the Standard & Poor's 500 Composite Index. The S&P 500 Index is considered a growth and value index; this fund competes with other funds in that category, and its performance is compared against the category returns. The table is taken from the *Morningstar Mutual Fund Survey* and provides quite a bit of valuable information. The fund has a beta equal to 1.00 as you would expect. Notice that the expense ratio averages between 0.18 and 0.20 percent (18 to 20 basis points) versus a normal .75 to 1.25 percent for managed funds, and this demonstrates the low-cost nature of an index fund that needs no research analysts or huge databases.

Bond Funds Income-oriented investors have always been attracted to bonds. Because bonds represent a contractual obligation on the part of the issuer to the bondholder, they normally offer a certain return. But as pointed out in Chapter 12, rising interest rates can undercut the market value of all classes of fixed-income securities. During the early 1980s and early 1990s, times of intense interest-rate fluctuations, many bondholders watched the principal value of even their "safe" government bonds drop to 75 percent of face value. Bonds held in bond mutual funds were affected by the same market forces. Returns from bonds are historically lower than those from stocks, and bond funds are no exception.

Bond mutual funds can be roughly subdivided into corporate, government, and municipal funds.

Some corporate bond funds are particularly targeted to low-rated, high-yielding bonds. These funds are termed *junk bond funds.* They may have a yield of 3 or 4 percent over the typical corporate bond fund but also possess greater risk in terms of potential default by the securities in the bond portfolio. Just how much greater that risk is was discovered in the fall of 1989 when a number of low-rated bonds in these funds defaulted on their interest payments and prices for all junk bonds fell.

Because municipal bond funds buy only tax-exempt securities, interest income to shareholders is free of federal tax. Special tax-exempt funds also have been established for the benefit of investors in states with high state and local income taxes. For example, fund managers of New York municipal bond funds establish portfolios of tax-exempt securities issued within the boundaries of that state. Under current tax law, interest income from these funds is exempt from federal, state, and local taxes for New York residents—a very appealing feature to high-bracket taxpayers.

TABLE 2–5 Sample Page for the Vanguard Idx: 500 Idx

Vanguard 500 Index

Ticker	Load	NAV	Yield	Total Assets	Mstar Category
VFINX	None	$84.83	1.5%	$76,998 mil	Large Blend

Manager Strategy

The core of the fund's strategy is simple: Manager Gus Sauter buys and holds the stocks that compose the S&P 500 index. Sauter attempts to add value on the margins by opportunistically buying futures contracts, among other techniques, and he actively tries to reduce trading costs.

Historical Profile

Return Above Avg
Risk Average
Rating ★★★★ Above Avg

Investment Style: Equity, Stock %: 100% 99% 99% 100% 100% 99% 100%

▼ Manager Change
▽ Partial Manager Change

Fund Performance vs. Category Average.
Quarterly Fund Return +/- Category Average
— Category Baseline

Performance Quartile (within Category)

Portfolio Manager(s)

George U. Sauter. Since 10-87. AB'76 Dartmouth C.; MBA'80 U. of Chicago. Other funds currently managed: Vanguard Explorer Adm, Vanguard Mid Capitalization Index Adm, Vanguard Reit Index Adm.

1991	1992	1993	1994	1995	1996	1997	1998	1999	2000	2001	08-02	History
39.32	40.97	43.83	42.97	57.60	69.17	90.07	113.95	135.33	121.86	105.89	84.83	NAV
30.22	7.42	9.89	1.18	37.45	22.88	33.19	28.62	21.07	-9.06	-12.02	-19.41	Total Return %
-0.26	-0.20	-0.17	-0.13	-0.09	-0.06	-0.16	0.04	0.03	0.04	-0.14	-0.01	+/-S&P 500
-2.81	-1.62	-0.26	0.79	-0.32	0.43	0.35	1.60	0.15	-1.27	0.43	-0.56	+/-Russ 1000
3.73	2.88	2.79	2.70	2.86	2.24	1.92	1.49	1.25	0.96	1.05	0.56	Income Return %
26.49	4.54	7.10	-1.52	34.59	20.64	31.27	27.13	19.82	-10.02	-13.07	-19.97	Capital Return %
54	50	53	23	12	27	14	16	38	59	41	48	Total Rtn % Rank Cat
1.15	1.12	1.13	1.17	1.22	1.28	1.32	1.33	1.41	1.30	1.28	0.59	Income $
0.12	0.10	0.03	0.20	0.13	0.25	0.59	0.42	1.00	0.00	0.00	0.00	Capital Gains $
0.20	0.19	0.19	0.19	0.20	0.20	0.19	0.18	0.18	0.18	0.18	—	Expense Ratio %
3.07	2.81	2.65	2.72	2.38	2.04	1.66	1.35	1.13	0.98	1.14	—	Income Ratio %
5	4	6	6	4	5	5	6	6	9	4	—	Turnover Rate %
4,345	6,518	8,273	9,356	17,372	30,332	49,358	74,229	104,652	90,486	73,151	63,889	Net Assets $mil

Performance 08-31-02

	1st Qtr	2nd Qtr	3rd Qtr	4th Qtr	Total
1998	13.91	3.29	-9.95	21.39	28.62
1999	4.98	7.00	-6.25	14.96	21.07
2000	2.25	-2.62	-0.93	-7.81	-9.06
2001	-11.90	5.82	-14.72	10.65	-12.02
2002	0.24	-13.43	—	—	—

Trailing	Total Return%	+/- S&P 500	+/- Russ 1000	%Rank All	%Rank Cat	Growth of $10,000
3 Mo	-13.74	0.05	0.04	60	43	8,626
6 Mo	-16.58	0.01	-0.45	75	51	8,342
1 Yr	-18.04	-0.05	-0.56	71	46	8,196
3 Yr Avg	-10.33	-0.01	-0.76	79	51	7,210
5 Yr Avg	1.72	-0.02	-0.08	61	32	10,891
10 Yr Avg	10.31	-0.07	-0.08	16	25	26,677
15 Yr Avg	9.53	-0.15	-0.19	17	30	39,161

Tax Analysis	Tax-Adj Rtn%	%Rank Cat	Tax-Cost Rat	%Rank Cat
3 Yr Avg	-10.75	42	0.48	15
5 Yr Avg	1.14	21	0.56	14
10 Yr Avg	9.44	11	0.78	9

Potential Capital Gain Exposure: 2% of assets

Rating and Risk

Time Period	Load-Adj Return %	Morningstar Rtn vs Cat	Morningstar Risk vs Cat	Morningstar Risk-Adj Rating
1 Yr	-18.04			
3 Yr	-10.33	Avg	Avg	★★★
5 Yr	1.72	+Avg	Avg	★★★★
10 Yr	10.31	+Avg	Avg	★★★★
Incept	12.19			

Other Measures	Standard Index S&P 500	Best Fit Index S&P 500
Alpha	0.0	0.0
Beta	1.00	1.00
R-Squared	100	100
Standard Deviation	15.82	
Mean	-10.33	
Sharpe Ratio	-0.96	

Portfolio Analysis 06-30-02

Share change since 03-02 Total Stocks:502	Sector	PE	YTD Ret%	% Assets
⊖ Microsoft	Software	34.8	-27.84	3.25
⊖ General Elec	Ind Mtrls	21.4	-28.63	3.16
⊖ ExxonMobil	Energy	23.0	-11.10	3.04
⊖ Wal-Mart Stores	Consumer	34.3	-8.06	2.68
⊖ Pfizer	Health	26.5	-22.01	2.40
⊖ Citigroup	Financial	10.7	-35.11	2.19
⊖ American Intl Grp	Financial	29.8	-24.98	1.95
⊖ Johnson & Johnson	Health	27.3	-6.12	1.72
⊖ Coca-Cola	Goods	40.2	6.64	1.52
⊖ IBM	Hardware	26.0	-39.16	1.35
⊖ Intel	Hardware	57.5	-48.29	1.34
⊖ Royal Dutch Petro NY ADR	Energy	11.0	-10.37	1.29
⊖ Procter & Gamble	Goods	28.7	15.98	1.27
⊖ Merck	Health	16.2	-15.74	1.26
⊖ Verizon Comms	Telecom	—	-35.47	1.20
⊖ Bank of America	Financial	15.4	13.02	1.19
⊖ Cisco Sys	Hardware	55.3	-28.05	1.12
⊖ SBC Comms	Telecom	16.5	-37.35	1.12
⊖ ChevronTexaco	Energy	—	-14.50	1.04
⊖ Philip Morris	Goods	11.5	3.89	1.02

Current Investment Style

Value Blnd Growth; Large Mid Small

Market Cap %	
Giant	48.6
Large	37.0
Mid	14.0
Small	0.5
Micro	0.0
Median $mil: 44,757	

Value Measures		Rel S&P 500
Price/Earnings	20.0	1.2
Price/Book	2.6	1.1
Price/Sales	1.2	1.1
Price/Cash Flow	6.7	1.1
Dividend Yield %	2.0	1.0

Growth Measures	%	Rel S&P 500
Projected Earnings	7.0	1.0
Book Value	8.0	0.9
Sales	9.0	1.0
Cash Flow	7.0	1.0
Trailing Earnings	15.0	1.0

Profitability	%	Rel S&P 500
Return on Equity	16.9	1.0
Return on Assets	9.0	1.0
Net Margin	8.7	1.0

Sector Weightings	% of Stocks	Rel S&P 500	3 Year High	3 Year Low
Info	21.0	1.0	41	21
Software	4.5	1.0	6	5
Hardware	9.0	1.0	22	9
Media	3.4	1.1	5	3
Telecom	4.1	1.1	7	4
Service	46.1	0.9	47	34
Health	13.8	0.9	14	11
Consumer	9.3	1.0	9	6
Business	3.4	0.8	3	2
Financial	19.7	0.9	20	14
Mfg	32.8	1.1	34	25
Goods	10.9	1.0	11	7
Ind Mtrls	11.4	1.0	12	10
Energy	7.4	1.2	7	5
Utilities	3.1	1.1	3	2

Composition

Cash	0.0
Stocks	99.6
Bonds	0.0
Other	0.3
Foreign (% of Stock)	2.3

Morningstar's Take by William Harding 08-22-02

Vanguard 500 Index doesn't shine as bright as it once did, but it remains a luminary large-cap option.

This fund had its share of critics when it launched 25 years ago, but it's safe to say that it has been a resounding success. Indeed, it has blossomed into the largest mutual fund on the planet. The fund's salient traits--low costs, superb tax efficiency and broad diversification--have been paramount to its superb long-term record. It also helps that the mega-cap stocks that dominate the fund's bogy, the S&P 500 index, enjoyed a remarkable rally during the 1990s.

But as the market's largest names, such as General Electric, have given way to small caps in recent years, the fund's returns have cooled. Indeed, the fund's 9.6% loss for the trailing three years ended Aug. 21, 2002, lands around the large-blend group's midpoint. Meanwhile, sibling Vanguard Total Stock Market Index, which tracks the Wilshire 5000 index, has posted an 8.5% annualized loss over that time. In fact, that fund is a better choice than 500 Index for investors looking for broad market exposure because it invests more assets outside of the large-cap arena.

That said, this fund has much to offer as a dependable large-cap holding. With a cheap 0.18% price tag, the fund's cost advantage gives it a big leg up on the competition. That's a big reason why the fund has managed to keep pace with most actively managed funds in the group even though its mega-cap tilt and lack of a cash cushion provided a head wind. In addition, the fund's diverse portfolio limits the effect a few big disasters can have on returns. Finally, Gus Sauter's indexing prowess is another point in its favor. Thanks to savvy trading and use of the futures market, he has been able to make up for most of the fund's expenses over time.

In short, this behemoth remains an attractive core holding.

Address:	Vanguard Financial Ctr. P.O. Box 2600 Valley Forge, PA 19482 800-662-7447
Web Address:	www.vanguard.com
Inception:	08-31-76
Advisor:	Vanguard Core Management Group
Subadvisor:	None
NTF Plans:	N/A

Minimum Purchase:	$3000	Add: $100	IRA: $1000
Min Auto Inv Plan:	$3000	Add: $50	
Sales Fees:	No-load		
Management Fee:	0.16%		
Actual Fees:	Mgt:0.16%	Dist: —	
Expense Projections:	3Yr:$58	5Yr:$101	10Yr:$230
Income Distrib:	Quarterly		
Total Cost (relative to category):	Low		

MORNINGSTAR® Mutual Funds EQ 289

Source: Reprinted by permission of Morningstar, Inc.

Sector Funds Special funds have been created to invest in specific sectors of the economy. Sector funds exist for such areas as energy, medical technology, computer technology, leisure, and defense.

Because stock performance of companies within a particular industry, or sector, tend to be positively correlated, these funds offer investors less diversification potential.

Investors should be cautious with regard to the initial offering of new sector funds. An initial offering usually occurs after the sector has already been the subject of intense interest based on recent spectacular performance. As a result, stocks in that sector are often fully priced or overpriced.

Foreign Funds Investors seeking participation in foreign markets and foreign securities confront a number of obstacles, but the rewards can be remarkable. The mutual fund industry has made overseas investing convenient by establishing foreign funds whose policies mandate investing on an international basis (Templeton World Fund), within the markets of a particular locale (Canadian Fund, Inc.), or within a region (Merrill Lynch Pacific). Some funds even specialize in Third World countries.

A listing of various types of international funds is presented in Table 2-6. The mutual fund industry distinguishes between global and international funds. Global funds have foreign stocks plus U.S. stocks, while international have only foreign stocks.

Specialty Funds Some mutual funds have specialized approaches that do not fit neatly into any of the preceding categories and so are called specialty funds. Their names are often indicative of their investment objectives or policies: the Phoenix Fund (rising from the ashes?), the Calvert Social Investment Fund, and United Services Gold Shares, to name just a few.

There is even a "fund of funds" (FundTrust) that manages a portfolio of different mutual fund shares.

Hedge Funds Hedge funds are products of the 1990s and became very popular in 2000–2003. Actually the name is somewhat misleading in that hedge funds do not restrict their activities to hedging or reducing risk. Rather the term is a generic name for funds that engage in a wide range of activities at one time in an attempt to generate a superior return. They normally are neither bullish nor bearish, but engage in buying, short selling, and transacting in puts and calls at the same time in the attempt to gain an edge. They tend to be highly leveraged and are usually in the form of a limited partnership.

Finally, funds are sometimes distinguished by the size of the market value (capitalization) of the firms in which they invest. Examples might be small-cap funds, which invest in firms with market values up to $1 billion; mid-cap funds, which invest in firms with market values up to $9 billion, and so on.[3]

---

3. The market value limitation for the small- or mid-cap fund designation varies from fund to fund.

TABLE 2–6 Internationally Oriented Funds

Name of Fund	Open- or Closed-End	Load (L) or No-Load (NL)	Where Invested
Dean Witter European Growth B	Open	5.00%	Europe
Central European Community	Closed	—	Europe
Invesco European	Open	None	Europe
France Growth	Closed	—	France
Mexico Equity and Income	Closed	—	Mexico
Latin American Discovery	Closed	—	Latin America
Chile Fund	Closed	—	Chile
Argentina Fund	Closed	—	Argentina
Scudder International Fund	Open	None	Mexico and Central America
Morgan Stanley Latin American A	Open	5.75%	Latin America
GT Latin America Growth A	Open	4.75%	Latin America
Fidelity Europe Capital Appreciation	Open	3.00%	Europe
Putnam Europe Growth A	Open	5.75%	Europe

Matching Investment Objectives with Fund Types

Investors must consider how much volatility of return they can tolerate. Investors who require safety of principal with very little deviation of returns should choose money market funds first and intermediate-term bond funds second. They should also expect to receive lower returns based on historical evidence. While aggressive growth stock funds provide the highest return, they also have the biggest risk.

Liquidity objectives are met by all mutual funds since redemption can occur any time. If investors need income, bond funds provide the highest annual current yield, while aggressive growth funds provide the least. Growth-income and balanced funds are most appropriate for investors who want growth of principal with moderate current income.

Many investors diversify by fund type. For example, at one stage in the business cycle, an investor may want to have 50 percent of assets in U.S. common stocks, 35 percent in bonds, 10 percent in money market funds, and 5 percent in an international stock fund. These percentages could change as market conditions change. If interest rates are expected to decline, it would be better to have a higher percentage of bonds and fewer money market securities since bond prices will rise as rates decline. Investing with a "family of funds" allows the investor a choice of many different types of funds and the privilege of switching between funds at no or low cost. Some of the larger families of funds are managed by American Capital, Dreyfus Group, Federated Funds, Fidelity Investments, T. Rowe Price Funds, and the Vanguard Group. In addition, most major retail brokerage firms, such as Merrill Lynch, Dean Witter, and Salomon Smith Barney, have families of mutual funds.

Each mutual fund has a unique history and management team. There is no guarantee that past performance will be repeated. Investors should check on a fund's longevity of management, historical returns, trading history, and management expenses. A very key instrument in providing information in this regard is the fund prospectus.

THE PROSPECTUS

The Investment Companies Act of 1940, which established the standard of practice for all investment companies, requires that the purchaser of fund shares be provided with a current prospectus. The prospectus contains information deemed essential by the SEC in providing "full disclosure" to potential investors regarding the fund's investment objectives and policies, risks, management, and expenses. The prospectus also provides information on how shares can be purchased and redeemed, sales and redemption charges (if any), and shareholders' services. Other fund documents are available to the public on request including the Statement of Additional Information and the fund's annual and quarterly reports.

While it is beyond the scope of this chapter to provide a complete discourse on interpreting a prospectus, investors need to understand the following essentials.

Investment Objectives and Policies This section is always found in the beginning of the prospectus. It usually describes the fund's basic objectives such as:

> The Fund will invest only in securities backed by the full faith and credit of the U.S. Government. At least 70 percent of the Fund's assets will be invested in certificates issued by the Government National Mortgage Association (GNMA). It may also purchase other securities issued by the U.S. Government, its agencies, or instrumentalities as long as these securities are backed by the full faith and credit of the U.S. Government.

The prospectus normally goes on to detail investment management policies under which it intends to operate—typically with regard to the use of borrowed money, lending of securities, or something like the following:

> The Fund may, under certain circumstances, sell covered call options against securities it is holding for the purpose of generating additional income.

Portfolio (or "Investment Holdings") This section lists the securities held by the fund as of the date indicated. Since investment companies are only required to publish their prospectuses every 14 months, the information is probably dated. Still, the portfolio should be compared with the stated objectives of the fund to see if they are consistent.

Management Fees and Expenses Besides sales and redemption charges, the prospectus also provides information and figures on fund managers' reimbursement and the fund's housekeeping expenses. Annual fees for the investment advisor are expressed as a percentage of the average daily net assets during the year (usually 0.50 percent). Other expenses include legal and auditing fees, the cost of preparing and distributing annual reports and proxy statements, directors' fees, and transaction expenses. When lumped together with investment advisory fees, a fund's total yearly expenses typically range from 0.75 to 1.25 percent of fund assets. Experienced mutual fund investors cast a jaundiced eye on funds with expense ratios that exceed this figure. It is required that all expenses appear on one page in a table format.

A controversial SEC ruling—Rule 12b-1—allows mutual funds to use fund assets for marketing expenses, which are included in the expense ratio. Since marketing expenses have nothing to do with advancing shareholders' interests and everything to do with increasing the managers' fees, investors should be alert to this in the prospectus.

Turnover Rate A number of mutual funds trade aggressively in pursuit of profits; others do just the opposite. In one year, the Fidelity Contrafund had a 243 percent turnover rate; the rate for the Oppenheimer Special Fund was 9 percent.

In reality, transaction costs amount to more than just commissions, and they are not accounted for in the expense ratio. When fund assets are traded over-the-counter, the dealer's spread between the bid and asked price is not considered. Nor is the fact that large block trades—the kind mutual funds usually deal in—are made at less favorable prices than are smaller volume transactions.

The prospectus also contains audited data on the turnover rate, the expense ratio, and other important data in the section on per-share income and capital changes. In 1998 the SEC ordered mutual funds to provide shortened forms of the prospectus to investors who do not want to be overwhelmed with data.

DISTRIBUTION AND TAXATION

The selling of securities by a mutual fund manager results in capital losses or gains for the fund. After netting losses against gains, mutual funds distribute net capital gains to shareholders annually.

Funds with securities that pay dividends or interest also have a source of investment income. The fund, in turn, distributes such income to shareholders either quarterly or annually.

A fund that distributes at least 90 percent of its net investment income and capital gains is not subject, as an entity, to federal income tax. It is simply acting as a "conduit" in channeling taxable sources of income from securities held in the portfolio to the fund's shareholders. Most funds operate this way. But while the mutual fund may not be subject to taxation, its shareholders are.

At the end of every calendar year, each fund shareholder receives a Form 1099-DIV. This document notifies the shareholder of the amount and tax status of his or her distributions.

When the investor actually sells (redeems) shares in a mutual fund, another form of taxable event occurs. It is precisely the same as if stocks, bonds, or other securities were sold. The investor must consider the cost basis, the selling price, and any gain or loss and appropriately report the tax consequences on his or her tax form.

Tax Differences between Mutual Funds and Individual Stock Portfolios

When you manage your own portfolio of common stocks, you can choose when to sell a specific stock, and by having that choice, you control when you pay capital gains taxes. When you own a mutual fund, the manager decides when to buy and sell, so you end up with a capital gain or loss at the manager's discretion. This difference might not seem significant, but if you receive a bonus this year, you might want to take losses this year to offset some of the bonus income and wait until next year to take your gains. You might also want to wait until the gain is long term and taxed at a lower rate.

The initial purchase of a common stock sets the cost basis; if the stock goes up you have a gain, and if it goes down you have a loss. At least if the stock stays the same you have no gain or loss. This is not so with a mutual fund. When you buy fund shares, a portfolio of stocks already exists, and these stocks are either held at a gain or loss. In rapidly rising bull markets, you may be buying into mutual funds that have large accumulated gains; if the manager decides to take those gains, you will have to pay the capital gains tax—even though the net asset value of your shares did not change. This would leave you with a negative return even though the price did not fall. This particular tax issue is what keeps more sophisticated investors from buying mutual funds during the last several months of the year.

SHAREHOLDER SERVICES

Most mutual funds offer a number of services to their shareholders. Some can be used in the investor's strategy. Common services include the following:

Automatic reinvestment. The fund reinvests all distributions (usually without sales charge). Shares and fractional shares are purchased at the net asset value. Purchases are noted on annual and periodic account statements.

Safekeeping. While shareholders are entitled to receive certificates for all whole shares, it is often convenient to let the fund's transfer agent hold the shares.

Exchange privilege. Many large management companies sponsor a family of funds. They may have five or more funds, each dedicated to a different investment objective. Within certain limits, shareholders are free to move their money between the different funds in the family on a net asset value basis. Transfers can often be done by telephone; a minimal charge is common to cover paperwork. These exchanges are taxable events.

Preauthorized check plan. Many people lack the discipline to save or invest regularly. Those who recognize this trait in themselves can authorize a management company to charge their bank account for predetermined amounts on a regular basis. The amounts withdrawn are used to purchase new shares.

Systematic withdrawal plan. Every shareholder plans to convert shares into cash at some time. The investor who wants to receive a regular amount of cash each month or quarter can do so by arranging for such a plan. The fund sells enough shares on a periodic basis to meet the shareholder's cash requirement.

Checking privileges. Most money market mutual funds furnish shareholders with checks that can be drawn against the account, provided that the account balance is above a minimum amount (usually $1,000). A per-check minimum of $250 to $500 is common.

INVESTMENT FUNDS, LONG-TERM PLANNING, AND DOLLAR-COST AVERAGING

Perhaps more than anything else, the liquidity and conveniences inherent in mutual funds lend themselves best to financial planning activities. The most important of these is the gradual accumulation of capital assets.

Using the preauthorized check plan, investors can have fixed amounts regularly withdrawn from their checking accounts to purchase fund shares. Just as savers can have their banks channel a specific amount from their paychecks into savings accounts, so too can investors make regular, lump-sum fund share purchases on an "out of sight, out of mind" basis. Reinvestment of distributions enhances this strategy.

What distinguishes the mutual fund from the bank savings strategy is the fact that fund shares are purchased at different prices. The investor can even use a passive strategy known as dollar-cost averaging. Under dollar-cost averaging, the investor buys a fixed dollar's worth of a given security at regular intervals regardless of the security's price or the current market outlook. By using such a strategy, investors concede they cannot outsmart the market. The intent of dollar-cost averaging is to avoid the common practice of buying high and selling low. In fact, investors are forced to do the opposite. Why? They commit a fixed-dollar amount each month (or year) and buy shares at the current market price. When the price is high, they are buying relatively fewer shares; when the price is low, they are accumulating more shares. An example is presented in Table 2-7. Suppose we use the preauthorized check plan to channel $200 per month into a mutual fund. The price ranges from a low of $12 to a high of $19.

Note that when the share price is relatively low, such as in January, we purchased a larger number of shares than when the share prices were high, as in April. In this case, the share price ended in June at the same price it was in January ($12).

What would happen if the price merely ended up at the average price over the six-month period? The values in column (3) total $88, so the average price over six months is $14.67 ($88/6). Actually, we would still make money under this assumption because the average *cost* is less than this amount. Consider that we invested $1,200 and purchased 83.95 shares. This translates to an average cost of only $14.29:

TABLE 2–7 Dollar-Cost Averaging

(1) Month	(2) Investment	(3) Share Price	(4) Shares Purchased
January	$ 200	$12	16.66
February	200	14	14.28
March	200	16	12.50
April	200	19	10.52
May	200	15	13.33
June	200	12	16.66
Totals	$1,200	$88	83.95 total shares
		Average price $14.67	Average cost $14.29

$$\frac{\text{Investment}}{\text{Shares purchased}} = \frac{\$1{,}200}{83.95} = \$14.29$$

The average cost ($14.29) is less than the average price ($14.67) because we bought relatively more shares at the lower price levels, and they weighed more heavily in our calculations. Thus, under dollar-cost averaging, investors can come out ahead over a period of investing fixed amounts, even if the share price ends up less than the average price paid on each transaction.[4]

The only time investors lose money is if the eventual price falls below the average cost ($14.29) and they sell at that point. While dollar-cost averaging has its advantages, it is not without criticism. Clearly, if the share price continues to go down over a long period, it is hard to make a case for continued purchases. However, the long-term performance of most diversified mutual funds has been positive, and long-term investors may find this strategy useful in accumulating capital assets for retirement, children's education funds, or other purposes.

EVALUATING FUND PERFORMANCE

Throughout this chapter, we referred to mutual fund performance with the Morningstar data presented in Figure 2–2 and the American Association of Individual Investors (AAII) performance evaluation presented in Table 2–5. The AAII examines performance in up and down (bull and bear) markets.

In the case of the *Morningstar Mutual Fund Survey* in Figure 2–2, the T. Rowe Price European Stock Fund is compared against both the S&P 500 Index and the MSCI Europe Index (Morgan Stanley Capital International Europe Index). This can be seen on the left side on the middle of the page under "Performance 04-30-01." In the second box under performance, we see a comparison for 3 months, 6 months, 1 year, 3 years, 5 years, and 10 years against the S&P 500 and

4. This does not consider any sales charges or commissions, which could be important but can generally be avoided.

the MSCI Europe. Because this is an international European fund, it makes sense to use the MSCI Europe Index as its benchmark for comparison purposes, and we find that on a 3-year basis, the T. Rowe Price European Stock Fund outperforms the MSCI Europe by 1.49 percent but underperforms by −0.36 percent for the 10-year time period.

Performance should always be measured against an appropriate benchmark. One common benchmark is the average performance of all competing mutual funds in the same fund category. Another and more rigorous performance comparison is against an index that measures the performance of a stock portfolio that matches the fund's investment objectives. That is why we compared the T. Rowe Price European Stock Fund against the MSCI Europe Index.

One warning: Past performance in no way guarantees future performance. A fund that did well in the past may do poorly in the future and vice versa. Nevertheless, all things being equal, investors generally prefer funds that have a prior record of good performance. Investors do not know whether the funds can reproduce the performance, but at least the funds have indicated the capacity for good returns in the past. The same cannot be said for underperformers.

Lipper Mutual Fund Performance Averages

As you can see in Table 2-8, mutual fund performance can also be broken down by type of fund. You can observe that certain types of funds did better or worse and how their performance changed with differing periods for measurement. The Lipper Mutual Fund Performance Averages shown in Table 2-8 are published weekly in *Barron's.*

Computing Total Return on Your Investment

Assume you own a fund for a year and want to determine the total return on your investment. There are three potential sources of return:

Change in net asset value (NAV).

Dividends distributed.

Capital gains distributed.[5]

Assume the following:

	$14.05	Beginning NAV
	15.10	Ending NAV
	1.05	Change in NAV (+)
0.72	0.40	Dividends distributed
	0.32	Capital gains distributed
	$ 1.77	Total return

5. This represents net capital gains that the fund actually had as a result of selling securities. They are distributed to shareholders.

TABLE 2–8

LIPPER MUTUAL FUND PERFORMANCE AVERAGES

Weekly Summary Report: Thursday, 5/22/2003
Cumulative Performances With Dividends Reinvested

NTA Mil.$	No. Funds		12/31/02-05/22/03	05/15/03-05/22/03	04/24/03-05/22/03	02/20/03-05/22/03	05/23/02-05/22/03
General Equity Funds							
451,933.5	1,094	Large-Cap Core Funds	+ 5.90%	– 1.49%	+ 2.25%	+ 10.97%	– 15.16%
206,043.4	680	Large-Cap Growth Funds	+ 7.47	– 1.86	+ 1.70	+ 11.18	– 15.30
185,476.9	422	Large-Cap Value Funds	+ 5.74	– 0.80	+ 3.58	+ 11.89	– 15.31
143,285.0	550	Multi-Cap Core Funds	+ 6.63	– 1.10	+ 3.52	+ 11.50	– 13.89
193,474.1	424	Multi-Cap Growth Funds	+ 9.54	– 1.39	+ 3.18	+ 12.53	– 14.79
166,161.4	534	Multi-Cap Value Funds	+ 6.99	– 0.54	+ 4.64	+ 13.03	– 13.91
60,703.0	319	Mid-Cap Core Funds	+ 7.24	– 0.83	+ 4.98	+ 12.99	– 14.45
80,225.2	530	Mid-Cap Growth Funds	+ 8.50	– 1.20	+ 4.16	+ 12.83	– 16.39
54,855.5	216	Mid-Cap Value Funds	+ 7.75	– 0.57	+ 5.66	+ 14.10	– 12.50
69,227.7	479	Small-Cap Core Funds	+ 6.96	– 1.53	+ 5.30	+ 13.97	– 16.17
35,611.0	472	Small-Cap Growth Funds	+ 8.05	– 1.71	+ 5.50	+ 14.51	– 17.71
36,775.9	268	Small-Cap Value Funds	+ 5.79	– 1.55	+ 5.18	+ 13.30	– 14.87
5,204.1	78	Specialty Dvsfd Eq Funds	– 5.07	+ 1.07	– 0.66	– 4.96	– 0.73
224,636.6	177	S&P 500 Funds	+ 6.40	– 1.56	+ 2.36	+ 11.62	– 14.06
82,965.5	201	Equity Income Funds	+ 4.74	– 0.70	+ 3.35	+ 10.93	– 13.46
1,996,578.8	6,444	Gen. Equity Funds Avg.	+ 6.87	– 1.25	+ 3.64	+ 12.14	– 14.93
Other Equity Funds							
35,873.2	193	Health/Biotechnology	+ 12.51%	– 0.34%	+ 6.44%	+ 16.79%	– 6.47%
5,854.3	80	Natural Resources	+ 8.09	+ 1.22	+ 7.74	+ 10.74	– 10.64
35,898.0	354	Science & Technol.	+ 15.01	– 2.51	+ 5.25	+ 14.18	– 18.19
2,085.7	43	Telecommunication Funds	+ 9.83	+ 0.70	+ 7.72	+ 15.29	– 12.71
12,784.9	92	Utility Funds	+ 7.50	+ 1.60	+ 5.73	+ 14.58	– 12.08
12,362.1	116	Financial Services	+ 7.16	– 1.32	+ 2.55	+ 12.33	– 9.94
18,142.3	176	Real Estate Fund	+ 12.02	+ 1.83	+ 5.45	+ 14.36	+ 6.40
3,949.8	79	Specialty/Misc.	+ 5.74	– 0.92	+ 4.18	+ 10.26	– 12.91
3,652.2	43	Gold Oriented Funds	– 1.78	+ 3.45	+ 11.79	+ 0.09	– 6.73
98,272.8	343	Global Funds	+ 4.95	– 0.62	+ 4.31	+ 10.03	– 15.18
12,307.8	56	Global Small Cap Funds	+ 7.69	– 0.50	+ 6.33	+ 12.46	– 15.35
174,683.5	883	International Funds	+ 3.67	– 0.22	+ 5.08	+ 8.79	– 16.28
8,265.1	111	Int'l Small Cap Funds	+ 10.19	+ 0.32	+ 7.85	+ 12.82	– 11.10
13,624.5	170	European Region Fds	+ 6.49	+ 0.16	+ 5.68	+ 13.62	– 12.78
2,862.1	55	Pacific Region Funds	– 2.67	– 0.39	+ 5.65	– 1.38	– 21.46
1,861.0	55	Japanese Funds	– 4.75	– 1.24	+ 4.29	– 4.24	– 27.38
2,526.3	63	Pacific Ex Japan Funds	– 1.41	– 0.26	+ 6.15	– 0.56	– 20.24
580.1	22	China Region Funds	+ 7.13	+ 3.13	+ 11.54	+ 1.39	– 16.27
30,963.9	194	Emerging Markets Funds	+ 5.84	– 0.25	+ 5.32	+ 7.53	– 11.89
893.8	29	Latin American Funds	+ 16.00	– 0.88	+ 5.02	+ 24.19	– 11.67
350,493.1	2,024	World Equity Funds Avg.	+ 4.34	– 0.17	+ 5.45	+ 8.65	– 15.37
2,474,022.2	9,601	All Equity Funds Avg.	+ 6.87	– 0.93	+ 4.23	+ 11.63	– 14.44
Other Funds							
47,974.3	320	Flexible Portfolio	+ 5.36%	– 0.60%	+ 2.69%	+ 8.23%	– 7.14%
16,893.0	99	Global Flex Port.	+ 6.35	– 0.36	+ 4.04	+ 9.22	– 5.77
186,492.1	550	Balanced Funds	+ 5.57	– 0.55	+ 2.75	+ 8.35	– 5.58
3,952.4	45	Balanced Target	+ 3.04	+ 0.30	+ 2.60	+ 3.68	+ 4.56
9,573.4	66	Conv. Securities	+ 9.75	– 0.09	+ 3.61	+ 9.44	+ 1.47
73,319.7	148	Income Funds	+ 5.39	+ 0.10	+ 2.60	+ 6.95	– 0.57
22,521.0	199	World Income Funds	+ 11.45	+ 1.19	+ 4.89	+ 8.34	+ 20.75
770,680.5	2,485	Fixed Income Funds	+ 5.11	+ 0.40	+ 1.88	+ 3.94	+ 9.51
3,605,428.6	13,513	Long-Term Average	+ 6.51	– 0.61	+ 3.68	+ 9.84	– 8.67
N/A		Long-Term Median	+ 5.95	– 0.63	+ 3.31	+ 10.34	– 12.92
N/A		Funds with a % Change	+ 13,297	+ 13,074	+ 13,374	+ 13,413	+ 12,476
Securities Market Indexes							
Value		**U.S. Equities**					
5,273.51		NYSE Composite P	+ 5.47	– 0.73	+ 3.70	+ 11.47	– 14.35
1,064.06		S&P Industrials	+ 5.79	– 1.64	+ 2.34	+ 10.79	– 15.01
931.87		S&P 500 P	+ 5.92	– 1.56	+ 2.24	+ 11.32	– 15.06
8,594.02		Dow Jones Ind. Avg. P	+ 3.03	– 1.37	+ 1.82	+ 8.58	– 15.88
		International Equities					
8,051.66		Nikkei 225 Average P	– 6.15	– 0.88	+ 2.51	– 6.93	– 32.79
3,990.40		FT S-E 100 Index	+ 1.27	– 0.52	+ 2.34	+ 8.22	– 22.90
2,865.21		DAX Index	– 0.95	– 4.15	– 0.91	+ 10.57	– 41.28
Fund Management Companies							
Value							
4,592.62		Stock-price Index	+ 2.57%	– 1.13%	+ 2.16%	+ 12.06%	– 23.21%

P-Price only index. Calculated without reinvestment of dividends.

Source: Lipper

Source: Republished with permission of Dow Jones & Company, Inc., from *Barron's*, May 26, 2003, p. F19; permission conveyed through Copyright Clearance Center, Inc.

In this instance, there is a total return of $1.77. Based on a beginning NAV of $14.05, the return is 12.60 percent:

$$\frac{\text{Total return}}{\text{Beginning NAV}} = \frac{\$1.77}{\$14.05} = 12.60\%$$

As a further consideration, assume that instead of taking dividends and capital gains income in cash, you decide to automatically reinvest the proceeds to purchase new mutual fund shares. To compute the percentage return in this instance, you must compare the total value of your ending shares to the total value of your beginning shares. Assume you owned 100 shares to start, and you received $0.72 in dividends plus capital gains per share (see prior example). This would allow you to reinvest $72 (100 shares × $0.72 per share). Further assume you bought new shares at an average price of $14.40 per share. This would provide you with five new shares.

$$\frac{\text{Dividends and capital gains allocated to the account}}{\text{Average purchase price of new shares}} = \frac{\$72}{\$14.40} = 5 \text{ new shares}$$

In comparing the ending and beginning value of the investment based on the example in this section, we show the following:

$$\text{Total return} = \frac{\begin{pmatrix}\text{Number of} \\ \text{ending shares} \\ \times \text{ Ending price}\end{pmatrix} - \begin{pmatrix}\text{Number of} \\ \text{beginning shares} \\ \times \text{ Beginning price}\end{pmatrix}}{\text{Number of beginning shares} \times \text{Beginning price}} \qquad (2\text{-}2)$$

$$= \frac{(105 \times \$15.10) - (100 \times \$14.05)}{(100 \times \$14.05)}$$

$$= \frac{\$1{,}585.50 - \$1{,}405}{\$1{,}405}$$

$$= \frac{\$180.50}{\$1{,}405} = 12.85\%$$

In determining whether the returns computed in this section are adequate, you must compare your returns with the popular market averages and with the returns on other mutual funds. While the returns might be considered quite good for a conservative fund, such might not be the case for an aggressive, growth-oriented fund. You must also consider the amount of risk you are taking in the form of volatility of returns.

UNIT INVESTMENT TRUSTS (UITS)

Unit investment trusts (UITs) are investment companies organized for the purpose of purchasing a pool of securities—usually tax-exempt municipal bonds.

UITs issue units to investors, representing a proportionate interest in the assets of the trust. Investors also receive a proportionate share in the interest or dividends received by the trust.

According to the Investment Company Institute, by the end of 2000 there were a total of 10,071 unit trusts with a market value of $88.75 billion. While this is not a lot of money compared with mutual funds, unit trusts do meet a market niche for specialized investors. Of the 10,000 trusts, more than 8,000 were tax-free bond trusts. While equity trusts only accounted for slightly more than 1,500 trusts, they made up the lion's share of the value with $62 billion.

Unit investment trusts are passive investments. They normally purchase assets and hold them for the benefit of owners for a specified period.

To understand UITs better, consider the following hypothetical example. Nuveen, Inc.—a prominent firm in this field—announces the formation of the next in its series of tax-exempt unit trusts: Nuveen Series 200. Through advertising and selling agents, Nuveen will raise $4 million; investors will pay approximately $1,000 per unit. After deducting 2 to 3 percent for sales commissions, Nuveen will use the remaining cash to purchase large blocks of municipal securities from 10 to 20 different issuers. Once this diversified pool of bonds is acquired, Nuveen will play a passive role. It will collect and pass on to unit holders all interest payments received and all principal repayments resulting from maturing or recalled bonds. While UITs usually hold bonds until maturity, the trust custodian may sell off bonds whose future ability to pay interest and principal is altered by events.

Often, trusts are formed to purchase tax-exempt securities from issuers in specific, high-tax states, such as New York, Massachusetts, and Minnesota. Unit holders residing in these states expect to receive a stream of income exempt from federal, state, and local taxation.

Even unit investment trusts dedicated to tax-exempt bonds have different investment objectives. Some deal strictly in long-term, high-rated issues. Others seek higher yields by purchasing issues with low ratings.

Units of a trust are redeemable under terms set forth in the prospectus. In most cases, this means a unit holder can sell units back to the trust at their net asset value, which is the current market value of each trust unit.

A secondary market for unit trusts is evolving among broker-dealers. Investors seeking to acquire or sell units can sometimes find a better deal in this market. However, most investors in UITs do not intend to redeem early.

Investors in UITs benefit by professional selection of securities, by diversification, and by avoiding the housekeeping chores of collecting coupon payments. As a large buyer, a UIT can usually purchase securities at a better price than the individual who buys in small lots.

Essential Difference between a Unit Investment Trust and a Mutual Fund

There is an important difference between UITs and mutual funds. UITs are formed with the intention of keeping all the initially purchased assets until maturity. The investment strategy, as described above, is strictly passive. A UIT of $4 million with a 10-year life will draw interest over that time period, while only cashing in bonds as they mature and returning the funds to the investors. The UIT will cease to exist after 10 years. Because of the features just described, there is very little interest-rate risk associated with UITs. Since all bonds are intended to be held until maturity, the investor can be reasonably well assured of recovering his initial investment (plus interest). The fact that interest rates and bond prices are changing at any point in time during the life of the UIT makes little difference.[6]

A bond-oriented mutual fund has no such assurance of recovering the initial investment. First, mutual funds have no stipulated life. Second, the bonds in the portfolio are actively managed and frequently sold off before their maturity dates at large profits or losses. Thus, the purchaser of a bond-oriented mutual fund may experience large capital gains or losses as well as receiving interest income.

The message is that if preservation of capital is of paramount importance to the investor, the UIT may be a better investment than a mutual fund. Of course, if one thinks interest rates are going down and bond prices up, the bond-oriented mutual fund would be a better investment.

6. Of course, if the investor needs to redeem shares before the end of the life of the trust, there will be fluctuations in value.

Chapter 3

Organization of Security Markets

THE MARKET ENVIRONMENT

The financial markets have changed dramatically during the last decade, and they continue to change at a rapid pace. This period has been one of deregulation, new laws, mergers, global consolidation, online (Internet) brokerage, and electronic communication networks (ECNs). These structural changes have been accompanied by 24-hour trading, decimalization of stock quotes, and intense global competition.

The last part of the 1990s was punctuated with mergers and consolidations both global and domestic. The 1998 merger between Citicorp (the parent of CitiBank) and Travelers Insurance (including the Salomon Smith Barney division) created Citigroup. This merger caused a significant change in the way competitors thought about financial services. For the first time since the 1930s we had an institution that was able to sell insurance, underwrite securities, perform brokerage functions, and offer commercial banking under the same roof. This had been prohibited by the Glass Steagall Act, which was enacted after the "Great Crash" of 1929 to keep one bank from being both a commercial bank and an investment bank. Citigroup legally had a three-year window to divest the insurance assets and was allowed like JPMorgan to keep its investment banking business in a holding company. However, the combination forced Congress to think about U.S. banks' ability to compete globally, and in 1999 the U.S. Congress passed the Gramm-Leach-Bliley Act allowing financial institutions to offer full financial services. Shortly after, Chase and JPMorgan merged and other commercial banks gobbled up smaller investment banks and brokerage firms. American financial institutions were starting to look more like European universal banks and would be able to compete more effectively around the globe during the 21st century.

The roaring bull market from 1995 through 1999 gave investors returns of more than 20 percent each year. This was unfortunately followed by a major market decline that began in 2000 and continued into the winter of 2003.

On September 11, 2001, the World Trade Center in New York City and the Pentagon in Washington, D.C., were attacked by terrorists. In New York both towers and many surrounding buildings were destroyed, and thousands of lives were lost. This act of terror caused significant physical damage to the financial system, but less than one week later the New York Stock Exchange opened with a record trading volume of more than 2.3 billion shares. Despite the significant decline in stock prices at the time, many thought that the ability to generate this much volume was an indication of the strength of our financial system. Trading occurred from satellite backup facilities in Connecticut, midtown Manhattan, and Jersey City, New Jersey. The New York Board of Trade opened up in a backup facility in Brooklyn, trading pits and all. It is clear that the markets could not have accomplished this feat without the technological improvements that have characterized the last decade.

Unfortunately, the economy was already in a recession, and the devastation both psychological and physical was enough to eliminate any chance for the economy to generate positive economic growth in the third quarter. The stock market had already declined significantly from its highs, with the Dow Jones Industrial Average falling from a high of 11,436 on May 21, 2001, to 8,376 on September 20, 2001, for a drop of 26.76 percent. At the same time the over-the-counter Nasdaq Composite Index dropped from 3,913 on September 20, 2000, to 1,451 one year later—a one-year drop of almost 63 percent (not including the fall from its high of over 5,000 in March 2000). The nature of these stock market indexes was more fully explored in Chapter 2.

During this period of great grief and turmoil, many e-mail messages, websites, and talk shows were asking Americans to buy common stock when the market opened on September 17, 2001. This would be the patriotic thing to do and would help the market from suffering declines. Most market professionals argued against this logic by stating that markets were here to reflect reality and expectations and that there was nothing that could be done artificially to keep markets from falling or rising if expectations were negative or positive. In fact the markets did fall. Some industry groups such as the airlines and hotels/motels plunged between 25 and 50 percent in one day. Other companies in the defense industry rose more than 50 percent. In the eyes of the market participants, the markets did their job in reflecting the new reality facing Americans and the rest of the civilized world. Markets have gone up and down throughout history, including periods of prosperity, recession, war, and other catastrophic events. What are markets supposed to do?

MARKET FUNCTIONS

Many times people will call their stockbroker and ask, "How's the market?" What they are referring to is usually the market for common stocks as measured by the Dow Jones Industrial Average, the New York Stock Exchange Index, or some other measure of common stock performance. The stock market is not the only market. There are markets for each different kind of investment that can be made.

A market is simply a way of exchanging assets, usually cash, for something of value. It could be a used car, a government bond, gold, or diamonds. There doesn't have to be a central place where this transaction is consummated. As long as there can be communication between buyers and sellers, the exchange can occur. The offering party does not have to own what he sells but can be an agent acting for the owner in the transaction. For example, in the sale of real estate, the owner usually employs a real estate broker/agent who advertises and sells the property for a percentage commission. Not all markets have the same procedures, but certain trading characteristics are desirable for most markets.

Market Efficiency and Liquidity

In general, an efficient market occurs when prices respond quickly to new information, when each successive trade is made at a price close to the preceding price, and when the market can absorb large amounts of securities or assets without changing the price significantly. The more efficient the market, the faster prices react to new information; the closer in price is each successive trade; and the greater the amount of securities that can be sold without changing the price.

For markets to be efficient in this context, they must be liquid. Liquidity is a measure of the speed with which an asset can be converted into cash at its fair market value. Liquid markets exist when continuous trading occurs, and as the number of participants in the market becomes larger, price continuity increases along with liquidity. Transaction costs also affect liquidity. The lower the cost of buying and selling, the more likely it is that people will be able to enter the market.

Competition and Allocation of Capital

An investor must realize that all markets compete for funds: stocks against bonds, mutual funds against real estate, government securities against corporate securities, and so on. The competitive comparisons are almost endless. Because markets set prices on assets, investors are able to compare the prices against their perceived risk and expected return and thereby choose assets that enable them to achieve their desired risk-return trade-offs. If the markets are efficient, prices adjust rapidly to new information, and this adjustment changes the expected rate of return and allows the investor to alter investment strategy. Without efficient and liquid markets, the investor would be unable to do this. This allocation of capital occurs on both secondary and primary markets.

Secondary Markets

Secondary markets are markets for existing assets that are currently traded between investors. These markets create prices and allow for liquidity. If secondary markets did not exist, investors would have no place to sell their assets. Without liquidity, many people would not invest at all. Would you like to own $10,000 of

Microsoft common stock but be unable to convert it into cash if needed? If there were no secondary markets, investors would expect a higher return to compensate for the increased risk of illiquidity and the inability to adjust their portfolios to new information.

Primary Markets

Primary markets are distinguished by the flow of funds between the market participants. Instead of trading between investors as in the secondary markets, participants in the primary market buy their assets directly from the source of the asset. A common example would be a new issue of corporate bonds sold by AT&T. You would buy the bonds through a brokerage firm acting as an agent for AT&T's investment bankers. Your dollars would flow to AT&T rather than to another investor. The same would be true of buying a piece of art directly from the artist rather than from an art gallery.

Primary markets allow corporations, government units, and others to raise needed funds for expansion of their capital base. Once the assets or securities are sold in the primary market, they begin trading in the secondary market. Price competition in the secondary markets between different risk-return classes enables the primary markets to price new issues at fair prices to reflect existing risk-return relationships. So far, our discussion of markets has been quite general but applicable to most free markets. In the following sections, we will deal with the organization and structure of specific markets.

ORGANIZATION OF THE PRIMARY MARKETS: THE INVESTMENT BANKER

The most active participant in the primary market is the investment banker. Since corporations, states, and local governments do not sell new securities daily, monthly, or even annually, they usually rely on the expertise of the investment banker when selling securities.

Underwriting Function

The investment banker acts as a middleman in the process of raising funds and, in most cases, takes a risk by underwriting an issue of securities. Underwriting refers to the guarantee the investment banking firm gives the selling firm to purchase its securities at a fixed price, thereby eliminating the risk of not selling the whole issue of securities and having less cash than desired. The investment banker may also sell the issue on a best-efforts basis where the issuing firm assumes the risk and simply takes back any securities not sold after a fixed period. A very limited number of securities are sold directly by the corporation to the public. Of the three methods of distribution, underwriting is far and away the most widely used.

With underwriting, once the security is sold, the investment banker will usually make a market in the security, which means active buying and selling to ensure a continuously liquid market and wider distribution. In the case of best efforts and for direct offerings by the issuer, which are even smaller than best efforts, the firm assumes the risk of not raising enough capital and has no guarantees that a continuous market will be made in the company's securities.

Corporations may also choose to raise capital through private placements rather than through a public offering. With a private placement, the company may sell its own securities to a financial institution such as an insurance company, a pension fund, or a mutual fund, or it can engage an investment banker to find an institution willing to buy a large block of stock or bonds. Most private placements involve bonds (debt issues) instead of common stock.

Table 3-1 presents a historical picture of private and public bond offerings. Beginning in the 1980s, the economic recovery and falling interest rates stimulated a huge increase in the volume of bonds issued. Between 1980 and 1985, new debt issues tripled and then doubled again in one year from 1985 to 1986 as companies overdosed on debt to finance mergers, acquisitions, leveraged buyouts, and stock repurchases. From 1986 through 1990, new debt issues remained in a narrow band, but falling interest rates in 1993 again caused an increased period of bond financing and a peak in debt funds raised. During the 1990s publicly offered

TABLE 3–1 Gross Proceeds of Corporate Bonds Publicly Offered and Privately Placed in the United States

		Publicly Offered		Privately Placed	
Year	Total Issues	Amount	Percentage of Total	Amount	Percentage of Total
1970	30,315	25,384	83.73	4,931	16.27
1975	42,755	32,583	76.21	10,172	23.79
1980	53,206	41,587	78.16	11,619	21.84
1985	165,754	119,559	72.13	46,195	27.87
1986	312,697	231,936	74.17	80,761	25.83
1987	301,349	209,279	69.45	92,070	30.55
1988	329,919	202,215	61.29	127,704	38.71
1989	298,813	181,393	60.70	117,420	39.30
1990	276,259	189,271	68.51	86,988	31.49
1991	389,822	286,930	73.61	102,892	26.39
1992	471,502	378,058	80.18	93,444	19.82
1993	608,255	487,029	80.07	121,226	19.93
1994	441,287	365,222	82.76	76,065	17.24
1995	496,296	408,804	82.37	87,492	17.63
1996	469,172	386,280	82.33	82,892	17.67
1997	566,766	467,130	82.42	99,636	17.58
1998	611,290	489,390	80.06	121,900	19.94
1999	686,320	551,284	80.32	135,036	19.68
2000	767,805	623,762	81.24	144,043	18.76

bonds approximated 80 percent of the funds raised with private placements accounting for about 20 percent. Table 3-1 demonstrates that publicly offered bonds issued through underwriters as opposed to privately placed issues are by far the most popular method of raising debt capital.

Distribution

In a public offering, the distribution process is extremely important, and on some large issues, an investment banker does not undertake this alone. Investment banking firms will share the risk and the burden of distribution by forming a group called a syndicate. The larger the offering in dollar terms, the more participants there generally are in the syndicate. For example, the tombstone advertisement in Figure 3-1 for the Sprint Corporation's $3.697 billion combined issue of PCS common stock (cell phone division) and Sprint Capital Corporation Equity Units illustrates the participation of investment banks in the syndicate and the globalization of the investment banking community.

JPMorgan was the lead-managing underwriter and was joined by Merrill Lynch and UBS Warburg as major partners in the underwriting syndicate. Several foreign banks were part of the international syndicate. UBS Warburg and Credit Suisse First Boston are Swiss-owned investment banks, while ABN AMRO Rothschild LLC is a Dutch investment bank. These three international banks are both commercial banks and investment banks, and for years they have had the flexibility to compete against U.S. commercial banks and investment banks on unequal footing. As discussed earlier, the U.S. Congress passed the Gramm-Leach-Bliley Act in 1999, repealing the Glass Steagall Act, which prohibited banks from offering both investment banking services and commercial banking services. Now U.S. banks can offer commercial and investment banking services as well as insurance and brokerage.

Firms are listed in the tombstone advertisement from the lead banker on the upper left, JPMorgan in this case, to the smallest banker in the bottom right. The firms at the top of the advertisement have agreed to underwrite the largest number of shares and the firms on the bottom have taken the smallest number of shares. The actual number of shares allocated to each investment banker is listed in the prospectus filed with the Securities and Exchange Commission (SEC). It should be noted that the investment bankers make a commitment to purchase (at a discount from the public price) and sell their allotted shares. If the PCS common stock price falls below the intended offering price of $24.50 while the shares are still being sold to the public, the investment bankers in the syndicate will not make their original estimated profit on the issue. If the stock price drops too much below $24.50, perhaps to $23.00, the investment bankers could lose money on the offering.

For most original offerings, the investment banker is extremely important as a link between the original issuer and the security markets. By taking much of the risk, the investment banker enables corporations and others to find needed capital and also allows investors an opportunity to participate in the ownership of securities through purchase in the secondary market. The Sprint Corporation

FIGURE 3–1 Tombstone Advertisement

These announcements are neither an offer to sell nor a solicitation of an offer to buy any of these Securities. The offer is made only by the Prospectuses and the related Prospectus Supplements, which may be obtained in any State from only such of the undersigned as may legally offer these Securities in compliance with the securities laws of such State.

$3,697,250,000

Sprint Corporation

80,500,000 Shares

PCS Common Stock, Series 1

Price $24.50 Per Share

Joint Book-Running Managers

JPMorgan **Merrill Lynch & Co.** **UBS Warburg**

ABN AMRO Rothschild LLC **Banc of America Securities LLC**

Credit Suisse First Boston **Lehman Brothers**

Dain Rauscher Wessels **First Union Securities, Inc.** **Robertson Stephens** **The Williams Capital Group, L.P.**

Sprint Corporation

Sprint Capital Corporation

69,000,000 Equity Units

Price $25.00 Per Unit

Joint Book-Running Managers

JPMorgan **Merrill Lynch & Co.** **UBS Warburg**

ABN AMRO Rothschild LLC **Banc of America Securities LLC**

Credit Suisse First Boston **Lehman Brothers**

August 10, 2001

lists 80.5 million shares for its PCS cell phone division and 69 million shares for its Sprint Capital Corporation division. The total raised by the sale of the common stock and equity units was $3.7 billion. The offering included more than 50 million shares of Sprint PCS held by Deutsche Telekom. After the issue was completed, Sprint was expected to keep about $2 billion.

The demand for the offering was strong for a stock market that was certainly in a bear market by most measures (August 2001). Sprint had originally intended to offer 70 million shares but had given the underwriters an additional 10.5 million shares as an overallotment option for the common stock. The bankers exercised all these extra shares, and the total soared to 80.5 million shares.

The passage of the Gramm-Leach-Bliley Act is expected to have a significant effect on the structure of the investment and commercial banking industries. One continuing trend of the act will be the increased willingness of large financial institutions to take more risk. To consider that in our Sprint example, only 11 investment banking firms were able to absorb $3.7 billion of risk is an indication of the trend. Ten years ago the number of bankers would have been more than triple that number, and the offering size would have been no more than $1 billion.

More mergers—creating firms such as Citigroup with its Travelers Insurance Division and its Salomon Smith Barney brokerage and investment banking business—will occur. Chase Bank and JPMorgan merged as well as many other commercial banks and investment banks. The insurance industry is in the process of moving from mutual companies owned by their policyholders to stock companies owned by their stockholders. By moving to a stock company, the insurance companies will have the ability to merge with other financial companies through an exchange of stock. Expect continued mergers between insurance companies and other financial service companies over the next decade.

Another change that has affected the distribution and underwriting process is the increased use of shelf registration under SEC Rule 415. A shelf registration allows issuing firms to register their securities with the SEC and then sell them at will as funds are needed in the future. Over time, this allows bankers to buy portions of the shelf issue and immediately resell the securities to institutional clients without forming the normal syndicate or tying up capital for several weeks. Shelf registration is more popular with bond offerings than common stock offerings, where the traditional syndicated offering tends to dominate.

Investment Banking Competition

Table 3-2 shows the top 10 lead underwriters of U.S. debt and equity offerings for the year 2001 from January 1 to September 14, three days after the World Trade Center terrorist act. The list of bankers remains relatively the same from year to year with some bankers moving up or down the list due to mergers and the fund-raising activities of their clients. The total market share of the top 10 bankers has remained fairly stable over time, creeping up from 81 percent of the total funds in 1995 to 83.4 percent during this 2001 period. With 10 bankers accounting for 83.4 percent of the total, hundreds of smaller bankers are left to fight for the other 16.6 percent.

TABLE 3–2 Top 10 Underwriters of U.S. Debt and Equity by Proceeds January 1, 2001, through September 14, 2001

Manager	Amount (in billions)	Market Share	Number of Deals
Merrill Lynch & Co.	$ 279.7	14.2%	1,446
Citigroup/Salomon Smith Barney	256.3	13.0	969
Credit Suisse First Boston	199.1	10.1	1,146
JPMorgan	168.2	8.5	788
Lehman Brothers	157.7	8.0	730
Morgan Stanley	143.0	7.2	595
Goldman Sachs & Co.	138.4	7.0	600
Banc of America Securities LLC	117.9	6.0	707
UBS Warburg	99.5	5.0	416
Deutsche Bank AG	87.5	4.4	408
	$1,647.3	83.4	7,805
Industry totals	$1,977.2	100.0%	11,248

Source: Republished with permission of Dow Jones & Company, Inc., from Dow Jones News Retrieval, September 17, 2001; permission conveyed through Copyright Clearance Center, Inc.

While investment bankers want to be on the top 10 underwriters list, they are more concerned about underwriting fees than about the number of issues in which they were the lead underwriter. Table 3-3 shows a slightly different ranking when looking at fees versus gross proceeds from underwriting. The reason for this difference is that some underwriting business, such as the sale of common stock, has higher fees than the sale of debt. Investment banks specializing in common stock or other high margin products can make more money with a smaller number of offerings and with lower proceeds. This is demonstrated by Goldman Sachs ranked seventh in Table 3-2 but third in Table 3-3. The same could be said for Merrill Lynch, ranked first in Table 3-2 but fourth in Table 3-3. Merrill Lynch dominates the amount of proceeds as lead underwriter, but they do a lot of lower risk business, thus reaping smaller underwriting fees.

Bringing private companies public for the first time is called an initial public offering (IPO), and distribution costs to the selling company are much higher than offerings of additional stock by companies that are already public. Average fees from IPOs are usually between 1.5 and 2.0 percent higher than the fees for secondary offerings of publicly traded stock. The Sprint Corporation offering in Figure 3-1 is called a secondary offering because the shares were already listed on the New York Stock Exchange. The fees for the Sprint offering were lower than if the offering had been an IPO.

Underwriting competition is like a decathlon; there are many events for each contestant. Table 3-4 provides a list of the categories in which investment bankers compete. While Merrill Lynch is the dominant player in many of the segments, firms such as Goldman Sachs dominate the common equity category, and DLJ (now

TABLE 3–3 Top 10 Managers of U.S. Debt and Equity Disclosed Fees from New Issue Underwriting January 1, 2001, through September 14, 2001

Manager	Amount (in billions)	Market Share	Number of Deals
Citigroup/Salomon Smith Barney	$1.301	17.1%	506
Morgan Stanley	1.155	15.2	289
Goldman Sachs & Co.	1.040	13.7	229
Merrill Lynch & Co.	0.961	12.7	427
Credit Suisse First Boston	0.737	9.7	332
Lehman Brothers	0.527	7.0	269
JPMorgan	0.482	6.4	399
Banc of America Securities LLC	0.370	4.9	200
UBS Warburg	0.256	3.4	155
Deutsche Bank AG	0.204	2.7	176
	$7.033	92.8%	2,982
Industry totals	$7.593	100.0%	3,296

Source: Republished with permission of Dow Jones & Company, Inc., from Dow Jones News Retrieval, September 17, 2001; permission conveyed through Copyright Clearance Center, Inc.

TABLE 3–4 Underwriting Market Segments

U.S. domestic
Straight debt
Convertible debt
Junk bonds
Investment grade debt
Mortgage debt
Collateralized securities
Preferred stock
Common stock
IPOs
International debt
U.S. issuers
Municipal new issues

part of Bear Stearns) dominates the junk bond market. Each firm competes on its expertise.

The worldwide market is becoming more important to all investment bankers, and Table 3-5 looks at the top 25 global underwriters of debt and equity. As in Table 3-2, the top 10 have the lion's share of the market, but there are many well-

TABLE 3–5 Top 25 Underwriters of Global Debt and Equity by Proceeds January 1, 2001, through September 14, 2001

Manager	Amount (in billions)	Market Share	Number of Deals
Merrill Lynch & Co.	$ 331.9	12.0%	1,494
Citigroup/Salomon Smith Barney	309.6	11.2	985
Credit Suisse First Boston	240.4	8.7	957
JPMorgan	215.6	7.8	775
Morgan Stanley	200.7	7.3	634
Lehman Brothers	181.1	6.6	642
Goldman Sachs & Co.	176.9	6.4	573
UBS Warburg	156.4	5.7	634
Deutsche Bank AG	149.2	5.4	528
Banc of America Securities LLC	120.1	4.3	548
Bear Stearns & Co. Inc.	79.2	2.9	303
ABN AMRO	64.4	2.3	571
Barclays Capital	52.6	1.9	213
Dresdner Kleinwort Wasserstein	40.6	1.5	187
HSBC Holdings PLC	34.6	1.3	227
Royal Bank of Scotland Group	31.3	1.1	109
Nomura Securities	21.9	0.8	135
Société Générale	20.0	0.7	65
Countrywide Securities Corp.	16.4	0.6	306
BANK ONE Corp.	15.7	0.6	89
Commerzbank AG	14.7	0.5	86
First Union Corp.	14.1	0.5	99
HypoVereinsbank AG	13.6	0.5	66
Westdeutsche Landesbank Giro	12.3	0.4	68
	$2,513.1	91.0%	10,294
Industry totals	$2,764.7	100.0%	11,930

Source: Republished with permission of Dow Jones & Company, Inc., from Dow Jones News Retrieval, September 17, 2001; permission conveyed through Copyright Clearance Center, Inc.

known names in the bottom 15 companies. Throughout the table there are four German underwriters, three Swiss, two British, one Dutch, one Japanese, one French, and one Scottish investment banking underwriter. The top 10 underwriters account for more than 75 percent of the total proceeds. As global combinations continue, the bottom 15 underwriters will either be forced to merge with smaller banks to enhance economies of scale and increase their competitive power or be absorbed by the bigger banks looking for an ever-larger market share. The European markets are more fragmented than the U.S. markets, and a competitive environment with less regulation is emerging in countries such as Germany and France.

ORGANIZATION OF THE SECONDARY MARKETS

Once the investment banker or the Federal Reserve (for U.S. government securities) has sold a new issue of securities, it begins trading in secondary markets that provide liquidity, efficiency, continuity, and competition. The organized exchanges fulfill this need in a central location where trading occurs between buyers and sellers. The over-the-counter markets also provide markets for exchange but not in a central location. A new type of market that has developed in the last several years is the ECN or electronic communication network. In the next sections we will present an overview of each market.

Organized Exchanges

Organized exchanges are either national or regional, but both are organized in a similar fashion. Exchanges have a central trading location where securities are bought and sold in an auction market by brokers acting as agents for the buyer and seller. Stocks usually trade at various trading posts on the floor of the exchange. Brokers are registered members of the exchanges, and their number is fixed by each exchange. The national exchanges are the New York Stock Exchange (NYSE) and the American Stock Exchange (AMEX). Both these exchanges are governed by a board of directors consisting of one-half exchange members and one-half public members.

The regional exchanges began their existence trading securities of local firms. As the firms grew, they became listed on the national exchanges, but they also continued to trade on the regionals. Many cities, such as Chicago, Cincinnati, Philadelphia, and Boston, have regional exchanges. Today, most of the trading on these exchanges is done in nationally known companies. Trading in the same companies is common between the NYSE and such regionals as the Chicago Stock Exchange, the Pacific Coast Exchange in San Francisco and Los Angeles, and the smaller regionals. More than 90 percent of the companies traded on the Chicago and Pacific Coast exchanges are also listed on the NYSE. This is referred to as dual trading.

October 20, 1987, the day after the crash of '87, was the busiest day in the history of the New York Stock Exchange until October 28, 1997, the day after the next crash. On October 27, 1997, the stock market moved down significantly and ranked as one of the 10 worst days in market history. What did make history however, was the 1.2 billion shares traded on the New York Stock Exchange the next day. This compares to 685 million shares on October 27, 1987. Perhaps the greatest triumph, however, was the record number of shares traded on the first day the New York Stock Exchange opened after being closed for almost one week after the attacks on the World Trade Center. The 2.368 billion shares set a record for the NYSE. The other markets (such as Chicago, Nasdaq, and Boston) also showed significant increases in volume from the previous record days. This data can be examined in Table 3-6.

TABLE 3–6 Data on Trading Volume (Breakdown of Trading in NYSE Stocks)

By Market	Tuesday 27-Oct-87	Tuesday 28-Oct-97	Monday 17-Sep-01
New York	685,496,330	1,195,836,620	2,368,326,910
Chicago	28,857,300	40,187,200	95,613,840
CBOE	56,600	74,000	6,300
Pacific	20,331,100	20,001,000	8,512,700
NASD/Nasdaq Intermarket	59,636,200	85,585,150	157,846,400
Philadelphia	9,009,600	10,619,700	14,530,700
Boston	10,793,100	13,995,100	43,359,000
Cincinnati	9,605,000	8,432,100	10,205,400
Composite	823,785,230	1,374,731,570	2,698,401,250

Source: Various issues of *The Wall Street Journal.*

Consolidated Tape

Although dual listing and trading have existed for some time, it was not until June 16, 1975, that a consolidated ticker tape was instituted. This allows brokers on the floor of one exchange to see prices of transactions on other exchanges in the dually listed stocks. Any time a transaction is made on a regional exchange or over-the-counter in a security listed on the NYSE, this transaction and any made on the floor of the NYSE are displayed on the composite tape. The composite price data keep markets more efficient and prices more competitive between exchanges at all times.

The NYSE and AMEX are both national exchanges and for years did not allow dual listing of companies traded on their exchanges, but as of August 1976, securities were able to be dually listed between these exchanges. There doesn't seem to be any advantage to this since both are located in New York City, and traditionally, shares that trade on one exchange are not traded on the other.

Table 3-7 displays the number of trades (not number of shares) on all markets participating in the consolidated tape. Trading volume has steadily increased from 1988 to 2000, doubling almost every four years. Market share has been relatively stable between the major players with the New York Stock Exchange increasing its market share dramatically in 2001 and 2002.

Listing Requirements for Firms

Securities can be traded on an exchange only if they have met the listing requirements of the exchange and have been approved by the board of governors of that exchange. All exchanges have minimum requirements that must be met before trading can occur in a company's common stock. Since the NYSE is the biggest exchange and generates the most dollar volume in large, well-known companies, its listing requirements are the most restrictive.

TABLE 3–7 Consolidated Tape Trades by Market, by Year

	Consolidated Tape Trades by Market								
	NYSE*	PSE	CHX**	PHLX	BSE	CSE	NASD***	CBOE	Total
2002	544,229,948	1,352,780	15,559,045	2,070,170	13,653,725	2,713,460	39,395,436	86	618,974,650
2001	338,097,835	1,834,977	14,664,576	2,538,291	9,419,755	5,003,102	28,053,473	658	399,612,667
2000	220,739,392	6,910,943	16,825,364	3,214,078	9,091,805	7,324,681	31,455,042	444	295,561,749
1999	169,405,684	8,279,262	13,758,573	2,692,976	7,323,563	4,437,849	26,994,867	629	232,893,403
1998	135,897,193	6,604,518	10,055,265	2,426,065	4,942,783	3,322,434	19,255,326	1,641	182,505,225
1997	102,601,803	5,712,875	6,375,353	2,392,148	2,850,194	3,443,128	14,463,766	2,388	137,841,655
1996	75,200,205	4,816,909	4,403,600	2,053,439	1,847,777	3,370,843	11,027,891	512	102,721,176
1995	58,630,094	4,443,064	4,281,216	1,784,669	2,096,402	3,263,961	8,994,455	0	83,493,861
1994	49,121,044	3,549,380	3,890,119	1,693,062	1,640,202	2,167,923	6,466,497	0	68,528,227
1993	46,476,295	3,806,226	4,050,348	1,851,256	1,687,649	1,704,590	6,351,196	0	65,929,861
1992	30,557,805	3,541,541	3,909,578	1,554,026	1,485,169	867,926	4,957,152	0	46,886,467
1991	27,167,350	3,274,499	3,240,894	1,147,522	1,361,572	298,665	3,847,067	0	40,349,111
1990	19,148,610	2,355,273	2,810,029	875,100	1,090,871	181,470	2,468,490	0	28,939,640
1989	19,727,062	2,378,200	2,970,627	965,448	900,529	125,215	1,419,914	0	28,494,789

*Data after 1988 include rights and warrants.

**MSE changed its name to CHX on July 8, 1993.

***INST totals included in NASD after March 1, 1993.

	Distribution of Consolidated Tape Trades, 1989–2002								
Year	NYSE*	PSE	CHX**	PHLX	BSE	CSE	NASD***	CBOE	Total
2002	87.9%	0.2%	2.5%	0.3%	2.2%	0.4%	6.4%	0.0%	100.00%
2001	84.6	0.5	3.7	0.6	2.4	1.3	7.0	0.0	100.00
2000	74.7	2.3	5.7	1.1	3.1	2.5	10.6	0.00	100.00
1999	72.7	3.6	5.9	1.2	3.1	1.9	11.6	0.00	100.00
1998	74.5	3.6	5.5	1.3	2.7	1.8	10.6	0.00	100.00
1997	74.4	4.1	4.6	1.7	2.1	2.5	10.5	0.00	100.00
1996	73.2	4.7	4.3	2.0	1.8	3.3	10.7	0.00	100.00
1995	70.2	5.3	5.1	2.1	2.5	3.9	10.8	0.00	100.00
1994	71.7	5.2	5.7	2.5	2.4	3.2	9.4	0.00	100.00
1993	70.5	5.8	6.1	2.8	2.6	2.6	9.6	0.00	100.00
1992	65.2	7.6	8.3	3.3	3.2	1.9	10.6	0.00	100.00
1991	67.3	8.1	8.0	2.8	3.4	0.7	9.6	0.00	100.00
1990	66.2	8.1	9.7	3.0	3.8	0.6	8.6	0.00	100.00
1989	69.2	8.4	10.4	3.4	3.2	0.4	5.0	0.00	100.00

*Data after 1988 include rights and warrants.

**MSE changed its name to CHX on July 8, 1993.

***INST totals included in NASD after March 1, 1993.

Participating markets: NYSE, New York; PSE, Pacific; CHX, Chicago; PHLX, Philadelphia; BSE, Boston; CSE, Cincinnati; NASD, National Association of Securities Dealers; CBOE, Chicago Board Options Exchange; INST, Instinet.

Source: NYSE Website, 2003. Reprinted by permission. This series includes every transaction in NYSE-listed issues as reported to the Consolidated Tape.

Initial Listing Although each case is decided on its own merits, there are minimum requirements that are specified by the exchanges. These requirements set minimums for the net income of the firm, the market value of publicly held shares, the number of shares publicly held, and the number of stockholders owning at least a round lot of 100 shares. Other exchanges such as the Chicago Stock Exchange have similar requirements, but the amounts are smaller.

Corporations desiring to be listed on exchanges have decided that public availability of the stock on an exchange will benefit their shareholders by providing liquidity to owners or by allowing the company a more viable means for raising external capital for growth and expansion. The company must pay annual listing fees to the exchange and additional fees based on the number of shares traded each year.

Delisting The New York Stock Exchange also has the authority to remove (delist) a security from trading when the security fails to meet certain criteria. There is much latitude in these decisions, but generally, a company's security may be considered for delisting if there are fewer than 1,200 round-lot (100 shares) owners, 600,000 shares or fewer in public hands, and the total market value of the security is less than $5 million. A company that easily exceeded these standards on first being listed may fall below them during hard times.

Membership for Market Participants

We've talked about listing requirements for corporations on the exchange, but what about the investment houses or traders that service the listed firms or trade for their own account on the exchanges? These privileges are reserved for a select number of people. The NYSE has 1,366 members who own "seats," which may be leased or sold with the approval of the NYSE. Multiple seats are owned by many member firms such as Merrill Lynch, so the number of member organizations totals 1,192. In recent years, the price of NYSE seats ranged from a low of $35,000 in 1977 to a high of $2,650,000 in early 1999. Prices fluctuate with market trends, going up in bull markets and down in bear markets. The members owning these seats can be divided into five distinct categories, each with a specific job.

Commission Brokers The commission brokers represent commission houses, such as Merrill Lynch, that execute orders on the floor of the exchange for customers of that firm. Many of the larger retail brokerage houses have more than one commission broker on the floor of the exchange. If you call your account executive (stockbroker) and place an order to buy 100 shares of ExxonMobil, the account executive will send your order to the NYSE where it will be transmitted to one of the firm's commission brokers who will go to the appropriate trading post and execute the order.

Floor Brokers You can imagine that commission brokers could get very busy running from post to post on a heavy volume day. In times like these, they will rely on some help from floor brokers, who are registered to trade on the exchange but are not employees of a member firm. Instead, floor brokers own their own seat and charge a small fee for services.

Registered Traders The registered traders own their own seats and are not associated with a member firm (such as Merrill Lynch). They are registered to trade for their own accounts and do so with the objective of earning a profit. Because they are members, they don't have to pay commissions on these trades; but in so trading, they help to generate a continuous market and liquidity for the market in general. There is always the possibility that these traders could manipulate the market if they acted in mass, and for that reason, the exchanges have rules governing their behavior and limiting the number of registered traders at one specific trading post.

Odd-Lot Dealers Odd lots (less than 100 shares) are not traded on the main floor of the exchange, so if a customer wants to buy or sell 20 shares of AT&T, the order will end up being processed by an odd-lot dealer. Dealers own their own inventory of the particular security and buy and sell for their own accounts. If they accumulate 100 shares, they can sell them in the market, or if they need 20 shares, they can buy 100 in the market and hold the other 80 shares in inventory. A few very large brokerage firms, such as Merrill Lynch, make their own odd-lot market in actively traded securities, and it is expected that this trend will become common at other large commission houses. Odd-lot trading on other exchanges is usually handled by the specialist in the particular stock.

Specialists The specialists are a very important segment of the exchange and make up about one-fourth of total membership. Each stock traded has a specialist assigned to it, and most specialists are responsible for more than one stock. Specialists have two basic duties with regard to the stocks they supervise. First, they must handle any special orders that commission brokers or floor brokers might give. For example, a special order could limit the price someone is willing to pay for AOL-Time Warner stock to $45 per share for 100 shares. If the commission broker reaches the AOL trading post and AOL is selling at $46 per share, the broker will leave the order with the specialist to execute if and when the stock of AOL falls to $45 or less. The specialist puts these special limit orders in his "book" with the date and time entered so he can execute orders at the same price by the earliest time of receipt. A portion of the broker's commission is then paid to the specialist.

The second major function of specialists is to maintain continuous, liquid, and orderly markets in their assigned stocks. This is not a difficult function in actively traded securities, such as General Motors, Du Pont, and AT&T, but it becomes more difficult in those stocks where there are no large, active markets. For example, suppose you placed an order to buy 100 shares of Brush Engineering at the market price. If the commission broker reaches the Brush Engineering trading post and no seller is present, the broker can't wait for one to appear since he has other orders to execute. Fortunately, the broker can buy the shares from the specialist who acts as a dealer—in this case buying for and selling from his own inventory. To ensure ability to maintain continuous markets, the exchange requires a specialist to have $500,000 or enough capital to own 5,000 shares of the assigned stock, whichever is greater. At times, specialists are under tremendous pressure to make a market for securities. A classic case occurred when President Reagan was shot in the 1980s, and specialists stabilized the market by absorbing wave after wave of sell orders.

The New York Stock Exchange keeps statistics on specialist performance and their ability to maintain price continuity, quotation spreads, market depth, and price stabilization. These data are given in Table 3-8. Price continuity is measured by the size of the price variation in successive trades. Column 1 is the percentage of transactions with no change in price or a minimum change of ⅛ of a dollar. Column 2 presents the percentage of the quotes where the bid and asked prices were equal to or less than ¼ of a point. Market depth (Column 3) is displayed as a percentage of the time that 1,000 to 3,000 shares of volume failed to move the price of the stock more than ⅛ of a point. Finally, the NYSE expects specialists to stabilize the market by buying and selling from their own accounts against the prevailing trend. This is measured in Column 4 as the percentage of shares purchased below the last different price and the percentage of shares sold above the last different price.

While these statistics are not 100 percent, it would be quite unreasonable for us to expect specialists to maintain that kind of a record in all types of markets. However, some critics of the specialist system on the NYSE think these performance measures could be improved by having more than one specialist for each stock. Many market watchers believe competing dealers on the over-the-counter

TABLE 3–8 Market Quality and Specialists' Stabilization

	NYSE Market Quality and Specialists' Stabilization, 1990–2002			
	Price Continuity	Quotation Spreads	Market Depth*	Stabilization Rate
2002	98.9%	97.7%	87.4%	80.8%
2001	98.6	96.3	89.5	82.7
2000	97.2	92.4	91.7	81.1
1999	98.1	94.2	88.4	82.8
1998	97.4	92.2	85.3	82.7
1997	97.7	93.5	86.9	80.0
1996	98.2	93.6	90.0	75.0
1995	98.2	93.1	90.8	74.6
1994	97.4	90.8	88.6	76.3
1993	97.1	88.9	88.3	77.6
1992	96.4	86.4	87.1	78.3
1991	95.9	84.6	85.5	80.9
1990	95.8	84.5	84.4	83.1

*After 1988 based on 3,000 shares of volume—all other years on 1,000 shares of volume.

Source: NYSE Website, 2003. Reprinted by permission.

market provide more price stability and fluid markets than the NYSE specialist system.

Somewhat in response to these criticisms, the New York Stock Exchange created computer systems that help the specialists manage order inflows more efficiently. Super Dot (designated order transfer system) allows NYSE member firms to electronically transmit all market and limit orders directly to the specialist at the trading post or the member trading booth. This order routing system takes orders and communicates executions of the orders directly back to the member firm on the same electronic circuit.

As a part of Super Dot, specialists are informed through OARS (Opening Automated Report Service) of market orders received before the opening bell. This preopening knowledge allows specialists to know whether the supply and demand for a stock is in balance because OARS pairs the buy and sell orders. If a sell imbalance exists, the specialist knows before opening that the price will open lower than yesterday's closing price.

The NYSE reports that 98.5 percent of all market orders on Super Dot were received, processed, and reported back to the originator within two minutes. Another feature of Super Dot that greatly aids the specialist is the Electronic Book. This database covers stocks listed on the NYSE and keeps track of limit orders and market orders for the specialist. You can imagine the great improvement in recording, reporting, and error elimination over the old manual entry in the "specialist's book."

OTHER ORGANIZED EXCHANGES

The American Stock Exchange

The American Stock Exchange trades in smaller companies than the NYSE, and except for one dually listed company on the NYSE in 1983, the stocks traded on the AMEX are different from those on any other exchange. Because many of the small companies on the AMEX do not meet the liquidity needs of large institutional investors, the AMEX has been primarily a market for individual investors.

In an attempt to differentiate itself from the NYSE, the AMEX traded warrants in companies for many years before the NYSE allowed them. Even now, the AMEX has warrants listed for stocks trading on the NYSE. The AMEX also trades put and call options on approximately 200 stocks, with most of the underlying common stocks being listed on the NYSE. This market has been a stabilizing force for the AMEX.

To become more innovative and to attract more business, the American Stock Exchange announced plans in 1991 to trade options in foreign stock indexes. By 1997 the AMEX was trading put and call options on the indexes of the stock markets of Mexico, Hong Kong, and Japan. Additionally they also made markets in puts and calls for specific industry indexes such as computer technology, consumer companies, high-tech Internet companies, and pharmaceutical companies. After merging with Nasdaq in the late 1990s, it appears that a divorce is on the horizon.

The Chicago Board Options Exchange

Trading in call options started on the Chicago Board Options Exchange (CBOE) in April 1973 and proved very successful. The number of call options listed grew from 16 in 1973 to more than 500 in 2000. A call option gives the owner the right to buy 100 shares of the underlying common stock at a set price for a certain period. The CBOE standardized call options into three-month, six-month, and nine-month expiration periods on a rotating monthly series. Other sequences have since been developed. The CBOE and the AMEX currently have many options that are dually listed, and the competition between them is fierce. The two exchanges also trade put options (options to sell). A number of smaller regional exchanges also provide for option trading, and the New York Stock Exchange sold its option business to the CBOE in 1997.

A new wrinkle in the options game has been options on stock market indexes or industry groupings (called subindexes). The CBOE offers puts and calls on the Standard & Poor's 500 Index and the Dow Jones Industrial Average; the AMEX has options on the AMEX Market Value Index, and so on.

Futures Markets

Futures markets have traditionally been associated with commodities and, more recently, also with financial instruments. Purchasers of commodity futures own the right to buy a certain amount of the commodity at a set price for a specified period. When the time runs out (expires), the futures contract will be delivered unless sold before expiration. One major futures market is the Chicago Board of Trade, which trades corn, oats, soybeans, wheat, silver, plywood, and Treasury bond futures. There are also other important futures markets in Chicago, Kansas City, Minneapolis, New York, and other cities. These markets are very important as hedging markets and help set commodity prices. They are also known for their wide price swings and volatile speculative nature.

In recent years, trading volume has increased in foreign exchange futures such as the German mark, Japanese yen, and British pound as well as in Treasury bill and Treasury bond futures. One important product having a direct effect in the stock market is the development of futures contracts on stock market indexes. The Chicago Mercantile Exchange, Chicago Board of Trade, New York Futures Exchanges (a division of the NYSE), and the Kansas City Board of Trade have all developed contracts in separate market indexes such as the Standard & Poor's 500, the Dow Jones Industrial Average, and the Value Line Index. Market indexes will be presented in the following chapter.

OVER-THE-COUNTER MARKETS

Unlike the organized exchanges, the over-the-counter (OTC) markets have no central location where securities are traded. Being traded over-the-counter implies the trade takes place by telephone or electronic device and dealers stand ready to buy or sell specific securities for their own accounts. These dealers will buy at a bid price and sell at an asked price that reflects the competitive market conditions. By contrast, brokers on the organized exchanges merely act as agents who process orders. The National Association of Securities Dealers (NASD), a self-policing organization of dealers, requires at least two market makers (dealers) for each security, but often there are 5 or 10 or even 20 for government securities. As previously mentioned, the multiple-dealer function in the over-the-counter market is an attractive feature for many companies in comparison to the single specialist arrangement on the NYSE and other organized exchanges.

OTC markets exist for stocks, corporate bonds, mutual funds, federal government securities, state and local bonds, commercial paper, negotiable certificates of deposits, and various other securities. These securities make the OTC the largest of all markets in the United States in dollar terms.

In the OTC market, the difference between the bid and asked price is the spread; it represents the profit the dealer earns by making a market. For example, if XYZ common stock is bid 10 and asked 10.50, this simply means the dealer will buy at least 100 shares at $10 per share or will sell 100 shares at $10.50 per share. If prices are too low, more buyers than sellers will appear, and the dealer will run out of inventory unless he raises prices to attract more sellers and balances the supply and demand. If his price is at equilibrium, he will match an equal number of shares bought and sold, and for his market-making activities, he will earn 50 cents per share traded.

Nasdaq

Nasdaq stands for the National Association of Securities Dealers Automated Quotations system. This system is linked by a computer network and provides up-to-the-minute quotations on approximately 6,000 of the OTC stocks traded on the Nasdaq system. These Nasdaq stocks are divided between national market issues and small cap issues. Each is presented separately in *The Wall Street Journal* and other newspapers.[1]

As the name implies, the national market issues represent larger Nasdaq companies that must meet higher listing standards than the small cap market. The standards are not as high as those on the NYSE but cover most of the same areas: net tangible assets, net income, pretax income, public float (shares outstanding in the hands of the public), operating history, market value of the float, a minimum share price, the number of shareholders, and the number of market makers.

Because the listing requirements are lower than those of the NYSE, many small public companies begin trading on the Nasdaq and many decide to stay there even after they far exceed the requirements for the NYSE. Companies such as Intel, Microsoft, Oracle, and Sun Microsystems trade on the Nasdaq Stock Market; as the names may suggest, this market is popular with technology stocks.

1. Publicly traded firms that are not listed on organized exchanges or by the Nasdaq are normally not quoted in newspapers but may be shown on special pink sheets put out by investment houses.

Nasdaq is currently in the middle of several significant transformations. It is changing its structure from a fully owned subsidiary of NASD (National Association of Security Dealers) to a privately held company. By August 2001, the NASD's stake in Nasdaq had been reduced to less than 30 percent. Nasdaq intends to eventually become a publicly traded company when market conditions make sense. The Nasdaq Stock Market is also registering as a securities exchange under the federal securities laws, which is primarily a legal move. The actual operations of the market will stay the same.

Over the last decade, the Nasdaq Stock Market has taken its place in world equity markets based on its dollar volume of trading activity. The NYSE is first followed by Nasdaq, London, and then Tokyo. This is a dramatic change for a market that was in fifth place in 1990. The U.S. equity market for small-growth companies boomed in the 1990s, and this helped to increase Nasdaq's volume. Additionally, its multiple-dealer system, efficient computerized quotation systems, and enhanced reporting capability are other reasons for the increased competitive nature. To add to its worldwide status, Nasdaq has begun to create Nasdaq stock markets in foreign cities such as Hong Kong.

Debt Securities Traded Over-the-Counter

Debt securities also trade over-the-counter. Actually, government securities of the U.S. Treasury provide the largest dollar volume of transactions on the OTC and account for billions of dollars in trades each week. These securities are traded by government securities dealers who are often associated with a division of a large financial institution, such as a New York, Chicago, or West Coast money market bank or a large brokerage house such as Merrill Lynch. These dealers make markets in government securities, such as Treasury bills and Treasury bonds, or federal agency securities such as Federal National Mortgage Association issues.

Municipal bonds of state and local governments are traded by specialized municipal bond dealers who, in most cases, work for large commercial banks. Commercial paper, representing unsecured, short-term corporate debt, is traded directly by *finance* companies, but a large portion of commercial paper sold by *industrial* companies is handled by OTC dealers specializing in this market. Every security has its own set of dealers and its own distribution system. On markets where large dollar trades occur, the spread between the bid and asked price could be as little as 1⁄16 or 1⁄32 of $1 per $1,000 of securities.

ELECTRONIC COMMUNICATION NETWORKS

A new competitor on the block for the exchanges and Nasdaq are the electronic communication networks, or ECNs. These are electronic trading systems that automatically match buy and sell orders at specified prices. ECNs are also known as alternative trading systems (ATSs) and have been given SEC approval to be more fully integrated into the national market system by choosing to either act as a broker–dealer or as an exchange. An ECN's subscribers can include retail and institutional investors, market makers, and broker–dealers. If a subscriber wants to buy a stock through an ECN, but there are no sell orders to match the buy order, the order cannot be executed. The ECN can wait for a matching sell order to arrive, or if the order is received during normal trading hours, the order can be routed to another market for execution. Some ECNs will let their subscribers see their entire order books, and some will even make their order books available on the web. ECNs bid and asked prices are included in Nasdaq's quotation montage with the best bid and asked price being shown. This helps create more efficient and transparent market prices and demonstrates how Nasdaq's open architecture allows firms with different computer technologies to compete in the same market.

Links to Other Markets ECNs lower the cost of trading by creating better executions and more price transparency, and they are able to trade after the markets are closed in what is known as "after-hours trading." There are nine ECNs, with the four largest being Instinet (www.instinet.com) owned by Reuters, Archipelago (www.tradearca.com), REDIBook (www.redibook.com), and Island (www.isld.com). These four accounted for 85 percent of the ECN trading volume during the first half of 2001. For example, in terms of Nasdaq volume, as of June 2001, Island had 600 subscribers and executed almost one out of every six trades on Nasdaq, or 16.2 percent of Nasdaq's volume. The other five ECNs are Bloomberg Tradebook (www.bloomberg.com/products/trdbk.html), Brut/Strike (www.ebrut.com), NexTrade (www.nestrade.org), Attain (www.attain.com), and MarketXT (www.marketxt.com). These nine ECNs collectively accounted for approximately 23 percent of the 2000 Nasdaq volume but only 3 percent of the NYSE volume. The disparity between markets occurs because ECNs were not able to trade NYSE-listed stocks through the Intermarket Trading System (ITS) that links the NYSE to the NASD and regional exchanges. The ECNs are, however, linked to Nasdaq and can display their best orders for Nasdaq securities in the Nasdaq system. On August 8, 2000, Archipelago began trading 11 exchange-listed securities and quickly expanded the list. With the repeal of Rule 390, the New York Stock Exchange has given ECNs the right to make markets in all NYSE issues. (Rule 390 prohibited off-exchange trading of listed NYSE securities.) It is expected that each ECN will take advantage of this rule change.

Shortly after revoking Rule 390 the New York Stock Exchange announced plans to develop its own Internet-based electronic stock trading system. This is a defensive move to protect it from the expected loss of volume as more trading on the NYSE moves to ECNs. If the ECNs can capture the same amount of volume from the NYSE as they did from Nasdaq, the loss would definitely be felt. In an attempt to compete after hours, the NYSE will also use its electronic trading system to extend its trading hours into the evening during 2001.

After-Hours Trading Trading after the markets have closed is not something new. Both the New York Stock Exchange and the American Stock Exchange have the ability to trade after the 4:00 P.M. Eastern Standard Time close. The NYSE has two crossing sessions that allow trades to be made until 6:30, when the consolidated tape is turned off. Investors trading after the market closes subject themselves to the risk of price volatility and low liquidity. With the advent of ECNs, trading after hours has in fact increased liquidity, and because ECNs usually take orders at a set price to buy and sell, the order process takes some of the risk out of the business. At first ECNs traded several hundred thousand shares after hours, but by summer 2001, they were trading millions of shares after hours. Using consolidated tape data until 6:30 P.M. an SEC study found that the New York Stock Exchange accounts for most of the after-hours volume in NYSE stocks. However, in the top 10 stocks traded on the Nasdaq after hours, ECNs accounted for between 20 to 66 percent of share volume on the various days of the SEC study.

INSTITUTIONAL TRADING

Financial institutions, such as banks, pension funds, insurance companies, and investment companies (mutual funds), have always invested and traded in securities. However, the growth of these institutions and their participation in the capital markets has been rather stable for the past 20 years. In fact, if we look at the last column of Table 3-9 on institutional trading activity, we can see that block trades of 10,000 shares or more carried out by financial institutions has averaged close to 53 percent since 1984. The highest percentage was 57 percent in 1995, and the lower percentage was 44.4 percent in 2002. It doesn't show up in the table, but in 1965, block trades only accounted for 3.1 percent of total trades.

Over this same time, individual investors have been putting their money into the market through intermediaries such as mutual funds, pension funds, profit-sharing plans, and individual retirement accounts (IRAs). Individuals who directly invest in the stock market have gone up and down with consumer sentiment and market returns. In 1987 the market crash scared many individual investors out of the market, but they came back during the bull market of the 1990s. This increased participation by the individual investor was made easier by the rise of electronic trading on the Internet with prices as low as $5 per trade. Brokerage firms such as Charles Schwab, Fidelity Investments, E-Trade, Ameritrade, and others offered small investors low-cost trades. This was a great benefit. As is always the case, bear markets and recessions cause individuals to move to the sidelines. However, with the demographics of the baby boom generation reaching the high-income-savings years, it is expected that the individual investor will continue to have a significant place in our stock markets.

THE NATIONAL MARKET SYSTEM AND THE FUTURE

Since 1975 the future of the markets was dictated by government regulations, institutional investors, and technology. A national market system was mandated by Congress in the Securities Amendments Act of 1975. This was envisioned as a coordinated national system of security trading with no barriers between the various exchanges or the over-the-counter markets. One of the first links between these markets was the composite tape that reflects trades on all exchanges for listed

TABLE 3–9 NYSE Block Transactions (10,000 shares or more)

	Transactions		Shares	Percentage of
	Total	Daily Average	(thousands)	Reported Volume
1979	97,509	385	2,164,726	26.5%
1980	133,597	528	3,311,132	29.2
1981	145,564	575	3,771,442	31.8
1982	254,707	1,007	6,742,481	41.0
1983	363,415	1,436	9,842,080	45.6
1984	433,427	1,713	11,492,091	49.8
1985	539,039	2,139	14,222,272	51.7
1986	665,587	2,631	17,811,335	49.9
1987	920,679	3,639	24,497,241	51.2
1988	768,419	3,037	22,270,680	54.5
1989	872,811	3,464	21,316,132	51.1
1990	843,365	3,333	19,681,849	49.6
1991	981,077	3,878	22,474,383	49.6
1992	1,134,832	4,468	26,069,383	50.7
1993	1,477,859	5,841	35,959,117	53.7
1994	1,654,505	6,565	40,757,770	55.5
1995	1,963,889	7,793	49,736,912	57.0
1996	2,348,457	9,246	58,510,323	55.9
1997	2,831,321	11,191	67,832,129	50.9
1998	3,518,200	13,961	82,656,678	48.7
1999	4,195,721	16,650	102,293,458	50.2
2000	5,529,152	21,941	135,772,004	51.7
2001	5,892,022	23,758	148,056,277	48.1
2002	6,267,128	25,271	161,075,119	44.4

Source: NYSE Website, 2003. Reprinted by permission.

NYSE companies. This was in Table 3-7. The composite tape helps create competition between specialists in different markets, making markets in the same stock through dual trading on the regional markets.

The future becomes the past quickly and it is sometimes easier to go back in time and look forward. If we consider the changes in the use of computer technology and the rise of electronic trading systems through ECNs and Internet-based trading, we can see that the future has arrived. How the market will evolve over the next decade is always an interesting question that depends on many things, including regulation.

Our view is that the electronic markets will continue to make inroads on traditional markets such as the New York Stock Exchange. There will be more international companies seeking capital across their home country's borders, and this need for global capital will stimulate global markets to merge. There has already been talk of a merger between Nasdaq and the London market. As markets and exchanges such as Nasdaq and the NYSE have publicly traded stock, they could be purchased by other international exchanges unless, of course, the government does not allow cross-border mergers of exchanges.

Individual investors will trade online through the Internet not only on discount broker sites such as E-Trade and Ameritrade, but also on the site of mainline old retail brokers such as Merrill Lynch and Salomon Smith Barney. This is already happening, but the volume will increase. Technology will bring the costs of trading even lower, and market volumes will continue to rise. Global companies such as Sony, McDonalds, Coca-Cola, and Daimler-Chrysler will trade 24 hours a day on the world's exchanges. Most of what we predicted in previous editions of this text has already occurred; only time will tell if the trend will extend.

REGULATION OF THE SECURITY MARKETS

Organized securities markets are regulated by the Securities and Exchange Commission (SEC) and by the self-regulation of the exchanges. The OTC market is controlled by the National Association of Securities Dealers. Three major laws govern the sale and subsequent trading of securities. The Securities Act of 1933 pertains to new issues of securities, while the Securities Exchange Act of 1934 deals with trading in the securities markets. The Securities Acts Amendments of 1975 is the last major piece of legislation, and its main emphasis is on a national securities market. The primary purpose of these laws was to protect unwary investors from fraud and manipulation and to make the markets more competitive and efficient.

Securities Act of 1933

The Securities Act of 1933 was enacted after congressional investigations of the abuses present in the securities markets during the 1929 crash and again in 1931. The act's primary purpose was to provide full disclosure of all pertinent investment information whenever a corporation sold a new issue of securities. It is sometimes referred to as the "truth in securities" act. The Securities Act has several important features:

1. All offerings except government bonds and bank stocks that are to be sold in more than one state must be registered with the SEC.[2]
2. The registration statement must be filed 20 days in advance of the date of sale and include detailed corporate information. If the SEC finds the information misleading, incomplete, or inaccurate, it will delay the offering until the registration statement is corrected. The SEC in no way certifies that the

2. Actually, the SEC did not come into existence until 1934. The Federal Trade Commission had many of these responsibilities before the formation of the SEC.

security is fairly priced but only that the information seems to be factual and accurate. Under certain circumstances, the previously mentioned shelf registration is being used to modify the 20-day waiting period concept.

3. All new issues of securities must be accompanied by a *prospectus,* a detailed summary of the registration statement. Included in the prospectus is usually a list of directors and officers; their salaries, stock options, and shareholdings; financial reports certified by a certified public accountant (CPA); a list of the underwriters; the purpose and use for the funds to be provided from the sale of securities; and any other reasonable information that investors may need to know before they can wisely invest their money. A preliminary prospectus may be distributed to potential buyers before the offering date, but it will not contain the offering price or underwriting fees. It is called a red herring because stamped on the front in red letters are the words "Preliminary Prospectus."
4. Officers of the company and other experts preparing the prospectus or registration statement can be sued for penalties and recovery of realized losses if any information presented was fraudulent or factually wrong or if relevant information was omitted.

Securities Exchange Act of 1934

This act created the Securities and Exchange Commission to enforce the securities laws. It was empowered to regulate the securities markets and those companies listed on the exchanges. Specifically, the major points of the 1934 act are as follows:

1. Guidelines for insider trading were established. Insiders must hold securities for at least six months before they can sell them. This is to prevent them from taking quick advantage of information that could result in a short-term profit. All short-term profits were payable to the corporation. Insiders were generally thought to be officers, directors, major stockholders, employees, or relatives of key employees. In the last two decades, the SEC widened its interpretation to include anyone having information that was not public knowledge. This could include security analysts, loan officers, large institutional holders, and many others who had business dealings with the firm.
2. The Federal Reserve Board of Governors became responsible for setting margin requirements to determine how much credit one had available to buy securities.
3. Manipulation of securities by conspiracies between investors was prohibited.
4. The SEC was given control over the proxy procedures of corporations (a proxy is an absent stockholder vote).
5. In its regulation of companies traded on the markets, it required certain reports to be filed periodically. Corporations must file quarterly financial statements with the SEC, send annual reports to the stockholders, and file 10-K

reports with the SEC annually. The 10-K report has more financial data than the annual report and can be very useful to an investor or loan officer. Most companies will now send 10-K reports to stockholders on request. The SEC also has company filings available on the Internet under its retrieval system called EDGAR.

6. The act required all securities exchanges to register with the SEC. In this capacity, the SEC supervises and regulates many pertinent organizational aspects of exchanges such as listing and trading mechanics.

The Securities Acts Amendments of 1975

The major focus of the Securities Acts Amendments of 1975 was to direct the SEC to supervise the development of a national securities market. No exact structure was put forth, but the law did assume that any national market would make extensive use of computers and electronic communication devices. Additionally, the law prohibited fixed commissions on public transactions and also prohibited banks, insurance companies, and other financial institutions from buying stock exchange memberships to save commission costs for their own institutional transactions. This is a worthwhile addition to the securities laws since it fosters greater competition and more efficient prices.

Other Legislation

In addition to these three major pieces of legislation, a number of other acts deal directly with investor protection. For example, the Investment Advisor Act of 1940 is set up to protect the public from unethical investment advisers. Any adviser with more than 15 public clients (excluding tax accountants and lawyers) must register with the SEC and file semiannual reports. The Investment Company Act of 1940 provides similar oversight for mutual funds and investment companies dealing with small investors. The act was amended in 1970 and currently gives the NASD authority to supervise and limit commissions and investment advisory fees on certain types of mutual funds.

Another piece of legislation dealing directly with investor protection is the Securities Investor Protection Act of 1970. The Securities Investor Protection Corporation (SIPC) was established to oversee liquidation of brokerage firms and to insure investors' accounts to a maximum value of $500,000 in case of bankruptcy of a brokerage firm. It functions much the same as the Federal Deposit Insurance Corporation. SIPC resulted from the problems encountered on Wall Street from 1967 to 1970 when share volume surged to then all-time highs, and many firms were unable to process orders fast enough. A back-office paper crunch caused Wall Street to shorten the hours the exchanges were formally open for new business, but even this didn't help. Investors lost large sums, and for many months, they were unable to use or get possession of securities held in their names. Even though SIPC insures these accounts, it still does not cover market value losses suffered while waiting to get securities from a bankrupt brokerage firm.

Insider Trading

The Securities Exchange Act of 1934 established the initial restrictions on insider trading. However, over the years, these restrictions have often proved to be inadequate. As previously indicated, the definition of *insider* may go beyond officers, directors, and major stockholders to include anyone with special insider knowledge. Both the Congress and the SEC are attempting to grapple with the issue of making punitive measures severe enough to discourage the illegal use of nonpublic information for profits.[3] Current and future legislation is likely to include tougher civil penalties and stiffer criminal prosecution. Also, the penalties for improper action will expand beyond simple recovery of profits to a penalty three or more times the profits involved.

The 1980s saw a rash of insider trading scandals involving major investment banking houses, traders, analysts, and investors. Ivan Boesky and Dennis Levine were the first of the well-known investors to end up in jail, and Michael Milken was not far behind. These insider trading scandals have plagued Wall Street and tarnished its image as a place where investors can get a fair deal.

On balance, all the legislation we have discussed has tended to increase the confidence of the investing public. In an industry where public trust is so critical, some form of supervision, whether public or private, is necessary and generally accepted.

Program Trading and Market Price Limits

Program trading is identified by some market analysts as the primary culprit behind the 508-point market crash on October 19, 1987. Program trading simply means computer-based trigger points are established in which large volume trades are initiated by institutional investors. For example, if the Dow Jones Industrial Average (or some other market measure) hits a certain point, a large sale or purchase may automatically occur. When many institutional investors are using program trading simultaneously, this process can have a major cumulative effect on the market. This was thought to be the case not only in the 1987 crash but also for many other highly volatile days in the market.

Rule 80A After the crash of 1987, several studies of the role of program trading in creating market volatility were undertaken. In response to concerns that program trading might create market volatility, the NYSE instituted Rule 80A. Under Rule 80A as amended by the SEC, all daily up or down movements in the Dow Jones Industrial Average (DJIA) of 50 points or more cause a tick test to go into effect.[4] In down markets, sell orders can only be executed on an increase in price

3. Insiders, of course, may make proper long-term investments in a corporation.

4. The rule specifically applies to stocks in the Standard & Poor's 500 Stock Index to protect against index arbitrage, that is, trading in stocks and stock index futures at the same time in order to profit from price differences between the two.

(a plus tick) and buy orders can only be executed on a decrease in price (a minus tick).

Circuit Breakers In 1989 circuit breakers were also put in place; circuit breakers shut down the market for a period of time if there is a dramatic drop in stock prices. Under the initial provisions implemented by the NYSE, the exchange agreed to initiate a 30-minute halt in trading if the Dow Jones Industrial Average went down by 250 points during a given day and a one-hour halt in case of a 400-point decline.

As the market continued to go up during the 1990s, the circuit breakers were raised in February 1997 to a 350-point decline for a 30-minute halt and a 550-point decline for a one-hour break. Both circuit breakers were triggered by the 500-point-plus decline on October 27, 1997. The SEC has informed the New York Stock Exchange that it expects the exchange to continually evaluate the size of the circuit breakers as market conditions change.

Other markets, such as the Nasdaq, the American Stock Exchange, and the Chicago Board of Trade (for stock index futures), have also agreed to discontinue trading if there is a halt on the NYSE.

Internet Resources

Website Address	Comments
www.nyse.com	Provides information on regulations and market operations
www.nasdaq.com	Provides information about the Nasdaq market
www.cboe.com	Provides information about options traded on the Chicago Board Options Exchange
www.ipo.com	Contains information, FAQs, and glossary about initial public offerings
www.individualinvestor.com	Contains information about current market conditions and stock information

Chapter 4

Participating in the Market

Many different kinds of investors participate in the market, from the individual to the professional, and each participant needs to know about the structure and mechanics of the market in which he or she might invest. In this chapter, we examine the use of indexes to gauge market performance, the rules and mechanics of opening and trading in an account, and basic tax considerations for the investor.

MEASURES OF PRICE PERFORMANCE: MARKET INDEXES

We first look at tracking market performance for stocks and bonds. Each market has several market indexes published by Dow Jones, Standard & Poor's, Value Line, and other financial services. These indexes allow investors to measure the performance of their portfolios against an index that approximates their portfolio composition; thus, different investors prefer different indexes. While a professional pension fund manager might use the Standard & Poor's 500 Stock Index, a mutual fund specializing in small, over-the-counter stocks might prefer the Nasdaq (National Association of Securities Dealers Automated Quotations) Index, and a small investor might use the Value Line Average or Russell 2000 as the best approximation of a portfolio's performance.

INDEXES AND AVERAGES

Dow Jones Averages

Since there are many stock market indexes and averages, we will cover the most widely used ones. Dow Jones, publisher of *The Wall Street Journal* and *Barron's,* publishes several market averages of which the Dow Jones Industrial Average (DJIA) is the most popular. This average consists of 30 large industrial companies and is considered a "blue-chip" index (stocks of very high quality). Many people criticize the DJIA for being too selective and representing too few stocks. Nevertheless, the Dow Industrials do follow the general trend of the market, and these 30 common stocks comprise more than 25 percent of the market value of the 3,000 firms listed on the New York Stock Exchange. Figure 4-1 shows a listing of the 30 stocks in the Dow Jones Industrial Average as well as the daily price movement for the average over a six-month period.

Dow Jones also publishes an index of 20 transportation stocks and 15 utility stocks. At the top of Table 4-1, you see a listing of the daily changes for the three Dow Jones Averages on May 20, 2003. It also shows a Dow Jones 65-stock composite average that summarizes the performance of the Dow Jones industrial, transportation, and utility issues as well as the Dow Jones indicator for the total U.S. market. Many other market averages are presented in the table, which we will discuss later.

For now, let's return to the Dow Jones Industrial Average of 30 stocks. The Dow Jones Industrial Average used to be a simple average of 30 stocks, but when a company splits its stock price, the average has to be adjusted. For the Dow Jones Industrials, the divisor in the formula has been adjusted downward from the original 30 to below 1. Each time a company splits its shares of stock (or provides a stock dividend), the divisor is reduced to maintain the average at the same level as before the stock split. If this were not done, the lower-priced stock after the split would reduce the average, giving the appearance that investors were worse off.

The Dow Jones Industrial Average is a price-weighted average, which means each stock in the average is weighted by its price. To simplify the meaning of price weighted: if you had three stocks in a price-weighted average that had values of 10, 40, and 100, you would add the prices and divide by three. In this case, you would get an average of 50 (150 divided by 3). A price-weighted average is similar to what you normally use in computing averages. Price-weighted averages tend to give a higher weighting bias to high-price stocks than to low-price stocks. For example, in the above analysis, if the $100 stock goes up by 10 percent, with all else the same, the average will go up over three points from 50 to 53.3. However, if the $10 stock goes up by 10 percent, with all else the same, the average will only go from 50 to 50.3.

In mid-2001 IBM was trading at 110 while Disney was at 28. Clearly, a 10 percent price movement up or down in IBM would have a greater impact on the Dow Jones Industrial Average than a 10 percent movement in Disney. Thus, we see the bias toward high-priced stocks in the Dow Jones Industrial Average.

Standard & Poor's Indexes

Standard & Poor's Corporation publishes a number of indexes. The best known is the Standard & Poor's 500 Stock Index. This index is widely followed by profes-

FIGURE 4–1 Dow Jones Industrial Average

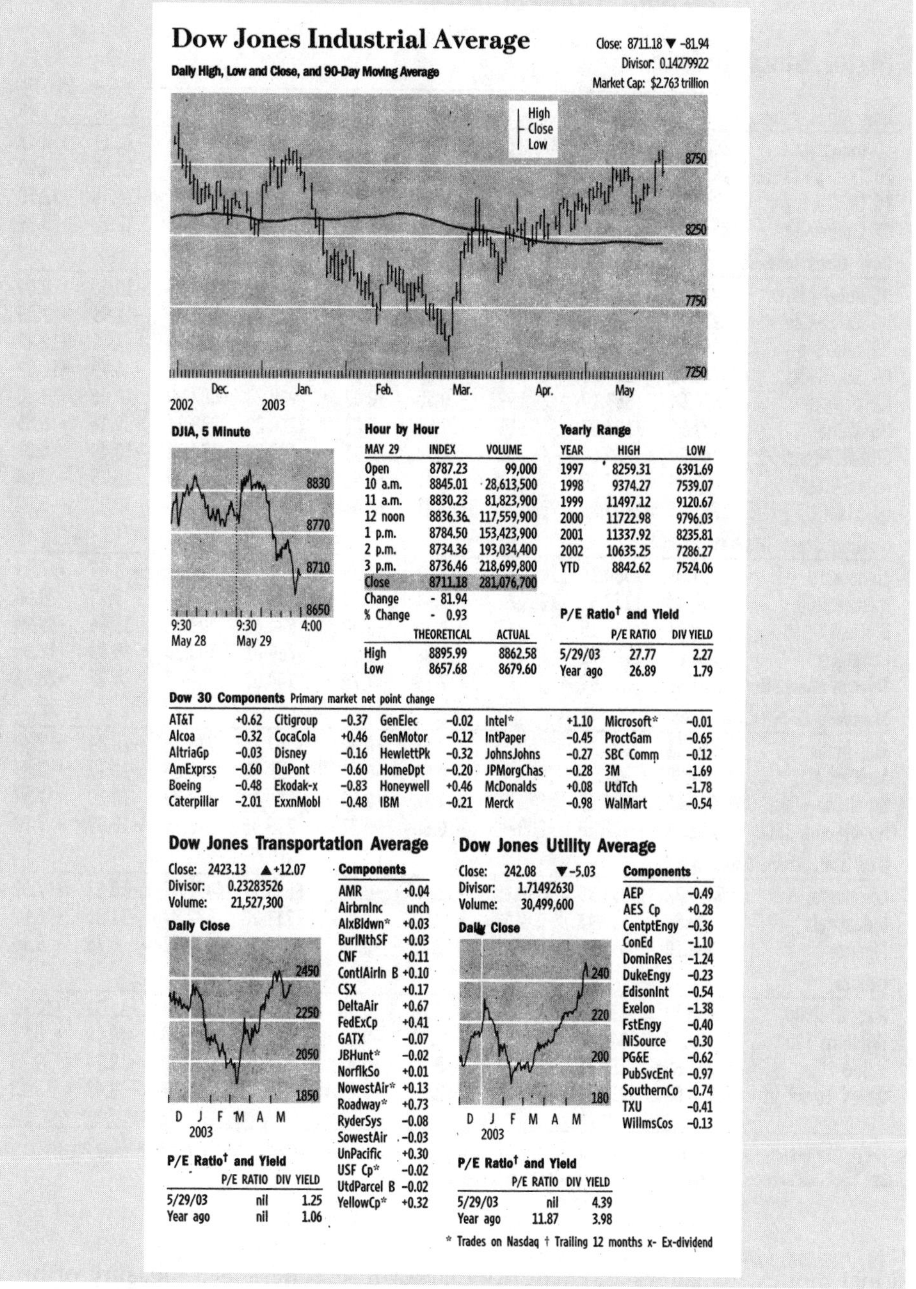

Dow Jones Industrial Average

Daily High, Low and Close, and 90-Day Moving Average

Close: 8711.18 ▼ -81.94
Divisor: 0.14279922
Market Cap: $2.763 trillion

DJIA, 5 Minute

Hour by Hour

MAY 29	INDEX	VOLUME
Open	8787.23	99,000
10 a.m.	8845.01	28,613,500
11 a.m.	8830.23	81,823,900
12 noon	8836.36	117,559,900
1 p.m.	8784.50	153,423,900
2 p.m.	8734.36	193,034,400
3 p.m.	8736.46	218,699,800
Close	8711.18	281,076,700
Change	- 81.94	
% Change	- 0.93	

	THEORETICAL	ACTUAL
High	8895.99	8862.58
Low	8657.68	8679.60

Yearly Range

YEAR	HIGH	LOW
1997	8259.31	6391.69
1998	9374.27	7539.07
1999	11497.12	9120.67
2000	11722.98	9796.03
2001	11337.92	8235.81
2002	10635.25	7286.27
YTD	8842.62	7524.06

P/E Ratio† and Yield

	P/E RATIO	DIV YIELD
5/29/03	27.77	2.27
Year ago	26.89	1.79

Dow 30 Components Primary market net point change

AT&T	+0.62	Citigroup	-0.37	GenElec	-0.02	Intel*	+1.10	Microsoft*	-0.01
Alcoa	-0.32	CocaCola	+0.46	GenMotor	-0.12	IntPaper	-0.45	ProctGam	-0.65
AltriaGp	-0.03	Disney	-0.16	HewlettPk	-0.32	JohnsJohns	-0.27	SBC Comm	-0.12
AmExprss	-0.60	DuPont	-0.60	HomeDpt	-0.20	JPMorgChas	-0.28	3M	-1.69
Boeing	-0.48	Ekodak-x	-0.83	Honeywell	+0.46	McDonalds	+0.08	UtdTch	-1.78
Caterpillar	-2.01	ExxnMobl	-0.48	IBM	-0.21	Merck	-0.98	WalMart	-0.54

Dow Jones Transportation Average

Close: 2423.13 ▲+12.07
Divisor: 0.23283526
Volume: 21,527,300

Daily Close

P/E Ratio† and Yield

	P/E RATIO	DIV YIELD
5/29/03	nil	1.25
Year ago	nil	1.06

Components

AMR	+0.04
AirbrnInc	unch
AlxBldwn*	+0.03
BurlNthSF	+0.03
CNF	+0.11
ContlAirln B	+0.10
CSX	+0.17
DeltaAir	+0.67
FedExCp	+0.41
GATX	-0.07
JBHunt*	-0.02
NorflkSo	+0.01
NowestAir*	+0.13
Roadway*	+0.73
RyderSys	-0.08
SowestAir	-0.03
UnPacific	+0.30
USF Cp*	-0.02
UtdParcel B	-0.02
YellowCp*	+0.32

Dow Jones Utility Average

Close: 242.08 ▼-5.03
Divisor: 1.71492630
Volume: 30,499,600

Daily Close

P/E Ratio† and Yield

	P/E RATIO	DIV YIELD
5/29/03	nil	4.39
Year ago	11.87	3.98

Components

AEP	-0.49
AES Cp	+0.28
CentptEngy	-0.36
ConEd	-1.10
DominRes	-1.24
DukeEngy	-0.23
EdisonInt	-0.54
Exelon	-1.38
FstEngy	-0.40
NiSource	-0.30
PG&E	-0.62
PubSvcEnt	-0.97
SouthernCo	-0.74
TXU	-0.41
WillmsCos	-0.13

* Trades on Nasdaq † Trailing 12 months x- Ex-dividend

Source: Republished with permission of Dow Jones & Company, Inc., from *The Wall Street Journal*, May 31, 2003, p. C2; permission conveyed through Copyright Clearance Center, Inc.

TABLE 4–1 Indexes and Averages Found in *The Wall Street Journal*

Major Stock Indexes

	DAILY					52-WEEK			YTD
Dow Jones Averages	HIGH	LOW	CLOSE	NET CHG	% CHG	HIGH	LOW	% CHG	% CHG
30 Industrials	8862.58	8679.60	8711.18	-81.94	-0.93	9925.25	7286.27	-12.11	+ 4.43
20 Transportations	2431.84	2408.23	2423.13	+12.07	+0.50	2755.64	1942.19	-10.85	+ 4.90
15 Utilities	249.18	240.83	242.08	- 5.03	-2.04	289.86	167.57	-16.48	+12.50
65 Composite	2554.40	2508.29	2517.29	-19.84	-0.78	2891.06	2033.44	-12.72	+ 5.99
Dow Jones Indexes									
US Total Market	225.07	221.48	222.28	- 0.75	-0.34	248.91	179.60	-10.50	+ 8.69
US Large-Cap	210.93	207.40	208.17	- 0.83	-0.40	235.78	172.31	-11.55	+ 7.39
US Mid-Cap	257.37	253.63	254.39	- 0.67	-0.26	276.63	192.15	- 7.69	+12.29
US Small-Cap	280.90	277.28	278.66	+ 0.15	+0.05	299.89	209.81	- 6.99	+12.82
US Growth	876.94	863.19	866.92	+ 0.58	+0.07	968.23	687.99	-10.46	+11.80
US Value	1171.55	1151.23	1154.55	- 9.56	-0.82	1280.29	938.11	- 9.44	+ 6.85
Global Titans 50	161.70	159.69	160.36	+ 0.34	+0.21	179.09	134.76	-10.45	+ 6.07
Asian Titans 50	79.35	77.88	79.34	+ 1.41	+1.81	106.97	71.25	-25.75	- 3.84
DJ STOXX 50	2335.75	2305.82	2320.29	+ 1.41	+0.06	3357.70	1909.05	-30.06	- 3.62
Nasdaq Stock Market									
Composite	1591.26	1564.14	1574.95	+11.71	+0.75	1631.92	1114.11	- 3.49	+17.93
Nasdaq 100	1198.43	1172.52	1181.82	+ 8.51	+0.73	1227.90	804.64	- 3.75	+20.06
Biotech	678.93	661.15	665.45	- 4.70	-0.70	674.63	403.98	+11.66	+33.93
Computer	738.03	719.92	728.77	+ 7.80	+1.08	769.81	503.26	- 5.33	+17.05
Telecommunications	141.42	137.99	140.02	+ 2.39	+1.74	140.02	81.43	+ 4.95	+28.71
Standard & Poor's Indexes									
500 Index	962.11	946.36	949.64	- 3.58	-0.38	1067.14	776.76	-10.80	+ 7.94
MidCap 400	467.85	462.29	463.55	- 0.52	-0.11	528.58	372.88	-12.12	+ 7.85
SmallCap 600	212.16	210.13	211.50	+ 1.18	+0.56	244.10	170.73	-13.10	+ 7.57
SuperComp 1500	212.16	208.80	209.54	- 0.68	-0.32	235.96	171.10	-10.99	+ 7.92
New York Stock Exchange									
Composite	5425.72	5351.35	5366.23	-11.50	-0.21	6035.27	4452.49	-10.62	+ 7.32
Industrials	629.89	620.43	622.59	- 2.50	-0.40	711.28	532.37	-11.89	+ 6.62
Finance	564.10	555.59	557.15	- 3.81	-0.68	599.49	437.72	- 6.76	+ 9.15
Others									
Russell 2000	435.12	430.01	432.64	+ 2.16	+0.50	487.83	327.04	-11.31	+12.93
Wilshire 5000	9185.93	9046.32	9078.11	-25.74	-0.28	10106.49	7342.84	-10.00	+ 8.81
Value Line	291.85	288.45	289.65	+ 0.90	+0.31	354.14	219.50	-18.14	+ 9.73
Amex Composite	934.02	930.30	933.83	+ 2.54	+0.27	961.58	771.87	- 2.48	+13.28

Source: Republished with permission of Dow Jones & Company, Inc., from *The Wall Street Journal*, May 30, 2003, p. C2; permission conveyed through Copyright Clearance Center, Inc.

sional money managers and security market researchers as a measure of broad stock market activity. In 2001, the S&P 500 Stock Index included 371 industrial firms, plus 15 transportation firms, 49 utilities, and 65 financial firms. The Standard

& Poor's 500 Index and two of its component parts, the industrials and utilities, can be seen in Table 4–1. The stocks in the S&P 500 Stock Index are equivalent to approximately 75 percent of the total value of the 3,000 firms listed on the New York Stock Exchange.[1]

In the summer of 1991, Standard & Poor introduced its MidCap Index. The Standard & Poor's 400 MidCap Index is composed of 400 middle-sized firms that have total market values between $1.2 billion and $9 billion. The index was intended to answer the complaint that the S&P 500 Stock Index shows only the performance of larger firms. For example, Microsoft, which is part of the S&P 500 Index, had a total market value of more than $350 billion in June 2001. By creating an index of middle-sized firms, portfolio managers with comparable-sized holdings could more accurately track their performance against an appropriate measure. The same is true for the Standard & Poor's 600 SmallCap Index, which provides an opportunity for comparison of stocks that are smaller than the MidCap. The Standard & Poor's 1500 Stock Index, also shown in Table 4–1, combines the S&P 500, the S&P 400 MidCap, and the S&P SmallCap 600.

Standard & Poor's also has other special purpose indexes, some of which are not shown in Table 4–1. For example, the Standard & Poor's 100 Index is composed of 100 blue-chip stocks on which the Chicago Board Options Exchange has individual option contracts. (This terminology will become clearer when we study options later in the text.) The S&P 100 Index closely mirrors the performance of the S&P 500 Stock Index.

All the S&P measures are true indexes in that they are linked to a base value. For the S&P 500 Stock Index, the base period is 1941–43. The base period price in 1941–43 was 10, so the S&P 500 Stock Index price of 949.64 on May 30, 2003, as previously shown in Table 4–1, represents an increase of 9486.4 percent over this 61-year period. For the newer indexes, the base period does not go back as far.

Regardless of the base period, the important consideration is how much the index changed over a given time period (such as a day, month, or year) rather than the absolute value. For example, looking back at Table 4–1, you can see that the Dow Jones Industrial Average is up 4.43 percent for the last 52 weeks (look at the last column to see the percentage change from the prior year) and that the Standard and Poor's 500 Stock Index is up 7.94 percent over a comparable time period. One might observe that this was not a particularly good period for market performance as further indicated in the 12-month percent change column. The average annual increase over the long term is 10 to 12 percent.

The Standard & Poor's Indexes are value-weighted indexes, which means each company is weighted in the index by its own total market value as a percentage of the total market value for all firms. For example, in a value-weighted index comprising the following three firms, the weighting would be:

1. Actually, some large Nasdaq firms are also in the S&P indexes, although the indexes are predominantly made up of NYSE firms.

Stock	Shares	Price	Total Market Value	Weighting
A	150	$10	$ 1,500	12.0%
B	200	20	4,000	32.0
C	500	14	7,000	56.0
			$12,500	100.0%

In each case, the weighting is determined by dividing the total market value of the stock by the total market value for all firms. In the case of stock A, that would be $1,500 divided by $12,500, or 12 percent. The same procedure is followed for stocks B and C.

Even though stock C has only the second highest price, it makes up 56 percent of the average because of its high total market value based on 500 shares outstanding. This same basic effect carries through in the Standard & Poor's 500 Index, with large companies such as GE, Exxon, and AT&T having a greater impact on the index than smaller companies. Value-weighted indexes do not require special adjustments for stock splits because the increase in the number of shares automatically compensates for the decline in the stock value caused by the split.

Standard & Poor's also compiles value-weighted indexes for more than 100 different industries, and they are reported in the *Standard & Poor's Security Price Index Record.*

Value Line Average

The Value Line Average represents 1,700 companies from the New York and American stock exchanges and the Nasdaq market. Some individual investors use the Value Line Average because it more closely corresponds to the variety of stocks small investors may have in their portfolios.

Unlike the previously discussed price-weighted average (the Dow Jones Industrial Average) and value-weighted indexes (S&P 500), the Value Line Average is an equal-weighted index. This means each of the 1,700 stocks, regardless of market price or total market value, is weighted equally. It is as if there were $100 to be invested in each and every stock. In this case, IBM or Exxon is weighted no more heavily than Wendy's International or Mattel Inc. This equal-weighting characteristic also more closely conforms to the portfolio of individual investors.

Other Market Indexes

Indexes are also computed and published by the New York Stock Exchange, American Stock Exchange, and the Nasdaq. Each index is intended to represent the performance of stocks traded in a particular exchange or market. As is seen in Table 4-1, the NYSE publishes a composite index as well as an industrial and financial index. Each index represents the stocks of a broad group or type of company.

The Nasdaq also publishes a number of indexes, including the Nasdaq Composite, the Nasdaq 100, and other indexes that represent various sectors of the economy. The Nasdaq 100 is made up of the 100 largest firms in its market and is heavily populated by high-tech firms such as Microsoft, Intel, Oracle, and Cisco.

The Nasdaq Composite Index has become particularly popular in the last decade and is often featured along with the Dow Jones Industrial Average and the Standard and Poor's 500 Index on the nightly news.

The American Exchange (AMEX) Composite Index is composed of all stocks trading on the American Stock Exchange. This index is also shown in Table 4-1 in the "Others" category.

The indexes of the New York Stock Exchange, Nasdaq, and the American Stock Exchange are all value-weighted indexes.[2]

Another important index is the Wilshire 5000 Equity Index. It represents the *total dollar value* of 5,000 stocks, including all NYSE and AMEX issues and the most active Nasdaq issues. By the very fact of including total dollar value, it is value weighted. On May 30, 2003, the Wilshire Index had a value of $9,185.93 billion ($9.18 trillion). The index tells you the total value of virtually all important equities daily.

The Russell indexes have also become popular in recent times. There are three separate but overlapping value-weighted indexes provided by Frank Russell Company, a money management consulting firm in Tacoma, Washington.[3] The Russell 3000 Index is comprised of 3,000 U.S. stocks as measured by market capitalization (market value times shares outstanding). The other two indexes allow you to see whether larger or smaller stocks are performing better. For example, the Russell 1000 Index includes only the largest 1,000 firms out of the Russell 3000, while the Russell 2000 specifically includes the smallest 2,000 out of the Russell 3000. If the Russell 2000 is outperforming the Russell 1000, you can generally assume that smaller stocks are outperforming larger firms. The reverse would obviously be true if there is a superior performance by the Russell 1000.

International Stock Averages As the internationalization of investments has become progressively more important in the 1990s, so have international market indexes. In January 1993, Dow Jones & Company introduced the Dow Jones Global Indexes. As shown in Table 4-2, they cover 33 countries in three major sectors of the world (Americas, Europe/Africa, and Asia/Pacific). Furthermore, the bottom two rows of the table show the World Index excluding the United States and the overall Dow Jones (DJ) World Stock Index. Note that in the last column, the World (excluding the United States) increased 5.06 percent from year-end while the Dow Jones World Stock Index (which includes the United States) increased 6.02 percent. In this particular time period, the inclusion of the United States aided the overall performance of world stock markets.

---

2. Until October 1973, the American Stock Exchange Index was price weighted.

3. Frank Russell Company has other indexes as well.

TABLE 4–2 World Stock Market Average

DOW JONES GLOBAL INDEXES

Region/ Country	DJ Global Indexes, Local Curr. Latest Fri.	Wkly % Chg.	DJ Global Indexes, U.S. $ Latest Fri.	Wkly % Chg.	DJ Global Indexes, U.S. $ on 12/31/02	Point Chg. From 12/31/02	% Chg. From 12/31/02
Americas			214.55	− 0.81	199.80	+ 14.76	+ 7.39
Brazil	1544036.66	− 0.56	208.93	+ 0.36	161.23	+ 47.70	+29.59
Canada	220.59	+ 0.63	185.50	+ 0.26	157.52	+ 27.98	+17.76
Chile	268.11	− 1.18	142.28	− 1.35	117.84	+ 24.44	+20.74
Mexico	480.33	+ 0.31	143.55	+ 0.72	133.55	+ 10.01	+ 7.49
U.S.	218.42	− 0.88	218.42	− 0.88	204.51	+ 13.91	+ 6.80
Venezuela	661.45	+16.24	25.57	+16.24	24.76	+ 0.80	+ 3.24
Latin America			**140.28**	**+ 0.36**	**119.46**	**+ 20.82**	**+ 17.42**
Europe			**162.26**	**− 0.92**	**152.59**	**+ 9.67**	**+ 6.34**
Austria	142.05	− 1.41	130.96	+ 0.70	104.38	+ 26.58	+25.46
Belgium	185.05	− 1.87	170.69	+ 0.23	154.34	+ 16.35	+10.59
Denmark	204.88	− 0.38	193.24	+ 1.95	160.05	+ 33.18	+20.73
Finland	841.50	− 6.16	693.84	− 4.15	671.54	+ 22.30	+ 3.32
France	175.69	− 3.29	164.17	− 1.22	153.79	+ 10.38	+ 6.75
Germany	133.20	− 5.25	122.41	− 3.23	112.13	+ 10.28	+ 9.17
Greece	134.95	− 3.52	91.83	− 1.46	83.99	+ 7.85	+ 9.34
Ireland	318.67	− 1.46	287.00	+ 0.64	236.66	+ 50.35	+21.27
Italy	187.21	− 1.76	141.80	+ 0.34	123.57	+ 18.23	+14.75
Netherlands	211.37	− 4.74	194.35	− 2.71	199.45	− 5.10	− 2.56
Norway	129.27	− 1.98	116.24	− 0.07	110.78	+ 5.46	+ 4.93
Portugal	156.28	− 0.16	125.08	+ 1.97	117.20	+ 7.89	+ 6.73
Spain	245.10	− 2.04	169.84	+ 0.05	142.60	+ 27.24	+19.10
Sweden	243.88	− 2.97	185.23	− 1.22	163.29	+ 21.94	+13.44
Switzerland	260.96	− 0.29	274.69	+ 1.12	259.06	+ 15.63	+ 6.03
United Kingdom	162.95	− 1.64	142.57	− 0.79	137.92	+ 4.65	+ 3.37
South Africa			**97.71**	**− 0.31**	**101.38**	**− 3.67**	**− 3.62**
Pacific Region			**66.83**	**+ 0.84**	**66.51**	**+ 0.32**	**+ 0.48**
Australia	200.96	+ 1.44	174.59	+ 2.48	149.43	+ 25.16	+16.84
Hong Kong	157.15	+ 2.96	156.72	+ 2.97	156.33	+ 0.40	+ 0.25
Indonesia	165.04	+ 0.87	39.75	+ 3.19	33.14	+ 6.61	+19.95
Japan	51.63	+ 0.84	55.13	+ 0.15	56.45	− 1.32	− 2.35
Malaysia	122.89	+ 2.21	88.00	+ 2.21	86.07	+ 1.93	+ 2.24
New Zealand	130.52	+ 1.60	141.08	+ 2.14	119.84	+ 21.23	+17.72
Philippines	94.64	− 1.54	46.58	− 2.10	43.25	+ 3.33	+ 7.70
Singapore	105.14	+ 1.53	98.90	+ 1.73	97.75	+ 1.15	+ 1.18
South Korea	121.94	+ 0.09	77.40	+ 0.54	80.98	− 3.58	− 4.42
Taiwan	109.19	+ 1.50	81.21	+ 1.36	82.93	− 1.72	− 2.07
Thailand	70.89	+ 3.63	39.90	+ 4.19	33.50	+ 6.40	+19.11
Euro Zone			**158.57**	**− 1.51**	**146.55**	**+ 12.02**	**+ 8.20**
Europe (ex.U.K.)			**171.23**	**− 1.01**	**158.20**	**+ 13.03**	**+ 8.24**
Nordic Region			**233.31**	**− 1.75**	**212.25**	**+ 21.06**	**+ 9.92**
Pacific Region (ex. Japan)			**132.53**	**+ 2.02**	**125.51**	**+ 7.02**	**+ 5.59**
World (ex. U.S.)			**109.82**	**− 0.26**	**104.53**	**+ 5.29**	**+ 5.06**
DOW JONES WORLD STOCK INDEX			**148.99**	**− 0.60**	**140.54**	**+ 8.46**	**+ 6.02**

Indexes based on 12/31/91=100.

Source: Republished with permission of Dow Jones & Company, Inc., from *Barron's*, May 30, 2003, p. MW26; permission conveyed through Copyright Clearance Center, Inc.

Besides the Dow Jones World Stock Market Index, there are other important global indexes such as the Morgan Stanley Capital International Indexes and the Solomon-Russell World Equity Index. The advantage of the Dow Jones World Stock

Index is that it is available to the typical investor on a daily basis in *The Wall Street Journal.*

In terms of averages for *specific countries* outside the United States, the Tokyo Nikkei 225 Average is probably the most actively watched. Many sophisticated U.S. investors look to the Japanese market immediately after checking local market conditions.

Bond Market Indicators Performance in the bond market is not widely followed by an index or average but is usually gauged by interest-rate movements. Because rising interest rates mean falling bond prices and falling rates signal rising prices, investors can usually judge the bond market performance by yield-curve changes or interest-rate graphs. Nevertheless, there is still a wide menu to choose from in *The Wall Street Journal* when tracking the performance of bond prices as indicated in Table 4-3. At the top of the table, yields are given for various maturities of Treasury and municipal issues. The indexes are then broken down by different types of bonds: Treasury securities, corporate debt, tax-exempt issues, and mortgage-backed securities. (All of these securities are discussed in Chapters 11-14 of the text.)

Mutual Fund Averages Lipper Analytical Services publishes the Lipper Mutual and Investment Performance Averages shown in Table 4-4. While mutual funds were considered in depth in Chapter 2, it is interesting to observe the various categories that the funds are broken into to compute measures of performance. Also, observe in the next few columns of Table 4-4 that the starting point of the measurement period is very important in relation to relative performance.

Direction of Indexes The directions of the indexes are closely related, but they do not necessarily move together. If a pension fund manager is trying to "outperform the market," then the choice of index may be as crucial as to whether the fund manager maintains his or her accounts. The important thing for you, as well as for a professional, when measuring success or failure of performance is to use an index that represents the risk characteristics of the portfolio being compared with the index.

BUYING AND SELLING IN THE MARKET

Once you are generally familiar with the market and perhaps decide to invest directly in common stocks or other assets, you will need to set up an account with a retail brokerage house. Some of the largest and better-known retail brokers are Merrill Lynch, Salomon Smith Barney, and UBS PaineWebber, but there are many other good houses, both regional and national. When you set up your account, the account executive (often called stockbroker or financial consultant) will ask you to fill out a card listing your investment objectives, such as conservative, preservation of capital, income oriented, growth plus income, or growth. The account

TABLE 4–3 Bond Indexes

INTEREST RATES & BONDS

Consumer Rates

Benchmark personal borrowing rate vs. Federal-funds target rate, the interest rate on overnight loans between banks.

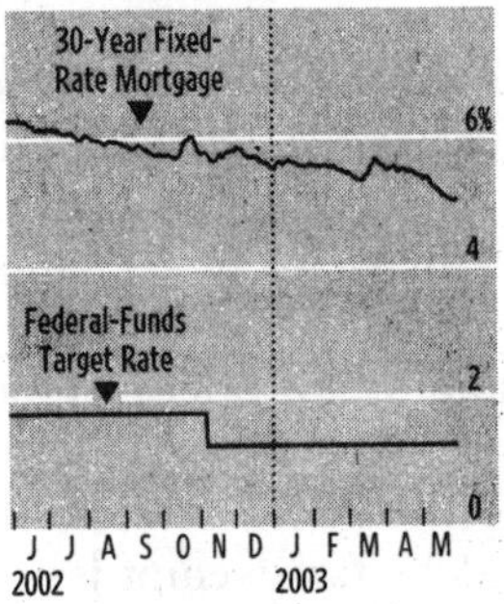

30-Year Fixed-Rate Mortgage

Federal-Funds Target Rate

6% 4 2 0

J J A S O N D J F M A M
2002 2003

	NAT'L AVG	WK'S CHG
Credit card	13.74%	+0.02
Money market ann. yield	1.44	−0.01
Five-year CD ann. yield	3.21	−0.04
New-car loan	5.39	−0.02
30-yr. fixed-rate mortgage	5.05	−0.01
15-yr. fixed-rate mortgage	4.49	+0.02
Jumbo mortgages*	5.40	+0.02
One-year ARM	3.58	+0.04
Home-equity loan	6.83	−0.01

*Over $322,700

Most Competitive Rates

30-yr. fixed-rate mortgage

Pure Platinum Realty & Mrtges ..4.64% APR
Carlsbad, CA, 760-431-7595

Old America Financial Services......4.70%
Tustin, CA, 714-505-9161

Capital Funding Mortgage...............4.77%
Houston, TX, 800-900-9456

Direct Funding..................................4.78%
Winter Springs, FL, 800-834-7188

J & K Mortgage..............................4.78%
Clearwater, FL, 727-524-2869

Source: Bankrate.com

Treasury Yield Curve

Yield to maturity of current bills, notes and bonds.

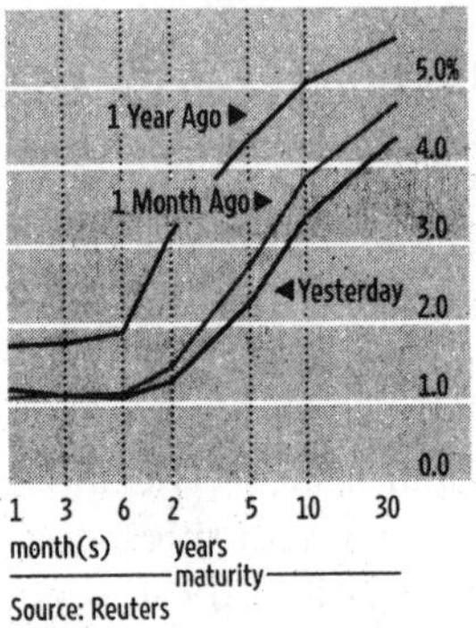

1 Year Ago ▶
1 Month Ago ▶
◀ Yesterday

5.0% 4.0 3.0 2.0 1.0 0.0

1 3 6 2 5 10 30
month(s) years
maturity

Source: Reuters

Libor/Swap Curve

Counterparty receives (mid-market) semi-annual swap rates for 2 to 30 years and pays floating 3-month Libor.

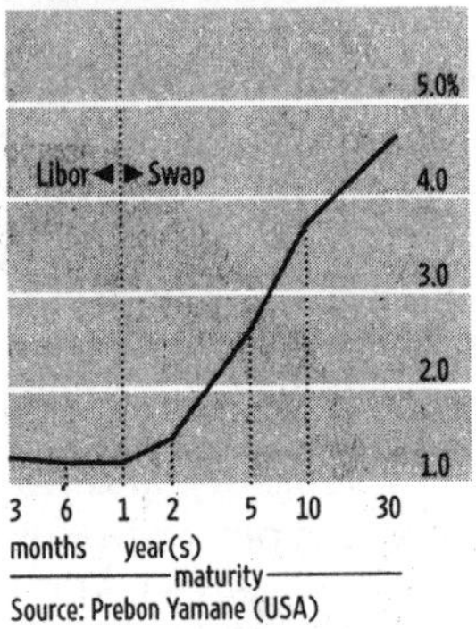

Libor ◀ ▶ Swap

5.0% 4.0 3.0 2.0 1.0

3 6 1 2 5 10 30
months year(s)
maturity

Source: Prebon Yamane (USA)

Major Bond Indexes

U.S. Treasury Securities Lehman Brothers	CLOSE	NET CHG	% CHG	52-WEEK HIGH	52-WEEK LOW	52-WEEK % CHG	YTD % CHG
Intermediate	7514.91	+9.88	+ 0.13	7514.91	6845.72	+ 9.75	+ 2.49
Long-term	12594.28	+105.50	+ 0.84	12697.51	10185.65	+23.60	+ 8.04
Composite	8653.64	+32.05	+ 0.37	8674.30	7571.18	+14.27	+ 4.32
Broad Market Lehman Brothers (preliminary)							
U.S. Aggregate	1058.88	+3.52	+ 0.30	1058.88	938.06	+11.73	+ 4.14
U.S. Gov't/Credit	1239.52	+5.99	+ 0.45	1239.52	1068.46	+14.81	+ 5.67
U.S. Corporate Debt Issues Merrill Lynch							
Corporate Master	1432.56	+ 6.41	+ 0.45	1432.56	1218.54	+16.59	+ 7.85
High Yield	584.93	+ 2.22	+ 0.38	585.59	466.65	+ 9.33	+13.97
Yankee Bonds	1053.43	+ 3.90	+ 0.37	1053.43	903.81	+16.40	+ 6.64
Mortgage-Backed Securities current coupon; Merrill Lynch: Dec. 31, 1986=100							
Ginnie Mae	433.62	+0.19	+ 0.04	433.62	386.02	+11.89	+ 3.53
Fannie Mae	434.20	+1.24	+ 0.29	434.20	381.73	+13.34	+ 4.84
Freddie Mac	265.21	+0.74	+ 0.28	265.21	232.78	+13.52	+ 4.93
Tax-Exempt Securities Merrill Lynch; Dec. 22, 1999							
6% Bond Buyer Muni	114.06	−4.84	− 4.07	118.91	103.94	+ 9.74	+ 4.20
7-12 Yr G.O.	194.74	+0.21	+ 0.11	195.16	174.30	+11.73	+ 4.92
12-22 Yr G.O.	204.69	+0.40	+ 0.20	205.27	181.56	+12.74	+ 5.31
22+ Yr Revenue	192.39	+0.24	+ 0.12	193.05	171.90	+11.90	+ 4.37

Source: Republished with permission of Dow Jones & Company, Inc., from *The Wall Street Journal*, May 30, 2003, p. C2; permission conveyed through Copyright Clearance Center, Inc.

executive will also ask for your Social Security number for tax reporting, the level of your income, net worth, employer, and other information. Basically, the account executive needs to know your desire and ability to take risk in order to give good advice and proper management of your assets. Later in this chapter, we will also talk about discount brokers and online brokers, that is, brokers who charge very

TABLE 4–4 Lipper Mutual Fund Performance Indexes

LIPPER MUTUAL FUND PERFORMANCE INDEXES

Weekly Summary Report: Thursday, 5/22/2003
Cumulative Performances With Dividends Reinvested

Current Value	No. Funds		12/31/02-05/22/03	05/15/03-05/22/03	04/24/03-05/22/03	02/20/03-05/22/03	05/23/02-05/22/03
General Equity Indexes							
1,868.69	30	Capital Apprec Index	+ 7.67%	− 0.88%	+ 3.51%	+ 11.85%	− 13.87%
6,011.35	30	Growth Fund Index	+ 7.64	− 1.31	+ 2.97	+ 12.13	− 12.88
700.66	30	Mid Cap Fund Indx	+ 7.58	− 0.76	+ 4.80	+ 12.82	− 15.32
168.43	30	Micro Cap Fund IX	+ 9.40	− 1.27	+ 5.78	+ 15.08	− 13.63
627.66	30	Small Cap Fund Index	+ 6.92	− 1.57	+ 5.09	+ 13.77	− 15.28
6,196.15	30	Growth & Income Index	+ 5.92	− 0.83	+ 3.33	+ 11.81	− 12.87
353.94	10	S&P 500 Fund Indx	+ 6.56	− 1.55	+ 2.39	+ 11.73	− 13.73
3,379.52	30	Equity Income Index	+ 4.88	− 0.74	+ 3.29	+ 11.14	− 13.50
Specialized Equity Indexes							
279.15	10	Hlth/Biotch Fd IX	+ 11.07%	− 0.26%	+ 6.13%	+ 15.36%	− 6.57%
479.11	10	Sci & Tech Index	+ 14.07	− 2.51	+ 4.92	+ 13.59	− 17.87
287.31	30	Utility Fund Indx	+ 7.23	+ 1.39	+ 5.57	+ 14.39	− 11.59
456.65	10	Fincl Svs Fd Indx	+ 5.79	− 1.34	+ 2.44	+ 11.13	− 11.86
204.67	10	Real Estate Fd IX	+ 12.41	+ 1.75	+ 5.42	+ 15.06	+ 6.44
117.54	10	Gold Fund Index	− 1.59	+ 3.53	+ 11.49	+ 0.45	− 6.18
570.96	30	Global Fund Index	+ 4.71	− 0.42	+ 4.60	+ 10.01	− 14.67
579.65	30	International Index	+ 3.88	− 0.10	+ 5.59	+ 8.80	− 14.93
237.07	10	European Fd Index	+ 6.90	+ 0.40	+ 6.18	+ 14.05	− 12.24
66.13	10	Pac Ex-Jpn Fd IX	+ 1.16	+ 0.12	+ 7.08	+ 1.39	− 19.02
104.93	10	Pacific Reg Fd IX	+ 0.46	+ 0.08	+ 6.19	+ 1.19	− 18.16
69.19	30	Emerg Mkt Fd Indx	+ 6.07	− 0.20	+ 4.98	+ 7.69	− 11.06
Other Equity Indexes							
336.64	30	Flex Port Fd Indx	+ 6.00%	− 0.66%	+ 3.20%	+ 9.39%	− 7.76%
232.78	10	Glbl Flx Fund IX	+ 6.07	− 0.40	+ 3.98	+ 8.67	− 4.55
4,325.17	30	Balanced Fund Index	+ 5.68	− 0.57	+ 2.79	+ 8.58	− 5.01
406.25	10	Conv Secur Index	+ 8.59	− 0.22	+ 3.38	+ 8.40	− 1.35
347.76	10	Income Fund Index	+ 5.54	+ 0.05	+ 2.50	+ 6.71	+ 0.28
Fixed-Income Indexes							
180.37	10	Intl Inc Fd IX	+ 10.09%	+ 1.47%	+ 5.60%	+ 6.54%	+ 24.93%
268.62	30	Global Inc Fd IX	+ 9.05	+ 1.27	+ 4.60	+ 6.45	+ 18.91
143.91	10	Ultra Short Fd Ix	+ 1.03	+ 0.02	+ 0.25	+ 0.58	+ 2.71
721.49	30	Gen Muni Dbt Indx	+ 4.13	+ 0.58	+ 2.69	+ 4.03	+ 9.99
402.19	30	Gen US Govt Fd IX	+ 3.12	+ 0.69	+ 2.17	+ 2.52	+ 11.04
427.89	10	GNMA Fund Index	+ 1.09	− 0.01	+ 0.30	+ 0.47	+ 6.32
225.63	10	US Mortgage Fd IX	+ 1.19	− 0.01	+ 0.25	+ 0.63	+ 6.35
1,066.28	30	A Rated Bnd Fd IX	+ 4.84	+ 0.74	+ 2.53	+ 3.78	+ 11.85
483.68	30	BBB Rated Fd IX	+ 7.09	+ 0.74	+ 3.00	+ 5.48	+ 13.25
259.90	10	Gen Bond Fd Index	+ 4.50	+ 0.46	+ 2.16	+ 3.82	+ 9.10
785.35	30	HI Yld Bond Fd IX	+ 12.07	− 0.25	+ 1.63	+ 9.36	+ 8.78
342.31	10	Ins Muni Fd Index	+ 4.56	+ 0.55	+ 2.76	+ 4.40	+ 10.97
321.27	10	HY Muni Dbt Fd IX	+ 3.57	+ 0.49	+ 2.48	+ 3.25	+ 7.28
143.54	10	Sh Muni Dbt Fd IX	+ 1.43	+ 0.13	+ 0.62	+ 0.96	+ 3.87
152.29	10	Sh-In Mun Dbt IX	+ 2.58	+ 0.41	+ 1.61	+ 2.08	+ 6.91
302.99	30	Intmdt Muni Fd IX	+ 3.74	+ 0.48	+ 2.25	+ 3.42	+ 9.27
251.09	30	Sht Inv Grd Fd IX	+ 1.81	+ 0.17	+ 0.71	+ 1.21	+ 4.93
229.24	30	Sh-In Inv Grd IX	+ 3.53	+ 0.60	+ 1.84	+ 2.72	+ 9.23
298.32	30	Intmdt Inv Grd IX	+ 4.76	+ 0.62	+ 2.20	+ 3.63	+ 11.30
220.87	10	Sh US Govt Fd IX	+ 1.09	+ 0.13	+ 0.46	+ 0.71	+ 4.74
265.17	30	Sh-In US Govt IX	+ 2.41	+ 0.38	+ 1.39	+ 1.83	+ 8.57
256.68	30	Intmdt US Govt IX	+ 3.08	+ 0.63	+ 2.05	+ 2.49	+ 10.93
162.21	10	CA Intmdt Muni IX	+ 3.14	+ 0.53	+ 2.15	+ 3.41	+ 8.26
408.52	30	CA Muni Dbt Fd IX	+ 3.96	+ 0.65	+ 2.67	+ 4.19	+ 9.76
199.91	10	FL Muni Dbt Fd IX	+ 3.98	+ 0.39	+ 2.23	+ 3.68	+ 9.41
181.29	10	MD Muni Dbt Fd IX	+ 3.88	+ 0.45	+ 2.16	+ 3.46	+ 9.65
294.84	10	MA Muni Dbt Fd IX	+ 4.45	+ 0.47	+ 2.57	+ 4.11	+ 10.86
222.02	10	MI Muni Dbt Fd IX	+ 4.03	+ 0.42	+ 2.28	+ 3.66	+ 9.97
283.72	10	MN Muni Dbt Fd IX	+ 4.48	+ 0.51	+ 2.39	+ 3.91	+ 10.18
222.96	10	NJ Muni Dbt Fd IX	+ 4.05	+ 0.51	+ 2.38	+ 3.79	+ 9.52
402.24	30	NY Muni Dbt Fd IX	+ 3.98	+ 0.53	+ 2.67	+ 3.86	+ 10.11
295.62	10	OH Muni Dbt Fd IX	+ 4.35	+ 0.50	+ 2.66	+ 4.08	+ 10.20
298.59	10	PA Muni Dbt Fd IX	+ 4.29	+ 0.46	+ 2.43	+ 3.91	+ 10.30
199.85	10	Muni Dbt VA Fd IX	+ 4.35	+ 0.53	+ 2.59	+ 4.19	+ 10.03

For a number of the indexes no long-term historical data exist. Source: Lipper

Source: Republished with permission of Dow Jones & Company, Inc., from *Barron's*, May 26, 2003, p. F19; permission conveyed through Copyright Clearance Center, Inc.

low commissions but give stripped-down service. These brokers are also very important (particularly the latter), and a comparative analysis will be provided at that point in the chapter.

Cash or Margin Account

Your broker will need to know if you want a cash account or margin account. Either account allows you three business days to pay for any purchase. A cash account requires full payment, while a margin account allows the investor to borrow a percentage of the purchase price from the brokerage firm. The percentage of the total cost the investor must pay is called the margin and is set by the Federal Reserve Board. During the great crash in the 1920s, margin on stock was only 10 percent, but it was as high as 80 percent in 1968. It has been at 50 percent since January 1974. The margin percentage is used to control speculation. Historically, when the Board of Governors of the Federal Reserve System thinks markets are being pushed too high by speculative fervor, it raises the margin requirement, which means more cash must be put up. The Fed has been hesitant to take action in this area in recent times.

Margin accounts are used mostly by traders and speculators or by investors who think their long-run return will be greater than the cost of borrowing. Most brokerage houses require a $2,000 minimum in an account before lending money, although many brokerage houses have higher limits. Here is how a margin account works. Assume you purchased 100 shares of Hershey Foods at $60 per share on margin and that margin is 50 percent:

Purchase: 100 shares at $60 per share	$6,000
Borrow: Cost × (1 − margin percentage)	−3,000
Margin: Equity contributed (cash or securities)	$3,000

You can borrow $3,000 or the total cost times (1 − margin percentage). The cost of borrowing is generally 1 to 2 percent above the prime rate, depending on the size of the account. Rather than putting up $3,000 in cash, a customer could put $3,000 of other approved financial assets into the account to satisfy the margin. Not all stocks may be used for margin purchases. The Securities and Exchange Commission publishes a list of approved securities that may be borrowed against.

One reason people buy on margin is to leverage their returns. Assume that Hershey stock rises to $80 per share. The account would now have $8,000 in stock and an increase in equity from $3,000 to $5,000:

100 shares at $80	$8,000
Loan	−3,000
Equity (margin)	$5,000

This $2,000 increase in equity creates a 67 percent return on the initial $3,000 of equity. The 67 percent return was accomplished on the basis of only a 33 percent increase in the price of stock ($60 to $80). With the increased equity in the account, the customer could now purchase additional securities on margin.

Margin is a two-edged sword, however, and what works to your advantage in up markets works to your disadvantage in down markets. If Hershey stock had gone to $40, your equity would decrease to $1,000:

100 shares at $40	$4,000
Borrowed	−3,000
Equity (margin)	$1,000

Minimum requirements for equity in a margin account are called *minimum maintenance standards* (usually 25 percent). Your equity would now be at minimum maintenance standards where the equity of $1,000 equals 25 percent of the current market value of $4,000. A fall below $1,000 would bring a margin call for more cash or equity. Many brokerage firms have maintenance requirements above 25 percent, and when margin calls are made, the equity often needs to be increased to 35 percent or more of the portfolio value. Normally, you must maintain a $2,000 minimum in your account, so you would have been called for more equity when the stock was at $50 even though the minimum maintenance requirement had not yet been reached.

One feature of a margin account is that margined securities may not be delivered to the customer. In this case, the Hershey stock would be kept registered in the street name of your retail brokerage house (e.g., Merrill Lynch), and your account would show a claim on 100 shares held as collateral for the loan. It is much like an automobile loan; you don't hold title to the car until you have made the last payment. In the use of margin, however, there is no due date on the loan. The use of margin increases risk and is not recommended for anyone who cannot afford large losses or who has no substantial experience in the market.

Long or Short?—That Is the Question

Once you have opened the account of your choice, you are ready to buy or sell. When investors establish a position in a security, they are said to have a long position if they purchase the security for their account. It is assumed the reason they purchased the security was to profit on an increase in price over time and/or to receive dividend income.

Sometimes investors anticipate that the price of a security may drop in value. If they are long in the stock, some may sell out their position. Those who have no position at all may wish to take a short position to profit from the expected decline. When you short a security, you are borrowing the security from the broker and selling it with the obligation to replace the security in the future. How you can sell something you don't own is an obvious question. Your broker will simply lend you the security from the brokerage house inventory. If your brokerage house doesn't have an inventory of the particular stock you want to short, the firm will borrow the stock from another broker.

Once you go short, you begin hoping and praying that the price of the security will go down so that you can buy it back and replace the security at a lower price. In a perverse way, bad news starts to become good news. When you read the morning paper, you look for signs of unemployment, high inflation, and rising interest rates in hopes of a stock market decline.

A short sale can only be made on a trade where the price of the stock advances (an uptick), or if there is no change in price, the prior trade must have been positive. These rules are intended to stop a snowballing decline in stock values caused by short sellers.

A margin requirement is associated with short selling, and it is currently equal to 50 percent of the securities sold short. Thus, if you were to sell 100 shares of Microsoft short at $70 per share, you would be required to put up $3,500 in margin (50 percent of $7,000). In a short sale, the margin is considered to be good-faith money and obviously is not a down payment toward purchase. The margin protects the brokerage house in case you start losing money on your account.

You would lose money on a short sales position if the stock you sold short starts going up. Assume Microsoft goes from $70 to $80. Since you initially sold 100 shares short at $70 per share, you have suffered a $1,000 paper loss. Your initial margin or equity position has been reduced from $3,500 to $2,500:

Initial margin (equity)	$3,500
Loss	−1,000
Current margin (equity)	$2,500

We previously specified that there is a minimum 25 percent margin maintenance requirement in buying stock. A similar requirement exists in selling short. The equity position must equal at least 30 percent of the *current* value of the stock that has been sold short. In the present example, the equity position is equal to $2,500, and the current market value of Microsoft is $8,000 ($80 × 100). Your margin percentage is 31.25 percent ($2,500 ÷ $8,000) or slightly above the minimum requirement. However, if the stock goes up another point or two and your losses increase, you will be asked to put up more margin to increase your equity position.

Of course, if the value of Microsoft stock goes down from its initial base of $70, you would be making profits off the bad news. A 20-point drop in Microsoft would mean a $2,000 profit on your 100 shares. Most market observers agree that it requires a "special breed of cat" to be an effective short seller. You often need nerves of steel and a contrarian outlook that cannot be easily shaken by good news.

One final point on selling short. In the last 10 or 15 years, some investors have chosen to use other ways to take a negative position in a security. These normally involve put and call options. Both selling short and option transactions can be effectively utilized for strategic purposes.

TYPES OF ORDERS

When an investor places an order to establish a position, he or she has many different kinds of orders from which to choose. When the order is placed with the broker on a NYSE-listed stock, it is teletyped to the exchange where it is executed by the company's floor broker in an auction market. Each stock is traded at a specific trading post on the floor of the exchange, so the floor broker knows exactly where to go to find other brokers buying and selling the same company's shares.

Most orders placed will be straightforward market orders to buy or sell. The market order will be carried by the floor broker to the correct trading post and will usually trade close to the last price or within 0.25 of a point.[4] For example, if you want to sell 100 shares of AT&T at market, you would probably have no trouble finding a ready buyer since AT&T may be trading a few million shares per day. But if you wanted to sell 100 shares of Bemis, as few as 1,000 shares might be traded in a day, and no other broker would be waiting at the Bemis post to make a transaction with the floor broker. If the broker finds no one else wishing to buy the shares, he will transact the sale with the specialist who is always at the post ready to buy and sell 100-share round lots. If the broker wants to sell, the specialist will either buy the shares for her own account at 0.125 or 0.25 less than the last trade or will buy out of her book in which special orders of others are kept.

Two basic special orders are the limit order and the stop order. A limit order limits the price at which you are willing to buy or sell and ensures you will pay no more than the limit price on a buy or receive no less than the limit price on a sell. Assume you are trying to buy a thinly traded stock that fluctuates in value and you are afraid that with a market order you might risk paying more than you want. So you would place a limit order to buy 100 shares of Allied Waste Industries, as an example, at 16.50 or a better price. The order will go to the floor broker who goes to the post to check the price. The broker finds Allied Waste trading at its high for the day of 16.80, and so he leaves the limit order with the specialist who records it in his book. The entry will record the price, date, time, and brokerage firm. There may be other orders in front of yours at 16.50, but once these are cleared, and assuming the stock stays in this range, your order will be executed at 16.50 or less. Limit orders are used by investors to buy or sell thinly traded stocks or to buy securities at prices thought to be at the low end of a price range and to sell securities at the high end of the price range. Investors who calculate fundamental values have a basic idea of what they think a stock is worth and will often set a limit to take advantage of what they view to be discrepancies in values.

---

4. Since the NYSE has gone to decimals, the difference could be less.

Many traders are certain they want their order to be executed if a certain price is reached. A limit order does not guarantee execution if orders are ahead of you on the specialist's book. In cases where you want a guaranteed "fill" of the order, a stop order is placed. A stop order is a two-part mechanism. It is placed at a specific price like a limit order, but when the price is reached, the stop turns into a market order that will be executed at close to the stop price but not necessarily at the exact price specified. Often, many short-term traders will view a common stock price with optimism for a certain trading strategy. When the stock hits the price, it may pop up on an abundance of buy orders or decline sharply on a large volume of sell orders, and your "fill" could be several dollars away from the top price. Assume AXE Corporation stock has been trading between $25 and $40 per share over the last six months, reaching both these prices three times. A trader may follow several strategies. One strategy would be to buy at $25 and sell at $40 using a stop buy and a stop sell order. Some traders may put in a stop buy at $41 thinking that if the stock breaks through its peak trading range it will go on to new highs, and finally some may put in a stop sell at $24 to either eliminate a long position or establish a short position with the assumption the stock has broken its support and will trend lower. When used to eliminate a long position, a stop order is often called a *stop-loss order.*

Limit orders and stop orders can be "day orders" that expire at the end of the day if not executed, or they can be GTC (good till canceled) orders. GTC orders will remain on the specialist's books until taken off by the brokerage house or executed. If the order remains unfilled for several months, most brokerage houses will send reminders that the order is still pending so that the client does not get caught buying stock for which he or she is unable to pay.

COST OF TRADING

Nowhere has the field of investments changed more than in the means and cost of trading. A decade ago, the basic choice was between full-service brokerage firms such as Merrill Lynch, PaineWebber (now UBS PaineWebber), and Dean Witter (now Morgan Stanley Dean Witter) and discount brokers such as Charles Schwab, Quick & Reilly, and Olde. The discount brokers provided bare bones service and generally charged 25 to 75 percent of the commissions charged by full-service brokers, who willingly provided research and stock analysis to clients, tax information, and help in establishing goals and objectives.

The nature of the landscape changed radically with the emergence of the Internet. Now, an investor can merely access an online broker's website to open an account, review the operating procedures and commission schedule, and initiate a trade. Confirmation of an electronic trade can take as little as 10 seconds and almost all trades are completed within a minute.

Online brokers such as Ameritrade and E-trade have become household names—and why not? A recent study by the American Association of Individual Investors indicated that for a 100-share trade, the average online broker charged $15. In comparison, the average discount broker charged $42, while a full-service broker charged $100.

To examine the effect of the pricing differential, assume 100 shares are traded at $40 per share for a total value of $4,000. Note the difference in percentage costs between the three types of brokers.

Online broker	$15/$4,000 = 0.37%
Discount broker	$42/$4,000 = 1.05%
Full-service broker	$100/$4,000 = 2.50%

Because of the intense competition provided by online brokers, in the late 1990s, many full-service and deep discount brokers began offering their clients the alternative of online trading. Merrill Lynch was the first major full-service broker to go this route, and Charles Schwab led the way among discount brokers (over half of Schwab's trades are now online). All others in the industry have followed the same path, so the landscape is blurred between full-service and deep discount brokers that offer an online alternative and pure online brokers. Even banks and mutual funds offer online trading through brokerage subsidiaries.

While online trading is a very attractive trading alternative because of the low commission rate, it is not for everyone. For the less sophisticated investor or computer novice, full service (or even the discount broker) may be the way to go. The importance of explanations about capital gains tax implications, potential merger tender offers, retirement and estate planning, etc., may outweigh savings in commissions. That is why most major traditional houses offer alternative ways to go. Nevertheless, for the sophisticated investor who knows his or her own mind, it is impractical to pay for additional unused and unnecessary services. While 10 to 15 percent of all trades are currently online, the number will undoubtedly double or triple in the next few years.

The Internet has not only influenced the way trades are executed, but has given the individual investor access to instant information that was once in the private domain of large institutional investors such as mutual funds or bank trust departments. Individual investors can download balance sheets, income statements, up-to-the-minute press releases, and so on. They can also participate in chat rooms and e-mail the company for immediate answers to questions.

All of these options certainly represents progress, with one caveat. The intoxication of it all has led to a new class of "day traders," who attempt to beat the market on an hourly or by-the-minute basis. While some with exceptional skill have profited by this activity, all too many others were badly hurt when the ever-climbing bull market of CISCO Systems, Intel, and Microsoft came to an end. Surgeons and trial lawyers suddenly decided the market was not as easy a play toy as they once thought and returned to their "day jobs."

TAXES

In making many types of investments, an important consideration will be the tax consequences of your investment (taxes may be more significant than the brokerage commissions just discussed).

This section is intended only as a brief overview of tax consequences. For more information, consult a tax guide. Consultation with a CPA, CFP (Certified Financial Planner), or similar sources may also be advisable.

Before we specifically talk about the tax consequences of investment *gains and losses,* let's briefly look at the tax rates that were in place at year-end 2003 for overall taxable income. The rates are presented in Table 4-5. Incredible as it sounds, the rates will revert back to their *pre-tax-law* level in 2011 under the sunset provision of the tax act unless the law is reenacted by then. This is so unpredictable, we will not specifically deal with that issue.

Refer to Table 4-5 and assume you have appropriately computed your taxable income after all deductions as $34,000. Further assume you are single so that you fall into the upper portion of the table. How much is your tax obligation? The answer is shown below:

	Amount	Rate	Tax
First	$ 7,000	10%	$ 700.00
Next	20,050*	15	3,007.50
Next	6,950**	25	1,737.50
	$34,000		$5,445.00

*$27,050 − 7,000
**$34,000 − 27,050

TABLE 4–5 Tax Rates 2003

Taxable Income	Rate (%)
Single	
$ 0–$ 7,000	10
7,000– 27,050	15
27,050– 65,550	25
65,550– 136,750	28
136,750– 297,350	33
Over 297,350	35
Married (joint return)	
$ 0–$ 14,000	10
12,000– 45,200	15
45,200– 109,250	25
109,250– 166,500	28
166,500– 297,350	33
Over 297,350	35

The total tax is $5,445. The rates of 10, 15, and 25 percent are referred to as marginal tax rates. The average tax is a slightly different concept. It is simply the amount of taxes paid divided by taxable income, or 16.01 percent in this case:

$$\frac{\text{Taxes paid}}{\text{Taxable income}} = \frac{\$5{,}445}{\$34{,}000} = 16.01\%$$

Capital Gains

A capital gain or loss occurs when an asset held for investment purposes is sold. A long-term capital gain takes place when an asset is held for more than a year, and the maximum tax rate is 15 percent on long-term capital gains. This rate falls to 5 percent for those in the lowest tax bracket. These rates went into effect with the Tax Act of 2003 and apply to sales of securities made after May 5, 2003 and before January 1, 2009.

If an asset is not held for more than 12 months, its sale represents a short-term capital gain or loss, and the tax treatment is exactly the same as ordinary income. This means it is taxed at the rates shown in Table 4-5. For example, if a person is in the 35 percent tax bracket and sells a stock owned for only six months, the tax on gain would be 35 percent. If he or she had held the asset for 12 months, the long-term capital gains tax rate on the gain would have only been 15 percent.

As you can see, there are some strong inducements to go for the longer term capital gains treatment. Assume an investor is in a 35 percent tax bracket and sells a stock at a $10,000 profit. Note the different amounts of taxes owed based on the holding period:

Holding Period	Profit	Tax Rate	Taxes
6 months	$10,000	35%	$3,500
Over 12 months	10,000	15	1,500

Because of the incentive to get preferential longer term capital gains, it is thought by some that the tax code leads many investors to pick investments that have long-term growth potential.

The new Tax Act of 2003 also lowered the tax on dividends so that the tax on dividends is now the same as the tax on long-term capital gains of 15 percent and 5 percent for taxpayers at the 10 percent ordinary income tax rate. However, not all dividends will receive the same treatment. For example, dividends on Real Estate Investment Trusts will be taxed at a different rate. Please check with your tax adviser. We merely bring up the issues of taxes to impress upon you that taxes are an important part of your investment decision process.

For investors putting their money into tax-deferred investments [such as an IRA or 401(k)], these tax considerations during the holding period are not relevant. Furthermore, taxes are only one of the many variables that should influence an investment decision.

It should also be pointed out that when you have net investment losses in any one year, you can write off up to $3,000 of these losses against other taxable income (salary, interest income, etc.). Any unused balance can be carried forward into the future to be written off against future capital gains from investments or other forms of income.

Internet Resources

Website Address	Comments
www.msci.com	Provides information on bond and stock indexes
www.barra.com	Provides information on various modified indexes
www.edgar-online.com	Provides access to SEC filings
www.quicken.com	Provides access to company SEC filings
www.my.yahoo.com	Profile pages on stock quotes provide access to company SEC filings
www.standardandpoors.com	Contains information about S&P indexes and the markets
www.dowjones.com	Provides information about the Dow Jones indexes

Chapter 5

Economic Activity

To determine the value of the firm, fundamental analysis relies on long-run forecasts of the economy, the industry, and the company's financial prospects. Short-run changes in business conditions are also important in that they influence investors' required rates of return and expectations of corporate earnings and dividends. This chapter presents the basic information for analysis of the economy, while the following chapters focus on industry analysis and the individual firm.

Figure 5–1 presents an overview of the top-down valuation process as an inverted triangle. The process starts with a macroanalysis of the economy and then moves into industry variables. Next, common stocks are individually screened according to expected risk-return characteristics, and finally the surviving stocks are combined into portfolios of assets. This figure is not inclusive of all variables considered by an analyst, but is intended to indicate representative areas applicable to most industries and companies.

ECONOMIC ACTIVITY AND THE BUSINESS CYCLE

An investor begins the valuation process with an economic analysis. The hope is that an accurate forecast and examination of economic activity will provide the basis for accurate stock market predictions and indicate which industries may prosper. The analyst needs information on present and expected interest rates, monetary and fiscal policy, government and consumer spending patterns, and other economic data. To be successful, investors must understand business cycles and be able to forecast accurately. Unfortunately, these are not easy tasks, but the rewards can be significant if the timing is right.

Whether analysts use statistical methods, such as regression analysis and probability theory, or simply seat-of-the-pants judgment, they are still basing their forecast on expectations related to past data and experiences. Past information usually is not extrapolated into the future without being adjusted to conform with the subjective beliefs of the decision maker. Even when highly sophisticated statistical methods are used, subjectivity enters into the decision in some fashion.

Most likely, past knowledge will be helpful, but modifications for the present effects of worldwide currency fluctuations, international debt obligations, and

FIGURE 5–1 Top-Down Overview of the Valuation Process

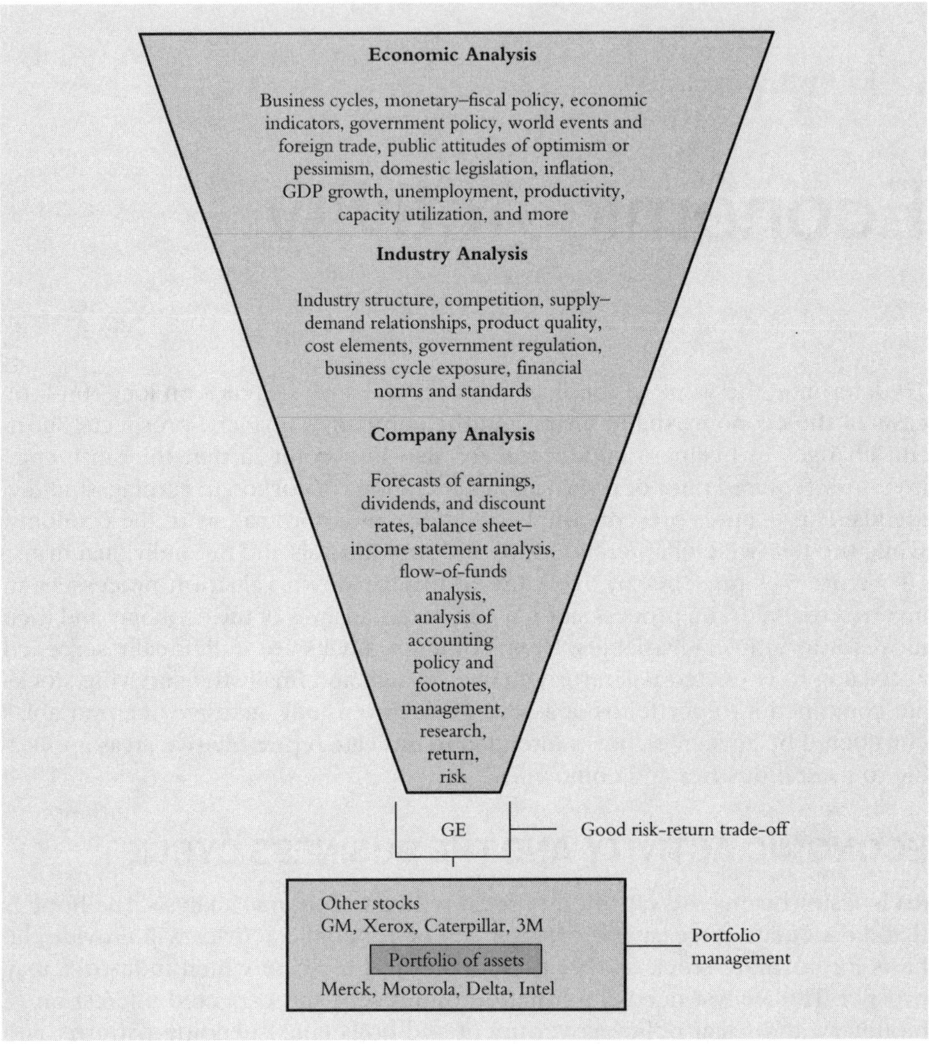

Economic Analysis

Business cycles, monetary–fiscal policy, economic indicators, government policy, world events and foreign trade, public attitudes of optimism or pessimism, domestic legislation, inflation, GDP growth, unemployment, productivity, capacity utilization, and more

Industry Analysis

Industry structure, competition, supply–demand relationships, product quality, cost elements, government regulation, business cycle exposure, financial norms and standards

Company Analysis

Forecasts of earnings, dividends, and discount rates, balance sheet–income statement analysis, flow-of-funds analysis, analysis of accounting policy and footnotes, management, research, return, risk

GE — Good risk-return trade-off

Other stocks
GM, Xerox, Caterpillar, 3M
Portfolio of assets
Merck, Motorola, Delta, Intel
— Portfolio management

other factors, which were not so important previously, need to be included in any forecast now. Since most companies are influenced to some degree by the general level of economic activity, a forecast will usually start with an analysis of the government's economic program.

Federal Government Economic Policy

Government economic policy is guided by the Employment Act of 1946 and subsequent position statements by the Federal Reserve Board, the President's

Council of Economic Advisors, and other acts of Congress. The goals established by the Employment Act still hold and cover four broad areas. These goals, the focus of monetary and fiscal policy, are as follows with a second interpretation in parentheses:

1. Stable prices (a low inflation rate).
2. Business stability at high levels of production (low levels of unemployment).
3. Sustained real growth in gross domestic product (actual economic growth after deducting inflation).
4. A balance in international payments (primarily a balance of exports and imports but also including cash flows in and out of the United States).

These goals are often conflicting in that they do not all respond favorably to the same economic stimulus. Therefore, goal priorities and economic policies change to reflect current economic conditions. In the 1950s and early 1960s, the United States did not have an international trade problem or spiraling inflation, so economic policy focused on employment and economic growth. The economy grew rapidly between 1961 and 1969, and, because of the Vietnam War, unemployment reached very low levels. The demand for goods and competition for funds were very high during the war, and eventually war expenditures, large budget deficits, full employment, and large increases in the money supply caused many problems. Inflation accelerated to high levels, interest rates reached record heights, and an imbalance of international payments finally resulted in two devaluations of the U.S. dollar in the early 1970s.

By the time Jimmy Carter took office in January 1977, the primary goals were once again to reduce unemployment, control inflation, and create a moderate level of economic growth that could be sustained without causing more inflation (a very difficult task!). The achievement of these goals was thrown into the hands of the Federal Reserve Board. The Fed's tight money policy caused a rapid increase in interest rates to control inflation, and these high rates depressed common stock prices as the required rate of return by investors reached record levels.

Ronald Reagan inherited most of the problems Carter faced but tried new ways of reaching the goals. As the 1980s began, Reagan instituted a three-year tax cut to increase disposable income and stimulate consumption and thus economic growth, and, at the same time, he negotiated reductions in government spending. These policies were successful in sharply reducing inflation and creating strong growth in the gross domestic product (GDP), but they were accomplished with record government deficits. George H. Bush followed most of Reagan's domestic policies but focused more on international issues. In the middle of President Bush's term, the 90-month peacetime expansion came to an end with the start of a recession in July 1990. In looking back, the expansion that began in November 1982 created record employment, reduced unemployment percentages, and lowered interest rates and inflation from the high levels of 1980 and 1981. The stock market began a major bull market in 1982 in response to these improved conditions but also sustained the biggest one-day crash ever on October 19, 1987.

Unfortunately, the recession that began in July 1990 was extremely painful. Major companies such as IBM, AT&T, TRW, General Motors, and hundreds of others announced employee reductions totaling more than one-half million employees. In November 1992, President Clinton was elected to office on the promise of more jobs and universal health coverage. The economy was already benefiting from the recovery started in March 1991, and Clinton persuaded Congress to pass an increase in personal and corporate income taxes. Many economists thought the tax increase would create a "fiscal drag" on the economy by reducing spending. By the third quarter of 1992, the economy had slowed down considerably and stagnated at minimal real GDP growth. However, by year end 1993, real GDP growth in the fourth quarter was more than 7 percent, and by the end of 1994 had stabilized at between 3.0 and 3.5 percent real growth. A Republican Congress was elected in 1994 and came into office in January 1995. President Clinton was elected for a second term in 1996, and he and Congress went to work on a balanced budget proposal. Spending was held in check, and tax revenues rose to record levels as a result of the long-term healthy growth of the economy.

The combination of these factors created large surpluses and projections of even larger surpluses in the coming years. Between 1997 and 2001 the U.S. Treasury was able to retire several hundred billion dollars of government debt. One of the results of deficit reduction is the loss of a fiscal stimulus created by government spending, and this can cause a drag on the economy if consumers don't pick up the slack. Consumers were more than happy to spend, and the economy rolled along until about 2000 when it slowed a little. The stock market started to decline in April 2000, and when George W. Bush took office in January 2001, he inherited a crumbling economy that had run out of steam after years of exceptional growth. By summer 2001, the economy managed to squeeze out a 0.2 percent growth in second quarter GDP, and the surplus was shrinking fast due to declining tax revenues and the tax cuts passed in the early days of the Bush administration. The third quarter of 2001, punctuated by the September 11th terrorist attack, generated a negative growth rate and the NBER declared a recession with a starting date of March 2001. By the fourth quarter of 2001, the economy was once again growing but at a low rate.

Unfortunately, at the same time, Japan was still suffering from more than a decade of economic decline, and Europe (especially Germany) was also beginning to experience an economic slowdown. The new European currency, the euro, was officially introduced in January 2002, but the economic impact of the 11 countries forming the European Monetary System was still in its early stages of economic transformation. Many former communist countries such as Russia, Poland, the Czech Republic, and Hungary were growing but still struggling to become capitalistic economies, and a slowdown in the industrialized world economies deprived them of investors and economic growth.

The international landscape is changing rapidly, and this includes economic changes in North America, South America, and Asia. As we enter this new era of the global economy, we cannot always rely on the past for indications about the future. The rising tide of capitalistic economies, China's emergence as an economic power, and world trade agreements will change the way the world's political and economic systems interact. The knowledge of economic theory and its applications will increase in importance to investors pursuing international strategies or to U.S. companies making foreign investments. The ability to interpret these events could have significant financial implications on investment returns for both investors and companies.

Fiscal Policy

Fiscal policy can be described as the government's taxing and spending policies. These policies can have a great impact on the direction of economic activity. One must realize at the outset that fiscal policy is cumbersome. It has a long implementation lag and is often motivated by political rather than economic considerations since Congress must approve budgets and develop tax laws. Figure 5-2 presents a historical picture of government income and expenditures. When the government spends more than it receives, it runs a deficit that must be financed by the Treasury.

A forecaster must pay attention to the size of the deficit and how it is financed to measure its expected impact on the economy. If the deficit is financed by the Treasury selling securities to the Federal Reserve, it is very expansive. The money supply will increase without having any significant short-run effects on interest rates. If the deficit is financed by selling securities to banks and individuals, there is not the same expansion in the money supply, and short-term interest rates will rise unless the Federal Reserve intervenes with open-market trading.

A look at Figure 5-2 shows that surpluses, in which revenues exceed expenditures, have been virtually nonexistent from 1966 to 1997, and the annual deficit increased dramatically during the 1980s. Surpluses tend to reduce economic growth as the government slows its demand for goods and services relative to its income. In an analysis of fiscal policy, the important consideration for the investor is the determination of the flow of funds. In a deficit economy, the government usually stimulates GDP by spending on socially productive programs or by increasing spending on defense, education, highways, or other government programs. The Reagan administration instituted budget cuts in education and social programs at the same time it reduced tax revenues through tax cuts. This strategy was one that attempted to shift GDP growth from the government sector into the private sector. In the George H. Bush administration, there was inconsistent fiscal policy. Clinton made it clear with his new tax increases that he would use fiscal policy to increase tax revenues to help shrink the fiscal deficit. He instituted a more progressive tax policy in 1993 by raising rates and reducing deductions for high-income people. His hope was that the wealthy would not slow down their spending and that the increased tax revenues would help decrease the fiscal deficit. He was right. Although Clinton and the Republican Congress passed further legislation in 1997 to reduce the deficit, cut taxes, and reduce entitlements, the deficit was already well in check by then (and moving toward a surplus) because of greatly increased tax revenue in a prospering economy. The increasing

FIGURE 5–2 Federal Budget Seasonally Adjusted Annual Rates

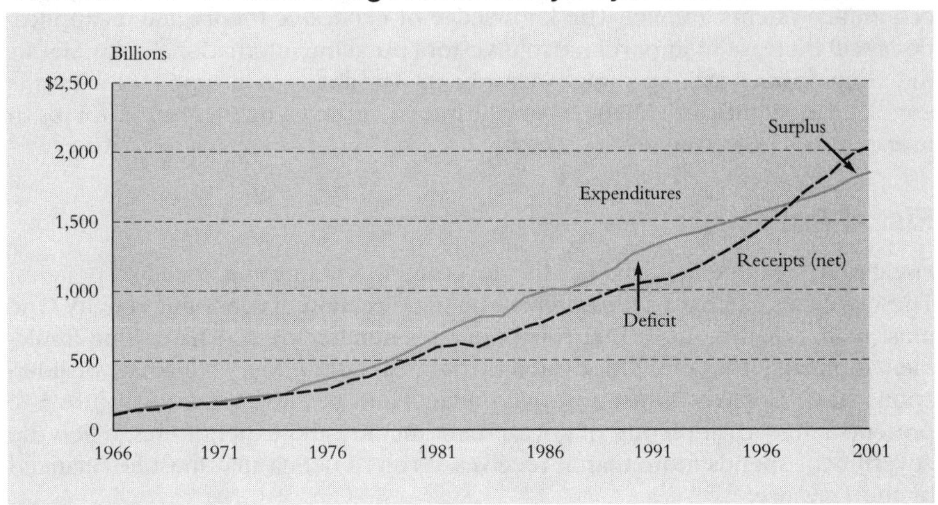

surplus from 1997 to 2001 is quite visible in Figure 5-2. Unfortunately, the government expenditures following September 11th pushed the government into a deficit spending budget for fiscal year 2002.

One other area of fiscal policy deals with the government's ability to levy import taxes or tariffs on foreign goods. As a free market economy, we have fought for years with our trading partners to open their countries' markets to U.S. goods. Figure 5-3 depicts the annual trade deficits that started piling up beginning in 1982. This deficit occurred because U.S. consumers purchased more foreign goods than U.S. companies sold to foreigners. This occurred for several reasons; one was a lack of free markets with some of our trading partners, specifically Japan, and the robust health of the U.S. economy. The United States has been trying to open markets for U.S. goods with Japan, China, and other countries for the last several decades. The World Trade Organization (WTO) and its round of tariff negotiations have been instrumental in breaking down trade barriers during the last half of the 1990s, and in 2001 China was approved for membership in the WTO, which should have long-term positive effects on world trade.

Countries can create trade barriers by either setting up import tariffs or taxes that raise the price of foreign goods and make them less competitive with domestic goods. This is a common way to protect domestic industries. The WTO deals with these issues through negotiations and if necessary through a world court to arbitrate complaints from one country against another.

As Figure 5-3 shows, the U.S. trade deficit increased quite rapidly from 1996 to 2000, rising from a negative $89.4 billion in 1997 to a negative $364 billion in 2000. By 2001 the United States had the largest trading deficit with China, followed by Japan in second place.

The rising trade deficit during this time period was a function of the healthy U.S. economy and a strong dollar. When a country's economy is healthy with high employment and income, its citizens spend more in general and import more

FIGURE 5–3 Imports and Exports in Current Dollars

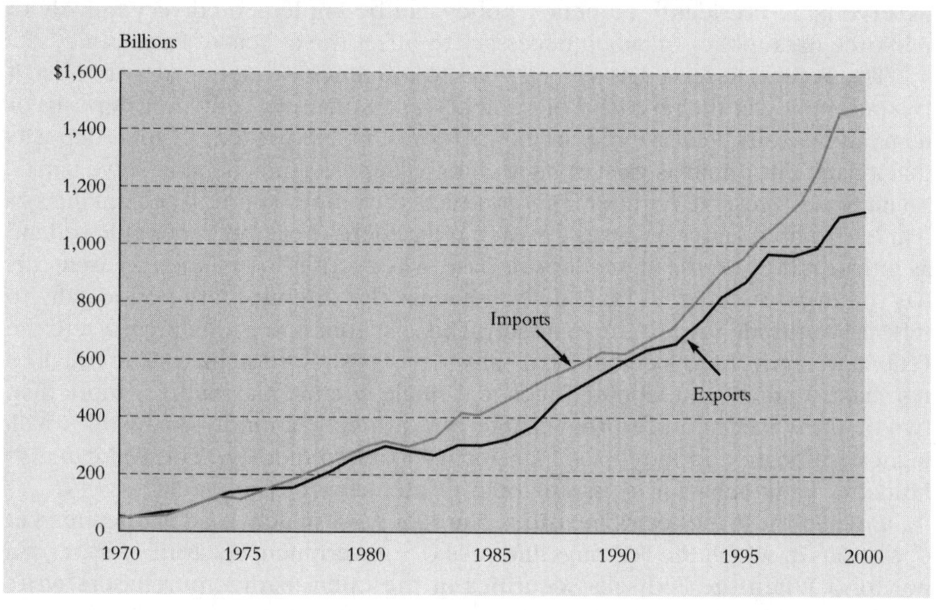

goods (especially high-priced luxury goods) from other countries. When a recession is occurring, people spend less, look for less expensive items, and import fewer goods. The second factor is the exchange rate between two currencies. For example, if the U.S. dollar rises against the British pound, U.S. goods become more expensive for British citizens, and British goods become less expensive for U.S. citizens. If the dollar exchange rate stays high or continues to rise, eventually British citizens change their buying habits and buy fewer U.S. goods, and U.S. citizens buy more British goods. This effect can also be seen in the U.S.-Japanese automobile market. As the Japanese yen rose against the dollar, in the early 1990s, Americans bought fewer Japanese cars and more U.S. domestic cars. The Japanese consumer did the opposite. The pattern reversed itself in 1996–97 with an increase in the dollar versus the yen. Short-term swings in exchange rates have little effect on imports and exports, but changes in long-term currency relationships eventually change import-export balances between countries. It usually takes more than a year before the effects of exchange rates on prices show up at the retail level and influence the buying patterns of consumers. As world trade increases, exchange rates and economic trends around the world become more important. While exchange rates and economic activity are influenced by fiscal policy, they are also affected by monetary policy, as discussed in the next section.

Monetary Policy

Monetary policy determines the "appropriate" levels for the money supply and interest rates that accomplish the economic goals of the Employment Act of 1946. Monetary policy is determined by the Federal Open Market Committee (FOMC), which includes the Federal Reserve Board of Governors and the 12 Federal Reserve bank presidents. Monetary policy can be implemented very quickly to reinforce fiscal policy or, when necessary, to offset the effects of fiscal policy.

The Federal Reserve has several ways to influence economic activity. First, it can raise or lower the reserve requirements on commercial bank time deposits or demand deposits. Reserve requirements represent the percent of total deposits that a bank must hold as cash in its vault or as deposits in Federal Reserve banks. An increase in reserve requirements contracts the money supply. The banking system has to hold larger reserves for each dollar deposited and is not able to lend as much money on the same deposit base. A reduction in reserve requirements has the opposite effect. The Fed also changes the discount rate periodically to reflect its attitude toward the economy. This discount rate is the interest rate the Federal Reserve charges commercial banks on very short-term loans. The Fed does not make a practice of lending funds to a single commercial bank for more than two or three weeks, and so this charge can influence an individual bank's willingness to borrow money for expansionary loans to industry. The Fed can also influence bank behavior by issuing policy statements, or jawboning.

Beyond these monetary measures, the tool most widely used is open-market operations in which the Fed buys and sells U.S. government securities for its own portfolio. When the Fed sells securities in the open market, purchasers write checks to pay for their securities, and demand deposits fall, causing a contraction in the money supply. At the same time, the increase in the supply of Treasury bills sold by the Fed forces prices down and interest rates up to entice buyers to part with their money. The Fed usually accomplishes its adjustments by selling securities to commercial banks, government securities dealers, or individuals.

If the Fed buys securities, the opposite occurs; the money supply increases, and interest rates go down. This tends to encourage economic expansion. As you will see in Chapter 7, the interest rate is extremely important in determining the required rate of return, or discount rate for a stock.

Table 5-1 summarizes the monetary policy goals and their impact on the economic goals presented earlier in the chapter.

As chairman of the Federal Reserve, Alan Greenspan exercised unusual power over the economy in the last decade. The Fed not only carefully managed monetary policy, but his semiannual appearances before the House Banking Committee, as mandated by federal legislation, drew attention on Wall Street and throughout the world financial capitals. A good portion of the success of the U.S. economy during the 1990s is attributed to Greenspan and his carefully crafted economic policy. Whether future historians will be as generous only time will tell.

Government Policy, Real Growth, and Inflation

In November 1991, the U.S. Commerce Department's Economic Bureau of Analysis shifted from gross national product to gross domestic product as the measure of economic activity for the U.S. economy. The gross domestic product (GDP) measurement makes us more compatible with the rest of the world and measures only output from U.S. factories and consumption within the United States. Gross

TABLE 5–1 Economic Policy Goals and Monetary Policy

Policy Goals	Raise Rates	Lower Rates
1. Sustainable growth in real GDP	Reduces economic growth	Stimulates economic growth
2. Business stability at high levels of production (low levels of unemployment)	Dampens employment	Stimulates employment
3. Balance in international payments		
a) Balance of trade (imports and exports)	Strengthens domestic currency (imports up, exports down)	Decreases domestic currency (imports down, exports up)
b) Cash flows between countries	Foreign investment inflows	Foreign investment outflows
4. Stable prices (a low inflation rate)	Reduces inflationary impact	Increases inflationary impact
Monetary Tools	**Raise Rates**	**Lower Rates**
Bank reserve requirements	Raise reserve requirements (takes money out of banking system—creates less loanable funds)	Lower reserve requirements (puts money into banking system—creates more loanable funds)
Discount rate	Raises the rate at which banks can borrow from the federal reserve bank	Lowers the rate at which banks can borrow from the federal reserve bank
Federal open market committee activity	Sells treasury securities (lowers prices and raises rates—takes money out of economy)	Buys treasury securities (raises prices and lowers rates—puts money into economy)
Jawboning (talking rates up or down in markets)	Say good things about GDP	Say bad things about GDP

domestic product does not include products made by U.S. companies in foreign countries, but gross national product did. Other U.S. economic measures such as employment, production, and capacity are also measured within the boundaries of the United States, and, with the switch to GDP, we now measure economic output consistently with these other variables.

Figure 5-4 depicts 40 years of real gross domestic product (GDP) and the consumer price index. Real GDP reflects gross domestic product in constant dollars, which eliminates the effects of inflation from GDP expressed in current dollars. Real GDP measures output in physical terms rather than in dollars that are inflated by price increases.

This information in Figure 5-4 needs to be looked at in context with the annual percentage change in the consumer price index (CPI), which is used as a proxy for inflation. Notice the relationship between real GDP and the CPI. The change in real GDP is inversely related to the rate of inflation. As inflation rises, real GDP falls (as indicated in 1970, 1975, 1980–81, and 1989–90), and as inflation subsides, as in 1982–83 and 1985–86, real GDP rises. Because real GDP is the measure of economic output in real physical terms, it does not do any good to stimulate the economy only to have all the gains eroded by inflation.

To understand the major sectors of the economy and the relative influence of each sector, we divide gross domestic product into its four basic areas: personal consumption expenditures, government purchases, gross private investment, and net exports. Figure 5-5 shows the contribution of each one to the total GDP over the past four decades. It becomes clear from Figure 5-5 that personal consumption is growing faster than the other sectors and is the driving force behind economic growth. In fact consumer spending accounts for more than 60 percent of GDP. For this reason economic forecasters pay close attention to the mood of the consumer.

The University of Michigan surveys consumer expectations on a monthly basis and reports whether consumers are becoming more or less optimistic. Consumer expectation is a leading indicator of economic activity—when consumer confidence increases, this bodes well for spending; when consumer confidence decreases, this indicates a possible contraction in spending. Figure 5-6 presents a historical view of the index of consumer expectation. It is easy to spot the recessions of 1973–75, 1980–81, and 1990–91. In all cases consumer expectations turned down before the recession began. In looking at the period 1990–2001, we can see the large rise in confidence with many short-term reversals on the downside. The index peaked in the first quarter of 2000, dropping from 111.3 to 92 by the first quarter of 2001. In the next section we look at the cyclical nature of gross domestic product.

BUSINESS CYCLES AND CYCLICAL INDICATORS

The economy expands and contracts through a business cycle process. By measuring GDP and other economic data, we can develop a statistical picture of the economic growth pattern. The National Bureau of Economic Research (NBER) is the final authority in documenting cyclical turning points. The NBER defines recessions as two or more quarters of negative real GDP growth and documents the beginning and end of a recession. Table 5-2 presents a historical picture of business cycle expansions and contractions in the United States. While the modern-day data may be more relevant, it is interesting to see that economic cycles have existed and been defined for more than 140 years.

Table 5-2 measures each contraction and expansion and then presents summary data at the bottom of the table for all business cycles and for cycles in peacetime only. A trough represents the end of a recession and the beginning of an expansion, and a peak represents the end of an expansion and the beginning of a recession. In general, we see on the last line of Table 5-2 that during peacetime cycles between 1945 and 2001, contractions (recessions) lasted an average of

FIGURE 5–4 Real Gross Domestic Product and the Consumer Price Index

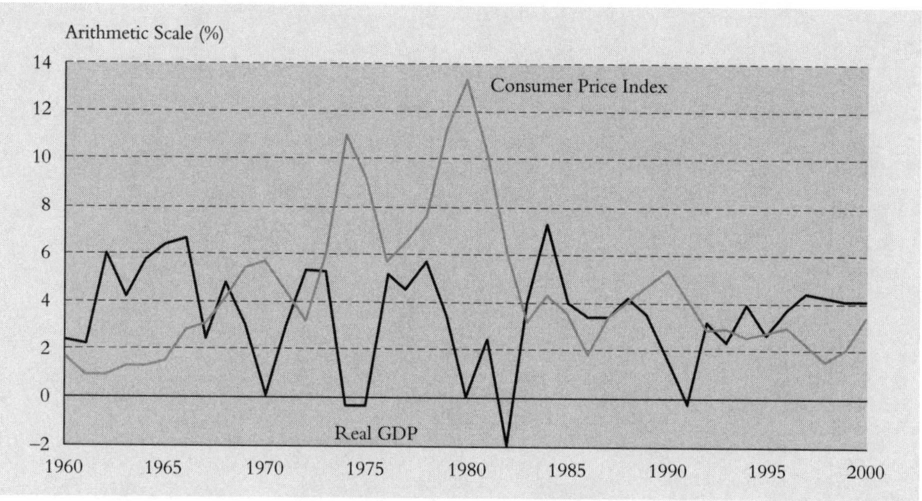

FIGURE 5–5 Breakdown of Gross Domestic Product in Current Dollars

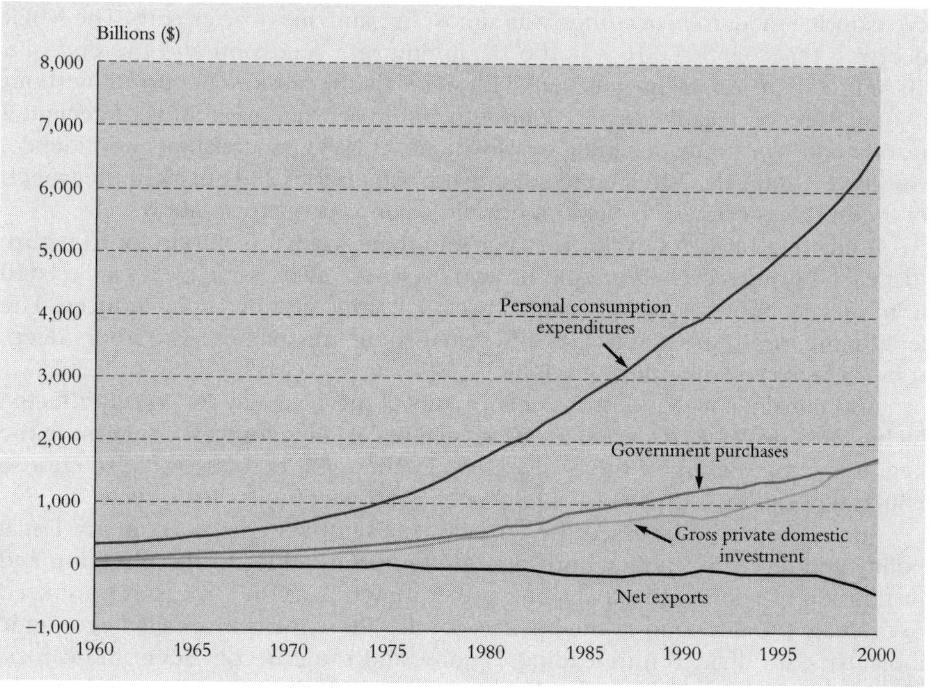

FIGURE 5–6 Consumer Expectations, University of Michigan (Index: 1966:1 = 100)

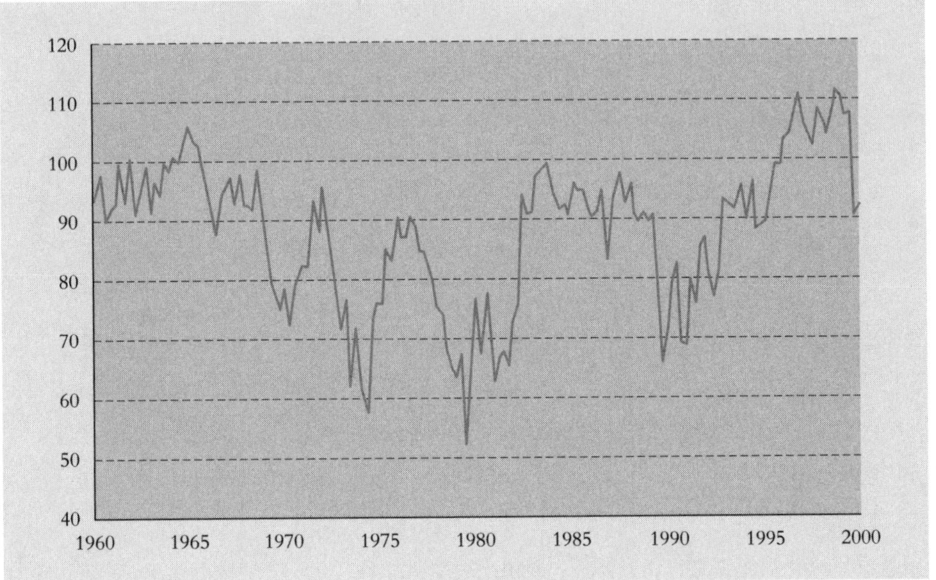

11 months, while expansions averaged 52 months. Thus, one *complete* business cycle during modern *peacetimes* lasts almost five and one-quarter years. The NBER declared that March 2001 was the beginning of a recession and the end of a 10-year expansion. This unusual dating of the recession occurred without two quarters of negative real GDP growth, but in the face of months of declining manufacturing output, declining employment, and sagging consumer confidence. On July 17, 2003, the NBER concluded that November of 2001 marked the trough of the business cycle. The eight-month recession was relatively short.

Predicting business cycles is easier said than done. It is important to realize that each business cycle is unique; no two cycles are alike. Some cycles are related to monetary policy; some are demand related; some are inventory induced. The length and depth of each is also different—some are shallow, and others deep; some are short, while others are long.

Additionally, not all industries or segments of the economy are equally affected by business cycles. However, if investors can make some forecast concerning the beginning and ending of the business cycle, they will be better able to choose which types of investments to hold over the various phases of the cycle.

So far, we have discussed the government's impact on the economy. Fiscal policy and monetary policy both provide important clues to the direction and magnitude of economic expansions and contractions. Other measures are used to evaluate the direction of the business cycle. These measures, called economic indicators, are divided into leading, lagging, and roughly coincident indicators. The NBER classifies indicators relative to their performance at economic peaks and troughs. Leading indicators change direction in advance of general business

TABLE 5–2 Business Cycle Expansions and Contractions in the United States

Business Cycle Reference Dates		Duration in Months Cycle			
Trough	Peak	Contraction (Trough from previous peak)	Expansion (Trough to peak)	Trough from Previous Trough	Peak from Previous Peak
December 1854	June 1857	—	30	—	—
December 1858	October 1860	18	22	48	40
June 1861	April 1865	8	46	30	54
December 1867	June 1889	32	18	78	50
December 1870	October 1873	18	34	36	52
March 1879	March 1882	65	36	99	101
May 1885	March 1887	38	22	74	60
April 1888	June 1890	13	27	35	40
May 1891	January 1893	10	20	37	30
June 1894	December 1895	17	18	37	35
June 1897	June 1899	18	24	36	42
December 1900	September 1902	18	21	42	39
August 1904	May 1907	23	33	44	56
June 1908	January 1910	13	19	46	32
January 1912	January 1913	24	12	43	36
December 1914	August 1918	23	44	35	67
March 1919	January 1920	7	10	51	17
July 1921	May 1923	18	22	28	40
July 1924	October 1926	14	27	36	41
November 1927	August 1929	13	21	40	34
March 1933	May 1937	43	50	64	93
June 1938	February 1945	13	80	63	93
October 1945	November 1948	8	37	88	45
October 1949	July 1953	11	45	48	56
May 1954	August 1957	10	39	55	49
April 1958	April 1960	8	24	47	32
February 1961	December 1969	10	106	34	116
November 1970	November 1973	11	36	117	47
March 1975	January 1980	16	58	52	74
July 1980	July 1981	6	12	64	18
November 1982	July 1990	16	**92**	28	108
March 1991	March 2001	8	120	100	128
November 2001		8			
Average, all cycles:					
1854–1982 (30 cycles)		18	33	51	51[a]
1854–1919 (16 cycles)		22	27	48	49[b]
1919–1945 (6 cycles)		18	35	53	53
1945–2001 (10 cycles)		10	57	63	67
Average, peacetime cycles:					
1854–1982 (25 cycles)		19	27	46	46[c]
1854–1919 (14 cycles)		22	24	46	47[d]
1919–1945 (5 cycles)		20	26	46	45
1945–2001 (8 cycles)		**11**	**52**	**53**	**63**

Note: Underscored figures are the wartime expansions (Civil War, World Wars I and II, Korean War, and Vietnam War), the postwar contractions, and the full cycles that include the wartime expansions.

[a]29 cycles. [b]15 cycles. [c]24 cycles. [d]13 cycles.

Source: NBER, *Business Conditions Digest* (U.S. Department of Commerce Bureau of Economic Analysis, July 1988, Nov. 1994).

conditions and are of prime importance to the investor who wants to anticipate rising corporate profits and possible price increases in the stock market. Coincident indicators move approximately with the general economy, and lagging indicators usually change directions after business conditions have turned around.

The leading, lagging, and coincident indicators of economic activity are published by the Conference Board in its publication called *Business Cycle Indicators.* This publication includes moving averages, turning dates for recessions and expansions, cyclical indicators, composite indexes and their components, diffusion indexes,[1] and information on rates of change. Many of the series are seasonally adjusted and are maintained on a monthly or quarterly basis. This information is also available on its website www.conference-board.org for a fee.

Table 5-3 presents a summary of cyclical indicators by cyclical timing with Part A of the table presenting timing at business cycle peaks and Part B showing timing at business cycle troughs. Thus, in the first part, we see the leading, coincident, and lagging indicators for business cycle peaks, and in the second part, similar indicators for the bottoming out of business cycles (troughs). While we would not expect you to study or learn all the leading or lagging indicators for a cyclical peak or trough, it is important that you know they are relied on by economists and financial analysts. Let's look more specifically at how they are used.

Economic Indicators

Of the 108 leading indicators shown in Parts A and B of Table 5-3, 61 lead at peaks and 47 lead at troughs. Of these, 10 basic indicators have been reasonably consistent in their relationship to the business cycle and are considered most important. These 10 leading indicators have been standardized and used to compute a composite index that is widely followed. It is a much smoother curve than each individual component since erratic changes in one indicator are offset by movements in other indicators. The same can be said for a similar index of four coincident indicators and six lagging indicators.

Figure 5-7 shows the performance of the composite index of leading, lagging, and coincident indicators over several past business cycles. The shaded areas are recessions as defined by the NBER. The minus figures indicate how many months the index preceded the economy. (Lagging indicators have plus signs.)

While the composite index of leading indicators (top of Figure 5-7) has been a better predictor than any single indicator, it has varied widely over time. Table 5-4 presents the components for the 10 leading, 4 roughly coincident, and 7 lagging indicators.

Studies have found that the 10 leading indicators do not exhibit the same notice at peaks as they do at troughs. The notice before peaks is quite long, but the warning before troughs is very short, which means it is very easy to miss a turnaround to the upside, but on the downside you can be more patient waiting

1. A diffusion index shows the pervasiveness of a given movement in a series. If 100 units are reported in a series, the diffusion index indicates what percentage followed a given pattern.

TABLE 5–3 Cross Classification of Cyclical Indicators by Economic Process and Cyclical Timing

Cyclical Timing / Economic Process	I. Employment and Unemployment (15 series)	II. Production and Income (10 series)	III. Consumption, Trade Orders, and Deliveries (13 series)	IV. Fixed Capital Investment (19 series)	V. Inventories and Inventory Investment (9 series)	VI. Price, Costs, and Profits (18 series)	VII. Money and Credit (28 series)
A. Timing at Business Cycle Peaks							
Leading (L) Indicators (61 series)	Marginal employment adjustments (3 series) Job vacancies (2 series) Comprehensive employment (1 series) Comprehensive unemployment (3 series)	Capacity utilization (2 series)	Orders and deliveries (6 series) Consumption and trade (2 series)	Formation of business enterprises (2 series) Business investment commitments (5 series) Residential construction (3 series)	Inventory investment (4 series) Inventories on hand and on order (1 series)	Stock prices (1 series) Sensitive commodity prices (2 series) Prices and profit margins (7 series) Cash flows (2 series)	Money (5 series) Credit flows (5 series) Credit difficulties (2 series) Bank reserves (2 series) Interest rates (1 series)
Roughly Coincident (C) Indicators (24 series)	Comprehensive employment (1 series)	Comprehensive output and income (4 series) Industrial production (4 series)	Consumption and trade commitments (1 series)	Business investment Business investment expenditures (6 series)		Velocity of money (2 series)	Interest rate (2 series)
Lagging (Lg) Indicators (19 series)	Comprehensive unemployment (2 series)			Business investment expenditures (1 series)	Inventories on hand and on order (4 series)	Unit labor costs and labor share (4 series)	Interest rate (4 series) Outstanding debt (4 series)
Timing Unclassified (U) (8 series)	Comprehensive employment (3 series)		Consumption and trade (1 series)	Business investment commitments (1 series)		Sensitive commodity prices (1 series) Profits and profit margins (1 series)	Interest rates (1 series)
B. Timing at Business Cycle Troughs							
Leading (L) Indicators (47 series)	Marginal employment adjustments (1 series)	Industrial production (1 series)	Orders and deliveries (5 series) Consumption and trade (4 series)	Formation of business enterprises (2 series) Business investment commitments (4 series) Residential construction (3 series)	Inventory investment (4 series)	Stock prices (1 series) Sensitive commodity prices (3 series) Profit and profit margins (6 series) Cash flows (2 series)	Money (4 series) Credit flows (5 series) Credit difficulties (2 series)
Roughly Coincident (C) Indicators (23 series)	Marginal employment adjustments (2 series) Comprehensive employment (4 series)	Comprehensive output and income (4 series) Industrial production (3 series) Capacity utilization (2 series)	Consumption and trade (3 series)	Business investment commitments (1 series)		Profits and profit margins (2 series)	Money (1 series) Velocity of money (1 series)
Lagging (Lg) Indicators (41 series)	Job vacancies (2 series) Comprehensive employment (1 series) Comprehensive unemployment (5 series)		Orders and deliveries (1 series)	Business investment commitments (2 series) Business investment expenditures (7 series)	Inventories on hand and on order (5 series)	Unit labor costs and labor share (4 series)	Velocity of money (1 series) Bank reserves (1 series) Interest rates (8 series) Outstanding debt (4 series)
Timing Unclassified (U) (1 series)							Bank reserves (1 series)

Source: NBER, *Business Conditions Digest* (U.S. Department of Commerce Bureau of Economic Analysis, July 1988).

for confirmation from other indicators. Indicators occasionally give false signals. Sometimes the indicators give no clear signal, and with the large variability of leads and lags versus the average lead time, an investor is lucky to get close to predicting economic activity within three or four months of peaks and troughs. Despite economic indicators and forecasting methods, investors cannot escape uncertainty in an attempt to manage their portfolios.

FIGURE 5–7 Composite Indexes (Leading, Lagging, and Coincident Indexes)

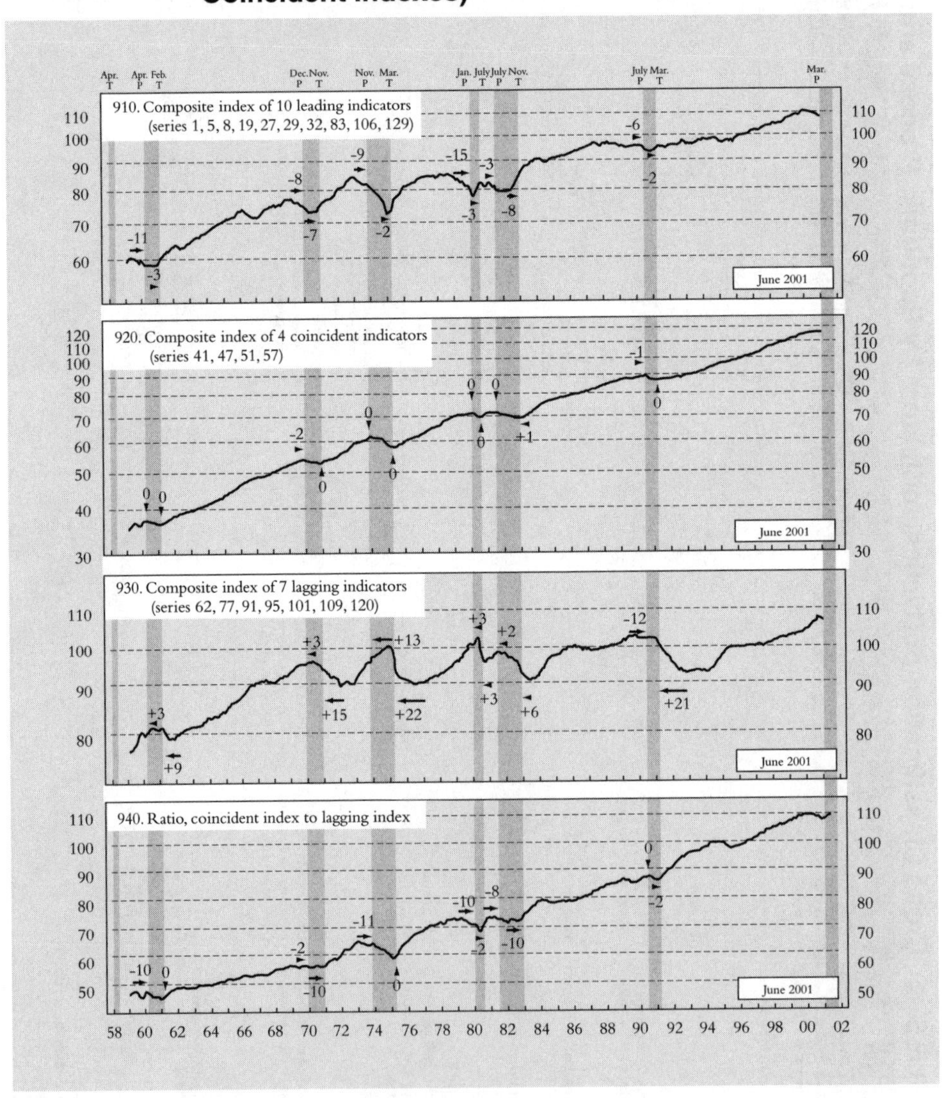

Source: *Business Cycle Indicators*, Conference Board, August 2001.

One very important fact is that the stock market is the most reliable and accurate of the 10 leading indicators. This presents a very real problem for us because our initial objective is to forecast (as well as we are able) changes in common stock prices. To do this, we are constrained by the fact that the stock market is anticipatory and, in fact, has worked on a lead time of nine months at peaks and five months at troughs.

MONEY SUPPLY AND STOCK PRICES

One variable that has been historically popular as an indicator of the stock market is the money supply. The money supply is supposed to influence stock prices in several ways. Studies of economic growth and the money supply by Milton

TABLE 5–4 Components of the Leading, Coincident, and Lagging Indicators

BCI No.	Series
Leading index components:	
1.	Average weekly hours, manufacturing
5.	Initial claims for unemployment insurance, thousands
8.	Mfrs.' new orders, consumer goods and materials
32.	Vendor performance, slower deliveries diffusion index
27.	Mfrs.' new orders, nondefense capital goods
29.	Building permits, new private housing units
19.	Stock prices, 500 common stocks
106.	Money supply, M2
129.	Interest rate spread, 10-year Treasury bonds less federal funds
83.	Index of consumer expectations
Coincident index components:	
41.	Employees on nonagricultural payrolls
51.	Personal income less transfer payments
47.	Industrial production
57.	Manufacturing and trade sales
Lagging index components:	
91.	Average duration of unemployment, weeks
77.	Ratio, mfg. and trade inventories to sales
62.	Change in labor cost per unit of output, mfg.
109.	Average prime rate charged by banks
101.	Commercial and industrial loans outstanding
95.	Ratio, consumer installment credit outstanding to personal income
120.	Changes in Consumer Price Index for services

Source: *Business Cycle Indicators,* Conference Board, August 2001.

Friedman and Anna Schwartz found a long-term relationship between these two variables.[2]

Why does money matter? If you are a monetarist, money explains much of economic behavior. The quantity theory of money holds that as the supply of money increases relative to the demand for money, people will make adjustments in their portfolios of assets. If they have too much money, they will first buy bonds (a modification of the theory would now include Treasury bills or other short-term monetary assets), stocks, and finally, real assets. This is the direct effect of money on stock prices sometimes referred to as the *liquidity effect.*

The indirect effect of money on stock prices would flow through the GDP's impact on corporate profits. As money influences economic activity, it will eventually influence corporate earnings and dividends and thus returns to the investors. Many studies have found that a significant relationship exists between the money supply variable and stock prices. However, even here, there have been some conflicting patterns in the last 10 to 20 years as shown in Figure 5-8. Note that in the first half of 1982, the money supply (M2) was increasing slightly while stock prices were declining sharply. This goes against the historical norm of comparable movements that can be seen in the same figure. Also note that from 1987 to 1995, the money supply (M2) has been relatively flat and has not coincided with increasing stock prices. Since 1995, however, the trend on both has been up.

There are many important predictors of economic patterns and stock market movements, but an investor must be flexible and consider as many variables as possible rather than simply relying on one or two factors. You may wish to acquaint yourself with many of the leading, coincident, and lagging indicators presented previously in Table 5-4 as you become active in the stock market.

BUSINESS CYCLES AND INDUSTRY RELATIONSHIPS

Each industry may be affected by the business cycle differently. Industries where the underlying demand for the product is consumer oriented will quite likely be sensitive to short-term swings in the business cycle. These industries would include durable goods such as washers and dryers, refrigerators, electric and gas ranges, and automobiles. Changes in the automobile industry will also be felt in the tire and rubber industry as well as by auto glass and other automobile component suppliers.

Table 5-5, which appeared in the *Chicago Tribune,* demonstrates the impact of this ripple effect through many industries. The automobile industry purchases 77 percent of the output from the natural rubber industry (tires and bumpers), 67 percent of the output from the lead industry (batteries), and so on to 10 percent of the copper output (electrical and tubing). Additionally, the automobile industry accounts for more than 4 percent of the GDP. The U.S. automobile industry employs 800,000 people, and one in seven workers (15 million) in America has a job in an industry somewhat dependent on the automobile industry.

---

2. Milton J. Friedman and Anna J. Schwartz, "Money and Business Cycles," *Review of Economics and Statistics,* Supplement, February 1963.

FIGURE 5–8 Relationship of Stock Prices to Money Supply

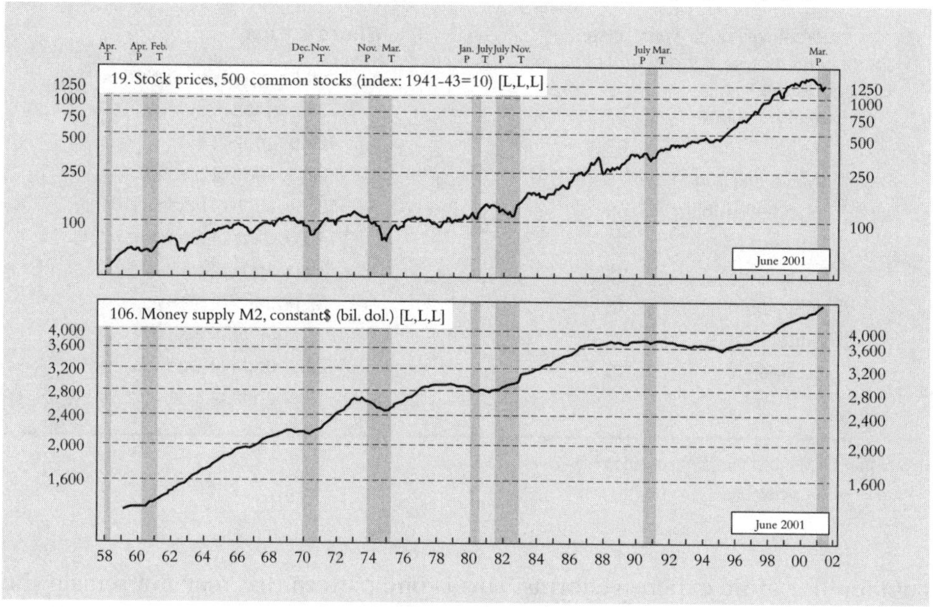

19. Stock prices, 500 common stocks (index: 1941-43=10) [L,L,L]

106. Money supply M2, constant$ (bil. dol.) [L,L,L]

Source: *Business Cycle Indicators,* Conference Board, August 2001.

The top of Figure 5-9 shows the automobile quarterly sales from 1967 to 2001 relative to GDP's growth rate (bottom of figure). Notice the similarity of the pattern. The peaks and troughs of economic activity mostly correspond with peaks in the auto industry. Perhaps the recessions of 1974–75 and 1981 are most easily identified as coinciding with auto sales. From about 1992, auto sales and GDP both maintained consistent performance.

The data do not include vehicles produced abroad but sales by foreign manufacturers such as Toyota, Honda, Volkswagen, and BMW would also be influenced by the growth in United States GDP, and additionally they would be affected by foreign currency exchange rates. When the U.S. dollar is strong against foreign currencies, foreign manufacturers have the ability to lower their prices and still maintain their profit margins relative to Ford and General Motors. When the U.S. dollar falls, the opposite effect is true, and foreign car sales suffer.

Not all industries are so closely related to the business cycle. Necessity-oriented industries, such as food and pharmaceuticals, are consistent performers since people have to eat, and illness is not dependent on the economy. Industries that have products with low price elasticities[3] that are habitual in nature, such as cigarettes and alcohol, do not seem to be much affected by business cycles either. In fact, some industries do better during a recession. The movie industry traditionally prospers during a recession as more people substitute low-cost enter-

3. Price elasticity represents the sensitivity of quantity purchased to price.

TABLE 5–5 Automobile Industry and Its Impact on Other Industries

The automotive industry purchases these percentages of the output of other U.S. industries.[a]		What's in a car — A typical American car includes:[b]
Natural rubber	77%	1,774 pounds of steel
Lead	67	460 pounds of iron
Malleable iron	63	222 pounds of plastic
Synthetic rubber	50	183 pounds of fluids
Platinum	39	146 pounds of aluminum
Zinc	23	135 pounds of rubber
Aluminum	18	86 pounds of glass
Steel	12	25 pounds of copper
Copper	10	24 pounds of lead
		18 pounds of zinc

[a]Motor Vehicle Manufacturers Association.

[b]*World Book Encyclopedia.*

tainment for more expensive forms. This is one pattern that may not remain the same, however. As cable television, VCRs, and DVDs continue to come into their own, people may find it even more convenient to stay at home than to go to the movies when money is tight. This is one thing that makes investments exciting, the ever-changing environment.

Housing is another example of an industry that historically has done well in recessionary environments. As the economy comes to a standstill, interest rates tend to come down, and prospective home purchasers are once again able to afford mortgage rates on a home. After the period of extremely high mortgage rates in the early 1980s, a precipitous drop in mortgage rates helped to stimulate growth in the housing market. The Federal Reserve followed such a policy again in the early 1990s by pushing interest rates down to their lowest level in decades. This happened again in 2001. Sales of existing housing units picked up, and people refinanced their mortgages at lower rates, giving them more disposable income. As mortgage costs came down, housing became more affordable to more people. For example, if interest rates declined 3 percentage points on a $120,000 loan, the same priced house would now cost $300 per month less in interest expense.

Sensitivity to the business cycle may also be evident in industries that produce *capital* goods for other business firms (rather than consumer goods). Examples would be manufacturers of business plant and equipment, machine tools, or pollution-control equipment. A lag often exists between the recovery from a recession and the increased purchase of capital goods, so recoveries within these industries may be delayed.

Service industries have also become extremely important in our economy. While service-oriented business firms (doctors, lawyers, accountants) are generally less susceptible to the business cycle, there are exceptions. Examples of cyclically

FIGURE 5–9 New Vehicle Sales and Real GNP Quarterly Percentage Change

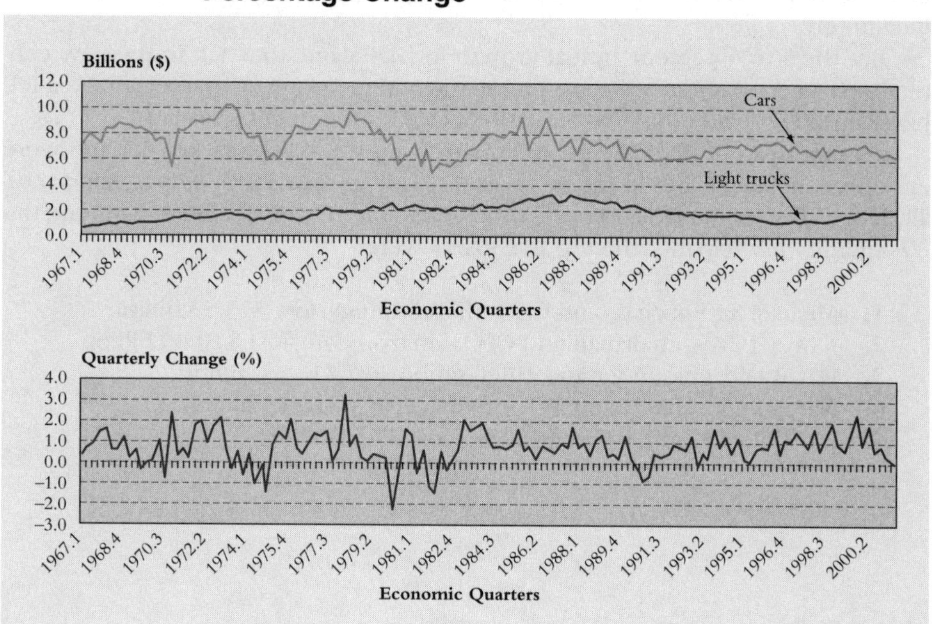

oriented service providers include architects, civil engineers, and auto repair shops.

One industry that has taken on increased importance is high technology. Companies in high technology generally include computer hardware and software producers; information technology, networking, database management firms; and other related fields. Examples of firms in these areas are Microsoft, Intel, CISCO, Oracle, IBM, and Sun Microsystems. These firms are also somewhat cyclical in that they depend on a high volume of business activity to continue an ever-expanding need for their products. Many of the newer high-tech firms are being severely tested in the economic slowdown of the early 2000s.

As a general statement, we do not mean to imply that cyclical industries are bad investments or that they should be avoided. We merely point out the cyclical influence of the economy. Often cyclical industries are excellent buys in the stock market because the market does not look far enough ahead to see a recovery and its impact on cyclical profits. We develop these ideas more completely in the next chapter.

THE NEW ECONOMY: GOING FROM GAIN TO PAIN

According to some economists, there was supposed to be very little pain in the new economy. After a decade of uninterrupted growth in the 1990s, some went so far as to suggest the business cycle had been repealed. The reasoning was that ever-increasing productivity fueled by technology in the new economy would increase output per man(woman)-hour to the point where growth could continue indefinitely.

But the 3 to 4 percent annual growth in GDP came to a halt in the new century, and so did the decade-long bull market. Many popular market indexes fell between 20 percent (S&P 500 Stock Index) and 60 percent (Nasdaq).

Among those to feel the greatest pain from the stock market decline were entrepreneurs and CEOs in the Internet/technology area. *Fortune* magazine actually listed "The Billion Dollar Losers Club" in its June 11, 2001, edition.[4] Among the 20 unhappy participants, the top five losers were:

1. Michael Saylor, chair and CEO, MicroStrategy; lost $13.53 billion.
2. Jeffrey Bezos, chairman and CEO, Amazon.com; lost $10.80 billion.
3. David Filo, cofounder and chief, Yahoo; lost $10.31 billion.
4. Navaan Jain, chair and CEO, IntoSpace; lost $10.13 billion.
5. Jay Walker, founder, Pipeline.com; lost $7.51 billion.

Can you feel their pain?

4. Julia Boorstein and Mathew Boyle, "The Billion Dollar Losers Club," *Fortune*, July 11, 2001, pp. 127–28.

Internet Resources

Website Address	Comments
www.economy.com	Provides access to economic data—some sources are fee based
finance.yahoo.com	Provides information about the economy
www.dismal.com	Contains articles on economies and tracks information from U.S. and global sources
www.fedstats.gov	Has links to economic data
www.freelunch.com	Has links to other economic sites, has listings of economic reports and news events, and provides access to economic data
www.smartmoney.com	Has information and news about U.S. economy
www.bea.doc.gov	Provides links to sources of U.S. government economic data
www.ny.frb.org	Contains links to New York Federal Reserve Bank analyses and data
www.stls.frg.org/fred	Contains historical interest rate, bond and economic data—site is free
www.mworld.com	Provides industry and economic data as well as data on money flows into stock funds
www.stat-usa.gov	Provides general information about the U.S. economy
www.bos.frb.org	Home page of the Federal Reserve of Boston providing economic information
www.ita.doc.gov	Provides access to U.S. government reports on international trade with reports being fee based

Chapter 6

Industry Analysis

We saw in Chapter 5 that *economic analysis* is the first step in the valuation process. Figure 5–1 is funnel shaped and leads from the economy to industry analysis and then to company analysis. This method of choosing common stocks is called the top-down approach because it goes from the macroeconomic viewpoint to the individual company. The opposite approach is the bottom-up approach, which starts with picking individual companies and then looks at the industry and economy to see if there is any reason an investment in the company should not be made. People who follow the bottom-up approach are sometimes referred to as stock pickers, as opposed to industry analysts.

Industry analysis is the second step in the top-down approach used in this text, and it focuses on industry life cycles and industry structure. Industries can be affected by government regulation, foreign and domestic competition, and the economic business cycle. As we shall also see, industry competition is affected by product quality, the cost structures within the industry, and the competitive strategies among companies in the industry. A starting point for industry analysis is determining where an industry's current position is in its industry life cycle.

INDUSTRY LIFE CYCLES

Industry life cycles are created because of economic growth, competition, availability of resources, and the resultant market saturation by the particular goods and services offered. Life-cycle growth influences many variables considered in the valuation process. The particular phase in the life cycle of an industry or company determines the growth of earnings, dividends, capital expenditures, and market demand for products.

An analysis of industry financial data helps place an industry on the life-cycle curve and, in turn, guides the analyst toward decisions on industry growth, the duration of growth, profitability, and potential rates of return. The analyst can determine whether all companies in the industry are in the same stage of the life cycle and translate company differences into various assumptions that will affect their individual valuations.

Figure 6–1 shows a five-stage industry life cycle (although it could very well be a company life cycle) and the corresponding dividend policy most likely to be found at each stage. The vertical scale on this graph is logarithmic, which means that a straight line on this scale represents a constant growth rate. The steeper the line, the faster the growth rate, and the flatter the line, the smaller the growth rate. The slope of the line in the life-cycle curve and how it changes over time is very important in the analysis of growth and its duration. We will examine each stage separately and learn why the dividend policy is important in placing an industry or company in a particular stage.

Development—Stage I

The development stage includes companies that are getting started in business with a new idea, product, or production technique that makes them unique. Firms in this stage are usually privately owned and are financed with the owner's money as well as with capital from friends, family, and a bank. If the company has some success, there is a probability that outside money from a venture capital group may increase the financing available to the company. In this stage, the company is also the industry or a subset of an existing industry. For example, when Steve Jobs started Apple Computer in the early 1970s, it was a development startup company that created an entirely new industry. In the beginning, Apple was certainly not taken seriously by IBM, but by the early 2000s the personal computer (PC) industry and its related software products represented a sizable multibillion dollar industry much bigger than the old mainframe business of IBM and others.

The pharmaceutical industry has been around for a long time, but in the 1970s and 1980s many small biotechnology firms were founded that created drugs using

FIGURE 6–1 Industry Life Cycle

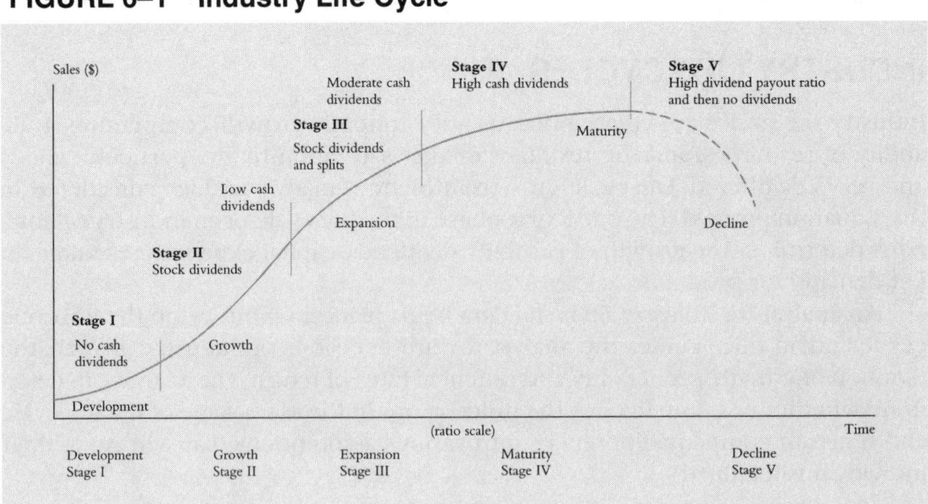

different production and research techniques. Hundreds of small biotech firms using genetic techniques were created by entrepreneurs in medical research. This focus on medical research created a subset of the pharmaceutical industry, and, eventually, large companies such as Merck and Eli Lilly created joint partnerships with these companies. Some biotech firms such as Genentech eventually produced successful drugs and became large companies themselves.

One thing all these firms have in common is their need for capital. A small firm in the initial stages of development (Stage I) pays no dividends because it needs all of its profits (if there are any) for reinvestment in new productive assets. If the firm is successful in the marketplace, the demand for its products will create growth in sales, earnings, and assets, and the industry or company will move into Stage II.

Growth—Stage II

Stage II growth represents an industry or company that has achieved a degree of market acceptance for its products. At this stage, earnings will be retained for reinvestment, and sales and returns on assets will be growing at an increasing rate. The increasing growth can be seen from the increasing slope of the line in Figure 6-1.

By 1978 Apple Computer's PC was so successful that Apple needed more capital for expansion than could be generated internally, so it made an initial public offering of common stock to finance a major expansion. The success of the personal computer enticed IBM to enter this segment of the market, and, eventually, the IBM PC—with its open architecture—was copied and cloned by companies such as Compaq, Gateway, Dell, and Micron. All these firms are now publicly traded in U.S. markets and control more than 90 percent of the PC market.

Companies such as IBM entered the developing PC industry with a small amount of their total assets targeted at this market and were able to fund the move into this market with internal sources of capital. However, the other companies entering this market were "pure plays"; in other words, all they did was make personal computers. These companies were in the early part of Stage II, and they still needed to reinvest their cash flow back into research and development and into new plant and equipment.

In general, companies in Stage II become profitable, and, in their early stage of growth, they want to acknowledge to their shareholders that they have achieved profitability. Because they still need their internal capital, they often pay stock dividends (distributions of additional shares). A stock dividend preserves capital but often signals to the market that the firm made a profit. In the latter part of Stage II, low cash dividends may be paid out when the need for new capital declines as new sources of capital appear. A cash dividend policy is sometimes necessary to attract institutional investors to the company stock since some institutions cannot own companies that pay no dividends.

Obviously, industries in Stage I or early Stage II are very risky, and the investor does not really know if growth objectives will be met or if dividends will ever be paid. But if you want to have a chance to make an investment (after careful research) in a high-growth industry with large potential returns, then Stage I or II industries will provide you with opportunities for large gains or losses. Since actual dividends are irrelevant in these stages, an investor will be purchasing shares for capital gains based on expected growth rather than on current income.

Expansion—Stage III

In Stage III, sales expansion and earnings continue but at a decreasing rate. As the industry crosses from the growth stage to the expansion stage, the slope of the line in Figure 6-1 becomes less steep, signaling slower growth. It is this crossover point that is important to the analyst who will also be evaluating declining returns on investment as more competition enters the market and attempts to take away market share from existing firms. The industry has grown to the point where asset expansion slows in line with production needs, and the firms in the industry are more capable of paying cash dividends. Stock dividends and stock splits are still common in Stage III, and the dividend payout ratio usually increases from a low level of 5 to 15 percent of earnings to a moderate level of 25 to 30 percent of earnings by Stage III.

Because industries and companies do not grow in a nice smooth line, it is often difficult to tell when the industry or company has crossed from Stage II growth to Stage III expansion. Determining the crossover point is extremely important to investors who choose to invest in growth companies. Once investors recognize that the past growth rate will not be extrapolated and, instead, is in decline, stock prices can take a sizable tumble as price-earnings ratios collapse because of slower growth expectations. Figure 6-2 demonstrates this relationship.

Maturity—Stage IV

Maturity occurs when industry sales grow at a rate equal to the economy as measured by the long-term trend in gross domestic product (GDP). Some analysts like to use the growth rate of the Standard & Poor's 500 Index for comparison because the growth rate of these 500 large companies sets the norm for mature companies. Figure 6-3 graphs sales for the S&P Industrials and the GDP using a logarithmic graph. The use of a logarithmic graph (sometimes called a ratio scale) allows a comparison of growth rates between trend lines since a straight line on a vertical logarithmic scale represents a constant growth rate. The steeper the slope of the line, the faster the growth rate. Notice that on the graph, the S&P Industrials' sales and GDP seem to have similar long-term growth rates (slope).

Automobiles are a good example of a mature industry. You may remember that, in Chapter 5, we looked at the automobile industry as it related to the business cycle. Figure 5-9 showed an industry that was very cyclical and where the number of automobiles sold seemed to be closely related to real GDP. Figure 6-4 shows the relationship between sales of the automobile industry and GDP in current dollars. While automobile sales do not have the relatively smooth line of GDP,

FIGURE 6–2 The Crossover Point

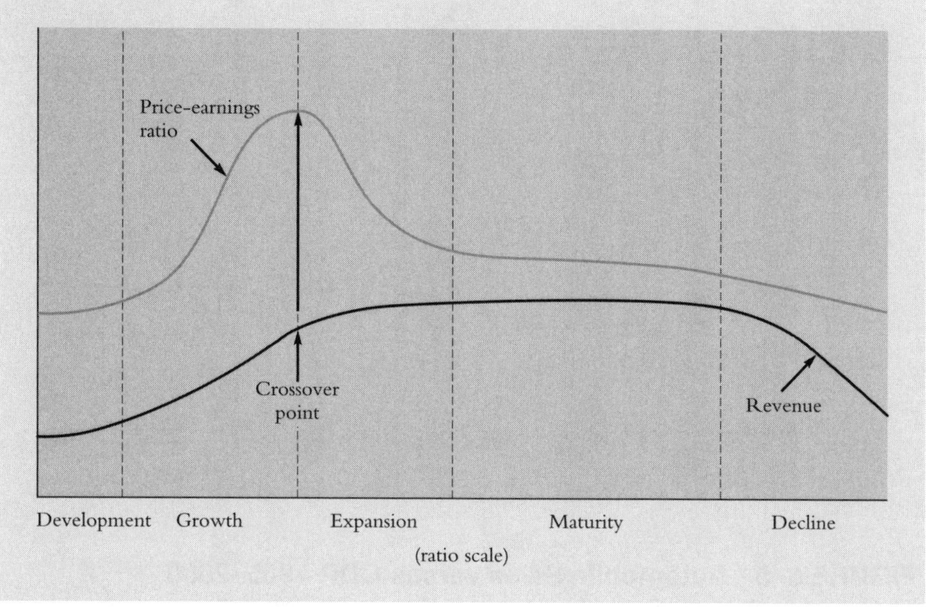

FIGURE 6–3 S&P Industrials versus GDP

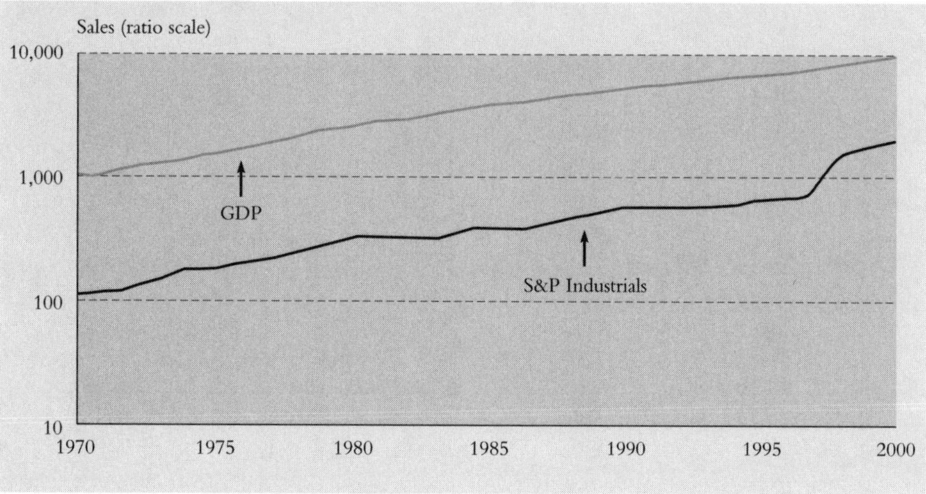

the slope of the two lines appears similar. Figure 6-5 plots sales for the auto industry against the GDP for the years 1965 through 2000. The scatter diagram again depicts the cyclical nature of automobile sales and a close relationship to that of GDP.

FIGURE 6–4 Automobile Industry versus GDP

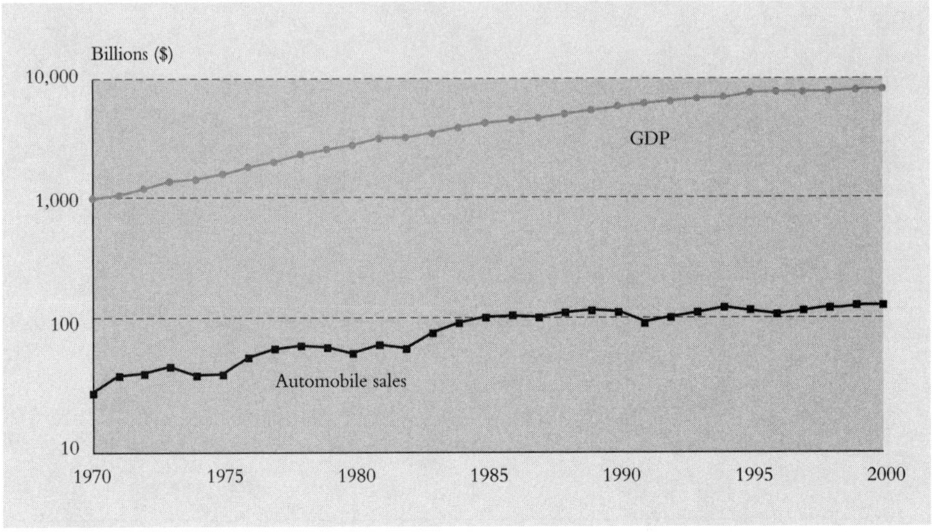

FIGURE 6–5 Automobile Sales versus GDP, 1965–2000

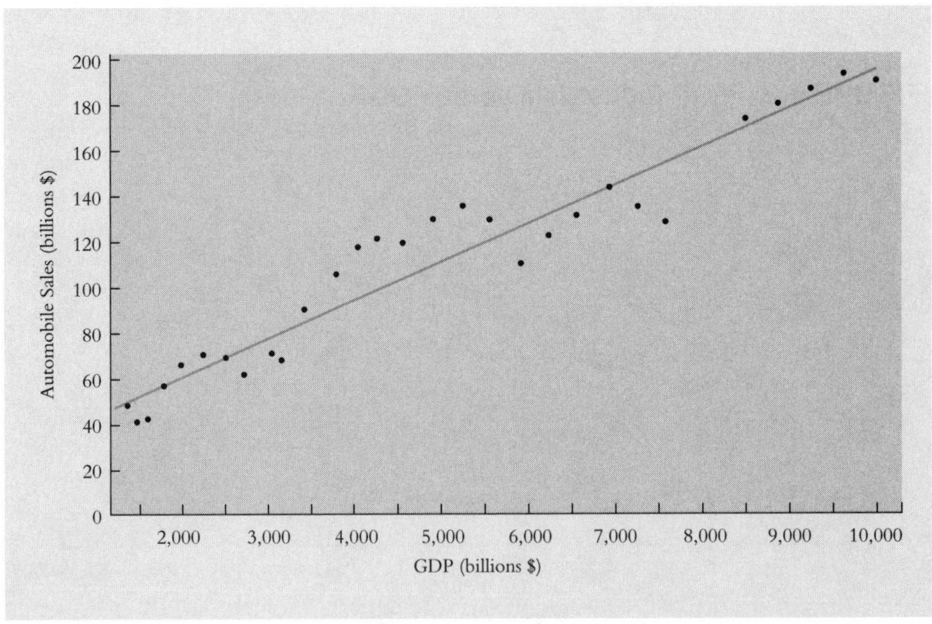

By the time an industry or firm reaches maturity, plant and equipment are in place, financing alternatives are available domestically and internationally, and the cash flow from operations is usually more than enough to meet the growth requirements of the firm. Under these conditions, dividends will usually range from

45 to 50 percent of earnings. These percentages will be different from industry to industry, depending on individual characteristics.

Decline—Stage V

In unfortunate cases, industries suffer declines in sales if product innovation has not increased the product base over the years. Declining industries may be specific to a country; passenger trains are such an example. In Europe, passenger trains are common forms of transportation, while in the United States, passenger trains have been in decline for many decades because competition from automobiles, buses, and airplanes has cut into the market. Besides the famous buggy whip example, black-and-white television, vacuum tubes, and transistor radios are examples of products within an industry that have been in decline. In some cases, the companies producing these products repositioned their resources into growth-oriented products, and, in other cases, the companies went out of business.

Often it is not a whole industry that goes into decline but the weakest company in the industry that cannot compete. Currently, industries such as banks, airlines, and breweries are undergoing consolidation. The number of banks has been declining, and this trend is expected to accelerate as national banking takes hold in the United States. The airline industry has been in consolidation for decades with famous names such as Braniff, Eastern, and Pan Am defunct and others such as TWA and Continental continually on the brink of bankruptcy. Apple Computer represents an extreme case of a leading company in the early stages of development that fell on hard times during the later stages because of intense competition and its inability to meet that competition in pricing and product development. Only time will tell whether its alliance with Microsoft will help save the company.

Dividend payout ratios of firms in decline often rise to 100 percent or more of earnings. Often, the firm does not want to signal stockholders that it is in trouble, so it maintains its dividends in the face of falling earnings. This causes the payout ratio to soar until management realizes that the firm is bleeding to death and needs to conserve cash. Then either drastic dividend cuts follow, or there is an elimination of dividends entirely.

Dividend Policy and the Life-Cycle Curve The dividend payout ratio has an important effect on company growth. As previously pointed out, the more funds a firm retains—and, thus, the lower the dividend payout—the greater the opportunity for growth. The dividend policy followed by management often provides the analyst with management's view of the company's ability to grow and some indication of where the company is on the life-cycle curve. For example, a firm paying out 50 percent of earnings in dividends is probably not in Phase I, II, or III of the life-cycle curve.

Growth in Nongrowth Industries

It is also important to realize that growth companies can exist in a mature industry and that not all companies within an industry experience the same growth path in sales, earnings, and dividends. Some companies are simply better managed, have better people, have more efficient assets, and have put more money into productive research and development that has created new or improved products.

Many U.S. companies, such as Coca-Cola and McDonald's, have found growth by expansion abroad. While their domestic markets are saturated and growing at the rate of GDP or less, the international demand for their products in Asia, Europe, Eastern Europe, Russia, and China has allowed these two companies to maintain double-digit growth rates. This may also be true of other marketing-oriented companies with global trademarks such as Sony, Pepsi, Heineken, and Nike.

Electric utilities are generally considered mature, but utilities in states such as Florida, Arizona, and the Carolinas, which have undergone rapid population explosions over the last decade, would still have higher growth rates than the industry in general.

Computer companies such as IBM were fast approaching maturity until technical innovations created new markets. Unfortunately for IBM, demand for its mainframe computers declined worldwide as personal computers and local area networks increased in flexibility and power. To combat this decline in its major product line, IBM restructured in an effort to revive growth from its personal computer, software, and service divisions. Some analysts would place the PC industry in the expansion stage, but IBM as the dominant player in the computer industry is playing catch-up to other PC makers who dominate the growth segments.

The warning to the investor is not to become enamored with a company just because it is in a "growth industry." Its time of glory may have passed. Other investors improperly ignore companies that are in the process of revitalization because they no longer carry the growth-stock tag. More will be said about growth stocks in Chapter 7.

INDUSTRY STRUCTURE

The structure of the industry is another area of importance for the analyst. Industry structure determines whether the companies in the industry are profitable, whether there are special considerations such as government regulations that positively or negatively affect the industry, and whether cost advantages and product quality create a dominant company within the industry.

A financial analyst may want to evaluate other significant factors for a given industry. For example, is the industry structure monopolistic like a regulated utility, oligopolistic like the automobile industry, partially competitive like the pharmaceutical industry, or very competitive like the industry for farm commodities? Questions of industry structure are very important in analyzing pricing structures and price elasticities that exist because of competition or the lack of it.

Economic Structure

We often look at the economic structure of an industry to determine how companies compete within the industry. Monopolies are generally not common in the

United States because of our antitrust laws, but they have existed by government permission in the area of public utilities. In return for the monopoly, the government has the right to regulate rates of return on equity and assets and to approve customer fees. This sets the limits of growth and profitability and creates minimums and maximums for the analyst. Monopolies are almost always in mature industries, although the government may occasionally grant a monopoly on emerging technologies and even offer subsidies for the development of new technologies, especially in the defense industry.

Oligopolies have few competitors and are quite common in large mature U.S. industries such as automobiles, steel, oil, airlines, and aluminum to name a few. The competition between companies in an oligopoly can be intense, and profitability can suffer as a result of price wars and battles over market share. Increasingly, oligopolistic industries are facing international competition, which has altered their competitive strategies. Note that many of the industries mentioned earlier have competition from other industrial countries such as Japan, Germany, the Netherlands, Britain, and France.

Pure competition in manufacturing is not widely found in the United States. The food processing industry may be the closest example of this economic form. Generally, companies in pure competition do not have a differentiated product such as corn, soybeans, and other commodities. Firms will often compete by trying to create perceived differences in product quality or service.

Other Economic Factors to Consider Questions of supply and demand relationships are very important because they affect the price structure of the industry and its ability to produce quality products at a reasonable cost. The cost variable can be affected by many factors. For example, high relative hourly wages in basic industries such as steel, autos, and rubber are somewhat responsible for the inability of the United States to compete in the world markets for these products. Availability of raw material is also an important cost factor. Industries such as aluminum and glass need to have an abundance of low-cost bauxite and silicon to produce their products. Unfortunately, the aluminum industry uses very large amounts of electricity in the production process, so the low cost of bauxite may be offset by the high cost of energy. Energy costs are of concern to all industries, but the availability of reasonably priced energy sources is particularly important to the airline and trucking industries. The list could go on and on, but as analysts become familiar with a specific industry, they learn the crucial variables.

Government Regulation Most industries are also affected by government regulation. This applies to the automobile industry where safety and exhaust emissions are regulated and to all industries where air, water, and noise pollution are of concern. Many industries engaged in interstate commerce—such as utilities, railroads, and telephone companies—have been strongly regulated by the government, but even these have begun to feel the effects of deregulation and competition. The telephone companies have begun a global expansion with international partners that is changing the face of competition for long-distance calling worldwide. Industries such as airlines, trucking, and natural gas production have been deregulated and are still undergoing structural changes within the industry as new competitive forces emerge. Most industries are affected by government expenditures; this is especially true for industries involved in defense, education, health care, and transportation.

These are but a few examples to alert you to the importance of having a thorough understanding of your industry. This is why in many large investment firms, trust departments, and insurance companies, analysts are assigned to only one industry or to several related industries so that they may concentrate their attention on a given set of significant factors. Perhaps one of the most important aspects of industry analysis is the competitive structure of the industry.

Competitive Structure

Industries consist of competing firms; some industries have many firms, others have few. Nevertheless, the existing firms compete with each other and employ different strategies for success. Increasingly, the competition is among large international companies where cultural values and production processes are different. It becomes important for the investment analyst to know the attractiveness of industries for long-term profitability and what factors determine an industry's long-term outlook.

As we discussed previously, just because an industry as a whole is in a certain life-cycle stage, all companies within that industry may not be in the same position. An individual company within the industry may have chosen a poor competitive position or an excellent competitive position. While the industry outlook is important, a company may be able to create a competitive position that shapes the industry environment. There are profitable firms in poor industries and unprofitable firms in good industries.

Perhaps one of the most efficient ways to indicate competitive issues is to consider Michael Porter's elements of industry structure.[1]

Porter divides the competitive structure of an industry into five basic competitive forces: (1) threat of entry by new competitors, (2) threat of substitute goods, (3) bargaining power of buyers, (4) bargaining power of suppliers, and (5) rivalry among existing competitors. All affect price and profitability. The first is the threat of entry by new competitors. If competitors can easily enter the market, firms may have to construct barriers to entry that raise the cost to the firm. This threat places a limit on prices that can be charged and affects profitability. A second force, as we know from economics, is the threat of substitute goods. If we can easily substitute one good for another, this will again affect the price that can be charged and profit margins. An example of this would be in the beverage industry. We can drink water (tap or bottled), beer, soft drinks, fruit juice, and so on. If not for the tremendous advertising expenditures from companies trying to get us to drink their beverages, the cost would be considerably lower.

1. Professor Porter is a leading business strategist at Harvard University.

Two other competitive forces are the bargaining power of buyers and the bargaining power of suppliers. A large buyer of goods (Wal-Mart) can influence the price suppliers can charge for their goods. Firms such as McDonald's have stringent requirements for their suppliers, and, because it is a powerful buyer, McDonald's expects and gets cost-efficient service and quality control from its suppliers. This behavior restricts the prices that suppliers can charge. On the other hand, there are many powerful suppliers, such as the Middle East oil cartel or De Beers, the company that controls more than 70 percent of the worldwide diamond market. These suppliers control the cost of raw materials to their customers, and their behavior determines a major part of their customers' profitability.

The last competitive force is the rivalry among existing competitors. The extent of the rivalry affects the costs of competition—from the investment in plant and equipment, to advertising and product development. The automobile industry is a reasonable example of intense rivalry that eventually caused Japanese auto manufacturers, for political reasons, to limit their exports to the United States and instead start producing automobiles in the United States. Because the threat of entry was thought to be small, U.S. automobile companies were complacent for years and did not modernize their production processes with new technology or work flow techniques. Once the Japanese took a large market share, the rivalry intensified and caused a restructuring of the whole U.S. automobile industry. The impact of intense rivalry, therefore, has the same effect as the threat of new entrants.

These five forces vary from industry to industry and directly affect the return on assets and return on equity. The importance of each factor is a function of industry structure or the economic and technical characteristics of an industry. These forces affect prices, costs, and investment in plants, equipment, advertising, and research and development. While each industry has a set of competitive forces that are most important to it in terms of long-run profitability, competitors will devise strategies that may change the industry structure. Strategies that change the environment may improve or destroy the industry structure and profitability. Sometimes it takes several years to see the impact of competitive strategies.

IN ANALYZING AN INDUSTRY OR COMPANY, WHAT'S A BRAND NAME WORTH?

In our modern economy, a brand name is often worth as much as brick or mortar. In recognizing this fact, in August 2001, *Business Week* began publishing its ranking of the 100 most valuable brand names in the world and their value.[2]

The first question is, "How do you establish the value?" For this purpose, *Business Week* engaged the services of Interbrand Corp., a pioneering brand consulting firm in New York. The value is based on the power to increase sales and

2. "The Best Global Brands," *Business Week*, August 6, 2001, pp. 50–55.

earnings and is quantified through taking the present value of the future impact on these variables. While intangible assets such as brand name recognition are normally not quantified in the United States because of rulings by the Financial Accounting Standards Board, financial analysts recognize their essential nature in valuing a firm. The lack of inclusion of intangible assets on the balance sheet (with the exception of postmerger goodwill) is one reason firms in the S&P 500 Stock Index, on average, trade at five times their accounting determined book value. For companies in Great Britain and Australia, brand name value *must* be included on the balance sheet.

Having said all this, which U.S. company had the most valuable brand name recognition? The envelope please. And the answer is Coca-Cola with a value of $68.9 billion. The top 10 in the *Business Week* 2001 survey are:

	(in billions)		(in billions)
Coca-Cola	$68.9	Intel	$34.7
Microsoft	65.1	Disney	32.6
IBM	52.8	Ford	30.1
GE	42.4	McDonald's	25.3
Nokia	35.0	AT&T	22.8

Because this chapter is on industry analysis, we also show the top-ranked brand names in two industries where brand recognition is particularly important:

Automotive	(in billions)	Technology	(in billions)
Ford	$30.1	IBM	$52.8
Mercedes	21.7	Intel	34.7
Toyota	18.6	Hewlett-Packard	18.0
Honda	14.6	CISCO	17.2
BMW	13.9	Compaq	12.4
Volkswagen	7.3	Dell	8.3

The story is not positive for all companies. According to the survey, due to unfortunate events or poor performance, Xerox lost 38 percent of its brand name value in 2001, and Yahoo! and Amazon.com each lost 31 percent.

INDUSTRY TREND ANALYSIS

In this section, we expand the horizon by shifting our attention to two industries—the pharmaceutical industry and the chemical industry. We look at their returns on equity and long-term debt-to-equity ratios over a 10-year period. By studying these important industries, the analyst develops a feel for comparative performance in our economy.

The return on equity (ROE) for the two industries shown in Table 6-1 indicates wide differences in profitability. These data are graphed in Figure 6-6 and the trends are more visible. The very strong economy of the mid-1990s has created a healthy earnings environment for both industries, and returns on equity are higher at the end of the period than at the beginning for both chemicals and pharmaceuticals. Since the 1996-97 period, however, the industry trend for ROE is up in the pharmaceutical industry, while the industry trend for ROE in the chemical industry is down.

The pharmaceutical industry is relatively stable as an industry, but individual companies go through cycles as their patents expire and popular drugs such as Prozac for Eli Lilly go off patent (August 2001). When a drug goes off patent and becomes manufactured by generic drug companies, profits plummet and returns on equity follow. The true test of sustainability in the pharmaceutical industry is the ability of the company's research and development team to generate new products that solve medical problems and can get approved by the U.S. Food and Drug Administration.

The past decade has seen several major mergers in the pharmaceutical industry. Pfizer merged with Warner Lambert; Glaxo merged with Welcome and then several years later with SmithKline Beecham. A merger occurs in this industry for several reasons. The buying company needs a more comprehensive product line, or their pipeline of new drugs is rather bare and they need to buy research. In some cases, international companies are looking for better distribution because they are limited to one geographic area.

Some companies in this industry feel that they need to be very large to compete on an international playing field, and the pharmaceutical industry is truly a global industry. Often when mergers occur, profitability falls because of integration problems. If the merger occurred because of patent expirations, profits could decline until new drugs enter the market. Both these phenomena were true of Glaxo SmithKline in 1995-96 when Glaxo bought Welcome and in 2000-01 when Glaxo bought SmithKline.

TABLE 6–1 Return on Equity

	1991	1992	1993	1994	1995	1996	1997	1998	1999	2000	2001
Pharmaceutical Industry	**27.2%**	**28.1%**	**26.7%**	**25.5%**	**25.3%**	**24.7%**	**28.5%**	**30.0%**	**31.9%**	**33.5%**	**35.0%**
Glaxo SmithKline	25.3	27.2	24.2	23.7	6.0	11.0	11.4	12.5	13.6	55.0	28.0
Eli Lilly	26.5	28.5	29.5	23.7	24.1	23.9	37.2	49.1	50.4	48.0	42.5
Merck & Co.	43.2	48.9	26.8	26.9	28.4	32.4	36.6	41.0	44.5	46.0	43.5
Pfizer	18.2	23.2	30.5	30.0	28.2	27.7	27.9	29.9	38.2	40.4	41.0
Schering-Plough	48.0	45.1	52.2	58.6	64.9	58.9	51.2	43.9	40.9	39.6	33.5
Chemical Industry	**12.7%**	**14.2%**	**12.4%**	**20.1%**	**33.3%**	**28.6%**	**31.2%**	**20.1%**	**19.1%**	**18.3%**	**21.5%**
Dow Chemical	10.2	7.1	6.9	13.2	28.8	23.9	23.6	18.4	16.7	16.5	8.5
Du Pont	10.3	14.4	14.8	21.6	40.4	34.0	36.3	20.9	22.1	21.5	12.5
Olin Corp.	10.7	7.4	6.7	12.1	16.6	18.3	17.4	9.9	5.5	24.6	8.5

FIGURE 6–6 Return on Equity—Pharmaceutical and Chemical Industries

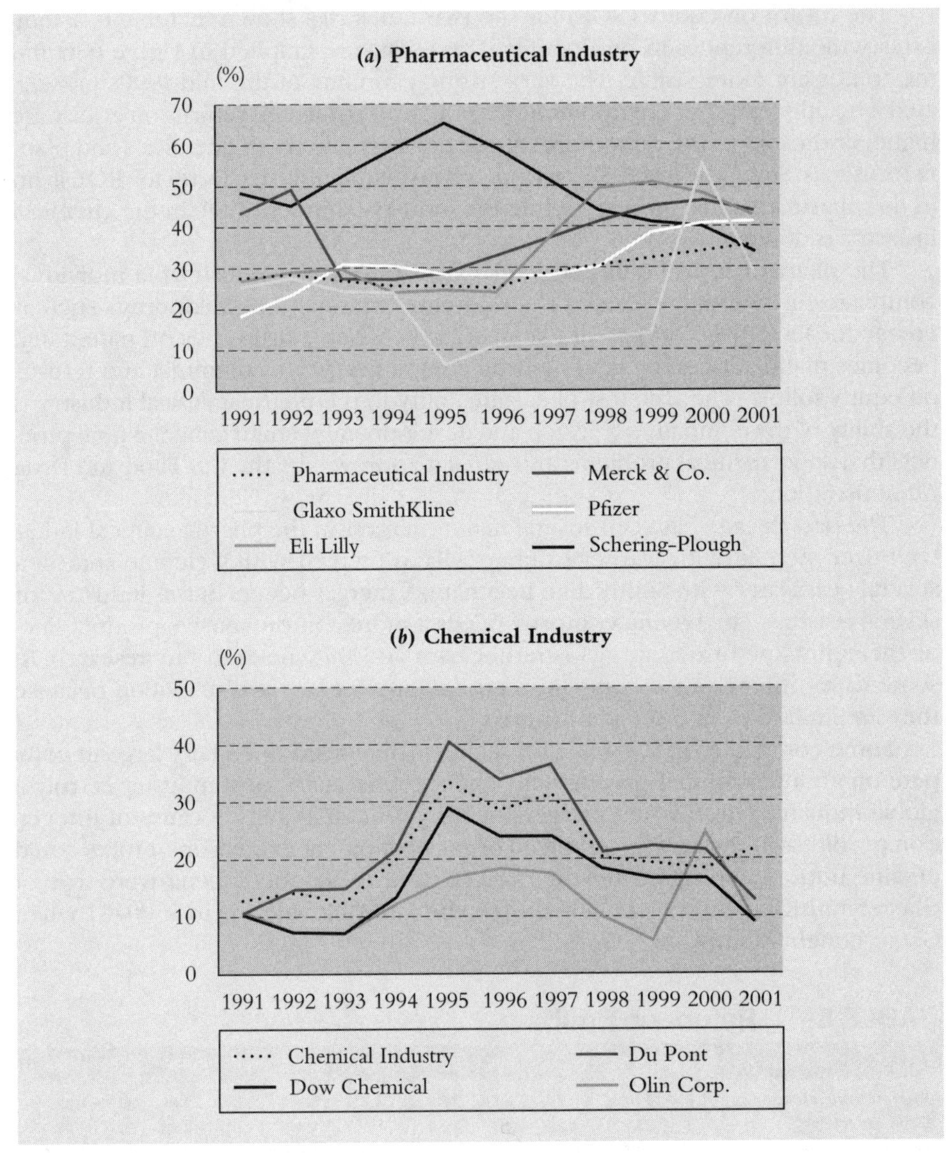

International regulation is also a problem for pharmaceutical companies. Government health care plans put tremendous pressure on drug companies to maintain prices at low levels, and many countries have price controls on prescription drugs. In the United States, large health maintenance organizations (HMOs) have very powerful buying power and can bargain for low prices with large quantity purchases.

Traditionally pharmaceutical companies have relatively low long-term debt-to-equity ratios. Table 6–2 and Figure 6–7 show that the long-term debt-to-equity ratios have fluctuated widely for the industry as well as for individual companies. Pfizer and Schering-Plough have very low debt-to-equity ratios, while Merck and Glaxo have ratios less than 30 percent. Eli Lilly's debt-to-equity ratio soared in 1995 because they spent many billions of dollars to purchase a pharmaceutical distribution business that in the end turned out to be a bad purchase. They divested this company several years later. Lilly has continued to spend large amounts of money on their research and development program in an effort to generate new drugs to replace Prozac. This is another reason for the increase in debt. However, since 1999 Lilly's debt-to-equity ratio has begun to approach the industry mean.

The basic chemical industry is cyclical in that it follows the ups and downs of the economy. Its returns are more cyclical than the pharmaceutical industry, and all companies in the industry seem to follow the same pattern even though not at the same level of profitability. We can see that this industry is very much influenced by the business cycle by looking at the low returns in 1991 (Figure 6–6b), during a time of economic recession. The good economic times in the 1990s raised the returns on equity for several years but eventually price competition in the late 1990s and the economic struggles of 2000–2001 caused another challenge to profitability.

Commodity prices greatly affect the profitability of the chemical industry worldwide. Many fibers and plastics are derived from petroleum and natural gas, and prices of these commodities have a big effect on their profits. The demand for the output produced by the chemical industry is influenced by the general level of economic activity, and companies in the industry seem to perform more efficiently when capacity is fully utilized.

This industry has gone through several mergers and restructuring in the last decade as pricing pressures have forced larger economies of scale on all companies. Du Pont sold off its ownership of Conoco Oil and used the funds from the

TABLE 6–2 Long-Term Debt-to-Equity Ratios

	1991	1992	1993	1994	1995	1996	1997	1998	1999	2000	2001
Pharmaceutical Industry	**12.0%**	**12.0%**	**16.0%**	**32.0%**	**48.0%**	**40.0%**	**24.7%**	**26.6%**	**32.5%**	**28.5%**	**25.5%**
Glaxo SmithKline	4.2	3.7	4.5	5.1	17.9	20.8	23.4	22.2	16.9	22.7	23.9
Eli Lilly	8.0	11.9	18.3	39.7	47.7	41.3	50.1	49.3	56.1	43.6	35.0
Merck & Co.	10.0	9.9	11.2	10.3	11.7	9.7	10.7	25.2	23.7	24.3	21.2
Pfizer	7.9	12.1	14.8	14.0	15.1	9.9	9.2	6.0	5.9	7.0	7.3
Schering-Plough	56.0	11.5	11.5	11.8	5.4	2.3	1.6	0.1	0.0	0.0	0.0
Chemical Industry	**61.0%**	**82.0%**	**68.0%**	**58.0%**	**66.0%**	**57.0%**	**59.8%**	**67.0%**	**86.7%**	**85.2%**	**90.7%**
Dow Chemical	64.4	76.7	73.3	64.4	61.1	52.5	54.7	54.2	60.0	53.0	43.2
Du Pont	38.6	61.1	58.2	49.7	67.3	47.5	52.6	32.2	51.5	50.3	47.4
Olin Corp.	78.1	64.4	75.3	55.8	48.9	29.2	30.5	29.1	74.1	69.3	88.2

FIGURE 6–7 Long-Term Debt-to-Equity Ratios—Pharmaceutical and Chemical Industries

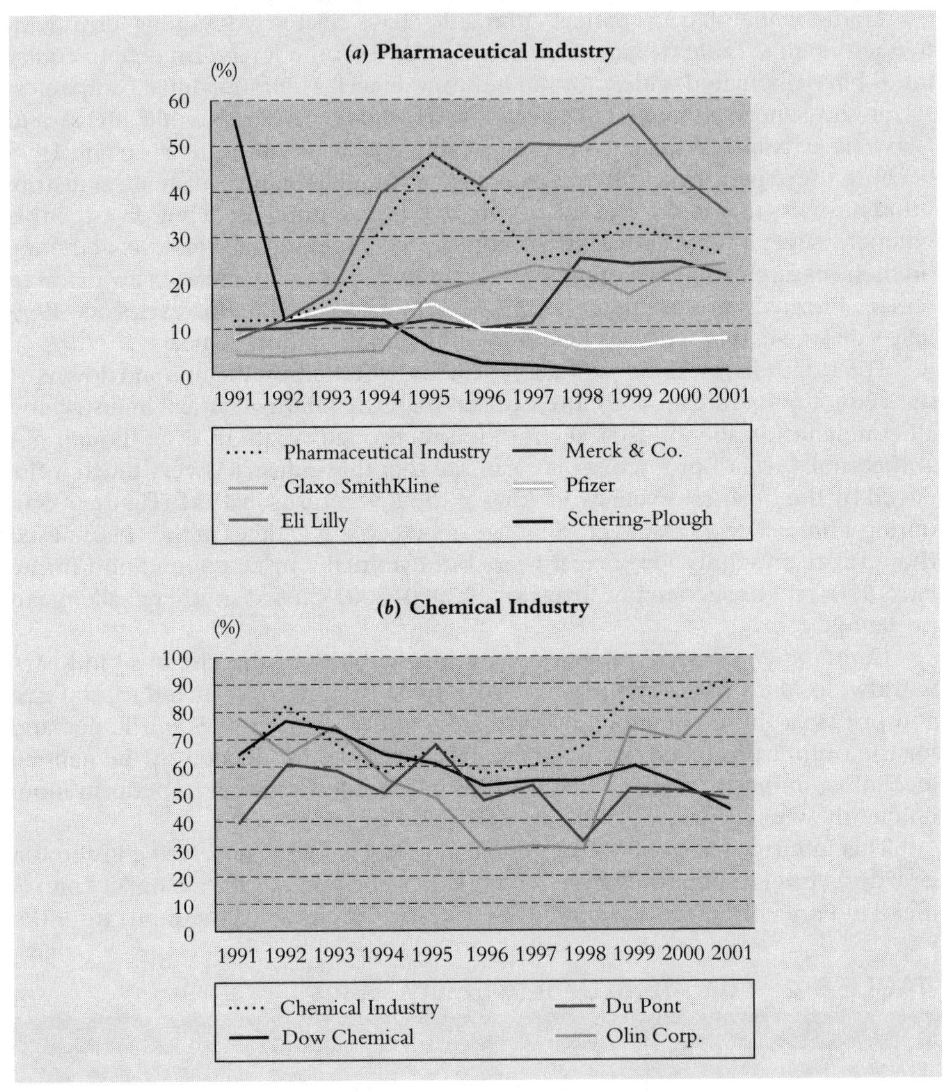

sale to reduce debt, repurchase common stock, and make significant investments in pharmaceuticals and other higher growth industries. Dow Chemical bought Union Carbide and Monsanto, moved into biochemical agriculture, and moved out of basic chemicals.

Du Pont and Dow Chemical are the two dominant powerhouses in the basic chemical industry, and Olin is a much smaller player. Both Dow and Du Pont had peak ROEs in 1995 (Figure 6-6b). Declining earnings due to competitive pricing pressures, sagging demand, and rising oil prices have followed this robust period. As the economy struggles in 2003, all three companies exhibit significant declines in profitability. The pharmaceutical industry (except for Glaxo) will be much less affected by the sluggish economy.

Du Pont has traditionally had the lowest long-term debt-to-equity ratio in the chemical industry (Figure 6–7b), which is why it has been considered a blue chip. During the mid-1990s, however, Dow had a lower long-term debt-to-equity ratio than Du Pont, but its purchase of Union Carbide caused a significant increase in its debt. The irony of the debt ratios between the pharmaceutical industry and the chemical industry is that the pharmaceutical industry—because of its sales stability and higher profitability—can manage a higher debt-to-equity ratio than the chemical industry. The lower profitability and higher cost of plant and equipment in the chemical industry forces them to use more debt in their capital structure.

These tables and figures only cover two ratios, but they should show that industry comparisons allow one to pick the quality companies and find the potential losers. These two ratios (return on equity and long-term debt to equity) can be extremely important when making risk-return choices among common stocks. By comparing the two tables, we see a distinct relationship between the ratios. This trend analysis demonstrates that by analyzing just two ratios and looking across companies in the industry, an analyst can learn quite a bit about the structure of the industry and the competitive environment. A closer look at many other variables would add to the knowledge base.

INDUSTRY GROUPS AND ROTATIONAL INVESTING

One strategy of investment used by institutional investors and occasionally by individual investors is the concept of rotational investing. Rotational investing refers to the practice of moving in and out of various industries over the business cycle. As the business cycle moves from a trough to a peak, different industries benefit from the economic changes that accompany the cycle. Table 6–3 lists ten Dow Jones Industry Groups; industries are classified into groups that are related in some form and that may exhibit similar behavior during different phases of the business cycle.

For example, as interest rates bottom out, houses become more easily financed and cost less per month to purchase. Because of this, housing stocks, home builders, lumber, and housing-related industries such as household durable goods benefit from the lower interest rates. Earnings of companies in these fields are expected to rise, and investors start buying the common stocks of these companies before any profits are actually visible. The same could be said for the automobile industry because of the effect of low-cost financing.

Once an economic recovery is under way, the unemployment rate declines, personal income starts growing, and consumers start spending more. It may take six quarters or more of growth from the recessionary trough, but investors usually anticipate when the consumer will start spending again and bid prices of consumer cyclical stocks up before earnings increases appear. While automobiles are

TABLE 6–3 Dow Jones Industry Groups

Basic Materials
Chemicals
Chemicals, commodity
Chemicals, specialty
Forest products
Paper products
Aluminum
Mining, diversified
Other nonferrous (e.g., aluminum)
Precious metals
Steel

Consumer, Cyclical
Advertising
Broadcasting
Publishing
Auto manufacturers
Auto parts
Casinos
Entertainment
Recreation products and services
Restaurants
Toys
Home construction
Furnishings
Retailers
Retailers, apparel
Retailers, broadline
Retailers, drug-based
Retailers, specialty (e.g., drug and apparel)
Clothing and fabrics
Footwear
Airlines
Lodging

Consumer, Noncyclical
Consumer services
Cosmetics and personal care
Distillers and brewers
Food products
Soft drinks
Food retailers and wholesalers
Consumer products
Household products, durables
Household products, nondurables
Tobacco

Energy
Coal
Oil and gas
Oil, drilling
Oil, integrated majors
Oil, secondary
Oilfield equipment and services
Pipelines

Financial
Banks
Insurance, composite
Insurance, full line
Insurance, life
Insurance, property and casualty
Specialty finance
Real estate investment
Financial services, diversified
Savings and loans
Securities brokers

Health Care
Health care providers
Medical products
Advanced medical devices
Medical supplies
Pharmaceutical and biotech
Biotechnology
Pharmaceuticals

Industrial
Aerospace and defense
Building materials
Heavy construction
Containers and packaging
Industrial diversified
Industrial equipment
Advanced industrial equipment
Electrical components and equipment
Factory equipment
Heavy machinery
Industrial services
Pollution control and waste management
Industrial transportation
Air freight and couriers
Marine transportation
Railroads
Trucking
Transportation equipment

Technology
Hardware and equipment
Communications technology
Computers
Office equipment
Semiconductor and related
Software

Telecommunications
Fixed line communications
Wireless communications

Utilities
Electric
Gas
Water

affected by the lower interest rates, they also get a second boost from healthier consumers.

When interest rates begin to rise, this is not good news for utility stocks. Utilities generate high dividend payouts and usually sell based on their dividend yield. As interest rates rise, utility stock prices fall along with prices of bonds. Another group that eventually loses favor after rates have risen somewhat from their bottom and are expected to continue rising is the banking sector. Rising rates eventually reduce bank lending and squeeze bank margins, which are small anyway.

Investors fearful of rising rates and a potential economic slowdown will often retreat into consumer noncyclical goods such as food, pharmaceuticals, beverages, and tobacco. A move into these industries is often considered defensive because the industries are not much influenced by economic downturns, so their earnings do not suffer nearly as much as cyclical industries.

Eventually, as the economy moves through its business cycle, inflation fears return as demand for products pushes up prices of goods. One possible move is into basic materials and energy. The pricing pressures in the economy spill over into rising prices for these commodities and rising profits for aluminum, oil, steel, and other companies in these industries. A move into these industry groups usually occurs later in the business cycle.

While we do not necessarily endorse buying and selling common stocks in a rotational manner throughout the business cycle, many investors follow this approach, and you should be well aware of this strategy.

Internet Resources

Website Address	Comments
www.hoovers.com	Provides limited free information about sectors and industries
cbs.marketwatch.com	Contains news and industry performance on daily basis
www.smartmoney.com	Provides sector and market performance—feature is map of market
www.wsj.com	Provides limited information about industry data; has searchable archive on articles about companies and industries
www.corporateinformation.com	Provides links to information on industries and by country
www.ita.doc.gov	Provides access to industry reports that are fee based
www.investorguide.com	Has links to sites providing sector and industry information

Chapter 7

Valuation of the Individual Firm

Valuation is based on economic factors, industry variables, an analysis of the financial statements, and the outlook for the individual firm. Valuation determines the long-run fundamental economic value of a company's common stock. In the process, we try to determine whether a common stock is undervalued, overvalued, or fairly valued relative to its market price. The orientation in this chapter is mostly toward long-run concepts of valuation rather than toward determining short-term market pricing factors.

BASIC VALUATION CONCEPTS

The valuation of common stock can be approached in several ways. Some models rely solely on dividends expected to be received during the future, and these are usually referred to as dividend valuation models. A variation on the dividend model is the earnings valuation model, which substitutes earnings as the main income stream for valuation. Earnings valuation models may also call for the determination of a price-earnings ratio, or multiplier of earnings, to determine value. Some models rely on long-run historical relationships between market price and sales per share, or market price and book value per share. Other methods may include the market value of assets, such as cash and liquid assets, replacement value of plant and equipment, and other hidden assets, such as undervalued timber holdings. For the first part of our discussion, we develop the dividend valuation model and then go to earnings-related approaches.

REVIEW OF RISK AND REQUIRED RETURN CONCEPTS

Before moving to the valuation models, it would be helpful to review and consolidate the concepts of risk and required return presented in Chapter 1. Calculation of the required rate of return is extremely important because it is the rate at which future cash flows are discounted to reach a valuation. An investor needs to know the required rate of return on the various risk classes of assets to reach intelligent decisions to buy or sell.

Chapter 1 examined rates of returns for various assets and returns based on Ibbotson Associates data and explained how the risk-free rate is a function of both the real rate of return and an inflation premium. The required return was a function of the risk-free rate plus a risk premium for a specific investment.

In this section, we develop a simple methodology based on the capital asset pricing model for determining a required rate of return when valuing common stocks in a diversified portfolio. First, we determine the risk-free rate. The risk-free rate (R_F) is a function of the real rate of return and the expected rate of inflation. Some analysts express the risk-free rate as simply the addition of the real rate of return and the expected rate of inflation, while a more accurate answer is found as follows:

$$R_F \text{ (risk-free rate)} = (1 + \text{Real rate})(1 + \text{Expected rate of inflation}) - 1 \qquad (7\text{-}1)$$

We now add a risk component to the risk-free rate to determine K_e, the total required rate of return. We show the following relationships.

$$K_e = R_F + b(K_M - R_F) \qquad (7\text{-}2)$$

where:

K_e = Required rate of return

R_F = Risk-free rate

b = Beta coefficient

K_M = Expected return for common stocks in the market

$(K_M - R_F)$ = Equity risk premium (ERP)

The risk-free rate, in practice, is normally assumed to be the return on U.S. Treasury securities. Beta measures individual company risk against the market risk (usually the S&P 500 Stock Index). Companies with betas greater than 1.00 have more risk than the market, companies with betas less than 1.00 have less risk than the market, and companies with betas equal to 1.00 have the same risk as the market. It stands to reason then that high beta stocks ($b > 1.00$) would have higher required returns than the market.

The last term ($K_M - R_F$) in Formula 7-2, the equity risk premium (ERP), is not observable from current market information because it is based on investor expectations. The equity risk premium represents the extra return or premium the stock market must provide compared with the rate of return an investor can earn on U.S. Treasury securities. If we observe the historical relationship between stocks and Treasury bills from Figure 1-4, we see that large stocks have returned an average of 10.4 percent over the 78-year period 1926–2003, and Treasury bills have returned an average of 3.7 percent over the same time, or an equity risk premium of 6.7 percent (10.4% − 3.7%).

Because K_M is not observable from the market, an analyst calculating K_e usually thinks of $(K_M - R_F)$ as one number, expressed as the equity risk premium (ERP).

The raging bull market of the 1990s increased the equity risk premium from 6.5 percent in the period 1926–94 to 6.9 percent in seven years' time. It takes a powerful bull market to raise 68 years of history by 0.4 percent over seven years. If it were not for the stock market's negative returns in 2000, this equity risk premium would have risen even higher. The subsequent decline in the market from 2000 to 2003 brought the risk premium back to 6.7 percent. We use a 7.0 percent equity risk premium in our calculations below but recognize that this risk premium for investing in common stocks instead of risk-free government securities is also dependent on perceptions of the future and an individual's propensity to accept risk. Let's compute a required rate of return for a sample company with a beta of 1.00 (beta equals the market risk) when the Treasury bill rate is 5.0 percent and the ERP is 7.0 percent. We should have a required return as follows:

$$\begin{aligned} K_e &= R_F + b(\text{ERP}) \\ &= 5.0\% + 1.00(7.0\%) \\ &= 12.00\% \end{aligned}$$

Now, K_e, the required rate of return, can be used as a discount rate for future cash flows from an investment. This methodology will be helpful as you work through the dividend valuation models and other valuation models for common stock.

DIVIDEND VALUATION MODELS

The value of a share of stock may be interpreted by the shareholder as the present value of an expected stream of future dividends. Although in the short run, stockholders may be influenced by a change in earnings or other variables, the ultimate value of any holding rests with the distribution of earnings in the form of dividend payments. Although the stockholder may benefit from the retention and reinvestment of earnings by the corporation, at some point, the earnings must generally be translated into cash flow for the stockholder.[1] While dividend valuation models are theoretical in nature and subject to many limitations, they are the most frequently used models in the literature of finance. Perhaps this is because they demonstrate so well the relationship between the major variables affecting common stock prices.

General Dividend Model

A generalized stock valuation model based on future expected dividends can be stated as follows:

$$P_0 = \frac{D_1}{(1 + K_e)^1} + \frac{D_2}{(1 + K_e)^2} + \frac{D_3}{(1 + K_e)^3} + \ldots + \frac{D_\infty}{(1 + K_e)^\infty} \qquad (7\text{-}3)$$

1. Some exceptions to this principle are noted later in the chapter.

where:

P_0 = Present value of the stock price

D_i = Dividend for each year, for example, 1, 2, 3 . . . ∞

K_e = Required rate of return (discount rate)

This model is very general and assumes the investor can determine the right dividend for each and every year as well as the annualized rate of return an investor requires.

Constant Growth Model

Rather than predict the actual dividend each year, a more widely used model includes an estimate of the growth rate in dividends. This model assumes a constant growth rate in dividends to infinity.

If a constant growth rate in dividends is assumed, then Formula 7-3 can be rewritten as:

$$P_0 = \frac{D_0(1+g)^1}{(1+K_e)^1} + \frac{D_0(1+g)^2}{(1+K_e)^2} + \frac{D_0(1+g)^3}{(1+K_e)^3} + \ldots + \frac{D_0(1+g)^\infty}{(1+K_e)^\infty} \qquad (7\text{-}4)$$

where:

$D_0(1+g)^1$ = Dividends in the initial year

$D_0(1+g)^2$ = Dividends in year 2, and so on

g = Constant growth rate in the dividend

The current price of the stock should equal the present value of the expected stream of dividends. If we can correctly predict the growth of future dividends and determine the discount rate, we can estimate the true value of the stock.

For example, assume we wanted to determine the present value of ABC Corporation common stock based on this model. We shall assume ABC anticipates an 8 percent growth rate in dividends per share, and we use a 12 percent discount rate as the required rate of return. The required rate of return is intended to provide the investor with a minimum real rate of return, compensation for expected inflation, and a risk premium. Twelve percent is sufficient to fulfill that function in this example.

Rather than project the dividends for an extremely long period and then discount them back to the present, we can reduce previously presented Formula 7-4 to a more usable form:

$$P_0 = D_1/(K_e - g) \qquad (7\text{-}5)$$

This formula is appropriate as long as two conditions are met. The first is that the growth rate must be constant. For the ABC Corporation, we are assuming that to be the case. It is a constant 8 percent. Second, K_e (the required rate of return) must exceed g (the growth rate). Since K_e is 12 percent and g is 8 percent for the ABC Corporation, this condition is also met. Let's further assume D_1 (the expected dividend at the end of period 1) is \$3.38.

Using Formula 7-5, we determine a stock value of:

$$\begin{aligned} P_0 &= D_1/(K_e - g) \\ &= \$3.38/(0.12 - 0.08) \\ &= \$3.38/0.04 \\ &= \$84.50 \end{aligned}$$

This value, in theory, represents the present value of all future dividends. The meaning is further illustrated in Table 7-1, in which we take the present value of

TABLE 7–1 Present Value Analysis of ABC Corporation

Year	Expected Dividends g = 8%	Present Value Factor K_e = 12%	Present Value of Dividends
2002	\$ 3.38	0.893	\$ 3.02
2003	3.65	0.797	2.91
2004	3.94	0.712	2.81
2005	4.26	0.636	2.71
2006	4.60	0.567	2.61
2007	4.97	0.507	2.52
2008	5.37	0.452	2.43
2009	5.80	0.404	2.34
2010	6.26	0.361	2.26
2011	6.76	0.322	2.18
2012	7.30	0.287	2.10
2013	7.88	0.257	2.03
2014	8.51	0.229	1.95
2015	9.19	0.205	1.87
2016	9.93	0.183	1.81
2017	10.72	0.163	1.75
2018	11.58	0.146	1.69
2019	12.51	0.130	1.63
2020	13.51	0.116	1.57
2021	14.59	0.104	1.52
PV of dividends for years 2002–2021			\$43.71
PV of dividends for years 2022 to infinity			40.79
Total present value of ABC common stock			\$84.50[a]

[a] Notice that this value is the same as that found above using Formula 7–5.

the first 20 years of dividends ($43.71) and then add in a figure of $40.79 to arrive at the present value of all future dividends of $84.50 as previously determined by Formula 7-5. The $40.79 value represents the present value of dividends occurring between 2022 and infinity (i.e., after 2021).

We must be aware that several things could be wrong with our analysis. First, our expectations of dividend growth may be too high for an infinite period. Perhaps 6 percent is a more realistic estimate of expected dividend growth. If we substitute our new estimate into Formula 7-5, we can measure the price effect as dividend growth changes from an 8 percent rate to a 6 percent rate:

$$\begin{aligned} P_0 &= \$3.38/(0.12 - 0.06) \\ &= \$3.38/0.06 \\ &= \$56.33 \end{aligned}$$

A 6 percent growth rate (a 2 percent change) cuts the present value down substantially from the prior value of $84.50.

We could also misjudge our required rate of return, K_e, which could be higher or lower. A lower K_e would increase the present value of ABC Corporation, whereas a higher K_e would reduce its value. We have made these points to show how sensitive stock prices are to the basic assumptions of the model. Even though you may go through the calculations, the final value is only as accurate as your inputs. This is where a security analyst's judgment and expertise are important—in justifying the growth rate and required rate of return.

A Nonconstant Growth Model

Many analysts do not accept the premise of a constant growth rate in dividends or earnings. As we examined in Chapter 6, industries go through a life cycle in which growth is nonlinear. Growth is usually highest in the infancy and early phases of the life cycle, and as expansion is reached, the growth rate slows until the industry reaches maturity. At maturity, a constant, long-term growth rate that approximates the long-term growth of the macro economy may be appropriate for a particular industry.

Some companies in an industry may not behave like the industry in general. Companies constantly try to avoid maturity or decline, and so they strive to develop new products and markets to maintain growth.

In situations where the analyst wants to value a company without the constant-growth assumption, a variation of the constant-growth model is possible. Growth is simply divided into several periods with each period having a present value. The present value of each period is summed to attain the total value of the firm's share price. An example of a two-period model may illustrate the concept. Assume that JAYCAR Corporation is expected to have the growth pattern shown in Figure 7-1.

It is assumed that JAYCAR will have a dividend growth rate of 20 percent for the next 10 years and an 8 percent perpetual growth rate after that. JAYCAR's div-

FIGURE 7–1 JAYCAR Growth Pattern

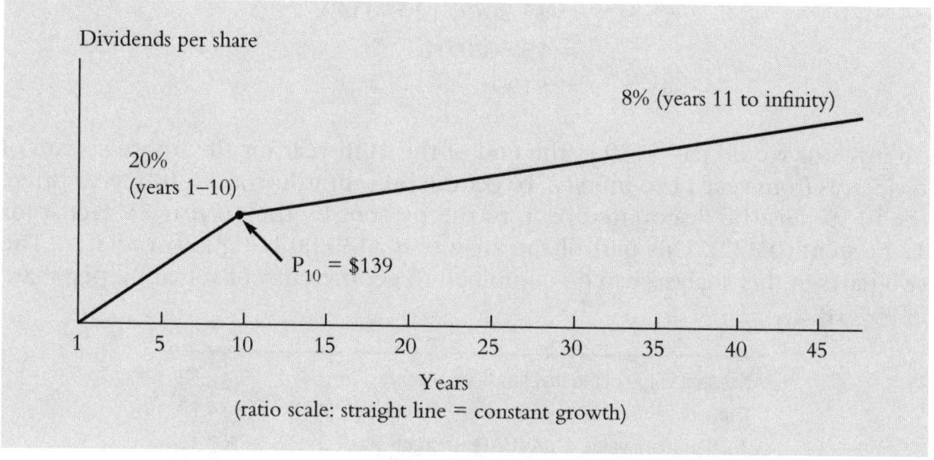

idend is expected to be $1 at the end of year one, and the appropriate required rate of return (discount rate) is 12 percent. Taking the present value for the first 10 years of dividends and then applying the constant dividend growth model for years 11 through infinity, we can arrive at an answer. First, we find the present value of the initial 10 years of dividends:

Year	Dividends (20% growth)	PV Factor (12%)	Present Value of Dividends First 10 Years
1	$1.00	0.893	$ 0.89
2	1.20	0.797	0.96
3	1.44	0.712	1.03
4	1.73	0.636	1.10
5	2.07	0.567	1.17
6	2.48	0.507	1.26
7	2.98	0.452	1.35
8	3.58	0.404	1.45
9	4.29	0.361	1.55
10	5.15	0.322	1.66
			$12.42

We then determine the present value of dividends after the 10th year. The dividend in year 11 is expected to be $5.56, or $5.15 (for year 10) compounded at the new, lower 8 percent growth rate ($5.15 × 1.08). Because the rest of the dividend stream will be infinite, Formula 7-5 can provide the value of JAYCAR at the end of year 10, based on a discount rate of 12 percent and an expected growth rate of 8 percent.

$$
\begin{aligned}
P_{10} &= D_{11}/(K_e - g) \\
&= \$5.56/(0.12 - 0.08) \\
&= \$5.56/0.04 \\
&= \$139
\end{aligned}
$$

An investor would pay $139 at the end of the 10th year for the future stream of dividends from year 11 to infinity. To get the present value of the 10th year price, the $139 must be discounted back to the present by the 10-year PV factor for 12 percent (0.322). This part of the answer is $139.00 × 0.322, or $44.76. The two parts of this analysis can be combined to get the current valuation per share of $57.18.

Present value of the dividends from years 1 to 10	$12.42
Present value of 10th year price ($139.00 × 0.322)	44.76
Total present value of JAYCAR common stock	$57.18

EARNINGS VALUATION MODELS

Dividend valuation models are best suited for companies in the expansion or maturity life-cycle phase. Dividends of these companies are more predictable and usually make up a larger percentage of the total return than capital gains. Earnings-per-share models are also used for valuation. For example, the investor may take the present value of all future earnings to determine a value. This might be appropriate where the firm pays no cash dividend and has no immediate intention of paying one.

The Combined Earnings and Dividend Model

Another, more comprehensive valuation model relies on earnings per share (EPS) and a price-earnings (P/E) ratio (earnings multiplier) combined with a finite dividend model. The value of common stock can be viewed as a dividend stream plus a market price at the end of the dividend stream. We have selected Johnson & Johnson from the health care and pharmaceutical industry as our sample company for the valuation models that follow. Assuming that we start our valuation at the beginning of 2002, we develop a present value for the common stock listed on the New York Stock Exchange. The numbers are shown in Table 7-2.

The present value of the common stock for Johnson & Johnson is shown at the bottom of Table 7-2 to be $55.26. Note that Part A of Table 7-2 calculates the present value of the future dividends, while Part B is used to determine the present value of the future stock price at the end of 2006. These are assumed to be the two variables that determine the current stock price under this model.

In Part A, earnings per share are first projected for the next five years. Johnson & Johnson's payout ratio fluctuated between 34 and 37 percent from 1992 to

TABLE 7–2 Johnson & Johnson Combined Dividend and Earnings Present Value Analysis

Part A: Present Value of Dividends for 5 Years					
Year	(1) Estimated EPS Growth = 13.61%	(2) Estimated Payout Ratio	(3) Estimated Dividends per Share	(4)* Present Value Factor at K_e = 10.00%	(5) Present Value of Cash Flows
2002	$2.20	36%	$0.79	0.909	$ 0.72
2003	2.50	36	0.90	0.826	0.74
2004	2.84	36	1.02	0.751	0.77
2005	3.23	36	1.16	0.683	0.79
2006	3.67	36	1.32	0.621	0.82
				PV Dividends	$ 3.84
Part B: Present Value of Johnson & Johnson's 2006 Common Stock Price					
	EPS	P/E	$Price_{2006}$	PV Factor	
2006	$3.67	22.56	$82.80	0.621	$51.42
A + B = Present Value of Johnson & Johnson at beginning of 2002					$55.26

*$K_e = R_F + b(K_M - R_F)$ $R_F = 3.62$ $b = 0.85$ $K_M - R_F = 7.5\%$ $K_e = 10.00\%$

2001 and averaged 35.74 percent over this 10-year period. Because we see no dramatic shift in the company's need for retained earnings, we estimate the payout ratio will average 36 percent over the next five years. The earnings are then multiplied by the company's estimated payout ratio of 36 percent to determine anticipated dividends per share for those five years. At the time of the analysis, Johnson & Johnson had a beta of 0.85, one-year U.S. government securities had a 3.62 percent yield, and we selected an equity risk premium ($K_M - R_F$) of 7.5 percent for a total required rate of return of 10.00 percent. You need to recognize that this required rate of return changes continuously with changes in interest rates, betas, and equity risk premiums. The present value of dividends from 2002 through 2006 is shown in Column 5 of Part A to equal $3.84.

In Part B, we multiply estimated 2006 earnings per share of $3.67 by the P/E ratio (earnings multiplier) of 22.56 to arrive at an anticipated price of $82.80 five years into the future. The P/E ratio we used to determine the price is the average P/E over the last 10 years. Evidence over the last seven years indicates that Johnson & Johnson always reached a P/E of at least this number. The future P/E could be affected by higher or lower expected growth rates of earnings, the risk characteristics of the stock in 2006, and other variables. The future price of $82.80 is then discounted for five years at 10 percent to arrive at a present value of $51.42. The total present value of the stock is equal to the present value of the dividend stream for five years ($3.84) plus the present value of the future stock price

($51.42) for a total present value of $55.26 at the beginning of 2002. The common stock was trading in the $54 to $55 range at the time of analysis.

This model can be used with your choice of time periods. Five years is not a magic number. As the time period used increases, the estimate of earnings per share becomes more uncertain for cyclical companies, and the future stock price based on an earnings multiplier (P/E ratio) becomes a risky forecast. Some companies in industries such as utilities or food have more predictable earnings streams than those in consumer-sensitive markets such as automobiles and furniture, but they still may exhibit fluctuating P/E ratios. The next section develops the concept of the price-earnings ratio, which was used as the earnings multiplier in Table 7-2.

EVA: THE HOT NEW VALUATION TERM OF THE CURRENT DECADE: WHAT DOES IT MEAN?

There is a new valuation concept that has garnered attention at leading U.S. corporations such as Coca-Cola, AT&T, Eli Lilly, Merrill Lynch, and Monsanto. These firms are not nearly so interested in generating earnings per share as they are in maximizing economic value added (EVA).

Economic value added is based on the concept that decisions should be made or projects accepted only if net operating profit after taxes (NOPAT) exceeds the capital costs to finance the investment. If this rule is followed, then economic value will be added. To many readers, this may sound like the capital budgeting principle you learned in the first course in corporate finance, warmed over and served again as a hot new idea.

Not so, say the founders of the EVA concept at Stern Stewart & Co. (www.sternstewart.com) in New York.[2] EVA is an overriding concept that is intended to be applied to every decision the corporation makes, from investing overseas to adding three more widgets in the stockroom. The question repeatedly asked is, "Is the firm earning an adequate return on the money investors entrusted to it?" Even at the lowest levels of the organization, this question cannot be escaped.

Proponents of EVA say that all too often chief financial officers evaluate projects based on net present value, but they modify recommendations to meet earnings growth targets of the firm. Business unit evaluations may not be based on either parameter but rather on return on assets or some other unrelated profit goal set by top management. Bonuses for operating managers may be linked to demand–supply conditions within an industry. New-product introductions may be based on gross profit margin. Furthermore, the analysis for some decisions may be based on cash flow, while other decisions are linked to earnings per share. There is no coherent theme or goal, and stockholder wealth may be harmed in the process.

---

2. *EVA, The Real Key to Creating Wealth* (New York: Stern Stewart & Co., 1996–97).

With EVA, the firm is assumed to always be working for the stockholder's benefit. Under the EVA concept, the firm will not accept a project or idea that does not earn back the cost of funds the stockholder provided. Economic value added is also intended to lead to market value added (MVA). MVA is another hot new topic and represents the total market value of the firm minus the total capital provided since day one (including the retained earnings). MVA requires a company's top managers to justify what they did with the money that was given to them. Did they increase the value and thereby produce a positive MVA, as expected, or did they destroy contributed capital and generate a negative MVA?

Based on the Stern Stewart & Co. report related to recent financial reports, Coca-Cola (www.cocacola.com) was the leading producer of market value over contributed capital with an MVA of $124.9 billion. General Motors (www.gm.com) was the largest destroyer of capital with a negative MVA of $20.7 billion.

MVA is thought to be linked to EVA because, according to Stern Stewart & Co., the way MVA increases is by consistently increasing EVA. In fact, MVA is intended to be the present value of all future EVAs.

Annual data on MVA and EVA for the 1,000 largest companies can be acquired directly from Stern Stewart & Co. of New York. *Fortune* magazine also publishes Stern Stewart & Co. data on the 200 top MVA creators toward the end of each year. (However, not all of these companies formally use EVA and MVA.)

Detractors of the EVA-MVA emphasis say it is not widely enough followed to truly affect value. They suggest that earnings per share is still the "king" on Wall Street. In spite of EVA, it is still quarterly earnings estimates that drive investors crazy. Only time will tell whether this hot new concept can permanently compete. Today, there are 300 to 350 firms that use EVA in their strategic development.

THE PRICE-EARNINGS RATIO

Mathematically, the price-earnings ratio (P/E) is simply the price per share divided by earnings per share, and it is ultimately set by investors in the market as they bid the price of a stock up or down in relation to its earnings. Price-earnings ratios are often expressed in the financial press as historical numbers using today's price divided by the latest 12-month earnings.

For companies with cyclical earnings, a P/E using the latest 12-month earnings might be misleading because these earnings could be high. If investors expect earnings to fall back to a normal level, they will not bid the price up in relation to this short-term cyclical swing in earnings per share, and the P/E ratio will appear to be low. But if earnings are severely depressed, investors will expect a return to normal higher earnings, and the price will not fall an equal percentage with earnings, and the P/E will appear to be high.

In the Johnson & Johnson example in Table 7-2, we used a P/E of 22.56 in 2006. This P/E ratio of 22.56 is determined by historical analysis and by other factors such as expected growth in earnings per share. The P/E of a company is also affected by overall conditions in the stock market. At the time of this writing Johnson & Johnson had a P/E of 31, but its 5-year average P/E was 26.62. In our judgment, we choose to use the more conservative 10-year average of 22.56.

Even though the current P/E ratio for a stock is known, investors may not agree it is appropriate. Stock analysts and investors probably spend more time examining P/E ratios and assessing their appropriate level than any other variable. Although the use of P/E ratios in valuation approaches lacks the theoretical underpinning of the present value-based valuation models previously discussed in the chapter, P/E ratios are equally important. The well-informed student of investments should have a basic understanding of both the theoretically based present value approach and the more pragmatic, frequently used P/E ratio approach.

What determines whether a stock should have a high or low P/E ratio? Let's first talk about the market for stocks in general, and then we will look at individual securities.

Stocks generally trade at a relatively high P/E ratio (perhaps 20 or greater) when there are strong growth prospects in the economy. However, inflation also plays a key role in determining P/E ratios for the overall market.

To illustrate the latter point, Figure 7–2 presents the relationship between the year-end Standard & Poor's 500 composite P/E ratio and the annual rate of inflation measured by the change in the consumer price index (CPI). The graphical relationship between these two variables shows they are inversely related. The price-earnings ratio goes down when the change in the CPI goes up, and the reverse is also true.

The dramatic drop in the P/E ratio in 1973–74 can be attributed in large measure to the rate of inflation increasing from 3.4 percent in 1972 to 12.2 percent

FIGURE 7–2 Inflation and Price-Earnings Ratios

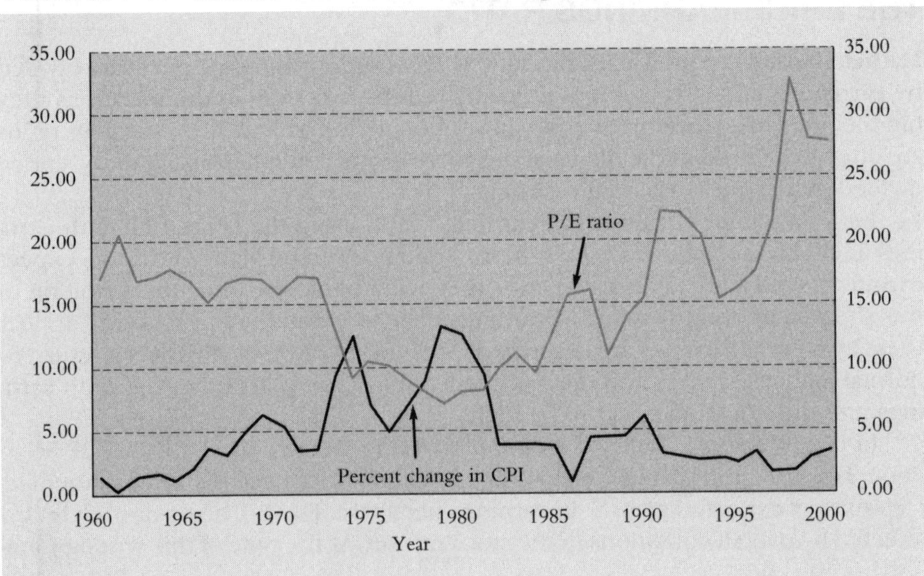

in 1974, or a change of more than three times its former level. For a brief period in 1976, inflation decreased to an annual rate of less than 5 percent, only to soar to 13.3 percent by 1979. The average rate of inflation for 1982 was reduced to 3.8 percent, and the market responded by paying higher share prices for one dollar of earnings (that is, higher P/E ratios).

From 1983 through 1985, the consumer price index hovered around 3 to 4 percent, but in 1986, inflation subsided to 1.1 percent, and the S&P price-earnings ratio soared. In 1987, the S&P 500 P/E ratio remained high until the crash of October 1987 brought stock prices down to lower levels. During the sobering and risk-averse period after the crash, market prices were fairly stable.

As fears of higher inflation rose during 1989, the S&P 500 P/E ratio came back to the low-midrange of its 40-year history shown in Figure 7-2. The higher price-earnings ratios in 1991-93 reflect both the impact of falling inflationary expectations and depressed earnings suffered by corporations during the recessionary period of 1990-91 and the slow recovery in 1992 and 1993. As earnings grew quickly in 1994, 1995, and 1996, the Standard & Poor's 500 P/E ratio fell below 20 again. The economy in 1997 saw low inflation, strong economic growth, low unemployment, and reduced government deficits. This economy was described as a dream economy, one that was perfectly balanced with GDP growth of 3.8 percent and inflation of 1.8 percent. In response, P/E ratios again soared above 21 times earnings, and the raging bull market, lasting through 1999, pushed P/E ratios over 30. Collapsing earnings in 2000 and 2001 kept P/E ratios higher than normal for an economic slowdown as the market waited for earnings to recover and hoped for a return to above-average GDP growth.

As was pointed out in Chapter 1 and earlier in this chapter, required rates of return are directly influenced by the rate of inflation. As inflation changes, the required rate of return on common stock, K_e, changes, and prices go up or down. This is the basic mechanism that causes inflation to influence P/E ratios.

Other factors besides inflationary considerations and growth factors influence the P/E ratio for the market in general. Federal Reserve policy and interest rates, federal deficits, the government's leading indicators, the political climate, the mood of the population, international considerations, and many other factors affect the P/E ratio for the overall market. The astute analyst constantly studies a multitude of variables that could cause P/E ratios to move higher or lower.

The P/E Ratio for Individual Stocks

Although the overall market P/E ratio is the collective average of individual P/Es, those factors that influence the market P/E do not necessarily affect P/E ratios of individual companies consistently from one industry to another. An individual firm's P/E ratio is heavily influenced by its growth prospects and the risk associated with its future performance. Table 7-3 shows examples of growth rates and P/E ratios for different industries and firms. Generally, a strong expected future growth rate for 2001-2006 (Column 3) is associated with a reasonably high P/E for mid-2001 (Column 4) and vice versa.

TABLE 7–3 P/E and Growth in EPS

(1) Industry	(2) Company	(3) Expected 5-Year Growth in EPS 2001–2006	(4) P/E July 2001
Electric utility	First Energy	6.50%	11.1
Auto parts	Genuine Parts	7.50	13.6
Telecom services	Bell South	13.50	16.7
Paper/forest products	Weyerhaeuser	13.50	20.9
Pharmacy services	Walgreens	17.50	39.4
Telecom equipment	Qualcomm	29.00	52.4
Semiconductors	Intel*	9.00	51.0

*Intel's P/E is inflated because earnings declined faster than the stock price, and the market expects this high-quality technology company to eventually recover but grow at a slower rate.

Source: Selected issues of *Value Line Investment Survey*; reproduced with the permission of Value Line Publishing, Inc.

In addition to the future growth of the firm and the risk associated with that growth, investors and analysts also consider a number of other factors that influence a firm's P/E ratio. These cannot be easily quantified, but they affect a broad range of stocks. Included in this category are the debt-to-equity ratio and the dividend policy of the firm. All things being equal, the less debt a firm has, the more likely it is to be highly valued in the marketplace.

The dividend policy is more elusive. For firms that show superior internal reinvestment opportunities, low cash dividends may be desired. But maturing companies may be expected to pay a high cash dividend. For the latter group, a reduction in cash dividends may be associated with a lower P/E ratio if the dividend cut signals falling earnings per share.

Certain industries also traditionally command higher P/E ratios than others. Investors seem to prefer industries that have a high technology and research emphasis. Thus, firms in computers, medical research and health care, and sophisticated telecommunications often have higher P/E ratios than the market in general. This does not mean firms in these industries represent superior investments, but merely that investors value their earnings more highly.[3] Also, fads and other factors can cause a shift in industry popularity. For example, because Ronald Reagan emphasized military strength, defense-oriented stocks were popular during his administration. Jimmy Carter stressed the need for environmental control, and stocks dealing in air and water pollution control traded at high P/E ratios during his tenure. Bill Clinton's health care proposals lowered P/Es of pharmaceutical stocks dramatically until a Republican Congress killed his proposals. Tobacco stocks rallied under George W. Bush.

3. William Kittrell, Geoffrey A. Hirt, and Roger Potter, "Price-Earnings Multiples, Investors' Expectations, and Rates of Return: Some Analytical and Empirical Findings" (Paper presented at the 1984 Financial Management Association meeting).

The quality of management as perceived by those in the marketplace also influences a firm's P/E ratio. If management is viewed as being highly capable, clever, or innovative, the firm may carry a higher P/E ratio. Investors may look to magazines such as *Forbes* or *Business Week,* which highlight management strategies by various companies, or to management-oriented books. Of course, it is possible that today's trendsetters may represent tomorrow's failures.

Not only is the quality of management important to investors in determining the firm's P/E ratio, but the quality of earnings is also. There are many interpretations of a dollar's worth of earnings. Some companies choose to use very conservative accounting practices so their reported earnings can be interpreted as being very solid by investors (they may even be understated). Other companies use more liberal accounting interpretations to report maximum earnings to their shareholders, and they, at times, overstate their true performance (e.g., Enron). It is easy to see that a dollar's worth of conservatively reported earnings (high quality earnings) may be valued at a P/E ratio of 20 to 25 times, whereas a dollar's worth of liberally reported earnings (low quality earnings) should be valued at a much lower multiple.

All of these factors affect a firm's P/E ratio. Thus, investors will consider growth in sales and earnings, future risk, the debt position, the dividend policy, the quality of management and earnings, and a multitude of other factors in arriving at the P/E ratio. The P/E ratio, like the price of the stock, is set by the interaction of the forces of demand and supply. Those firms that are expected to provide returns greater than the overall economy, with equal or less risk, generally have superior P/E ratios.

The Pure, Short-Term Earnings Model

Often investors/speculators take a very short-term view of the market and ignore present value analysis with its associated long-term forecasts of dividends and earnings per share. Instead, they only use earnings per share and apply an appropriate multiplier to compute the estimated value.

Applying this approach to Johnson & Johnson's financial data initially presented in Table 7-2, we can arrive at a value of \$58.56 based on an earnings per share estimate of \$2.20 for 2002 and a P/E ratio of 26.62 reflecting the five-year average P/E from 1997 through 2001:

$$
\begin{aligned}
P_0 &= \text{EPS}_{2002} \times \text{P/E}_{\text{5-year average}} \\
&= \$2.20 \times 26.62 \\
\text{P}_{2002} &= \$58.56
\end{aligned}
$$

Every valuation method has its limitations. Although this method is simplified by ignoring dividends and present value calculations, earnings need to be correctly estimated, and the appropriate price-earnings multiplier must be applied. Unfortunately, even if the estimated EPS is correct, you have no assurance that the market will agree with your P/E ratio.

Relating an Individual Stock's P/E Ratio to the Market

Johnson & Johnson is the leading producer of health care products and pharmaceuticals. Everyone has probably used at least one of their products, such as Band-Aids, Q-tips, baby oil, or Tylenol, but you may not be familiar with the financial data presented in Table 7-4. This table provides an historical summary and an estimate of sales per share (SPS), dividends per share (DPS), earnings per share (EPS), cash flow per share (CFPS), and book value per share (BVPS). It also indicates Johnson & Johnson's high and low stock prices and the high and low P/E ratios for the company and the Standard & Poor's 500 Index.

In the last three columns, the high and low P/E ratios for Johnson & Johnson are compared with the high and low P/E ratio for the S&P 500. For example, in the first row for 1992, Johnson & Johnson's high P/E ratio was 23.71 and the S&P 500 high P/E was 23.40. When Johnson & Johnson's high P/E ratio is divided by the S&P 500 high P/E, a relative P/E of 1.01 is calculated in the high relative P/E column. This indicates that Johnson & Johnson's high P/E ratio was at 101 percent of the market or selling at a 1 percent premium to the S&P Index. Over the 10 years listed we can see that Johnson & Johnson's high P/E relative to the S&P 500 sold as high as a 34 percent premium in 1995 (shown as 1.34) and as low as a 15 percent discount in 1993 when it sold at only 85 percent of the index.

For each year, a high and low relative was calculated for Johnson & Johnson with the 10-year average of the high and low shown on the last line. Over this time period, Johnson & Johnson's high relative P/E averaged 1.09 (a 9 percent premium to the market's high P/E) and its low relative P/E averages 0.93 (a 7 percent discount to the market's low P/E). When we add the high and low and divide by 2, we get an average of 1.01, which indicates that Johnson & Johnson historically sells at 101 percent of the S&P 500 P/E ratio.

TABLE 7–4 Johnson & Johnson

Year	Sales per Share (SPS)	Dividends per Share (DPS)	Earnings per Share (EPS)	Cash Flow per Share (CFPS)	Book Value per Share (BVPS)	Stock Price High	Stock Price Low	P/E Ratio High	P/E Ratio Low	S&P 500 P/E Ratio High	S&P 500 P/E Ratio Low	Relative P/E Ratios High	Relative P/E Ratios Low
1992	$ 5.25	$0.22	$0.62	$0.85	$1.97	$14.70	$10.80	23.71	17.42	23.40	20.92	1.01	0.83
1993	5.50	0.25	0.69	0.93	2.17	12.60	8.90	18.26	12.90	21.55	19.64	0.85	0.66
1994	6.12	0.28	0.78	1.06	2.77	14.10	9.00	18.08	11.54	16.12	14.57	1.12	0.79
1995	7.27	0.32	0.93	1.26	3.49	23.10	13.40	24.84	14.41	18.50	13.66	1.34	1.05
1996	8.11	0.37	1.09	1.46	4.07	27.00	20.80	24.77	19.08	19.55	15.45	1.27	1.24
1997	8.41	0.43	1.21	1.62	4.59	33.70	24.30	27.85	20.08	24.77	18.56	1.12	1.08
1998	8.80	0.49	1.34	1.83	5.06	44.90	31.70	33.51	23.66	32.93	24.60	1.02	0.96
1999	9.88	0.55	1.49	2.03	5.83	53.40	38.50	35.84	25.84	30.50	25.16	1.18	1.03
2000	10.47	0.62	1.70	2.27	6.76	53.00	33.10	31.18	19.47	30.00	25.30	1.04	0.77
2001	11.40	0.70	1.95	2.55	7.70	54.98	40.30	28.19	20.67	30.10	24.10	0.94	0.86
10-year average	$ 8.12	$0.42	$1.18	$1.59	$4.44	$33.15	$23.08	26.62	18.51	24.74	20.20	1.09	0.93
2002 estimates	$12.55	$0.80	$2.20	$2.90	$8.55	$28.11 average stock price for 1992–2001							

Notice that Table 7–4 also gives us estimates for SPS, DPS, EPS, CFPS, and BVPS. We will use these estimates for our valuation models. Table 7–4 indicates that earnings per share (fourth column) for 2002 will be $2.20.

At the time of the analysis, the S&P 500 Stock Index was selling at a P/E ratio of 26.65 times earnings. In Table 7–5, the relative P/E model uses the high, low, and average P/E times the S&P 500 P/E to calculate the appropriate price-earnings ratio for Johnson & Johnson based on its relationship to the current market level. When applied to the $2.20 EPS estimate, we find that Johnson & Johnson should be selling between $54.52 at its low price and $63.91 at its high price. This would indicate that at a market price in the range of $54 to $55, Johnson & Johnson is selling at the low end of its historical valuation relative to the S&P 500.

OTHER VALUATION MODELS USING AVERAGE PRICE RATIOS AND 10-YEAR AVERAGES

Using the 10-year averages for price and per share data from Table 7–4, we can use the average price of $28.11 (bottom line) as the average per-share data to determine the historical relationships. These models will simply determine whether the current stock price is selling above or below its historical valuation. It is up to the analyst to determine if the results are warranted by expectations.

Using the data in Table 7–4 we develop these five models in Table 7–6. In each case in Table 7–6, we calculate the historical price ratios and multiply the result times the value estimated for 2002. The answer provides an estimated value of the common stock based on history. For example in Part A of Table 7–6, Johnson & Johnson exhibits a price-to-sales ratio of 3.46, which indicates that over the 10 years covered, Johnson & Johnson stock sold at 346 percent of its sales per share. Multiplying this ratio times estimated sales per share of $12.55 for 2002 produces a value of $43.42. This is quite a bit below the current market price of $54 to $55. On the other hand the price-to-book value model in Part E generates a value of $54.12, almost identical to the current market price.

TABLE 7–5 Projected Earnings and Relative P/E Valuation Model

	Relative P/E	S&P 500 Current P/E	Johnson & Johnson's Expected P/E	Johnson & Johnson's Estimated EPS_{2002}	Johnson & Johnson's Value in 2002 Based on Relative P/E
Average high P/E	1.09	26.65	29.05	$2.20	$63.91
Average low P/E	0.93	26.65	24.78	2.20	54.52
Average P/E	1.01	26.65	26.92	2.20	59.22

TABLE 7–6 Other Valuation Models Using Average Price Ratios and 10-Year Averages

A. Price to sales per share

Average Price	÷	Average Sales per Share	=	Price-to-SPS Ratio	×	Estimated 2002 SPS	=	Projected 2002 Price
$28.11		$8.12		3.46		$12.55		$43.42

B. Price to dividend per share

Average Price	÷	Average Dividends per Share	=	Price-to-DPS Ratio	×	Estimated 2002 DPS	=	Projected 2002 Price
$28.11		$0.42		66.93		$0.80		$53.54

C. Price to earnings per share

Average Price	÷	Average Earnings per Share	=	Price-to-EPS Ratio	×	Estimated 2002 EPS	=	Projected 2002 Price
$28.11		$1.18		23.82		$2.20		$52.40

D. Price to cash flow per share

Average Price	÷	Average Cash Flow per Share	=	Price-to-CFPS Ratio	×	Estimated 2002 CFPS	=	Projected 2002 Price
$28.11		$1.59		17.68		$2.90		$51.27

E. Price to book value per share

Average Price	÷	Average Book Value per Share	=	Price-to-BVPS Ratio	×	Estimated 2002 BVPS	=	Projected 2002 Price
$28.11		$4.44		6.33		$8.55		$54.12

The analyst needs to look at the results of these models as information. In the case of Johnson & Johnson, all the models show that the current stock price of $54 to $55 is probably a fair value. Several models in the chapter indicate that the company could be slightly undervalued by $4 to $8 per share. It is the analyst's job to make a judgment based on experience, expectations, and an in-depth knowledge of the company. These models do not provide foolproof values, only information that can be used to make a financial judgment.

VALUING COMPANIES WITHOUT EARNINGS: EBITDA AND FREE CASH FLOW

In the high-tech, "new economy" era of the late 1990s and early 2000s, many popular companies did not achieve consistent earnings (or earnings at all). Examples include Ebay, WorldCom, Oracle, and virtually every high-tech or telecommunications start-up firm.

For a firm with negative earnings per share, the concept of a price-earnings ratio is hardly applicable. For example, a company that has a loss of $0.75 a share and is assigned a P/E ratio of 20 by analysts would have a negative value of $15. No such concept exists in finance. For that reason, analysts looked for other values to track besides earnings. Some developed stock price to revenue, stock price to website hits, stock price to actual website sales (as opposed to just hits), and so on. All of these were done on a per-share basis. While these new "metrics" were popular, sophisticated analysts looked for greater depth in their analysis.

The term EBITDA fits the bill. EBITDA stands for earnings before interest, taxes, depreciation, and amortization. Companies that have negative earnings may well have a positive EBITDA.

An example of computing EBITDA is shown here for a company with reported negative earnings of $5 million and 1 million shares outstanding:

Earnings	−$5,000,000
+ Amortization	1,000,000
+ Depreciation	6,000,000
+ Taxes	0
+ Interest	2,000,000
Earnings before interest, taxes, depreciation, and amortization (EBITDA)	$4,000,000
− Shares outstanding	1,000,000
EBITDA per share	$4.00

Amortization (line 2) usually represents the write-off of intangible assets (perhaps goodwill), while depreciation represents the write-off of physical assets (such as plant and equipment). The other terms are self-explanatory. EBITDA per share is very close to the concept of cash flow per share, but in addition to depreciation and amortization, taxes and interest are added back to earnings. What the analyst ends up with is operating income per share. In other words, this tells the analyst how much the company is making purely from its operations out in the plant before financing charges and taxes as well as noncash charges. While the latter items are important in a traditional sense, the analyst needs to get a handle on something, and what better than how it's doing on its actual day-to-day operations.

Once EBITDA is determined for a firm in a given industry, analysts look to other companies in the same industry to determine their stock price to EBITDA multiplier. Because this often is not commonly available data, the analyst may have to do the work on his or her own. Assume in this example that the industry average stock price/EBITDA ratio was 12×, then the firm with $4 in EBITDA per share might be valued at $48. If the firm has unusually bright prospects, it might be higher and the opposite would also be true.

Analysts may also use a slightly different concept of free cash flow per share by adding depreciation and amortization to earnings and subtracting out necessary capital expenditures and dividends (and dividing by the number of shares outstanding). Once again, an industry multiplier of stock price to free cash flow is developed and applied to free cash flow per share.

FORECASTING EARNINGS PER SHARE

The other side of choosing an appropriate P/E ratio is forecasting the earnings per share of a company with the proper growth rate. Investors can get earnings forecasts in several ways. They can rely on professional brokerage house research, investment advisory firms such as Value Line or Standard & Poor's, or financial magazines such as *Forbes, Business Week, Worth,* or *Money,* or they can do it themselves.

Least Squares Trendline

One of the most common ways of forecasting earnings per share is to use regression or least squares trend analysis. The technique involves a statistical method whereby a trendline is fitted to a time series of historical earnings. This trendline, by definition, is a straight line that minimizes the distance of the individual observations from the line. Figure 7-3 depicts a scattergram for the earnings per share of XYZ Corporation. The earnings of this company have been fairly consistent, and so we get a good trendline with a minimum of variation. The compounded growth rate for the whole 10-year period was 16.5 percent, with 9.8 percent for the first 5 years and 20.4 percent for the second 5 years. This shows up in Figure 7-3 as two distinct five-year trendlines. There are many statistical programs on PCs and mainframes that run regression analysis, and even handheld calculators have the ability to compute a growth rate from raw data.

Whenever a mechanical forecast is made, subjectivity still enters the decision in choosing the data that will be considered in the regression plot. If we compare two companies, one with consistent growth and one with cyclical growth, we find that the cyclical companies (e.g., autos, chemicals, airlines, forest products) are much more difficult to forecast than the consistent growth companies (e.g., pharmaceuticals, food, beverages). Cyclical companies are much more sensitive to swings in the economy and are likely to be in industries with high-priced durable goods where consumers can postpone purchases or where the economy has a direct effect on their products. Do not confuse cyclical with seasonal. Seasonal companies show earnings variability because their products have seasonal demand, such as fuel oil for winter heating and electricity for summer air conditioning or snowmobiles for winter. Cyclical companies have earnings related to

FIGURE 7–3 Least Squares Trendline for EPS of XYZ Corporation

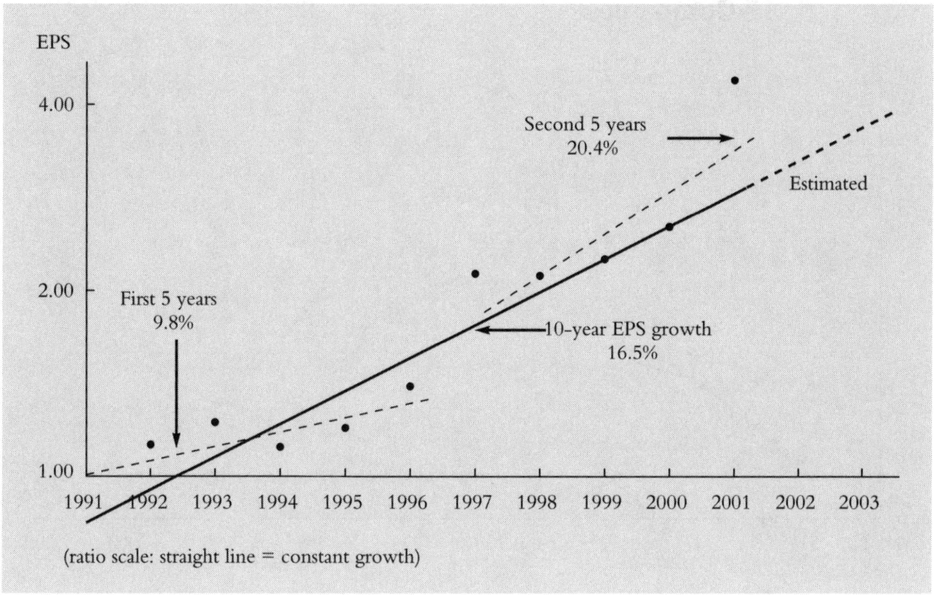

(ratio scale: straight line = constant growth)

Source: Reproduced with the permission of Value Line Publishing, Inc.

the economy and exhibit variability over many years rather than three-month seasons.

Consistently growing companies often have higher P/E ratios on average than cyclical companies because investors are more confident in their future earnings. We compare two growth trends in Figure 7-4.

With cyclical companies you have to be careful not to start your forecast at a peak or trough period because you will get either biased-downward or -upward forecasts. Instead it is important to forecast cyclical companies throughout several business cycles with several peaks and troughs. Often the forecast for cyclical firms will cover 10 to 15 years of historical data, while the forecast for consistently growing firms might be based on five years of data.

The Income Statement Method

A more process-oriented method of forecasting earnings per share is to start with a sales forecast and create a standardized set of financial statements based on historical relationships. The sales forecast must be accurate if the earnings estimates are to have any significance. This method can be involved and provides a student with a very integrated understanding of the relationships that go into the creation of earnings.

Several important factors are included in this method of forecasting. The analyst is forced to examine profitability and the resultant fluctuations in profit mar-

FIGURE 7–4 Trendlines for Cyclical and Consistent Growth Companies

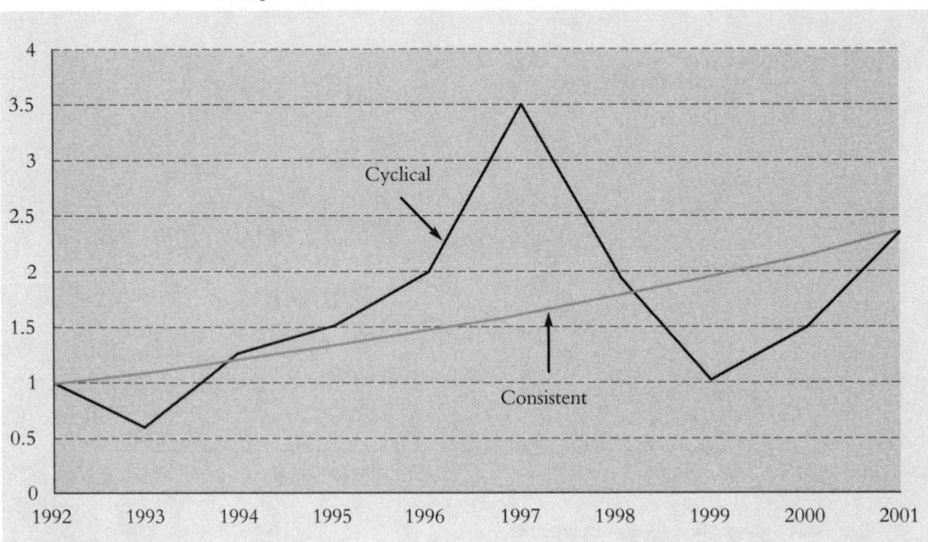

gins before and after taxes. The impact of short-term interest expense and any new bond financing can be factored into the analysis as well as any increase in shares of common stock from new equity financing.

Some analysts use an abbreviated method of forecasting earnings per share. They use a sales forecast combined with after-tax profit margins. For example, let us assume the Hutchins Corporation has a sales and profit margin history as set forth in Table 7-7. The sales have been growing at a 10 percent growth rate, so the forecast is a simple extrapolation. However, the profit margin has fluctuated between 6.7 and 9.1 percent, with 8.2 percent being the average. Common stock outstanding has also grown by an average of 1.4 million shares per year. Given the cyclical nature of the profit margin, 8.2 percent was used for 2002, which is expected to be an average year. Nine percent was used for 2003, a year expected to be economically more robust for the firm. Multiplying the profit margin times the estimated sales produced an estimate of earnings that was divided by the number of shares outstanding to find the earnings per share. Once the EPS is found, it still must be plugged into an earnings valuation model to determine an appropriate value.

GROWTH STOCKS AND GROWTH COMPANIES

In assessing the worth of an investment, stockholders, analysts, and investors often make reference to such terms as growth stock and growth companies. As part of the process of improving your overall valuation skills, you should have some familiarity with these terms.

TABLE 7–7 Abbreviated Income Statement Method—Hutchins Corporation

Year	Sales ($000s)	×	After-Tax Profit Margin	=	Earnings ($000s)	–	Shares (000s)	=	Earnings per Share
1996	$1,250,000		7.9%		$ 98,750		30,000		$3.29
1997	1,375,000		9.1		125,125		31,500		3.97
1998	1,512,500		8.5		128,562		33,200		3.87
1999	1,663,750		6.7		111,471		35,000		3.18
2000	1,830,125		8.3		151,900		35,200		4.31
2001	2,013,137		8.5		171,117		37,000		4.62
2002e	2,214,452		8.2		181,585		38,400		4.73
2003e	2,435,896		9.0		219,230		39,800		5.50

e = Estimated.

A growth stock may be defined as the common stock of a company generally growing faster than the economy or market norm. These companies are usually predictable in their earnings growth. Many of the more popular growth stocks, such as Disney, Coca-Cola, and McDonald's, are really in the middle-to-late stages of the expansion phase. They tend to be fully valued and recognized in the marketplace.

Growth companies, on the other hand, are those companies that exhibit rising returns on assets each year and sales that are growing at an increasing rate (growth phase of the life-cycle curve). Growth companies are found in stage 1 and 2 of the life-cycle curve discussed in Chapter 6. Growth companies may not be as well-known or recognized as growth stocks. Companies that may be considered to be growth companies might be in such industries as computer networking, cable television, cellular telephones, biotechnology, medical electronics, and so on. These companies are growing very rapidly, and extrapolations of growth trends can be very dangerous if you guess incorrectly. Growth companies have many things in common. Usually, they have developed a proprietary product that is patented and protected from competition like the original Xerox process. This market protection allows a high rate of return and generates cash for new-product development.

There are also other indicators of growth potential. Companies should have sales growth greater than the economy by a reasonable margin. Increasing sales should be translated into similar earnings growth, which means consistently stable and high profit margins. Additionally, the earnings growth should show up in earnings per share growth (no dilution of earnings through unproductive stock offers). The firm should have a low labor cost as a percentage of total cost since wages are prone to be inflexible on the downside but difficult to control on the upside.

The biggest error made in searching for growth-oriented companies is that the price may already be too high. By the time you identify the company, so has everyone else, and the price is probably inflated. If the company has one quarter where earnings do not keep up with expectations, the stock price could tumble. The trick is to find growth companies before they are generally recognized in the market, and this requires taking more risk in small companies trading over-the-counter.

ASSETS AS A SOURCE OF STOCK VALUE

Until now, our emphasis has been primarily on earnings and dividends as the source of value. However, in certain industries, asset values may have considerable importance. These assets may take many forms—cash and marketable securities, buildings, land, timber, old movies, oil, and other natural resources. At times, any one of these assets may dominate a firm's value. Furthermore, companies with heavy cash positions are attractive merger and acquisition candidates because of the possibility that a firm with highly liquid assets could be taken over and its own cash used to pay back debt incurred in the takeover.

In the last two decades, natural resources also had an important influence on value. Let's briefly examine this topic.

Natural Resources

Natural resources such as timber, copper, gold, and oil often give a company value even if the assets are not producing an income stream. This is because of the present value of the future income stream that is expected as these resources are used up. Companies such as International Paper, Weyerhaeuser, and other forest product companies have timberlands with market values far in excess of their book values and, in some cases, in excess of their common stock prices.

Oil companies with large supplies of oil in the ground may have to wait 20 years before some of it is pumped, but there may be substantial value there. In the case of natural gas pipeline companies, increasing reserves have changed the way these companies are viewed by the market. They were previously considered similar to utilities because of their natural gas transmission system, but now they are also being valued based on their hidden assets (energy reserves). The term hidden assets refers to assets that are not readily apparent to investors in a traditional sense but that add substantial value to the firm.

Investors should not overlook hidden assets because of naive extrapolation of past data or failure to understand an industry or company. Furthermore, assets do not always show up on the books of a company. They may be fully depreciated, like the movies *Sound of Music, 101 Dalmatians,* or *Star Wars,* but still have substantial value in the television or VCR/DVD market.

Internet Resources

Website Address	Comments
my.yahoo.com	Provides portfolio and stock tracking and screening
cbs.marketwatch.com	Provides stock information, screening, and evaluation
www.quicken.com	Provides stock screening and analysis; has intrinsic value calculator
www.valuepro.net	Has free intrinsic value calculator—other services fee based
www.morningstar.com	Provides stock screening and detailed evaluation with Quick Quotes
www.fool.com	Contains stock evaluation and information from Motley Fool
www.wjs.com	Provides company information along with news
www.finportfolio.com	Has portfolio tracker
moneycentral.msn.com	Has portfolio tracker, company information, investment information
www.valuengine.com	Provides stock analyses and forecasts, mainly fee based
www.411stocks.com	Provides information on stocks and portfolio tracking
www.bestsignals.com	Provides stock research; has interactive research tools
www.pcquote.com	Provides stock quotes, portfolio tracking, and news
www.validea.com	Provides fee-based valuation of stocks
www.stockworm.com	Provides stock analysis and screening

Chapter 8

Financial Statement Analysis

Financial statements present a numerical picture of a company's financial and operating health. Since each company is different, an analyst needs to examine the financial statements for industry characteristics as well as for differences in accounting methods. The major financial statements are the balance sheet, the income statement, and the statement of cash flows. A very helpful long-term financial overview also is provided by a 5- or 10-year summary statement found in the corporate annual report. One must further remember that the footnotes to these statements are an integral part of the statements and provide a wealth of in-depth explanatory information. More depth can often be found in additional reports such as the 10-K filed with the Securities and Exchange Commission and obtainable on request (free) from most companies or the SEC's Edgar website.

Fundamental analysis depends on variables internal to the company, and the corporate financial statements are one way of measuring fundamental value and risk. Financial statement analysis should be combined with economic and industry analysis before a final judgment is made to purchase or sell a specific security. Chapter 7 presented methods of valuation that used forecasts of dividends and earnings per share. Earnings per share combined with an estimated price-earnings ratio was also used to get a future price. Careful study of financial statements provides the analyst with much of the necessary information to forecast earnings and dividends, to judge the quality of earnings, and to determine financial and operating risk.

THE MAJOR FINANCIAL STATEMENTS

In the first part of this chapter, we examine the three basic types of financial statements—the income statement, the balance sheet, and the statement of cash flows—with particular attention paid to the interrelationships among these three measurement devices. In the rest of the chapter, ratio analysis is presented in detail, and deficiencies of financial statements are discussed along with the role of the security analyst in interpreting financial statements.

Income Statement

The income statement is the major device for measuring the profitability of a firm over a period of time. An example of the income statement is presented in Table 8–1 for the Coca-Cola Company. Note that the income statement is for a defined period, whether it be one month, three months, or a year. The statement is presented in a stair-step fashion so that we may examine the profit or loss after each type of expense item is deducted.

TABLE 8–1 Coca-Cola Income Statement

THE COCA-COLA COMPANY AND SUBSIDIARIES
Consolidated Statements of Income
for the Years Ended December 31, 1998, 1999, 2000
(Dollars in Millions Except Per Share Data, Ratios, and Growth Rates)

	Year Ended December 31		
	2000	1999	1998
Net Operating Revenues	**$20,458**	$19,805	$18,813
Cost of goods sold	**6,204**	6,009	5,562
Gross Profit	**14,254**	13,796	13,251
Selling, administrative and general expenses	**9,120**	9,001	8,211
Other operating charges	**1,443**	813	73
Operating Income	**3,691**	3,982	4,967
Interest income	**345**	260	219
Interest expense	**447**	337	277
Equity income (loss)	**(289)**	(184)	32
Other income-net	**99**	98	230
Gains on issuances of stock by equity investees	**—**	—	27
Income Before Income Taxes	**3,399**	3,819	5,198
Income taxes	**1,222**	1,388	1,665
Net Income	**$ 2,177**	$ 2,431	$ 3,533
Basic Net Income per Share	**$ .88**	$ .98	$ 1.43
Diluted Net Income per Share	**$ .88**	$ .98	$ 1.42
Average Shares Outstanding	**2,477**	2,469	2,467
Dilutive effect of stock options	**10**	18	29
Average Shares Outstanding Assuming Dilution	**2,487**	2,487	2,496

Source: *Coca-Cola Annual Report 2000.*

For 2000, the Coca-Cola Company had net operating revenues (sales) of approximately $20.5 billion. After subtracting the cost of goods sold, and selling, administrative, and general expenses, the firm's operating income was about $3.7 billion. Because of a high level of cash, cash equivalents, and marketable securities during 2000, Coca-Cola had interest income that was 77.2 percent of its interest expense. This is an uncommonly high ratio of interest income to interest expense, but this pattern occurred in all three years shown in the consolidated income statements. An analyst might conclude that Coca-Cola has a policy of keeping a high level of cash as a current asset. Coca-Cola also had losses of $289 million from equity interests in other publicly held companies. These companies are mostly Coca-Cola bottlers located around the world.

Altogether, Coca-Cola reported income from before income taxes of $3.4 billion, down from $5.2 billion in 1998. After paying taxes of $1.2 billion, net income available to common stockholders was approximately $2.2 billion. Coca-Cola's net income declined in 1999 and 2000.

We can see from an examination of diluted net income per share that Coca-Cola suffered a steady decline from $1.42 in 1998, to $0.98 in 1999, and $0.88 in 2000. In previous years 1994–97, Coca-Cola had been repurchasing shares of common stock, which helped increase earnings per share. In this three-year period however, the number of shares of common stock outstanding has stayed relatively the same. An analyst forecasting earnings per share would be interested in knowing if a share repurchase program will be implemented again.

Are these good income figures or bad? As we shall see later, the analyst's interpretation of the numbers will depend on historical figures, on industry data, and on the relationship of income to balance sheet items such as assets and net worth.

Balance Sheet

The balance sheet indicates what the firm owns and how these assets are financed in the form of liabilities or ownership interest. While the income statement purports to show the profitability of the firm, the balance sheet delineates the firm's holdings and obligations. Together, these statements are intended to answer two questions: How much did the firm make or lose, and what is a measure of its worth? A balance sheet for the Coca-Cola Company is presented in Table 8–2.

Note that the balance sheet is given at one point in time, in this case December 31, 2000. It does not represent the result of transactions for a specific month, quarter, or year but rather is a cumulative chronicle of all transactions that have affected the corporation since its inception. This is in contrast to the income statement, which measures results only over a short, quantifiable period. Generally, balance sheet items are stated on an original cost basis rather than at market value.

The Coca-Cola Company was chosen for analysis because of its international scope and its well-known soft drinks such as Coca-Cola, Sprite, and Diet Coke. Its food division's major product is Minute Maid orange juice.

Coca-Cola invests in many of its bottling companies and has either a noncontrolling ownership interest or a controlling ownership interest. For example Coca-

Cola owns an interest in Coca-Cola Amatil Limited, Coca-Cola HBC S.A., Coca-Cola West Japan Company Ltd., and many other bottlers. These ownership interests show up on the balance sheet under Investments and Other Assets.

TABLE 8–2 Coca-Cola Balance Sheet

THE COCA-COLA COMPANY AND SUBSIDIARIES
Consolidated Balance Sheets
for the Years Ended December 31, 1999 and 2000
(Dollars in Millions Except Per Share Data)

	Year Ended December 31	
	2000	1999
Assets		
Current		
Cash and cash equivalents	$ 1,819	$ 1,611
Marketable securities	73	201
	1,892	1,812
Trade accounts receivable, less allowances of $62 in 2000 and $26 in 1999	1,757	1,798
Inventories	1,066	1,076
Prepaid expenses and other assets	1,905	1,794
Total Current Assets	6,620	6,480
Investments and Other Assets		
Equity method investments		
Coca-Cola Enterprises Inc.	707	728
Coca-Cola Amatil Limited	617	1,133
Coca-Cola HBC S.A.	758	788
Other, principally bottling companies	3,164	3,793
Cost method investments, principally bottling companies	519	350
Marketable securities and other assets	2,364	2,124
	8,129	8,916
Property, Plant, and Equipment		
Land	225	215
Buildings and improvements	1,642	1,528
Machinery and equipment	4,547	4,527
Containers	200	201
	6,614	6,471
Less allowances for depreciation	2,446	2,204
	4,168	4,267
Goodwill and Other Intangible Assets	1,917	1,960
Total Assets	$20,834	$21,623

Statement of Cash Flows

The third required financial statement, along with the balance sheet and income statement, is the statement of cash flows. Referred to as *Statement of Financial Accounting Standards (SFAS) No. 95,* it replaced the old statement of changes in financial position (and the sources and uses of funds statement).

The purpose of the statement of cash flows is to emphasize the critical nature of cash flow to the operations of the firm. Cash flow generally represents cash or cash-equivalent items that can easily be converted into cash within 90 days (such as a money market fund).

The income statement and balance sheet are normally based on the accrual method of accounting, in which revenues and expenses are recognized as they

TABLE 8–2 Coca-Cola Balance Sheet *(concluded)*

	Year Ended December 31	
	2000	**1999**
Liabilities and Shareowners' Equity		
Current		
Accounts payable and accrued expenses	**$ 3,905**	$ 3,714
Loans and notes payable	**4,795**	5,112
Current maturities of long-term debt	**21**	261
Accrued income taxes	**600**	769
Total Current Liabilities	**9,321**	9,856
Long-Term Debt	**835**	854
Other Liabilities	**1,004**	902
Deferred Income Taxes	**358**	498
Total Liabilities	**11,518**	12,110
Shareowners' Equity		
Common stock, $.25 par value		
Authorized: 5,600,000,000 shares		
Issued: 3,481,882,834 shares in 2000; 3,466,371,904 shares in 1999	**870**	867
Capital surplus	**3,196**	2,584
Reinvested earnings	**21,265**	20,773
Accumulated other comprehensive income and unearned compensation on restricted stock	**(2,722)**	(1,551)
	22,609	22,673
Less treasury stock, at cost (997,121,427 shares in 2000; 994,796,786 shares in 1999)	**13,293**	13,160
Total Equity	**9,316**	9,513
Total Liabilities and Equity	**$20,834**	$21,623

Source: *Coca-Cola Annual Report 2000.*

occur, rather than when cash actually changes hands. For example, a $100,000 credit sale may be made in December 2001 and shown as revenue for that year—despite the fact the cash payment would not be received until March 2002. When the actual payment is finally received under accrual accounting, no revenue is recognized (it has already been accounted for previously). The primary advantage of accrual accounting is that it allows us to match revenues and expenses in the period in which they occur to appropriately measure profit; but a disadvantage is that adequate attention is not directed to the actual cash flow position of the firm.

One can think of situations in which a firm made a $1 million profit on a transaction but will not receive the actual cash payment for two years. Or perhaps the $1 million profit is in cash, but the firm increased its asset purchases by $3 million (a new building). If you merely read the income statement, you might assume the firm is in a strong $1 million cash position; but if you go beyond the income statement to cash flow considerations, you would observe the firm is $2 million short of funds for the period.

As a last example, a firm might show a $100,000 loss on the income statement; but if it had a depreciation expense write-off of $150,000, the firm would actually have $50,000 in cash. Since depreciation is a noncash deduction, the $150,000 deduction in the income statement for depreciation can be added back to net income to determine cash flow.

The statement of cash flows addresses these issues by translating income statement and balance sheet data into cash flow information. A corporation that has $1 million in accrual-based accounting profits can determine whether it can actually afford to pay a cash dividend to stockholders, buy new equipment, or undertake new projects.

The three primary sections of the statement of cash flows are:

1. Cash flows from operating activities.
2. Cash flows from investing activities.
3. Cash flows from financing activities.

After each of these sections is completed, the results are added to compute the net increase or decrease in cash flow for the corporation. An example of this process is shown in Figure 8-1. This statement informs us about how the cash was created (operations, investing, financing), where it was spent, and the net increase or decrease of cash for the entire year.

Let's look at Coca-Cola's statement of cash flows in Table 8-3. Cash provided from operating activities (top one-third of the statement) was approximately $3.5 billion in 2000. The major items were net income, depreciation and amortization, and other operating charges. Second, investing activities used approximately $1.165 billion of cash.

In 2000, financing activities used $2.072 billion of cash. Coca-Cola issued new debt to raise $3.671 billion but then paid off $4.256 billion of debt, sold new common stock for $331 million (mostly for corporate stock options), retired common stock valued at $133 million, and paid dividends of $1.685 billion. Because Coca-Cola is an international company, they also include the effects of changing

FIGURE 8–1 Illustration of Concepts behind Statement of Cash Flows

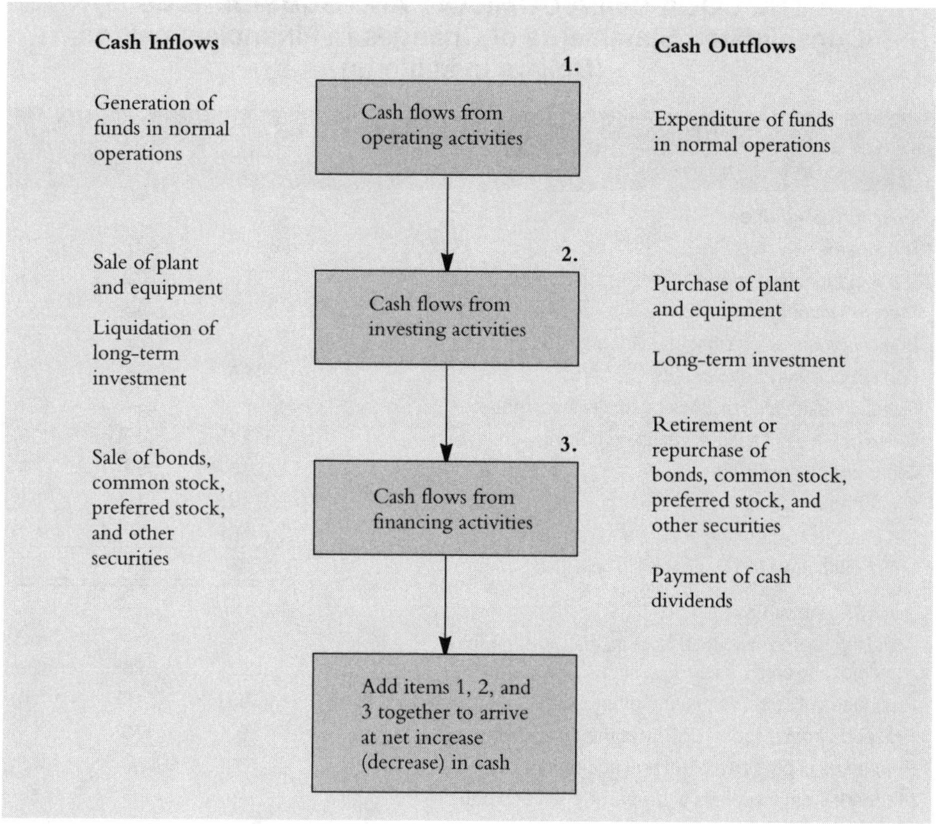

exchange rates on their worldwide cash positions. In 2000, foreign currency exchange rates reduced their cash flow by $140 million.

An analysis of this statement can pinpoint strengths or weaknesses in a company's cash flow. We can see that for 1998 and 1999, Coca-Cola had decreases in cash flow (third line from the bottom). These decreases were relatively modest and were more than covered by its positive performance in 2000. If we add cash flow from operating, investing, and financing activities we arrive at the following figures in millions of dollars for 2000:

Net cash provided by operating activities	$3,585*
Net cash provided by (used in) investing activities	(1,165)
Net cash used in financing activities	(2,072)
Increase in cash before exchange rate adjustment	$ 348

*In millions of dollars.

TABLE 8–3 Coca-Cola Statement of Cash Flows

THE COCA-COLA COMPANY AND SUBSIDIARIES
Consolidated Statements of Changes in Financial Position
(Dollars in Millions)

	Year Ended December 31		
	2000	**1999**	**1998**
Operating Activities			
Net income	**$2,177**	$2,431	$3,533
Depreciation and amortization	**773**	792	645
Deferred income taxes	**3**	97	(38)
Equity income or loss, net of dividends	**380**	292	31
Foreign currency adjustments	**196**	(41)	21
Gains on issuances of stock by equity investees	**—**	—	(27)
Gains on sales of assets, including bottling interests	**(127)**	(49)	(306)
Other operating charges	**916**	799	73
Other items	**119**	119	51
Net change in operating assets and liabilities	**(852)**	(557)	(550)
Net cash provided by operating activities	**3,585**	3,883	3,433
Investing Activities			
Acquisitions and investments, principally trademarks and bottling companies	**(397)**	(1,876)	(1,428)
Purchases of investments and other assets	**(508)**	(518)	(610)
Proceeds from disposals of investments and other assets	**290**	176	1,036
Purchases of property, plant and equipment	**(733)**	(1,069)	(863)
Proceeds from disposals of property, plant and equipment	**45**	45	54
Other investing activities	**138**	(179)	(350)
Net cash used in investing activities	**(1,165)**	(3,421)	(2,161)
Financing Activities			
Issuances of debt	**3,671**	3,411	1,818
Payments of debt	**(4,256)**	(2,455)	(410)
Issuances of stock	**331**	168	302
Purchases of stock for treasury	**(133)**	(15)	(1,563)
Dividends	**(1,685)**	(1,580)	(1,480)
Net cash used in financing activities	**(2,072)**	(471)	(1,333)
Effect of Exchange Rate Changes on Cash and Cash Equivalents	**(140)**	(28)	(28)
Cash and Cash Equivalents			
Net increase (decrease) during the year	**208**	(37)	(89)
Balance at beginning of year	**1,611**	1,648	1,737
Balance at end of year	**$1,819**	$1,611	$1,648

Source: *Coca-Cola Annual Report 2000.*

From this $348 million figure, we subtract $140 million to indicate the effect of exchange rate changes on cash and cash equivalents. This leaves Coca-Cola with a net increase in cash and cash equivalents of $208 million in 2000, as shown on the third line from the bottom of Table 8-3. This figure can be added to the $1.611 billion balance at the beginning of the year (2000) to arrive at a balance at the end of the year of $1.819 billion. This number is also the same as the cash balance shown on the first line of the balance sheet for 2000 as previously presented in Table 8-2.

Many companies are not as fortunate as Coca-Cola in generating cash. For example, a number of hard-pressed firms in the energy industry in the 1980s and early 1990s had insufficient earnings to pay dividends or to maintain or expand long-term asset commitments. In such cases, short-term borrowing is required to meet long-term needs. This can lead to a reduction of short-term working capital and a dangerous operating position.

In the booming 1996–99 period, some firms built up large cash positions and repurchased shares with excess cash rather than increasing their dividends. This may be partially motivated by the higher tax rate on dividends than capital gains.

KEY FINANCIAL RATIOS FOR THE SECURITY ANALYST

We just summarized the three major financial statements that will be the basis of your analysis in this section emphasizing financial ratios. Ratio analysis brings together balance sheet and income statement data to permit a better understanding of the firm's past and current health, which will aid you in forecasting the future outlook.

Ratio Analysis

Ratios are used in much of our daily life. We buy cars based on miles per gallon, we evaluate baseball players by their earned run averages and batting averages and basketball players by field goal and foul shooting percentages, and so on. These are all ratios constructed to judge comparative performance. Financial ratios serve a similar purpose, but you must know what is being measured to construct a ratio and to understand the significance of the resultant number.

Financial ratios are used to weigh and evaluate the operating performance and capital structure of the firm. While an absolute value such as earnings of $50,000 or accounts receivable of $100,000 may appear satisfactory, its acceptability can be measured only in relation to other values.

For example, are earnings of $50,000 actually good? If a company earned $50,000 on $500,000 of sales (10 percent profit-margin ratio), that might be quite satisfactory, whereas earnings of $50,000 on $5 million could be disappointing (a meager 1 percent return). After we have computed the appropriate ratio, we must compare our firm's results to the achievement of similar firms in the industry as well as to our own firm's past performance. Even then, this "number-crunching" process is not always adequate because we are forced to supplement our financial findings with an evaluation of company management, physical facilities, and numerous other factors.

Ratio analysis will not uncover "gold mines" for the analyst. It is more like a physical exam at the doctor's office. You hope you are all right, but if not, you may be content to know what is wrong and what to do about it. Just as with medical illness where some diseases are easier to cure than others, the same is true of financial illness. The analyst is the doctor. He or she determines the illness and keeps track of management to see if they can administer the cure. Sometimes ailing companies can be very good values. Penn-Central went into bankruptcy, and its common stock could have been purchased at $2 per share for several years. In the 1990s, Penn-Central traded in the $17 to $27 range after a three-for-two stock split in 1982 and a two-for-one stock split in 1988. Chrysler (now DaimlerChrysler) and Lockheed (now Lockheed Martin) were both on the brink of bankruptcy in the 1970s until the government made guaranteed loans available. Both Chrysler and Lockheed could have been bought at less than $3 per share. After recovering and generating higher stock prices, they both split their common stock. These were all sick companies that returned to health, and any investor willing to take such great risk would have been well rewarded.

Bankruptcy Studies

In a sense, ratio analysis protects an investor from picking continual losers more than it guarantees picking winners. Several studies have used ratios as predictors of financial failure. The most notable studies are by William Beaver and Edward Altman. Beaver found that ratios of failing firms signal failure as much as five years ahead of bankruptcy, and as bankruptcy approaches, the ratios deteriorate more rapidly, with the greatest deterioration in the last year. The Beaver studies also found (a) "Investors recognize and adjust to the new solvency positions of failing firms," and (b) "The price changes of the common stocks act as if investors rely upon ratios as a basis for their assessments, and impound the ratio information in the market prices."[1]

The first Altman research study indicated that five ratios combined were 95 percent accurate in predicting failure one year ahead of bankruptcy and were 72 percent accurate two years ahead of failure, with the average lead time for the ratio signal being 20 months.[2] Altman developed a Z score that was an index developed through multiple discriminate analysis that could predict failure. Altman modified and improved his model's accuracy even further by increasing the number of ratios to seven.[3] This service is currently sold to institutional investors by Zeta Services Inc. The Z (zeta) score relies on the following variables:

---

1. William H. Beaver, "Market Prices, Financial Ratios, and the Prediction of Failure," *Journal of Accounting Research*, Autumn 1968, p. 192.
2. Edward I. Altman, "Financial Ratios, Discriminant Analysis, and the Prediction of Corporate Bankruptcy," *Journal of Finance*, September 1968, pp. 589–609.
3. Edward I. Altman, *Corporate Financial Distress* (New York: John Wiley & Sons, 1983).

1. Retained earnings/total assets (cumulative profitability).
2. Standard deviation of operating income/total assets (measure of earnings stability during the last 10 years).
3. Earnings before interest and taxes/total assets (productivity of operating assets).
4. Earnings before interest and taxes/interest (leverage ratio, interest coverage).
5. Current assets/current liabilities (liquidity ratio).
6. Market value of common stock/book value of equity (a leverage ratio).
7. Total assets (proxy for size of the firm).

The greater the firm's bankruptcy potential, the lower its Z score. The ratios are not equally significant, but together they separate the companies into a correct bankruptcy group and nonbankruptcy group a high percentage of the time. Retained earnings/total assets has the heaviest weight in the analysis, and leverage is also very important. In the next section, we present six classifications of ratios that are helpful to the analyst. Many more would be used, but these represent the most widely used measures.

Classification System

We divide 20 significant ratios into six primary groupings:

A. Profitability ratios:
- 1. Operating margin.
- 2. After-tax profit margin.
- 3. Return on assets.
- 4. Return on equity.

B. Asset-utilization ratios:
- 5. Receivables turnover.
- 6. Inventory turnover.
- 7. Fixed-asset turnover.
- 8. Total asset turnover.

C. Liquidity ratios:
- 9. Current ratio.
- 10. Quick ratio.
- 11. Net working capital to total assets.

D. Debt-utilization ratios:
- 12. Long-term debt to equity.
- 13. Total debt to total assets.
- 14. Times interest earned.
- 15. Fixed charge coverage.

E. Price ratios:
- 16. Price to earnings.
- 17. Price to book value.
- 18. Dividends to price (dividend yield).

F. Other ratios:
   19. Average tax rate.
   20. Dividend payout.

The users of financial statements will attach different degrees of importance to the six categories of ratios. To the potential investor, the critical consideration is profitability and debt utilization. For the banker or trade creditor, the emphasis shifts to the firm's current ability to meet debt obligations. The bondholder, in turn, may be primarily influenced by debt to total assets—while also eyeing the profitability of the firm in terms of its ability to cover interest payments in the short term and principal payments in the long term. Of course, the shrewd analyst looks at all the ratios, with different degrees of attention.

A. Profitability Ratios The profitability ratios allow the analyst to measure the ability of the firm to earn an adequate return on sales, total assets, and invested capital. The profit-margin ratios (1, 2) relate to income statement items, while the two return ratios (3, 4) relate the income statement (numerator) to the balance sheet (denominator). Many of the problems related to profitability can be explained, in whole or in part, by the firm's ability to effectively employ its resources. We shall apply these ratios to Coca-Cola's income statement and balance sheet for 2000, which were previously presented in Tables 8-1 and 8-2.

Profitability ratios (Coca-Cola, 2000—in millions):

1. Operating margin $= \dfrac{\text{Operating income}}{\text{Sales (revenue)}} = \dfrac{\$3{,}691}{\$20{,}458} = 18.04\%$

2. After-tax profit margin $= \dfrac{\text{Net income}}{\text{Sales}} = \dfrac{\$2{,}177}{\$20{,}458} = 10.64\%$

3. Return on assets

(a) $\dfrac{\text{Net income}}{\text{Total assets}} = \dfrac{\$2{,}177}{\$20{,}834} = 10.45\%$

(b) $\dfrac{\text{Net income}}{\text{Sales}} \times \dfrac{\text{Sales}}{\text{Total assets}} = 10.64\% \times .982 = 10.45\%$

4. Return on equity

(a) $\dfrac{\text{Net income}}{\text{Stockholders' equity}^4} = \dfrac{\$2{,}177}{\$9{,}316} = 23.37\%$

(b) $\dfrac{\text{Return on assets}}{(1 - \text{Debt/Assets})^5} = \dfrac{10.45\%}{1 - .5528} = 23.37\%$

4. A working definition of stockholders' equity is the preferred and common stock accounts plus retained earnings. Coca-Cola also has a few other adjustments. The total can be found on the second line from the bottom at the end of Table 8-2.

5. Debt/Assets = \$11,518/\$20,834 = .5528.

The profitability ratios indicate that Coca-Cola is quite profitable, but the analysis of its return on equity using 4(b) indicates that its high return on stockholders' equity is largely a result of heavy total debt to assets. The disparity between return on assets and return on equity is the result of financing 55.28 percent of assets with debt.

Du Pont Analysis Notice that the return on assets and return on equity have parts (a) and (b), or two ways to determine the ratio. The methods employed in (b), which arise from the Du Pont Company's financial system, help the analyst see the relationship between the income statement and the balance sheet. The return on assets is generated by multiplying the after-tax profit margin (income statement) by the asset-turnover ratio (combination income statement–balance sheet ratio).

The Du Pont Company was a forerunner in stressing that satisfactory return on assets may be achieved through high profit margins or rapid turnover of assets, or a combination of both. The Du Pont system causes the analyst to examine the sources of a company's profitability. Since the profit margin is an income statement ratio, a high profit margin indicates good cost control, whereas a high asset turnover ratio demonstrates efficient use of the assets on the balance sheet. Different industries have different operating and financial structures. For example, in the heavy capital goods industry (machinery and equipment), the emphasis is on a high profit margin with a low asset turnover, while in food processing, the profit margin is low, and the key to satisfactory returns on total assets is a rapid turnover of assets.

Du Pont analysis further stresses that the return on equity stems from the return on assets adjusted for the amount of financial leverage by using the total debt-to-asset ratio. About 55 percent of the Coca-Cola Company's assets are financed by debt, and the return on equity reflects a high level of debt financing because the return on equity of 23.37 percent is more than twice as large as return on assets of 10.45 percent. As a detective, the financial analyst can judge how much debt a company employs by comparing these two measures of return. Of course, you will want to check this clue with the debt-utilization ratios. The total relationship between return on assets and return on equity under the Du Pont system is depicted in Figure 8-2.

In computing return on assets and equity, the analyst must also be sensitive to the age of the assets. Plant and equipment purchased 15 years ago may be carried on the books far below its replacement value. A 20 percent return on assets that were purchased in the late 1980s may be inferior to a 15 percent return on newly purchased assets.

B. Asset-Utilization Ratios With asset-utilization ratios, we measure the speed at which the firm is turning over accounts receivable, inventory, and longer-term assets. In other words, asset-utilization ratios measure how many times per year a company sells its inventory or collects its accounts receivable. For long-term assets, the utilization ratio tells us how productive the fixed assets are in terms of sales generation.

FIGURE 8–2 Du Pont Analysis

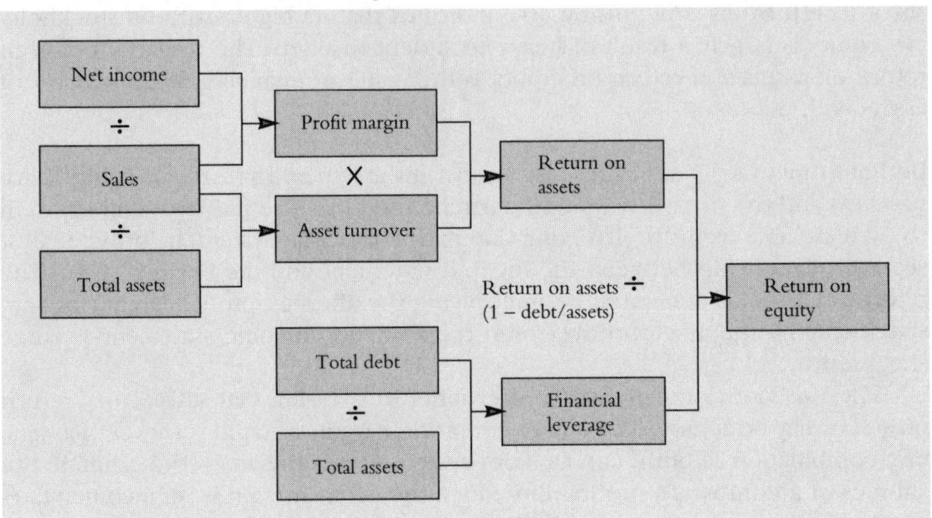

Asset-utilization ratios (Coca-Cola, 2000—in millions):

$$\textbf{5.}\ \text{Receivables turnover} = \frac{\text{Sales}}{\text{Receivables}} = \frac{\$20{,}458}{\$1{,}757} = 11.64\times$$

$$\textbf{6.}\ \text{Inventory turnover} = \frac{\text{Sales}}{\text{Inventory}} = \frac{\$20{,}458}{\$1{,}066} = 19.19\times$$

$$\textbf{7.}\ \text{Fixed-asset turnover} = \frac{\text{Sales}}{\text{Fixed assets}} = \frac{\$20{,}458}{\$6{,}614} = 3.09\times$$

$$\textbf{8.}\ \text{Total asset turnover} = \frac{\text{Sales}}{\text{Total assets}} = \frac{\$20{,}458}{\$20{,}834} = 0.982\times$$

The asset-utilization ratios relate the income statement (numerator) to the various assets on the balance sheet. Given that Coca-Cola's primary products are soft drinks and food, the receivables-turnover and inventory-turnover ratios reflect high turnover.

The receivables are collected almost once per month. Because the cost of Coca-Cola syrup sold to the bottlers has a small cost relative to the sales price, the inventory turnover is very high. It takes a little bit of syrup to make a lot of Coke. The fact that the company's consumable assets are nonperishable is also favorable. The large amount of cash and marketable securities as well as the investment in bottlers creates a very low total asset turnover.

C. Liquidity Ratios The primary emphasis of the liquidity ratios is a determination of the firm's ability to pay off short-term obligations as they come due.

These ratios can be related to receivables and inventory turnover in that a faster turnover creates a more rapid movement of cash through the company and improves liquidity. Again remember that each industry will be different. A jewelry store chain will have much different ratios from a grocery store chain.

Liquidity ratios (Coca-Cola, 2000—in millions):

9. Current ratio

$$\frac{\text{Current assets}}{\text{Current liabilities}} = \frac{\$6{,}620}{\$9{,}321} = 0.7102$$

10. Quick ratio

$$\frac{\text{Current assets} - \text{Inventory}}{\text{Current liabilities}} = \frac{\$6{,}620 - \$1{,}066}{\$9{,}321} = 0.596$$

11. Net working capital to total assets

$$\frac{\text{Current assets} - \text{Current liabilities}}{\text{Total assets}} = \frac{\$6{,}620 - \$9{,}321}{\$20{,}834} = -0.1296$$

The first two ratios (current and quick) indicate whether the firm can pay off its short-term debt in an emergency by liquidating its current assets. The quick ratio looks only at the most-liquid assets, which include cash, marketable securities, and receivables. Cash and securities are already liquid, but receivables usually will be turned into cash during the collection period. If there is concern about the firm's liquidity, the analyst will want to cross-check the liquidity ratios with receivable and inventory turnover to determine how fast the current assets are turned into cash during an ordinary cycle.

The last liquidity ratio is a measure of the percentage of current assets (after short-term debt has been paid) to total assets. This indicates the liquidity of the assets of the firm. The higher the ratio, the greater the short-term assets relative to fixed assets, and the safer a creditor is. Net working capital to total assets is negative but small for Coca-Cola. In some firms, this would indicate serious trouble, but for Coca-Cola it is probably not a problem. The total borrowing power of the firm remains strong, but this ratio, along with the low current ratio, indicates a high reliance on short-term borrowing, which could be a disadvantage to the firm if interest rates increase. The quick ratio probably indicates most correctly in Coca-Cola's case that liquidity is not a problem. Because the company holds more than $1.8 billion in cash and marketable securities, the quick ratio is adequate. Also consider that the firm generated net cash flow of $208 million in 2000. Remember, ratios are pieces of the puzzle, and you cannot tell by looking at one piece whether the firm is healthy.

D. Debt-Utilization Ratios The debt-utilization ratios provide an indication of the way the firm is financed between debt (lenders) and equity (owners) and therefore helps the analyst determine the amount of financial risk present in the firm. Too much debt cannot only impair liquidity with heavy interest payments but can also damage profitability and the health of the firm during an economic recession or industry slowdown.

Debt-utilization ratios (Coca-Cola, 2000—in millions):

$$\textbf{12. } \text{Long-term debt to equity} = \frac{\text{Long-term debt}}{\text{Stockholders' equity}} = \frac{\$835}{\$9{,}316} = 8.96\%$$

$$\textbf{13. } \text{Total debt to total assets} = \frac{\text{Total debt}}{\text{Total assets}} = \frac{\$11{,}518}{\$20{,}834} = 55.28\%$$

$$\textbf{14. } \text{Times interest earned} = \frac{\text{Income before interest and taxes}^{6}}{\text{Interest}} = \frac{\$3{,}691}{\$447} = 8.26\times$$

$$\textbf{15. } \text{Fixed-charge coverage} = \frac{\text{Income before fixed charges and taxes}^{7}}{\text{Fixed charges}^{8}} = \frac{\$3{,}691}{\$447} = 8.26\times$$

We have already discussed the impact of financial leverage on return on equity, and the first two ratios in this category indicate to the analyst how much financial leverage is being used by the firm. The more debt, the greater the interest payments and the more volatile the impact on the firm's earnings. Companies with stable sales and earnings such as utilities can afford to employ more debt than those in cyclical industries such as automobiles or airlines. Ratio 12, long-term debt to equity, provides information concerning the long-term capital structure of the firm. In the case of Coca-Cola, long-term liabilities represent only 8.96 percent of the stockholders' equity base provided by the owners of the firm. Ratio 13, total debt to total assets, looks at the total assets and the use of debt. Each firm must consider its optimum capital structure, and the analyst should be aware of industry fluctuations in assessing the firm's proper use of leverage. Coca-Cola seems safe, given that its business is not subject to large swings in sales.

The last two debt-utilization ratios indicate the firm's ability to meet its cash payments due on fixed obligations such as interest, leases, licensing fees, or sinking-fund charges. The higher these ratios, the more protected the creditor's position. Use of the fixed-charge coverage is more conservative than interest earned since it includes all fixed charges. Now that most leases are capitalized and show up on the balance sheet, it is easier to understand that lease payments are similar in importance to interest expense. Charges after taxes such as sinking-fund payments must be adjusted to before-tax income. For example, if a firm is in the 40 percent tax bracket and must make a $60,000 sinking-fund payment, the firm would have

---

6. Income before interest and taxes is the same as operating income as shown in Table 8–1.

7. Because there are no other fixed charges besides interest, the numerators are the same in Formulas 14 and 15.

8. The denominators are also the same in Formulas 14 and 15.

had to generate $100,000 in before-tax income to meet that obligation. The adjustment would be as follows:

$$\text{Before-tax income required} = \frac{\text{After-tax payment}}{1 - \text{Tax rate}}$$
$$= \frac{\$60{,}000}{1 - 0.40} = \$100{,}000$$

Coca Cola's fixed-charge coverage is the same as its interest-earned ratio because it has no fixed charges other than interest expense.

E. Price Ratios The price ratios relate the internal performance of the firm to the external judgment of the marketplace in terms of value. What is the firm's end result in market value? The price ratios indicate the expectations of the market relative to other companies. For example, a firm with a high price-to-earnings ratio has a higher market price relative to $1 of earnings than a company with a lower ratio.

Price ratios (Coca-Cola, 2000—in millions):

16. Price to earnings $= \dfrac{\text{Common stock price}}{\text{Earnings per share}} = \dfrac{\$60.94}{\$0.88} = 69.25\times$

17. Price to book value $= \dfrac{\text{Common stock price}}{\text{Book value per share}^{9}} = \dfrac{\$60.94}{\$3.75} = 16.25\times$

18. Dividends to price (Dividend yield) $= \dfrac{\text{Dividends per share}}{\text{Common stock price}} = \dfrac{\$0.68}{\$60.94} = 1.12\%$

Coca-Cola's price-earnings ratio indicates that the firm's stock price represents $69.25 for every $1 of earnings. This number can be compared with that of other companies in the soft-drink industry and/or related industries. As indicated in Chapter 7, the price-earnings ratio (or P/E ratio) is influenced by the earnings and the sales growth of the firm and also by the risk (or volatility in performance), the debt-equity structure of the firm, the dividend-payment policy, the quality of management, and a number of other factors. The P/E ratio indicates expectations about the future of a company. Firms that are expected to provide greater returns than those for the market in general, with equal or less risk, often have P/E ratios higher than the overall market P/E ratio. However, in Coca-Cola's case, EPS has declined faster than the price, inflating the P/E.

Expectations of returns and P/E ratios do change over time, as Table 8–4 illustrates. Price-earnings ratios for a selected list of U.S. firms in 1981, 1988, 1997, and 2001 show that during this 20-year period, price-earnings ratios generally rose between 1981 and 2001.

---

9. Book value per share $= \dfrac{\text{Stockholders' equity}}{\text{Number of shares}} = \dfrac{\$9{,}316}{\$2{,}487} = \$3.75$

The P/E ratios are more complicated than they may appear at first glance. The level of the market was higher in 2001, but not all companies exhibited higher P/E ratios. A high P/E ratio can result from many sets of assumptions. P/E ratios can be high because of high expected growth in earnings per share. For a company in a cyclical industry, the P/E ratio can be high because of low earnings, and a stock price that has not declined as rapidly as earnings. This is true of Texas Instruments in 2001.

The price-to-book-value ratio relates the market value of the company to the historical accounting value of the firm. In a company that has old assets, this ratio may be quite high, but in one with new, undepreciated fixed assets, the ratio might be lower. This information needs to be combined with a knowledge of the company's assets and of industry norms.

The dividend yield is part of the total return that an investor receives along with capital gains or losses. It is usually calculated by annualizing the current quarterly dividend since that is the cash value a current investor is likely to receive over the next year.

The price-to-earnings and price-to-book-value ratios are often used in computing stock values. The simple view of these ratios is that when they are relatively low compared with a market index or company history, the stock is a good buy. In the case of the dividend yield, the opposite is true. When dividend yields are relatively high compared with the company's historical data, the stock may be undervalued. Of course, the application of these simple models is much more complicated. The analyst has to determine if the company is performing the same as it was when the ratios were at what the analyst considers a normal level.

F. Other Ratios The other ratios presented in category F are to help the analyst spot special tax situations that affect the profitability of an industry or company

TABLE 8–4 Price-Earnings Ratios for Selected U.S. Corporations

		P/E Ratio[a]			
Corporation	Industry	12/31/81	10/24/88	8/13/97	8/10/01
Exxon	International oil	5	12	19	15
Bank America	Banking	7	9	17	14
Halliburton	Oil service	11	26	30	21
Winn-Dixie	Retail	8	15	21	71
IBM	Computers	9	14	20	22
McDonald's	Restaurant franchise	10	15	22	20
Texas Instruments	Semiconductors	15	13	cc[b]	45
S&P 500	Market index	8	13	21	25

[a]P/E ratio is calculated by taking the market price and dividing by the previous 12 months' earnings per share.

[b]cc indicates that the P/E ratio is 100 or more.

Source: Selected issues of *Barron's*.

and to determine what percentage of earnings are being paid to the stockholder and what is being reinvested for internal growth.

Other ratios (Coca-Cola, 2000—in millions):

$$\textbf{19.}\ \text{Average tax rate} = \frac{\text{Income tax}}{\text{Taxable income}} = \frac{\$1{,}222}{\$3{,}399} = 35.95\%$$

$$\textbf{20.}\ \text{Dividend payout} = \frac{\text{Dividends per share}}{\text{Earnings per share}} = \frac{\$0.68}{\$0.88} = 77.27\%$$

These other ratios are calculated to provide the analyst with information that may indicate unusual tax treatment or reinvestment policies. For example, the tax ratio for forest products companies will be low because of the special tax treatment given timber cuttings. A company's tax rate may also decline in a given year as a result of special tax credits. Thus, earnings per share may rise, but we need to know if it is from operations or favorable tax treatment. If it is from operations, we will be more sure of next year's forecast, but if it is from tax benefits, we cannot normally count on the benefits being continued into the future.

The dividend-payout ratio provides data concerning the firm's reinvestment strategies. It represents dividends per share divided by earnings per share. A high payout ratio tells the analyst that the stockholder is receiving a large part of the earnings and that the company is not retaining much income for investment in new plant and equipment. High payouts are usually found in industries that do not have great growth potential, while low payout ratios are associated with firms in growth industries. Coca-Cola's earnings per share have fallen from $1.42 in 1998 to $0.88 in 2000 and, accompanied by rising dividends, has created an unsustainable dividend payout, unless Coca-Cola can increase earnings per share.

USES OF RATIOS

The previous section presented 20 ratios that may be helpful to the analyst when evaluating a firm. How can we further use the data gathered to check the health of companies we are interested in analyzing?

One way is to compare the company with the industry. This is becoming more difficult as companies diversify into several industries. Twenty years ago, many firms competed in only one industry, and ratio comparisons were more reliable. Now companies have a wide range of products and markets.

In the early 1990s Coca-Cola was divided by soft drinks and food. Coca-Cola is now divided into operating segments by geographical areas to reflect the more local control of each region: North America, Africa and Middle East, Europe and Eurasia, Latin America, and Asia Pacific.

Companies in oligopolies such as the soft-drink industry are hard to evaluate on a ratio basis because one or two firms (Pepsi and Coke) dominate the industry, so industry ratios are not very helpful measures of performance. Nevertheless,

Table 8–5 looks at Coca-Cola compared with Pepsi, Cadbury Schweppes Plc., and the soft-drink industry. Sales for the industry total $75 billion and Coke and Pepsi have almost equal dollar sales and account for over 50 percent of the industry's total sales. One foreign company, Cadbury Schweppes from England, is a distant third with $6.8 billion in sales with brands such as Schweppes ginger ale, Dr. Pepper, Hawaiian Punch, and Snapple.

Coca-Cola used to dominate Pepsi in the ratio game, but Pepsi divested itself of its bottlers and restaurants. Pepsi does have a much larger presence in snack food with its Frito-Lay Division. Snack foods accounted for 63 percent of sales and 73 percent of operating profits in 2000.

Coke and Pepsi have comparable operating margins and after-tax margins, but Pepsi has a higher return on equity because of more debt in the capital structure. Dividend yields and the average tax rates for both Coke and Pepsi are also similar. The large discrepancy is between the P/E ratios and the much higher payout ratio for Coke. Both of these high ratios are caused by depressed earnings per share for Coca-Cola due to restructuring costs. A lower EPS caused both the P/E and the payout ratio to be extremely high. As management continues to raise the dividends, the message is clear: Management expects earnings to rebound.

Cadbury Schweppes, the smaller competitor, does manage to compare well on operating margin but falls short on the after-tax profit margin and return on equity. Its dividend yield is higher than both Coke and Pepsi, but it should be pointed out that British investors historically demand high dividend yields from their companies.

In general, after reviewing all the financial statements and ratios, Coca-Cola looks to be in good financial shape. Coca-Cola needs to use more long-term debt in its capital structure to replace short-term debt that has more volatile interest rates and therefore may carry more risk as a financing vehicle.

It is important to realize that Coca-Cola is an international company that may be affected by political and economic events abroad. Foreign revolts and a rising

TABLE 8–5 Selected Ratio Comparisons for the Coca-Cola Company, 2000

	Coca-Cola	Pepsi	Cadbury-Schweppes Plc.	Soft-Drink Industry
Sales	$20.5 billion	$20.4 billion	$6.8 billion	$75 billion
Operating margin	18.04%	21.20%	19.40%	21.00%
After-tax profit margin	10.64%	10.70%	8.30%	9.30%
Return on equity	23.37%	30.10%	11.20%	24.90%
Long-term debt to equity	8.96%	32.36%	11.34%	72.86%
Price-to-earnings ratio	69.25	27.4	21.7	33
Dividend yield	1.12%	1.30%	2.80%	1.20%
Average tax rate	35.95%	32.00%	34.70%	30.00%
Payout ratio	77.27%	36.00%	56.00%	41.00%

Source: Data from *Value Line Investment Survey,* May 11, 2001, and company annual reports.

dollar can hurt Coca-Cola's earnings. Unfortunately, its earnings during 1992, 1993, 1997, and 2000 suffered from a rising dollar. This made the translation of foreign profits less valuable in dollars and reduced Coca-Cola's earnings per share. Coca-Cola does partially hedge its currency risk in the international currency market by using derivatives such as currency options and financial futures. These hedging transactions have partially smoothed out Coca-Cola's EPS over time.

Figure 8-3 shows the breakdown of the company's worldwide revenues and profitability by region for the years 1998, 1999, and 2000. Using the 2000 data for comparisons, all North American products account for about 39 percent of net operating revenues, but they account for only 29 percent of operating income. We can see that Asia Pacific is second in revenues but third in operating income, while Europe and Eurasia is third in revenues but first in operating income. While we don't think of Coca-Cola as a cyclical company, their dependence on international markets for growth was short-circuited by the economic downturn in Asia. Americans may think of Coke as a low-cost alternative to water, but in developing coun-

FIGURE 8–3 Operating Revenues and Income by Operating Segment

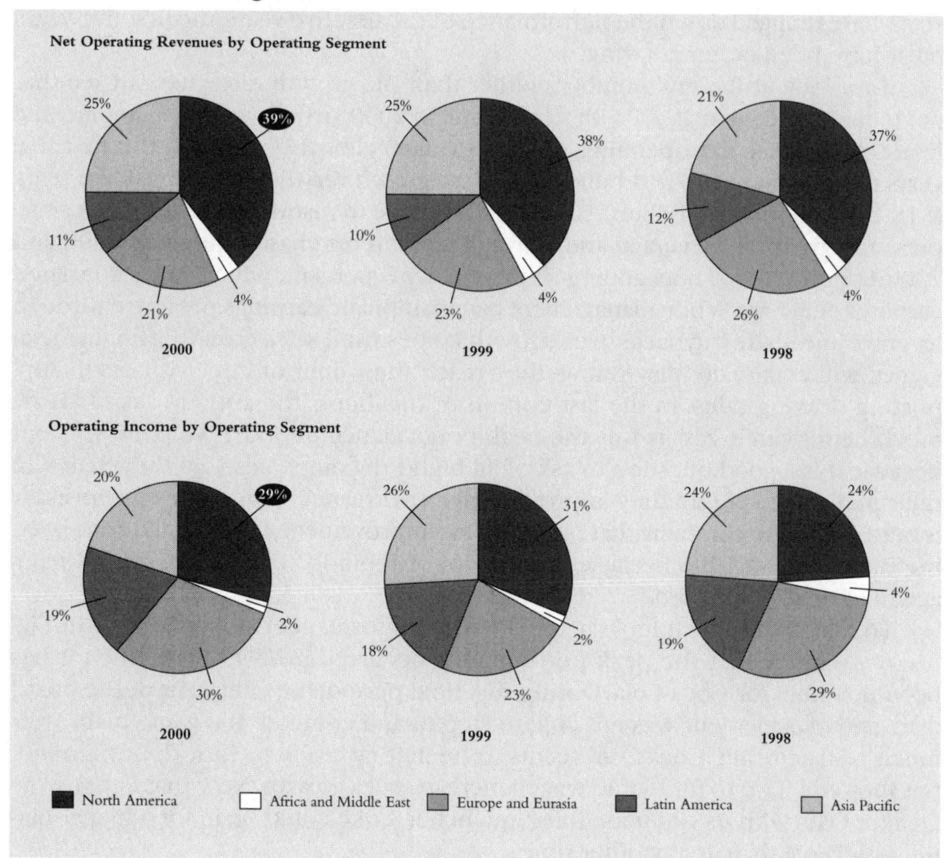

tries such as China, Thailand, and the Philippines, Coke is more of a luxury that can be postponed when economic times are difficult.

Coke's growth is occurring in the international markets, but it must be aware that competitors such as Pepsi, Cadbury Schweppes, Gatorade, and bottled water companies are entering their foreign markets and attempting to take away market share. The result could be continued pressure on Coke's profit margins, which would translate into slower earnings growth and a lower P/E ratio. Time will tell.

COMPARING LONG-TERM TRENDS

Over the course of the business cycle, sales and profitability may expand and contract, and ratio analysis for any one year may not present an accurate picture of the firm. Therefore, we look at trend analysis of performance over a number of years to examine long-term performance.

Table 8-6, presents the 10-year summary of selected financial data for Coca-Cola. We can see a big difference in performance between the first five years and the second five years. Looking under the two compound growth rates in the first two columns, we can see that the 10-year column is filled with positive numbers, while the 5-year column is filled with negative numbers. Given that the last five years have dragged down the performance of the first five years, the first five years must have been rather amazing.

If we look at the raw numbers rather than the growth rates, we can see that net income peaked in 1997, with net income in 2000 virtually equaling net income in 1993. Likewise net operating revenues (sales) almost doubled in the first five years ($10.2 billion to $18.1 billion) but have grown very little in the last five years ($18.7 billion to $20.5 billion). Coca-Cola was able to maintain growth in earnings per share by use of leverage and through share repurchases. Between 1990 and 2000 the number of outstanding shares fell by 8 percent, which in turn inflated earnings per share. While management can manipulate earnings per share through leverage and share buybacks, true growth comes from sales growth. The financial games will eventually play out as they reach their limit of effectiveness in supporting slowing sales. In the last edition of this book, the authors asked, "How much better can it get? Is this the peak performance period?" We point this out because it is a good question to ask of all high P/E companies. Can they maintain their performance? Can they improve their performance? Sometimes the investor is better with the company that has room for improvement. Pepsi would have been the better buy in 1996 because it had a lot of room for improvement, and management finally delivered.

To take a graphical look at the 10-year performance, look at trends in Figure 8-4. Notice that the peak performance occurred in 1997; since then it has been downhill for Coca-Cola. During this time period, the chairman of the board died, and management was not able to step in and continue the game plan. After much restructuring, Coca-Cola seems to be getting ready to turn things around, but they will have to find some way to increase sales growth. Now that Pepsi owns Quaker Oats with its Gatorade thirst quencher, Coke could be in for a bigger battle with Pepsi than at any other time.

FIGURE 8–4 Selected Ratios from Coca-Cola

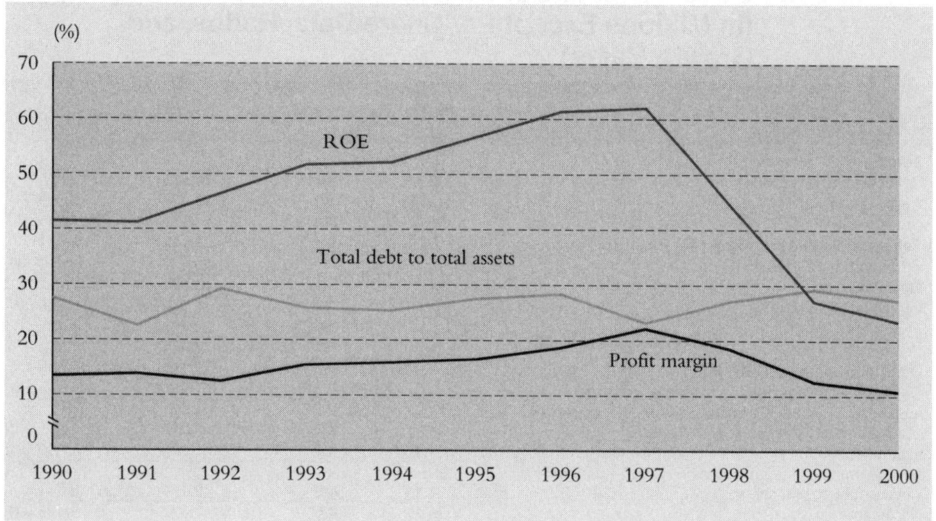

DEFICIENCIES OF FINANCIAL STATEMENTS

Several differences occur between companies and industries, and, at times, inflation has additionally clouded the clarity of accounting statements. Some of the more important difficulties occur in the area of inflation-adjusted accounting statements, inventory valuation, depreciation methods, pension fund liabilities, research and development, deferred taxes, and foreign exchange accounting. We do not have space to cover all of them, but we will touch on the most important ones.

Inflation Effects

While inflation has been extremely mild in the last decade, the student who is preparing for a long-term career in finance should be aware of its potential effects for the future.

Inflation causes phantom sources of profit that may mislead even the most alert analyst. Revenue is almost always stated in current dollars, whereas plant and equipment or inventory may have been purchased at lower price levels. Thus, profit may be more a function of increasing prices than of satisfactory performance.

Distortion of inflation also shows up on the balance sheet since most of the values on the balance sheet are stated on a historical or original-cost basis. This may be particularly troublesome in the case of plant and equipment and inventory, which may now be worth two or three times the original cost or—from a negative viewpoint—may require many times the original cost for replacement.

The accounting profession has been groping with this problem for decades, and the discussion becomes particularly intense each time inflation rears its ugly

TABLE 8–6 Selected Financial Data for the Coca-Cola Company (in Millions Except Per Share Data, Ratios, and Growth Rates)

	Compound Growth Rates		Year Ended December 31	
	5 Years	10 Years	2000	1999
Summary of Operations				
Net operating revenues	2.4%	7.1%	$ 20,458	$ 19,805
Cost of goods sold	(2.2)	4.0	6,204	6,009
Gross profit	5.0	8.9	14,254	13,796
Selling, administrative and general expenses	5.2	8.4	9,120	9,001
Other operating charges			1,443	813
Operating income	(1.7)	6.6	3,691	3,982
Interest income			345	260
Interest expense			447	337
Equity income (loss)			(289)	(184)
Other income (deductions)-net			99	98
Gains on issuances of stock by equity investees			—	—
Income from continuing operations before income taxes and changes in accounting principles	(4.7)	5.4	3,399	3,819
Income taxes	(1.9)	6.8	1,222	1,388
Income from continuing operations before changes in accounting principles	(6.1)	4.6	$ 2,177	$ 2,431
Net income	(6.1)	4.6	$ 2,177	$ 2,431
Preferred stock dividends			—	—
Net income available to common share-owners	(6.1)	4.8	$ 2,177	$ 2,431
Average common shares outstanding			2,477	2,469
Average common shares outstanding assuming dilution			2,487	2,487
Per Common Share Data				
Income from continuing operations before changes in accounting principles—basic	(5.7)	5.6	$ 0.88	$ 0.98
Income from continuing operations before changes in accounting principles—diluted	(5.5)	5.8	0.88	0.98
Basic net income	(5.7)	5.6	0.88	0.98
Diluted net income	(5.5)	5.8	0.88	0.98
Cash dividends	9.1	13.0	0.68	0.64
Market price on December 31	10.4	18.0	60.94	58.25
Total Market Value of Common Stock	10.2	17.2	$151,421	$143,969
Balance Sheet Data				
Cash, cash equivalents and current marketable securities			$ 1,892	$ 1,812
Property, plant and equipment-net			4,168	4,267
Depreciation			465	438
Capital expenditures			733	1,069
Total assets and liabilities			20,834	21,623
Long-term debt			835	854
Total debt			5,651	6,227
Share-owners' equity			9,316	9,513
Total capital			14,967	15,740
Other Key Financial Measures				
Total debt-to-total capital			37.8%	39.6.%
Net debt-to-net capital			29.4%	32.2%
Return on common equity			23.1%	27.1%
Return on capital			16.2%	18.2%
Dividend payout ratio			77.4%	65.0%
Free cash flow[f]			$ 2,806	$ 2,332
Economic profit			$ 861	$ 1,128

(continued)

[a]In 1998, we adopted SFAS No. 132, "Employers' Disclosures about Pensions and Other Postretirement Benefits."

[b]In 1994, we adopted SFAS No. 115, "Accounting for Certain Investments in Debt and Equity Securities."

[c]In 1993, we adopted SFAS No. 112, "Employers' Accounting for Postemployment Benefits."

TABLE 8–6 Selected Financial Data for the Coca-Cola Company *(concluded)*

1998[a]	1997[a]	1996[a]	1995[a]	1994[a,b]	1993[a,c]	1992[a,d,e]	1991[a,e]	1990[a,e]
$ 18,813	$ 18,868	$ 18,673	$18,127	$16,264	$14,030	$13,119	$11,599	$10,261
5,562	6,015	6,738	6,940	6,168	5,160	5,055	4,649	4,208
13,251	12,853	11,935	11,187	10,096	8,870	8,064	6,950	6,053
8,211	7,792	7,635	7,075	6,459	5,721	5,317	4,628	4,054
73	60	385	86	—	50	—	13	49
4,967	5,001	3,915	4,026	3,637	3,099	2,747	2,309	1,950
219	211	238	245	181	144	164	175	170
277	258	286	272	199	168	171	192	231
32	155	211	169	134	91	65	40	110
230	583	87	86	(25)	7	(59)	51	15
27	363	431	74	—	12	—	—	—
5,198	6,055	4,596	4,328	3,728	3,185	2,746	2,383	2,014
1,665	1,926	1,104	1,342	1,174	997	863	765	632
$ 3,533	$ 4,129	$ 3,492	$ 2,986	$ 2,554	$ 2,188	$ 1,883	$ 1,618	$ 1,382
$ 3,533	$ 4,129	$ 3,492	$ 2,986	$ 2,554	$ 2,176	$ 1,664	$ 1,618	$ 1,382
—	—	—	—	—	—	—	1	18
$ 3,533	$ 4,129	$ 3,492	$ 2,986	$ 2,554	$ 2,176	$ 1,664	$ 1,617	$ 1,364
2,467	2,477	2,494	2,525	2,580	2,603	2,634	2,666	2,674
2,496	2,515	2,523	2,549	2,599	2,626	2,668	2,695	2,706
$ 1.43	$ 1.67	$ 1.40	$ 1.18	$ .99	$ .84	$ .72	$ .61	$ .51
1.42	1.64	1.38	1.17	.98	.83	.71	.60	.50
1.43	1.67	1.40	1.18	.99	.84	.63	.61	.51
1.42	1.64	1.38	1.17	.98	.83	.62	.60	.50
.60	.56	.50	.44	.39	.34	.28	.24	.20
67.00	66.69	52.63	37.13	25.75	22.31	20.94	20.06	11.63
$165,190	$164,766	$130,575	$92,983	$65,711	$57,905	$54,728	$53,325	$31,073
$ 1,807	$ 1,843	$ 1,658	$ 1,315	$ 1,531	$ 1,078	$ 1,063	$ 1,117	$ 1,492
3,669	3,743	3,550	4,336	4,080	3,729	3,526	2,890	2,386
381	384	442	421	382	333	310	254	236
863	1,093	990	937	878	800	1,083	792	593
19,145	16,881	16,112	15,004	13,863	11,998	11,040	10,185	9,245
687	801	1,116	1,141	1,426	1,428	1,120	985	536
5,149	3,875	4,513	4,064	3,509	3,100	3,207	2,288	2,537
8,403	7,274	6,125	5,369	5,228	4,570	3,881	4,236	3,662
13,552	11,149	10,638	9,433	8,737	7,670	7,088	6,524	6,199
38.0%	34.8%	42.4%	43.1%	40.2%	40.4%	45.2%	35.1%	40.9%
28.1%	22.0%	31.6%	32.3%	25.5%	29.0%	33.1%	24.2%	24.6%
45.1%	61.6%	60.8%	56.4%	52.1%	51.8%	46.4%	41.3%	41.4%
30.2%	39.5%	36.8%	34.9%	32.8%	31.2%	29.4%	27.5%	26.8%
41.9%	33.6%	35.7%	37.2%	39.4%	40.6%	44.3%	39.5%	39.2%
$ 1,876	$ 2,951	$ 2,215	$ 2,460	$ 2,356	$ 1,857	$ 875	$ 881	$ 844
$ 2,480	$ 3,325	$ 2,718	$ 2,291	$ 1,896	$ 1,549	$ 1,300	$ 1,073	$ 920

[d]In 1992, we adopted SFAS No. 106, "Employers' Accounting for Postretirement Benefits Other Than Pensions."

[e]In 1992, we adopted SFAS No. 109, "Accounting for Income Taxes," by restating financial statements beginning in 1989.

[f]All years presented have been restated to exclude net cash flows related to acquisitions.

Source: *Coca-Cola Annual Report 2000.*

head. In October 1979, the Financial Accounting Standards Board (FASB) issued a ruling that required about 1,300 large companies to disclose inflation-adjusted accounting data in their annual reports. This information shows the effects of inflation on the financial statements of the firm. The ruling on inflation adjustment was extended for five more years in 1984 but was later made optional. As inflation temporarily slowed, many companies chose not to disclose inflation-adjusted statements in addition to the historical cost statements.

From a study of 10 chemical firms and 8 drug companies using current-cost (replacement-cost) data found in the financial 10-K statements these companies filed with the SEC, it was found that the changes shown in Table 8-7 occurred in their assets, income, and other selected ratios. The impact of these changes is important as an example of the changes that take place on ratio analysis during periods of high inflation.

The comparison of replacement-cost and historical-cost accounting methods in Table 8-7 shows that replacement cost increases assets but at the same time reduces income. This increase in assets lowers the debt-to-assets ratio since debt is a monetary asset that is not revalued because it is paid back in current dollars.

The decreased debt-to-assets ratio would indicate that the financial leverage of the firm decreased, but a look at the interest-coverage ratio tells a different story. Because the interest-coverage ratio measures the operating income available to cover interest expense, the declining income penalizes the ratio, and the firm shows a decreased ability to cover its interest cost.

As long as prices continue to rise in an inflationary environment, profits appear to feed on themselves. The main objection is that when prices do level off, management and unsuspecting stockholders have a rude awakening as expensive inventory is charged against softening retail prices. A 15 to 20 percent growth rate in earnings may be little more than an "inflationary illusion." Industries most sensitive to inflation-induced profits are those with cyclical products, such as lumber, copper, rubber, and food products, as well as those in which inventory is a signif-

TABLE 8–7 Comparison of Replacement-Cost Accounting to Historical-Cost Accounting

	10 Chemical Companies		8 Drug Companies	
	Replacement Cost	Historical Cost	Replacement Cost	Historical Cost
Increase in assets	28.4%	—	15.4%	—
Decrease in net income before taxes	(45.8)	—	(19.3)	—
Return on assets	2.8	6.2%	8.3	11.4%
Return on equity	4.9	13.5	12.8	19.6
Debt-to-assets ratio	34.3	43.8	30.3	35.2
Interest-coverage ratio (times interest earned)	7.1×	8.4×	15.4×	16.7×

Note: Replacement cost is but one form of current cost. Nevertheless, it is widely used as a measure of current cost.

Source: Jeff Garnett and Geoffrey A. Hirt, "Replacement Cost Data: A Study of the Chemical and Drug Industry for Years 1976 through 1978."

icant percentage of sales and profits. Reported profits for the lumber industry have been influenced as much as 50 percent by inventory pricing, and profits of a number of other industries have been influenced by 15 to 20 percent.

Inventory Valuation

The income statement can show considerable differences in earnings, depending on the method of inventory valuation. The two basic methods are FIFO (first-in, first-out) and LIFO (last-in, first-out). In an inflationary economy, a firm could be reporting increased profits even though no actual increase in physical output occurred. The example of the Rhoades Company will illustrate this point. We first observe its income statement for 2001 in Table 8-8. It sold 1,000 units for $20,000 and shows earnings after taxes of $4,200 and an operating margin and after-tax margin of 35 percent and 21 percent, respectively.

Assume that in 2002 the number of units sold remains constant at 1,000 units. However, inflation causes a 10 percent increase in price, from $20 to $22 per unit as shown in Table 8-9. Total sales will go up to $22,000, but with no actual increase in physical volume. Further assume the firm uses FIFO inventory pricing so that inventory first purchased will be written off against current sales. We will assume that 1,000 units of 2001 inventory at a cost of $10 per unit are written off against 2002 sales revenue. If Rhoades used LIFO inventory and if the cost of goods sold went up 10 percent also, to $11 per unit, income will be less than under FIFO. Table 8-9 shows the 2002 income statement of Rhoades under both inventory methods.

The table demonstrates the difference between FIFO and LIFO. Under FIFO, Rhoades Corporation shows higher profit margins and more income even though

TABLE 8–8 Rhoades Corporation Income Statement

RHOADES CORPORATION
First-Year Income Statement
Net Income for 2001

Sales	$20,000 (1,000 units at $20)
Cost of goods sold	10,000 (1,000 units at $10)
Gross profit	10,000
Selling and administrative expense	2,000
Depreciation	1,000
Operating profit	7,000
Taxes (40 percent)	2,800
Earnings after taxes	$ 4,200
Operating margin	$ 7,000/$20,000 = 35%
After-tax margin	$ 4,200/$20,000 = 21%

TABLE 8–9 Rhoades Corporation Income Statement

RHOADES CORPORATION
Second-Year Income Statement Using FIFO and LIFO
Net Income for 2002

	FIFO	LIFO
Sales	$22,000 (1,000 at $22)	$22,000 (1,000 at $22)
Cost of goods sold	10,000 (1,000 at $10)	11,000 (1,000 at $11)
Gross profit	12,000	11,000
Selling and administrative expense	2,200 (10% of sales)	2,200 (10% of sales)
Depreciation	1,000	1,000
Operating profit	8,800	7,800
Taxes (40 percent)	3,520	3,120
Earnings after taxes	$ 5,280	$ 4,680
Operating margin	$ 8,800/$22,000 = 40%	$ 7,800/$22,000 = 35.4%
After-tax margin	$ 5,280/$22,000 = 24%	$ 4,680/$22,000 = 21.2%

no physical increase in sales occurs. This is because FIFO costing lags behind current prices, and the company generates "phantom profits" due to capital gains on inventory. Unfortunately, this inventory will need to be replaced next period at higher costs. When and if prices turn lower in a recessionary environment, FIFO will have the opposite effect and drag down earnings. LIFO inventory costing, on the other hand, relates current costs to current prices, and although profits rise in dollar terms from 2001, the margins stay basically the same. The only problem with LIFO inventory accounting is that low-cost layers of inventory build up on the balance sheet of the company and understate inventory. This will cause inventory turnover to appear higher than under FIFO.

While many companies shifted to LIFO accounting in the past, FIFO inventory valuation still exists in some industries, and the analyst must be alert to the consequences of both methods.

Extraordinary Gains and Losses

Extraordinary gains and losses may occur from the sale of corporate fixed assets, lawsuits, or similar events that would not be expected to occur often, if ever, again. Some analysts argue that such extraordinary events should be included in computing the current income of the firm, while others would leave them off when assessing operating performance. The choice can have a big impact on ratios that rely on earnings or earnings per share. Extraordinary gains can inflate returns and lower payout ratios if they are included in earnings. The analyst concerned about forecasting should include only those earnings from continuing operations; otherwise, the forecast will be seriously off its mark. Unfortunately, there is some inconsistency in the manner in which nonrecurring losses are treated despite determined attempts by the accounting profession to ensure uniformity.

Pension Fund Liabilities

One area of increasing concern among financial analysts is the unfunded liabilities of corporate pension funds. These funds eventually will have to pay workers their retirement income from the pension fund earnings and assets. If the money is not available from the pension fund, the company is liable to make the payments. These unfunded pensions may have to come out of earnings in future years, which would penalize shareholders and limit the corporation's ability to reinvest in new assets.

Foreign Exchange Transactions

Foreign currency fluctuations have a major impact on the earnings of those companies heavily involved in international trade. The drug industry is significantly affected. Coca-Cola, with more than 70 percent of operating income coming from foreign operations in 2000, is a prime example of a company affected by swings in the currency markets. For example, when the dollar declines relative to foreign currencies, earnings from foreign subsidiaries get translated into more U.S. dollars and help the earnings of U.S. companies such as Coca-Cola. The opposite is true when the dollar increases in value. Coca-Cola's foreign exchange currency transactions had a negative effect of $140 million in 2000. Because Coca-Cola is available in almost 200 countries, the firm has a diversification effect with some currencies rising and others falling. However, a major change in a given part of the world could cause this diversification effect to lose its impact, as was the case in 2000.

Other Distortions

Other problems exist in accounting statements and methods of reporting earnings. A mention of some of them might provide you with areas that require further investigation. Additional areas for detective work are in accounting methods for the following: off balance sheet financing (e.g., Enron), research and development expenditures, deferred taxes, tax credits, merger accounting, intangible drilling and development costs, and percentage depletion allowances. As you can see, many issues cause analysts to dig further and to be cautious about accepting bottom-line earnings per share.

AGGRESSIVE ACCOUNTING TACTICS

The stock market is tough on companies that, in the parlance of Wall Street, "don't make their numbers." If your parents expect you to make an A in investments and you make a C, you're likely to hear about it. The same type of discipline exists on Wall Street.

Just ask a couple of IBM's competitors (www.ibm.com). In the year 2000, Compaq (www.compaq.com) and Unisys (www.unisys.com) issued warnings about not meeting their earnings goals, and their stocks plummeted 50 to 75 percent.

IBM fortunately did not have to issue such negative news to investors, but many question the firm's very aggressive financial reporting techniques. For the year 2000, IBM reported $8.1 billion in earnings, which translated into earnings per share of $4.44. That represented a 5 percent increase in EPS over the prior year that, on the surface, looked very good for a firm in the computer industry, which was going through a mini-recession of its own during this period.

But how did IBM get such commendable numbers? Bradley Rexford, a financial analyst at the Center for Financial Research and Analysis, implies IBM took the low road.[10]

He says $1.02 should be backed out of IBM's 2000 reported earnings per share of $4.44 to arrive at a more realistic value of $3.42 for IBM's earning power for the year. While there is no specific contention that IBM violated accounting or SEC rules, there is no question that IBM employed "a very aggressive offense" in reporting its numbers.

Rexford says that among IBM's questionable techniques was a gain in its pension fund value. Because the stock market had been steadily increasing for the last decade and also because of other related pension fund policy changes, IBM was able to claim $0.43 in pension fund gain. This represented almost 10 percent of IBM's entire earnings per share of $4.44. Of course, the pension fund gains had absolutely nothing to do with IBM's ability to manufacture and sell computer hardware, software, or related service.

IBM also posted a $0.15 gain by reversing prior reserve accounts entries for accounts receivable, inventory, and a reserve related to the sale of its Micrus semiconductor business. Reserves or changes against income are sometimes set up in good times and then reversed to bolster income during bad times. This so-called dipping into the cookie jar can be used to smooth out income.

A further $0.28 boost to IBM's earnings came from an assumption of a lower tax rate for the year 2000. In 1999, income was taxed at 34.4 percent, while in 2000, the rate was 29.9 percent.

Other minor items, related to share repurchases and capitalizing rather than expensing website expenses, added $0.16 more to earnings per share. Once again, none of these items had anything to do with IBM's ability to generate profit from its basic computer business. As stipulated earlier, all the cited transactions added $1.02 to IBM's reported earnings per share and allowed the firm to make its numbers.

The question to you as a future financial analyst is, "How much credit do you want to give to IBM for increasing earnings per share?" A firm that uses more conservative accounting practices might not have shown an increase in earnings per share, but you might have more confidence in valuing the earnings and in computing the profitability ratios. IBM is now in the position of having to use very

10. "Recurring Gains," *Forbes*, May 14, 2001, pp. 86–88.

aggressive accounting practices in the future to match prior earnings, which were based on a similar premise. Once you get started, it is hard to stop. You can also ask the former top officers of Enron about this principle.

Internet Resources

Website Address	Comments
www.zacks.com	Provides detailed company financial information and ratios—mostly free
www.multexinvestor.com	Provides detailed financial information, including ratios and statements
www.morningstar.com	Provides financial information and ratios for free, some information fee based
www.investors.com	Provides financial information from *Investor's Business Daily*
www.valueline.com	Is a web version of print information source
www.investopedia.com	Provides tutorials on financial ratios
www.ventureline.com	Allows access to financial ratios and other analytics, requires registration for access, and is fee based

Chapter 9

Technical Analysis and Market Efficiency

In the preceding four chapters, we followed a fundamental approach to security analysis. That is, we examined the fundamental factors that influence the business cycle, the performance of various industries, and the operations of the individual firms. We further examined the financial statements and tools of measurement that are available to the security analyst. In following a fundamental approach, one attempts to evaluate the appropriate worth of a security and perhaps ascertain whether it is under- or overpriced.

In this chapter, we examine a technical approach to investment timing. In this approach, analysts and market technicians examine prior price and volume data, as well as other market-related indicators, to determine past trends in the belief that they will help forecast future ones. Technical analysts place much more emphasis on charts and graphs of *internal market data* than on such fundamental factors as earnings reports, management capabilities, or new-product development. They believe that even when important fundamental information is uncovered, it may not lead to profitable trading because of timing considerations and market imperfections.

We also devote much time and attention in this chapter to the concept of market efficiency; that is, the ability of the market to adjust very rapidly to the supply of new information in valuing a security. This area of study has led to the efficient market hypothesis, which states that all securities are correctly priced at any point.

At the outset, be aware there are many disagreements and contradictions in the various areas we examine. As previously implied, advocates of technical analysis do not place much emphasis on fundamental analysis, and vice versa. Even more significant, proponents of the efficient market hypothesis would suggest that neither works.

In light of the various disagreements that exist, we believe it is important that the student be exposed to many schools of thought. For example, we devote the first part of the chapter to technical analysis and then later offer research findings that relate to the value of the technical approach as well as the fundamental approach. Our philosophy throughout the chapter is to recognize that there sometimes is a gap between practices utilized by brokerage houses (and on Wall Street) and beliefs held in the academic community, yet the student should be exposed to both.

TECHNICAL ANALYSIS

Technical analysis is based on a number of basic assumptions:

1. Market value is determined solely by the interaction of demand and supply.
2. It is assumed that though there are minor fluctuations in the market, stock prices tend to move in trends that persist for long periods.
3. Reversals of trends are caused by shifts in demand and supply.
4. Shifts in demand and supply can be detected sooner or later in charts.
5. Many chart patterns tend to repeat themselves.

For our purposes, the most significant items to note are the assumptions that stock prices tend to move in trends that persist for long periods, and these trends can be detected in charts. The basic premise is that past trends in market movements can be used to forecast or understand the future. The market technician generally assumes there is a lag between the time he perceives a change in the value of a security and when the investing public ultimately assesses this change.

In developing the tools of technical analysis, we shall divide our discussion between (a) the use of charting and (b) the key indicator series to project future market movements.

THE USE OF CHARTING

Charting is often linked to the development of the Dow theory in the late 1890s by Charles Dow. He was the founder of the Dow Jones Company and editor of *The Wall Street Journal.* Many of his early precepts were further refined by other market technicians, and it is generally believed the Dow theory was successful in signaling the market crash of 1929.

Essential Elements of the Dow Theory

The Dow theory maintains that there are three major movements in the market: daily fluctuations, secondary movements, and primary trends. According to the theory, daily fluctuations and secondary movements (covering two weeks to a month) are only important to the extent they reflect on the long-term primary trend in the market. Primary trends may be characterized as either bullish or bearish in nature.

In Figure 9-1, we look at the use of the Dow theory to analyze a market trend. Note that the primary movement in the market is positive despite two secondary movements that are downward. The important facet of the secondary movements is that each low is higher than the previous low and each high is higher than the previous high. This tends to confirm the primary trend, which is bullish.

FIGURE 9–1 Presentation of the Dow Theory

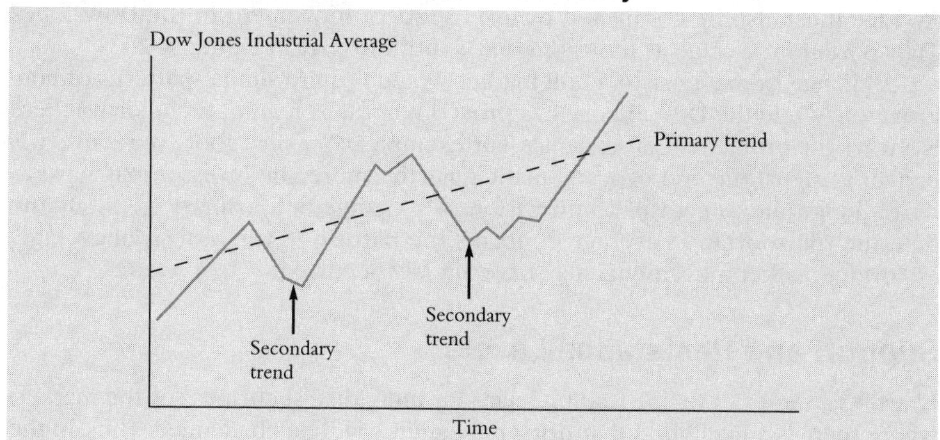

Under the Dow theory, it is assumed that this pattern will continue for a long period, and the analyst should not be confused by secondary movements. However, the upward pattern must ultimately end. This is indicated by a new pattern in which a recovery fails to exceed the previous high (abortive recovery) and a new low penetrates a previous low as indicated in Figure 9-2. For a true turn in

FIGURE 9–2 Market Reversal and Confirmation

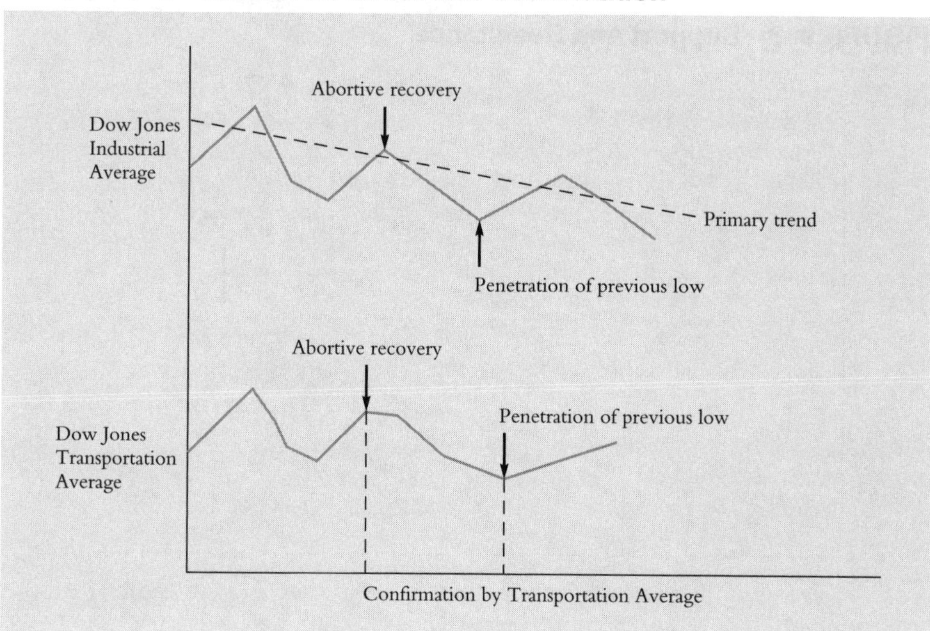

the market to occur, the new pattern of movement in the Dow Jones Industrial Average must also be confirmed by a subsequent movement in the Dow Jones Transportation Average as indicated on the bottom part of Figure 9-2.

A change from a bear to a bull market would require similar patterns of confirmation. While the Dow theory has proved helpful to market technicians, there is always the problem of false signals. For example, not every abortive recovery is certain to signal the end of a bull market. Furthermore, the investor may have to wait a long time to get full confirmation of a change in a primary trend. By the time the transportation average confirms the pattern in the industrial average, important market movements may have already occurred.

Support and Resistance Levels

Chartists attempt to define trading levels for individual securities (or the market) where there is a likelihood that price movements will be challenged. Thus, in the daily financial press or on television, the statement is often made that the next barrier to the current market move is at 11,000 (or some other level). This assumes the existence of support and resistance levels. As indicated in Figure 9-3, a support level is associated with the lower end of a trading range and a resistance level with the upper end.

Support may develop each time a stock goes down to a lower level of trading because investors who previously passed up a purchase opportunity may now choose to act. It is a signal that new demand is coming into the market. When a stock reaches the high side of the normal trading range, resistance may develop

FIGURE 9–3 Support and Resistance

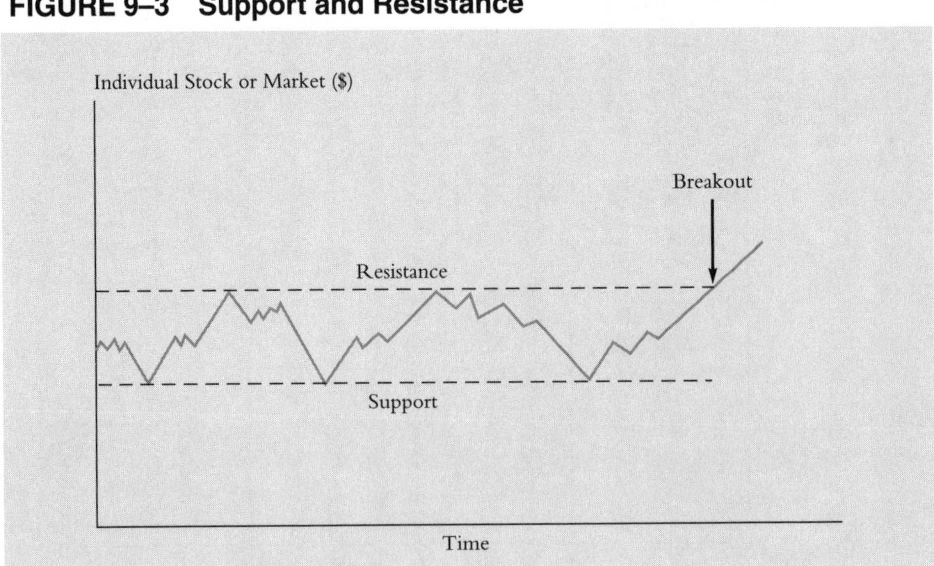

because some investors who bought in on a previous wave of enthusiasm (on an earlier high) may now view this as a chance to get even. Others may simply see this as an opportunity to take a profit.

A breakout above a resistance point (as indicated in Figure 9-3) or below a support level is considered significant. The stock is assumed to be trading in a new range, and higher (lower) trading values may now be expected.

A good example of support and resistance levels can be found in the trading pattern of IBM in the 1990s. After trading in the $150 to $170 range in the early 1990s, the stock hit rock bottom in mid-1993 at $40 per share. Part of the decline was due to a loss in EPS in 1993 for the first time in decades. However, the stock did find support at $40 per share as investors began to purchase the stock in anticipation of a possible comeback. Lou Gerstner, Jr., a highly respected executive, had come on board as chairman and CEO. He immediately began eliminating redundant operations as well as implementing a strategic pattern for future growth. By 1996, the stock was in the 90s range and made a number of attempts to break through a resistance point of 100. After several tries, the stock finally crossed the 100 resistance barrier and then made an almost uninterrupted run up to $200 in mid-1997. The stock then split two for one. By March 2002 it was still in the post split $100 range. IBM will undoubtedly continue to face new support and resistance levels in the future.

Volume

The amount of volume supporting a given market movement is also considered significant. For example, if a stock (or the market in general) makes a new high on heavy trading volume, this is considered to be bullish. Conversely, a new high on light volume may indicate a temporary move that is likely to be reversed.

A new low on light volume is considered somewhat positive because of the lack of investor participation. When a new low is established on the basis of heavy trading volume, this is considered to be quite bearish.

In the early 2000s, the New York Stock Exchange averaged a volume of 900 million to 1 billion shares daily. When the volume jumped to 1.5 billion shares, analysts took a very strong interest in the trading pattern of the market.

For an individual stock, the same principles also apply. In 2001, Intel normally traded 40 to 50 million shares daily. However, upward movements on volumes of 75 to 100 million shares or more were considered significant.

Types of Charts

Until now, we have been using typical line charts to indicate market patterns. Technicians also use bar charts and point and figure charts. We shall examine each.

Bar Chart A bar chart shows the high and low price for a stock with a horizontal dash along the line to indicate the closing price. An example is shown in Figure 9-4.

FIGURE 9–4 Bar Chart

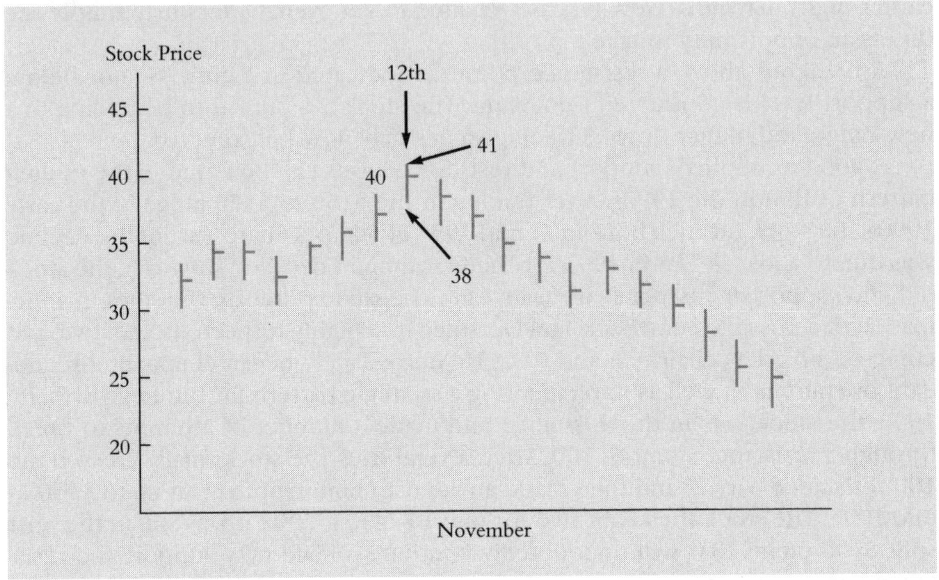

We see on November 12 the stock traded between a high of 41 and a low of 38 and closed at 40. Daily information on the Dow Jones Industrial Average is usually presented in the form of a bar chart, with daily volume shown at the bottom as indicated in Figure 9–5.

Trendline, published through a division of Standard & Poor's, provides excellent charting information on a variety of securities traded on the major exchanges and is available at many libraries and brokerage houses. Market technicians carefully evaluate the charts, looking for what they perceive to be significant patterns of movement. For example, the pattern in Figure 9–4 might be interpreted as a head-and-shoulder pattern (note the head in the middle) with a lower penetration of the neckline to the right indicating a sell signal. In Figure 9–6 we show a series of the price-movement patterns presumably indicating market bottoms and tops.

Although it is beyond the scope of this book to go into interpretation of chart formations in great detail, special books on the subject are suggested at the end of our discussion of charting.

Point and Figure Chart A point and figure chart (PFC) emphasizes significant price changes and the reversal of significant price changes. Unlike a line or bar chart, it has no time dimension. An example of a point and figure chart is presented in Figure 9–7.

The assumption is that the stock starts at 30. Only moves of two points or greater are plotted on the graph (some may prefer to use one point). Advances are indicated by Xs, and declines are shown by Os. A reversal from an advance to a decline or vice versa calls for a shift in columns. Thus, the stock initially goes from

FIGURE 9–5 Bar Chart of Market Average

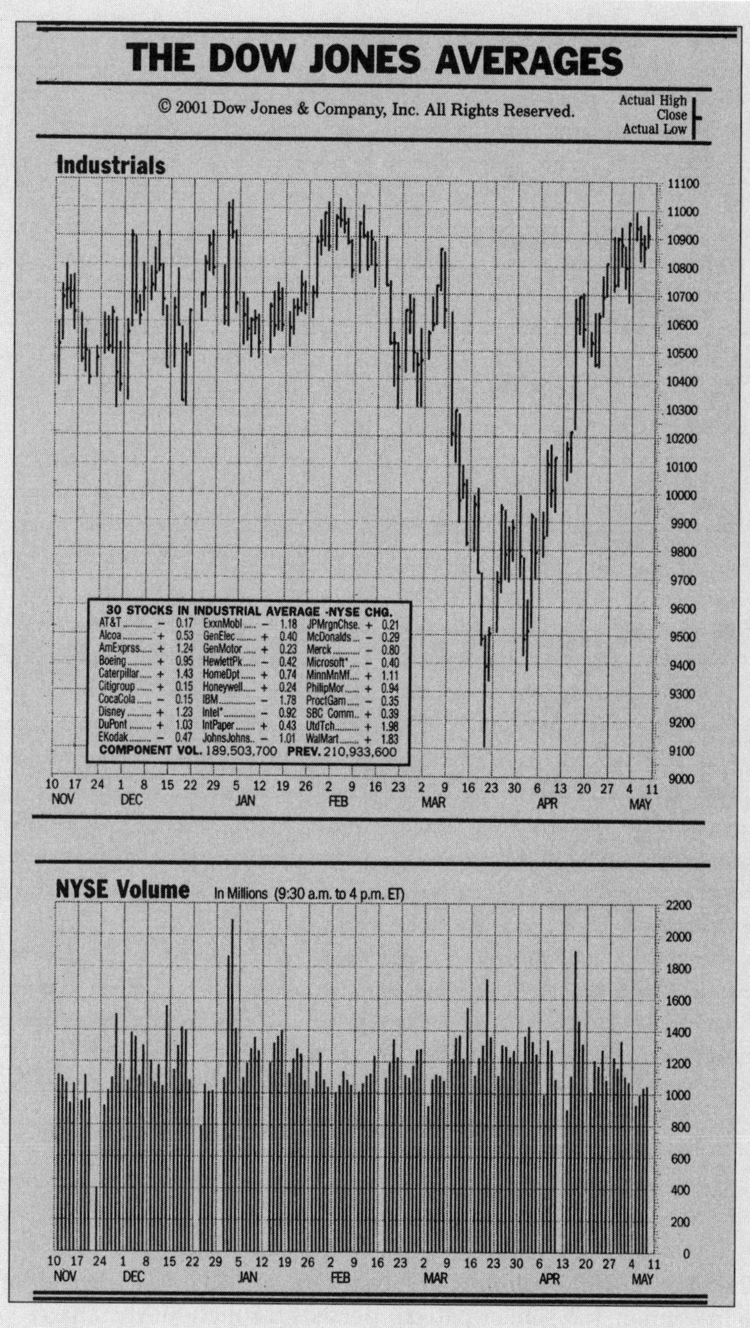

30 STOCKS IN INDUSTRIAL AVERAGE -NYSE CHG.

AT&T	–	0.17	ExxnMobl	–	1.18	JPMrgnChse.	+	0.21
Alcoa	+	0.53	GenElec	+	0.40	McDonalds	–	0.29
AmExprss	+	1.24	GenMotor	+	0.23	Merck	–	0.80
Boeing	+	0.95	HewlettPk	–	0.42	Microsoft*	–	0.40
Caterpillar	+	1.43	HomeDpt	+	0.74	MinnMnMf	+	1.11
Citigroup	+	0.15	Honeywell	+	0.24	PhilipMor	+	0.94
CocaCola	–	0.15	IBM	–	1.78	ProctGam	–	0.35
Disney	+	1.23	Intel*	–	0.92	SBC Comm.	+	0.39
DuPont	+	1.03	IntPaper	+	0.43	UtdTch	+	1.98
EKodak	–	0.47	JohnsJohns.	–	1.01	WalMart	+	1.83

COMPONENT VOL. 189,503,700 **PREV.** 210,933,600

Source: Republished with permission of Dow Jones & Company, Inc., from *The Wall Street Journal*, May 11, 2003, p. C3; permission conveyed through Copyright Clearance Center, Inc.

FIGURE 9–6 Chart Representation of Market Bottoms and Tops

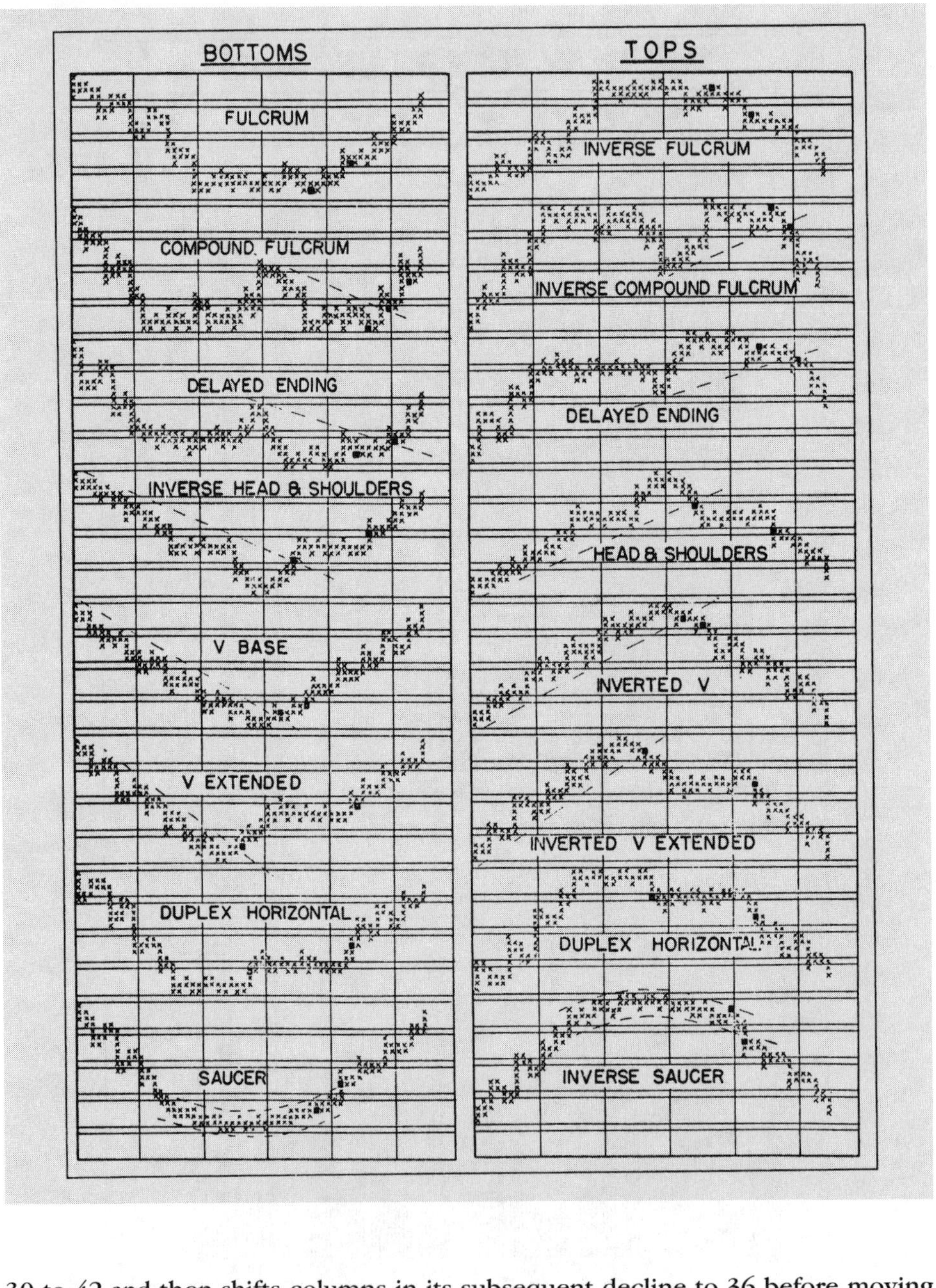

30 to 42 and then shifts columns in its subsequent decline to 36 before moving up again in column 3. A similar pattern persists throughout the chart.

Chartists carefully read point and figure charts to observe market patterns (where there is support, resistance, breakouts, congestion, and so on). Students

FIGURE 9–7 Point and Figure Chart

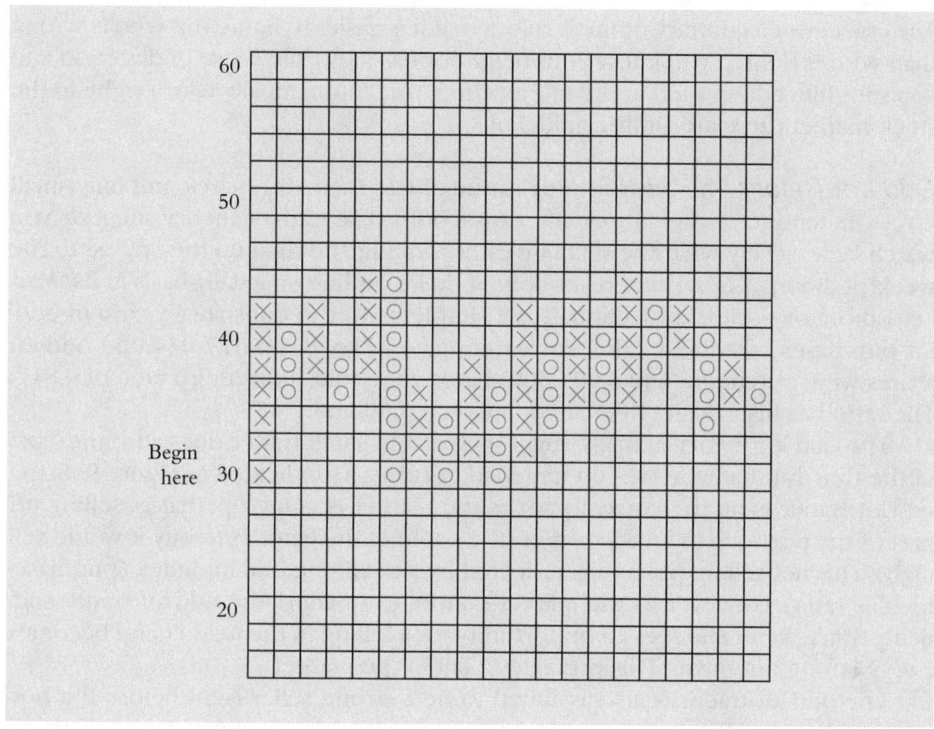

with a strong interest in charting may consult such books as Colby and Meyers, *The Encyclopedia of Technical Market Indicators,*[1] and DeMark, *The New Science of Technical Analysis.*[2] The problem in reading charts has always been to analyze patterns in such a fashion that they truly predict stock market movements before they unfold. To justify the effort, one must assume there are discernible trends over the long term.

KEY INDICATOR SERIES

In the television series "Wall Street Week," former host Louis Rukeyser traditionally watched a number of indicators on a weekly basis and compared the bullish and bearish indicators to determine what the next direction of the market might be.

In this section, we examine bullish and bearish technical indicator series. We first look at contrary opinion rules, then smart money rules, and finally, overall market indicators.

1. Robert W. Colby and Thomas A. Meyers, *The Encyclopedia of Technical Market Indicators* (Homewood, IL: Business One Irwin, 1988).
2. Thomas R. DeMark, *The New Science of Technical Analysis* (New York: John Wiley & Sons, 1994).

Contrary Opinion Rules

The essence of a contrary opinion rule is that it is easier to figure out who is wrong than who is right. If you know your neighbor has a terrible sense of direction and you spot him taking a left at the intersection, you automatically take a right. In the stock market there are similar guidelines.

Odd-Lot Theory An odd-lot trade is one of less than 100 shares, and only small investors tend to engage in odd-lot transactions. The odd-lot theory suggests you watch very closely what the small investor is doing and then do the opposite. The weekly edition of *Barron's* breaks down odd-lot trading on a daily basis in its "Market Laboratory—Stocks" section. It is a simple matter to construct a ratio of odd-lot purchases to odd-lot sales. For example, on May 8, 2001, 7,034,000 odd-lot shares were purchased, and 8,604,300 shares were sold, indicating a ratio of 0.817. The ratio has historically fluctuated between 0.50 and 1.45.

The odd-lot theory actually suggests that the small trader does all right most of the time but badly misses on key market turns. As indicated in Figure 9–8, the odd-lot trader is on the correct path as the market is going up; that is, selling off part of the portfolio in an up market (the name of the game is to buy low and sell high). This net selling posture is reflected by a declining odd-lot index (purchase-to-sales ratio). However, as the market continues upward, the odd-lot trader suddenly thinks he or she sees an opportunity for a killing in the market and becomes a very strong net buyer. This precedes a fall in the market.

The odd-lot trader is also assumed to be a strong seller right before the bottom of a bear market. Presumably, when the small trader finally gets grandfather's

FIGURE 9–8 Comparing Standard & Poor's 500 Index and the Odd-Lot Index

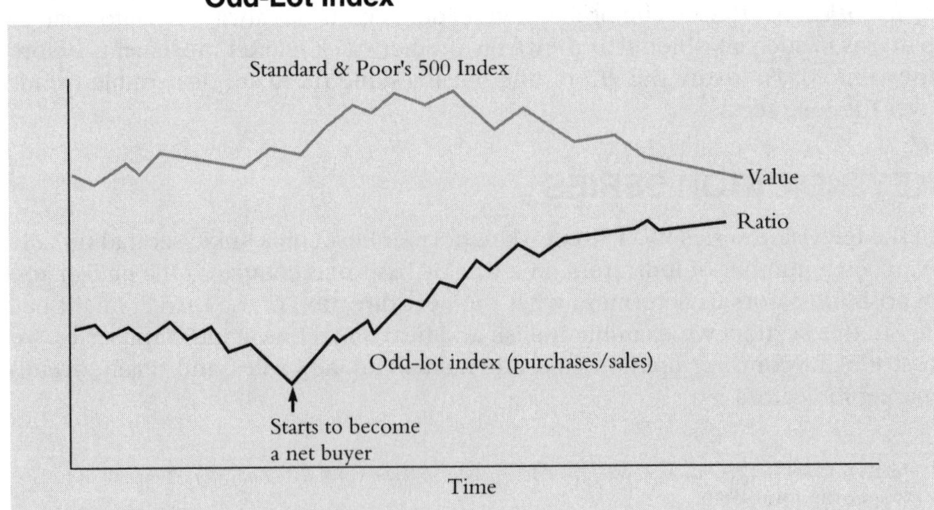

50 shares of AT&T out of the lockbox and sells them in disgust, it is time for the market to turn upward.

As if to add injury to insult, a corollary to the odd-lot theory says one should be particularly sensitive to what odd-lot traders do on Monday because odd-lotters tend to visit each other over the weekend, confirm each other's opinions or exchange hot tips, and then call their brokers on Monday morning. The assumption is that their chatter over the barbecue pit or in the bowling alley is even more suspect than their own individual opinions.

While the odd-lot theory appeared to have some validity in the 1950s and 1960s, it was not a particularly valuable tool in the last three decades. For one thing, the odd-lotters outguessed many of the professional money managers in selling off before the stock market debacle of the mid-1970s and late 1980s, and they began buying in advance of a recovery. The same is true in the 500 plus point market decline of October 1997.

Short Sales Position A second contrary opinion rule is based on the volume of short sales in the market. As you recall from Chapter 4, a short sale represents the selling of a security you do not own with the anticipation of purchasing the security in the future to cover your short position. Investors would only engage in a short sale transaction if they believed the security would, in fact, be going down in price in the near future so they could buy back the security at a lower price to cover the short sale. When the aggregate number of short sellers is large (that is, they are bearish), this is thought to be a bullish signal.

The contrary opinion stems from two sources: first, short sellers are sometimes emotional and may overreact to the market; second and more important, there now is a built-in demand for stocks that have been sold short by investors who will have to repurchase the shares to cover their short positions.

Daily short sale totals for the New York Stock Exchange are recorded in *The Wall Street Journal.* Also once a month (around the 20th), *The Wall Street Journal* reports on total short sale figures for the two major exchanges as well as securities traded on those exchanges (based on midmonth data). This feature usually contains comments about current trends in the market.

Technical analysts compute a ratio of the total short sales positions on an exchange to average daily exchange volume for the month. The normal ratio is between 2.0 and 3.0. A ratio of 2.5 indicates that the current short sales position is equal to two and a half times the day's average trading volume.

As the short sales ratio (frequently called the short interest ratio) approaches the higher end of the normal trading range, this would be considered bullish (remember this is a contrary opinion trading rule). As is true with many other technical trading rules, its use in predicting future performance has produced mixed results.[3]

3. Joseph Vu and Paul Caster, "Why All the Interest in Short Interest?" *Financial Analysts Journal,* July–August 1987, pp. 77–79.

Applied to individual stocks, the same type of principles apply. If traders are aggressively short-telling MMM, CISCO systems, or Novell, it may be time to buy.

Investment Advisory Recommendations A further contrary opinion rule states that you should watch the predictions of the investment advisory services and do the opposite. This has been formalized by Investors Intelligence (an investment advisory service itself) into the Index of Bearish Sentiment. When 60 percent or more of the advisory services are bearish, you should expect a market upturn. Conversely, when only 15 percent or fewer are bearish, you should expect a decline.[4]

Figure 9-9 gives a summary of bullish and bearish sentiments as published in the "Market Laboratory—Economic Indicators" section of *Barron's.* Investors Intelligence as well as three other sources of sentiments are presented. Let's concentrate our attention on Investors Intelligence. Since the percentage of bears was declining in the "last week" to 23.2 percent from 28.6 percent "two weeks ago," this indicates a possible sell under contrary opinion rules.

FIGURE 9–9 Investor Sentiment Readings

INVESTOR SENTIMENT READINGS

High bullish readings in the Consensus stock index or in the Market Vane stock index usually are signs of Market tops; low ones, market bottoms.

	Last Week	2 Weeks Ago	3 Weeks Ago
Consensus Index			
Bullish Opinion	*	50%	67%

Source: Consensus Inc., P.O. Box 520526,Independence, Mo.
* Data available at (800) 383-1441. editor@consensus-inc.com

	Last Week	2 Weeks Ago	3 Weeks Ago
AAII Index			
Bullish	57.6%	50.0%	57.3%
Bearish	23.2	28.6	22.3
Neutral	19.2	21.4	20.4

Source: American Association of Individual Investors, 625 N. Michigan Ave., Chicago, Ill. 60611 (312) 280-0170.

	Last Week	2 Weeks Ago	3 Weeks Ago
Market Vane			
Bullish Consensus	57%	50%	56%

Source: Market Vane, P.O. Box 90490, Pasadena, CA 91109 (626) 395-7436.

Source: Republished with permission of Dow Jones & Company, Inc., from *Barron's*, October 13, 2003, p. MW41; permission conveyed through Copyright Clearance Center, Inc.

4. John R. Dortman, "The Stock Market Sign Often Points the Wrong Way," *The Wall Street Journal*, January 26, 1989, p. C1.

Lest one take investment advisory services too lightly, however, observe the market impact of a recommendation by Joseph Granville, publisher of the *Granville Market Letter.* On Tuesday, January 6, 1981, Granville issued a late-evening warning to his subscribers to "sell everything." He helped cause a $40 billion decline in market values the next day. Although subsequent events proved Granville wrong in his prediction of an impending bear market, the fact that one man could trigger such a reaction is an indication of the number of people who are influenced by the suggestions of advisory services. Granville has been followed by many other so-called gurus in the 1980s and 1990s, most of whom have their day in the sun and then eventually fall into disrepute as they fail to call a major turn in the market or begin reversing their positions so often that investors lose confidence. No doubt a new series of such stars will appear in 2004 and after.

Put-Call Ratio A final contrary opinion rule applies to the put-call ratio. Puts and calls represent options to sell or buy stock over a specified time period at a given price. A put is an option to sell, and a call is an option to buy. Options have become very popular since they began trading actively on organized exchanges in 1973. There are many sophisticated uses for options to implement portfolio strategies (particularly to protect against losses). However, there is also a great deal of speculation by individual investors in the options market. Because some of this speculation is ill conceived, ratios based on options may tell you to do the opposite of what option traders are doing.

The ratio of put (sell) options to call (buy) options is normally about 0.60. There are generally fewer traders of put options than call options. However, when the ratio gets up to 0.65 to 0.70 or higher, this indicates increasing pessimism by option traders. Under a contrary opinion rule, this indicates a buy signal (he turned left so you turn right). If the put-call ratio goes down to 0.40, the decreasing pessimism (increasing optimism) of the option trader may indicate that it is time to sell if you are a contrarian. The put-call ratio has a better than average record for calling market turns. Put-call ratio data can be found in the "Market Week—Options" section of *Barron's.*

Smart Money Rules

Market technicians have long attempted to track the pattern of sophisticated traders in the hope that they might provide unusual insight into the future. We briefly observe theories related to bond market traders and stock exchange specialists.

Barron's Confidence Index The *Barron's* Confidence Index is used to observe the trading pattern of investors in the bond market. The theory is based on the premise that bond traders are more sophisticated than stock traders and pick up trends more quickly. The theory suggests that a person who can figure out what bond traders are doing today may be able to determine what stock market investors will be doing in the near future.

Barron's Confidence Index is actually computed by taking the yield on 10 top-grade corporate bonds, dividing by the yield on 40 intermediate-grade bonds,[5] and multiplying by 100:

$$\text{Barron's Confidence Index} = \frac{\text{Yield on 10 top-grade corporate bonds}}{\text{Yield on 40 intermediate-grade bonds}} \times 100 \qquad (9\text{-}1)$$

The index is published weekly in the "Market Laboratory—Bonds" section of *Barron's.* What does it actually tell us? First, we can assume that the top-grade bonds in the numerator always have a smaller yield than the intermediate-grade bonds in the denominator. The reason is that the higher quality issues can satisfy investors with smaller returns. The bond market is very representative of a risk-return trade-off environment in which less risk requires less return and higher risk necessitates a higher return.

With top-grade bonds providing smaller yields than intermediate-grade bonds, the Confidence Index is always less than 100 (percent). The normal trading range is between 80 and 96, and it is within this range that technicians look for signals on the economy. If bond investors are bullish about future economic prosperity, they are rather indifferent between holding top-grade bonds and holding intermediate-grade bonds, and the yield differences between these two categories is relatively small. This would indicate the Confidence Index may be close to 96. An example is presented below in which top-grade bonds are providing 8.4 percent and intermediate-grade bonds are yielding 9.1 percent:

$$\text{Barron's Confidence Index} = \frac{\text{Yield on 10 top-grade corporate bonds}}{\text{Yield on 40 intermediate-grade bonds}} \times 100$$

$$= \frac{8.4\%}{9.1\%} \times 100 = 92(\%)$$

Now let us assume that investors become quite concerned about the outlook for the future health of the economy. If events go poorly, some weaker corporations may not be able to make their interest payments, and thus, bond market investors will have a strong preference for top-quality issues. Some investors continue to invest in intermediate- or lower-quality issues but only at a sufficiently high yield differential to justify the risk. We might assume that the *Barron's* Confidence Index will drop to 83 because of the increasing spread between the two yields in the formula:

$$\text{Barron's Confidence Index} = \frac{\text{Yield on 10 top-grade corporate bonds}}{\text{Yield on 40 intermediate-grade bonds}} \times 100$$

$$= \frac{8.9\%}{10.7\%} \times 100 = 83(\%)$$

5. The 40 bonds compose the Dow Jones 40 bond averages.

The yield on the intermediate-grade bonds is now 1.8 percentage points higher than that on the 10 top-grade bonds, and this is reflected in the lower Confidence Index reading. As confidence in the economy is once again regained, the yield spread differential narrows, and the Confidence Index goes up.

Market technicians assume there are a few months of lead time between what happens to the Confidence Index and what happens to the economy and stock market. As is true with other such indicators, it has a mixed record of predicting future events. One problem is that the Confidence Index is only assumed to consider the impact of investors' attitudes on yields (their demand pattern). We have seen in the 1980s and 1990s that the supply of new bond issues can also influence yields. Thus, a very large bond issue by General Electric or ExxonMobil may drive up high-grade bond yields even though investor attitudes indicate they should be going down.

Short Sales by Specialists Another smart money index is based on the short sales positions of specialists. Recall from Chapter 3 that specialists make markets in various securities listed on the organized exchanges. Because of the uniquely close position of specialists to the action on Wall Street, market technicians ascribe unusual importance to their decisions. One measure of their activity that is frequently monitored is the ratio of specialists' short sales to the total amount of short sales on an exchange.

When we previously mentioned short sales in this chapter, we suggested that a high incidence of short selling might be considered bullish because short sellers often overreact to the market and provide future demand potential to cover their short position. In the case of market specialists, this is not necessarily true. These sophisticated traders keep a book of limit and stop orders on their securities so that they have a close feel for market activity at any given time, and their decisions are considered important.

The normal ratio of specialist short sales to short sales on an exchange is about 45 percent. When the ratio goes up to 50 percent or more, market technicians interpret this as a bearish signal. A ratio under 40 percent is considered bullish.

Overall Market Rules

Our discussion of key indicator series has centered on both contrary opinion rules and smart money rules. We now briefly examine two overall market indicators: the breadth of the market indicator series and the cash position of mutual funds.

Breadth of the Market A breadth of the market indicator attempts to measure what a broad range of securities is doing as opposed to merely examining a market average. The theory is that market averages, such as the Dow Jones Industrial Average of 30 stocks or the Standard & Poor's 500 Stock Index, are weighted toward large firms and may not be representative of the entire market. To get a broader perspective of the market, an analyst may examine all stocks on an exchange.

The technician often compares the advance-declines with the movement of a popular market average to determine if there is a divergence between the two. Advances and declines usually move in concert with the popular market averages but may move in the opposite direction at a market peak or bottom. One of the possible signals for the end of a bull market is when the Dow Jones Industrial Average is moving up but the number of daily declines consistently exceeds the number of daily advances on the New York Stock Exchange. This indicates that conservative investors are investing in blue-chip stocks but that there is a lack of broad-based confidence in the market. In Table 9–1, we look at an example of divergence between the advance-decline indicators on the New York Stock Exchange and the Dow Jones Industrial Average (DJIA).

In Column 4, we see the daily differences in advances and declines. In Column 5, we look at the cumulative pattern by adding or subtracting each new day's value from the previous total. We then compare the information in Column 4 and Column 5 to the Dow Jones Industrial Average (DJIA) in Column 6. Clearly, the strength in the Dow Jones Industrial Average is not reflected in the advance-decline data, and this may be interpreted as signaling future weakness in the market.

Breadth of the market data can also be used to analyze upturns in the market. When the Dow Jones Industrial Average is going down but advances consistently lead declines, the market may be positioned for a recovery. Some market technicians develop sophisticated weighted averages of the daily advance-declines to go along with the data in Table 9–1. Daily data on the Dow Jones Industrial Average and advancing and declining issues can be found in the "Stock Market Data Bank" section of *The Wall Street Journal.*

While a comparison of advance-decline data to market averages can provide important insights, there is also the danger of false signals. Not every divergence between the two signals a turn in the market, so analysts must be careful in their interpretation. The technical analyst must look at a wide range of variables. With the advent of decimalization of stock prices in 2001, many technicians think this

TABLE 9–1 Comparing Advance-Decline Data and the Dow Jones Industrial Average (DJIA)

Day	(1) Advances	(2) Declines	(3) Unchanged	(4) Net Advances or Declines	(5) Cumulative Advances or Declines	(6) DJIA
1	1607	1507	201	+100	+100	+33.38
2	1550	1560	188	−10	+90	+20.51
3	1504	1602	194	−98	−8	+13.08
4	1499	1506	295	−7	−15	+35.21
5	1530	1573	208	−43	−58	−12.02
6	1550	1562	186	−12	−70	+50.43
7	1455	1650	200	−155	−225	+30.10
8	1285	1815	212	−530	−755	+21.30

indicator has lost some of its usefulness because now stocks only have to advance or decline a penny to make the list.

Mutual Fund Cash Position Another overall market indicator is the cash position of mutual funds. This measure indicates the buying potential of mutual funds and is generally representative of the purchasing potential of other large institutional investors. The cash position of mutual funds, as a percentage of their total assets, generally varies between 5 and 20 percent.[6]

At the lower end of the boundary, it would appear that mutual funds are fully invested and can provide little in the way of additional purchasing power. As their cash position goes to 15 percent or higher, market technicians assess this as representing significant purchasing power that may help to trigger a market upturn. While the overall premise is valid, there are problems in identifying just what is a significant cash position for mutual funds in a given market cycle. It may change in extreme market environments.

EFFICIENT MARKET HYPOTHESIS

We shift our attention from technical analysis to that of examining market efficiency. As indicated at the beginning of the chapter, we now view any contradictions between the assumptions of fundamental or technical analysis and findings of the efficient market hypothesis (EMH).

Earlier in the text, we said that an efficient market is one in which new information is very rapidly processed so that securities are properly priced at any given time.[7] An important premise of an efficient market is that a large number of profit-maximizing participants are concerned with the analysis and valuation of securities. This would seem to describe the security market environment in the United States. Any news on IBM, AT&T, an oil embargo, or tax legislation is likely to be absorbed and acted on very rapidly by profit-maximizing individuals. For this reason, the efficient market hypothesis assumes that no stock price can be in disequilibrium or improperly priced for long. There is almost instantaneous adjustment to new information. The EMH applies most directly to large firms trading on the major security exchanges.

The efficient market hypothesis further assumes that information travels in a random, independent fashion and that prices are an unbiased reflection of all currently available information.

More generally, the efficient market hypothesis is stated and tested in three different forms: the weak form, the semistrong form, and the strong form. We shall

---

6. The cash dollars are usually placed in short-term credit instruments as opposed to stocks and bonds.

7. A slightly more precise definition is that securities are priced in an unbiased fashion at any given time. Because information is assumed to travel in a random, independent fashion, there is no consistent upside or downside pricing bias mechanism. Although the price adjustment is not always perfect, it is unbiased and cannot be anticipated in advance.

examine each of these and the related implications for technical and fundamental analysis.

WEAK FORM OF THE EFFICIENT MARKET HYPOTHESIS

The weak form of the efficient market hypothesis suggests there is no relationship between past and future prices of securities. They are presumed to be independent over time. Because the efficient market hypothesis maintains that current prices reflect all available information and information travels in a random fashion, it is assumed that there is little or nothing to be gained from studying past stock prices.

The weak form of the efficient market hypothesis has been tested in two different ways—tests of independence and trading rule tests.

Tests of Independence

Tests of independence have examined the degree of correlation between stock prices over time and have found the correlation to be consistently small (between +0.10 and −0.10) and not statistically significant. This indicates that stock price changes are independent.[8] A further test is based on the frequency and extent of runs in stock price data. A run occurs when there is no difference in direction between two or more price changes. An example of a series of data and some runs is presented below:

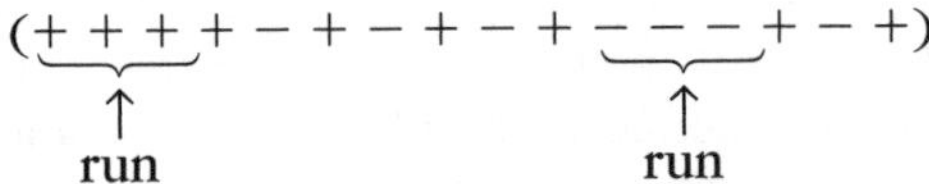

Runs can be expected in any series of data through chance factors, but an independent data series should not produce an unusual amount of runs. Statistical tests have indicated that security prices generally do not produce any more runs than would be expected through the process of random number generation.[9] This also tends to indicate that stock price movements are independent over time.[10]

Trading Rule Tests

A second method of testing the weak form of the efficient market hypothesis (that past trends in stock prices are not helpful in predicting the future) is through trading rule tests. Because practicing market technicians maintain that tests of inde-

8. Sidney S. Alexander, "Price Movements in Speculative Markets: Trends or Random Walks," *Industrial Management Review*, May 1961, p. 26; and Eugene F. Fama, "The Behavior of Stock Market Prices," *Journal of Business*, January 1965, pp. 34–105.
9. Ibid.
10. A possible exception to this rule was found in small stocks. A sample study is Jennifer Conrad and Gantam Kaul, "Time Variation and Expected Returns," *Journal of Business*, October 1988, pp. 409–25.

pendence (correlation studies and runs) are too rigid to test the assumptions of the weak form of the efficient market hypothesis, additional tests by academic researchers have been developed. These are known as trading rule or filter tests. These tests determine whether a given trading rule based on past price data, volume figures, and so forth can be used to beat a naive buy-and-hold approach. The intent is to simulate the conditions under which a given trading rule is used and then determine if superior returns were produced after considering transaction costs and the risks involved.

As an example of a trading rule, if a stock moves up 5 percent or more, the rule might be to purchase it. The assumption is that this represents a breakout and should be considered bullish. Similarly, a 5 percent downward movement would be considered bearish and call for a sell strategy (rather than a buy-low/sell-high strategy, this is a follow-the-market-trend strategy). Other trading rule tests might be based on advance-decline patterns, short sales figures, and similar technical patterns. Research results have indicated that in a limited number of cases, trading rules may produce slightly positive returns, but after commission costs are considered, the results are neutral and sometimes negative in comparison to a naive buy-and-hold approach.[11]

Implications for Technical Analysis

The results of the *tests of independence* and *trading rules* would seem to uphold the weak form of the efficient market hypothesis. Security prices do appear to be independent over time or, more specifically, move in the pattern of a random walk.

Some challenge the research on the basis that academic research in this area does not capture the personal judgment an experienced technician brings forward in reading charts. There is also the fact that there are an infinite number of trading rules, and not all of them can or have been tested. Nevertheless, research on the weak form of the EMH still seems to suggest that prices move independently over time, that past trends cannot be used to easily predict the future, and that charting and technical analysis may have limited value.

SEMISTRONG FORM OF THE EFFICIENT MARKET HYPOTHESIS

The semistrong form of the efficient market hypothesis maintains that all public information is already impounded into the value of a security, and therefore, one cannot use fundamental analysis to determine whether a stock is undervalued or overvalued.

11. Eugene F. Fama and Marshall Blume, "Filter Rules and Stock Market Trading Profits," *Journal of Business*, supplement, January 1966, pp. 226–41; and George Pinches, "The Random Walk Hypothesis and Technical Analysis," *Financial Analysts Journal*, March–April 1970, pp. 104–10.

Basically, the semistrong form of the efficient market hypothesis supports the notion that there is no learning lag in the distribution of public information. When a company makes an announcement, investors across the country assess the information with equal speed. Also, a major firm listed on the New York Stock Exchange could hardly hope to utilize some questionable accounting practice that deceptively leads to higher reported profits and not expect sophisticated analysts to pick it up. (This may not be equally true for a lesser known firm that trades over-the-counter and enjoys little investor attention.)

Researchers have tested the semistrong form of the EMH by determining whether investors who acted on the basis of newly released public information have been able to enjoy superior returns. If the market is efficient in a semistrong sense, this information is almost immediately impounded in the value of the security, and little or no trading profits would be available. The implications are that one could not garner superior returns by trading on public information about stock splits, earnings reports, or other similar items.

Tests on the semistrong form of the efficient market hypothesis have generally been on the basis of risk-adjusted returns. Thus, the return from a given investment strategy must be compared with the performance of popular market indicators with appropriate risk adjustments. The risk measurement variable is usually the beta. After such adjustments are made, the question becomes: Are there abnormal returns that go beyond explanations associated with risk? If the answer is yes and can be shown to be statistically significant, then the investment strategy may be thought to refute the semistrong form of the efficient market hypothesis. The investor must also cover transaction costs in determining that a given strategy is superior.

For example, assume a stock goes up 15 percent. The security is 20 percent riskier than the market. Further assume the overall market goes up by 10 percent. On a risk-adjusted basis, the security would need to go up in excess of 12 percent (the 10 percent market return × 1.2 risk factor) to beat the market. In the above case, the stock with the 15 percent gain beat the market on a risk-adjusted basis.

Tests examining the impact of such events as stock splits and stock dividends, corporate announcements, and changes in accounting policy indicate that the market is generally efficient in a semistrong sense. For example, a study by Fama, Fisher, Jensen, and Roll indicated that almost all of the market impact of a stock split occurs before a public announcement.[12] There is little to be gained from acting on the announcement.

According to the semistrong form of the efficient market hypothesis, investors not only digest information very quickly, but they also are able to see through mere changes in accounting information that do not have economic consequences. For example, the switching from accelerated depreciation to straight-line depreciation for financial reporting purposes (but not tax purposes) tends to make earnings

---

12. Eugene F. Fama, Lawrence Fisher, Michael G. Jensen, and Richard Roll, "The Adjustment of Stock Prices to New Information," *International Economic Review,* February 1969, pp. 2–21.

per share look higher but provides no economic benefit for the firm. Research studies indicate this has no positive impact on valuation.[13]

Similarly, investors are not deceived by mere accounting changes related to inventory policy, reserve accounts, exchange translations, or other items that appear to have no economic benefits. The corporate treasurer who switches from LIFO to FIFO accounting to make earnings look better in an inflationary economy will probably not see the firm's stock price rise because investors look at the economic consequences of higher taxes associated with the action and disregard the mere financial accounting consequences of higher reported profits.[14] Under this circumstance, the effect on stocks may be neutral or negative.

Implications for Fundamental Analysis

If stock values are already based on the analysis of all available public information, it may be assumed that little is to be gained from additional fundamental analysis. Under the semistrong form of the efficient market hypothesis, if General Motors is trading at $55, the assumption is that every shred of public information about GM has been collected and evaluated by thousands of investors, and they have determined an equilibrium price of $55. The assumption is that anything you read in *The Wall Street Journal* or Standard & Poor's publications has already been considered many times over by others and is currently impounded in the value of the stock. If you were to say you think GM is really worth $57 because of some great new product, proponents of the semistrong form of the efficient market hypothesis would suggest that your judgment cannot be better than the collective wisdom of the marketplace in which everyone is trying desperately to come out ahead.

Ironically, although many suggest that fundamental analysis may not lead to superior profits in an efficient market environment, it is fundamental analysis itself that makes the market efficient. Because everyone is doing fundamental analysis, there is little in the way of unabsorbed or undigested information. Therefore, one extra person doing fundamental analysis is unlikely to achieve superior insight.

Although the semistrong form of the efficient market hypothesis has research support, there are exceptions. These are referred to as anomalies or deviations from the basic proposition that the market is efficient. For example, Basu has found that stocks with low P/E ratios consistently provide better returns than stocks with high P/E ratios on both a non-risk-adjusted and risk-adjusted basis.[15] Because a

13. T. Ross Archibald, "Stock Market Reaction to Depreciation Switch-Back," *Accounting Review*, January 1972, pp. 22–30; and Robert S. Kaplan and Richard Roll, "Investor Evaluation of Accounting Information: Some Empirical Evidence," *Journal of Business*, April 1972, pp. 225–57.

14. Shyam Sunder, "Stock Price and Risk Related to Accounting Changes in Inventory Valuation," *Accounting Review*, April 1975, pp. 305–15.

15. S. Basu, "Investment Performance of Common Stocks in Relation to Their Price-Earnings Ratios: A Test of the Efficient Market Hypothesis," *Journal of Finance*, June 1977, pp. 663–82. Also, S. Basu, "The Information Content of Price-Earnings Ratios," *Financial Management*, Summer 1975, pp. 53–64.

P/E ratio is publicly available information that may be used to generate superior returns, this flies in the face of the more common conclusions on the semistrong form of the efficient market hypothesis. Banz[16] and Reinganum's[17] research indicates that small firms tend to provide higher returns than larger firms even after considering risk. Perhaps fewer institutional investors in smaller firms make for a less-efficient market and superior potential opportunities.

Additional evidence of this nature continues to accumulate, and in Chapter 10, covering special situations, we present an extended discussion of some of these items and other possible contradictions to the acceptance of the semistrong version of the efficient market hypothesis. We also comment on measurement problems in that chapter.

Thus, even if the semistrong form of the efficient market hypothesis appears to be generally valid, exceptions can be noted. Also, it is possible that while most analysts may not be able to add additional insight through fundamental analysis, there are exceptions to every rule. It can be assumed that some analysts have such *extraordinary* insight and capability in analyzing publicly available information that they can perceive what others cannot. Also, if you take a very long-term perspective, the fact that a stock's value is in short-term equilibrium may not discourage you from taking a long-term position or attempting to find long-term value.

Before we move on, it is also appropriate to point out that there is not only debate about whether the market is efficient in a semistrong sense but also over whether market researchers are appropriately testing for efficiency. For example, if risk is not properly measured, then conclusions about research studies can be questioned. This is an issue that cannot be easily settled and is discussed again at the end of Chapter 10.

STRONG FORM OF THE EFFICIENT MARKET HYPOTHESIS

The strong form of the efficient market hypothesis goes beyond the semistrong form to state that stock prices reflect not only all public information but *all* information. Thus, it is hypothesized that insider information is also immediately impounded into the value of a security. In a sense, we go beyond the concept of a market that is highly efficient to one that is perfect.

The assumption is that no group of market participants or investors has monopolistic access to information. If this is the case, then no group of investors can be expected to show superior risk-adjusted returns under any circumstances.

Unlike the weak and semistrong forms of the efficient market hypothesis, major test results are not supportive of the strong form of the hypothesis. For

16. Rolf W. Banz, "The Relationship between Returns and Market Value of Common Stocks," *Journal of Financial Economics,* March 1981, pp. 3–18.

17. Marc R. Reinganum, "Misspecification of Capital Asset Pricing—Empirical Anomalies Based on Earnings Yield and Market Values," *Journal of Financial Economics,* March 1981, pp. 19–46.

example, specialists on security exchanges have been able to earn superior rates of return on invested capital. The book they keep on unfilled limit orders appears to provide monopolistic access to information. A SEC study actually found that specialists typically sell above their latest purchase 83 percent of the time and buy below their latest sell 81 percent of the time.[18] This implies wisdom that greatly exceeds that available in a perfect capital market environment. Likewise, an institutional investor study, also sponsored by the SEC, indicated that specialists' average return on capital was more than 100 percent.[19] While these returns have decreased somewhat recently in a more competitive environment, specialists still appear to outperform the market.

Another group that appears to use nonpublic information to garner superior returns is corporate insiders. As previously described, an insider is considered to be a corporate officer, member of the board of directors, or substantial stockholder. The SEC requires that insiders report their transactions to that regulatory body. A few weeks after reporting to the SEC, the information becomes public. Researchers can then go back and determine whether investment decisions made by investors appeared, on balance, to be wise. Did heavy purchases by insiders precede strong upward price movements, and did sell-offs precede poor market performance? The answer appears to be yes. Research studies indicate insiders consistently achieve higher returns than would be expected in a perfect capital market.[20] Although insiders are not allowed to engage in short-term trades (of six months or less) or illegal transactions to generate trading profits, they are allowed to take longer-term positions, which may prove to be profitable. It has even been demonstrated that investors who follow the direction of inside traders after information on their activity becomes public may enjoy superior returns.[21] (This, of course, represents contrary evidence to the semistrong form of the efficient market hypothesis as well.)

Even though there is evidence on the activity of specialists and insiders that would cause one to reject the strong form of the efficient market hypothesis (or at least not to accept it), the range of participants with access to superior information is not large. For example, tests on the performance of mutual fund managers have consistently indicated they are not able to beat the market averages over the long term.[22] Although mutual fund managers may get the first call when news is breaking, that is not fast enough to generate superior returns.

---

18. Securities and Exchange Commission, *Report of the Special Study of the Security Markets*, part 2 (Washington, D.C.: U.S. Government Printing Office).

19. Securities and Exchange Commission, *Institutional Investor Study Report* (Washington, D.C.: U.S. Government Printing Office).

20. For an overview, see Alexandra Peers, "Insiders Reap Big Gains from Big Trades," *The Wall Street Journal*, September 23, 1992, pp. C1, C12.

21. Michael S. Rozeff and Mir A. Zaman, "Market Efficiency and Insider Trading: New Evidence," *Journal of Business*, January 1988, pp. 24–25.

22. Richard A. Ippolito, "On Studies of Mutual Fund Performance, 1962–1991," *Financial Analysts Journal*, January–February 1993, pp. 42–50.

While the strong form of the efficient market hypothesis suggests more opportunity for superior returns than the weak or semistrong forms, the premium is related to monopolistic access to information rather than other factors.

It should also be pointed out that those who act *illegally* with insider information may initially achieve superior returns from their special access to information, but the price of their actions may be high. For example, Ivan Boesky and Michael Milken, convicted users of illegal insider information in the late 1980s, were forced to give up their gains, pay heavy fines, and serve jail sentences. In their particular cases, they traded on insider information about mergers well before the public was informed. Although they were not officers of the companies or on the boards, they had special fiduciary responsibilities as money managers that they violated.

Internet Resources

Website Address	Comments
www.bigcharts.com	Provides data, charts, and technical indicators, free
cbs.marketwatch.com	Has technical charts and information
www.quicken.com	Contains some technical analytical data and charts
www.stockworm.com	Has technical charts
www.stockcharts.com	Provides free technical charts and education on technical analysis
www.investopedia.com	Has primer on technical analysis
www.stocksites.com	Contains links to technical analysis sites and related finance sites

Chapter 10

Special Situations and Market Anomalies

In a previous discussion of market efficiency in Chapter 9, we suggested that while the security markets were generally efficient in the valuing of securities, there were still opportunities for special returns in a number of circumstances. Just what these circumstances are is subject to debate.

In most instances, special or abnormal returns refer to gains beyond what the market would normally provide after adjustment for risk. Transactions costs must also be covered. In this chapter, we explore such topics as market movements associated with mergers and acquisitions, the underpricing of new stock issues, the effect of an exchange listing on a stock's valuation, the stock market impact of a firm repurchasing its own shares, and the small-firm and low-P/E effects.

MERGERS AND ACQUISITIONS

Many stocks that were leaders in daily volume and price movement in the last decade represented firms that were merger candidates—that is, companies that were being acquired or anticipated being acquired by other firms. The stocks of these acquisition candidates often increased by 60 percent or more over a relatively short period. The list of acquired companies includes such well-known names as Duracell, Turner Broadcasting, Chemical Bank, and Quaker Oats.

Premiums for Acquired Company

The primary reason for the upward market movement in the value of the acquisition candidate is the high premium that is offered over current market value in a merger or acquisition. The merger price premium represents the difference between the offering price per share and the market price per share for the candidate (before the impact of the offer). For example, a firm that is selling for $25 per share may attract a purchase price of $40 per share. Quite naturally, the stock goes up in response to the offer and the anticipated consummation of the merger.

As expected, researchers have consistently found that there are abnormal returns for acquisition candidates.[1] A study has indicated the average premium paid in a recent time period was approximately 60 percent, and there was an associated upward price movement of a similar magnitude.[2] This is a much larger average premium than in prior time periods and may be attributed to the recognition of high replacement value in relationship to market value. The premium was based on the difference between the price paid and the value of the acquisition candidate's stock *three months* before announcement of the merger. Some examples of premiums paid during the last decade are presented in Table 10-1.

The only problem from an investment viewpoint is that approximately two-thirds of the price gain related to large premiums occurs before public announcement. It is clear that people close to the situation are trading on information leaks. In the 1980s, the highly prestigious investment banking house of Morgan Stanley was embarrassed by charges brought by the U.S. Attorney's Office that two of its former merger and acquisition specialists were conspiring to use privileged information on takeovers to make profits on secret trading accounts.[3] Also in the 1980s, notorious insider traders Ivan Boesky, Michael Milken, and Dennis Levine served jail sentences for their misuse of information related to unannounced mergers.

Those who attempt to legitimately profit by investing in mergers and acquisitions can follow a number of routes. First, some investors try to identify merger candidates before public announcement to capture maximum profits. This is

TABLE 10–1 Premiums Paid in Mergers and Acquisitions

Acquiring Firm	Acquired Firm	Price Paid in Cash for Acquired Company's Stock	Value of Acquired Firm Three Months before Announcement	Premium Paid (percent)
Roche	Syntex	$24.00	$15.25	57.38%
Beatrice Food Co.	Harmon International Inc.	35.25	20.00	76.25
Parker Pen Co.	Manpower, Inc.	15.20	11.50	32.18
Colt Industries	Menaso Manufacturing	26.60	15.00	77.33
Pepsico, Inc.	Pizza Hut, Inc.	38.00	22.375	69.83
Walter Kidde & Co.	Victor Comptometer	11.75	7.375	59.32
Dana Corporation	Weatherford Co.	14.00	9.375	49.33
Allis Chalmers Corporation	American Air Filter	34.00	19.50	74.36
Time, Inc.	Inland Containers	35.00	20.75	68.67
Chemical Bank	Texas Commerce Bank	32.75	20.25	61.73

1. Gershon Mandelker, "Risk and Return: The Case of Merging Firms," *Journal of Financial Economics,* December 1974, pp. 303-35; Donald R. Kummer and J. Ronald Hoffmeister, "Valuation Consequences of Cash Tender Offers," *Journal of Finance,* May 1978, pp. 505-6; Peter Dodd, "Merger Proposals, Management Discretion and Stockholder Wealth," *Journal of Financial Economics,* December 1980, pp. 105-38; and Steven Kaplan, "The Effect of Management Buyouts on Operating Performance and Value," *Journal of Financial Economics,* October 1989, pp. 217-54.
2. Henry Oppenheimer and Stanley Block, "An Examination of Premiums and Exchange Ratios Associated with Merger Activity during the 1975-78 Period" (Financial Management Association Meeting, 1980).
3. "Two Former Morgan Stanley Executives Accused of Plot Involving Takeover Data," *The Wall Street Journal,* February 4, 1981, p. 2.

difficult. While researchers have attempted to identify financial and operating characteristics of acquisition candidates, the information is often contradictory and may even change over time.[4] In prior time periods, acquisition candidates were often firms with sluggish records of performance, whereas many of the recent acquirees are high-quality companies that have unusually good records of performance (Time Warner, Cellular Communications, Pillsbury, and Wachovia Bank Corp.).

Some alert analysts keep a close eye on securities undergoing unusual volume or pricing patterns (this could be for any number of reasons). Other investors identify industries where companies are being quickly absorbed and attempt to guess which firm will be the next to be acquired. Prime examples of such industries in recent times were banking, telecommunications, pharmaceuticals, and energy.

While trying to guess an acquisition candidate before public announcement can be potentially profitable, it requires that an investor tie up large blocks of capital in betting on an event that may never come to pass. Others prefer to invest at the time of announcement of a merger or acquisition. A gain of the magnitude of 15 percent or more may still be available (over a few months' time period). Perhaps a stock that was $25 before any consideration of merger moves up to $35 on announcement. If the acquisition price is $40, there may still be a nice profit to be made. The only danger is that the announced merger may be called off, in which case the stock may sharply retreat in value. This happened to Kemper in 1994 when General Electric made a bid for its shares only to be outbid by Conseco Insurance at $62 per share. When Conseco could not arrange financing, the bid fell through and the stock plunged into the low $40s until Zurich Insurance offered $49 per share in 1995. Examples of other price drops associated with merger cancellations are shown in Table 10-2.

The wise investor must carefully assess the likelihood of cancellation. Special attention must be given to such factors as the possibility of antitrust action, the attitude of the target company's management toward the merger, the possibility of unhappy stockholder suits, and the likelihood of poor earnings reports or other negative events. In a reasonably efficient market environment, the potential price gain that exists at announcement may be well correlated with the likelihood of

TABLE 10–2 Stock Movement of Potential Acquirees in Canceled Mergers

Acquirer–Potential Acquiree	Preannouncement	One Day after Announcement	One Day after Cancellation
Mead Corporation–Occidental Petroleum	20⅜	33¼	23¼
Olin Corp.–Celanese	16	23¾	16¾
Chicago Rivet–MITE	20¾	28⅛	20¾

4. Robert J. Monroe and Michael A. Simkowitz, "Investment Characteristics of Conglomerate Targets: A Discriminant Analysis," *Southern Journal of Business,* November 1971, pp. 1–15; and Donald J. Stevens, "Financial Characteristics of Merger Firms: A Multivariate Analysis," *Journal of Financial and Quantitative Analysis,* March 1973, pp. 149–58.

the merger being successfully consummated. That is to say, if it appears the merger is almost certain to go through, the stock may be up to $38.50 at announcement based on an anticipated purchase price of $40. If a serious question remains, the stock may only be at $33. When a merger becomes reasonably certain, arbitrageurs come in and attempt to lock in profits by buying the acquisition candidate at a small spread from the purchase price.

One of the most interesting features of the latest merger movement was the heavy incidence of unfriendly takeovers, that is, the bidding of one company for another against its will. Such events often lead to the appearance of a third company on the scene, referred to as a white knight, whose function is to save the target company by buying it out, thus thwarting the undesired suitor. The new suitor is generally deemed to be friendly to the interests of the target company and may be invited by it to partake in the process. Examples of white knights occurred when Gulf Oil thwarted an offer from Mesa Petroleum and went with Standard Oil of California (renamed Chevron). Similarly, Marathon Oil rejected an offer from Mobil to merge with U.S. Steel.

These multiple-suitor bidding wars often lead to unusually attractive offers. A 40 to 60 percent premium may ultimately parlay into an 80 to 100 percent gain or more. For example, the bidding for Gulf Oil sent the stock from $38 to $80.

Acquiring Company Performance

What about the acquiring company's stock in the merger and acquisition process? Is this a special situation; that is, does this stock also show abnormal market gains associated with the event? A study by Mandelker indicated that it did not.[5] Long-term economic studies indicate that many of the anticipated results from mergers may be difficult to achieve.[6] There is often an initial feeling of optimism that is not borne out in reality. The synergy, or "2 + 2 = 5," effect associated with broadening product lines or eliminating overlapping functions may be offset by the inability of management to mesh divergent philosophies. However, companies do appear to be more adept at the process than in prior periods; conservatively managed firms, such as Disney, Du Pont, and AT&T, have replaced the funny-money conglomerate gunslingers of another era. Nevertheless, most investors prefer to position themselves with the acquired firm, which is certain to receive a high premium, rather than with the acquiring firm, which has to pay it.

Form of Payment

Another consideration in a merger is the form of payment. Cash offers usually carry a slightly higher premium than stock offers because of the immediate tax conse-

5. Mandelker, "Risk and Return," pp. 303–35. Also see Anup Agrawal, Jeffrey F. Jaffe, and Gershon Mandelker, "The Post-Merger Performance of Acquiring Firms," *Journal of Finance,* September 22, 1992, pp. 1605–21.

6. T. Hogarty, "The Profitability of Corporate Managers," *Journal of Business,* July 1970, pp. 317–27. For a contrary opinion, see Paul M. Healy, Krisha G. Paleps, and Richard S. Ruback, "Does Corporate Performance Improve after Mergers?" *Journal of Financial Economics,* April 1992, pp. 132–65.

quences to the acquired firm's shareholders. When stock is offered, the tax obligation may be deferred by the acquired company's stockholders until the stock of the acquiring firm is actually sold, relatively soon or many years in the future.

While cash was the popular medium of payment in the late 1980s, this is no longer the case. With the great bull market of the 1990s, acquiring firms have shown a strong preference for trading their shares for that of the merger candidate.[7] Examples of recent mergers in which stock for stock trades took place include the Gillette acquisition of Duracell and the Chase Manhattan-Chemical Bank merger.

Leveraged Buyouts

Some corporations are also taken over through leveraged buyouts (LBOs). Here, either the management of the company or some other investor group borrows the needed cash to repurchase all the shares of the company. The balance sheet of the company serves as the collateral base to make the borrowing possible. After the leveraged buyout, the company may be taken private for a period, in which unprofitable assets are sold and debts reduced. The intent is then to bring the company to the public market once again (or resell it to another company) at a large profit over the initial purchase price. Successful leveraged buyouts, in which profits of 50 percent or more were made, include those of Blue Bell, Leslie Fay, Metromedia, SFN, and Uniroyal. The largest leveraged buyout involved RJR Nabisco in 1988. The price tag was in excess of $25 billion.

Not all leveraged buyouts are successful. Sometimes the debt burden associated with the transaction is so large that a company has difficulty recovering after an LBO. A classic case is the Southland Corporation (former owners of 7-Eleven convenience stores), which found itself in bankruptcy court after putting an unmanageable amount of debt on its books.

NEW STOCK ISSUES

Another form of a special situation is the initial issuance of stock by a corporation. There is a belief in the investment community that securities may be underpriced when they are issued to the public for the first time. That is to say, when a company goes public by selling formerly privately held shares to new investors in an initial public offering, the price may not fully reflect the value of the security.

Why does this so-called underpricing occur, and what is the significance to the investor? The underpricing may be the result of the investment banker's firm commitment to buy the shares when distributing the issue. That is, the investment banker normally agrees to buy the stock from Company A at a set price and then resells it to the public (along with other investment bankers, dealers, and brokers). The investment banker must be certain the issue will be fully subscribed to at the

---

7. For further justification of type of payment, see Kenneth J. Martin, "The Method of Payment in Corporate Acquisitions, Investment Opportunities and Management Ownership," *Journal of Finance*, September 1996, pp. 1227–46.

initial public market price or the banker (and others) will absorb losses or build up unwanted inventory. To protect his position, the investment banker may underprice the issue by 5 to 10 percent to ensure adequate demand.

Studies by Miller and Reilly;[8] Ibbotson, Sindelar, and Ritter;[9] Muscarella and Vetsuypens;[10] and others have indicated positive excess returns are related to the issue of the stock. Miller and Reilly, for example, observed positive excess returns of 9.9 percent one week after issue. However, the efficiency of the market comes into play after the stock is actively trading on a regular basis, and any excess returns begin to quickly disappear. Excess returns represent gains above the market averages after adjusting for the relative risk of the investment. The lesson to be learned is that, on average, the best time to buy a new, unseasoned issue is on initial distribution from the underwriting syndicate (investment bankers, dealers, brokers), and the best time to sell is shortly after. These new issues may actually underperform the market over the long term.[11]

The point has been strongly made by recent research by Barry and Jennings.[12] They calculated positive excess returns of 8.69 percent on the first date of trading for new issues but discovered that 90 percent of that gain occurred on the opening transaction.

Participating in the distribution of a new issue is not always as easy as it sounds. A really hot new issue may be initially oversubscribed, and only good customers of a brokerage house may be allocated shares. Such was the case in the feverish atmosphere that surrounded the initial public trading of NexGen, Netscape, Microsoft, Apple Computer, and Genentech. Genentech actually went from $35 to $89 in the first 20 minutes of trading (only to quickly come back down). For the most part, customers with a regular brokerage account and a desire to participate in the new-issues market can find adequate opportunities for investment, though perhaps in less spectacular opportunities than those described above.

Performance of Investment Bankers

Research studies indicate that large, prestigious investment banking houses do not generally provide the highest initial returns to investors in the new issues they underwrite.[13] The reason for this is that the upper-tier investment bankers tend

8. Robert E. Miller and Frank K. Reilly, "An Examination of Mispricing Returns, and Uncertainty for Initial Public Offerings," *Financial Management,* Winter 1987, pp. 33–38.

9. Roger G. Ibbotson, J. Sindelar, and Jay R. Ritter, "Initial Public Offerings," *Journal of Applied Corporate Finance,* Fall 1988, pp. 37–45.

10. Chris Muscarella and Mike Vetsuypens, "A Simple Test of Barron's Model of IPO Underpricing," *Journal of Financial Economics,* September 1989, pp. 125–35.

11. Jay Ritter, "The Long-Term Performance of Initial Public Offerings," *Journal of Finance,* March 1991, pp. 3–27.

12. Christopher B. Barry and Robert H. Jennings, "The Opening Performance of Initial Offerings of Common Stock," *Financial Management,* Spring 1993, pp. 54–63.

13. Brian M. Neuberger and Carl T. Hammond, "A Study of Underwriters' Experience with Unseasoned New Issues," *Journal of Financial and Quantitative Analysis,* March 1974, pp. 165–74. Also, see Dennis E. Logue, "On the Pricing of Unseasoned New Issues, 1965–1969," *Journal of Financial and Quantitative Analysis,* January 1973, pp. 91–103; and Brian M. Neuberger and Chris A. La Chapelle, "Unseasoned New Issue Price Performance on Three Tiers: 1976–1980," *Financial Management,* Autumn 1983, pp. 23–28.

to underwrite the issues of the strongest firms coming into the market. Less uncertainty is associated with these strong firms.[14] These firms generally shop around among the many investment bankers interested in their business and eventually negotiate terms that would allow for very little underpricing when they reach the market. (They want most of the benefits to go to the corporation, not to the initial stockholders.)

Factors to Consider in a New Issue

Although the best strategy in a new public offering is often to sell the stock soon after it becomes public, some investors may choose to take a longer-term position. In this case, the investor should consider the management of the firm and its performance record. In most cases, a firm that is going public will have past sales and profit figures that can be compared with others in the industry. In one study, the average sales volume for a firm approaching the new issues market was $22.9 million with $1.8 million in after-tax profits and $14.6 million in assets.[15]

The investor also should take a close look at the intended use of funds from the public distribution. There are many legitimate purposes, such as the construction of new plant and equipment, the expansion of product lines, or the reduction of debt. The investor should be less enthusiastic about circumstances in which funds are being used to buy out old stockholders or to acquire property from existing shareholders.

EXCHANGE LISTINGS

A special situation of some interest to investors is an exchange listing, in which a firm trading over-the-counter now lists its shares on an exchange (such as the American or New York Stock Exchange). Another version of a listing is for a firm to step up from an American Stock Exchange listing to a New York Stock Exchange listing.

An exchange listing may generate interest in a security (particularly when a company moves from the over-the-counter market to an organized exchange). The issue will now be assigned a specialist who has responsibility for maintaining a continuous and orderly market.[16] Furthermore, there may be greater marketability for the issue as well as more readily available price quotes. An exchange listing may also make the issue more acceptable for margin trading and short selling.

---

14. Richard Carter and Steven Manaster, "Initial Public Offerings and Underwriter Reputation," *Journal of Finance*, September 1990, pp. 1045–67.

15. Stanley Block and Marjorie Stanley, "The Financial Characteristics and Price Movement Patterns of Companies Approaching the Unseasoned Securities Market in the Late 1970s," *Financial Management*, Winter 1980, pp. 30–36.

16. This is not always a superior arrangement to having multiple market makers in the over-the-counter market. It depends on how dedicated the specialist is to maintaining the market. Some banks and smaller industrial firms may choose the competitive dealer system in the over-the-counter market in preference to the assigned specialist. For a truly extensive overview of research on stock listings, see H. Kent Baker and Sue E. Meeks, "Research on Exchange Listings and Delistings: A Review and Synthesis," *Financial Practice and Education*, Spring 1991, pp. 57–71.

Large institutional investors and foreign investors may also consider a listed security more appropriate for inclusion in their portfolios.

Listed firms must meet certain size and performance criteria provided in Table 10-3 (and previously mentioned in Chapter 3 for the NYSE). Although the criteria are not highly restrictive, meeting these standards may still signal a favorable message to investors.

A number of research studies have examined the stock market impact of exchange listings. As might be expected, a strong upward movement is associated with securities that are to be listed, but there is also a strong sell-off after the event has occurred. Research by Van Horne,[17] Fabozzi,[18] and others[19] indicates that the total effect may be neutral. Research by Ying, Lewellen, Schlarbaum, and Lease (YLSL) would tend to indicate an overall gain.[20]

The really significant factor is that regardless of whether a stock has a higher net value a few months after listing as opposed to a few months before listing, there still may be profits to be made. This would be true if the investor simply bought the stock four to six weeks before listing and sold it on listing. Because an application approval for listing is published in the weekly bulletin of the New York Stock Exchange well before the actual date of listing, a profit is often possible. The study by YLSL, cited above, indicates there may be an opportunity for abnormal returns on a risk-adjusted basis in the many weeks between announcement of listing and actual listing (between 4.40 and 16.26 percent over normal market returns, depending on the time period). In this case, YLSL actually reject the semi-strong form of the efficient market hypothesis by suggesting there are substantial profits to be made even after announcement of a new listing. The wise investor may wish to sell on the eventual date of listing because sometimes a loss in value may occur at that point.

The reader should also be aware of the potential impact of delisting on a security, that is, the formal removal from a New York Stock Exchange or American Stock Exchange listing, and a resumption of trading over-the-counter. This may occur because the firm has fallen substantially below the requirements of the exchange. As you would expect, this has a large negative effect on the security. Merjos found that 48 of the 50 firms in her study declined between the last day of trading on an exchange and the resumption of trading over-the-counter.[21] The average decline was 17 percent. While the value was not risk adjusted, it is large enough to indicate the clear significance of the event. Other studies have found similar results.[22]

---

17. James C. Van Horne, "New Listings and Their Price Behavior," *Journal of Finance,* September 1970, pp. 783–94.
18. Frank J. Fabozzi, "Does Listing on the AMEX Increase the Value of Equity?" *Financial Management,* Spring 1981, pp. 43–50.
19. Richard W. Furst, "Does Listing Increase the Market Value of Common Stock?" *Journal of Business,* April 1970, pp. 174–80; and Waldemar M. Goulet, "Price Changes, Managerial Accounting and Insider Trading at the Time of Listing," *Financial Management,* Spring 1974, pp. 303–6.
20. Louis K. W. Ying, Wilbur G. Lewellen, Gary G. Schlarbaum, and Ronald C. Lease, "Stock Exchange Listing and Securities Returns," *Journal of Financial and Quantitative Analysis,* September 1977, pp. 415–32.
21. Anna Merjos, "Stricken Securities," *Barron's,* March 4, 1963, p. 9.
22. Gary C. Sanger and James D. Paterson, "An Empirical Analysis of Common Stock Delistings," *Journal of Financial and Quantitative Analysis,* June 1990, pp. 261–72.

TABLE 10–3 Minimum Requirements for NYSE* Listing

Round-lot holders (number of holders of a unit of trading—generally 100 shares)	2,000 U.S.
or:	
Total shareholders	2,200
. . . together with:	
Average Monthly Trading Volume (for the most recent six months)	100,000 shares
or:	
Total shareholders	500
. . . together with:	
Average Monthly Trading Volume (for the most recent 12 months)	1,000,000 shares
Public shares	1,100,000 outstanding
Market value of public shares	
Public companies	$100,000,000
IPOs, spin-offs, carve-outs	$60,000,000
Minimum Quantitative Standards: Financial Criteria	
Earnings	
Aggregate pretax earnings (D) over the last three years of $6,500,000 achievable as:	
Most recent year	$2,500,000
Each of two preceding years	$2,000,000
or:	
Most recent year (All three years must be profitable)	$4,500,000
or:	
Operating Cash Flow	
For companies with not less than $500 million in global market capitalization and $200 million in revenues in the last 12 months:	
Aggregate for the three years operating cash flow (each year must report a positive amount)	$25,000,000
Global Market Capitalization	
Revenues for the last fiscal year	$100,000,000
Average global market capitalization	$1,000,000,000
REITs (less than 3 years operating history)	$60,000,000
stockholders' equity	
Funds (less than 3 years operating history)	$60,000,000
Net assets	

*www.nyse.com.

STOCK REPURCHASE

The repurchase by a firm of its own shares provides for an interesting special situation. The purchase tends to increase the demand for the shares while decreasing the effective supply. Before we examine the stock market effects of a repurchase, we briefly examine the reasons behind the corporate decision.

Reasons for Repurchase

In some cases, management believes the stock is undervalued in the market. Prior research studies indicated that repurchased securities generally underperformed the popular market averages before announcement of repurchase.[23] Thus, management or the board of directors may perceive this to be an excellent opportunity because of depressed prices. Others, however, might see the repurchase as a sign that management is not creative or that it lacks investment opportunities for the normal redeployment of capital.[24] Past empirical studies indicated that firms that engage in repurchase transactions often have lower sales and earnings growth and lower return on net worth than other, comparable firms.[25] However, in the bull market of the 1990s, many of the firms repurchasing their own shares were among the strongest and most respected on Wall Street. Examples include Exxon, GE, IBM, Merck, and Monsanto.

Actual Market Effect

From the viewpoint of a special situation, the key question is, What is the stock market impact of the repurchase? Is there money to be made here or not? Much of the earlier research said no.[26] A number of studies based on data from the 1970s and 1980s took a more positive viewpoint.[27] The latest important research, published in 1995, by Ikenberry, Lakonishok, and Vermaelen (ILV) gives only a conditionally positive response.[28]

The researchers found that the immediate reaction to share repurchase announcements was only minimal. For the 1,239 repurchases included in the study, the average gain was only 3.5 percent. One reason for the small increase might be the skepticism with which share repurchases are often viewed. Approximately 90 percent of stock repurchases are announced as future intentions to make open market purchases rather than firm commitments (so-called tender offers). Many analysts are hesitant to accept the premise that there will be a follow-through. A 50 million share repurchase program might be announced, but only 15 million shares might actually be repurchased over time.

---

23. Richard Norgaard and Connie Norgaard, "A Critical Evaluation of Share Repurchase," *Financial Management,* Spring 1974, pp. 44–50; and Larry Y. Dann, "Common Stock Repurchases: An Analysis of Returns to Bondholders and Stockholders," *Journal of Financial Economics,* June 1981, pp. 113–38.
24. Charles D. Ellis and Allen E. Young, *The Repurchase of Common Stock* (New York: The Ronald Press, 1971), p. 61.
25. Norgaard and Norgaard, "A Critical Evaluation."
26. A good example is Ellis and Young, *The Repurchase of Common Stock,* p. 156.
27. Terry E. Dielman, Timothy J. Nantell, and Roger L. Wright, "Price Effects of Stock Repurchasing: A Random Coefficient Regression Approach," *Journal of Financial and Quantitative Analysis,* March 1980, pp. 175–89; Larry Y. Dann, "Common Stock Repurchases: An Analysis of Returns to Bondholders and Stockholders," *Journal of Financial Economics,* June 1981, pp. 113–38; Theo Vermaelen, "Common Stock Repurchases and Market Signaling: An Empirical Study," *Journal of Financial Economics,* June 1981, pp. 139–83; and R. W. Masulis, "Stock Repurchase by Tender Offer: An Analysis of the Causes of Common Stock Price Changes," *Journal of Finance,* May 1980, pp. 305–19.
28. David Ikenberry, Josef Lakonishok, and Theo Vermaelen, "Market Underreaction to Open Market Share Repurchases," *Journal of Financial Economics,* October 1995, pp. 181–208.

Nevertheless, in the latest study, the researchers did find large positive returns over a long period of time following a stock repurchase announcement, even though the initial reaction was muted. Over a four-year time period following the month of announcement, the stocks in the study had an average abnormal return of 12.1 percent (return over and above comparable firms with equal risk).

While there was undoubtedly skepticism about follow-through at time of announcement, the most important factor influencing future market performance was the type of stock involved in the repurchase. For value-oriented stocks with solid fundamentals, the average abnormal return was 45.3 percent over the four-year time horizon.[29] For high-flying "glamour stocks," the returns were neutral to slightly negative (in comparison to similar firms).

The predominant argument for the beneficial effects of the repurchase is that management knows what it is doing when it purchases its *own* shares. In effect, management is acting as an insider for the benefit of the corporation, and we previously observed in Chapter 9 that insiders tend to be correct in their investment decisions. This factor may provide positive investment results. Of course, these are merely average results over many transactions, and not all tender offers will prove to be beneficial events. The investor must carefully examine the number of shares to be repurchased, the reasons for repurchase, and the future impact on earnings and dividends per share.

THE SMALL-FIRM AND LOW-P/E-RATIO EFFECT

Two University of Chicago doctoral studies in the early 1980s contended that the true key to superior risk-adjusted rates of return rests with investing in firms with small market capitalizations. (Market capitalization refers to shares outstanding times stock price.) In a study of New York Stock Exchange firms, covering from 1936 to 1975, Banz indicates that the lowest quintile (bottom 20 percent) of firms in terms of market capitalization provide the highest returns even after adjusting for risk. Banz suggests, "On average, small NYSE firms have had significantly larger risk-adjusted returns than larger NYSE firms over a 40-year period."[30]

Some criticized Banz for using only NYSE firms in his analysis and for using a time period that included the effects of both a depression and a major war. Small firms had incredibly high returns following the Depression. A similar type study, produced by Reinganum[31] at about the same time, overcame these criticisms. Reinganum examined 2,000 firms that were traded on the New York Stock Exchange or the American Stock Exchange between 1963 and 1980. He annually divided the 2,000 firms into 10 groupings based on size, with the smallest category repre-

29. The most important valuation measure used by Ikenberry, Lakonishok, and Vermaelen was book-to-market value, a topic covered in a later section of the chapter.

30. Rolf W. Banz, "The Relationship between Returns and Market Value of Common Stocks," *Journal of Financial Economics,* March 1981, pp. 3–18.

31. Marc R. Reinganum, "Misspecification of Capital Asset Pricing—Empirical Anomalies Based on Earnings Yield and Market Values," *Journal of Financial Economics,* March 1981, pp. 19–46. Also, "A Direct Test of Roll's Conjecture on the Firm Size Effect," *Journal of Finance,* March 1982, pp. 27–35; and "Portfolio Strategies Based on Market Capitalization," *Journal of Portfolio Management,* Winter 1983, pp. 29–36.

senting less than $5 million in market capitalization and the largest grouping representing a billion dollars or more.

A synopsis of the results from the Reinganum study is presented in Table 10–4.

Column 2 indicates the median value of the market capitalization for the firms in each group. Column 3 is the median stock price for firms in each group, while Column 4 indicates average annual return associated with that category.

As observed in Column 4, the smallest capitalization group (MV 1) outperformed the largest capitalization group (MV 10) by more than 23 percentage points per year. Although not included in the table, in 14 out of the 18 years under study, the MV 1 group showed superior returns to the MV 10 group. In another similar analysis, Reinganum found that $1 invested in the smallest capitalization group would have grown to $46 between 1963 and 1980, while the same dollar invested in the largest capitalization group would have only grown to $4. As did Banz, Reinganum adjusted his returns for risk and continued to show superior risk-adjusted returns.

Such superior return evidence drew criticisms from different quarters. Roll suggested that small-capitalization studies underestimate the risk measure (beta) by failing to account for the infrequent and irregular trading patterns of stocks of smaller firms.[32] Stoll and Whaley maintained that transaction costs associated with dealing in smaller capitalization firms might severely cut into profit potential.[33] They indicated the average buy-sell spread on small-capitalized, low-priced stocks might be four or five times that of large-capitalization firms. Reinganum has maintained that even after accounting for these criticisms, small-capitalization firms continue to demonstrate superior risk-adjusted returns.[34]

Given that there might be advantages to investing in smaller firms, why haven't professional money managers picked up on the strategy? This, in part, is a catch-22. Part of the reason for the inefficiency in this segment of the market that allows for superior returns is the absence of institutional traders. This absence means less information is generated on the smaller firms, and the information that is generated is reacted to in a less immediate fashion. Studies suggest an important linkage between the absence of organized information and superior return potential.[35]

Advocates of the small-firm effect argue that it is this phenomenon alone, rather than others, such as the low-P/E-ratio effect, that leads to superior risk-adjusted returns. Peavy and Goodman argued that the low-P/E-ratio effect is also important.[36] In following up on the earlier work of Basu[37] on the importance of

32. Richard Roll, "A Possible Explanation of the Small Firm Effect," *Journal of Finance*, September 1981, pp. 879–88.

33. H. A. Stoll and R. E. Whaley, "Transaction Costs and the Small Firm Effect," *Journal of Financial Economics*, March 1985, pp. 121–43.

34. Reinganum, "Misspecification of Capital Asset Pricing," pp. 19–46.

35. Avner Arbel and Paul Strebel, "Pay Attention to Neglected Firms," *Journal of Portfolio Management*, Winter 1983, pp. 37–42.

36. John W. Peavy III and David A. Goodman, "The Significance of P/Es for Portfolio Returns," *Journal of Portfolio Management*, Winter 1983, pp. 43–47.

37. S. Basu, "Investment Performance of Common Stocks in Relation to Their Price-Earnings Ratios: A Test of the Efficient Market Hypothesis," *Journal of Finance*, June 1977, pp. 663–82.

TABLE 10–4 Synopsis of Results—Reinganum Study

(1) Grouping[a]	(2) Median Market Value (Capitalization, in millions)	(3) Median Share Price	(4) Average Annual Return
MV 1	$ 4.6	$ 5.24	32.77%
MV 2	10.8	9.52	23.51
MV 3	19.3	12.89	22.98
MV 4	30.7	16.19	20.24
MV 5	47.2	19.22	19.08
MV 6	74.2	22.59	18.30
MV 7	119.1	26.44	15.64
MV 8	209.1	30.83	14.24
MV 9	434.6	34.43	13.00
MV 10	1,102.6	44.94	9.47

[a]MV = Market value.

Source: Marc R. Reinganum, "Portfolio Strategies Based on Market Capitalization," *Journal of Portfolio Management*, Winter 1983, pp. 29–36.

P/E ratios, they compensated for other factors that may have resulted in superior returns, such as the small size of the firm, the infrequent trading of stock, and the overall performance of an industry. They did this by using firms that had a market capitalization of at least $100 million, that had an active monthly trading volume of at least 250,000 shares, and that were in the same industry. Thus, none of these factors was allowed to be an intervening variable in the relationship between returns and the level of P/E ratios.

After following these parameters, Peavy and Goodman showed a significant relationship between the firm's P/E ratios and risk-adjusted returns. Firms were broken down into quintiles based on the size of their P/E ratios. Quintile 1 contained firms with the lowest P/E ratios, quintile 2 had the next lowest P/E ratios, and so on up the scale. A portion of their results is presented in Table 10–5.

Note that lower P/E stocks have higher risk-adjusted returns. While Table 10–5 shows data only for the electronics industry, a similar pattern was found for other industries.

In summarizing this section, some researchers such as Banz and Reinganum argue that small size is the primary variable leading to superior returns, while others argue that it is the low-P/E-ratio effect.

THE LATEST THEORY— THE BOOK VALUE TO MARKET VALUE EFFECT

Just to make sure that finance professors and their students do not sleep too soundly at night, we have yet another theory to explain why certain stocks out-

TABLE 10–5 P/E Ratios and Performance: The Electronics Industry (1970–1980)

Quintile	Average P/E	Average Quarterly Return (Risk-adjusted)	Average Beta
1	7.1	8.53	1.15
2	10.3	4.71	1.12
3	13.4	4.34	1.13
4	17.4	2.53	1.19
5	25.5	1.86	1.29

Source: John W. Peavy III and David A. Goodman, "The Significance of P/Es for Portfolio Returns," *Journal of Portfolio Management*, Winter 1983, pp. 43–47.

perform the market. Professors Fama and French maintain that the ratio of book value to market value and size are more important than P/E ratios, leverage, or other variables in explaining stock market performance. Since we've already discussed size, let's concentrate on book value to market value. The Fama-French study says that the higher the ratio of book value to market value (lower the ratio of market value to book value) the higher the potential return on the stock.[38]

This conclusion is somewhat surprising to students who have been taught that book value, which is based on historical cost rather than current replacement value, is not an important variable. The newer logic is that stocks that have a book value that approaches market value are more likely to be undervalued than stocks that have book values that are perhaps only 20 percent of market value. The latter figure implies that the stock is trading at five times its book value (or net worth) as shown on the corporate books:

$$\frac{\text{Book value}}{\text{Market value}} \quad \frac{\text{Market value}}{\text{Book value}}$$
$$0.20 = 5\times$$

The high ratio of 5× means the company may be due for a correction as opposed to a stock that is trading at very close to book value.

With this third theory in mind, the investor may wish to keep his or her eye on stocks that meet some or all of the attributes previously discussed, that is, small size, low P/E ratios, and a high book-to-market value ratio.

38. Eugene F. Fama and Kenneth R. French, "The Cross Section of Stock Returns," *Journal of Finance*, June 1992, pp. 427–65. The Fama and French study dealt with nonfinancial firms. A similar study with financial firms produced the same type of results. See Brad M. Barber and John D. Lyon, "Firm Size, Book-to-Market Ratio, and Security Returns: A Holdout Sample of Financial Firms," *Journal of Finance*, June 1997, pp. 875–83.

OTHER STOCK-RELATED SPECIAL SITUATIONS

Although the authors have attempted to highlight the major special situations related to stocks in the preceding pages, there are other opportunities as well. While only brief mention will be made in this section, the student may choose to follow up the footnoted references for additional information.

The January Effect Because stockholders may sell off their losers in late December to establish tax losses, these stocks are often depressed in value in early January and may represent bargains and an opportunity for high returns.[39] In fact, the January effect and the potential for high returns has attracted so much attention that it often is used as a variable to explain other phenomena as well as itself. For example, Keim has found that roughly half the small-firm effect for the year occurs in January.[40] Actually, as more and more investors begin anticipating and playing the January effect, it has moved up in time (everyone wants to be the first one to arrive). Part of the January effect may be viewed in December now.

The Weekend Effect Research evidence indicates that stocks tend to peak in value on Friday and generally decline in value on Monday. Thus, the theory is that the time to buy is on late Monday and the time to sell is on late Friday. While over many decades this observation is valid,[41] generally the price movement is too small to profitably cover transaction costs. However, if you *know* you are going to sell a stock that you have held for a long time, you may prefer to do so later in the week rather than early in the week.

The Value Line Ranking Effect The *Value Line Investment Survey* contains information on approximately 1,700 stocks. Using a valuation model, each company is rated from 1 through 5 for profitable market performance over the next 12 months. One is the highest possible rating, and 5 is the lowest. One hundred stocks are always in category 1. Researchers have generally indicated that category 1 stocks provide superior risk-adjusted returns over the other four categories and the market in general.[42] Of course, frequent trading may rapidly cut into these profits. Table 10-6 presents the strong performance of the Value Line group 1 category compared with the other four categories.

---

39. Ben Branch and J. Ryan, "Tax-Loss Trading: An Inefficiency Too Large to Ignore," *Financial Review*, Winter 1980, pp. 20–29.

40. Donald B. Keim, "Size-Related Anomalies and Stock Return Seasonality," *Journal of Financial Economics*, March 1983, pp. 13–32. Also see Richard Roll, "Vas ist das? The Turn of the Year Effect and the Return Premium of Small Firms," *Journal of Portfolio Management*, Winter 1983, pp. 18–28.

41. Frank Cross, "The Behavior of Stock Prices on Fridays and Mondays," *Financial Analysts Journal*, November–December 1973, pp. 67–69; Kenneth R. French, "Stock Returns and the Weekend Effect," *Journal of Financial Economics*, March 1980, pp. 55–69; and Lawrence Harris, "A Transaction Data Study of Weekly and Interdaily Patterns in Stock Returns," *Journal of Financial Economics*, May 1986, pp. 99–117.

42. Fisher Black, "*Yes*, Virginia, There Is Hope: Test of the Value Line Ranking System," *Financial Analysts Journal*, September–October 1973, pp. 10–14; Clark Holloway, "A Note on Testing an Aggressive Strategy Using Value Line Ranks," *Journal of Finance*, June 1981, pp. 711–19; and Scott E. Stickel, "The Effect of *Value Line Investment Survey* Rank Changes on Common Stock Prices," *Journal of Financial Economics*, March 1985, pp. 121–43.

TABLE 10–6 Performance of Value Line Groups

Record of Value Line Rankings for Timeliness (allowing for changes in rank each week)

April 16, 1965 to December 31, 2001

Group	'65	'66	'67	'68	'69	'70	'71	'72	'73	'74
1	28.8%	−5.5%	53.4%	37.1%	−10.4%	7.3%	30.6%	12.6%	−19.1%	−11.1%
2	18.5	−6.2	36.1	26.9	−17.5	−3.2	13.7	7.4	−28.9	−29.5
3	6.7	−13.9	27.1	24.0	−23.8	−8.0	9.3	3.5	−33.6	−34.1
4	−0.4	−15.7	23.8	20.9	−33.3	−16.3	8.4	−7.1	−37.9	−40.6
5	−3.2	−18.2	21.5	11.8	−44.9	−23.3	−5.5	−13.4	−43.8	−55.7
Group	**'84**	**'85**	**'86**	**'87**	**'88**	**'89**	**'90**	**'91**	**'92**	**'93**
1	−2.1%	47.0%	22.9%	5.4%	9.5%	27.9%	−10.4%	55.4%	10.0%	13.4%
2	−0.8	30.7	14.4	−2.4	20.4	26.5	−10.2	34.1	14.3	12.4
3	−5.6	22.8	7.7	−12.6	16.1	13.7	−24.4	18.9	11.0	9.8
4	−17.4	11.4	−6.8	−15.8	17.6	2.6	−33.7	16.7	6.2	8.5
5	−31.0	−5.6	−19.6	−28.0	11.4	−19.2	−45.5	25.5	15.4	0.3

The Surprise-Earnings Effect As indicated in Chapter 9 in the discussion of efficient markets, accounting information tends to be quickly impounded in the value of a stock, and there appears to be little opportunity to garner superior returns from this data. Even if a firm reports a 20 percent increase in earnings, there is likely to be little market reaction to the announcement if the gain was generally anticipated. However, an exception to this rule may relate to truly *unexpected* earnings announcements.[43] If they are very positive, the stock may go up for a number of days after the announcement and thus provide a superior investment opportunity. The opposite would be true of a totally unexpected negative announcement.

The latter factor was particularly evident in the momentum market of the mid- to late 1990s. Stock that had superior market performance, such as Microsoft, Intel, and Hewlett-Packard, were expected to produce ever-increasing earnings to justify their high valuation. If they did not, the punishment was swift and strong. For example, when Intel announced that its earnings would be below predictions for the second quarter of 1997, its stock dropped 25 points in the first hour of trading.

TRULY SUPERIOR RETURNS OR MISMEASUREMENT?

In our discussion in the previous chapter and in this chapter, we pointed out the possibility that high returns may be the result of a superior strategy in a less than efficient capital market. It also may be the result of mismeasurement thus showing that you got a superior risk-adjusted return when you did not. You simply misspecified the extent of the risk (beta) component or used the wrong model. If all

43. Richard Rendleman, Charles Jones, and Henry A. Latane, "Empirical Anomalies Based on Unexpected Earnings and the Importance of Risk Adjustments," *Journal of Financial Economics,* November 1982, pp. 269–87.

TABLE 10–6 Performance of Value Line Groups *(concluded)*

Record of Value Line Rankings for Timeliness (allowing for changes in rank each week)

April 16, 1965 to December 31, 2001								
'75	'76	'77	'78	'79	'80	'81	'82	'83
75.6%	54.0%	26.6%	32.6%	54.7%	52.6%	13.6%	50.6%	40.9%
47.4	31.2	13.4	18.3	38.0	35.6	1.8	31.0	19.1
40.7	29.0	1.3	3.0	20.7	15.4	−3.3	17.9	20.2
39.3	28.8	−6.9	−3.8	12.8	7.4	−8.7	5.1	25.0
−40.9	26.7	−17.6	−3.2	10.4	2.9	−21.4	−10.9	19.0
'94	'95	'96	'97	'98	'99	'00	'01	Cumulative
−2.6%	22.8%	20.4%	11.3%	8.2%	24.1%	10.4%	−20.3%	46,862%
−2.2	28.1	19.0	24.0	0.1	−0.5	−4.4	−3.8	4,084
−6.9	16.6	12.3	21.5	−3.9	−3.3	−3.2	−0.8	281
−9.9	17.1	7.1	14.5	−11.0	−7.5	−3.7	5.9	−49
−15.2	5.2	7.5	16.6	−11.5	−1.3	−19.7	−7.2	−98

Source: *Value Line Selection and Opinion,* January 24, 2002. Reproduced with the permission of Value Line Publishing, Inc.

risk-adjusted superior return studies were the result of misspecification, we could then once again assume the market is perfectly efficient.

The predominant view is that while there is some mismeasurement, many opportunities truly reflect market inefficiencies. There are "special situations" that if properly analyzed provide an opportunity for abnormally high risk-adjusted returns. The most literal and unbending interpretations of efficient markets no longer carry the weight they did two decades ago.[44]

Internet Resources

Website Address	Comments
www.ipo.com	Provides initial public offering information
www.redherring.com	Provides free information on public offerings and links to related sites
www.thehfa.com	Website for the Hedge Fund Association providing information about the industry
www.hedgefundcenter.com	Education site on hedge funds

44. Eugene F. Fama, "Efficient Capital Markets: II," *Journal of Finance,* December 1991, pp. 1575–1617.

Chapter 11

Bond and Fixed-Income Fundamentals

As the reader will observe in various sections of this chapter, bonds actually represent a more substantial portion of new offerings in the capital markets than common stock. Some of the most financially rewarding jobs on Wall Street go to sophisticated analysts and dealers in the bond market.

In this chapter, we examine the fundamentals of the bond instrument for both corporate and government issuers, with an emphasis on the debt contract and security provisions. We also look at the overall structure of the bond market and the ways in which bonds are rated. The question of bond market efficiency is also considered. While most of the chapter deals with corporate and government bonds, other forms of fixed-income securities also receive attention. Thus, there is a brief discussion of short-term, fixed-income investments (such as certificates of deposit and commercial paper) as well as preferred stock.

In Chapter 12, we shift the emphasis to actually evaluating fixed-income investments and devising strategies that attempt to capture profitable opportunities in the market. In Chapter 13, we look at the interesting concept of *duration.* We begin our discussion by considering the key elements that go into a bond contract.

THE BOND CONTRACT

A bond normally represents a long-term contractual obligation of the firm to pay interest to the bondholder as well as the face value of the bond at maturity. The major provisions in a bond agreement are spelled out in the bond indenture, a complicated legal document often more than 100 pages long, administered by an independent trustee (usually a commercial bank). We shall examine some important terms and concepts associated with a bond issue.

The par value represents the face value of a bond. Most corporate bonds are traded in \$1,000 units, while many federal, state, and local issues trade in units of \$5,000 or \$10,000.

Coupon rate refers to the actual interest rate on the bond, usually payable in semiannual installments. To the extent that interest rates in the market go above or below the coupon rate after the bond is issued, the market price of the bond will change from the par value. A bond initially issued at a rate of 8 percent will sell at a substantial discount from par value when 12 percent is the currently demanded rate of return. We will eventually examine how the investor makes and loses large amounts of money in the bond market with the swings in interest rates. A few corporate bonds are termed variable-rate notes or floating-rate notes, meaning the coupon rate is fixed for only a short period and then varies with a stipulated short-term rate such as the rate on U.S. Treasury bills. In this instance, the interest payment rather than the price of the bond varies up and down. In recent times, zero-coupon bonds have also been issued at values substantially below maturity value. With zero-coupon bonds, the investor receives return in the form of capital appreciation over the life of the bond since no semiannual cash interest payments are received.

The maturity date is the date on which final payment is due at the stipulated par value.

Methods of bond repayment can occur under many different arrangements. Some bonds are never paid off, such as selected perpetual bonds issued by the Canadian and British governments, and have no maturity dates. A more normal procedure would simply call for a single-sum lump payment at the end of the obligation. Thus, the issuer may make 40 semiannual interest payments over the next 20 years plus one lump-sum payment of the par value of the bond at maturity. There are also other significant means of repayment.

The first is the serial payment in which bonds are paid off in installments over the life of the issue. Each serial bond has its own predetermined date of maturity and receives interest only to that point. Although the total bond issue may span more than 20 years, 15 to 20 maturity dates are assigned. Municipal bonds are often issued on this basis. Second, there may be a sinking-fund provision in which semiannual or annual contributions are made by a corporation into a fund administered by a trustee for purposes of debt retirement. The trustee takes the proceeds and goes into the market to purchase bonds from willing sellers. If no sellers are available, a lottery system may be used to repurchase the required number of bonds from among outstanding bondholders.

Third, debt may also be retired under a call provision. A call provision allows the corporation to call or force in all of the debt issue prior to maturity. The corporation usually pays a 3 to 5 percent premium over par value as part of the call provision arrangement. The ability to call is often *deferred* for the first 5 or 10 years of an issue (it can only occur after this time period).

The opposite side of the coin for a bond investor is a put provision. The put provision enables the bondholder to have an option to sell a long-term bond back to the corporation at par value after a relatively short period (such as three to five years). This privilege can be particularly valuable if interest rates have gone up since the initial issuance and if the bond is currently trading at 75 to 80 percent of par. A put bond generally carries a lower interest rate than conventional bonds (perhaps 1 to 2 percent lower) because of this protective put privilege. If one buys a put bond and interest rates go down and bond prices up (perhaps to $1,200), the privilege is unnecessary and is merely ignored.

SECURED AND UNSECURED BONDS

We have discussed some of the important features related to interest payments and retirement of outstanding issues. At least of equal importance is the nature of the security provision for the issue. Bond market participants have a long-standing practice of describing certain issues by the nature of asset claims in liquidation. In actuality, pledged assets are sold and the proceeds distributed to bondholders only infrequently. Typically, the defaulting corporation is reorganized, and existing claims are partially satisfied by issuing new securities to the participating parties. Of course, the stronger and *better secured* the initial claim, the higher the quality of the security to be received in a reorganization.

A number of terms are used to denote secured debt, that is, debt backed by collateral. Under a mortgage agreement, real property (plant and equipment) is pledged as security for a loan. A mortgage may be senior or junior in nature, with the former requiring satisfaction of claims before payment is given to the latter. Bondholders may also attach an after-acquired property clause requiring that any new property be placed under the original mortgage.

A very special form of a mortgage or collateralized debt instrument is the equipment trust certificate used by firms in the transportation industry (railroads, airlines, etc.). Proceeds from the sale of the certificate are used to purchase new equipment, and this new equipment serves as collateral for the trust certificate.

Not all bond issues are secured or collateralized by assets. Most federal, state, and local government issues are unsecured. A wide range of corporate issues also are unsecured. There is a set of terminology referring to these unsecured issues. A corporate debt issue that is unsecured is referred to as a debenture. Even though the debenture is not secured by a specific pledge of assets, there may be priorities of claims among debenture holders. Thus, there are senior debentures and junior or subordinated debentures.

If liquidation becomes necessary because all other avenues for survival have failed, secured creditors are paid off first out of the disposition of the secured assets. The proceeds from the sale of the balance of the assets are then distributed among unsecured creditors, with those holding a senior ranking being satisfied before those holding a subordinate position (subordinated debenture holders).[1]

Unsecured corporate debt may provide slightly higher yields because of the greater suggested risk. However, this is partially offset by the fact that many unsecured debt issuers have such strong financial statements that security pledges may not be necessary.

---

1. Those secured creditors who are not fully satisfied by the disposition of secured assets may also participate with the unsecured creditors in the remaining assets.

Companies with less favorable prospects may issue income bonds. Income bonds specify that interest is to be paid only to the extent that it is earned as current income. There is no legally binding requirement to pay interest on a regular basis, and failure to make interest payments cannot trigger bankruptcy proceedings. These issues appear to offer the corporation the unusual advantage of paying interest as a tax-deductible expense (as opposed to dividends) combined with freedom from the binding contractual obligation of most debt issues. But any initial enthusiasm for these issues is quickly reduced by recognizing that they have very limited appeal to investors. The issuance of income bonds is usually restricted to circumstances where new corporate debt is issued to old bondholders or preferred stockholders to avoid bankruptcy or where a troubled corporation is being reorganized.

THE COMPOSITION OF THE BOND MARKET

Having established some of the basic terminology relating to the bond instrument, we are now in a position to take a more comprehensive look at the bond market. Corporate issues must vie with offerings from the U.S. Treasury, federally sponsored credit agencies, and state and local governments (municipal offerings). The relative importance of the four types of issues is indicated in Figure 11-1.

Over the 20-year period presented in Figure 11-1, the two fastest growing users of funds (borrowers) were the U.S. government and corporations. The former's needs can be attributed to persistent federal deficits that must be financed by increased borrowing. It should also be pointed out that as the government began running surpluses in the late 1990s to early 2000s, the need for such financing diminished.

In the case of corporations, strong growth combined with the need to finance mergers and leveraged buyouts has led to increased borrowing requirements. State and local governments have been active participants with municipal bond issues used to finance local growth and cover local deficits. Finally, federally sponsored credit agencies must call on the long-term funds market. Please observe the explosive growth in long-term borrowing by all sectors of the economy since 1980.

U.S. Government Securities

U.S. government securities take the form of Treasury bills, Treasury notes, and Treasury bonds (only the latter two are considered in Figure 11-1). The distinction among the three categories relates to the life of the obligation. A fourth category, termed Treasury strips, has other attributes and is also discussed.

Treasury bills (T-bills) have maturities of 91 and 182 days. Treasury bills trade on a discount basis, meaning the yield the investor receives occurs as a result of the difference between the price paid and the maturity value (and no actual interest is paid). A further discussion of this is presented later in the chapter.

Treasury bills trade in minimum units of $1,000, and there is an extremely active secondary, or resale, market for these securities. Thus, an investor buying a

FIGURE 11–1 Long-Term Funds Raised by Business and Government

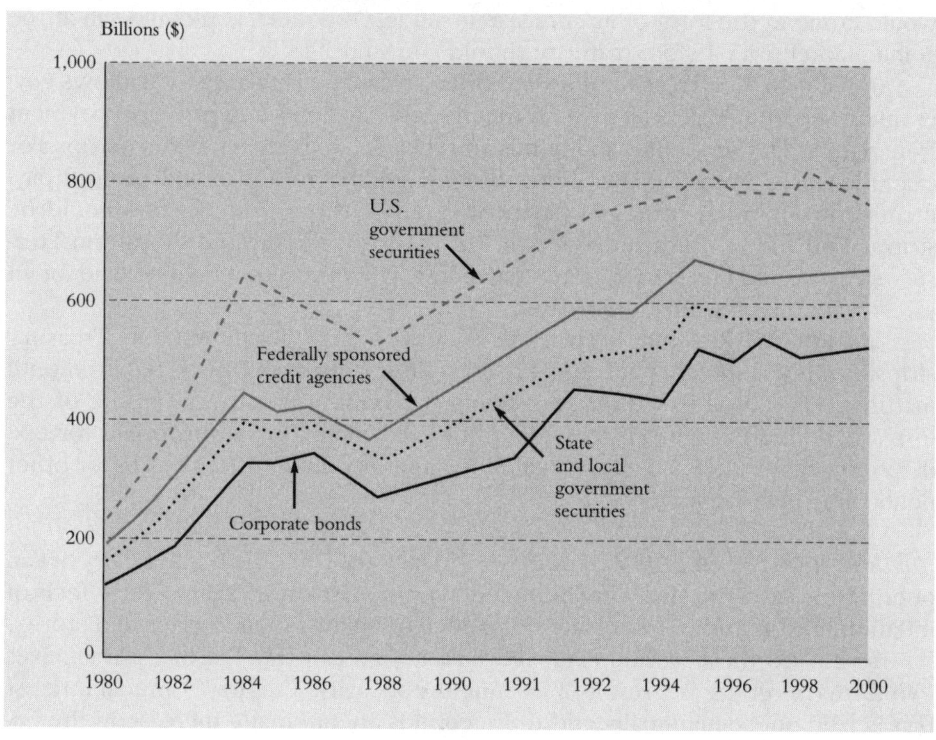

Treasury bill from the government with an initial life of approximately six months would have no difficulty selling it to another investor after two or three weeks. Because the T-bill now has a shorter time to run, its market value would be a bit closer to par.

A second type of U.S. government security is the Treasury note, which is considered to be of intermediate term and generally has a maturity of 1 to 10 years. Finally, Treasury bonds are long term in nature and mature in 10 to 30 years. Unlike Treasury bills, Treasury notes and bonds provide direct interest and trade in units of $1,000 and higher. Because there is no risk of default (unless the government stops printing money or the ultimate bomb explodes), U.S. government securities provide lower returns than other forms of credit obligations. Interest on U.S. government issues is fully taxable for IRS purposes but is exempt from state and local taxes.

Treasury securities may also trade in the form of Treasury strips (strip-Ts). Treasury strips pay no interest, and all returns to the investor come in the form of increases in the value of the investment (as is true of Treasury bills also). Treasury strips are referred to as zero-coupon securities because of the absence of interest payments.

As an example, 25-year Treasury strips might initially sell for 19 percent of par value. You could buy a 25-year, $10,000 Treasury strip for $1,900.[2] All your return would come in the form of an increase in value. Of course, you could sell at the going market price before maturity should you so desire.

Actually the U.S. Treasury does not offer Treasury strips directly. It allows government security dealers to strip off the interest payments and principal payment from regular Treasury notes and bonds and repackage them as Treasury strips. For example, on a 25-year Treasury bond, there would be 50 semiannual interest payments and one final principal payment. Each of these 51 payments could be stripped off and sold as a zero-coupon strip.[3] Those who desired short-term Treasury strips would buy into the early payments. The opposite would be true for an investor with a long-term orientation.

The Internal Revenue Service taxes zero-coupon bonds, such as Treasury strips, as if interest were paid annually even though no cash flow is received until maturity. The tax is based on amortizing the built-in gain over the life of the instrument. For tax reasons, zero coupons are usually only appropriate for tax-deferred accounts such as individual retirement accounts, 401(k) plans, or other nontaxable pension funds.

Inflation-Indexed Treasury Securities In January 1997, the U.S. Treasury began offering 10-year notes that were intended to protect investors against the effects of inflation. The maturities were later expanded to include longer terms to maturity.

Here's how these inflation-indexed Treasury notes work. The investor receives two forms of return as a result of owning the security. The first is annual interest that is paid out semiannually, and the second is an automatic increase in the initial value of principal to account for inflation.

These securities are formally called Treasury Inflation Protection Securities (TIPS). TIPS might pay 3.5 percent in annual interest and, assuming a 3 percent rate of inflation, an additional 3 percent to compensate for inflation. As implied in the preceding paragraph, the 3 percent inflation adjustment is not paid in cash but is added on to the principal value of the bond. Assume the bond had an initial par value of $1,000. At the end of the first year, the principal value would go up to $1,030. Thus, during the first year, the investor would receive $35 (3.5 percent) in cash as interest payments, plus enjoy a $30 increase in principal. On a 10-year indexed Treasury security, this procedure continues for each of the remaining nine years and at maturity, the security is redeemed at the indexed value of the principal by the Treasury. If the investor needs to sell before the maturity date, he or she can sell it in the secondary market to other investors at a value approximating the appreciated principal value.[4]

2. The yield is approximately 6¾ percent. Zero-coupon securities are also offered by corporations and are discussed more fully in Chapter 13.

3. Any one payment, such as the first, may be stripped from many hundreds of Treasury bonds at one time to provide a $10,000 Treasury strip.

4. Other factors can come into play in pricing this security, but they unnecessarily complicate this basic example.

The reader should be aware that the base against which the 3.5 percent annual interest is paid is the inflation-adjusted value of the security. Thus, in the second year, the interest payment would be $36.05 (3.5% × $1,030). In each subsequent year, there is a similar adjustment depending on the prior year's rate of inflation.

Assuming inflation remains at 3 percent over the 10-year time period, the inflation-adjusted value of the principal will increase to $1,344 (10 periods compounded at 3 percent). The investor is effectively getting a return of 6.5 percent in the form of interest and appreciation of principal. Of course, if inflation averages 6 percent over the life of the investment, the investor will get a return of 9.5 percent. The interest payment (real return) will remain at 3.5 percent, but the inflation adjustment will supply the extra return.

Through inflation-indexed Treasury notes, the investor is protected against the effect of inflation. This may be quite a benefit if inflation is high, but the security can provide an inferior return compared with other investments in a low-inflation environment.

Also, the investor should be aware that the annual adjustment in principal is treated as taxable income each year even though no cash is received until redemption at maturity. For this reason, inflation-indexed Treasury securities are more appropriate for tax-deferred or nontaxable accounts.

Federally Sponsored Credit Agency Issues

Referring back to Figure 11-1, the second category represents securities issued by federal agencies. The issues represent obligations of various agencies of the government such as the Federal National Mortgage Association and the Federal Home Loan Bank. Although these issues are authorized by an act of Congress and are used to finance federal projects, they are not direct obligations of the Treasury but rather of the agency itself.

Although the issues are essentially free of risk (there is always the implicit standby power of the government behind the issues), they carry a slightly higher yield than U.S. government securities simply because they are not directly issued by the Treasury. Agency issues have been particularly active as a support mechanism for the housing industry. The issues generally trade in denominations of $5,000 and up and have varying maturities of from 1 to 40 years, with an average life of approximately 15 years. Examples of some agency issues are presented below:

	Minimum Denomination	Life of Issue
Federal Home Loan Bank	$10,000	12–25 years
Federal Intermediate Credit Banks	5,000	Up to 4 years
Federal Farm Credit Bank	50,000	1–10 years
Export-Import Bank	5,000	Up to 7 years

Interest on agency issues is fully taxable for IRS purposes and is generally taxable for state and local purposes although there are exceptions. (For example, interest on obligations issued by the Federal Farm Credit Bank are subject to state and local taxes, but those of the Federal Home Loan Bank are not.)

One agency issue that is of particular interest to the investor because of its unique features is the GNMA (Ginnie Mae) pass-through certificate. These certificates represent an undivided interest in a pool of federally insured mortgages. Actually, GNMA, the Government National Mortgage Association, buys a pool of mortgages from various lenders at a discount and then issues securities to the public against these mortgages. Security holders in GNMA certificates receive monthly payments that essentially represent a pass through of interest and principal payments on the mortgages. These securities come in minimum denominations of $25,000, are long term, and are fully taxable for federal, state, and local income tax purposes. A major consideration in this investment is that the investor has fully consumed his or her capital at the end of the investment. (Not only has interest been received monthly but also all principal has been returned over the life of the certificate, and therefore, there is no lump-sum payment at maturity.)

Because mortgages that are part of GNMA pass-through certificates are often paid off early as a result of the sale of a home or refinancing at lower interest rates, the true life of a GNMA certificate tends to be much less than the quoted life. For example, a 25-year GNMA certificate may actually be paid off in 12 years. This feature can be a negative consideration because GNMA certificates are particularly likely to be paid off early when interest rates are going down and homeowners are refinancing. The investor in the GNMA certificate is then forced to reinvest the proceeds in a low interest rate environment.

State and Local Government Securities

Debt securities issued by state and local governments are referred to as municipal bonds. Examples of issuing agencies include states, cities, school districts, toll roads, or any other type of political subdivision. The most important feature of a municipal bond is the tax-exempt nature of the interest payment. Dating back to the U.S. Supreme Court opinion of 1819 in *McCullough v. Maryland,* it was ruled that the federal government and state and local governments do not possess the power to tax each other. An eventual by-product of the judicial ruling was that income from municipal bonds cannot be taxed by the IRS. Furthermore, income from municipal bonds is also exempt from state and local taxes if bought within the locality in which one resides. Thus, a Californian buying municipal bonds in that state would pay no state income tax on the issue. However, the same Californian would have to pay state or local income taxes if the originating agency were in Texas or New York.

We cannot overemphasize the importance of the federal tax exemption that municipal bonds enjoy. The consequences are twofold. First, individuals in high tax brackets may find highly attractive investment opportunities in municipal bonds.[5] The formula used to equate interest on municipal bonds to other taxable investments is:

$$Y = \frac{i}{(1 - T)} \tag{11-1}$$

where:

Y = Equivalent before-tax yield on a taxable investment
i = Yield on the municipal obligation
T = Marginal tax rate of the investor

If an investor has a marginal tax rate of 35 percent and is evaluating a municipal bond paying 6 percent interest, the equivalent before-tax yield on a taxable investment would be:

$$\frac{6\%}{(1 - 0.35)} = \frac{6\%}{0.65} = 9.23\%$$

Thus, the investor could choose between a *non*-tax-exempt investment paying 9.23 percent and a tax-exempt municipal bond paying 6 percent and be indifferent between the two. Table 11-1 presents examples of trade-offs between tax-exempt and non-tax-exempt (taxable) investments at various interest rates and marginal tax rates. Clearly, the higher the marginal tax rate, the greater the advantage of tax-exempt municipal bonds.

A second significant feature of municipal bonds is that the yield the issuing agency pays on municipal bonds is lower than the yield on taxable instruments. Of course, a municipal bond paying 6 percent may be quite competitive with taxable instruments paying more. Average differentials are presented in Table 11-2. You should notice in Table 11-2 that the yield differences between municipal bonds and corporate bonds were normally 2 to 4 percentage points. A major distinction that is also important to the bond issuer and investor is whether the bond is of a general obligation or revenue nature.

General Obligation versus Revenue Bonds A general obligation issue is backed by the full faith, credit, and "taxing power" of the governmental unit. For a revenue bond, on the other hand, the repayment of the issue is fully dependent on the revenue-generating capability of a specific project or venture, such as a toll road, bridge, or municipal colosseum.

Because of the taxing power behind most general obligation (GO) issues, they tend to be of extremely high quality. Approximately three-fourths of all municipal bond issues are of the general obligation variety, and very few failures have

5. It should be noted that any capital gain on a municipal bond is taxable as would be the case with any investment.

TABLE 11–1 Marginal Tax Rates and Return Equivalents

Yield on Municipal	27% Bracket	35% Bracket	38.6% Bracket
5%	6.85%	7.69%	8.14%
6	8.22	9.23	9.77
7	9.59	10.77	11.40
8	10.96	12.31	13.03
9	12.32	13.85	14.66
10	13.70	15.38	16.28

occurred in the post–World War II era. Revenue bonds tend to be of more uneven quality, and the economic soundness of the underlying revenue-generating project must be carefully examined (though most projects are quite worthwhile).

Municipal Bond Guarantee A growing factor in the municipal bond market is the third-party guarantee. Whether dealing with a general obligation or revenue bond, a fee may be paid by the originating governmental body to a third-party insurer to guarantee that all interest and principal payments will be made. There are four private insurance firms that guarantee municipal bonds, the largest of which are the Municipal Bond Investors Assurance (MBIA) and the American Municipal Bond Assurance Corporation (AMBAC). Municipal bonds that are guaranteed carry the highest rating possible (AAA) because all the guaranteeing insurance companies are rated AAA. Approximately 30 percent of municipal bond issues are guaranteed.

A municipal bond that is guaranteed will carry a lower yield and have a better secondary or resale market. This may be important because municipal bonds, in general, do not provide as strong a secondary market as U.S. government issues. The market for a given municipal issue is often small and fragmented, and high indirect costs are associated with reselling the issue.

Corporate Securities

Corporate bonds are the dominant source of new financing for corporations in the United States.

Bonds normally supply 80 to 85 percent of firms' external financial needs. Even during the great bull stock market of the 1990s, corporations looked as heavily as ever to the debt markets to provide financing (this was justified by the decreasing interest rates during this period).

The corporate market may be divided into a number of subunits, including *industrials, public utilities, rails and transportation,* and *financial issues* (banks, finance companies, etc.). The industrials are a catchall category that includes everything from high-technology companies to discount chain stores. Public utilities represent the largest segment of the market and have issues that run up to 40 years

TABLE 11–2 Comparable Yields on Long-Term Municipals and Taxable Corporates (Yearly Averages)

Year	Municipals Aa	Corporates Aa	Yield Difference
2001	5.80%	7.14%	1.34%
2000	6.01	7.80	1.79
1999	5.48	7.36	1.88
1998	5.13	6.80	1.67
1997	5.52	7.48	1.96
1996	5.90	7.72	1.82
1995	5.60	7.55	1.95
1994	6.40	8.60	2.20
1993	5.51	7.40	1.89
1992	6.30	8.46	2.16
1991	6.80	9.09	2.29
1990	7.15	9.56	2.41
1989	7.51	9.46	1.95
1988	8.38	9.66	1.28
1987	8.50	9.68	1.18
1986	7.35	9.47	2.12
1985	8.81	11.82	3.01
1984	9.95	12.25	2.30
1983	9.20	12.42	3.22
1982	11.39	14.41	3.02
1981	10.89	14.75	3.86
1980	8.06	12.50	4.44
1979	6.12	9.94	3.82
1978	5.68	8.92	3.24
1977	5.39	8.24	2.85
1976	6.12	8.75	2.63

Source: *Moody's Municipal & Government Manual, Moody's Industrial Manual,* and *Mergent Bond Record* (published by Mergent, Inc., New York, NY), selected issues.

in maturity. Because public utilities are in constant need of funds to meet ever-expanding requirements for power generation, telephone services, and other essential services, they are always in the bond market to raise new funds. The needs associated with rails and transportation as well as financial issues tend to be less than those associated with public utilities or industrials. Table 11-3 shows comparative yields for the two main categories.[6]

The higher yields on public utility issues represent a supply-demand phenomenon more than anything else. A constant stream of new issues to the market can only be absorbed by a higher yield pattern. In other cases, the higher required

6. Financial and transportation issues are generally not broken out of the published data.

TABLE 11–3 Comparative Yields on Aa Bonds among Corporate Issuers

Year	Industrial	Public Utility
2001	7.14%	7.89%
2000	7.80	8.05
1999	7.36	7.92
1998	6.80	7.12
1997	7.48	8.00
1996	7.55	7.70
1995	7.72	7.84
1994	8.41	8.74
1993	7.05	7.19
1992	8.24	8.65
1991	9.01	9.25
1990	9.41	9.65
1989	9.35	9.55
1988	9.41	10.20
1987	9.73	9.83
1986	9.49	9.44
1985	11.57	12.02
1984	12.39	13.02
1983	11.94	12.74
1982	15.01	16.48
1981	13.01	14.03
1980	11.16	11.95
1979	9.24	9.70
1978	8.42	8.76
1977	7.90	8.41
1976	8.87	9.39

Source: *Mergent Bond Record* (published by Mergent, Inc., New York, NY), selected issues.

return may also be associated with quality deterioration as measured by profitability and interest coverage. During 1983–84, the default of the Washington State Power Authority on bonds issued to construct power-generating facilities sent waves through the bond market. Again in 1984, when Public Service of Indiana canceled construction of a partially complete nuclear power plant, nuclear utility issues (both stocks and bonds) suffered severe price erosion, and the bond market demanded high risk premiums on bonds of almost all nuclear utilities. In 2001, the public utility bond market was once again "spooked" by the energy crisis and blackouts in northern California.

Corporate bonds of all types generally trade in units of $1,000, and this is a particularly attractive feature to the smaller investor who does not wish to purchase in units of $5,000 to $10,000 (which is necessary for many Treasury and federally sponsored credit agency issues). Because of higher risk relative to government issues, the investor will generally receive higher yields on corporates as well. All income from corporates is taxable for federal, state, and local purposes. Finally, corporate issues have the disadvantage of being subject to calls. When buying a bond during a period of high interest rates, the call provision must be considered a negative feature because the high-yielding bonds may be called in for early retirement as interest rates go down.

BOND MARKET INVESTORS

Having considered the issuer or supply side of the market, we now comment on the investor or demand side. The bond market is dominated by large institutional investors (insurance companies, banks, pension funds, mutual funds) even more than the stock market. Institutional investors account for 80 to 85 percent of the trading in key segments of the bond market. However, the presence of the individual investor is partially felt in the corporate and municipal bond market where the incentives of low denomination ($1,000) corporate bonds or tax-free municipal bonds have some attraction. Furthermore, in the last decade individual investors have made their presence felt in the bond market through buying mutual funds that specialize in bond portfolios. The activities of individuals in mutual funds were covered in detail in Chapter 2, so for now we concentrate on institutional investors.

Institutional investors' preferences for various sectors of the bond market are influenced by their tax status as well as by the nature of their obligations or liabilities to depositors, investors, or clients. For example, banks traditionally have been strong participants in the municipal bond market because of their substantial tax obligations. Their investments tend to be in short- to intermediate-term assets because of the short-term nature of their deposit obligations (the funds supplied to the banks). One problem that banks find in their bond portfolios is that such investments are often preferred over loans to customers when the economy is weak and loan demand is sluggish. Not so coincidentally, this happens to be the time period when interest rates are low. When the economy improves, interest rates go up, and so does loan demand. To meet the loan demand of valued customers, banks liquidate portions of their bond portfolios. The problem with this recurring process is that banks are buying bonds when interest rates are *low* and selling them when interest rates are *high*. This can cause losses in the value of the bank portfolio.

The bond investor must be prepared to deal in a relatively strong primary market (new issues market) and a relatively weak secondary market (resale market). While the secondary market is active for many types of Treasury and agency issues, such is not the case for corporate and municipal issues. Thus, the investor must look well beyond the yield, maturity, and rating to determine if a purchase is acceptable. The question that must be considered is: How close to the going market price can I dispose of the issue if that should be necessary? If a 5 or 10 percent discount is involved, that might be unacceptable. Unlike the stock market, the secondary market in bonds tends to be dominated by over-the-counter transactions (although listed bonds are traded as well).

A significant development in the last decade has been the heavy participation of foreign investors in U.S. bond markets. Foreign investors now bankroll between 10 to 15 percent of the U.S. government's debt. While these investors have helped to finance the U.S. government's deficits, they can be a disruptive factor in the market when they decide to partially withdraw their funds. This happened in the mid-1990s when the declining value of the dollar and fear of inflation in the United States caused many foreign investors to temporarily cash in their investments. Because the U.S. government fears the flight of funds provided by foreign investors, it is sensitive to their needs and desires.

DISTRIBUTION PROCEDURES

In February 1982, the Securities and Exchange Commission began allowing a process called shelf registration under SEC Rule 415. Shelf registration permits large companies to file one comprehensive registration statement that outlines the firm's plans for future long-term financing. Then, when market conditions seem appropriate, the firm can issue the securities through an investment banker without further SEC approval. Future issues are said to be sitting on the shelf, waiting for the most advantageous time to appear. An issue may be on the shelf for up to two years.

Approximately half of the new public bond issues are distributed through the shelf registration process. The rest are issued under more traditional procedures in which the bonds are issued shortly after registration by a large syndicate of investment bankers in a highly structured process.

Private Placement

A number of bond offerings are sold to investors as a private placement; that is, they are sold privately to investors rather than through the public markets. Private placements are most popular with investors such as insurance companies and pension funds, and they are primarily offered in the corporate sector by industrial firms rather than public utilities. The lender can generally expect to receive a slightly higher yield than on public issues to compensate for the extremely limited or nonexistent secondary market and the generally smaller size of the borrowing firm in a private placement.

BOND RATINGS

Bond investors tend to place much more emphasis on independent analysis of quality than do common stock investors. For this reason, both corporate financial management and institutional portfolio managers keep a close eye on bond rating procedures. The difference between an AA and an A rating may mean the corporation will have to pay ¼ point more interest on the bond issue (perhaps 8½ percent rather than 8¼ percent). On a $100 million, 20-year issue, this represents $250,000 per year (before tax), or a total of $5 million over the life of the bond.

The two major bond-rating agencies are Moody's Investors Service and Standard & Poor's (a subsidiary of McGraw-Hill, Inc.). They rank thousands of corporate and municipal issues as well as a limited number of private placements, commercial paper, preferred stock issues, and offerings of foreign companies and governments. U.S. government issues tend to be free of risk and therefore are given no attention by the bond-rating agencies. Moody's, founded in 1909, is the older of the two bond-rating agencies and covers twice as many securities as Standard & Poor's (particularly in the municipal bond area). Fitch Investors Service, Inc., acquired Duff & Phelps, another rating agency, in an attempt to diversify and expand its rating coverage.

The bond ratings, generally ranging from an AAA to a D category, are decided on a committee basis at both Moody's and Standard & Poor's. There are no fast and firm quantitative measures that specify the rating a new issue will receive. Nevertheless, measures pertaining to cash flow and earnings generation in relationship to debt obligations are given strong consideration. Of particular interest are coverage ratios that show the number of times interest payments, as well as all annual contractual obligations, are covered by earnings. A coverage of 2 or 3 may contribute to a low rating, while a ratio of 5 to 10 may indicate the possibility of a strong rating. Operating margins, return on invested capital, and returns on total assets are also evaluated along with debt-to-equity ratios.[7] Financial ratio analysis makes up perhaps 50 percent of the evaluation. Other factors of importance are the nature of the industry in which the firm operates, the relative position of the firm within the industry, the pricing clout the firm has, and the quality of management. Decisions are not made in a sterile, isolated environment. Thus, it is not unusual for corporate management or the mayor to make a presentation to the rating agency, and on-site visitations to plants or cities may occur.

The overall quality of the work done by the bond-rating agencies may be judged by the agencies' acceptance in the business and academic community. Their work is very well received. Although UBS PaineWebber and some other investment houses have established their own analysts to shadow the activities of the bond-rating agencies and look for imprecisions in their classifications (and thus potential profits), the opportunities are not great. Academic researchers have generally found that accounting and financial data were well considered in the bond ratings and that rational evaluation appeared to exist.[8]

---

7. Similar appropriate measures can be applied to municipal bonds, such as debt per capita or income per capita within a governmental jurisdiction.

8. James O. Horrigan, "The Determination of Long-Term Credit Standing with Financial Ratios," *Empirical Research in Accounting: Selected Studies,* supplement to *Journal of Accounting Research* 4 (1966), pp. 44–62; Thomas F. Pogue and Robert M. Soldofsky, "What's in a Bond Rating?" *Journal of Financial and Quantitative Analysis,* June 1969, pp. 201–8; and George E. Pinches and Kent A. Mingo, "A Multivariate Analysis of Industrial Bond Ratings," *Journal of Finance,* March 1973, pp. 1–18.

One item lending credibility to the bond-rating process is the frequency with which the two major rating agencies arrive at the same grade for a given issue (this occurs well over 50 percent of the time). When "split ratings" do occur (different ratings by different agencies), they are invariably of a small magnitude. A typical case might be AAA versus AA rather than AAA versus BBB. While one can question whether one agency is looking over the other's shoulder or "copying its homework," this is probably not the case in this skilled industry.

Nevertheless, there is room for criticism. While initial evaluations are quite thorough and rational, the monitoring process may not be wholly satisfactory. Subsequent changes in corporate or municipal government events may not trigger a rating change quickly enough. One sure way a corporation or municipal government will get a reevaluation is for them to come out with a new issue. This tends to generate a review of all existing issues.

Actual Rating System

Table 11-4 shows an actual listing of the designations used by Moody's and Standard & Poor's. Note that Moody's combines capital letters and small *a*'s, and Standard & Poor's uses all capital letters.

TABLE 11–4 Description of Bond Ratings

Quality	Moody's	Standard & Poor's	Description
High grade	Aaa	AAA	Bonds that are judged to be of the best quality. They carry the smallest degree of investment risk and are generally referred to as "gilt edge." Interest payments are protected by a large or exceptionally stable margin, and principal is secure.
	Aa	AA	Bonds that are judged to be of high quality by all standards. Together with the first group, they comprise what are generally known as high-grade bonds. They are rated lower than the best bonds because margins of protection may not be as large.
Medium grade	A	A	Bonds that possess many favorable investment attributes and are to be considered as upper-medium-grade obligations. Factors giving security to principal and interest are considered adequate.
	Baa	BBB	Bonds that are considered as medium-grade obligations—they are neither highly protected nor poorly secured.
Speculative	Ba	BB	Bonds that are judged to have speculative elements; their future cannot be considered as well assured. Often the protection of interest and principal payments may be very moderate.
	B	B	Bonds that generally lack characteristics of the desirable investment. Assurance of interest and principal payments or of maintenance of other terms of the contract over any long period may be small.
Default	Caa	CCC	Bonds that are of poor standing. Such issues may be in default, or there may be elements of danger present with respect to principal or interest.
	Ca	CC	Bonds that represent obligations that are speculative to a high degree. Such issues are often in default or have other marked shortcomings.
	C		The lowest-rated class in Moody's designation. These bonds can be regarded as having extremely poor prospects of attaining any real investment standing.
		C	Rating given to income bonds on which interest is not currently being paid.
		D	Issues in default with arrears in interest and/or principal payments.

Sources: *Mergent Bond Record* (published by Mergent, Inc., New York, NY) and *Bond Guide* (Standard & Poor's).

The first four categories are assumed to represent investment-grade quality. Large institutional investors (insurance companies, banks, pension funds) generally confine their activities to these four categories. Moody's also modifies its basic ratings with numerical values for categories Aa through B. The highest in a category is 1, 2 is the midrange, and 3 is the lowest. A rating of Aa2 means the bond is in the midrange of Aa. Standard & Poor's has a similar modification process with pluses and minuses applied. Thus, AA+ would be on the high end of an AA rating, AA would be in the middle, and AA− would be on the low end.

It is also possible for a corporation to have issues outstanding in more than one category. For example, highly secured mortgage bonds of a corporation may be rated AA, while unsecured issues carry an A rating.

The level of interest payment on a bond is inverse to the quality rating. If a bond rated AAA by Standard & Poor's pays 7.5 percent, an A quality bond might pay 8.0 percent; a BB, 9.0 percent; and so on. The spread between these yields changes from time to time and is watched closely by the financial community as a barometer of future movements in the financial markets. A relatively small spread between two rating categories would indicate that investors generally have confidence in the economy. As the yield spread widens between higher and lower rating categories, this may indicate loss of confidence. Investors are demanding increasingly higher yields for lower rated bonds. Their loss of confidence indicates they will demand progressively higher returns for taking risks. This logic was previously covered in Chapter 9 as part of the discussion of the *Barron's* Confidence Index.

POWER OF THE RATING AGENCIES

When Shell Canada (www.shellcanada.com), an integrated oil company with many U.S. investors, decided to sell its coal business, it called Moody's and Standard & Poor's first. Although its own financial analysis indicated the move was appropriate, it would not have made the decision without the blessings of the two major U.S. bond-rating agencies as well as similar rating agencies in Canada. The sell-off provided a $120 million write-off that could have caused a downgrading of Shell Canada's double-A rating, and the firm was not about to take a chance.

The firm's concern was well justified. Its action was taken in June 1991 (a recession year). During the first six months of 1991, 422 corporations suffered a downgrading in ratings while only 88 had an increase. In the prior decade, the big causes for downgradings were the effects of acquisitions or attempts by corporations to defend themselves against takeovers. In the 1990s, these factors were less important, and the major concern was poor earnings performance.

Three good rules for firms to follow in dealing with bond-rating agencies is never surprise the agencies, tell all, and show good intent. A number of years ago, Manville Corporation (www.jm.com) was severely downgraded not for poor performance, but because it took Chapter 11 bankruptcy protection as a way to face asbestos damage litigation. The decision may have been right at the time, but the firm did not have the blessings of the bond-rating agencies.

JUNK BONDS

Lower quality bonds are sometimes referred to as junk bonds or high yield bonds. Any bond that is not considered to be of investment quality by Wall Street analysts is put in the junk bond category. As previously indicated, investment quality means the bond falls into one of the four top investment-grade categories established by Moody's and Standard & Poor's. This indicates investment-grade bonds extend down to Baa in Moody's and BBB in Standard & Poor's (Table 11-4). A wide range of quality is associated with junk bonds. Some are very close to investment quality (such as the Ba and BB bonds), while others carry ratings in the C and D category.

Bonds tend to fall into the junk bond category for a number of reasons. First are the so-called fallen angel bonds issued by companies that once had high credit rankings but now face hard times. Second are emerging growth companies or small firms that have not yet established an adequate record to justify an investment-quality rating. Finally, a major part of the junk bond market is made of companies undergoing a restructuring either as a result of a leveraged buyout or as part of fending off an unfriendly takeover offer. In both these cases, equity capital tends to be replaced with debt and a lower rating is assigned.

Many junk bonds behave more like common stock than bonds and rally on good news, actual interest payments, or improving business conditions. Several institutions such as Merrill Lynch and Fidelity Investments manage mutual funds with a junk bond emphasis.

The main appeal of junk bonds historically is that they provided yields 300 to 800 basis points higher than that for AAA corporate bonds or U.S. Treasury securities. Also, until the recession of 1990-91, there were relatively few defaults by junk bond issuers. Thus, the investor got a substantially higher yield with only a small increase in risk.

However, in the 1990-91 recession, junk bond prices tumbled by 20 to 30 percent, while other bond values stayed firm. Examples of junk bond issues that dropped sharply in value included those issued by Rapid-American Corporation, Revco, Campeau Corporation, and Resorts International. Many of these declines were due to poor business conditions. However, the fall of Drexel Burnham Lambert, the leading underwriter of junk bond issues, also contributed to the difficulties in the market. That problem was further compounded when Michael Milken, the guru of junk bond dealers, was sentenced to 10 years in prison for illegal insider trading.

As the economy came out of the recession of 1990-91, junk bonds once again gained in popularity. Many of these issues had their prices battered down so low that they appeared to be bargains. As a result, junk bonds recovered and continued to perform exceptionally well throughout the 1990s—so much so that the spread between the yield on junk bonds and AAA corporates or U.S. Treasury securities was half of its historical spread in 1997. While these securities took a hit in 2001 as the economy slowed down, they still appear to have a place in the portfolio of investors with a higher than average risk tolerance. This is particularly true for bonds that are in the low- to mid-B rating categories.

BOND QUOTES

Barron's and a number of other sources publish bond values on a daily basis. Table 11-5 provides an excerpt from the daily quote sheet for corporate bonds.

In the third column, the company name is followed by the annual coupon rate and maturity date. For example, the table shows Bell South Telecommunications (BellsoT) bonds with a coupon rate of 7 percent maturing in 25 (the year 2025). The current yield (Cur Yld) represents the annual interest or coupon payment divided by the price and is 6.4 percent. The bond quote does not represent actual dollars but percent of par value. Because corporate bonds trade in units of $1,000, 110 represents $1100 ($1,000 × 110%).

A student interested in further information on a bond could proceed to *Mergent Bond Record* published by Mergent, Inc. or the *Bond Guide,* published by Standard & Poor's. For example, using *Mergent Bond Record,* as shown in Table 11-6, the reader could determine information about a firm. Let's look at May Department Stores, 8.375s of 2024. The designation in the left margin indicates the industry classification of the firm. The firm has a Moody's bond rating of A1 and a call price of 104.19 percent of par or $1,041.90 ($1,000 × 104.19%). *Mergent Bond Record* further indicates that interest is payable on February 1 and

TABLE 11–5 Daily Quotes on Corporate Bonds

52-Weeks High	52-Weeks Low	Name and Coupon	Cur Yld	Sales $1,000	Weekly High	Weekly Low	Weekly Last	Net Chg
NEW YORK EXCHANGE								
94⅝	17⅞	AES Cp 4½05	cv	428	94¼	93¼	94¼	+ ¾
97	34	AES Cp 8s8	8.3	498	96⅞	94⅛	96	+ ½
77⅞	13	AMR 9s16	11.6	1739	77⅞	73¾	77⅞	+ 3⅜
104¾	99	AT&T 6¾04	6.6	30	102	102	102	− 1/32
104⅝	101	AT&T 7½04	7.3	168	102 11/32	102 5/16	102 5/16	− 1/32
107	93⅛	AT&T 7s05	6.6	351	106½	105⅝	106⅜	+ ¼
111¼	92⅞	AT&T 7½06	6.8	78	110⅞	110⅛	110⅛	− ⅞
113¾	92⅛	AT&T 7¾07	6.9	147	113¼	111¾	112⅝	+ ⅞
109¼	88⅜	AT&T 6s09	5.7	558	106¾	105¾	105⅞	− ⅛
110	88⅛	AT&T 6½13	6.3	187	104⅜	104	104	− ½
109⅜	77⅜	AT&T 8.35s25	7.8	1266	108⅝	107	107	+ ¼
101¼	78	AT&T 6½29	6.6	839	100	98	98½	− 1⅛
128⅞	100½	ATTBdb 8⅜13	6.9	147	121⅞	120⅜	120⅞	+ ¼
141⅝	108½	ATTBdb 9.45s22	7.0	103	135½	133⅛	134	− 1
69½	58	AForP 5s30	7.5	30	66½	66½	66½	− 1½
108	91⅛	AmFnGp 7⅛07	6.7	225	107½	106	106	− 2
107	87½	AmFnGp 7⅛09	6.8	95	105⅝	105	105	− ¾
111⅛	103⅝	AnheusB 6½28	6.3	2	103⅝	103⅝	103⅝	− 1½
122	114	ARch 10⅞05	9.5	27	114⅛	114⅛	114⅛	+ ⅛
54⅛	31⅛	Avaya zr21	...	3	54⅛	54⅛	54⅛	+ ⅛
105¼	99	BauschL 6¾04	6.4	118	105	104⅝	104¾	+ ½
101⅞	78½	BauschL 7⅛28	7.0	22	101⅞	100½	101⅞	+ 1⅛
116½	95½	Bellso 6⅜28	6.2	189	104⅞	103½	103½	− 1⅝
106½	102 5/16	BellsoT 6⅜04	6.2	16	103	103	103	− 1
109⅝	106¼	BellsoT 6½05	6.1	30	107¼	107¼	107¼	+ ⅜
115⅛	101¾	BellsoT 5⅞09	5.4	269	109⅝	109¼	109½	− 1
103⅞	91	BellsoT 6.3s15rp	...	118	98	98	98	...
116½	101⅛	BellsoT 7s25	6.4	10	110	110	110	− 1⅞
104⅝	94	BellsoT 6¾33	6.6	832	102¼	102	102	+ ¼
112	102½	BellsoT 7⅝35	7.2	60	107⅛	106⅝	106⅝	− ⅜
104⅜	75	Bevrly 9s06	8.8	45	102¼	101	102¼	+ ⅞
107½	102	BlockF 6¾04	6.4	10	104⅞	104⅞	104⅞	...
89⅜	43	BordCh 8⅜16	9.5	217	89⅜	86⅜	88½	+ 2½
120	109⅛	BurN 8.15s20N	7.1	20	116	115¼	115¼	+ 5¼
111½	95	CIT Gp 5⅞08	5.5	6	106¾	106¾	106¾	− 4¾
102	79	CallonP 11s05	11.0	40	101¼	100½	100½	...
103	79	CallonP 10¼04	10.1	5	101	101	101	+ ½
120	113¾	Caterplnc 9s06	7.9	11	113¾	113¾	113¾	− 1½
102⅝	88	Chkpnt 5¼05	cv	286	101½	101⅛	101½	+ ½

Source: Republished with permission of Dow Jones & Company, Inc., from *Barron's*, October 13, 2003, p. MW32; permission conveyed through Copyright Clearance Center, Inc.

TABLE 11–6 Background Data on Bond Issues

U.S. CORPORATE BONDS — Matt—MCN 99

CUSIP	ISSUE	MOODY'S® RATING	INTEREST DATES	CURRENT CALL PRICE	CALL DATE	SINK FUND PROV	CURRENT PRICE		YIELD TO MAT.	2001 HIGH	2001 LOW	AMT. OUTST. MIL. $	ISSUED	PRICE	YLD.
577081AN	Mattel, Inc. nt 6.00 2003[1]	Baa2	J&J 15	100.00 to	7-15-03		96⅞	sale	7.38	96⅞	93⅞	150	7-21-98	99.71	0.00
577081AP	nt 6.125 2005[1]	Baa2	J&J 15	100.00 to	7-15-05		93½	sale	7.88	93⅝	88¼	150	7-21-98	99.42	0.00
57722MAB	Mattress Discounters Corp sr nt ser B 12.625 2007	B2	J&J 15	106.31 fr	7-15-04		86	sale	16.18	91	86	140	8-6-99	96.36	0.00
577730AH	Maxus Energy Corp. nt 9.875 2002	B1 r	A&O 15	100.00 to	10-15-02	No	—	sale	—	—	—	247.8	9-21-92	100.00	9.88
577730AK	nt 9.50 2003	B1 r	F&A 1	100.00 to	2-15-03	No	—	sale	—	—	—	100	1-19-93	99.25	9.62
577730AL	nt 9.375 2003	B1 r	M&N 1	N.C.	—	No	103¼	sale	8.11	103¼	101⅜	200	10-20-93	100.00	9.38
577730AM	nt ser B 9.375 2003	B1	J&J 18		—		103¼	sale	7.61	103¼	101¼	60.0	1-10-94	—	—
577769AC	Maxxam Group Holdings Inc. sr secd nt 12.00 2003	Caa1	&		—		83½	sale	17.09	83½	77½	130	12-18-96	0.00	0.00
57777HAC	Maxxim Medical Group, Inc. sr sub disc nt 11.00 2009[2]	B3	M&N 15	106.88 fr	11-15-04		—	sale	—	—	—	144.552	11-12-99	0.00	0.00
577778AQ	May Department Stores Co nt 9.875 2002	A1 r	J&D 1	N.C.	—	No	107¾	sale	6.33	108	107	175	12-6-90	99.50	9.90
577778AY	nt 7.15 2004	A1 r	F&A 15	N.C.	—		104¾	sale	5.65	104¾	102½	125	8-15-95	99.09	7.20
577778BG	deb 6.875 2005	A1 r	M&N 1	N.C.	—		103⅜	sale	6.08	103⅝	101⅛	125	10-30-96	100.00	6.90
577778BP	deb 7.90 2007	A1	A&O 15	100.00 to	10-15-07		108⅞	sale	6.23	109⅛	103⅞	225	10-16-00	99.96	0.00
577778BJ	nt 5.95 2008	A1	M&N 1	100.00 to	11-1-08		96⅞	sale	6.46	97⅜	93⅛	150	10-27-98	99.89	0.00
577778AP	deb 10.625 2010	A1 r	M&N 1	N.C.	—	No	125½	sale	7.08	126⅝	122½	150	11-6-90	99.87	11.00
577778BE	nt 7.45 2011	A1 r	M&S 15	N.C.	—		108½	sale	6.34	108½	101¾	150	9-13-96	99.72	0.00
577778BN	deb 8.00 2012[3]	A1	J&J 15	100.00 to	7-15-12		112⅞	sale	6.40	112⅞	106⅜	200	7-14-00	99.90	0.00
577778BB	nt 7.625 2013	A1 r	F&A 15	N.C.	—		109¾	sale	6.52	109¾	101⅜	125	8-15-95	98.98	7.70
577778AX	nt 7.50 2015	A1 r	J&D 1	N.C.	—	No	108⅝	sale	6.58	108⅝	100	100	6-9-95	99.38	7.60
577778AG	deb 9.25 2016	A1 r	M&S 1	101.85 to	2-28-03	Yes	—	sale	—	—	—	111.7	2-28-86	100.00	9.30
577778BF	nt 7.45 2016	A1 r	A&O 15	N.C.	—		104⅞	sale	6.94	104⅞	96⅛	125	10-21-96	100.00	7.40
577778AM	deb 10.75 2018	A1 r	J&D 15	103.23 fr	6-15-02	Yes	—	sale	—	—	—	30.0	Ref fr. 06-15-1998 @ 105.		
577778BM	deb 8.50 2019	A1	J&D 1	100.00 to	6-1-19		110⅝	sale	7.43	112¼	104¼	200	6-5-00	99.81	0.00
577778AR	deb 10.25 2021	A1 r	J&J 1	N.C.	—	No	125⅞	sale	7.70	127	120⅞	100	1-9-91	99.53	10.00
577778AS	amort deb 9.75 2021	A1 r	F&A 15	N.C.	—	No	122⅛	sale	7.59	123	115½	125	2-12-91	99.52	9.80
577778AT	amort deb 9.50 2021	A1 r	A&O 15	N.C.	—	No	120½	sale	7.50	121½	113⅞	150	4-8-91	99.35	9.60
577778AU	deb 9.875 2021	A1 r	J&D 15	104.56 fr	6-15-01	Yes	105⅜	sale	9.29	106⅛	105⅜	100	6-19-91	99.25	9.90
577778AV	deb 8.375 2022	A1 r	A&O 1	104.04 fr	10-1-02	Yes	113	sale	7.19	113½	107½	200	10-1-92	99.71	8.40
577778AW	deb 8.375 2024	A1 r	F&A 1	104.19 fr	8-1-04	Yes	115¼	sale	7.04	116⅜	107	200	8-4-94	100.00	8.40
577778AZ	deb 7.60 2025	A1 r	J&D 1	N.C.	—		102	sale	7.44	103¾	95⅝	100	6-9-95	99.88	7.60
577778BA	deb 8.30 2026	A1 r	J&J 15	104.15 fr	7-15-06		104¼	sale	7.92	105¾	102½	200	7-12-96	100.00	8.30
577778BH	deb 6.70 2028	A1	M&S 15		—		92⅞	sale	7.31	94⅜	85	200	9-22-98	99.59	0.00
577778BL	deb 8.75 2029[3]	A1	M&N 15	100.00 to	5-15-29		116⅞	sale	7.33	117¼	106⅝	250	5-22-00	99.38	0.00
577778BK	deb 7.875 2030	A1	M&S 1	100.00 to	3-1-30		106¾	sale	7.31	106⅞	98¼	200	2-29-00	100.00	0.00
577778BC	deb 8.125 2035	A1 r	F&A 15	100.00 to	8-15-35		106⅛	sale	7.61	106⅛	99¼	150	8-15-95	99.93	8.10
577778BD	deb 7.875 2036	A1 r	F&A 15	100.00 fr	8-15-16		98½	sale	8.00	100	95⅝	200	8-19-96	98.75	0.00
578592AC	Maytag Co. nt 9.75 2002	A3 r	M&N 15	N.C.	—	No	104⅜	sale	6.67	104⅛	103⅜	200	5-16-90	99.55	9.81
	MBIA, Inc. bd 4.50 2010	Aa2			—		—		—	—	—	175	11-13-00	0.00	0.00
55262CAB	nt 9.375 2011	Aa2	F&A 15	N.C.	—	No	120		6.61	120¾	115⅜	100	2-12-91	99.25	9.46
55262CAC	deb 8.20 2022	Aa2	A&O 1	103.99 fr	10-1-02	No	104⅛		7.78	105	101⅞	100	10-1-92	99.87	8.22

Source: *Mergent Bond Record* (published by Mergent, Inc., New York, NY), April 2001, p. 99.

August 1 of each year (Interest Dates column). The current price of the bond is \$1,152.50 (\$1,000 × 115.25%).

Table 11-7 features quotes on U.S. government securities. Treasury notes and bonds are traded as a percentage of par value, similar to corporate bonds. Historically, price changes in the market have been rather small, and bonds are quoted in $\frac{1}{32}$ of a percentage point. For example, the price for the $5\frac{1}{4}$ Treasury note due August 2003 is quoted as 101.24 bid and 101.26 asked.[9] These prices translate into $101\frac{24}{32}$ and $101\frac{26}{32}$ percent of \$1,000.

The bid price on a \$1,000 note would be 101.67% × \$1,000 or \$1,016.70:

$$\begin{array}{r} 101.67\% \text{ (Same as } 101\tfrac{24}{32}) \\ \times \$1{,}000 \\ \hline \$1{,}016.70 \end{array}$$

The asked price is 101.8125% × \$1,000 or \$1,012.125:

$$\begin{array}{r} 101.8125\% \text{ (same as } 101\tfrac{26}{32}) \\ \times \$1{,}000 \\ \hline \$1{,}018.125 \end{array}$$

9. The bid price is the value at which the bond can be sold, and the asked price is the value at which it can be bought.

TABLE 11–7 Quotes on Government Issues—Treasury Bonds, Notes, and Bills

GOVT. BOND & NOTES

RATE	MATURITY MO/YR	BID	ASKED	CHG.	ASKED YLD.
5¼	May 01n	100:00	100:02	– 1	3.74
6½	May 01n	100:02	100:04	– 1	3.55
5¾	Jun 01n	100:07	100:09	....	3.45
6⅝	Jun 01n	100:10	100:12	....	3.57
5½	Jul 01n	100:11	100:13	....	3.52
6⅝	Jul 01n	100:18	100:20	– 1	3.60
7⅞	Aug 01n	101:00	101:02	– 1	3.59
13⅜	Aug 01	102:13	102:15	– 2	3.46
5½	Aug 01n	100:15	100:17	....	3.63
6½	Aug 01n	100:24	100:26	....	3.65
5⅝	Sep 01n	100:20	100:22	....	3.75
6⅜	Sep 01n	100:29	100:31	....	3.74
5⅞	Oct 01n	100:28	100:30	....	3.79
6¼	Oct 01n	101:02	101:04	+ 1	3.75
7½	Nov 01n	101:24	101:26	....	3.81
15¾	Nov 01	105:26	105:28	– 2	3.78
5⅞	Nov 01n	101:02	101:04	+ 1	3.76
6⅛	Dec 01n	101:12	101:14	+ 1	3.77
6¼	Jan 02n	101:20	101:22	+ 2	3.82
6⅜	Jan 02n	101:22	101:24	+ 1	3.85
14¼	Feb 02	107:19	107:21	– 1	3.83
6¼	Feb 02n	101:25	101:27	+ 1	3.86
6½	Feb 02n	101:31	102:01	+ 1	3.87
6½	Mar 02n	102:05	102:07	+ 1	3.90
6⅝	Mar 02n	102:08	102:10	+ 1	3.91
6⅜	Apr 02n	102:07	102:09	+ 2	3.93
6⅝	Apr 02n	102:14	102:16	+ 1	3.94
7½	May 02n	103:12	103:14	+ 1	3.96
6½	May 02n	102:16	102:18	+ 2	3.97
6⅝	May 02n	102:20	102:22	+ 1	3.97
6¼	Jun 02n	102:13	102:15	+ 2	3.98
6⅜	Jun 02n	102:17	102:19	+ 2	3.99
3⅝	Jul 02i	102:09	102:10	+ 3	1.62
6	Jul 02n	102:08	102:10	+ 2	4.02
6¼	Jul 02n	102:16	102:18	+ 2	4.06
6⅜	Aug 02n	102:23	102:25	+ 1	4.07
6⅛	Aug 02n	102:14	102:16	+ 1	4.11
6¼	Aug 02n	102:19	102:21	+ 1	4.11
5⅞	Sep 02n	102:08	102:10	+ 1	4.13
6	Sep 02n	102:13	102:15	+ 1	4.13
5¾	Oct 02n	102:05	102:07	+ 1	4.17
11⅝	Nov 02	110:19	110:23	....	4.18
5⅝	Nov 02n	102:02	102:04	+ 1	4.19
5¾	Nov 02n	102:08	102:10	+ 1	4.19
5⅛	Dec 02n	101:12	101:14	+ 1	4.20
5⅝	Dec 02n	102:05	102:07	....	4.20
4¾	Jan 03n	100:24	100:26	+ 2	4.25
5½	Jan 03n	102:00	102:02	+ 1	4.23
6¼	Feb 03n	103:07	103:09	+ 2	4.28
10¾	Feb 03	110:20	110:24	....	4.31
4⅝	Feb 03n	100:16	100:18	+ 1	4.29
5½	Feb 03n	102:00	102:02	+ 1	4.29
4¼	Mar 03n	99:29	99:30	+ 3	4.28
5½	Mar 03n	102:02	102:04	+ 1	4.31
4	**Apr 03n**	**99:14**	**99:15**	**+ 2**	**4.28**
5¾	Apr 03n	102:19	102:21	+ 2	4.32
10¾	May 03	111:31	112:03	....	4.37
5½	May 03n	102:06	102:08	+ 2	4.34
5⅜	Jun 03n	102:00	102:02	+ 2	4.35
5¼	Aug 03n	101:24	101:26	+ 3	4.39
5¾	Aug 03n	102:25	102:27	+ 1	4.41
11⅛	Aug 03	114:00	114:04	+ 1	4.46
4¼	Nov 03n	99:12	99:14	+ 3	4.49
11⅞	Nov 03	117:01	117:05	+ 1	4.54
4¾	Feb 04n	100:13	100:15	+ 4	4.56
5⅞	Feb 04n	103:09	103:11	+ 3	4.57
5¼	May 04n	101:18	101:20	+ 3	4.66
7¼	May 04n	107:02	107:04	+ 2	4.68
12⅜	May 04	121:01	121:07	+ 1	4.71
6	Aug 04n	103:24	103:26	+ 4	4.72
7¼	Aug 04n	107:14	107:16	+ 3	4.73
13¾	Aug 04	126:19	126:25	+ 3	4.77
5⅞	Nov 04n	103:12	103:14	+ 4	4.80
7⅞	Nov 04n	109:24	109:26	+ 5	4.80
11⅝	Nov 04	121:15	121:21	+ 3	4.83

TREASURY BILLS

MATURITY	DAYS TO MAT.	BID	ASKED	CHG.	ASKED YLD.
May 17 '01	2	3.47	3.39	–0.01	3.44
May 24 '01	9	3.62	3.54	–0.02	3.59
May 31 '01	16	3.75	3.67	–0.02	3.73
Jun 07 '01	23	3.57	3.49	–0.05	3.55
Jun 14 '01	30	3.60	3.56	–0.01	3.62
Jun 21 '01	37	3.60	3.56	–0.05	3.62
Jun 28 '01	44	3.60	3.56	–0.01	3.63
Jul 05 '01	51	3.60	3.56	–0.04	3.63
Jul 12 '01	58	3.60	3.56	–0.04	3.63
Jul 19 '01	65	3.58	3.56	–0.06	3.63
Jul 26 '01	72	3.58	3.56	–0.08	3.64
Aug 02 '01	79	3.61	3.59	–0.06	3.67
Aug 09 '01	**86**	**3.63**	**3.62**	**–0.05**	**3.70**
Aug 16 '01	93	3.63	3.61	–0.06	3.69
Aug 16 '01	93	3.63	3.62	–0.06	3.70
Aug 23 '01	100	3.62	3.60	–0.07	3.69
Aug 30 '01	107	3.60	3.58	–0.05	3.67
Sep 06 '01	114	3.58	3.56	–0.05	3.65
Sep 13 '01	121	3.58	3.56	–0.03	3.65
Sep 20 '01	128	3.56	3.54	–0.06	3.63
Sep 27 '01	135	3.56	3.54	–0.05	3.64
Oct 04 '01	142	3.61	3.59	–0.02	3.69
Oct 11 '01	149	3.61	3.59	–0.03	3.69
Oct 18 '01	156	3.62	3.60	–0.02	3.71
Oct 25 '01	163	3.60	3.58	–0.04	3.69
Nov 01 '01	170	3.62	3.60	–0.04	3.71
Nov 08 '01	**177**	**3.64**	**3.63**	**–0.03**	**3.75**
Nov 15 '01	184	3.64	3.63	–0.04	3.75
Nov 29 '01	198	3.60	3.58	–0.04	3.70
Feb 28 '02	289	3.61	3.60	–0.08	3.73

Source: Republished with permission of Dow Jones & Company, Inc., from *The Wall Street Journal*, May 15, 2001, p. C17; permission conveyed through Copyright Clearance Center, Inc.

The spread between the bid and asked price is $1.425:

Bid price	$1,016.700
Asked price	1,018.125
Spread	$1.425

While Treasury notes and bonds are quoted on the basis of price, Treasury bills are quoted on the basis of yield. Look at the Treasury bills on the right side of Table 11-7. These yields (ask. yld.) represent the return to the Treasury bill investor. How is the yield determined? First, you must understand that the interest on a Treasury bill is treated on a discount basis; that is, it is subtracted from the $1,000 face value to get the purchase price. On a six-month, $1,000 Treasury bill, paying 3 percent interest, the actual yield is 3.04 percent. Let's see how we arrive at this number:

> Interest = 3% × $1,000 × ½ year = $30 × ½ = $15.
>
> We multiply $30 by ½ in the second part of the above line to arrive at $15 because the Treasury bill is for half a year.
>
> The amount to be paid for the Treasury bill is $985 ($1,000 − $15).
>
> The true yield is $15/$985 × 2 = 1.52% × 2 = 3.04%.
>
> The reason 1.52% is multiplied by two is to translate a six-month return into an annual return.

The actual rate (3.04% in this case) is always higher than the quoted rate (3%) because you do not have to pay the full face value ($1,000), but rather a discounted value ($985).

Examples of Treasury strip quotes are shown in Table 11-8. Note the May 2019 strip is selling at 32.29 bid and 33.02 asked. The yield is 6.24 percent. What this means is that on May 17, 2001 (the date of the table), you could buy a Treasury strip maturing in May 2019 at slightly over 32 percent of par value and that would provide you with a yield of 6.24 percent. In the Type column (second column), there is a "ci." This means you are buying stripped coupon interest. A "bp" also appears in the Type column, indicating you are purchasing stripped principal.

BOND MARKETS, CAPITAL MARKET THEORY, AND EFFICIENCY

In many respects, the bond market appears to demonstrate a high degree of rationality in recognition of risk and return. Corporate issues promise a higher yield than government issues to compensate for risk, and furthermore, federally sponsored credit agencies pay a higher return than Treasury issues for the same reason. Also, lower rated bonds consistently trade at larger yields than higher quality bonds to provide a risk premium.

TABLE 11–8 Quotes on Treasury Strips

U.S. TREASURY STRIPS

MAT.		TYPE	BID	ASKED	CHG.	ASKED YLD.
May	14	ci	46:07	46:12	+ 2	6.00
Aug	14	ci	45:13	45:18	+ 2	6.02
Nov	14	ci	44:21	44:26	+ 2	6.04
Feb	15	ci	43:27	44:01	+ 4	6.06
Feb	15	bp	43:18	43:24	+ 5	6.11
May	15	ci	43:03	43:09	+ 4	6.08
Aug	15	ci	42:11	42:17	+ 4	6.09
Aug	15	bp	42:02	42:07	+ 5	6.14
Nov	15	ci	41:19	41:24	+ 4	6.12
Nov	15	bp	41:09	41:14	+ 6	6.17
Feb	16	ci	40:28	41:01	+ 5	6.13
Feb	16	bp	40:21	40:27	+ 7	6.16
May	16	ci	40:05	40:11	+ 6	6.15
May	16	bp	40:05	40:10	+ 5	6.15
Aug	16	ci	39:15	39:21	+ 7	6.16
Nov	16	ci	38:25	38:30	+ 6	6.18
Nov	16	bp	38:26	39:00	+ 8	6.17
Feb	17	ci	38:02	38:08	+ 6	6.20
May	17	ci	37:14	37:20	+ 7	6.21
May	17	bp	37:14	37:20	+ 7	6.21
Aug	17	ci	36:26	37:00	+ 6	6.22
Aug	17	bp	36:29	37:03	+ 7	6.20
Nov	17	ci	36:06	36:11	+ 6	6.23
Feb	18	ci	35:19	35:24	+ 6	6.24
May	18	ci	35:02	35:08	+ 6	6.23
May	18	bp	35:02	35:08	+ 6	6.23
Aug	18	ci	34:17	34:23	+ 6	6.23
Nov	18	ci	34:00	34:05	+ 6	6.24
Nov	18	bp	33:30	34:04	+ 6	6.24
Feb	19	ci	33:12	33:18	+ 6	6.25
Feb	19	bp	33:15	33:20	+ 7	6.24
May	19	ci	32:29	33:02	+ 6	6.24
Aug	19	ci	32:12	32:18	+ 6	6.24
Aug	19	bp	32:15	32:20	+ 6	6.23
Nov	19	ci	31:28	32:02	+ 6	6.25
Feb	20	ci	31:13	31:18	+ 7	6.24
Feb	20	bp	31:15	31:20	+ 7	6.24
May	20	ci	30:30	31:03	+ 7	6.24
May	20	bp	30:28	31:01	+ 7	6.26
Aug	20	ci	30:16	30:22	+ 7	6.24
Aug	20	bp	30:15	30:21	+ 7	6.24
Nov	20	ci	29:31	30:05	+ 7	6.25
Feb	21	ci	29:17	29:22	+ 8	6.24
Feb	21	bp	29:19	29:25	+ 8	6.23
May	21	ci	29:02	29:08	+ 8	6.24
May	21	bp	28:31	29:05	+ 8	6.26
Aug	21	ci	28:21	28:26	+ 8	6.24
Aug	21	bp	28:20	28:25	+ 8	6.24
Nov	21	ci	28:08	28:13	+ 7	6.24
Nov	21	bp	28:03	28:09	+ 7	6.26
Feb	22	ci	27:23	27:29	+ 7	6.25
May	22	ci	27:10	27:15	+ 7	6.25
Aug	22	ci	26:28	27:02	+ 7	6.25

Source: Republished with permission of Dow Jones & Company, Inc., from *The Wall Street Journal*, May 17, 2001, p. C20; permission conveyed through Copyright Clearance Center, Inc.

Taking this logic one step further, bonds should generally pay a lower return than equity investments since the equity holder is in a riskier position because of the absence of a contractual obligation to receive payment. As was pointed out in Chapter 1, researchers have attributed superior returns to equity investments relative to debt over the long term.

A number of studies have also investigated the efficiency of the bond market. A primary item under investigation was the extent of a price change that was associated with a change in a bond rating. If the bond market is efficient, much of the information that led to the rating change was already known to the public and should have been impounded into the value of the bond before the rating change. Thus, the rating change should not have led to major price movements. Major research has generally been supportive of this hypothesis.[10] Nevertheless, there is evidence that the bond market may still be less efficient than the stock market (as viewed in terms of short-term trading profits.)[11] The reason behind this belief is that the stock market is heavily weighted toward being a secondary market in which *existing* issues are constantly traded between investors. The bond market is more of a primary market, with the emphasis on new issues. Thus, bond investors are not constantly changing their portfolios with each new action of the corporation. Many institutional investors, such as insurance companies, are not active bond traders in existing issues but, instead, buy and hold bonds to maturity.

THE GLOBAL BOND MARKET

The global bond market is in excess of $30 trillion. The United States makes up approximately 48 percent of the market, with no one else even close. Japan has an 18 percent market position, followed by Germany at 13 percent, and Italy at 5 percent.

The astute U.S. investor may wish to scout the entire world bond market for investments. In certain years, foreign bonds perform better than U.S. bonds. For example, in 1996, the total return in the U.S. bond market was 1.4 percent, whereas it was 30.4 percent in Italy and 17.8 percent in the United Kingdom (these latter two values represent returns translated to U.S. dollars). Going back further to 1994, there was a negative return of 7.8 percent in the United States, while the return in Germany was 9.1 percent and 8.5 percent in Japan (once again the two latter returns are translated to U.S. dollars). The high foreign returns can be related to more favorable interest rate conditions (declining rates) and/or an increasing value of the currency against the dollar.

Of course, in many years the U.S. bond market is the best-performing market in the world. The U.S. investor must carefully assess world market conditions, but there are potential benefits to international diversification as explained in Chapter 15.

Dollar-Denominated Bonds

There are key terms associated with the international bond investments. Dollar-denominated bonds are bonds in which the payment is in dollars, and these may take the form of Yankee bonds or Eurodollar bonds. Yankee bonds are issued by

10. Steven Katz, "The Price Adjustment Process of Bonds to Rating Classifications: A Test of Bond Market Efficiency," *Journal of Finance*, May 1974, pp. 551–59; and George W. Hettenhouse and William S. Sartoris, "An Analysis of the Informational Content of Bond Rating Changes," *Quarterly Review of Economics and Business*, Summer 1976, pp. 65–78.

11. George E. Pinches and Clay Singleton, "The Adjustment of Stock Prices to Bond Rating Changes," *Journal of Finance*, March 1978, pp. 29–44.

foreign governments, corporations, or major agencies (such as the World Bank) and are traded in the United States and denominated (payable) in U.S. dollars. To the U.S. investor, they appear the same as any other domestically traded bond.

Eurodollar bonds are also denominated in dollars, but they are issued and traded outside the United States. The issuing firm is normally a major U.S. corporation raising money overseas. Even though the term *euro* is used in the title Eurodollar, it could be issued in any country outside the United States.

Foreign-Pay Bonds

Foreign-pay bonds are issued in a foreign country and payable in that country's currency. For example, a Japanese government bond payable in yen would represent a foreign-pay bond. There is currency exposure to a U.S. investor in a foreign-pay bond in that the yen (or some other currency) may go up or down against the dollar.

Examples of dollar-denominated Yankee and Eurodollar bonds and foreign-pay bonds are presented in Table 11-9.

OTHER FORMS OF FIXED-INCOME SECURITIES

Our interest so far in this chapter has been on fixed-income securities, primarily in the form of bonds issued by corporations and various sectors of the government. There are other significant forms of debt instruments from which the investor may choose, and they are primarily short term in nature.

Certificates of Deposit (CDs)

The certificates of deposit (CDs) are provided by commercial banks and savings and loans (or other thrift institutions) and have traditionally been issued in small amounts such as $1,000 or $10,000, or large amounts such as $100,000. The investor provides the funds and receives an interest-bearing certificate in return.

TABLE 11–9 Global Bonds

Issuer	Type	Coupon	Rating	Currency Denomination
Italy (Republic of)	Yankee	2005	Aa3	U.S. dollar
Petro-Canada	Yankee	2021	Baa1	U.S. dollar
Bank America Corp.	Eurodollar	2009	Aa2	U.S. dollar
North American Holdings	Eurodollar	2013	Baa3	U.S. dollar
Nippon Credit Bank	Foreign-pay	2004	Baa3	Yen
Robo Securities (European firm)	Foreign-pay	2003	Aaa	Euro

Source: *Mergent Bond Record* (published by Mergent, Inc., New York, NY), April 2001.

The smaller CDs usually have a maturity of anywhere from six months to eight years, and the large $100,000 CDs, 30 to 90 days.

The large CDs are usually sold to corporate investors, money market funds, pension funds, and so on, while the small CDs are sold to individual investors. One main difference between the two CDs, besides the dollar amount, is that there may be a secondary market for the large CDs, which allows these investors to maintain their liquidity without suffering an interest penalty. Investors in the small CDs have no such liquidity. Their only option when needing the money before maturity is to redeem the certificate to the borrowing institution and suffer an interest loss penalty.

Small CDs have been traditionally regulated by the government, with federal regulatory agencies specifying the maximum interest rate that can be paid and the life of the CD. In 1986, all such interest-rate regulations and ceilings were phased out, and the free market now determines return. Any financial institution is able to offer whatever it desires. Almost all CDs are federally insured for up to $100,000 in the event of the collapse of the financial institution offering the instrument. This feature became particularly important in the late 1980s and early 1990s as a result of the problems in the savings and loan and banking industries.

Commercial Paper

Another form of a short-term credit instrument is commercial paper, which is issued by large business corporations to the public. Commercial paper usually comes in minimum denominations of $25,000 and represents an unsecured promissory note. Commercial paper carries a higher yield than small CDs or government Treasury bills and is in line with the yield on large CDs. The maturity is usually 30, 60, or 90 days (though up to six months is possible).

Bankers' Acceptance

This instrument often arises from foreign trade. A bankers' acceptance is a draft drawn on a bank for approval for future payment and is subsequently presented to the bank for payment. The investor buys the bankers' acceptance from an exporter (or other third party) at a discount with the intention of presenting it to the bank at face value at a future date. Bankers' acceptances provide yields comparable to commercial paper and large CDs and have an active secondary or resale market.

Money Market Funds

Money market funds represent a vehicle to buy short-term fixed-income securities through a mutual fund arrangement.[12] An individual with a small amount to invest may pool funds with others to buy higher-yielding large CDs and other sim-

12. Most brokerage houses also offer money market fund options.

ilar instruments indirectly through the fund. There is a great deal of flexibility in withdrawing funds through check-writing privileges.

Money Market Accounts

Money market accounts are similar to money market funds but are offered by financial institutions rather than mutual funds. Financial institutions introduced money market accounts in the 1980s to compete with money market funds. These accounts pay rates generally competitive with money market funds and normally allow up to three withdrawals (checks) a month without penalty. One advantage of a money market account over a money market fund is that it is normally insured by the federal government for up to $100,000. However, because of the high quality of investments of money market funds, this advantage is not particularly important in most cases.

Both money market funds and money market accounts normally have minimum balance requirements of $500 to $1,000. Minimum withdrawal provisions may also exist. Each fund or account must be examined for its rules. In any event, both provide much more flexibility than a certificate of deposit in terms of access to funds with only a slightly lower yield.

PREFERRED STOCK AS AN ALTERNATIVE TO DEBT

Finally, we look at preferred stock as an alternative to debt because some investors may elect to purchase preferred stock to satisfy their fixed-income needs. Preferred stock pays a stipulated annual dividend but does not include an ownership interest in the corporation. A $50 par value preferred stock issue paying $4.40 in annual dividends would provide an annual yield of 8.8 percent.

Preferred stock as an investment falls somewhere between bonds and common stock as far as protective provisions for the investor. In the case of debt, the bondholders have a contractual claim against the corporation and may force bankruptcy proceedings if interest payments are not forthcoming. Common stockholders have no such claim but are the ultimate owners of the firm and may receive dividends and other distributions after all prior claims have been satisfied. Preferred stockholders, on the other hand, are entitled to receive a stipulated dividend and must receive the dividend before any payment to common stockholders. However, the payment of preferred stock dividends is not compelling to the corporation as is true in the case of debt. In bad times, preferred stock dividends may be omitted by the corporation.

While preferred stock dividends are not tax deductible to the corporation, as would be true with interest on bonds, they do offer certain investors unique tax advantages. The tax law provides that any corporation that receives preferred or common stock dividends from another corporation must add only 30 percent of such dividends to its taxable income. Thus, if a $5 dividend is received, only 30 percent of the $5, or $1.50, would be taxable to the corporate recipient.[13]

13. An individual investor does not enjoy the same tax benefit.

TABLE 11–10 Yields on Corporate Bonds and High-Grade Preferred Stock

Year	(1) High-Grade Bonds	(2) High-Grade Preferred Stock	(2) − (1) Spread
2001	7.07%	6.42%	−0.65%
2000	7.72	7.19	−0.53
1999	7.31	6.44	−0.87
1998	6.71	6.09	−0.62
1997	7.40	6.70	−0.70
1996	7.55	6.91	−0.64
1995	7.72	7.01	−0.71
1994	8.50	7.75	−0.75
1993	7.40	6.89	−0.51
1992	8.46	7.46	−1.00
1991	8.97	8.55	−0.42
1990	9.40	9.14	−0.26
1989	9.33	9.08	−0.25
1988	9.75	9.05	−0.70
1987	9.68	8.37	−1.31
1986	9.47	8.76	−0.71
1985	11.82	10.49	−1.33
1984	13.31	11.59	−1.72
1983	12.42	10.55	−1.87
1982	14.41	11.68	−2.73
1981	14.75	11.64	−3.11
1980	12.50	10.11	−2.39
1979	9.94	8.54	−1.40
1978	8.92	7.76	−1.16
1977	8.24	7.12	−1.12

Because of this tax feature, preferred stock may carry a slightly lower yield than corporate bond issues of similar quality as indicated in Table 11–10.

Features of Preferred Stock

Preferred stock may carry a number of features that are similar to a debt issue. For example, a preferred stock issue may be *convertible* into common stock. Also, preferred stock may be *callable* by the corporation at a stipulated price, generally slightly above par. The call feature of a preferred stock issue may be of particular interest in that preferred stock has no maturity date as such. If the corporation wishes to take preferred stock off the books, it must call in the issue or purchase the shares in the open market at the going market price.

An important feature of preferred stock is that the dividend payments are usually *cumulative* in nature. That is, if preferred stock dividends are not paid in any one year, they accumulate and must be paid before common stockholders can receive any cash dividends. If preferred stock carries an $8 dividend and dividends are not paid for three years, the full $24 must be paid before any dividends go to common stockholders. This provides a strong incentive for the corporation to meet preferred stock dividend obligations on an annual basis even though preferred stock does not have a fixed, contractual obligation as do bonds. If the corporation gets behind in preferred stock dividends, it may create a situation that is difficult to get out of in the future. Being behind or in arrears on preferred stock dividends can make it almost impossible to sell new common stock because of the preclusion of common stock dividends until the preferred stockholders are satisfied.

Examples of existing preferred stock issues are presented in Table 11-11. The issues are listed in *Standard & Poor's Security Owners Stock Guide,* and the daily price quotes may be found in the NYSE Composite Stock Transactions section of *The Wall Street Journal* or other newspapers.

TABLE 11–11 Examples of Outstanding Preferred Stock Issues, March 2001

Issuer	S&P Rating	Par Value	Call Price	Market Price	Yield
Consolidated Edison (www.coned.com) 5% cumulative preferred stock	A–	100	105	$71.00	7.04%
PPL Electric Utilities (www.pplweb.com) 4.40% cumulative preferred stock	BBB	100	102	60.00	7.32
Texaco Corp. (www.texaco.com) 6.875% cumulative preferred stock	A–	25	25	25.20	6.82

Internet Resources

Website Address	Comments
www.bondmarkets.com	Provides bond information and trading
www.moodys.com	Provides bond information; some is fee based
www.bondsonline.com	Provides bond information
www.smartmoney.com	Provides information on bond yields, bond investing, and related topics
www.briefing.com	Provides some bond trading information and general information about bonds
www.teachmefinance.com	Education site pertaining to finance and bonds
www.investorguide.com	Links to sites provide information on government and corporate bonds

Chapter 12

Principles of Bond Valuation and Investment

The old notion that a bond represents an inherently conservative investment can be quickly dispelled. A $1,000, 10 percent coupon rate bond with 25 years to maturity could rise $214.80 or fall $157.60 in response to a 2 percent change in interest rates in the marketplace. Investors enjoyed a total return of 43.79 percent on long-term, high-grade corporate bonds in 1982 and 25.37 percent in 1985. However, the same bond investors would have had a negative total return in 12 of the years between 1968 and 2001. Losses were as high as 10 percent.

In this chapter, we examine the valuation process for bonds, the relationship of interest-rate changes to the business cycle, and various investment and speculative strategies related to bond maturity, quality, and pricing.

FUNDAMENTALS OF THE BOND VALUATION PROCESS

The price of a bond at any given time represents the present value of future interest payments plus the present value of the par value of the bond at maturity. We say that:

$$V = \sum_{t=1}^{n} \frac{C_t}{(1 + i)^t} + \frac{P_n}{(1 + i)^n} \qquad (12\text{-}1)$$

where:

V = Market value or price of the bond
n = Number of periods
t = Each period
C_t = Coupon or interest payment for each period, t
P_n = Par or maturity value
i = Interest rate in the market

We can use logarithms and various mathematical calculations to find the value of a bond or simply use Tables 12–1 and 12–2 to determine the present value of C_t and P_n and add the two.

Assume a bond pays 10 percent interest or $100 ($C_t$) for 20 years ($n$) and has a par ($P_n$) or maturity value of $1,000. The interest rate (i) in the marketplace is assumed to be 12 percent. The present value of the bond, using annual compounding, is shown to be $850.90 as follows:

Present Value of Coupon Payments (C_t) (from Table 12–1)	Present Value of Maturity Value (P_n) (from Table 12–2)
$n = 20, i = 12\%$	$n = 20, i = 12\%$
$100 × 7.469 = $746.90	$1,000 × 0.104 = $104.00
Present value of coupon payments	= $746.90
Present value of maturity value	= 104.00
Value of bond	= $850.90

Because the bond pays 10 percent of the par value when the competitive market rate of interest is 12 percent, investors will pay only $850.90 for the issue. This bond is said to be selling at a discount of $149.10 from the $1,000 par value. The discount is determined by several factors, such as the years to maturity, spread between the coupon and market rates, and the level of the coupon payment. While the $850.90 price was calculated using annual compounding, coupon payments on most bonds are paid semiannually. To adjust for this, we *divide* the annual coupon payment and required interest rate in the market by two and *multiply* the number of periods by two. Using the same example as before but with the appropriate adjustments for semiannual compounding, we show a slightly lower price of $849.30 as follows:

Present Value of Coupon Payments (C_t) (from Table 12–1)	Present Value of Maturity Value (P_n) (from Table 12–2)
$n = 40, i = 6\%$	$n = 40, i = 6\%$
$50 × 15.046 = $752.30	$1,000 × 0.097 = $97.00
Present value of coupon payments	= $752.30
Present value of maturity value	= 97.00
Value of bond	= $849.30

We see a minor adjustment in price as a result of using the more exacting process. To check our answer, Table 12–3 presents an excerpt from a bond table indicating prices for 10 percent and 12 percent annual coupon rate bonds at various market rates of interest (yields to maturity) and time periods. Although the values are quoted on an annual basis, the assumption is that semiannual discounting, such as that shown in our second example, was utilized. Note that for a

TABLE 12–1 Present Value of an Annuity of $1 (Coupon Payments, C_t)

Number of periods (*n*)	Interest Rate (*i*)						
	4 Percent	5 Percent	6 Percent	8 Percent	9 Percent	10 Percent	12 Percent
1	0.962	0.952	0.943	0.926	0.917	0.909	0.893
2	1.886	1.859	1.833	1.783	1.759	1.736	1.690
3	2.775	2.723	2.673	2.577	2.531	2.487	2.402
4	3.630	3.546	3.465	3.312	3.240	3.170	3.037
5	4.452	4.329	4.212	3.993	3.890	3.791	3.605
10	8.111	7.722	7.360	6.710	6.418	6.145	5.650
15	11.118	10.380	9.712	8.559	8.061	7.606	6.811
20	13.590	12.462	11.470	9.818	9.129	8.514	7.469
30	17.292	15.372	13.765	11.258	10.274	9.427	8.055
40	19.793	17.160	15.046	11.925	10.757	9.779	8.244

TABLE 12–2 Present Value of a Single Amount of $1 (Par or Maturity value, P_n)

Number of periods (*n*)	Interest Rate (*i*)						
	4 Percent	5 Percent	6 Percent	8 Percent	9 Percent	10 Percent	12 Percent
1	0.962	0.952	0.943	0.926	0.917	0.909	0.893
2	0.925	0.907	0.890	0.857	0.842	0.826	0.797
3	0.889	0.864	0.840	0.794	0.772	0.751	0.712
4	0.855	0.823	0.792	0.735	0.708	0.683	0.636
5	0.822	0.784	0.747	0.681	0.650	0.621	0.567
10	0.676	0.614	0.558	0.463	0.422	0.386	0.322
15	0.555	0.481	0.417	0.315	0.275	0.239	0.183
20	0.456	0.377	0.312	0.215	0.178	0.149	0.104
30	0.308	0.231	0.174	0.099	0.075	0.057	0.033
40	0.208	0.142	0.097	0.046	0.032	0.022	0.011

TABLE 12–3 Excerpts from Bond Value Table

Yield to Maturity (percent)	Coupon Rate (10 percent)				Coupon Rate (12 percent)				Yield to Maturity (percent)
	1 Year	5 Years	10 Years	20 Years	1 Year	5 Years	10 Years	20 Years	
8%	101.89%	108.11%	113.50%	119.79%	103.77%	116.22%	127.18%	139.59%	8%
9	100.94	103.96	106.50	109.20	102.81	111.87	119.51	127.60	9
10	100.00	100.00	100.00	100.00	101.86	107.72	112.46	117.16	10
11	99.08	96.23	94.02	91.98	100.92	103.77	105.98	108.02	11
12	98.17	92.64	88.53	84.93	100.00	100.00	100.00	100.00	12
13	97.27	89.22	83.47	78.78	99.09	96.41	94.49	92.93	13
14	96.38	85.95	78.81	73.34	98.19	92.98	89.41	86.67	14

bond with a 10 percent coupon rate, a 12 percent market rate (yield to maturity), and 20 years to run, the value in the table is 84.93. This is assumed to represent 84.93 percent of par value. Since the par value of the bond in our example was \$1,000, the answer would be \$849.30 (\$1,000 × 84.93%). This is the answer we got in our second example. A typical modern bond table may be 1,000 pages long and cover time periods up to 30 years and interest rates from ¼ to 30 percent. For professionals working with bonds on a continual basis, financial calculators and computers are quite common and have a quicker response time.

RATES OF RETURN

Bonds are evaluated on a number of different types of returns, including current yield, yield to maturity, yield to call, and anticipated realized yield.

Current Yield

The current yield, which is shown in *The Wall Street Journal* and many daily newspapers, is the annual interest payment divided by the price of the bond. An example might be a 10 percent coupon rate \$1,000 par value bond selling for \$950. The current yield would be:

$$\frac{\$100}{\$950} = 10.53\%$$

The 10.53 percent indicates the annual cash rate of return an investor would receive in interest payments on the \$950 investment but does not include any adjustments for capital gains or losses as bond prices change in response to new market interest rates. Another problem with current yield is that it does not take into consideration the maturity date of a debt instrument. A bond with 1 year to run and another with 20 years to run would have the same current yield quote if interest payments were \$100 and the price were \$950. Clearly, the one-year bond would be preferable under this circumstance because the investor would not only get \$100 in interest but also a \$50 gain in value (\$1,000 − \$950) within a *one-year* period, as the price goes to its \$1,000 maturity value.

Yield to Maturity

Yield to maturity is a measure of return that considers the annual interest received, the difference between the current bond price and its maturity value, and the number of years to maturity. More importantly, yield to maturity is the same concept as the internal rate of return or true yield on an investment. That is, it is the interest rate (i) at which you can discount the future coupon payments (C_t) and maturity value (P_n) to arrive at a known current value (V) of the bond. Now, we are assuming that you know the current value (price) of the bond (perhaps from *The Wall Street Journal*), the coupon payments, the maturity value, and the number of periods to maturity and that you want to know what the true yield to maturity is on the bond.

Restating Formula 12-1 below, the unknown is now assumed to be *i*, the interest rate in the market. The interest rate in the market is always going to be the same as the yield to maturity (the bond will yield what the market dictates):

$$V = \sum_{t=1}^{n} \frac{C_t}{(1+ⓘ)^t} + \frac{C_t}{(1+ⓘ)^n}$$

Unknown

Let us compute the value of *i*. We will use annual analysis to facilitate the calculations. First, we do an easy problem to demonstrate the process, and then we extend the analysis to a more involved calculation.

Assume V (market value or price of the bond) is \$850.90, C_t (coupon or interest payment for each period) is \$100, P_n (par or maturity value) is \$1,000, and n (number of periods) is 20. What i will force the future cash inflows to equal \$850.90? Let's use 12 percent, and prove that it works:

Present Value of Coupon Payments (C_t) (from Table 12–1)	Present Value of Maturity Value (P_n) (from Table 12–2)
n = 20, i = 12%	n = 20, i = 12%
\$100 × 7.469 = \$746.90	\$1,000 × 0.104 = \$104.00
Present value of coupon payments	= \$746.90
Present value of maturity value	= 104.00
Value of bond	= \$850.90

An i of 12 percent gave us the \$850.90 we desired because we used the same *12 percent* we employed earlier in the chapter to get \$850.90. (We turned the problem around.) Thus, 12 percent is the yield to maturity.

Let us now go to a situation where we presumably do not know the answer in advance. We will introduce you to a trial-and-error method of solution. Please feel free to use a financial calculator if one is available.

Assume a bond is paying a 7 percent coupon rate (C_t), has 15 periods to maturity (n), is selling for \$839.27 (V), and has a par maturity value (P_n) of \$1,000. What is the value of i? Using a trial-and-error process, we will need to make a first guess at the value of i and try it out. Because the bond is selling for less than par value (\$1,000), we can assume that the interest rate is greater than 7 percent. Why? Anytime a bond is trading at an interest rate (i) greater than the coupon rate, it will sell for less than par value, and that is the case in this example. Of course, if the coupon rate were greater than the interest rate (i), the bond would sell for more than par value. It would be paying more than the market is demanding and would sell at a premium rather than a discount.

Remember that our first trial-and-error calculation in this example must be at an interest rate (i) greater than 7 percent. Let's try 8 percent for the 15 periods to maturity:

Present Value of Coupon Payments (C_t) (from Table 12–1)	Present Value of Maturity Value (P_n) (from Table 12–2)
$n = 15$, $i = 8\%$	$n = 15$, $i = 8\%$
$70 × 8.559 = $599.13	$1,000 × 0.315 = $315
Present value of coupon payments	= $599.13
Present value of maturity value	= 315.00
Value of bond	= $914.13

The answer of $914.13 is higher than our desired answer of $839.27. To bring the answer down, we use a higher interest rate. The next try is at 9 percent:

Present Value of Coupon Payments (C_t) (from Table 12–1)	Present Value of Maturity Value (P_n) (from Table 12–2)
$n = 15$, $i = 9\%$	$n = 15$, $i = 9\%$
$70 × 8.061 = $564.27	$1,000 × 0.275 = $275
Present value of coupon payments	= $564.27
Present value of maturity value	= 275.00
Value of bond	= $839.27

Obviously, 9 percent is the interest rate that equates the future coupon payments (C_t) and *maturity value* (P_n) to the bond value of $839.27. Thus, we say that 9 percent is the yield to maturity.

The Formula for Approximate Yield to Maturity Most textbooks present a formula for *approximate* yield to maturity, and we shall also. Although the formula gives a less precise answer than that determined by financial calculators, computers, or the trial-and-error method, it is an appropriate tool for getting an approximation for the yield on a bond.

The formula is:[1]

$$Y' = \frac{C_t + \dfrac{P_n - V}{n}}{(0.6)V + (0.4)P_n} \qquad (12\text{–}2)$$

1. This formula is recommended by Gabriel A. Hawawini and Ashok Vora, "Yield Approximations: A Historical Perspective," *Journal of Finance*, March 1982, pp. 145–56. It tends to provide the best approximation.

Plugging values into the formula on an annual basis, we find:

Y' = Approximate yield to maturity

C_t = Coupon payment = \$100

P_n = Par or maturity value = \$1,000

V = Market value = \$850.90

n = Number of periods = 20

$$Y' = \frac{\$100 + \dfrac{\$1{,}000 - \$850.90}{20}}{(0.6)\$850.90 + (0.4)\$1{,}000}$$

$$= \frac{\$100 + \dfrac{\$149.10}{20}}{\$510.54 + \$400}$$

$$= \frac{\$100 + 7.45}{910.54}$$

$$= \frac{\$107.45}{\$910.54} = 11.80\%$$

Actually, the true yield to maturity is 12.00 percent, so the approximate yield to maturity of 11.80 percent is 0.20 percent below the actual yield. In the jargon of bond trading, each 1/100 of 1 percent is referred to as a basis point, so the difference is 20 basis points. The approximate yield to maturity method tends to understate exact yield to maturity for issues trading at a discount (in this case, the bond is priced at \$850.90). The opposite effect occurs for bonds trading at a premium (above par value).[2]

In the interest of simplicity, we will use approximation formulas in the next two sections related to yield to call and anticipated realized yield, but keep in mind these are only estimates of the exact answers.

Yield to Call

As discussed in the preceding chapter on bond fundamentals, not all fixed-income securities are held to maturity. To the extent a debt instrument may be called in before maturity, a separate calculation is necessary to determine yield to the call date. The answer is termed the yield to call. Assume a 20-year bond was initially issued at 11.5 percent interest rate, and after two years, rates have dropped. Let us assume the bond is currently selling for \$1,180, and the yield to maturity on the bond is 9.48 percent. However, the investor who purchases the bond for \$1,180 may not be able to hold the bond for the remaining 18 years because the issue can be called. Under these circumstances, yield to maturity may not be the appropriate measure of return over the expected holding period.

2. In all our bond problems, we assume we buy the bond at the beginning of an interest payment period. To the extent there is accrued interest, we would have to modify our calculations slightly.

In the present case, we assume the bond can be called at $1,090 five years after issue. Thus, the investor who buys the bond two years after issue can have his bond called back after three more years at $1,090. To compute yield to call, we determine the approximate interest rate that will equate a $1,180 investment today with $115 (11.5 percent) per year for the next three years plus a payoff or call price value of $1,090 at the end of three years. We can adjust Formula 12-2 (approximate yield to maturity) to Formula 12-3 (approximate yield to call):

$$Y'_c = \frac{C_t + \dfrac{P_c - V}{n_c}}{(0.6)V + (0.4)P_c} \qquad (12\text{-}3)$$

On an annual basis, we show:

Y'_c = Approximate yield to call
C_t = Coupon payment = $115
P_c = Call price = $1,090
V = Market value = $1,180
n_c = Number of periods to call = 3

$$Y'_c = \frac{\$115 + \dfrac{\$1{,}090 - \$1{,}180}{3}}{(0.6)\$1{,}180 + (0.4)\$1{,}090}$$

$$= \frac{\$115 + \dfrac{-\$90}{3}}{\$708 + \$436}$$

$$= \frac{\$115 - \$30}{\$1{,}144}$$

$$= \frac{\$85}{\$1{,}144}$$

$$= 7.43\%$$

The yield to call figure of 7.43 percent is 205 basis points less than the yield to maturity figure of 9.48 percent cited on the previous page. Clearly, the investor needs to be aware of the differential, which represents the decrease in yield the investor would receive if the bond were called. Generally, any time the market price of a bond is equal to or greater than the call price, the investor should do a separate calculation for yield to call.[3]

In the case where market interest rates are much lower than the coupon, there is always the chance the company will call the bond. Because of this possibility, the call price often serves as an upper price limit, and further reductions in mar-

---

3. Bond tables may also be used to find the exact value for yield to call. A source is *Thorndike Encyclopedia of Banking and Financial Tables* (Boston: Warren, Gorham & Lamont, 1981).

ket interest rates will not cause this callable bond to increase in price. In other words, investors' capital gain potentials may be quite limited with bonds subject to a call.

Reinvestment Assumption

Throughout our analysis, when we have talked about yield to maturity, yield to call, and anticipated realized yield, we have assumed that the determined rate also represents an appropriate rate for reinvestment of funds. If yield to maturity is 11 or 12 percent, then it is assumed that coupon payments, as they come in, can also be reinvested at that rate. To the extent that this is an unrealistic assumption, investors will wish to temper their thinking. For example, if it is anticipated that returns can be reinvested at a higher rate in the future, this increases true yield, and the opposite effect would be present for a decline in interest rates. The reinvestment topic is more fully developed in Chapter 13.

THE MOVEMENT OF INTEREST RATES

In developing our discussion of bond valuation and investments, we observed that lower interest rates bring higher bond prices and profits. A glance back at Table 12-3 indicates a 12 percent coupon rate, 20-year bond will sell for $1,171.60 if yields to maturity on competitive bonds decline to 10 percent and for $1,276.00 when yields decline to 9 percent. The maturity of the bond is also important, with the impact on price being greater for longer-term obligations.

The investor who wishes to make a substantial profit in the bond market must try to anticipate the turns and directions of interest rates. While much of the literature on efficient markets indicates that this is extremely difficult,[4] Wall Street economists, bank economists, and many others rely on interest-rate forecasts to formulate financial strategies. The fact that short-term and long-term rates do not necessarily move in the same direction or move with the same magnitude makes the task even more formidable. Nevertheless, some historical analysis and knowledge of interest-rate patterns over the business cycle are useful in making investment decisions.

Interest rates have long been viewed as a coincident indicator in our economy; that is to say, they are thought to move in concert with industrial production, gross domestic product, and similar measures of general economic health. This is generally true, although in the last five recessions, the change in interest rates has actually lagged behind the decline in industrial production.

While inflationary expectations have the greatest influence on long-term rates, a number of other factors also influence overall interest rates. The demand for funds by individuals, businesses, and the government represents one side of the

4. Michael J. Prell, "How Well Do the Experts Forecast Interest Rates?" Federal Reserve Bank of Kansas City, *Monthly Review*, September–October 1973, pp. 3–13; Oswald D. Bowlin and John D. Martin, "Extrapolations of Yields over the Short Run: Forecast or Folly?" *Journal of Monetary Economics*, 1975, pp. 275–88; and Richard Roll, *The Behavior of Interest Rates* (New York: Basic Books, 1970).

equation, with the desire for savings and Federal Reserve policy influencing the supply side. A classic study by Feldstein and Eckstein found that bond yields were inversely related to the money supply (the slower the growth, the higher the interest rates) and directly related to economic activity, the demand for loanable funds by the government, the level of inflation, and changes in short-term interest rate *expectations.*[5]

Term Structure of Interest Rates

Of general importance to understanding the level of interest rates is the development of an appreciation for the relationship between the level of interest rates and the maturity of the debt obligation. There is no one single interest rate but, rather, a whole series of interest rates associated with the given maturity of bonds.

The term structure of interest rates depicts the relationship between maturity and interest rates. It is sometimes called a yield curve because yields on existing securities having maturities from three months to 30 years are plotted on a graph to develop the curve. To eliminate any business risk consideration, the securities analyzed are usually U.S. Treasury issues. Examples of four different types of term structures are presented in Figure 12-1.

In panel a, we see an ascending term structure pattern in which interest rates increase with the lengthening of the maturity dates. When the term structure is in this posture, it is a general signal that interest rates will rise in the future. In panel b, we see a descending pattern of interest rates, with this pattern generally predictive of lower interest rates. Panel c is a variation of panel b, with the hump representing intermediate-term interest rates. This particular configuration is an even stronger indicator that interest rates may be declining in the future. Finally, in panel d, we see a flat-term structure indicating investor indifference between debt instrument maturity. This generally indicates that there is no discernible pattern for the future of interest rates. Several theories of interest rates are used to explain the particular shape of the yield curve. We review three of these theories.

Expectations Hypothesis The dominant rationale for the shape of the term structure of interest rates rests on a phenomenon called the expectations hypothesis. The hypothesis is that any long-term rate is an average of the expectations of future short-term rates over the applicable time horizon. Thus, if lenders expect short-term rates to be continually increasing, they will demand higher long-term rates. Conversely, if they anticipate short-term rates to be declining, they will accept lower long-term rates. An example may be helpful. Suppose the interest rate on a one-year Treasury security is 6 percent, and that after one year, it is assumed that a new one-year Treasury security may be bought to yield 8 percent. At the end of year 2, it is assumed that a third one-year Treasury security may be bought to yield 10 percent. In other words, the investor can buy (this is sometimes

5. Martin Feldstein and Otto Eckstein, "The Fundamental Determinants of the Interest Rate," *The Review of Economics and Statistics,* November 1970, pp. 363–75.

FIGURE 12–1 Term Structure of Interest Rates

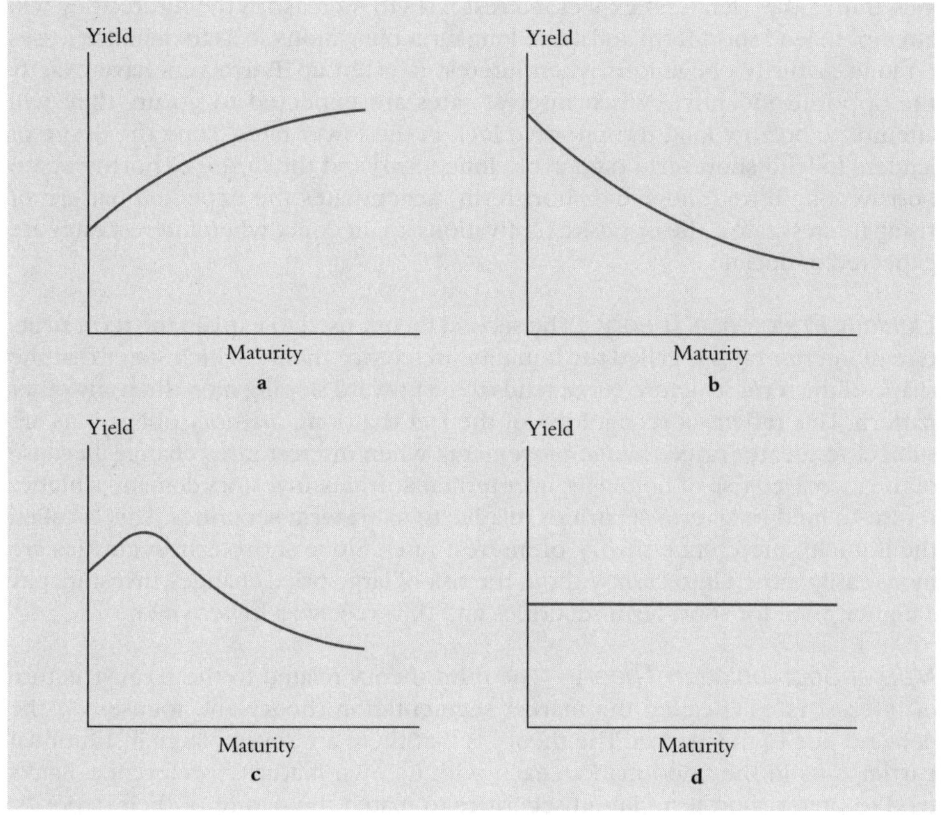

called roll over) three one-year Treasury securities in yearly succession, each with an expected one-year return.

But what about investors who buy one-, two-, or three-year securities today? The yield they will require will be based on expectations about the future. For the one-year security, there is no problem. The 6 percent return will be acceptable. But investors who buy a two-year security now will want the average of the 6 percent they could expect in the first year and the 8 percent expected in the second year, or 7 percent.[6] An investor who buys a three-year security will demand an average of 6, 8, and 10 percent, or an 8 percent return. Higher expected interest rates in the future will mean that longer maturities will carry higher yields than will shorter maturities. The reverse would be true if interest rates were expected to go down.

6. The expectations hypothesis actually uses the geometric mean (compound growth rate) rather than the arithmetic mean (simple average) used in the example. For a short number of years, the two means would be quite similar.

The expectations hypothesis tends to be reinforced by lender/borrower strategies. If investors (lenders) expect interest rates to increase in the future, they will attempt to lend short-term and avoid long-term obligations so as to diminish losses on long maturity obligations when interest rates go up. Borrowers have exactly the opposite incentive. When interest rates are expected to go up, they will attempt to borrow long term now to lock in the lower rates. Thus, the desire of lenders to lend short term (and avoid long term) and the desire of borrowers to borrow long term (and avoid short term) accentuates the expected pattern of rising interest rates. The opposite motivations are in effect when interest rates are expected to decline.

Liquidity Preference Theory The second theory used to explain the term structure of interest rates is called the liquidity preference theory, which states that the shape of the term structure curve tends to be upward sloping more than any other pattern. This reflects a recognition of the fact that long maturity obligations are subject to greater price-change movements when interest rates change. Because of the increased risk of holding longer-term maturities, investors demand a higher return to hold long-term securities relative to short-term securities. This is called the liquidity preference theory of interest rates. Since short-term securities are more easily turned into cash without the risk of large price changes, investors pay a higher price for short-term securities and thus receive a lower yield.

Market Segmentation Theory The third theory related to the term structure of interest rates is called the market segmentation theory and focuses on the demand side of the market. The theory is that there are several large institutional participants in the bond market, each with its own maturity preference. Banks tend to prefer short-term liquid securities to match the nature of their deposits, whereas life insurance companies prefer long-term bonds to match their long-run obligations. The behavior of these two institutions, as well as that of savings and loans, often creates pressure on short-term or long-term rates but very little in the intermediate market of five- to seven-year maturities. This theory helps to focus on the accumulation or liquidation of securities by institutions during the different phases of the business cycle and the resultant impact on the yield curve.

We have now covered all three explanations of the term structure of interest rates. As stated earlier, the expectations hypothesis is probably the most dominant theory, but all three theories have some part in the creation of the term structure of interest rates.

The question being asked in the first part of this decade was, What would be the next major movement in the term structure of interest rates? Would inflation rear its ugly head, causing a shift up in all levels of interest rates, or could the economy continue to grow at a relatively slow pace with no significant evidence of inflation? Of course, a recession is always a possibility as well.

Before concluding our discussion of the term structure of interest rates and proceeding to the development of investment strategies, one final observation is significant. Short-term rates, which are most influenced by Federal Reserve policy in attempting to regulate the money supply and economy, are much more volatile than long-term rates. An examination of Figure 12-2 indicates that *short-term* prime commercial paper rates move much more widely than *long-term,* high-grade corporate bond rates. It also demonstrates quite well the positive relationship between inflation as measured by the consumer price index and both long- and short-term interest rates.

INVESTMENT STRATEGY: INTEREST-RATE CONSIDERATIONS

Thus far in this chapter, we have examined the different valuation procedures for determining the price or yield on a bond and the methods for evaluating the future course of interest rates. We now bring this knowledge together in the form of various investment strategies.

When the bond investor believes interest rates are going to fall, he will take a bullish position in the market by buying long-term bonds and try to maximize the price movement pattern associated with a change in interest rates. The investor can do this by considering the *maturity, coupon rate,* and *quality* of the issue.

Because the impact of an interest-rate change is much greater on long-term securities, the investor generally looks for extended maturities. The impact of various changes in yields on bond prices for a 12 and a 6 percent coupon rate bond can be examined in Table 12-4. For example, looking at the −2% line for the 12 percent coupon bond, we see a 2 percent drop in competitive yields would cause a 1.86 percent increase in value for a bond with 1 year to maturity but an 18.93 percent increase in value for a bond with 30 years to maturity. For the same 2 percent drop in rates, the 6 percent coupon bond would increase 1.92 percent (1 year to maturity) and 34.59 percent (30 years to maturity). The relationship between these two bonds further shows that the lower 6 percent coupon bond is more price sensitive than the higher 12 percent coupon bond.

We can also observe that the effect of interest-rate changes is not symmetrical. Drops in interest rates cause proportionally greater gains than increases in interest rates cause losses, particularly as we lengthen the maturity. An evaluation of the 30-year column in Table 12-4 confirms that both bonds are more price sensitive to a decline in yields than to a rise in yields.[7]

Although we have emphasized the need for long maturities in maximizing price movement, the alert student will recall that short-term interest rates generally move up and down more than long-term interest rates as was indicated in Figure 12-2. What if short-term rates are more volatile—even though long-term rates have a greater price impact—which then do we choose? The answer is fairly direct. The mathematical impact of long maturities on price changes far outweighs the more volatile feature of short-term interest rates. A 1-year, 12 percent debt

7. A sophisticated investor would also consider the concept of *duration.* Duration is defined as the weighted average time to recover interest and principal. For a bond that pays interest (which includes most cases except zero-coupon bonds), duration will be shorter than maturity in that interest payments start almost immediately. Portfolio strategy may call for maximizing duration rather than maturity in order to achieve maximum movement. A complete discussion of this topic is presented in Chapter 13.

FIGURE 12–2 Relative Volatility of Short-Term and Long-Term Interest Rates

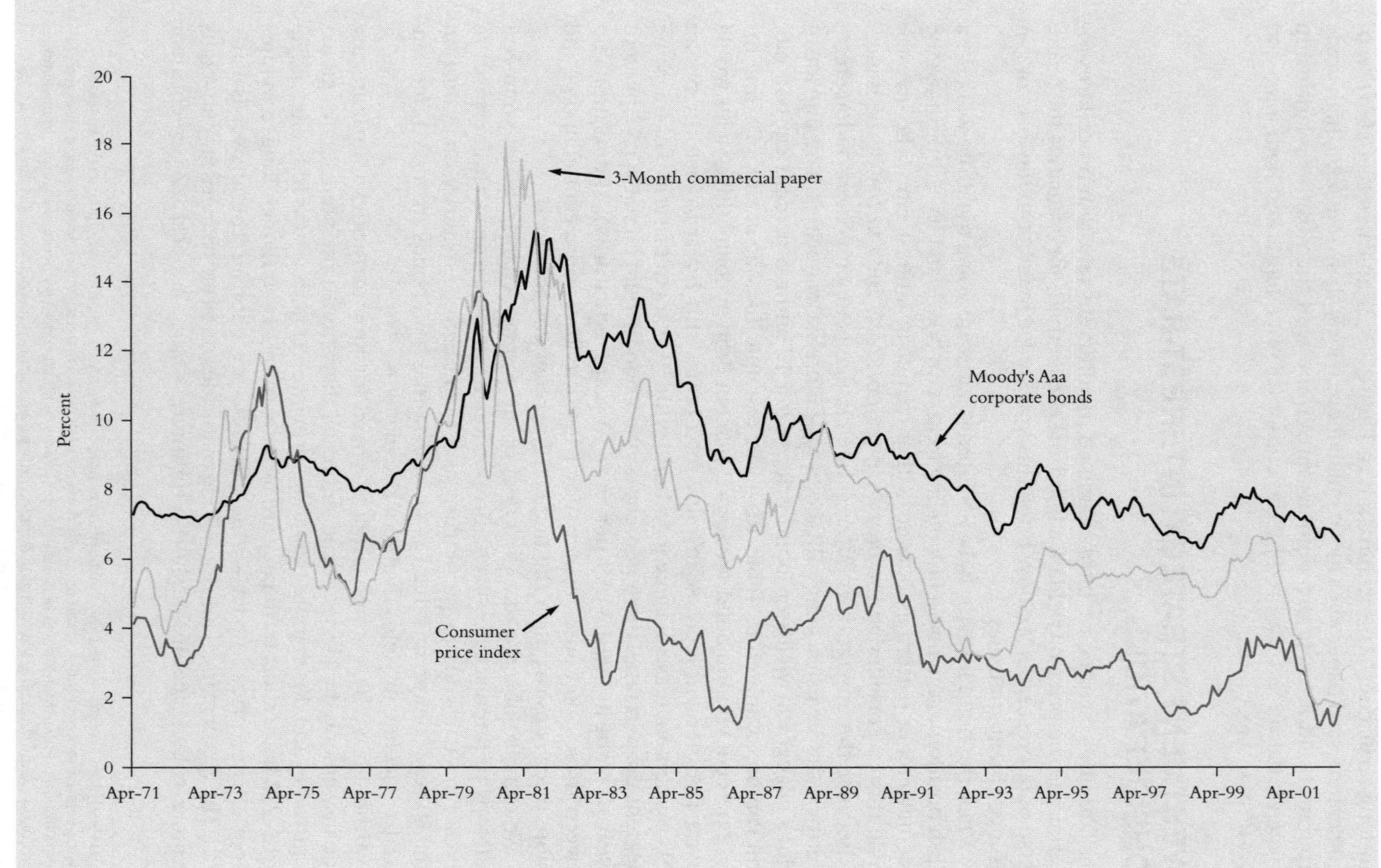

Note: Three-month commercial paper rate consists of the 3-month commercial paper rate between 1971 and 1997 and the 3-month AA financial commercial paper rate from 1997 to 2002.

Source: St. Louis Federal Reserve website: www.stls.frb.org/fred

instrument would need to have an interest-rate *change* of almost 9 *percent* to have the equivalent impact of a 1 percent change in a 30-year debt obligation.

Bond-Pricing Rules

The relationships we presented in this section can be summarized in a set of bond-pricing rules. Prices of existing bonds have a relationship to maturities, coupons, and market yields for bonds of equal risk. These relationships are evident from an examination of previously presented Table 12–4. If you look at the change in bond prices in Table 12–4, you may be able to describe many of the relationships presented in the following list:

1. Bond prices and interest rates are inversely related.
2. Prices of long-term bonds are more sensitive to a change in yields to maturity than short-term bonds.
3. Bond price sensitivity increases at a decreasing rate as maturity increases.
4. Bond prices are more sensitive to a decline in market yields to maturity than to a rise in market yields to maturity.
5. Prices of low-coupon bonds are more sensitive to a change in yields to maturity than high-coupon bonds.
6. Bond prices are more sensitive when yields to maturity are low than when yields to maturity are high.

TABLE 12–4 Change in Market Prices of Bonds for Shifts in Yields to Maturity

12 Percent Coupon Rate

	Maturity (Years)				
Yield Change	1	5	10	20	30
+3%	−2.69%	−10.30%	−15.29%	−18.89%	−19.74%
+2	−1.81	−7.02	−10.59	−13.33	−14.04
+1	−0.91	−3.57	−5.01	−7.08	−7.52
−1	+0.92	+3.77	+5.98	+8.02	+8.72
−2	+1.86	+7.72	+12.46	+17.16	+18.93
−3	+2.81	+11.87	+19.51	+27.60	+30.96

6 Percent Coupon Rate

	Maturity (Years)				
Yield Change	1	5	10	20	30
+3%	−2.75%	−11.67%	−19.25%	−27.39%	−30.82%
+2	−1.85	−7.99	−13.42	−19.64	−22.52
+1	−0.94	−4.10	−7.02	−10.60	−12.41
−1	+0.95	+4.33	+7.72	+12.46	+15.37
−2	+1.92	+8.90	+16.22	+27.18	+34.59
−3	+2.91	+13.74	+25.59	+44.63	+58.80

Understanding these six bond-pricing relationships is at the heart of creating bond trading and investment strategies. The next chapter on duration provides a more comprehensive analysis of price sensitivity, coupon rates, maturity, market rates, and their combined impact on bond prices.

Example of Interest-Rate Change

Assume we buy 20-year, $1,000 Aaa bonds at par providing a 12 percent coupon rate. Further assume interest rates on these bonds in the market fall to 10 percent. Based on Table 12–5, the new price on the bonds would be $1,171.60 ($1,000 × 117.16).

Although we could assume the gain in price from $1,000 to $1,171.60 occurred very quickly, even if the time horizon were one year, the gain is still 17.16 percent. This is only part of the picture. An integral part of many bond-interest-rate strategies is the use of margin or borrowed funds. For government securities, it is possible to use margin as low as 5 percent, and on high-quality utility or corporate bonds, the requirement is generally 30 percent. In the preceding case, if we had put down 30 percent cash and borrowed the balance, the rate of return on invested capital would have been 57.2 percent:

$$\frac{\text{Return}}{\text{Investment}} = \frac{\$171.60}{\$300.00} = 57.2\%$$

Although we would have had to pay interest on the $700 we borrowed, the interest on the bonds (which belongs to the borrower/investor) would have partially or fully covered this expense. Also, if interest rates drop further to 8 percent, our leveraged return could be over 100 percent on our original investment.

Lest the overanxious student sell all his or her worldly possessions to participate in this impressive gain, there are many admonitions. Even though we think interest rates are going down, they may do the opposite. A 2 percent *increase* in interest rates would cause a $133.30 loss or a negative return on a leveraged investment of $300 or a 44.4 percent loss. At the very time it appears that interest rates should be falling due to an anticipated or actual recession, the Federal Reserve

TABLE 12–5 Bond Value Table

Yield to Maturity	Coupon Rate 12 percent — Number of Years: 10	20	30
8%	127.18%	139.59%	145.25%
10	112.46	117.16	118.93
12	100.00	100.00	100.00
14	89.41	86.55	85.96

Source: Reprinted by permission from the *Thorndike Encyclopedia of Banking and Financial Tables,* 1981.

may generate the opposite effect by tightening the money supply as an anti-inflation weapon as it did in 1974, 1979, 1981, 1994, and 2001.

Deep Discount versus Par Bonds

Another feature in analyzing a bond is the current pricing of the bond in regard to its par value. Bonds that were previously issued at interest rates significantly lower than current market levels may trade at deep discounts from par. These are referred to as deep discount bonds. As an example, the Missouri Pacific 4¾ percent bonds due to mature in 2020 were selling at $645 in the summer of 2001. Their bond rating was Baa2, and the yield to maturity was 8.01 percent.

Deep discount bonds generally trade at a lower yield to maturity than bonds selling at close to par. There are two reasons for this. First, a deep discount bond has almost no chance to be called away. Even if prices go up because of falling interest rates, the price is still likely to be below par value. Because of this protection against a call, the investor in deep discount bonds accepts a lower yield. Second, investors in deep discount bonds have the potential for higher percentage price increases (because of the low price base at which the investment is made).

Yield Spread Considerations

As discussed in the previous chapter, different types or grades of bonds provide different yields. For example, the yield on Baa corporate bonds is always above that of corporate Aaa obligations to compensate for risk. Similarly, Aaa corporates pay a higher yield than long-term government obligations. In Figure 12-3, we observe the actual yield spread between Moody's corporate Baa's, Moody's corporate Aaa's, and long-term government securities.

Let's direct our attention to total spread between corporate Baa bonds and government securities (corporate Aaa's fall somewhere in between). Over the long term, the spread appears to be between 75 and 100 basis points.[8] Nevertheless, at certain phases of the business cycle, the yield spread changes. For example, in the early phases of a recession, confidence tends to be at a low ebb, and as a consequence, investors attempt to shift out of lower grade securities into stronger instruments. The impact on the yield spreads can be observed in the recessions of 1969–70, 1973–75, 1981–82, and 1990–91. In all cases, the yield spread between corporate Baa's and government securities went over 150 basis points, only to narrow again during the recovery. Remember that in Chapter 9, on technical analysis, one of the market indicators was the *Barron's* Confidence Index, which measured the ratio of high-grade bonds to medium-grade bonds. The closer the confidence index is to 1.00, the smaller the spread between rates and the more optimistic investors are about the economy. The further the index is below 1.00, the greater the spread in yields and the less the confidence.

8. The concept of higher yields on Baa bonds should not be confused with that of junk bonds. In the latter case, the yield is substantially higher, but so is the risk of default.

FIGURE 12–3 Yield Spread Differentials on Long-Term Bonds

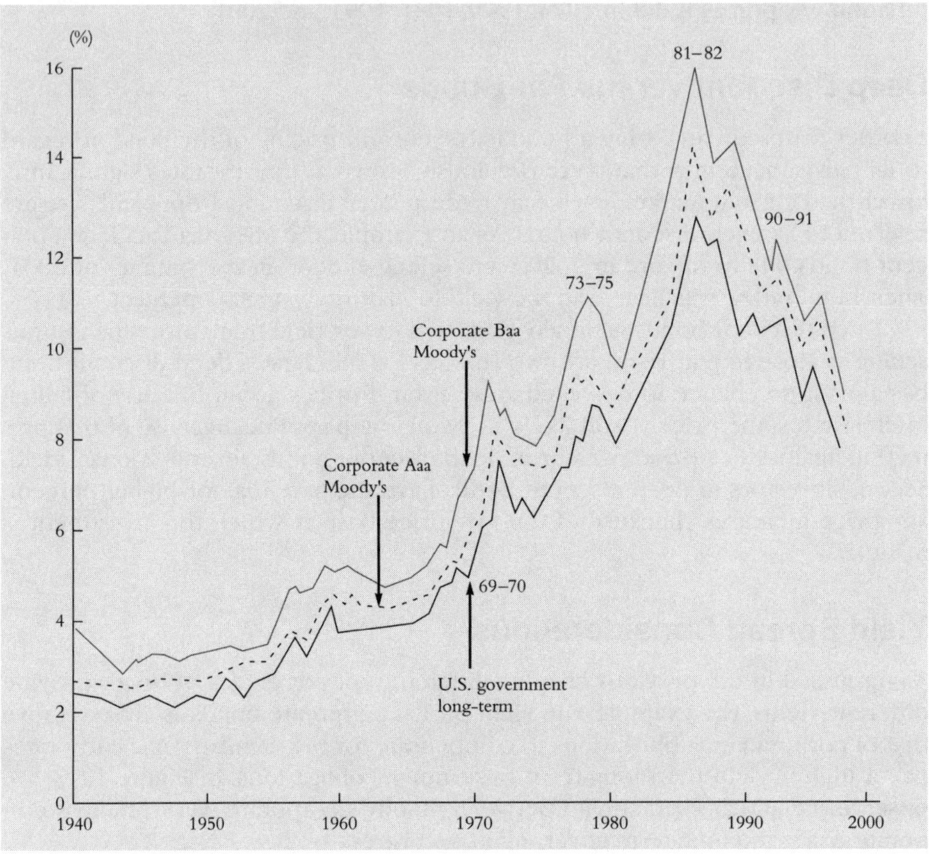

Source: *Federal Reserve Bulletins* (Washington, D.C.: Federal Reserve Board of Governors).

Investors must determine how the yield spread affects their strategy. If they do not need to increase the quality of the portfolio during the low-confidence periods of a recession, they can enjoy unusually high returns on lower-grade instruments relative to higher grades.

BOND SWAPS

The term bond swap refers to selling out of a given bond position and immediately buying into another one with similar attributes in an attempt to improve overall portfolio return or performance.[9]

9. Interest rate swaps are a somewhat different concept.

Often there are bonds that appear to be comparable in every respect with the exception of one characteristic. For example, ***newly issued bonds*** that are the equivalent in every sense to outstanding issues generally trade at a slightly higher yield.

Swaps may also be utilized for tax-adjustment purposes and are very popular at the end of the year. Assume you own a single A rated AT&T bond that you bought five months ago, and you are currently sitting on a 20 percent capital loss because of rising interest rates. You can sell the bond and claim the loss (up to $3,000) against other income.[10] This will save you taxes equal to the loss times your marginal tax rate. You can then take the proceeds from the sale and reinvest in a bond of equal risk, and you will have increased your total cash returns because of tax benefits.

Another common swap is the pure pickup yield swap in which a bond owner thinks he can increase the yield to maturity by selling a bond and buying a different bond of equal risk. The key to this swap is that the bond price of one or both bonds has to be in disequilibrium. This assumes that the market is less than totally efficient. By selling the bond that is overpriced and purchasing the bond that is underpriced, the investor is increasing the yield on the investment. If by chance the true quality and risk of the two bonds are different, the bond trader may have swapped for nothing or may even end up losing on the trade. Other types of swaps exist for arbitrages associated with interest-payment dates, call transactions, conversion privileges, or any quickly changing factor in the market.

Internet Resources

Website Address	Comments
www.smartmoney.com	Provides some bond information; unique feature is living yield curve
www.bondsonline.com	Provides trading, yield curve data
www.stls.frb.org	The St. Louis Federal Reserve Board website has a wealth of interest rate data.

10. Losses greater than $3,000 can be carried forward to future years.

Chapter 13

Duration and Reinvestment Concepts

REVIEW OF BASIC BOND VALUATION CONCEPTS

In Chapter 12, we discussed the principles of bond valuation. The value of a bond was established in Formula 12-1 as follows:

$$V = \sum_{t=1}^{n} \frac{C_t}{(1 = i)^t} + \frac{P_n}{(1 + i)^n}$$

where:

V = Market value or price of the bond
n = Number of periods
t = Each period
C_t = Coupon or interest payment for each period, t
P_n = Par or maturity value
i = Interest rate in the market

Based on this equation, as interest rates in the market rise, the price of the bond will decline because the present value of the cash flows is worth less at a higher discount rate. The opposite is true if interest rates decline. We also demonstrated in Table 12-4 that bonds with long-term maturities were generally more sensitive to changes in interest rates than were short-term bonds. Reproduction of part of Table 12-4 on the following page shows that a 30-year bond exhibits larger price changes in response to a change in yield than do shorter-term obligations. For example, a 2 percent drop in interest rates would cause a 1.86 percent increase in value for a bond with one year to maturity, but an 18.93 percent increase in value for a bond with 30 years to maturity. Given the relationship between the life of a bond and the price sensitivity just described, it is particularly important that we have an appropriate definition of the life or term of a bond.

The first inclination is to say that the term of a bond is an easily determined matter. One supposedly merely needs to look up the maturity date (such as 2010 or 2020) in a bond book, and the matter is settled. However, the notion of effective life of a bond is more complicated than this. The situation is somewhat analogous to the quoted coupon rate on the bond not really conveying the true yield on the obligation. Similarly, the maturity date on a bond may not convey all important information about the life of a bond.

In studying the true characteristics about the life of a bond, not only must the final date and amount of the maturity payment be considered but also the pattern of coupon payments that occurs in the interim. If you were to receive $1,000 after 20 years and no interest payments during the term of the obligation, clearly the effective life is 20 years. But suppose in addition to the $1,000, you were also to receive $100 per year for the next 20 years. Part of the payment is coming early and part of the payment is coming late, and the weighted average term of the payout is certainly less than 20 years. The higher the coupon payments relative to the maturity payment, the shorter the weighted average life of the payout. The weighted average life refers to the time period over which the coupon payments and maturity payment on a bond are recovered. In the next section, we shall go through the simple mathematics of computing the weighted average life of the payout; for now it is enough to know that such a concept exists.

The important consideration is that *bond price sensitivity* can be more appropriately related to *weighted average life* than to just the maturity date. While many bond analysts simply relate price sensitivity to maturity (and we did that also in Chapter 12), there is a more sophisticated approach that is related to weighted average life.

Before we move on to calculate weighted average life, there is an investment decision we wish you to consider. Assume you have to decide whether to invest in an 8 percent coupon rate bond with a 20-year maturity or a 12 percent coupon rate bond with a 25-year maturity. Which bond will have the larger increase in price if interest rates decline? You may choose the 25-year, 12 percent coupon rate bond

(Reproduction of Table 12–4) Change in Market Prices of Bonds for Shifts in Yields to Maturity (12 Percent Coupon Rate)

Yield	Maturity (Years)				
Change	1	5	10	20	30
+3%	−2.69%	−10.30%	−15.29%	−18.89%	−19.74%
+2	−1.81	−7.02	−10.59	−13.33	−14.04
+1	−0.91	−3.57	−5.01	−7.08	−7.52
−1	+0.92	+3.77	+5.98	+8.02	+8.72
−2	+1.86	+7.72	+12.46	+17.16	+18.93
−3	+2.81	+11.87	+19.51	+27.60	+30.96

because it has the longer maturity, but don't answer too quickly on this. Let's consider weighted average life and then come back to this question of price sensitivity.

DURATION

The concept of weighted average life of a bond falls under the general topic of duration. We shall first of all do a simple example of weighted average life and then more formally look at duration. Assume we have a five-year bond that provides \$80 per year for the next five years plus \$1,000 at the end of five years. For ease of calculation, we are using annual coupon payments in our analysis. Semiannual analysis would change the answer only slightly. An approach to computing weighted average life is presented in Table 13-1.

First, we see that the weighted average life of the bond, based on the annual cash flows, is 4.4290 years. Let's see how this is calculated. In column (1) is the year in which each cash flow falls, and in column (2) is the size of the cash flow for each year plus the total cash flow. Column (3) calls for dividing the annual cash flow in column (2) by the total cash flow at the bottom of column (2) to determine what percentage of the total it represents. For example, the annual cash flow of \$80 on the first line of column (2) represents 0.0571 of the total cash flow of \$1,400. (\$80 ÷ \$1,400 = 0.0571.) The same basic procedure is followed for all subsequent years. In column (4), each year is multiplied by the weights (percentages) developed in column (3). For example, year 1 is multiplied by 0.0571 to arrive at 0.0571 in column (4). Year 2 is multiplied by 0.0571 to arrive at 0.1142 in column (4). This procedure is followed for each year and each weight. The final answer is 4.4290 for the weighted average life of the bond.

If you can understand the approach presented in Table 13-1, you should have no difficulty following a more formal and appropriate definition of weighted average life called duration. Duration represents the weighted average life of a bond where the weights are based on the *present value* of the individual cash flows relative to the *present value* of the total cash flows. An example of duration is pre-

TABLE 13–1 Simple Weighted Average Life

(1) Year, t	(2) Cash Flow	(3) Annual Cash Flow (2) ÷ by Total Cash Flow	(4) Year × Weight (1) × (3)
1	\$80	0.0571	0.0571
2	80	0.0571	0.1142
3	80	0.0571	0.1713
4	80	0.0571	0.2284
5	80	0.0571	0.2855
5	1,000	0.7145	3.5725
Total cash flow →	\$1,400	1.0000	4.4290

sented in Table 13-2. Present value calculations are based on the market rate of interest (yield to maturity) for the bond, which in this case, we shall assume to be 12 percent.

The only difference between Tables 13-1 and 13-2 is that in Table 13-2, the cash flows are present valued before the weights are determined. Thus, the cash flows (2) are multiplied by the present value factors at 12 percent (3) to arrive at the present value of cash flows (4). The total present value of cash flows at the bottom of column (4) is also the same as the price of the bond. In column (5), weights for each year are determined by dividing the present value of each annual cash flow (4) by the total present value of cash flows [bottom of column (4)]. For example in year 1, the present value of the cash flow is $71.44, and this is divided by the total present value of cash flows of $855.40 to arrive at 0.0835 in column (5). Similarly, the weight in year 2, as shown in column (5), is determined by dividing $63.76 by $855.40 to arrive at 0.0745. In column (6), each year is multiplied by the weights developed in column (5). For example, year 1 is multiplied by 0.0835 to arrive at 0.0835 in column (6). Year 2 is multiplied by 0.0745 to arrive at 0.1490. This procedure is followed for each year, and the values are then summed.

The final answer for duration (the weighted average life based on present value) is 4.2498. This 4.2498 duration is referred to as Macaulay duration, named after Frederick Macaulay, who developed this concept more than 100 years ago. Duration, once determined, is the most representative value for effective bond life and the measure against which bond price sensitivity should be evaluated.

The formula for duration can be formally stated as:

$$\text{Macaulay duration (D)} = \underbrace{\frac{CF\,PV}{V}}_{\substack{\uparrow \\ \textit{Weight}}}\underbrace{(1)}_{\substack{\uparrow \\ \textit{Year}}} + \underbrace{\frac{CF\,PV}{V}}_{\substack{\uparrow \\ \textit{Weight}}}\underbrace{(2)}_{\substack{\uparrow \\ \textit{Year}}} + \underbrace{\frac{CF\,PV}{V}}_{\substack{\uparrow \\ \textit{Weight}}}\underbrace{(3)}_{\substack{\uparrow \\ \textit{Year}}} + \ldots + \underbrace{\frac{CF\,PV}{V}}_{\substack{\uparrow \\ \textit{Weight}}}\underbrace{(n)}_{\substack{\uparrow \\ \textit{Year}}} \qquad (13\text{-}1)$$

where:

CF = Yearly cash flow for each time period
PV = Present value factor for each time period
V = Total present value or market price of the bond
n = Number of periods to maturity[1]

1. Using the symbols from Formula 12-1, duration can also be stated as:

$$\text{Duration} = \sum_{t=1}^{n} \frac{C_t \dfrac{1}{(1+i)^t}}{V}(t) + \frac{P_n \dfrac{1}{(1+i)^n}}{V}(n)$$

If semiannual analysis is used throughout the calculation, the answer should be divided by two to convert the figure to annual terms.

TABLE 13–2 Duration Concept of Weighted Average Life

(1) Year, t	(2) Cash Flow (CF)	(3) PV Factor at 12 Percent	(4) PV of Cash Flow (CF)	(5) PV of Annual Cash Flow (4) ÷ by Total PV of Cash Flows	(6) Year × Weight (1) × (5)
1	$ 80	0.893	$ 71.44	0.0835	0.0835
2	80	0.797	63.76	0.0745	0.1490
3	80	0.712	56.96	0.0666	0.1998
4	80	0.636	50.88	0.0595	0.2380
5	80	0.567	45.36	0.0530	0.2650
5	$1,000	0.567	567.00	0.6629	3.3145
			Total PV of → cash flows (V) $855.40	1.0000	4.2498 ↑ Duration

In Table 13-3, we observe durations for an 8 percent coupon rate bond with maturities of 1, 5, and 10 years. The discount rate is 12 percent. The procedure used to compute duration in Table 13-3 is the same as that employed in Table 13-2. Although many calculations are involved, you should primarily direct your attention to the last value presented in column (6) for each of the three bonds. This value represents the duration of the issue.

We see in Table 13-3 that the duration for a one-year bond is 1.0. Since all cash flows are paid at the end of year 1, duration equals the maturity.[2] As maturity increases (to 5 and 10 years), duration increases but less than the maturity of the bond. With a 5-year bond, duration is 4.2498, and with a 10-year bond, duration is 6.8381. Duration is increasing at a decreasing rate because the principal repayment in the last year becomes a smaller percentage of the total present value of cash flow, and the annual coupon payments become more important.[3]

DURATION AND PRICE SENSITIVITY

Once duration is computed, its most important use is in determining the price sensitivity of a bond. In Table 13-4, we consider the maturity, duration, and percentage price change for an 8 percent coupon rate bond based on a 2 percent decrease and on a 2 percent increase in interest rates. The *market* rate of interest for computing duration in Table 13-4 is 8 percent. Duration is related not only to maturity but also to coupon rate and market rate of interest. For example, in Table 13-3, the coupon rate of interest was 8 percent, and the market rate of interest was 12 percent. In the calculations in Table 13-4, the coupon rate is 8 percent, and the initial market rate of interest is assumed to be 8 percent. Because of the different market rates of interest in Tables 13-3 and 13-4, the duration for a given maturity (such as 5 or 10 years) will be different. The point just discussed will be

2. If semiannual analysis were used, the duration would be slightly less than the maturity in the first year.

3. A sinking-fund provision can also have an effect on duration, causing the weighted average life of the bond to be shorter.

TABLE 13–3 Duration for an 8 Percent Coupon Rate Bond with Maturities of 1, 5, and 10 Years Discounted at 12 Percent

(1) Year, t	(2) Cash Flow (CF)	(3) PV Factor at 12 Percent	(4) PV of Cash Flow (CF)	(5) PV of Annual Cash Flow (4) ÷ by Total PV of Cash Flows	(6) Year × Weight (1) × (5)
1-Year Bond					
1	$ 80	0.893	$ 71.44	0.0741	0.0741
1	1,000	0.893	893.00	0.9259	0.9259
			Total PV of cash flows → $964.44	1.0000	1.0000 ↑ Duration
5-Year Bond					
1	$ 80	0.893	$ 71.44	0.0835	0.0835
2	80	0.797	63.76	0.0745	0.1490
3	80	0.712	56.96	0.0666	0.1998
4	80	0.636	50.88	0.0595	0.2380
5	80	0.567	45.36	0.0530	0.2650
5	1,000	0.567	567.00	0.6629	3.3145
			Total PV of cash flows → $855.40	1.0000	4.2498 ↑ Duration
10-Year Bond					
1	$ 80	0.893	$ 71.44	0.0923	0.0923
2	80	0.797	63.76	0.0824	0.1648
3	80	0.712	56.96	0.0736	0.2208
4	80	0.636	50.88	0.0657	0.2628
5	80	0.567	45.36	0.0586	0.2930
6	80	0.507	40.56	0.0524	0.3144
7	80	0.452	36.16	0.0467	0.3269
8	80	0.404	32.32	0.0418	0.3344
9	80	0.361	28.88	0.0373	0.3357
10	80	0.322	25.76	0.0330	0.3330
10	$1,000	0.322	322.00	0.4160	4.1600
			Total PV of cash flows → $774.08	1.0000	6.8381 ↑ Duration

further clarified later in the chapter, so even if you do not fully understand it, you should still continue to read on.

We see in Table 13-4 that the longer the maturity or duration, the greater the impact of a 2 percent change in interest rates on price. However, we shall also observe how much more closely the percentage change in price parallels the change in duration as compared with maturity. For example, between 25 and 50 years, duration increases very slowly [column (2)], and the same can be said for the increase in the percentage impact that a 2 percent decline in interest rates

TABLE 13–4 Duration and Price Sensitivity (8 Percent Coupon Rate Bond)

(1) Maturity	(2) Duration	(3) Impact of a 2 Percent Decline in Interest Rates on Price	(4) Impact of a 2 Percent Increase in Interest Rates on Price
1	1.0000	+1.89%	−1.81%
5	4.3121	+8.42	−7.58
10	7.2470	+14.72	−12.29
20	10.6038	+22.93	−17.03
25	11.5290	+25.57	−18.50
30	12.1585	+27.53	−18.85
40	12.8787	+30.09	−19.55
50	13.2123	+31.15	−19.83

has on price [column (3)]. This is true despite the fact that the maturity period has increased by 100 percent, from 25 to 50 years.

As a rough measure of price sensitivity, one can multiply duration times the change in interest rates to determine the percentage change in the value of a bond.

$$\text{Percentage change in the value of a bond approximately equals} \rightarrow \text{Duration} \times \text{Change in interest rates} \qquad (13\text{-}2)$$

The sign in the final answer is reversed because interest-rate changes and bond prices move in opposite directions. For example, if a bond has a duration of 7.2470 years, and interest rates go down by 2 percent, a rough measure of bond value appreciation is +14.494 percent (7.2470 × 2). Columns (2) and (3) in Table 13–4, across from 10 years maturity, indicate this is a good approximation. That is, when duration was 7.2470, a 2 percent drop in interest rates actually produced a 14.72 percent increase in bond prices (not too many basis points away from our formula value of +14.494 percent).[4] The approximation gets progressively less accurate as the term of the bond is extended. It is also a less valid measure for interest-rate increases (and the associated price decline). Even with these qualifications, one can observe a more useful relationship between price changes and duration than between price changes and maturity.

It is for this reason that the analyst must have a reasonable feel for the factors that influence duration. The length of the bond affects duration, but as previously mentioned, it is not the only variable. Duration is also influenced by market rate

4. The approximation can be slightly improved by using modified duration instead of actual duration.

of interest and the coupon rate on the bond. It is theoretically possible for these two factors to outweigh maturity in determining duration. That is to say, it is possible that a bond with a shorter maturity than another bond may actually have a longer duration and be more price sensitive to interest rate changes.

Duration and Market Rates

Market rates of interest (yield to maturity) and duration are inversely related. The higher the market rate of interest, the lower the duration. This is because of the present-value effect that is part of duration. Higher market rates of interest mean lower present values. For example, in Table 13-2, if the market rate of interest in column (3) had been 16 percent instead of 12 percent, the final answer for duration would have been 4.1859. The new value is computed in Table 13-5. Clearly, it is less than the 4.2498 duration value in Table 13-2.

To expand our analysis, in Table 13-6 we see the duration values for an 8 percent coupon rate bond at different market rates of interest. As market rates of interest increase, duration decreases. This can be easily seen in the 20-year row (reading across). At a 4 percent market rate of interest, duration for the 8 percent coupon rate bond is 12.3995. At 8 percent, it is 10.6038, and at 12 percent, 8.9390.

Also note in Table 13-6 that an equal change in market rates of interest will have a bigger impact on duration when rates move down than when they move up. For example, in the 50-year row, a 4 percentage point decrease in market rates of interest (say, from 8 percent to 4 percent) causes duration to increase by 7.0358 years, from 13.2123 to 20.2481 years. A similar increase from 8 percent to 12 percent would cause duration to decrease by only 3.8407 years, from 13.2123 to 9.3716 years.

Duration and Coupon Rates

In the previous section, we learned that duration is inversely related to the market rate of interest. We now look at the relationship between duration and the coupon rate on a bond. As the coupon rate rises, duration decreases. Why? The answer is that high coupon rate bonds tend to produce higher annual cash flows before maturity and thus tend to weight duration toward the earlier to middle years. On the other hand, low coupon rate bonds produce less annual cash flows before maturity and have less influence on duration. Duration is weighted more heavily toward the final payment at maturity, and duration tends to be somewhat closer to the actual maturity on the bond. At the extreme, a zero-coupon bond has the same maturity and duration.

The relationship between duration and coupon rates can be seen in Table 13-7. Here three different coupon rate bonds are presented. Each bond is assumed to have a maturity of 25 years. The best way to read the table is to pick a market rate of interest in the first column and then read across the table to determine the duration at various coupon rates. For example, at an 8 percent market rate of interest, duration is 13.2459 at a 4 percent coupon rate, 11.5290 at an 8 percent coupon

TABLE 13–5 Duration of an 8 Percent Coupon Rate Bond with a 16 Percent Market Rate of Interest

(1) Year, *t*	(2) Cash Flow (*CF*)	(3) *PV* Factor at 16 Percent	(4) *PV* of Cash Flow (*CF*)	(5) *PV* of Annual Cash Flow (4) ÷ by Total *PV* of Cash Flows	(6) Year × Weight (1) × (5)
1	$ 80	0.862	$ 68.96	0.0935	0.0935
2	80	0.743	59.44	0.0806	0.1612
3	80	0.641	51.28	0.0695	0.2085
4	80	0.552	44.16	0.0598	0.2392
5	80	0.476	38.08	0.0516	0.2580
5	1,000	0.476	476.00	0.6451	3.2255
		Total *PV* of → cash flows	$737.92	1.0000	4.1859 ↑ Duration

TABLE 13–6 Duration Values at Varying Market Rates of Interest (Based on 8 Percent Coupon Rate Bond)

	Market Rates of Interest				
Maturity (Years)	4 Percent	6 Percent	8 Percent	10 Percent	12 Percent
1	1.0000	1.0000	1.0000	1.0000	1.0000
5	4.3717	4.3423	4.3121	4.2814	4.2498
10	7.6372	7.4450	7.2470	7.0439	6.8381
20	12.3995	11.4950	10.6038	9.7460	8.9390
25	14.2265	12.8425	11.5290	10.3229	9.2475
30	15.7935	13.8893	12.1585	10.6472	9.3662
40	18.3274	15.3498	12.8787	10.9176	9.3972
50	20.2481	16.2494	13.2123	10.9896	9.3716

TABLE 13–7 Duration and Coupon Rates (25-Year Bonds)

	Coupon Rates		
Market Rate of Interest	4 Percent	8 Percent	12 Percent
4%	16.2470	14.2265	13.3278
6	14.7455	12.8425	12.0407
8	13.2459	11.5290	10.8396
10	11.8112	10.3229	9.7501
12	10.4912	9.2475	8.7844

rate, and 10.8396 at a 12 percent coupon rate. Clearly, the higher the coupon rate, the lower the duration (and vice versa).

The impact of coupon rates on duration is also demonstrated in Figure 13-1. Note that with a zero-coupon bond, the line is at a 45-degree angle; that is, duration and years to maturity are always the same value. There is only one payment, and it is at maturity.

You can also observe in Figure 13-1 that progressively higher coupon rates lead to a lower duration. As an example, go to point N on the horizontal axis and observe duration for 4 percent, 8 percent, and 12 percent interest. Clearly the higher the coupon rate, the lower the duration value.

Because the higher the duration, the greater the price sensitivity, it follows that an investor desiring maximum price movements will look toward lower coupon rate bonds. As previously demonstrated, low coupon rate and high duration go together, and high duration leads to maximum price sensitivity. The relationship of low coupon rates to price sensitivity was briefly discussed in Chapter 12 under investment strategy. We now see that the unnamed explanatory variable at that point was duration.

BRINGING TOGETHER THE INFLUENCES ON DURATION

The three factors that determine the value of duration are the maturity of the bond, the market rate of interest, and the coupon rate. Duration is positively correlated with maturity but moves in the opposite direction of market rates of interest and coupon rates; that is, the higher the market rate of interest or the coupon rate, the lower the duration. Earlier in this chapter, you were asked to consider whether you should invest in an 8 percent coupon rate, 20-year bond or a 12 percent coupon rate, 25-year bond. Since we were assuming interest rates were going to go down, you were looking for maximum price volatility. Had you not studied duration, you probably would have selected the bond with the longer maturity. This would generally be a valid assumption as indicated in Chapter 12. However, the primary emphasis to the sophisticated bond investor when assessing price volatility, or sensitivity, is duration.

Note that the bond with the longer maturity (25 years versus 20 years) also has a higher coupon rate (12 percent versus 8 percent). The first factor (longer maturity) would indicate higher duration, but the second factor (higher coupon rate) would indicate a lower duration. What is the net effect? The answer can be found in earlier tables in this chapter. Let's assume that the *market rate* of interest is 12 percent for both bonds. Table 13-6 presented information on 8 percent coupon rate bonds for varying maturities and market rates of interest. To determine the duration on the 8 percent coupon rate, 20-year bond, assuming a 12 percent market rate of interest, we read across the 20-year row to the last column in the table and see the answer is 8.9390. (Note that all bonds in Table 13-6 have an 8 percent coupon rate, so we must identify the value associated with 20 years and a 12 percent market rate of interest.)

To determine the duration for the 12 percent coupon rate, 25-year bond with a 12 percent market rate of interest, we must go to Table 13-7. Note that all bonds in this table have a 25-year maturity, so read down to a market rate of interest of

FIGURE 13–1 The Effect of Coupon Rates on Duration

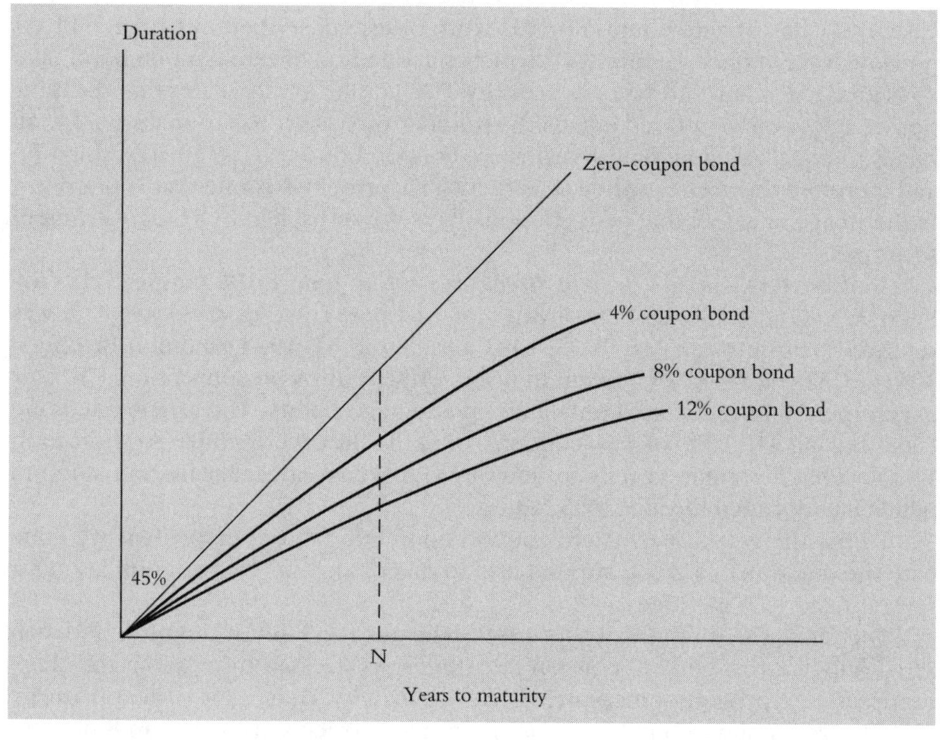

12 percent and across to a coupon rate of 12 percent. The value for duration on this bond is 8.7844.

Based on this analysis, the answer to the question posed earlier in the chapter is that the bond with the shorter maturity (8 percent coupon rate for 20 years) has a higher duration than the bond with the greater maturity (12 percent for 25 years) and thus is the most price sensitive.[5]

Bond	Duration
8%, 20 years	8.9390 ← greater price sensitivity
12%, 25 years	8.7844

In actuality, if interest rates went down by 2 percent, the 8 percent, 20-year bond would go up by 18.5 percent, while the 12 percent, 25-year bond would increase by only 17.9 percent.

5. As previously indicated, if we vary the market rate of interest, we can also influence the outcome to our question.

DURATION AND ZERO-COUPON BONDS

Characteristics of zero-coupon bonds were briefly described in Chapter 11. As previously mentioned, Figure 13-1 depicts the duration of zero-coupon bonds as a 45-degree line relative to years to maturity. This graphically indicates that the duration of a zero-coupon bond equals the number of years it has to maturity. For all bonds of equal risk and maturity, the zero-coupon bond has the greatest duration and therefore the greatest price sensitivity. This price risk is one that is often lost in the image of safety that zero-coupons have when backed by U.S. government securities.

A classic headline in *The Wall Street Journal* on June 1, 1984, appeared as follows: "Zero-Coupon Bonds' Price Swings Jolt Investors Looking for Security."[6] It was reported that between March 31, 1983 and March 31, 1984, Salomon Brothers' 30-year CATs declined 25 percent in price, while returns on conventional 30-year government bonds declined only a few percentage points. The article cited one client buying $100,000 of zero-coupons, thinking they were similar to short-term Treasury bill investments, only to find out four weeks later that his zero-coupon bonds had declined in value by $24,000.

To put the volatility of a zero-coupon bond into better perspective, we compare the duration of a zero-coupon bond to that of an 8 percent coupon bond for several maturities in Table 13-8.

The far right column in Table 13-8 indicates the ratio of duration between zero-coupon and 8 percent coupon rate bonds. As stressed throughout the chapter, duration represents a measure of price sensitivity. Thus, for a 10-year maturity period, a zero-coupon bond is almost 1½ times as price sensitive as an 8 percent coupon rate bond (the ratio in the last column is 1.4625). For a 20-year maturity period, it is over two times more price sensitive (2.2374), and for 50 years the price sensitivity ratio is over five times greater (5.3353). This might explain why zero-coupons were much more sensitive to rising interest rates during 1983-84 as described in the story in *The Wall Street Journal.* Of course, tremendous profits can be made in zero-coupon bonds when there is a sharp drop in interest rates as in early 1985 and again in 1997 and early 1998.

TABLE 13–8 Duration of Zero-Coupon versus 8 Percent Coupon Bonds (Market Rate of Interest Is 12 Percent)

(1) Years to Maturity	(2) Duration of Zero-Coupon Bond	(3) Duration of 8 Percent Coupon Bond	(4) Relative Duration of Zero-Coupon to 8 Percent Coupon Bonds (2) ÷ (3)
10	10	6.8374	1.4625
20	20	8.9390	2.2374
30	30	9.3662	3.2030
40	40	9.3972	4.2566
50	50	9.3716	5.3353

6. Randall Smith, "Zero-Coupon Bonds' Price Swings Jolt Investors Looking for Security," *The Wall Street Journal,* June 1, 1984, p. 19.

THE USES OF DURATION

Duration is primarily used as a measure to judge bond price sensitivity to interest-rate changes. Because duration includes information on several variables (maturity, coupon rate, and market rate of interest), it captures more information than any one of them. It therefore allows more accurate decisions for complex bond strategies. One such strategy involves the timing of investment inflows to provide a needed cash outlay at a known future date. Perhaps $1 million is needed after five years. Everything is tailored to this five-year time horizon. If interest rates go up, there will be a decline in the value of the portfolio but a higher reinvestment rate opportunity for inflows. Similarly, if interest rates go down, there will be capital appreciation for the portfolio but a lower reinvestment rate opportunity. By tying all the investment decisions to a duration period, the portfolio manager can take advantage of these counterforces to ensure a necessary outcome. This strategy is called immunization and is used by insurance companies, pension funds, and other institutional money managers to protect their portfolios against swings in interest rates. For a more comprehensive discussion of immunization strategies, an article by Fisher and Weil is an appropriate source.[7] For an excellent criticism of duration and immunization strategy, see Yawitz and Marshall.[8] One of the problems with duration analysis is that it often assumes a parallel shift in yield curves. Although long-duration bonds are clearly more price sensitive than shorter-duration bonds, there is no assurance that long- and short-term interest rates will move by equal amounts.

BOND REINVESTMENT ASSUMPTIONS AND TERMINAL WEALTH ANALYSIS

Reinvestment Assumptions

As indicated in the previous section, one concern an investor may have when purchasing bonds is that the interest income will not be reinvested to earn the same return the coupon payment represents. This may not be a problem for an individual consuming the interest payments, but it could be a serious concern for individuals building a retirement portfolio or a pension fund manager accumulating funds for future payout to retirees. The crucial issue is the amount of money accumulated at the time the retirement fund will be used to cover living expenses. One major determinant of the ending value of a retirement fund is the rate of return on coupon payments as they are reinvested.

Since the middle 1970s, interest rates have generally been more volatile than during previous periods. This has caused more emphasis on the management of fixed-income securities, not only in the selection of maturity but also in the switch-

7. Lawrence Fisher and Roman L. Weil, "Coping with Risk of Interest Rate Fluctuations: Returns to Bondholders from Naive and Optimal Strategies," *Journal of Business,* October 1971, pp. 408–31.

8. Jess B. Yawitz and William J. Marshall, "The Shortcomings of Duration as a Risk Measure for Bonds," *Journal of Financial Research,* Summer 1981, pp. 91–101.

ing from short- to long-term securities. These volatile rates have caused more emphasis on concepts such as duration to measure bond price sensitivity and on total return as a measure of bond management success. Given that interest rates change daily and by large amounts over a year, what impact would a lower or higher reinvestment assumption have on the outcome of your retirement nest egg?

First, let us look at Table 13-9. The material covers the compound sum of $1. All interest is reinvested at the stated rate in order to find the ending value of $1 invested to maturity. For our current analysis, we are assuming annual interest (though the answer changes only slightly if we use semiannual interest).

The table values are given in $1 amounts, so for a $1,000 bond we would just move the decimal three places to the right. A $1,000 bond having a 12 percent coupon rate with interest being reinvested at 12 percent would compound to $93,051 over 40 years, while a 7 percent coupon bond reinvested at 7 percent would compound to only $14,974 over a similar period. A difference of 5 points in the rates creates a total difference of $78,077. This is quite a large difference. Notice that the longer the compounding period, the larger the amount. From further inspection of Table 13-9, other comparisons can be made between years and total ending values.

The importance of the reinvestment assumption can also be viewed from the perspective of its contribution to total wealth. For example, an investor owning a 40-year bond with a 12 percent coupon rate and an assumed reinvestment rate of 12 percent will have an accumulated value of $93,051. In terms of payout, $4,800 (40 × $120) comes directly from 40 years of 12 percent interest payments, $1,000 comes from principal, and the balance of $87,251 comes from interest that is earned on the annual interest payments. In this case, interest on interest represents 93.8 percent of the overall return ($87,251/$93,051).

Terminal Wealth Analysis

Now, we will assume a reinvestment assumption different from the coupon rate. Take the two extreme values from Table 13-9 of 12 percent and 7 percent. Assume you buy a bond having a 12 percent coupon rate, but the interest can only be reinvested at 7 percent. To find the ending value of this investment, we will need to use a terminal wealth table.

Table 13-10 is called a terminal wealth table because it generates the ending value of the investment at the end of each year, assuming the bond has a *maturity* date corresponding to that year. Let's use 10 years as an example in examin-

TABLE 13–9 Compound Sum of $1.00

Period	7 Percent	8 Percent	9 Percent	10 Percent	11 Percent	12 Percent
10	$ 1.967	$ 2.159	$ 2.367	$ 2.594	$ 2.839	$ 3.106
20	3.870	4.661	5.604	6.727	8.062	9.646
30	7.612	10.063	13.268	17.449	22.892	29.960
40	14.974	21.725	31.409	45.259	65.001	93.051

TABLE 13–10 Terminal Wealth Table (12 Percent Coupon with 7 Percent Reinvestment Rate on Interest)

(1) Years to Maturity	(2) Principal	(3) Annual Coupon Interest	(4) Accumulated Interest[a]	(5) Reinvestment Rate on Interest	(6) Interest on Interest	(7) Total Annual Interest	(8) Portfolio Sum	(9) Compound Sum Factor	(10) Annual Percentage Return
0.0	$1,000.00								
1.0	1,000.00	$120.00	$ 0.00			$ 120.00	$ 1,120.00	1.12000	12.00%
2.0	1,000.00	120.00	120.00	0.07	$ 8.40	128.40	1,248.40	1.24840	11.73
3.0	1,000.00	120.00	248.40	0.07	17.39	137.39	1,385.79	1.38579	11.48
4.0	1,000.00	120.00	385.79	0.07	27.01	147.01	1,532.80	1.53280	11.26
5.0	1,000.00	120.00	532.80	0.07	37.30	157.30	1,690.10	1.69010	11.06
6.0	1,000.00	120.00	690.10	0.07	48.31	168.31	1,858.41	1.85841	10.86
7.0	1,000.00	120.00	858.41	0.07	60.90	180.09	2,038.50	2.03850	10.71
8.0	1,000.00	120.00	1,038.50	0.07	72.70	192.70	2,231.20	2.23120	10.55
9.0	1,000.00	120.00	1,231.20	0.07	86.18	206.18	2,437.38	2.43738	10.40
10.0	1,000.00	120.00	1,437.38	0.07	100.62	220.62	2,658.00	2.65800	10.26
11.0	1,000.00	120.00	1,658.00	0.07	116.06	236.06	2,894.06	2.89406	10.14
12.0	1,000.00	120.00	1,894.06	0.07	132.58	252.58	3,146.64	3.14664	10.02
13.0	1,000.00	120.00	2,146.64	0.07	150.26	270.26	3,416.90	3.41690	9.91
14.0	1,000.00	120.00	2,416.90	0.07	169.18	289.18	3,706.08	3.70608	9.80
15.0	1,000.00	120.00	2,706.08	0.07	189.43	309.43	4,015.51	4.01551	9.71
16.0	1,000.00	120.00	3,015.51	0.07	211.09	331.09	4,346.60	4.34660	9.61
17.0	1,000.00	120.00	3,346.60	0.07	234.26	354.26	4,700.86	4.70086	9.54
18.0	1,000.00	120.00	3,700.86	0.07	259.06	379.06	5,079.92	5.07992	9.44
19.0	1,000.00	120.00	4,079.92	0.07	285.59	405.59	5,485.51	5.48551	9.37
20.0	1,000.00	120.00	4,485.51	0.07	313.99	433.99	5,919.50	5.91950	9.29
21.0	1,000.00	120.00	4,919.50	0.07	344.37	464.37	6,383.87	6.38387	9.22
22.0	1,000.00	120.00	5,383.87	0.07	376.87	496.87	6,880.74	6.88074	9.16
23.0	1,000.00	120.00	5,880.74	0.07	411.65	531.65	7,412.39	7.41239	9.09
24.0	1,000.00	120.00	6,412.39	0.07	448.87	568.87	7,981.26	7.98126	9.04
25.0	1,000.00	120.00	6,981.26	0.07	488.69	608.69	8,589.95	8.58995	8.98
26.0	1,000.00	120.00	7,589.95	0.07	531.30	651.30	9,241.25	9.24125	8.92
27.0	1,000.00	120.00	8,241.25	0.07	576.89	696.89	9,938.14	9.93814	8.87
28.0	1,000.00	120.00	8,938.14	0.07	625.67	745.67	10,683.81	10.68381	8.82
29.0	1,000.00	120.00	9,683.81	0.07	677.87	797.87	11,481.68	11.48168	8.78
30.0	1,000.00	120.00	10,481.68	0.07	733.72	853.72	12,335.40	12.33540	8.73
31.0	1,000.00	120.00	11,335.40	0.07	793.48	913.48	13,248.88	13.24888	8.69
32.0	1,000.00	120.00	12,248.88	0.07	857.42	977.42	14,226.30	14.22630	8.65
33.0	1,000.00	120.00	13,226.30	0.07	925.84	1,045.84	15,272.14	15.27214	8.61
34.0	1,000.00	120.00	14,272.14	0.07	999.05	1,119.05	16,391.19	16.39119	8.57
35.0	1,000.00	120.00	15,391.19	0.07	1,077.38	1,197.38	17,588.57	17.58857	8.53
36.0	1,000.00	120.00	16,588.57	0.07	1,161.20	1,281.20	18,869.77	18.86977	8.50
37.0	1,000.00	120.00	17,869.77	0.07	1,250.88	1,370.88	20,240.65	20.24065	8.46
38.0	1,000.00	120.00	19,240.65	0.07	1,346.85	1,466.85	21,707.50	21.70750	8.43
39.0	1,000.00	120.00	20,707.50	0.07	1,449.53	1,569.53	23,277.03	23.27703	8.40
40.0	1,000.00	120.00	22,277.03	0.07	1,559.39	1,679.39	24,956.42	24.95642	8.37

[a]At beginning of year.

ing Table 13–10. If the bond matures in 10 years, the $1,000 principal in column (2) will be recovered. Also the investor will receive $120 in annual interest (12 percent of $1,000) in year 10 as indicated in column (3). In column (4), the accumulated interest up to the *beginning* of year 10 is shown. The reinvestment rate on this previously accumulated interest is a mere 7 percent as indicated in column (5). The interest on the previously accumulated interest is $100.62 (0.07 × $1,437.38). Finally, the total interest for year 10 is shown in column (7). This consists of the coupon interest of $120 and the interest on interest of $100.62 and totals to $220.62. The total ending value of the portfolio is shown in column (8). The ending value consists of the recovered principal of $1,000 plus the accumulated interest of $1,437.38 up to the beginning of year 10 plus the total interest paid in year 10 of $220.62. The ending wealth value (portfolio sum) thus shown in column (8) is $2,658.00. The value is summarized below:

Recovered principal	$1,000.00	Column (2)
Accumulated interest (beginning of year 10)	1,437.38	Column (4)
Total annual interest (during year 10)	220.62	Column (7)
Ending wealth value (portfolio sum)	$2,658.00	Column (8)

A $1,000 investment that grows to $2,658.00 after 10 years is the equivalent of a $1 investment that grows to 2.65800 as indicated in column (9). The annual percentage return for a $1 investment that grows to 2.65800 after 10 years is 10.26 percent as indicated in column (10).

A similar analysis can be done for all other maturity periods running from 1 to 40 years. One thing to notice from Table 13–10 is that the longer the maturity period of the bond, the greater the effect the low 7 percent reinvestment rate has on the bond. For 5 years, the annual percentage return [column (10)] is 11.06 percent; for 15 years, 9.71 percent; and for 40 years, 8.37 percent.

What is the actual difference between the ending value for a 40-year, 12 percent coupon rate bond assuming a *12 percent* reinvestment rate and the 40-year, *7 percent* reinvestment rate just presented in Table 13–10? Earlier in this section, Table 13-9 demonstrated that a 12 percent coupon rate bond with an assumed 12 percent reinvestment rate for 40 years would grow to $93,051. In Table 13–10, we see that a 12 percent coupon rate bond with a 7 percent reinvestment rate will grow to only $24,956.42 after 40 years. It should be evident that it is not only the coupon rate that matters but the reinvestment rate as well.

If the bond were not held to maturity in our analysis, then we would have to rely on the realized rate of return analysis developed in Chapter 12. The realized rate of return approach would assume that the bond is not held to maturity and that it is sold at either a gain or a loss. In the case of the bond analyzed in the terminal wealth table (Table 13–10), we know that since interest rates are assumed to decline, any sale of the bond before maturity should result in a capital gain. How large that capital gain would be will be dependent on its duration. Terminal wealth analysis is a way of analyzing the reinvestment assumption when bonds are held to maturity, while the realized yield approach assumes bonds are actively traded to take advantage of interest-rate swings.

Zero-Coupon Bonds and Terminal Wealth

One of the benefits of zero-coupon bonds is that they lock in a compound rate of return (or reinvestment rate) for the life of the bond *if held to maturity.* There are no coupon payments during the life of the bond to be reinvested, so the originally quoted rate holds throughout if held to maturity. If a $1,000 par value, 15-year zero-coupon bond is quoted at a price of $183 to yield 12 percent, you truly have locked in a 12 percent reinvestment rate. Some would say you have not only locked in 12 percent but have thrown away the key. In any event, zero-coupon bonds allow you to predetermine your reinvestment rate.

Of course, if a zero-coupon bond is sold before maturity, there could be large swings in the sales price of the bond because of its high duration characteristics. Under this circumstance, the locked-in reinvestment concept for the zero-coupon bond loses much of its meaning. It is valid only when the zero-coupon bond is held to maturity.

Chapter 14

Convertible Securities and Warrants

An investment in convertible securities or warrants offers the market participant special opportunities to meet investment objectives. For conservative investors, convertible securities can offer regular income and potential downside protection against falling stock prices. Convertibles also offer capital gains opportunities for an investor desiring the appreciation potential of an equity investment. Warrants are more speculative securities than convertibles and also offer the chance for leveraged returns.

These securities have been used as financing alternatives by corporations in periods of high interest rates or tight money. Also, convertibles have been utilized as a medium of exchange for acquiring other companies' stock in mergers and acquisitions. Convertibles and warrants have advantages to the corporation and to the owner of the security. It is important to realize as we go through this chapter that what is an advantage to the corporation is often a disadvantage to the investor, and vice versa. These securities involve trade-offs between the buyer and the corporation that are considered in the pricing of each security.

CONVERTIBLE SECURITIES

A convertible security is a bond or share of preferred stock that can be converted into common stock at the option of the holder. Thus, the owner has a fixed-income security that can be transferred to common stock if and when the performance of the firm indicates such a conversion is desirable.

For the last several editions of this book we have been following the 7.5 percent convertible bond of Telxon (pronounced Telzon). On December 1, 2000, Telxon was acquired by Symbol Technologies, Inc., in an exchange of stock. Even though a change of ownership occurred, the bond still exists and trades in the market under its Telxon name. As of the date of merger the bond became convertible into shares of Symbol Technologies, Inc., rather than Telxon. We will follow through on the Telxon bond from its offering date to its current status.

Telxon makes hand-held computers that are used to take inventory based on bar codes. You have probably seen them used by employees in grocery stores. The company has had an extremely volatile existence in sales, profits, and stock prices, reporting a loss of $19 million the quarter before its takeover. The Telxon convertible security was originally a 25-year long-term bond, and it demonstrates the benefits and perils of owning any convertible security. During the first 30 months of its existence (June 1, 1987, through December 15, 1989) the price of the convertible bond ranged between $1,000 and $555 while its 2001 high and low price ranged between $1,090 and $860. In the next several pages we will follow through on this example from its beginning through 2001.

In general, the best time to buy convertible bonds is when interest rates are high (bond prices are depressed) and when stock prices are relatively low. A purchase at times like these increases the probability of a successful investment because rising stock prices and falling interest rates both exert upward pressure on the price of a convertible security. This will become more apparent as we proceed through the chapter.

CONVERSION PRICE AND CONVERSION RATIO

The Telxon annual report states that this 7.5 percent convertible bond is a subordinated bond with a sinking fund and is due June 1, 2012. One bond is convertible into shares of common stock of the company at a conversion price of $26.75 per share. The bonds are currently redeemable by the company at the par value of $1,000.

While there is standard information about the coupon being 7.5 percent and the maturity date being June 1, 2012, one piece of information is not answered directly. How many shares of common stock are you entitled to receive on conversion? The annual report states that the bonds are convertible at $26.75 per share. This is called the conversion price.

The face value ($1,000) or par value never changes (the market price does), so by dividing the face value by the conversion price, we get the number of shares received on conversion of one $1,000 bond. This is called the conversion ratio:

$$\frac{\text{Face value}}{\text{Conversion price}} = \text{Conversion ratio} \qquad (14\text{-}1)$$

For the Telxon convertible bond, an investor would receive 37.38 shares for each bond:

$$\frac{1{,}000 \text{ (Face value)}}{\$26.75 \text{ per share (Conversion price)}} = 37.38 \text{ shares}$$

Value of the Convertible Bond

The Telxon bond was originally sold at $1,000, and the common stock price on the Nasdaq Stock Market on the day of this offering closed at $22. If the bondholder converted the bond into 37.38 shares of common stock, what would be the market value of the common stock received? We can find this by multiplying the conversion ratio by the market price per share of the common stock, and we get a value of $822.36.

$$\text{Conversion ratio} \times \text{Common stock price} = \text{Conversion value} \qquad (14\text{–}2)$$

$$37.38 \text{ shares} \times \$22 = \$822.36$$

This value is called the conversion value and indicates the value of the underlying shares of common stock each bond represents.

The convertible bond also has what is called a pure bond value. This represents its value as a straight bond (nonconvertible). In the case of Telxon, straight bonds of similar risk (B2 rating) had a yield to maturity of about 13 percent at the time of issue. A rating of B2 is considered a high-yield bond (junk bond), and considerable risk is associated with the 13 percent yield to maturity. If the Telxon 7.5 percent convertible bond were valued at 13 percent yield to maturity, the pure bond value would be $596.[1] This pure bond value is considered the floor value, or minimum value, of the bond. The conversion value and the pure bond value can be seen in Figure 14–1, which depicts the Telxon convertible bond. You should be aware that it is possible for the pure bond value to change if interest rates change. In other words, the pure bond value will be inversely related to changes in interest rates just like any other fixed-income security. This point is not reflected in Figure 14–1.

In examining Figure 14–1, you can see that the market price of the bond will not go below the pure bond value regardless of what happens to the price of the common stock. If the stock price went down to $10 and the conversion value fell to $373.80 ($10 × 37.38 shares), the market value of the bond would at least equal its pure bond value of $596. The convertibility of the bond loses much of its meaning at low stock prices, and the pure bond value is the controlling factor on price. Of course, if the common stock goes up to $35 or $40 per share, the market price of the bond will approach $1,500 because of the conversion feature. At a high bond price, the pure bond value of $596 loses much of its meaning. When a bond is selling at $1,500, it is little comfort to know the bond has a pure bond value or floor price of $596. You would lose $904 before the bond got down to the floor price.

In summary, you can see in Figure 14–1 that if the stock price is low or declining, pure bond value is very important in determining the bond price. When stock

1. Using present value procedures or a calculator, the pure bond value comes out to be $596 for a bond with 25 years to maturity and a yield to maturity of approximately 13 percent. We rounded to 13 percent in the text.

FIGURE 14–1 Telxon 7.5 Percent Convertible Bond on Day of Issue (June 1, 1987)

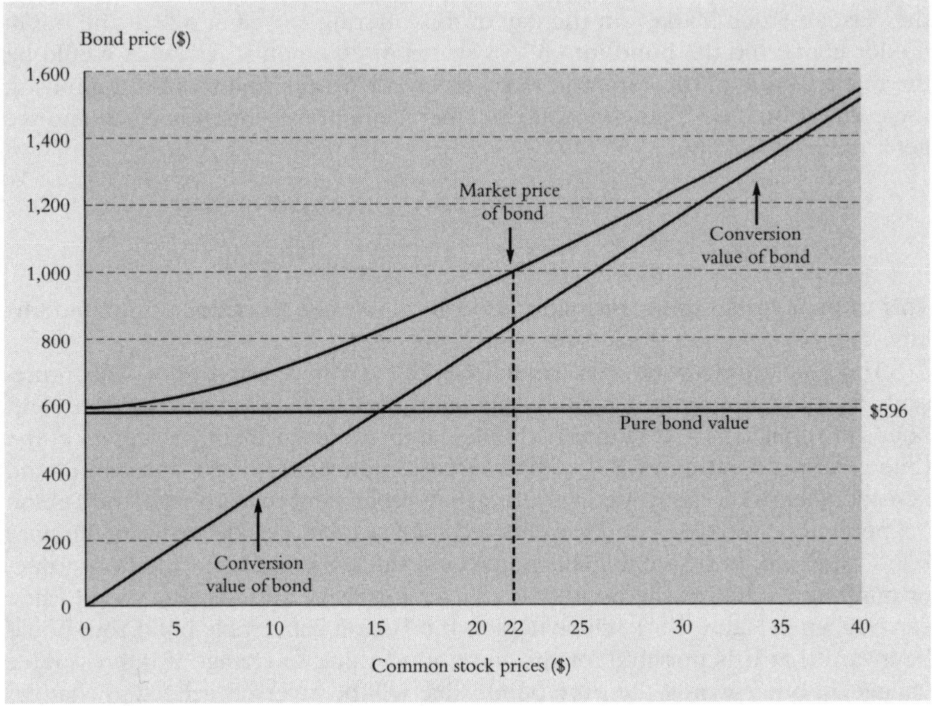

prices are booming, the conversion value is the controlling factor. The bond's minimum price will always be the pure bond value or the conversion value, whichever has the highest price.

Bond Price and Premiums

You may wonder how a company can originally sell a bond for $1,000 with both a conversion value of $822 (rounded) and a pure bond value of $596. Let's examine these values. The difference between the bond's market price ($1,000) and the conversion value ($822) is a premium of $178; it is usually expressed as a percentage of the conversion value and thus is called the conversion premium. In this case, the conversion premium at issue was 21.65 percent:

$$\text{Conversion premium} = \frac{\text{Market price of bond} - \text{Conversion value}}{\text{Conversion value}} \qquad (14\text{-}3)$$

$$= \frac{1{,}000 - 822}{\$822} = \frac{\$178}{\$822}$$

$$= 21.65\%$$

The $178 premium indicates the extra amount paid for the 37.38 shares of stock. Remember, in essence, you paid $26.75 per share for 37.38 shares by purchasing the bond at $1,000; you could have had the same number of shares purchased on the NYSE for $22 and had $178 in cash left. Instead, the investor buying the convertible security paid a premium for the benefits offered by this type of security.

People pay the conversion premium for several reasons. In the case of Telxon's convertible bond, the premium is about the usual 20 percent. First, at the time, Telxon common stock paid $0.01 per share in dividends or approximately $0.37 per year for 37.38 shares ($0.01 × 37.38 = $0.37). The bond paid $75 per year. If the bondholder owns the bond for approximately 2.5 years, he recovers the premium through the differential between interest and dividend income. This analysis of interest income versus dividend income is always important in comparing a stock purchase with a convertible bond purchase.

Additionally, the bond price will rise as the stock price rises because of the convertible feature, but there is a downside limit if the stock should decline in price. This downside limit is established by the pure bond value, which in this case is $596. This downside protection is further justification for the conversion premium. One way to compute this downside protection is to calculate the difference between the market price of the bond and pure bond value as a percentage of the market price. We call this measure downside risk.

$$\text{Downside risk} = \frac{\text{Market price of bond} - \text{Pure bond value}}{\text{Market price of bond}} \qquad (14\text{-}4)$$

$$= \frac{\$1{,}000 - 596}{\$1{,}000} = \frac{\$404}{\$1{,}000}$$

$$= 40.4\%$$

Telxon has a downside risk of 40.4 percent, which is the maximum percentage the bond will decline in value if the stock price falls. One important warning is necessary—the pure bond value is sensitive to market interest rates. If competitively rated B2 bond interest rates rise, the pure bond value will decline. Therefore, downside risk can vary with changing interest rates.

The conversion premium is also affected by several other variables. The more volatile the stock price as measured by beta or standard deviation of returns, the higher the conversion premium. This occurs because the potential for capital gains is larger than on less volatile stocks. The longer the term to maturity, the higher the premium—because there is a greater chance the stock price could rise, making the bond more valuable.

Figure 14-2 presents two graphs of the Telxon convertible bond and depicts the conversion premium in Panel (a) and the downside risk in Panel (b). Note in Panel (a) that as the stock price gets higher, the conversion premium the investor is willing to pay becomes lower. This is because the investor is getting almost no downside protection. This is confirmed by the presence of large downside risk at high stock prices in Panel (b).

FIGURE 14–2 Telxon Convertible Bond—7.5 Percent, 2012 Maturity (Convertible into 37.38 Shares of Common Stock)

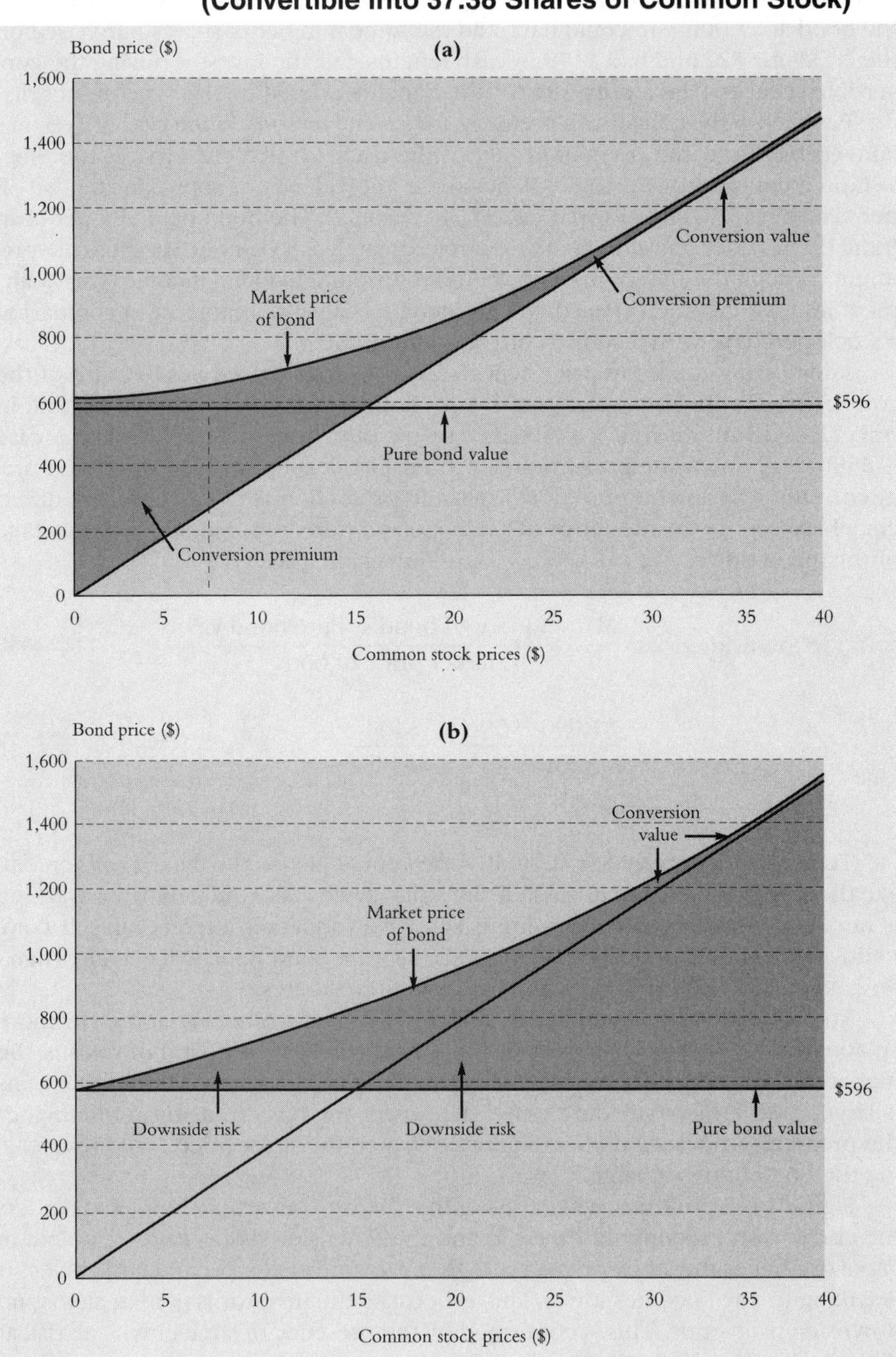

You can track the actual performance of the Telxon bond in Table 14–1. The analysis is over a 10-year period.

Note that between June 1, 1987, and December 15, 1989, the common stock price fell sharply from $22 to $7.50 per share—a decline of $14.50 or 65.9 percent. Because the conversion ratio remained constant at 37.38 shares, the conversion value fell by an equal percentage amount. However, the actual bonds only fell 44.5 percent from $1,000 to $555 because they had the security of a pure bond value on December 15, 1989, of $555 to back them up. The pure bond level had declined slightly from its previous level of $596 due to increasing interest rates.

By October 17, 1994, the stock had demonstrated an improved performance, increasing from $7.50 on December 15, 1989, to $13 on October 17, 1994, five years later. This increase in stock value helped trigger an increase in the convertible bond value to $865. Additionally, interest rates declined during this period, and the pure bond value increased to $770. Three years later, Telxon common stock continued to perform well and reached a price of $25.38 per share, which translated into a conversion price of $948.70 for a 9.5 percent conversion premium. Even though Telxon still maintained a credit rating of B2 by Moody's, interest rates continued to decline from 1994 to 1997, and the pure bond value rose to $930. Because the market value of the convertible bond rose to $1,038.80, the downside risk declined slightly to 10.47 percent.

Since Telxon's convertible bond became callable in 1995, let's see what happens if Telxon common stock reached $30 per share during 1998. This is not such a farfetched possibility since Telxon had a high stock price of $29.75 in 1997. If Telxon calls the bond at $1,000, what action would an owner take? Owners have the choice of receiving 37.38 shares worth $1,121.40 ($30 × 37.38 shares) or receiving $1,000 in cash. It should be obvious that the 37.38 shares are the best choice. If the company calls the bonds, all convertible bondholders would be "forced" to take the shares of common stock to maximize their value. This is called a forced conversion when the company calls the convertible security knowing that the owners will take stock and thus convert debt to equity. The advantage to the company's balance sheet is an obvious reduction in the debt-to-equity ratio and less financial risk. However, on the initial announcement of the call, the common stock usually declines somewhat because of the increased number of shares

TABLE 14–1 Telxon Convertible Bond Price Performance—7.5 Percent, 2012 Maturity

	June 1, 1987	December 15, 1989	October 17, 1994	October 13, 1997
Market price of bonds	$1,000.00	$555.00	$865.00	$1038.80
Common stock price	$ 22.00	$ 7.50	$ 13.00	$ 25.38
Conversion ratio	37.38	37.38	37.38	37.38
Conversion value	$ 822.36	$280.35	$485.94	$ 948.70
Conversion premium	21.65%	96.18%	78.01%	9.50%
Pure bond value	$ 596.00	$555.00	$770.00	$ 930.00
Downside risk	40.4%	0%	11%	10.47%

on the market and the potential for many bondholders to liquidate their shares for other fixed-income investments. This is why companies generally wait until the conversion price is well above the call price before forcing the call. If the price drops enough so that the conversion value falls below the call price, the company could get stuck having to come up with cash instead of shares of stock.

After the Merger with Symbol Technologies

Under the terms of the merger agreement, Telxon shareholders received 0.50 share of Symbol common stock (NYSE ticker SBL) for every share of Telxon stock. This exchange ratio doubled the conversion price to \$53.50 per Symbol share or reduced the conversion ratio to 18.69 shares calculated with Formula 14-1 as follows:

$$\frac{\$1{,}000 \text{ (Face value)}}{\$53.50 \text{ (Conversion price)}} = 18.69 \text{ shares (Conversion ratio)}$$

In May 2001, Symbol Technologies declared a three-for-two stock split, and so the terms of the convertible bond were once again adjusted. The 7.5 percent Telxon convertible bond now could be converted at a conversion price of \$35.67 (\$53.50/1.5) or into 28.04 shares (18.69 × 1.5) of Symbol Technologies common stock. Where does that leave the investor who owns the Telxon convertible bond? In Table 14-2 we update Table 14-1 using stock prices adjusted for the stock split, and we find that using the high and low stock prices for 2001 demonstrates quite nicely the advantages and disadvantages of convertible bonds when stock prices rise and fall.

The stock market for technology stocks had a rocky ride during 2001, and the attacks on the World Trade Center and Pentagon drove stock prices to their yearly lows. An investor in the Telxon convertible bond would have been able to sell the bond for \$1,090 on March 6, 2001, because the stock price was high, creating

TABLE 14–2 Telxon Convertible Bond Price Performance after Merger

	March 6, 2001	September 27, 2001
Market price of bonds	\$1,090.00	\$860.00
Common stock price	\$ 37.33	\$ 9.50
Conversion ratio	28.04 shares	28.04 shares
Conversion value	\$1,046.73	\$266.38
Conversion premium	4.13%	222.84%
Pure bond value	\$ 837.62	\$860.00
Downside risk	23.15%	0.0%

a conversion value of $1,046.73. However, the market for Symbol Technologies (the stock exchanged for Telxon convertibles) collapsed, and the stock price fell 74 percent in less than seven months. During this same time the bond price fell $230 or 21 percent. It should be pointed out that the conversion value fell by the exact same percentage as the common stock, but the investor was protected from the decline in the bond price by the pure bond value of $860.

Comparing the Convertible Bond with Common Stock Purchase

Would you have been better off putting $1,000 in Telxon common stock on June 1, 1987, or $1,000 in the convertible bond? Investing $1,000 in Telxon stock at $22 would have purchased 45.45 shares. These shares would now be the equivalent of 38.04 shares of Symbol Technologies after the merger and stock split. However, $1,000 invested in the bond would now be equivalent to 28.04 shares of Symbol Technologies as described in the previous section.

As shown in Table 14-3 on October 15, 2001 (at a common stock price of $14.30 per share), a stock investment would have been worth $549.47 (last column), and the bond investment would have been worth $1,910 (also last column). Notice that most of the bond value comes from the $1,050 in interest payments; this value would be even higher if we include the interest that could have been earned on the $75 coupon payments each and every year. The convertible bond investor definitely would have been better off under this situation. The longer it takes for a company to force the conversion of its convertible bonds, the more important are the interest payments received by the investor. Even if Symbol Technologies went up to a stock price of $50 per share, the bond investor would be better off because the bond investor will still reap the benefits of an increased conversion value. With only 10 extra shares of stock, the common stock has to rise enough to offset the interest payments.

The trade-off the investor makes in the stock versus convertible security decision is whether to buy stock (receiving more shares and a lower cash flow from dividends) or to buy the convertible security (with its option of fewer shares but higher cash flow from interest payments). In this case, the cash flow difference between dividends of $5.50 and interest ($1,050) was very high, and since the stock price did not go up substantially, the differential was impossible to make up.

TABLE 14–3 Comparative Telxon Corporation Investments, October 15, 2001

	Amount Invested, June 1987	Symbol Technologies Shares	Stock Prices, October 15, 2001	Ending Stock or Bond Value	Total Dividends or Interest	Total Value
Stock	$1,000	38.04	$14.30	$543.97	$ 5.50	$ 549.47
Bond	$1,000	28.04	14.30	860.00	1,050.00	1,910.00

Table 14–4 presents a selection of convertible bonds and preferred stock and helps illustrate basic points. While an occasional convertible bond such as the Automatic Data Processing zero-coupon 2012 bond carries an Aa1 Moody's bond rating, in general, convertible bonds are usually lower-quality bonds. However, in recent years, high-quality companies such as Johnson & Johnson (which would be rated at least Aa) have turned to the zero-coupon convertible market as a way of raising low-cost debt capital. This is a change from the past.

Turning our attention to the first bond on the list, Amazon.com, we see that this bond has a conversion premium of 341 percent (Column 9). This indicates that the stock price has fallen since the original issue and the bond price is trading based on its pure bond value (investment value) or interest-paying ability rather than the stock price.

Compare Amazon.com's conversion premium (Column 9) to the five bonds selling above $1,000 (Column 4). These bonds have conversion premiums of between 0 and 8 percent, which is consistent with what would be expected as the conversion value moves significantly above the bonds' pure bond value. In addition to the Automatic Data Processing bond and the Banco Bilbao bond, neither Cephalon nor Textron preferred stocks (bottom of table) have a conversion premium. The zero conversion premium indicates that these securities are selling at their conversion value. This occurs because the common stock price has risen so much since the convertible preferred was first issued that the pure value no longer creates downside protection if the stock price drops from its current levels.

Disadvantages of Convertibles

It has been said that everything has a price, and purchasing convertible securities at the wrong price can eliminate one of their main advantages. For example, once convertible bonds begin going up in value, or the pure bond value declines substantially, the downside protection becomes meaningless. In the case of the Banco Bilbao Vizcaya bonds in Table 14–4, the market price of the bond is $1,927.50 (Column 4, upper part of table), while the pure bond value is $890 (Column 10). If the investor buys the bond at $1,927.50 and the common stock declines significantly to its pure bond value of $890, the investor is exposed to a potential decline of $1,037.50 (hardly adequate protection for a true risk averter). Also don't forget that if market yields rise, the floor price or pure bond value could decline from $890, thus creating even greater downside risk. The same type of analysis could be applied to other bonds in the table.

Another drawback with convertible bonds is that the purchaser is invariably asked to accept below-market yields on the debt instrument. The interest rate on convertibles is generally one-third below that for instruments in a similar risk class (perhaps 6 percent instead of 9 percent).

From the institutional investor's standpoint, many convertible securities lack liquidity because of small trading volume or even the small amount of convertibles issued by one company. The institutions prefer to own convertible issues where the size of the total bond issue is $100 million or more.

TABLE 14–4 Selected Convertible Bonds and Preferred Stock

	(1) Coupon	(2) Maturity	(3) Moody's Bond Rating	(4) Bond Price	Conversion (5) Price	Conversion (6) Ratio	(7) Common Stock Price	Conversion (8) Value	Conversion (9) Premium	(10) Pure Bond Value	(11) Stock Dividend Yield	(12) Bond Current Yield	(13) Call Price
Convertible Bond Issues													
Amazon.com	4.75%	2009	Caa1	$ 421.20	$78.03	12.8160	$ 7.46	$ 95.60	341.00%	$421.00	Nil	11.30%	$1,033.30
Automatic Data Processing	0.00	2012	Aa1	1,163.50	38.69	25.8440	45.02	1,163.50	0.00	570.00	0.90%	0.00	565.50
Banco Bilbao Vizcaya	3.50	2006	Aa2	1,927.50	5.17	193.5030	9.92	1,919.50	0.00	890.00	4.00	1.80	1,192.70
First Data Corp.	2.00	2008	A1	980.00	81.90	12.2100	57.95	707.60	39.00	910.00	0.10	2.00	NCB
IDEC Pharmaceuticals	0.00	2019	NR	1,883.80	24.75	40.4040	45.34	1,831.90	3.00	290.00	Nil	0.00	NCB
Johnson & Johnson	0.00	2020	NR	753.40	72.74	13.7470	52.41	720.50	5.00	500.00	1.40	0.00	NCB
Kerr McGee Corp.	5.25	2010	Baa2	1,000.00	61.08	16.3730	49.44	809.50	24.00	780.00	3.60	5.30	NCB
Nextel Communications	6.00	2011	B1	842.50	23.84	41.9510	9.97	418.30	101.00	750.00	Nil	7.10	NCB
Scholastic Corp.	5.00	2005	Baa3	1,136.30	38.43	26.0220	40.38	1,050.80	8.00	940.00	Nil	4.40	1,000.00
Standard Motor Products	6.75	2009	B1	678.40	32.19	31.0680	11.85	368.20	84.00	770.00	3.00	9.90	NCB
Vector Group	6.25	2008	NR	1,276.30	34.41	29.0610	40.65	1,181.30	8.00	760.00	3.90	4.90	1,031.23

NR = not rated; Nil = zero; NCB = non callable bond

Source: *The Value Line Convertibles Survey,* October 1, 2001, and *Mergent Bond Survey,* September 2001. Reproduced with the permission of Value Line Publishing, Inc.

	(1) Dividend	(2) Call Date	(3) Preferred Stock Price	(4) Common Stock Price	(5) Conversion Ratio	Conversion (6) Value	Conversion (7) Premium	(8) Pure Value	(9) Common Dividend Yield	(10) Preferred Dividend Yield
Convertible Preferred Issues										
Cephalon	$3.63	30-Apr-04	$125.25	$45.00	2.790	$125.55	0.00%	$29.00	Nil	2.90%
Philippine Long Distance	3.50	callable	24.00	9.90	1.713	16.96	42.00	26.00	1.20%	14.60
Textron	2.08	callable	186.00	42.36	4.400	186.38	0.00	27.00	2.80	1.10
Unocal	3.13	callable	45.38	30.40	1.175	35.72	27.00	32.00	2.60	6.90
Williams Comms Group	3.38	15-Aug-05	10.25	1.54	1.761	2.71	278.00	6.00	Nil	65.90

Source: *The Value Line Convertibles Survey,* October 1, 2001. Reproduced with the permission of Value Line Publishing, Inc.

When to Convert into Common Stock

Convertible securities generally have a call provision, which gives the corporation the option of redeeming the bond at a specified price before maturity. The call price is usually at a premium over par value ($1,000) in the early years of callability, and it generally declines over time to par value. We know that as the price of the common stock goes up, the convertible security will rise along with the stock so the investor has no incentive to convert bonds into stock. However, the corporation may use the call privilege to force conversion before maturity. Companies usually force conversion when the conversion value is well above the call price. Investors will take the shares rather than the call price since the shares are worth more. This enables the company to turn debt into equity on its balance sheet and makes new debt issues a better risk for future lenders because of higher interest coverage and a lower debt-to-equity ratio.

Corporations may also encourage voluntary conversion by using a step-up in the conversion price over time. When the bond is issued, the contract may specify the following conversion provisions.

	Conversion Price	Conversion Ratio
First five years	$40	25.0 shares
Next three years	45	22.2 shares
Next two years	50	20.0 shares
Next five years	55	18.2 shares

At the end of each time period, there is a strong inducement to convert rather than accept an adjustment to a higher conversion price and a lower conversion ratio. This is especially true if the bond's conversion value is the dominating influence on the market price of the bond. In the case where the conversion value is below the pure bond value and where the interest income is greater than the dividend income, an investor will most likely not be induced to convert through the step-up feature.

About the only other reason for voluntary converting is if the dividend income received on the common stock is greater than the interest income on the bond. Even in this case, risk-averse investors may want to hold the bond because interest payments are legally required whereas dividends may be reduced.

ADVANTAGES AND DISADVANTAGES TO THE ISSUING CORPORATION

Having established the fundamental characteristics of the convertible security from the investor's viewpoint, let us now examine the factors a corporate financial officer must consider in weighing the advisability of a convertible offer for the firm.

It has been stated that the interest rate paid on convertible issues is normally lower than that paid on a straight debt instrument. Also, the convertible feature may be the only device for allowing smaller corporations access to the bond market.

Convertible bonds are also attractive to a corporation that believes its stock is undervalued. For example, assume a corporation's $1,000 bonds are convertible into 20 shares of common stock at a conversion price of $50. Also assume the company's common stock has a current price of $45, and new shares of stock might be sold at only $44.[2] Thus, the corporation will effectively receive $6 over current market price, assuming future conversion. Of course, one can also argue that if the firm had delayed the issuance of common stock or convertibles for a year or two, the stock might have gone up from $45 to $60 or $65, and new common stock might have been sold at this lofty price.

To translate this to overall numbers for the firm, if a corporation needs $10 million in funds and offers straight stock now at a new price of $44, it must issue 227,272 shares ($10 million/$44 per share). With convertibles, the number of shares potentially issued is only 200,000 shares ($10 million/$50 per share). Finally, if no stock or convertible bonds are issued now and the stock goes up to a level at which new shares can be offered at a price of $60, only 166,667 will be required ($10 million/$60).

Another matter of concern to the corporation is the accounting treatment accorded to convertibles. In the funny-money days of the 1960s' conglomerate merger movement, corporate management often chose convertible securities over common stock because the convertibles had a nondilutive effect on earnings per share. As indicated in the following section on reporting earnings for convertibles, the rules were changed.

ACCOUNTING CONSIDERATIONS WITH CONVERTIBLES

Before 1969, the full impact of the conversion privilege as it applied to convertible securities, warrants (long-term options to buy stock), and other dilutive securities was not adequately reflected in reported earnings per share. Because all of these securities may generate additional common stock in the future, the potential effect of this dilution (the addition of new shares to the capital structure) should be considered. The accounting profession has applied many different measures to earnings per share over the years, most recently replacing the concepts of primary earnings per share and fully diluted earnings per share with basic earnings per share and diluted earnings per share. In 1997, the Financial Accounting Standards Board issued "Earnings per Share" Statement of Financial Accounting Standards No. 128 that covered the adjustments that must be made when reporting earnings per share.

2. There is always a bit of underpricing to ensure the success of a new offering.

TABLE 14–5 XYZ Corporation

1. Capital section of balance sheet:	
Common stock (1 million shares at $10 par)	$10,000,000
4.5% convertible debentures (10,000 debentures of $1,000; convertible into 40 shares per bond, or a total of 400,000 shares)	10,000,000
Retained earnings	20,000,000
Net worth	$40,000,000
2. Condensed income statement:	
Earnings before interest and taxes	$ 2,950,000
Interest (4.5% of $10 million of convertibles)	450,000
Earnings before taxes	$ 2,500,000
Taxes (40%)	1,000,000
Earnings after taxes	$ 1,500,000
3. Basic earnings per share:	

$$\frac{\text{Earnings after taxes}}{\text{Shares of common stock}} = \frac{\$1{,}500{,}000}{1{,}000{,}000} = \$1.50$$

If we examine the financial statements of the XYZ Corporation in Table 14-5 we find that the earnings per share reported are not adjusted for convertible securities and are referred to as basic earnings per share.

Diluted earnings per share adjusts for all potential dilution from the issuance of any new shares of common stock arising from convertible bonds, convertible preferred stocks, warrants, or any other options outstanding. The comparison of basic and diluted earnings per share give the analyst or investor a measure of the potential effects of these securities.

We get diluted earnings per share for the XYZ Corporation by assuming that 400,000 new shares will be created from potential conversion, while at the same time, allowing for the reduction in interest payments that would occur as a result of the conversion of the debt to common stock. Since before-tax interest payments on the convertibles are $450,000, the after-tax interest cost ($270,000) will be saved and can be added back to income. After-tax interest cost is determined by multiplying interest payments by one minus the tax rate $(1 - 0.4)$ times $\$450{,}000 = \$270{,}000$. Making the appropriate adjustments to the numerator and denominator, we show diluted earnings per share as $1.26 in Formula 14-5.

$$\text{Diluted earnings per share} = \frac{\text{Adjusted earnings after taxes}}{\text{Shares outstanding} + \text{All convertible securities}} \qquad (14\text{-}5)$$

$$= \frac{\$1{,}500{,}000 \ \text{(Reported earnings)} + \$270{,}000 \ \text{(Interest savings)}}{1{,}000{,}000 + 400{,}000} = \frac{\$1{,}770{,}000}{1{,}400{,}000}$$

$$= \$1.26$$

We see a $0.24 reduction from the basic earnings per share figure of $1.50 in Table 14-5. The new figure is the value that a sophisticated security analyst would utilize.

INNOVATIONS IN CONVERTIBLE SECURITIES

Not all convertible securities are convertible into the common stock of the company issuing the convertible. Some convertibles are convertible into bonds, preferred stock, stock of another company, or another type of asset.

Another type of new convertible security bears mentioning. For many companies recovering from years of losses and having tax-loss carryforwards, "convertible exchangeable preferred stock" is a security that can improve the firm's balance sheet and provide high returns to investors. A firm with losses does not need tax-deductible interest expenses but does need balanced financing. Because no taxes are due, preferred dividends are no different from interest expenses to the issuing company. When the issuing firm becomes taxable again, it can exchange the preferred stock for debt with the same conversion ratio and can then utilize the tax savings from the deductible interest expense. The exchange occurs without the cost of new underwriting fees.

SPECULATING THROUGH WARRANTS

A warrant is an option to buy a stated number of shares of stock at a specified price over a given time period. The six warrants listed in Table 14-6 demonstrate the relationships discussed in the following sections. For example, U.S. Laboratories is a company specializing in quality control of building projects. It is a small company with a high stock price of $15 and a low stock price of $3.13 during the last 52 weeks. U.S. Laboratories has a warrant listed in Table 14-6 that allows the holder to buy one share of stock for $7.80 (Column 4) until February 23, 2004. The common stock (Column 3) is already selling above the option price and investors are willing to pay $1.88 (Column 2) for the warrant. Since investors have 2.5 years left to exercise their warrants at the time of this example, there is a possibility that the stock could rise back to its high of $15. If this were to happen the warrant would be worth at least $7.20 ($15 market price minus the $7.80 option price in Column 4). We will analyze this relationship after a few more examples.

Most warrants allow the holder to buy one share of common stock per warrant on the date of issue, but if the common stock performs well and stock splits occur, the warrant gets adjusted to reflect the stock splits. Five out of the six warrants listed in Table 14-6 have had stock splits, so the warrant carries with it the ability to buy more than one share. One of the most dynamic companies in the table is Micron Technology, a leading company in the computer memory-chip industry. This company has split so many times that its warrant allows the purchase of 26.163 shares (Column 7) of the underlying stock. If Micron common stock goes to $56 per share (option price), the intrinsic value will be zero, but if Micron common stock goes to $57 per share, the intrinsic value will be $26.163. Every dollar that the stock price is above $56 will generate one dollar of profit on 26.163 shares.

TABLE 14–6 Selected Warrants as of October 1, 2001

(1) Name of Firm, Place of Warrant Listing, and Stock Listing[a]	(2) Warrant Price	(3) Per Share Stock Price	(4) Per Share Option Price	(5) Intrinsic Value[b] [(3) − (4)]	(6) Speculative Premium [(2) − (5)]	(7) Shares per Warrant	(8) Due Date
ChinaB2BSourcing.com OTC, OTC	$ 1.63	$ 6.50	$ 5.00	$1.88[c]	−$ 0.25	1.250	4/23/2004
Micron Technology OTC, NYSE	17.25	22.30	56.00	0.00	17.25	26.163	5/15/2008
New Valley OTC, OTC	0.17	4.00	12.50	0.00	0.17	71.898	6/14/2004
Nexell Therapeutics OTC, OTC	0.20	1.13	5.42	0.00	0.20	2.399	6/20/2006
U.S. Laboratories OTC, OTC	1.88	8.75	7.80	0.95	0.93	1.000	2/23/2004
Video Network Communication OTC, OTC	0.18	0.54	4.00	0.00	0.18	4.000	6/15/2004

[a]OTC = over-the-counter; NYSE = New York Stock Exchange

[b]When Column (4) is larger than Column (3), the intrinsic value will calculate as a negative number. Because the intrinsic value of a warrant cannot be less than zero (worthless), we put a zero in Column (5).

[c]Indicates that the warrants are offered at a conversion ratio of more than one share per warrant. The difference between the stock price and option price must be multiplied by Column (7) to get the intrinsic value.

Source: *The Value Line Convertibles Survey,* October 1, 2001. Reproduced with the permission of Value Line Publishing, Inc.

Warrants are usually issued as a sweetener to a bond offering, and they may enable the firm to issue debt when this would not be feasible otherwise. The warrants allow the bond issue to carry a lower coupon rate and are usually detachable from the bond after the issue date. After being separated from the bond, warrants have their own market price and may trade on a different market from the common stock. After the warrants are exercised, the initial debt with which they were sold remains in existence.

The Bache Group, a financial company (now Prudential Securities), had a bond offering October 30, 1980. It offered 35,000 units of $1,000 debentures due in the year 2000 with a coupon interest rate of 14 percent. To each bond, 30 warrants were attached. Each warrant allowed the holder to buy one share of stock at $18.50 until November 1, 1985. At the time of issue, the warrant had no true value since the common stock was selling below $18.50. During 1981, however, the stock went up as several merger offers were made for retail brokerage companies. On May 29, 1981, Bache common stock was selling at 31½, and each warrant traded at 13⅝. The 30 warrants received with each bond were now worth $408.75 and provided the sweetener every bondholder had hoped for.

Because a warrant is dependent on the market movement of the underlying common stock and has no "security value" as such, it is highly speculative. If the common stock of the firm is volatile, the value of the warrants may change dramatically.

Valuation of Warrants

Because the value of a warrant is closely tied to the underlying stock price, we can develop a formula for the minimum or intrinsic value of a warrant:

$$I = (M - OP) \times N \qquad (14\text{-}6)$$

where:

I = The intrinsic or minimum value of the warrant
M = The market value of the common stock
OP = The option or exercise price of the warrant
N = The number of shares each warrant entitles the holder to purchase

Assume that the common stock of the Graham Corporation is $25 per share and that each warrant carries an option to purchase one share at $20 over the next 10 years. The purchase price stipulated in the warrant is the option or exercise price. Using Formula 14-6, the intrinsic value is $5 [($25 − 20) × 1]. The intrinsic value in this case is equal to the market price of the common stock minus the option price of the warrant. Because the warrant has 10 more years to run and is an effective vehicle for speculative trading, it may well trade for over $5. If the warrant were selling for $9, we would say it had an intrinsic value of $5 and a speculative premium of $4. The speculative premium is equal to the price of the warrant minus the intrinsic value.

Even if the stock were trading at less than $20 (the option price on the warrant), the warrant might still have some value in the market. Speculators might purchase the warrant in the hope that the common stock value would increase sufficiently to make the option provision valuable. If the common stock were selling for $15 per share, thus giving the warrant a negative intrinsic value of $5, the warrant might still command a value of $1 or $2 in anticipation of increased common stock value.

In many cases, warrants would have negative intrinsic values because the stock price is below the warrant's option price, but a warrant cannot be less than worthless, so a zero value is denoted for the intrinsic value, as shown in Table 14-6. In some cases, firms with zero intrinsic values still have large speculative premiums. This is true even when the stock price has to more than double in price by expiration before the warrant breaks even on the original investment.

The typical relationship between the market price and the intrinsic value of a warrant is depicted in Figure 14-3. We assume the warrant entitles the holder to purchase one new share of common stock at $20.

Although the intrinsic value of the warrant is theoretically negative at a common stock price between 0 and $20, the warrant still carries some value in the market. Also, observe that the difference between the market price of the warrant and its intrinsic value is diminished at the upper ranges of value. Two reasons may be offered for this declining premium.

First, the speculator loses the ability to use leverage to generate high returns as the price of the stock goes up. When the price of the stock is relatively low, say, $25, and the warrant is in the $5 to $10 range, a 10-point movement in the stock could mean a 200 percent gain in the value of the warrant, as indicated in part A of Table 14-7. At the upper levels of stock value, much of this leverage is lost, as

FIGURE 14–3 Market Price Relationships for a Warrant

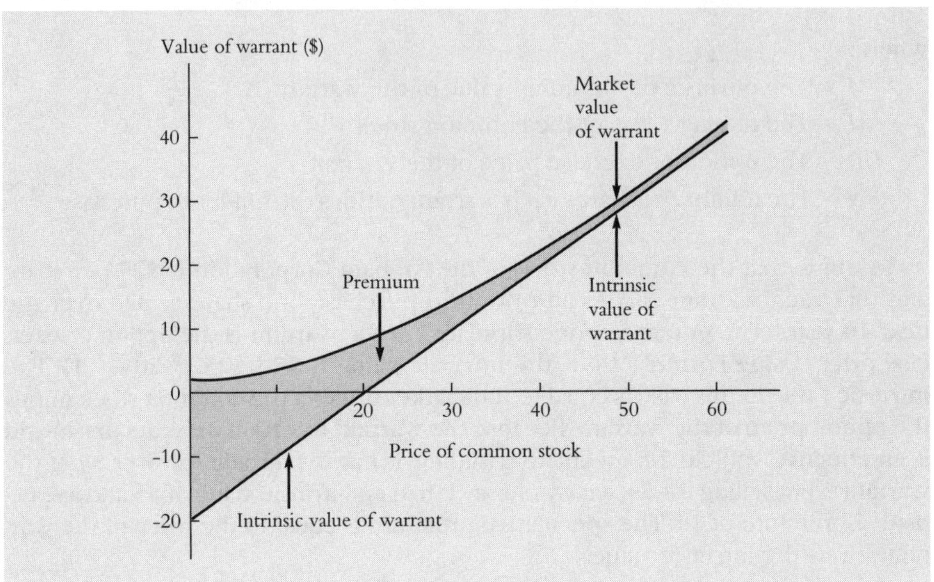

indicated in part B of the table. At a stock value of $50 and a warrant value of approximately $30, a 10-point movement in the stock would produce only a 33 percent gain in the warrant.

Another reason speculators pay a very low premium at higher stock prices is that there is less downside protection. A warrant selling at $30 when the stock price is $50 is more vulnerable to downside movement than is a $5 to $10 warrant when the stock is in the 20s.

Warrant premiums are also influenced by the same factors that affect convertible bond premiums. More volatile common stocks will have greater potential to create short-run profits for warrant speculators, so the higher the price volatil-

TABLE 14–7 Leverage in Valuing Warrants

(A)	(B)
Stock price = $25; warrant price = $5[a] + 10-point movement in stock price New warrant price = $15 (10-point gain)	Stock price = $50; warrant price = $30 + 10-point movement in stock price New warrant price = $40 (10-point gain)
Percentage gain in warrant $= \frac{\$10}{\$5} \times 100 = 200\%$	Percentage gain in warrant $= \frac{\$10}{\$30} \times 100 = 33\%$

[a]The warrant price would, of course, be greater than $5 because of a premium. Nevertheless, we use $5 for ease of computation.

ity, the greater the premium. Also, the longer the option has before expiration, the higher the premium will be. This "time premium" is worth more the longer the common stock has to reach and surpass the option price of the warrant.

Further Explanation of Intrinsic Value

For one of the warrants in previously shown Table 14-6, the formula for intrinsic value requires further explanation. You will recall the formula is

$$I = (M - OP) \times N \tag{14-6}$$

where:

I = The intrinsic or minimum value of the warrant

M = The market value of the common stock

OP = The option or exercise price of the warrant

N = The number of shares each warrant entitles the holder to purchase

Up until now we've simplified matters by assuming $N = 1$. But what about cases where it is equal to or greater than 1? Let's take ChinaB2BSourcing.com from Table 14-6 as an example; $N = 1.25$.

Using the formula for intrinsic value and the data from Table 14-6 for the firm, we would show:

$$\begin{aligned}\text{Intrinsic value} &= (\$6.50 - \$5.00) \times 1.25 \\ &= (\$1.50) \times 1.25 \\ &= 1.88\end{aligned}$$

This, of course, is the value shown for the intrinsic value of the firm in Table 14-6. Also, with a warrant price of \$1.63, there is a negative speculative premium of −\$0.25, which indicates the warrant is selling at a discount to its intrinsic value.

$$\text{Speculative premium} = \text{Warrant price} - \text{Intrinsic value}$$

$$\begin{aligned}&= \$1.63 - \$1.88 \\ &= -\$0.25\end{aligned}$$

Use of Warrants by Corporations

As previously indicated, warrants may allow for the issuance of debt under difficult circumstances. While a straight debt issue may not be acceptable or may be accepted only at extremely high rates, the same security may be well received because detachable warrants are included. Warrants may also be included as an add-on in a merger or acquisition agreement. A firm might offer \$20 million in cash plus 10,000 warrants in exchange for all the outstanding shares of the acquisition candidate.

The use of warrants has traditionally been associated with such aggressive, "high-flying" firms as biotechs, airlines, and conglomerates.

As a financing device for creating new common stock, warrants may not be as desirable as convertible securities. A corporation with convertible bonds outstanding may force the conversion of debt to common stock through a call, while no similar device is available to the firm with warrants. The only possible inducement might be a step-up in the option price—whereby the warrant holder must pay a progressively higher option price if he does not exercise by a given date.

The capital structure of the firm after the exercise of a warrant also is somewhat different from that created after the conversion of a debenture. In the case of a warrant, the original debt outstanding remains in existence after the detachable warrant is exercised, whereas the conversion of a debenture extinguishes the former debt obligation.

ACCOUNTING CONSIDERATIONS WITH WARRANTS

As with convertible securities, the potential dilutive effect of warrants must be considered. In calculating the earnings per share resulting from conversion of warrants, accountants use the Treasury stock method. Under this method the accountant must compute the number of new shares that could be created by the exercise of all warrants, with the provision that the total can be reduced by the assumed use of the cash proceeds to purchase a partially offsetting amount of shares at the market price. Assume that warrants to purchase 10,000 shares at $20 are outstanding and the current price of the stock is $50. We show the following:

1. New shares created	10,000
2. Reduction of shares from cash proceeds (computed below)	4,000
Cash proceeds—10,000 shares at $20 = $200,000	
Current price of stock—$50	
Assumed reduction in shares outstanding from cash proceeds = $200,000/$50 = 4,000	
3. Assumed net increase in shares from exercise of warrants (10,000 − 4,000)	6,000

In computing earnings per share, we will add 6,000 shares to the denominator with no adjustment to the numerator, which will lower earnings per share. If earnings per share had previously been $1 based on $100,000 in earnings and 100,000 shares outstanding, EPS would now be reduced to $0.943:

$$\frac{\text{Earnings}}{\text{Shares}} = \frac{\$100{,}000}{106{,}000} = \$0.943$$

With warrants included in computing diluted earnings per share, their impact on reported earnings is important from both the investor and corporate viewpoints.

Internet Resources

Website Address	Comments
www.convertbond.com	Fee-based source of information on convertible bond issues
www.numa.com	Provides calculator for convertible bonds
cbs.marketwatch.com	Personal finance section contains general information on convertible bonds
www.bondsonline.com	Provides information about convertible bonds

Chapter 15

International Securities Markets

In Chapter 1, we discussed the advantage of diversification in terms of risk reduction. To reduce risk exposure, the investor may desire a broad spectrum of securities from which to choose. An investor who lives in California would hardly be expected to limit all his investments to that geographic boundary. The same might be said for an investor living in the United States or Germany or Japan. The advantages of crossing international boundaries may be substantial in terms of diversification benefits.

Companies operating in different countries will be affected differently by international events such as crop failures, energy prices, wars, tariffs, trade between countries, and the value of local currencies relative to other currencies, especially the U.S. dollar. Furthermore, despite the up and down markets in the United States, there is almost certain to be a bull market somewhere in the world for the investor who likes to keep his chips on the table at all times.

Of course, there are some disadvantages to investing in international securities. The main drawback would appear to be the more complicated nature of the investment. Currently, one cannot simply pick up the phone and ask a broker to buy 100 shares of any stock listed on a foreign exchange. Some foreign markets have very low liquidity or require citizenship for ownership, or U.S. brokers may be restricted from dealing in these securities.

The primary focus of this chapter is international equities, although investments may certainly include fixed-income securities and real assets. We shall examine the composition of world equity markets, the diversification and return benefits that can be derived from foreign investments, the obstacles that are present, and finally, the methods of participating in foreign investments directly and indirectly.

THE WORLD EQUITY MARKET

The world equity markets have grown dramatically as shown in Table 15-1. At the end of 1999, the United States accounted for more than 50 percent of the world's securities markets in terms of total market value (second column from the right). Japan followed with 13.8 percent (down from 17 percent in 1996) and the United Kingdom (England) was in third place with 8.9 percent of total market value.

TABLE 15–1 Market Capitalization of Developed Countries (in Millions of U.S. Dollars)

Country	Year-End 1996	Percent of Total	Year-End 1999	Percent of Total
Australia	$ 311,981	1.73%	$ 427,683	1.30%
Austria	33,953	0.19	33,025	0.10
Belgium	119,831	0.67	184,942	0.56
Bermuda	0	0.00	1,300	0.00
Canada	486,268	2.70	800,914	2.43
Cyprus	2,355	0.01	8,075	0.02
Denmark	71,688	0.40	105,293	0.32
Finland	63,078	0.35	349,409	1.06
France	591,123	3.29	1,475,457	4.48
Germany	670,997	3.73	1,432,190	4.35
Hong Kong	449,381	2.50	609,090	1.85
Iceland	1,210	0.01	4,807	0.01
Ireland	12,242	0.07	42,458	0.13
Italy	258,160	1.44	728,273	2.21
Japan	3,088,850	17.18	4,546,937	13.80
Kuwait	21,840	0.12	18,814	0.06
Luxembourg	32,692	0.18	35,940	0.11
Netherlands	378,721	2.11	695,209	2.11
New Zealand	38,641	0.21	28,352	0.09
Norway	57,423	0.32	63,696	0.19
Portugal	24,660	0.14	66,488	0.20
Qatar	0	0.00	5,502	0.02
Singapore	150,215	0.84	198,407	0.603
Spain	242,779	1.35	431,668	1.31
Sweden	247,217	1.37	373,278	1.13
Switzerland	402,104	2.24	693,127	2.10
United Arab Emirates	0	0.00	28,211	0.09
United Kingdom	1,740,246	9.68	2,933,280	8.90
United States	8,484,433	47.18	16,635,114	50.48
Total	$17,982,088		$32,956,939	

Source: *Emerging Stock Markets Factbook*, 2000 (Washington, D.C.: International Finance Corporation, 2000), p. 17.

Going back further in time, the U.S. share of the market went from 45 percent in 1992 to 47 percent in 1996 and 50.5 percent in 1999. Japan has been in a prolonged economic slump since the early 1990s, and this has shown up in the market capitalization of their stock market. In 1990 Japan accounted for 33 percent of the world market and then decreased to 24 percent in 1992, 17 percent in 1996, and 13.8 percent in 1999. To some extent Japan demonstrates the economic truth that stock market growth is related to the overall growth in a country's economy. As Japan's economy has stagnated and profits declined so has the Nikkei 225 Index representing the Tokyo stock market.

You may be surprised by some of the countries listed in Table 15-1, but the International Monetary Fund defines developed countries by per-capita income not by the size of GDP or the population. That is why several small countries like Qatar and the United Arab Emirates with small stock markets, small economies, and small populations are included in the table. Figure 15-1 depicts the geographical breakdown of major developed markets showing Europe, North America, and the Pacific region.

While the developed world securities markets continue to expand, major growth in securities markets has also occurred in the "emerging" markets such as Argentina, Brazil, China, Taiwan, and Mexico. Additionally, the Eastern European countries of Poland, Hungary, the Czech Republic, Slovakia, and Slovenia have developed fledgling stock markets, with Poland leading the group with a market value of $29.5 billion, constituting 1 percent of the total emerging market. Table 15-2 lists the market capitalizations of the emerging markets. The total value in

FIGURE 15–1 Developed Markets by Geographical Region, 1999

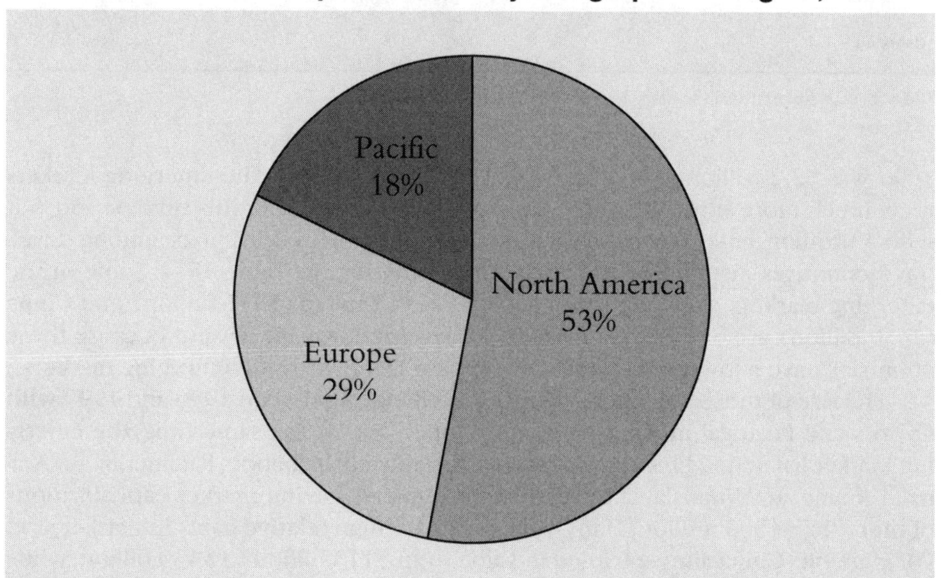

Source: *Emerging Stock Markets Factbook,* 2000 (Washington, D.C.: International Finance Corporation, 2000), p. 17.

TABLE 15–2 Market Capitalization of Emerging Markets Greater than $500 Million in Capitalization (in Millions of U.S. Dollars)

Country	Year-End 1996	Percent of Total	Year-End 1999	Percent of Total
Argentina	$ 44,679	1.99%	$ 83,887	2.74%
Bahrain	0	0.00	7,155	0.23
Bangladesh	4,551	0.20	865	0.03
Barbados	766	0.03	2,008	0.07
Brazil	216,990	9.67	227,962	7.43
Chile	65,940	2.94	68,228	2.22
China	113,755	5.07	330,703	10.78
Colombia	17,137	0.76	11,590	0.38
Costa Rica	782	0.03	2,303	0.08
Cote d'Ivoire	914	0.04	1,514	0.05
Croatia	2,975	0.13	2,584	0.08
Czech Republic	18,077	0.81	11,796	0.38
Ecuador	1,946	0.09	415	0.01
Egypt	14,173	0.63	32,838	1.07
El Salvador	452	0.02	2,141	0.07
Estonia	0	0.00	1,789	0.06
Ghana	1,492	0.07	916	0.03
Greece	24,178	1.08	204,213	6.66
Hungary	5,273	0.23	16,317	0.53
India	122,605	5.46	184,605	6.02
Indonesia	91,016	4.06	64,087	2.09
Iran	17,008	0.76	21,830	0.71
Israel	35,935	1.60	63,820	2.08
Jamaica	1,887	0.08	2,530	0.08
Jordan	4,551	0.20	5,827	0.19
Kazakhstan	0	0.00	2,260	0.07
Kenya	1,846	0.08	1,409	0.05
Korea	138,817	6.19	308,534	10.06
Lebanon	0	0.00	1,921	0.06

The eight countries that are in boldface type are new to the list since 1996.

1996 was $2.2 trillion, which grew to $3 trillion by 1999. The emerging markets grew much more slowly than the developed markets during this time period, but with $3 trillion, emerging markets in total would rank in third place among developed countries just edging out the United Kingdom in Table 15–1. Some of the emerging markets, such as Korea ($308 billion), Taiwan ($375 billion), and China ($330 billion), are bigger than markets in developed countries, but because these countries have a low per-capita GDP, they are listed with the emerging markets.

The size of the list of emerging markets changed between 1996 and 1999 with Cyprus and Portugal moving to the developed list. At the same time, the emerging market list added El Salvador, Estonia, Kazakhstan, Lebanon, Panama, Saudi Arabia, Ukraine, and Yugoslavia to the list of countries having market capitalizations of more than $500 million. Many countries had huge relative gains in market size. For example, China almost tripled in value from $113 billion to $330 billion, while Turkey grew from $30 billion to $112 billion. Some formerly large markets such

TABLE 15–2 Market Capitalization of Emerging Markets Greater than $500 Million in Capitalization (in Millions of U.S. Dollars) *(concluded)*

Country	Year-End 1996	Percent of Total	Year-End 1999	Percent of Total
Lithuania	$ 900	0.04%	$ 1,138	0.04%
Malaysia	307,179	13.69	145,445	4.74
Mauritius	1,676	0.07	1,642	0.05
Mexico	106,540	4.75	154,044	5.02
Morocco	8,705	0.39	13,695	0.45
Nigeria	3,560	0.16	2,940	0.10
Oman	2,673	0.12	4,302	0.14
Pakistan	10,639	0.47	6,965	0.23
Panama	1,279	0.06	3,584	0.12
Peru	12,291	0.55	13,392	0.44
Philippines	80,649	3.59	48,105	1.57
Poland	8,390	0.37	29,577	0.96
Russia	37,230	1.66	72,205	2.35
Saudi Arabia	45,861	2.04	60,440	1.97
South Africa	241,571	10.76	262,478	8.56
Slovakia	2,182	0.10	723	0.02
Slovenia	663	0.03	2,180	0.07
Sri Lanka	1,848	0.08	1,584	0.05
Taiwan	273,608	12.19	375,991	12.26
Thailand	99,828	4.45	58,365	1.90
Trinidad and Tobago	1,405	0.06	4,367	0.14
Tunisia	4,263	0.19	2,706	0.09
Turkey	30,020	1.34	112,716	3.68
Ukraine	0	0.00	1,121	0.04
Venezuela	10,055	0.45	7,471	0.24
Yugoslavia	0	0.00	10,817	0.35
Zimbabwe	3,635	0.16	2,514	0.08
Total	$2,244,395		$3,066,554	

Source: *Emerging Stock Markets Factbook*, 2000 (Washington, D.C.: International Finance Corporation, 2000), pp. 16–17.

as Malaysia had significant declines in value (from $307 billion to $145 billion) and Thailand lost almost half its market capitalization, falling from $99 billion to $58 billion. These changes indicate how economic fortunes and markets can change in a short period of time.

One way to keep emerging markets in perspective is to compare their size with some well-known U.S. companies. For example during a comparable time period, Colgate Palmolive ranked 200th in the list of *Fortune 500* companies and had a market capitalization of $31 billion, while General Electric, which ranked fifth in the *Fortune 500,* had a market capitalization of $407 billion. General Electric would lead the list of countries in Table 15-2 followed by Taiwan with $376 billion of market capitalization and Colgate Palmolive would be ranked 20th in the list. The small market size of many emerging markets explains the low liquidity of these markets and also explains why small capital flows in and out of these markets and can create wide price swings. When U.S. investors suddenly decide they want to own stocks in emerging market countries, money managers of mutual funds specializing in these countries have a difficult time placing all the money flows without driving prices up dramatically.

Investors often equate emerging markets to high growth, and there is some truth to this when taken in a portfolio context. Between 1992 and 1999 the developed countries increased in market capitalization from $9.9 trillion to $32.9 trillion, a 232 percent increase. The emerging markets increased in size from $882 billion to $3 trillion, an increase of 240 percent. While this is slightly higher than the developed countries, many individual emerging market countries increased at much higher rates than the average. China increased 1,733 percent over this same time, from $18 billion to $330 billion, and Poland increased 13,222 percent, from $222 million to $29.577 billion. Several other countries increased their market value by more than 500 percent during this time period, which far outdistanced any growth among the developed countries.

A geographical breakdown of the emerging markets is depicted in Figure 15-2 for 1996 and 1999. The relationships among the emerging countries have changed dramatically. Although Latin America and the Mideast and Africa stayed relatively the same, South Asia declined from 28 percent to 15 percent of the total emerging market capitalization; the economies of that region failed to recover from the currency crisis they encountered in 1997 and 1998. East Asia, with China and Korea growing, gained 8 percent, and Europe tripled its market share from 3 to 9 percent.

As emerging markets have grown, there are more opportunities to own equity positions in emerging markets. It is useful to look at the different market structures and institutional characteristics of these and other markets.

Markets are structured quite differently. For example, continuous auction markets are the standard in countries such as the United States, Japan, United Kingdom, Germany, Canada, Hong Kong, and others. In many smaller emerging markets, there is not enough continuous buying and selling of securities to create the liquid markets necessary for continuous auction markets; instead, exchanges may trade shares once or twice per day. Some markets have specialists, automated trading, and computer-directed trading, while others do not. Even in the developed markets, most exchanges do not allow trading in options and futures on the stock exchanges. While most exchanges do not have limits on price movements, some exchanges limit prices within a band of 5 or 10 percent on a daily basis. Transaction taxes can be significant on foreign exchanges, ranging from 0 percent in Mexico to 2.4 percent in the Netherlands. Taxes at very high levels can reduce trading, liquidity, and potential returns. Many exchanges allow some form of margin, which allows investors to purchase securities with a percentage of borrowed money, and some do not allow this practice at all. In some countries such as Korea, foreign investors may not be allowed to buy shares of companies at all. The moral is, do not assume that foreign markets function like those in the United States. Foreign markets usually have higher transactions costs, less liquidity, and are generally less efficient. Institutional practices around the world can have significant impacts on your rates of return.

FIGURE 15–2 Regional Weights of Emerging Markets (Based on Market Capitalization in U.S. Dollars)

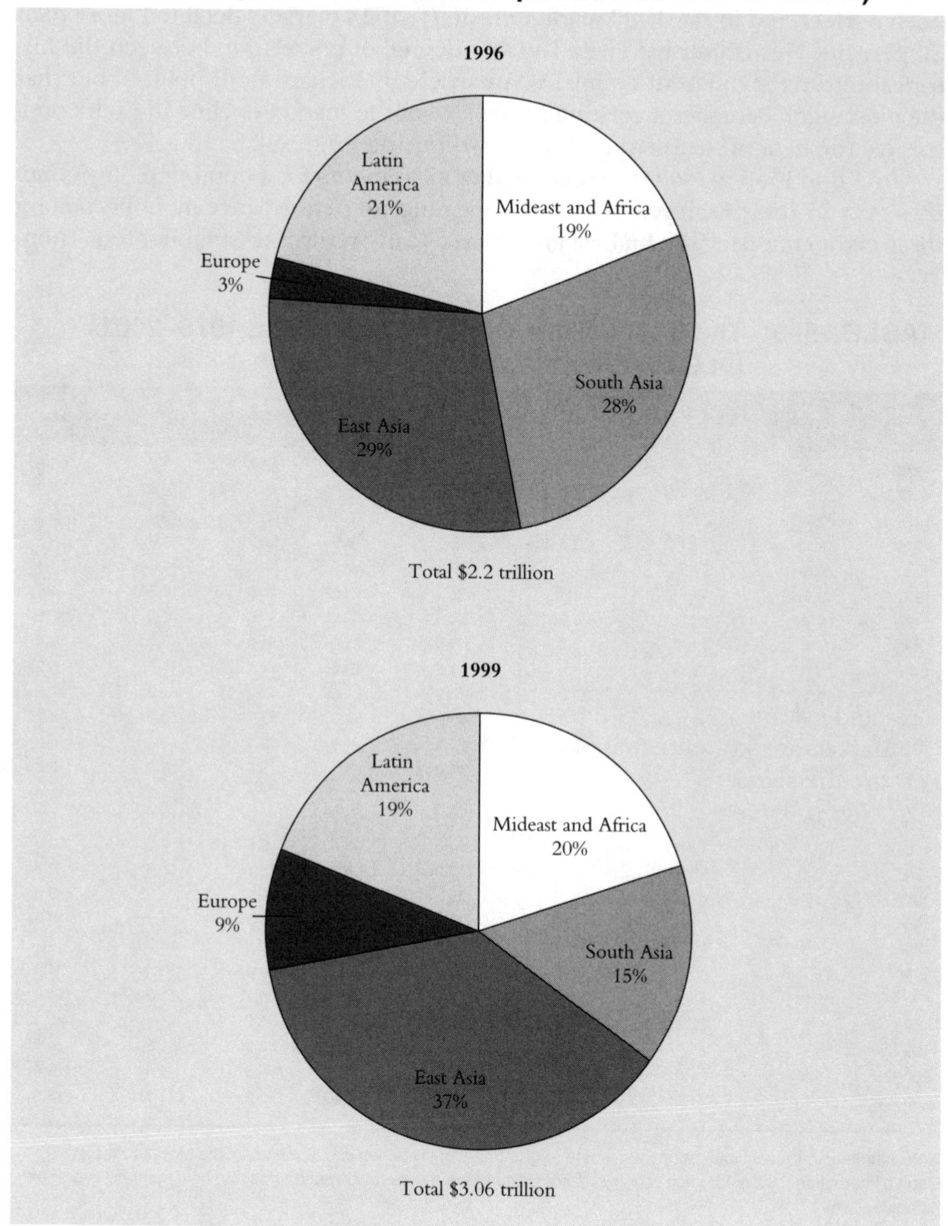

DIVERSIFICATION BENEFITS

One of the benefits of foreign investing is that not all foreign markets move in the same direction at any point in time, so a diversified portfolio consisting of stocks from many countries will have less volatility than a purely domestic portfolio of stocks and could even have a higher rate of return. This benefit has not always been perfect, and in the 1987 market crash, 19 of 23 markets declined more than 20 percent. This is unusual given the low degree of correlation between the historical returns of different countries. An article by Richard Roll[1] pointed out that the most significant factor relating to the size of the market decline in each country was the beta of that market to the world market index.

In Table 15-3 we see the stock market movements for a number of key countries over 25 years. Each year there is a wide range of performance numbers among these eight countries; the highest and lowest yearly returns are highlighted. There

TABLE 15–3 The Best Performing Equity Markets, 1976–2001 (in U.S. Dollars)

	Germany	Switzerland	United Kingdom	Australia	Hong Kong	Japan	Canada	United States
1976	6.6	10.5	*(12.70)*	(10.2)	**40.7**	25.6	9.7	23.8
1977	25.8	28.7	**58.0**	11.9	*(11.20)*	15.9	(2.1)	(7.2)
1978	26.9	21.9	14.6	21.8	18.5	**53.3**	20.4	*6.5*
1979	(2.2)	12.1	22.1	43.6	**83.5**	*(11.9)*	51.8	18.5
1980	*(9.1)*	(7.3)	41.1	55.3	**72.7**	30.3	22.6	32.4
1981	(8.2)	(9.5)	(10.6)	*(23.9)*	(15.8)	**15.8**	(10.7)	(4.9)
1982	12.3	3.4	9.2	(22.6)	*(44.5)*	(0.5)	2.4	**21.5**
1983	25.9	19.3	17.2	**56.0**	*(3.0)*	24.9	33.4	22.2
1984	(3.8)	(11.1)	5.4	*(12.6)*	**46.8**	17.1	(7.6)	6.2
1985	**139.2**	107.4	52.8	20.9	51.6	43.4	*15.9*	31.6
1986	37.2	34.3	27.1	43.8	56.0	**99.7**	*10.7*	18.2
1987	*(23.4)*	(8.8)	36.5	10.3	(4.1)	**43.2**	14.6	5.2
1988	23.1	*7.1*	*7.1*	**38.0**	28.0	35.5	18.0	16.5
1989	**48.8**	27.1	23.1	10.8	8.3	*1.8*	25.2	31.4
1990	(10.8)	(7.8)	**6.0**	(21.0)	3.7	*(36.4)*	(15.3)	(5.6)
1991	8.7	13.6	12.0	n.a.	**43.4**	*6.5*	8.7	30.3
1992	(13.2)	13.3	(6.2)	(16.2)	**28.3**	*(23.1)*	(15.7)	2.8
1993	33.7	47.5	*3.2*	36.3	**107.7**	25.3	17.0	9.0
1994	3.3	2.4	(4.7)	2.9	*(31.0)*	**20.7**	(4.9)	(0.9)
1995	14.8	**42.4**	17.2	8.3	18.2	*0.0*	16.1	34.7
1996	12.1	1.2	23.3	13.4	**28.9**	*(16.0)*	26.4	21.4
1997	23.3	**43.2**	19.1	(12.6)	*(28.8)*	(24.2)	11.2	31.7
1998	28.2	22.6	14.8	3.8	*(7.6)*	4.3	(7.4)	**28.8**
1999	18.7	*(7.8)*	9.7	15.2	54.9	**60.6**	51.8	20.9
2000	(16.5)	**4.9**	(13.6)	(12.0)	(17.0)	*(28.5)*	4.4	(13.6)
2001	(23.5)	(21.9)	(16.1)	**(0.6)**	(21.2)	*(29.9)*	(21.4)	(13.2)

Note: Numbers represent total return, assuming reinvestment of dividends in U.S. dollars of the Morgan Stanley Capital International Index for each country. (Italicized numbers represent lowest returns and bold numbers represent highest returns.)

Source: Templeton International; Morgan Stanley Capital International Perspective, Geneva, located in *Barron's* January issues; and year-end issues of *The Wall Street Journal,* local index returns in U.S. dollars.

1. Richard Roll, "The International Crash of 1987," *Financial Analysts Journal,* September–October 1988, pp. 19–35.

are several issues worth noting. No country continually outperforms the others on an annual basis. Hong Kong has the highest returns 8 out of 26 years and Japan had the lowest returns 9 out of 26 years. Canada has never had the highest return. In 15 of these years one of these countries had a loss.

Table 15-3 further shows that the developed markets in 2000 and 2001 were mostly in negative territory except for Switzerland and Canada in 2000. When markets move in the same direction, you sometimes hear that international markets don't provide any risk reduction. Occasionally markets move together because of some global economic force. In 1989 and 1997 during the October collapses of the U.S. markets and right after the September 11, 2001, attacks on New York's World Trade Center and the Pentagon in Washington, D.C., markets around the world reacted together as they fell in sympathy with the U.S. markets. International events that cause markets to move in unison have caused many market analysts to surmise that markets are more connected than they used to be for several reasons:

1. We have a global economy where international companies do business across borders. This phenomenon will cause economies across these geographical regions to become more intertwined and less diverse.
2. We have a new European Monetary Union with 25 countries (perhaps more by the time you read this) adopting the euro as the single currency. With the European Central Bank harmonizing monetary policy across the region, these European markets will behave more in line with each other.

While all these stories make sense, and even if they are true, we should recognize that over the long run, the world economies and their markets do not move directly with the U.S. economy on a consistent basis.

Let us look at a U.S. investor based on the data in Table 15-3. In 1976, a 23.8 percent return could be earned in the United States, while a 12.7 percent loss occurred in the United Kingdom. In 1977, this situation was reversed with a 7.2 percent loss in the United States and a 58 percent return in the United Kingdom. If an investor had held equal positions in both countries, returns would have been less volatile (risky), and a U.S. investor would have had a greater total return. Diversification reduces portfolio volatility and at the same time offers opportunities for higher returns than a single country portfolio.

One way to consider diversification benefits is to measure the extent of correlation of stock movements. The correlation coefficient measures the movement of one series of data over time to another series of data, in this case stock market returns. The correlation coefficient can be between −1 and +1. A coefficient of +1 indicates a perfect positive relationship as the two variables move together up and down. A coefficient of −1 indicates a perfect negative relationship as the two variables move opposite of each other. A zero coefficient describes a series that has no relationship. Any time you can diversify into assets that have a correlation coefficient of less than +1, you reduce the amount of risk assumed. Such a measure is presented in Table 15-4, in which stock movements for a number of developed countries are compared with those of the United States.

Three sets of correlation coefficients are presented: one long-term set from 1960 to 1980, and two short-term sets from June 1981 through September 1987 and from July 1991 through July 1996. The countries are listed from the highest correlation to the lowest based on 1960 to 1980 data. By comparing the three sets of correlations, we can see there is not a great amount of stability among the time periods, with some countries such as Italy going from 12th to 11th place to 4th place in the latest period. Canada, because of its close ties with the U.S. economy, is highly correlated with the U.S. markets.

The best risk-reduction benefits can be found by combining U.S. securities with those from countries having low correlations such as Germany and Japan. Countries with high correlations provide the least benefit from diversification. According to one researcher, Bruno Solnik, a well-diversified international portfolio can achieve the same risk-reduction benefits as a pure U.S. portfolio that is twice the size in terms of securities.[2]

In Table 15-4, we examined developed countries. Using Table 15-5 for emerging markets, we see correlations data for five years ending in 1999. Looking down the last column of numbers gives each country's correlation coefficient against

TABLE 15–4 Correlation of Foreign Stock Movements with U.S. Stock Movement

Country	Correlation 1960–80		Correlation June 1981–September 1987		Monthly Correlation July 1991–July 1996	
United States	1.000		1.000		1.000	
Netherlands	0.730	(1)	0.473	(4)	0.320	(5)
Canada	0.710	(2)	0.720	(1)	0.700	(1)
Australia	0.699	(3)	0.328	(7)	0.173	(9)
United Kingdom	0.617	(4)	0.513	(2)	0.318	(6)
Switzerland	0.454	(5)	0.500	(3)	0.184	(8)
Sweden	0.398	(6)	0.279	(9)	0.285	(7)
Belgium	0.389	(7)	0.250	(10)	0.338	(3)
Denmark	0.243	(8)	0.351	(6)	0.084	(11)
Japan	0.216	(9)	0.326	(8)	0.080	(12)
France	0.214	(10)	0.390	(5)	0.355	(2)
Germany	0.210	(11)	0.209	(12)	0.135	(10)
Italy	0.208	(12)	0.224	(11)	0.327	(4)

Source: Roger G. Ibbotson, Richard C. Carr, and Anthony W. Robinson, "International Equity and Bond Returns," *Financial Analysts Journal*, July–August 1982, p. 71; and Richard Roll, "The International Crash of 1987," *Financial Analysts Journal*, September–October 1988, pp. 20–21.

2. Bruno H. Solnik, "Why Not Diversify Internationally Rather than Domestically?" *Financial Analysts Journal*, July–August 1974, pp. 48–54.

the U.S. market as measured by the Standard & Poor's 500 Index. Two countries have a negative correlation with the United States. The highest positive correlation for the 60 months with the United States is Thailand with a correlation of 0.59 while the lowest one is Morocco with −0.36. Only three countries (Thailand, Philippines, and South Africa) are more than 50 percent correlated with the United States, 14 have correlations between 0.30 and 0.46, and 10 countries have correlation with the United States at 0.20 or below. It would appear that emerging market countries provide better diversification benefits than developed countries, but we must remember that the annual returns on these markets must also be considered whenever diversifying a portfolio to achieve a risk-return benefit.

TABLE 15–5 Statistics of the IFC Total Return Indexes (in U.S. Dollars, December 1994–December 1999)

Market	Number of Months	Mean of Percent Change	Standard Deviation	Annualized Mean	Annualized Standard Deviation	Correlation with S&P 500
Latin America						
Argentina	60	1.38	9.91	16.56	34.33	0.42
Brazil	60	1.48	12.80	17.76	44.34	0.40
Chile	60	0.16	7.51	1.92	26.02	0.40
Colombia	60	−0.60	9.56	−7.20	33.12	0.13
Mexico	60	1.35	10.91	16.20	37.79	0.44
Peru	60	0.38	8.45	4.56	29.27	0.18
Venezuela	60	1.23	15.60	14.76	54.04	0.17
Asia						
China	60	0.56	13.96	6.72	48.36	0.22
India	60	0.40	8.75	4.80	30.31	0.05
Indonesia	60	0.58	18.69	6.96	64.74	0.35
Korea	60	1.05	17.02	12.60	58.96	0.44
Malaysia	60	−0.06	14.69	−0.72	50.89	0.45
Pakistan	60	−0.47	13.06	−5.64	45.24	0.20
Philippines	60	−0.73	11.62	−8.76	40.25	0.52
Sri Lanka	60	−0.62	10.20	−7.44	35.33	0.36
Taiwan	60	0.61	9.29	7.32	32.18	0.31
Thailand	60	−1.11	15.29	−13.32	52.97	0.59
Europe						
Czech Republic	60	−0.25	8.71	−3.00	30.17	0.25
Greece	60	3.26	9.47	39.12	32.81	0.18
Hungary	60	2.15	12.36	25.80	42.82	0.46
Poland	60	1.41	12.23	16.92	42.37	0.42
Russia	34	2.87	26.43	34.44	91.56	0.41
Slovakia	34	−3.03	7.89	−36.36	27.33	−0.18
Turkey	60	4.21	18.25	50.52	63.22	0.20
Mideast/Asia						
Egypt	34	−0.22	7.27	−2.64	25.18	0.24
Israel	36	1.75	6.90	21.00	23.90	0.32
Jordan	60	0.82	3.73	9.84	12.92	0.12
Morocco	34	1.34	4.97	16.08	17.22	−0.36
South Africa	60	0.42	8.90	5.04	30.83	0.51
Zimbabwe	60	1.18	12.16	14.16	42.12	0.27

Source: *Emerging Market Factbook*, 2000. Published by Standard and Poor's.

RETURN POTENTIAL IN INTERNATIONAL MARKETS

Actually, risk reduction through effective international diversification is only part of the story. Not only does the investor have less risk exposure, but there is also the potential for higher returns in many foreign markets. Why? A number of countries have had long-term growth rates superior to those of the United States in terms of real GDP. These would include Norway, Singapore, and Hong Kong. Second, many countries have become highly competitive in traditional U.S. products such as automobiles, steel, and consumer electronics. Third, many nations (Germany, Japan, France, Canada) enjoy higher individual savings rates than the United States, and this leads to capital formation and potential investment opportunity. This is not to imply that the United States does not have the strongest and best regulated securities markets in the world. It clearly does. However, it is a more mature market than many others, and there may be abundant opportunities for high returns in a number of foreign markets.

We have already presented the annual returns for eight developed countries in Table 15-3. However, we present five different international indexes of investment performance in Figure 15-3, showing the wealth that would have accumulated by the end of 2001 from an investment of $1 in each index at the beginning of 1969. The Pacific region is more volatile than the other regions; it peaked in 1989 and 1999 and then took a dive. Europe on the other hand is ahead in the race because they have had smaller negative returns when they occurred while North America consisting of the U.S. and Canada ended up in the middle. Despite strong performances in 1995 through 1999, the market downturn in 2000 and 2001 took their toll on the final wealth numbers. The annualized rates of return for each index over this 32-year period are as follows:

Region	Annualized Rates of Return
Pacific	10.27%
EAFE[a]	10.68
Europe	11.47
World Index	11.37
North America	10.77

[a]Europe, Australasia, and Far East.

Figure 15-3 represents a long-term perspective. There are, of course, time periods when the United States outperforms foreign markets and foreign markets in turn outperform the U.S. markets. In the last edition of the text with data ending in 1996, the highest annualized return was 14.79 percent and the lowest was 12.32 percent. With an extra five years of data, the difference between the highest (Europe, 11.47%) and the lowest (Pacific, 10.27%) is only 1.2 percent and all annualized returns are rather close together. However when looking at the wealth values over 32 periods, Europe ($32.26) is almost $10 ahead of the Pacific region

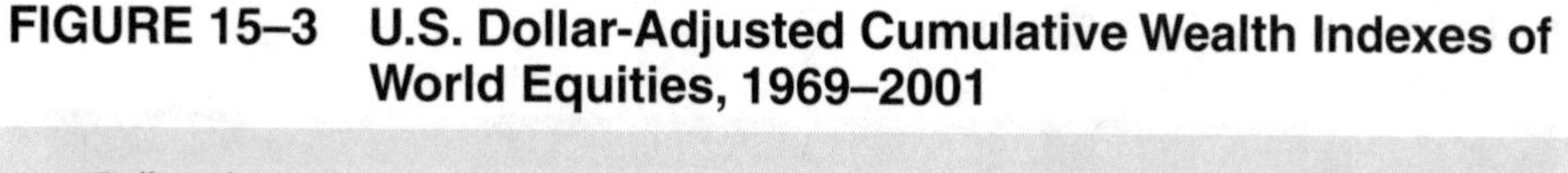

FIGURE 15–3 U.S. Dollar-Adjusted Cumulative Wealth Indexes of World Equities, 1969–2001

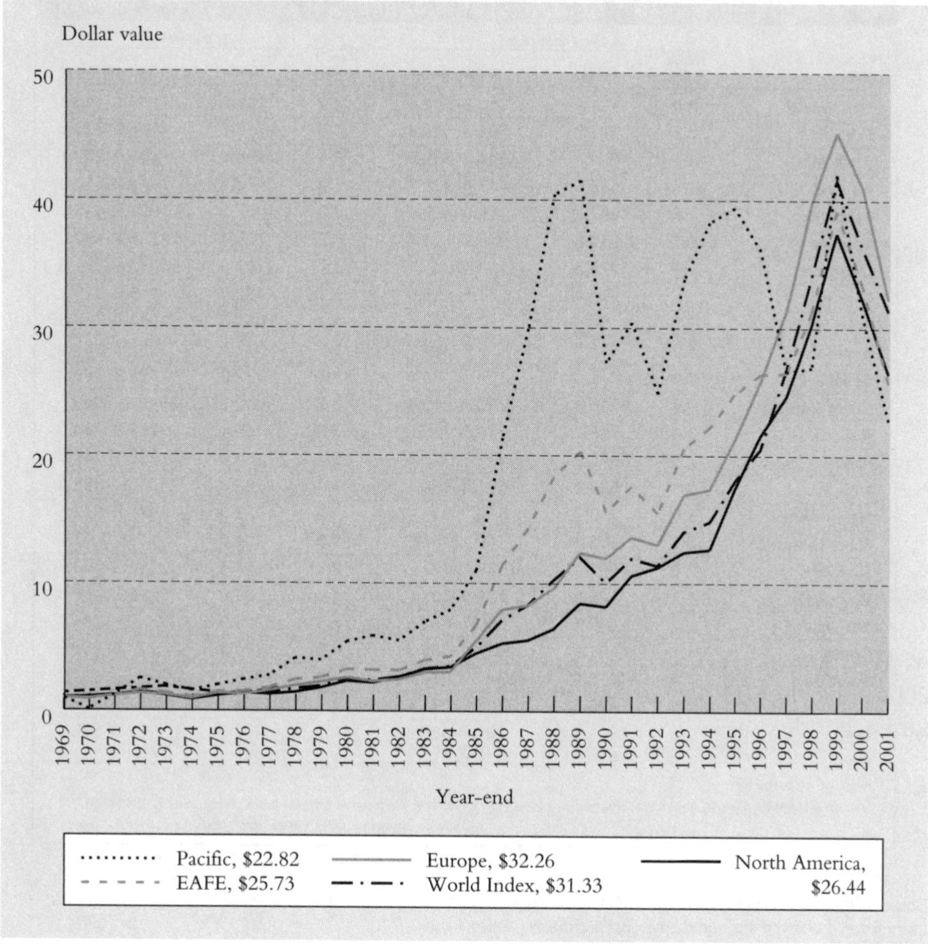

($22.82) with only a 1.2 percent better performance. This demonstrates the power of compounding.

Current Quotations of Foreign Market Performance

To track the current performance of selected world markets, *The Wall Street Journal* provides daily quotes of price movements, while *Barron's* presents a weekly summary of the major global markets. The closing quotes of October 9, 2003, for *Barron's* are presented in Table 15-6.

The quotes are shown in local currencies as well as in U.S. dollars. For a U.S. investor, the returns in U.S. dollars are the best comparative measure against an investment in U.S. stocks. Under the U.S. dollars columns, you can first observe the

TABLE 15–6 Global Stock Markets

GLOBAL STOCK MARKETS

Index	In Local Currencies Week's % Chg.	10/09	52-wk Range	In U.S. Dollars[1] Week's % Chg.	10/09	52-wk Range
The World	**2.0**	**735.2**	**740.3–562.4**	**2.2**	**953.8**	**953.8–710.8**
E.A.F.E.[2]	2.3	673.5	684.0–503.4	2.8	1166.9	1166.9–823.5
Australia	1.7	644.2	644.2–539.9	3.1	398.4	398.4–282.1
Austria	1.5	438.5	443.4–328.3	1.9	972.2	976.7–611.0
Belgium	1.6	692.7	715.0–467.0	2.0	1007.5	1007.5–637.9
Canada	0.7	944.5	950.7–721.4	1.2	765.4	765.4–490.2
Denmark	1.9	1773.3	1825.6–1245.8	2.3	2101.0	2103.5–1371.8
Finland	5.5	555.4	697.2–435.9	5.9	432.3	459.8–319.2
France	3.9	1090.6	1127.5–793.0	4.3	1081.8	1081.8–738.8
Germany	6.2	433.7	455.6–282.7	6.6	952.1	952.1–583.0
Greece	2.9	741.0	802.0–492.6	3.3	322.2	325.3–199.2
Hong Kong	− 0.7	6190.4	6329.2–4305.4	− 0.7	4449.6	4559.1–3065.6
Ireland	2.6	296.2	308.6–245.6	3.0	265.1	268.9–184.5
Italy	2.3	908.0	931.1–722.5	2.7	344.0	352.1–249.5
Japan	− 0.1	636.4	654.4–462.1	1.4	2103.8	2135.2–1385.4
Netherlands	3.0	738.2	834.0–537.1	3.4	1423.5	1423.5–972.8
New Zealand	0.6	102.8	102.8–86.6	1.0	94.0	94.0–67.1
Norway	2.8	1097.1	1139.5–762.2	2.3	1114.3	1114.3–763.7
Portugal[3]	1.1	129.9	129.9–103.7	1.5	99.9	99.9–66.3
Singapore	6.2	1000.7	1000.7–687.5	6.5	1785.9	1785.9–1204.8
Spain	4.1	661.8	687.0–506.3	4.5	326.7	327.6–209.8
Sweden	5.6	4412.5	4534.9–3017.4	6.0	2979.5	2979.5–1681.2
Switzerland	2.7	678.6	704.5–481.4	2.6	2208.6	2208.6–1552.8
U.K.	2.5	1301.9	1301.9–986.4	2.0	902.3	902.3–662.6
U.S.A.	1.8	975.4	976.6–752.3	1.8	975.4	976.6–752.3

Base Jan. 1, 1970=100

[1]Adjusted for foreign exchange fluctuations relative to the U.S. $. [2]Europe, Australasia, Far East Index. [3]Base: Jan. 1, 1988=100.

Source: Morgan Stanley Capital International Perspective, Geneva.

percentage change from the last weekly quote. Next observe the index values shown under the 10/09 column (second column from the right) for U.S. dollar values. The base value is 100, and the base period for the index is 1970. Over the 33-year period, the United States (last line) has been outperformed on a U.S. dollar basis by many countries. The United States, with an ending base number of 975.4, outperformed 12 countries and was outperformed by 10 countries. Hong Kong had an ending index of 4449.6, Sweden 2979.5, and Switzerland 2208.6. Numbers don't always tell the whole story. For example, L.M. Ericsson, a manufacturer of cell phones and telephone infrastructure equipment, accounts for more than 50 percent of Sweden's market capitalization, and its performance has been outstanding over this time period. By owning Ericsson, an investor would have diversified into the Swedish market.

Another variable that shows up in Table 15-6 is the return difference in local currencies versus U.S. dollars. Notice that 13 countries (for example, Sweden) have lower returns in U.S. dollars than in their local currencies because their currency declined against the dollar, while 9 countries (for example, Switzerland) have higher returns in U.S. dollars because their currency rose against the dollar. This 33-year time period covers many economic events and currency fluctuation that show up because of the 1970 base year used by Morgan Stanley Capital International Perspective of Geneva, Switzerland.

At the top of Table 15-6 is the World Index, at 953.8 in U.S. dollars, which is a value-weighted index of the performance in 23 major countries as compiled by Morgan Stanley Capital International Perspective. An investment in the U.S. markets would have outperformed a diversified value-weighted portfolio, but a comparison of raw returns excludes any risk adjustment that would have occurred from having a more diversified portfolio with the World Index. We should point out that Table 15-6 presents a very short-term view that may not be indicative of any five- or ten-year period.

Other Market Differences

There are large differences among cultures, including willingness to take risk, desire for dividend income versus growth in share value, the number and type of companies available to stockholders, and bureaucratic differences such as accounting conventions and government regulation of markets. In a book of this type, we do not intend to cover each issue but simply bring them to your attention. Table 15-7 presents differences in price-earnings ratios, price-to-book value ratios, and dividend yields from the *Emerging Stock Markets Factbook,* 2000, published by International Finance Corporation of Washington, D.C.

Many developing countries have higher price-earnings ratios in their stock markets than the rest of the world. For example, Argentina had an average P/E of 39.00 for 1999. However, the P/E ratios in Latin America vary widely from country to country ranging from 39.00 in Argentina to 10.52 in Venezuela. Clearly, individual country differences account for these disparities, but in all cases, those countries with high expected growth in "real" earnings and dividends will have higher price-earnings ratios than those with lower expected growth. This is the same impact found in the U.S. market as discussed in Chapter 7.

To some extent, the price-to-book-value ratio in each country corresponds to each country's P/E ratio. Countries with high P/Es generally have high P/BV ratios and vice versa. The dividend yields show a wide difference with Pakistan having a yield of 5.79 percent for 1999 and the Philippines having a 0.86 percent dividend yield. This wide difference is mostly attributable to country differences, inflation rates, different accounting methods, and risk-return preferences of the stockholders.

TABLE 15–7 Comparative Valuations of Emerging Countries[a]

Market	Price-Earnings Ratio			Price-Book Value Ratio			Dividend Yield		
	End 1999	Relative to World[a]	End 1998	End 1999	Relative to World[a]	End 1998	End 1999	Relative to World[b]	End 1998
Latin America									
Argentina	39.00	1.09	13.22	1.53	0.36	1.25	3.22	2.48	4.03
Brazil	25.07	0.70	7.08	1.55	0.37	0.60	3.02	2.32	7.23
Chile	37.70	1.06	14.77	1.81	0.43	1.17	2.99	2.30	4.20
Colombia	61.17	1.71	10.41	0.73	0.17	0.73	6.89	5.30	5.56
Mexico	14.12	0.40	21.31	2.18	0.52	1.44	0.85	0.65	2.97
Peru	26.10	0.73	21.07	1.54	0.36	1.56	2.02	1.55	3.83
Venezuela	10.52	0.29	5.46	0.46	0.11	0.53	6.23	4.79	4.43
Asia									
China	48.18	1.35	12.74	2.24	0.53	1.02	0.81	0.62	0.96
India	21.97	0.62	11.46	3.14	0.74	1.75	1.05	0.81	1.91
Indonesia	−10.48	−0.29	108.81	2.89	0.68	1.66	0.60	0.46	0.83
Korea	−27.74	−0.78	−50.69	2.03	0.48	0.92	0.53	0.41	0.62
Malaysia	−19.08	−0.53	19.89	1.88	0.44	1.29	1.35	1.04	2.53
Pakistan	17.54	0.49	5.73	1.87	0.44	1.22	5.79	4.45	14.69
Philippines	24.02	0.67	15.00	1.49	0.35	1.37	0.86	0.66	0.72
Sri Lanka	8.65	0.24	8.11	1.04	0.25	1.20	2.78	2.14	2.86
Taiwan	49.16	1.38	21.49	3.27	0.77	2.63	0.68	0.52	0.84
Thailand	−14.49	−0.41	−6.45	2.56	0.61	1.49	0.34	0.26	0.75
Europe/Mideast/Africa									
Czech Republic	−14.79	−0.41	48.17	1.22	0.29	0.81	1.65	1.27	0.17
Egypt	18.55	0.52	8.64	3.99	0.94	2.74	3.40	2.62	6.75
Greece	55.64	1.56	33.66	9.35	2.21	4.87	1.09	0.84	1.57
Hungary	18.16	0.51	17.02	3.64	0.86	3.21	1.05	0.81	1.07
Israel	17.95	0.50	13.18	1.77	0.42	1.21	3.26	2.51	1.91
Jordan	13.61	0.38	16.31	1.53	0.36	1.65	2.32	1.78	2.27
Morocco	18.37	0.51	19.52	3.05	0.72	3.37	1.99	1.53	2.03
Poland	22.02	0.62	10.74	1.95	0.46	1.54	0.85	0.65	1.52
Russia	98.40	2.76	10.39	2.27	0.54	0.62	0.10	0.08	1.12
Slovakia	−2.18	−0.06	7.37	0.55	0.13	0.31	0.56	0.43	3.83
South Africa	17.37	0.49	10.09	2.65	0.63	1.53	2.27	1.75	3.24
Turkey	33.84	0.95	7.80	8.77	2.07	2.74	1.07	0.82	4.34
Zimbabwe	12.47	0.35	5.36	5.38	1.27	2.38	2.28	1.75	3.43

[a]Relative to the MSCI World Index.

[b]The composite P/E and P/BV are averages of the companies in the IFC indexes weighted by market capitalization; the dividend yield represents a 12-month moving yield for the indexes.

Source: *Emerging Stock Markets Factbook,* 2000 (Washington, D.C.: International Finance Corporation, 2000), p. 38.

CURRENCY FLUCTUATIONS AND RATES OF RETURN

We must explicitly consider the effect of currency fluctuations (changes in currency values) as well as rates of return in different countries. For example, assume an investment in Switzerland produces a 10 percent return. But suppose at the same time the Swiss franc declines in value by 5 percent against the U.S. dollar. The Swiss franc profits are thus worth less in dollars. In the present case, the gain on the investment would be shown as follows:

110%	(Investment with 10% profit)
	(Adjusted value of Swiss franc relative to U.S. dollar)
× 0.95	(1.00 − 0.05 decline in currency)
104.5%	Percent of original investment

The actual return in U.S. dollars would be 4.5 instead of 10 percent. Of course, if the Swiss franc appreciated by 5 percent against the dollar, the Swiss franc profits converted to dollars would be worth considerably more than 10 percent. The values are indicated below:

110%	(Investment with 10% profit)
	(Adjusted value of Swiss franc relative to U.S. dollar)
× 1.05	(1.00 + 0.05 increase in currency)
115.5%	Percent of original investment

The 10 percent gain in the Swiss franc investment has produced a 15.5 percent gain in U.S. dollars. A U.S. investor in foreign securities must consider not only the potential trend of security prices but also the trend of foreign currencies against the dollar.

This point will become more apparent as we look at Table 15-8, which depicts rates of return on the J.P. Morgan Overseas Government Bond Index for 13 developed countries from January 1, 2003, through October 13, 2003. During this period, the U.S. dollar was relatively strong against the rest of the world. This can be seen by comparing the return in local dollars against the return in U.S. dollars (YTD change column). In every case, the return in U.S. dollars is lower than the returns in local currencies.

Let's examine the currency effects in Sweden year to date (YTD). In this instance, the return in the local currency was 3.66 percent (third column) while the return in U.S. dollars was 17.91 percent (sixth column). The change in the dollar versus the kroner caused a positive return in local currency to become even a bigger return in U.S. currency as the dollar fell over this period. If you were Swedish, this would not affect your return, but if you were an international investor translating returns to U.S. dollars, the positive return would definitely enhance your wealth. We would compute the returns as follows:

103.66%	(Investment with 3.66% profit)
	(Adjusted value of the Swedish kroner to the U.S. dollar)
× 1.1374	(1.000 + .1374 increase in currency)
117.91%	Percent of original investment

The ending value of 117.91 indicates a gain of 17.91 percent from the initial value of 100 percent.[3] If we were merely to add the foreign currency gain of 13.74

3. Due to rounding and other statistical adjustments, not all values adjusted to U.S. dollars come out as precisely as this.

TABLE 15–8 Overseas Government Bond Returns in Local Currency and U.S. Dollars (January 1 to October 13, 2003)

J.P. MORGAN OVERSEAS GOVERNMENT BOND INDEX

	Local Currency			U.S. Dollar			Yield	
Country	Index	Wkly % Chg	YTD % Chg	Index	Wkly % Chg	YTD % Chg	%	YTD Chg
Australia	487.24	-1.32	1.69	467.30	0.00	25.05	5.48	0.54
Belgium	350.84	-0.65	3.40	336.48	-0.26	15.63	3.95	-0.03
Canada	409.90	-1.12	3.89	399.25	-0.60	23.00	4.83	0.00
Denmark	403.51	-0.47	3.55	386.91	-0.09	15.78	3.92	-0.11
France	375.61	-0.62	2.94	357.32	-0.22	15.11	4.02	0.02
Germany	281.21	-0.63	2.91	264.71	-0.24	15.09	4.06	0.03
Italy	561.16	-0.61	3.02	394.28	-0.21	15.21	4.34	0.06
Japan	218.07	0.49	-0.88	242.01	2.05	7.84	0.95	0.30
Netherlands	302.31	-0.61	3.16	284.13	-0.21	15.36	3.98	-0.02
Spain	501.54	-0.68	3.17	379.55	-0.29	15.38	4.07	0.00
Sweden	449.89	-0.75	3.66	339.49	-0.39	17.91	4.33	-0.01
U.K.	417.99	-0.72	0.53	368.59	-1.14	3.86	4.77	0.37
U.S.	340.74	-1.54	1.06	340.74	-1.54	1.06	4.30	0.25
Non-U.S.	315.81	-0.24	1.49	284.33	0.54	12.02	3.10	0.19
Global	327.11	-0.55	1.38	314.73	0.04	9.21	3.39	0.16

YTD-Year to date. Yields-Semi-annual. Dec. 31, 1987=100. Source: J.P. Morgan Government Bond Index

Source: Republished with permission of Dow Jones & Company, Inc., from *Barron's*, October 13, 2003, p. MW40; permission conveyed through Copyright Clearance Center, Inc.

percent from the 3.66 percent profit, the answer would be a gain of 17.40 percent, but this is not the correct procedure. The gain of 3.66 percent was on an initial base of 100 percent, but the foreign currency gain of 13.74 percent was on an ending value of 103.66 percent. The resulting gain in U.S. dollar terms is the 17.91 percent, which leaves investors with 117.91 percent of their original investment.

You can see that several countries had their currency rise against the dollar by approximately 15 percent. These countries are all in the Monetary Union and have their currencies pegged to the euro. Those countries that are not in the Monetary Union, such as Australia, Canada, Japan, Sweden, and the United Kingdom all had different percentage upward valuations against the U.S. dollar.

Those who track the performance in foreign markets usually make adjustments so that the reported returns are in U.S. dollars that have already been adjusted for foreign currency effects. For example, most of the returns in prior tables of this chapter have already been adjusted for the foreign currency effect.

One might justifiably ask, how important is the foreign currency effect in relation to the overall return performance in the foreign currency? Do events in foreign exchange markets tend to overpower actual returns achieved in specific investments in foreign countries? Normally, the foreign currency effect is only about 10 to 20 percent as significant as the actual return performance in the foreign currency.[4] However, when the dollar is rising or falling rapidly over a short period, the impact can be much greater. For example, the returns to U.S. investors in Japanese securities between 1985 and 1988 were increased by 50 percent from the gain in the yen against the dollar.

In a well-diversified international portfolio, the changes in foreign currency values in one part of the world normally tend to cancel changes in other parts of the world. Also, those who do not wish to have foreign currency exposure of any sort may use forward exchange contracts, futures market contracts, or put options on foreign currency to hedge away the risk. Finally, there are those who believe in parity theories that suggest one should get additional compensation in local returns to make up for potential losses in foreign currency values. This latter point is a purely theoretical matter that provides little comfort in the short run.

The authors would suggest that those considering international investments be sensitive to the foreign currency effect, but not be overly discouraged by it. The superior return potentials from foreign investments previously shown in Figure 15-3 (and most other places in this chapter) are constructed *after* considering the foreign exchange effect on U.S. dollar returns. While foreign currency swings have been *wider* in recent times, they are still not a major deterrent to an internationally diversified portfolio.

OTHER OBSTACLES TO INTERNATIONAL INVESTMENTS

Other problems are peculiar to international investments. Let us consider some of them.

Political Risks

Many firms operate in foreign political climates that are more volatile than that of the United States. There is the danger of nationalization of foreign firms or the restriction of capital flows to investors. There also may be the danger of a violent overthrow of the political party in power. Furthermore, many countries have been unable to meet their foreign debt obligations, and this has important political implications.

The informed investor must have some feel for the political/economic climate of the foreign country in which he or she invests. Of course, problems sometimes create opportunities. Local investors may overreact to political changes occurring in their environment. Because all their eggs are in one basket, they may engage in an oversell in regard to political changes. A less impassioned outside investor may identify an opportunity for profit.

Nevertheless, political risk represents a potential deterrent to foreign investment. The best solution for the investor is to be sufficiently diversified around the world so that a political or economic development in one foreign country does

4. Bertrand Jacquillat and Bruno Solnik, "Multinationals Are Poor Tools for Diversification," *Journal of Portfolio Management,* Winter 1978, pp. 8–12.

not have a major impact on his or her portfolio (this can be accomplished through a mutual fund or through other means discussed later in the chapter).

Tax Problems

Many major foreign countries may impose a 15 to 30 percent withholding tax against the dividends or interest paid to nonresident holders of equity or debt securities. However, it is often possible for *tax-exempt* U.S. investors to secure an exemption or rebate on part or all of the withholding tax. Also, taxable U.S. investors can normally claim a U.S. tax credit for taxes paid in foreign countries. The problem is more likely to be one of inconvenience and paper shuffling rather than loss of funds.

Lack of Market Efficiency

U.S. capital markets tend to be the most liquid and efficient in the world. Therefore, an investor who is accustomed to trading on the New York Stock Exchange may have some difficulties adjusting to foreign markets. A larger spread between the bid (sell) and asked (buy) price in foreign countries is likely. Also, an investor may have more difficulty executing a large transaction (the seller may have to absorb a larger discount in executing the trade). Furthermore, as a general rule, commission rates are higher in foreign markets than in the United States.

Administrative Problems

There can also be administrative problems in dealing in foreign markets in terms of adjusting to the various local systems. For example, in the Hong Kong, Swiss, and Mexican stock markets, you must settle your account one day after the transaction; in London, there is a two-week settlement procedure; and in France, there are different settlement dates for cash and forward markets. The different administrative procedures of foreign countries simply add up to an extra dimension of difficulty in executing trades. (As implied throughout this chapter, there are ways to avoid most of these difficulties by going through mutual funds and other investment outlets.)

Information Difficulties

The U.S. securities markets are the best in the world at providing investment information. The Securities and Exchange Commission, with its rigorous requirements for full disclosure, is the toughest national regulator of investment information. Also, the United States has the Financial Accounting Standards Board (FASB) continually providing pronouncements on generally accepted accounting principles for financial reporting. Publicly traded companies are required to provide stockholders with fully audited annual reports. In the United States, we are further spoiled by the excellent evaluative reports and ratings generated by Moody's, Standard & Poor's, Value Line, and other firms. We also have extensive economic data provided by governmental sources such as the Department of Commerce and the Federal Reserve System.

Many international firms, trading in less sophisticated foreign markets, simply do not provide the same quantity or quality of data. This would be particularly true of firms trading in some of the smaller foreign markets. Even when the information is available, there may be language problems for the analyst who does not speak German, French, Portuguese, and so on.

Also, the analyst must be prepared to analyze the firm in light of the standards that are generally accepted in the foreign market in which the company operates. For example, Japanese companies often have much higher debt ratios than U.S. firms. A debt-to-equity ratio of three times is not unusual in Japan, whereas in the United States, the standard is closer to 1:1. The analyst may be inclined to "mark down" the Japanese firm for high debt unless he or she realizes the different features at play in the Japanese economy. For example, in Japan there are normally very close relationships between the lending bank and the borrower, with the lender perhaps having an equity position in the borrower and with interlocking boards between the two. This diminishes the likelihood of the lender calling in the loan in difficult economic periods. Also, the Japanese make extensive use of reserve accounts that tend to give the appearance of a smaller asset or equity base than actually exists. This pattern of understatement is further aided by a strict adherence to historical cost valuation. When appropriate adjustments are made for these effects on financial reporting, a Japanese debt-to-equity ratio of 3:1 may not be a matter of any greater concern than a U.S. debt-to-equity ratio of 1:1.

METHODS OF PARTICIPATING IN FOREIGN INVESTMENTS

The avenues to international investment include investing in firms in their own foreign markets, purchasing the shares of foreign firms trading in the United States, investing in mutual funds and closed-end funds with a global orientation, buying the shares of multinational corporations, and entrusting funds to private money managers who specialize in international equities. We shall examine each of these alternatives.

Direct Investments

The most obvious but least likely alternative would be to directly purchase the shares of a firm in its own foreign market through a foreign broker or an overseas branch of a U.S. broker. The investor might consider such firms as Toshiba or Fanuc on the Tokyo Stock Exchange, Consolidated Rutile on the Sydney Stock Exchange, or Hoechst on the Frankfurt Stock Exchange. This approach is hampered by all the difficulties and administrative problems associated with international investments. There could be information-gathering problems, tax problems, stock-delivery problems, capital-transfer problems, and communication difficulties in executing orders. Only the most sophisticated money manager would probably follow this approach (although this may change somewhat in the future as foreign markets become better coordinated).

A more likely route to direct investment would be to purchase the shares of foreign firms that actually trade in U.S. securities markets. Hundreds of foreign firms actively trade their securities in the United States. As of November 21, 2001, the New York Stock Exchange listed 461 companies from 53 countries. Table 15–9 lists the 53 countries and the number of companies traded on the NYSE from each country.

Firms such as Alcan Aluminum, Ltd., Campbell Resources, Inc., and Nortel Networks Corporation (all Canadian firms) trade their stocks *directly* on the New York Stock Exchange. Most of the other foreign firms trade their shares in the United States through American depository receipts (ADRs). The ADRs represent the ownership interest in a foreign company's common stock. If you go to the New York

TABLE 15–9 Foreign Countries with Firms Trading on the New York Stock Exchange

Argentina	12 ADR companies
Australia	10 ADR companies
Austria	1 ADR company
Bahamas	2 non-ADR companies
Belgium	1 ADR company
Bermuda	16 non-ADR companies and 1 preferred stock
Brazil	30 ADR companies
Canada	30 non-ADR companies and 1 preferred stock
Cayman Islands	2 non-ADR companies and 3 preferred stocks
Chile	21 ADR companies
China	12 ADR companies
Colombia	1 ADR company
Cyprus	1 non-ADR company
Denmark	2 ADR companies
Dominican Republic	1 ADR company
Finland	4 ADR companies
France	20 non-ADR companies and 1 preferred stock
Germany	12 ADR companies and 3 non-ADR companies
Ghana	1 ADR company
Global	1 non-ADR company
Greece	2 ADR companies and 1 non-ADR company
Guernsey	1 non-ADR company
Hong Kong, China	5 ADR companies and 4 non-ADR companies
Hungary	1 ADR company
India	9 ADR companies
Indonesia	2 ADR companies and 1 non-ADR company
Ireland	5 ADR companies

Stock Exchange website www.nyse.com and click on International, then on non-U.S. listed companies, you will then be able to access the entire list of 461 foreign companies traded on the NYSE. There are also American depository receipts listed on Nasdaq, with one of the most widely traded being L.M. Ericsson of Sweden.

An American depository receipt is created when the shares of a foreign company are purchased and put in trust in a foreign branch of a New York bank. The bank receives and can issue depository receipts to the American shareholders of the foreign firm. These ADRs allow foreign shares to be traded in the United States. Because many countries have securities priced higher or lower than the traditionally priced U.S. securities, each ADR may have a claim on more or less than one share of the foreign stock. For example, Switzerland is known for very high priced shares, and each ADR of the pharmaceutical firm Syngenta is exchangeable for one-fifth of a share of the common stock. While in the United Kingdom (Eng-

TABLE 15–9 Foreign Countries with Firms Trading on the New York Stock Exchange *(concluded)*

Israel	3 ADR companies and 2 non-ADR companies
Italy	11 ADR companies
Japan	15 ADR companies
Jersey, Channel Islands	1 ADR company
Korea	5 ADR companies
Liberia	1 non-ADR company
Luxembourg	1 ADR company
Mexico	26 ADR companies
Netherlands	18 ADR companies and 2 non-ADR companies
New Zealand	3 ADR companies
Norway	4 ADR companies and 1 preferred stock
Panama	3 non-ADR companies
Peru	2 ADR companies and 1 non-ADR company
Philippines	1 ADR company
Portugal	3 ADR companies
Commonwealth of Puerto Rico	4 non-ADR companies
Russian Federation	4 ADR companies
Singapore	2 non-ADR companies
South Africa	2 ADR companies and 1 non-ADR company
Spain	6 ADR companies and 1 preferred stock
Sweden	1 ADR company and 1 preferred stock
Switzerland	9 ADR companies and 2 non-ADR companies
Taiwan	3 ADR companies
Turkey	1 ADR company
Turks and Caicos	1 preferred stock
United Kingdom	48 ADR companies, 4 preferred ADRs and 1 preferred stock
Venezuela	2 ADR companies

land), share prices are low and 1 ADR in British Airways, for example, is exchangeable into 10 shares of British Air. The New York Stock Exchange website allows you to check out the exchange ratio for each ADR listed on the NYSE.

When you call your broker and ask to purchase Sony Corporation or Honda Motor Company, Ltd. (which are represented by ADRs), you will notice virtually no difference between this transaction and buying shares of General Motors or Eastman Kodak. You can receive a certificate that looks very much like a U.S. stock certificate. You will receive your dividends in dollars and get your reports about the company in English. Generally, you will pay your normal commission rates.

Table 15-10 shows a page from *Standard & Poor's Stock Guide* that includes Sony Corporation's ADRs. Note that the financial information is basically the same as that for other U.S. corporations trading on a major exchange or over-the-counter. The Sony ADRs also receive coverage from Value Line, Morningstar, and other reporting services. *The Wall Street Journal* has daily quotes just as it would have for any company. Since these ADRs trade on the New York Stock Exchange, the quote would be found in that section of the paper.

Indirect Investments

The forms of indirect investments in the international securities include (a) purchasing shares of multinational corporations, (b) purchasing mutual funds or

TABLE 15–10 Sample Page from Standard & Poor's Stock Guide

178 SMI-SOU — Standard & Poor's

¶ S&P 500 · # MidCap 400 · ◇ SmallCap 600 · • Options

Index	Ticker	Name of Issue (Call Price of Pfd. Stocks)	Market	Com. Rank. & Pfd. Rating	Inst. Hold Cos	Inst. Hold Shs. (000)	Principal Business	Price Range 1971-99 High	1971-99 Low	2000 High	2000 Low	2001 High	2001 Low	July, 2001 Sales in 100s	Last Sale Or Bid High	Last Sale Or Bid Low	Last Sale Or Bid Last	%Div Yield	P-E Ratio	EPS 5 Yr Growth	% Annualized Total Return 12 Mo	36 Mo	60 Mo
1	SRW	Smith(Charles E.)Res Rlty	NY,Ch,Ph	NR	174	16753	Real estate investment trust	35.87	21.75	48.25	34.00	50.40	42.90	19094	50.16	48.50	49.92	4.7	12	31	19.0	24.5	24.6
#2•[1]	SII	✓Smith Intl	NY,B,Ch,P,Ph	B	399	46758	Varied line drill,boring eq	87.87	1.25	88.50	45.00	84.52	48.55	340909	61.10	48.55	54.40	...	18	2	−23.8	27.7	10.2
3	SNN	✓Smith & Nephew plc ADS[52]	NY	NR	12	982	Mfr medical/healthcare prd	42.31	40.02	46.29	30.55	53.14	41.80	1338	53.14	50.65	51.40	...	18	...	52.3	...	...
◇4•[2]	SFD	✓Smithfield Foods	NY	↑B+	259	29722	Fresh pork,processed meats	36.37	0.02	31.75	14.87	44.99	27.20	56480	44.99	40.10	44.00	...	11	44	54.7	22.8	30.4
5	SMTX	✓SMTC Corp	NNM	NR	27	3501	Electronics manufacturing svc	....	....	30.12	8.68	17.37	1.50	25216	2.95	1.95	2.85	...	3	...	−84.2	...	...
6	SMTI	SMTEK Intl	NSC,P,Ph	C	4	3	Mfrs printed circuit boards	261.65	3.00	7.25	2.75	10.70	4.18	872	7.25	6.51	7.25	...	9	NM	75.8	−16.6	−25.9
#7	SJM	✓Smucker (J.M.)	NY,Ch,Ph	B+	149	10207	Preserves: jellies & fillings	39.00	0.52	29.00	15.00	29.00	22.61	5698	27.74	25.10	27.15	2.4	22	2	54.9	7.5	11.8
8•[3]	SSCC	✓Smurfit-Stone Container	NNM,Ch	NR	241	137604	Produce paperboard & pkg prd	25.75	9.00	25.00	9.12	17.80	12.25	326621	17.80	15.45	17.41	...	70	84	40.0	9.5	9.9
¶9•[4]	SNA	✓Snap-On Inc	NY,B,Ch,P,Ph	B+	359	41019	Hand tools: auto/ind'l maint	46.43	2.44	32.43	20.87	31.30	24.11	59390	27.60	24.11	27.00	3.6	14	15	−7.6	−5.9	0.8
10	SQM	✓Sociedad Quimica Y Minera ADS[55]	NY,Ch,P	NR	25	1842	Produce natural nitrates	67.75	20.00	35.12	17.37	24.60	17.25	4230	20.10	17.25	18.80	2.7	30	...	−5.4	−16.2	−16.9
11	SQM.A	Cl'A' ADS[56]	NY	NR	4	96		40.50	26.00	34.50	20.00	27.40	22.50	272	24.40	22.50	23.50e	2.1	9	24	8.9	...	...
12•[5]	SOFN	Softnet Systems	NNM	C	57	5718	Electronic info/mgmt sys	69.50	0.75	50.25	1.12	2.50	1.06	11087	2.10	1.66	1.70	...	d	Neg	−79.4	−53.8	−24.1
13•[6]	SWH	Software HOLDRs Tr Dep Receipt	AS	NR	..	...	Investment co-sofwtare ind	....	....	99.93	57.25	80.00	36.80	67876	57.50	44.90	48.15	...	..	...	...	...	...
◇14•[7]	SOL	✓Sola Intl	NY,Ch,P	NR	115	17647	Mfr plastic eyeglass lenses	43.75	9.87	14.00	3.50	15.20	4.00	18935	14.55	11.56	13.70	...	d	Neg	131	−22.2	−14.3
¶15•[1]	SLR	✓Solectron Corp	NY,Ph,P	B+	1001	531899	Mfr computer prod/subsys	49.00	0.18	52.62	24.54	41.95	14.71	894594	18.40	14.71	17.48	...	38	17	−56.6	13.4	34.7
#16•[8]	SOI	✓Solutia Inc	NY	NR	305	64879	Mfr chemical based materials	32.00	13.50	17.25	10.18	15.32	11.86	65239	14.29	12.74	13.58	0.3	17	1	−4.8	−22.8	...
17•[4]	SMRA	✓Somera Communications	NNM	NR	81	5064	Telecommun infrastructure eq	20.00	12.00	17.18	5.06	11.81	3.68	28595	7.10	5.14	6.30	...	14	...	−45.2	...	...
18	SNRA	Sonera Corp ADS[57]	NNM	NR	30	2439	Telecommunic svc,Finland	73.12	25.18	93.12	16.00	23.12	4.96	18851	8.07	4.96	6.29	1.0	4	...	−84.0	...	...
19	SONW	Song Networks ADS[58]	NNM	NR	42	2834	Broadband communic svcs	....	....	26.01	3.87	7.50	1.15	1368	2.19	1.15	1.65	...	d	...	−87.4	...	...
20	SAH	✓Sonic Automotive'A'	NY	NR	104	20380	Own/oper auto dealerships	18.93	4.68	12.25	5.68	20.20	6.00	56227	20.20	16.50	19.50	...	12	41	70.5	22.6	...
◇21•[4]	SONC	✓Sonic Corp	NNM	B+	187	22602	Oper fast food drive-in restr	22.58	3.62	27.00	15.20	32.10	21.50	29640	32.10	28.25	29.81	...	23	27	46.9	31.3	26.0
22•[4]	SOFO	✓Sonic Foundry	NNM	NR	39	1841	Computer software pds	12.75	2.68	84.96	0.90	6.00	1.12	8342	2.40	1.61	1.62	...	d	...	−87.0	−25.4	...
23	SNCI	✓Sonic Innovations	NNM	NR	53	3997	Mfr,mkt hearing aids	....	....	25.00	4.06	11.00	3.75	13962	8.70	4.00	4.01	...	4	...	−75.8	...	...
◇24•[9]	SBLU	✓SONICblue Inc	NNM	NR	157	49031	Mfr accelerators/software prd	23.75	1.53	24.81	3.50	8.75	2.40	79450	3.35	2.40	2.58	...	d	Neg	−74.8	−14.7	−27.9
25	SPO	Sonicport Inc	AS	NR	1	1.5	Internet marketing co	....	....	4.56	0.50	1.18	0.35	2528	0.60	0.44	0.48	...	d	...	−57.3	...	...
26•[10]	SNWL	✓SonicWALL Inc	NNM	NR	146	20502	Design internet security prd	22.81	7.00	66.68	11.00	26.00	8.50	193257	25.05	19.15	21.25	...	d	...	−51.0	...	...
#27•[2]	SON	✓Sonoco Products	NY,Ch,Ph,P	B+	242	44485	Mfr paper packaging products	40.00	0.52	23.50	16.56	26.00	19.20	27379	26.00	24.35	25.83	3.1	12	45	42.4	−0.8	4.1
28	SSN	✓Sonus Corp	AS	NR	1	1108	Own/oper hearing care clinics	9.87	2.75	5.50	1.25	3.10	1.75	518	3.10	2.30	3.10	...	d	...	3.3	−30.5	...
29•[1]	SONS	✓Sonus Networks	NNM	NR	277	107301	Provide communication equip	....	....	93.66	7.66	46.50	12.00	923743	24.80	16.82	21.94	...	d	...	−64.7	...	...
30•[11]	SNE	✓Sony Corp[59] ADR	NY,To,B,C,Ch,P,Ph,Mo	NR	270	37761	Color TV sets,tape rec,radio	147.93	1.33	157.37	67.00	85.75	46.25	119286	66.00	46.25	49.52	0.4	d	Neg	−47.1	5.6	9.6
#31•[6]	BID	✓Sotheby's Hldgs'A'	NY,Ch,P	C	143	37016	Worlds largest art auctioneer	47.00	7.68	30.18	14.50	27.68	15.53	19618	18.15	15.53	18.05	...	d	Neg	−3.7	−6.0	5.6
◇32•[12]	TSFG	✓South Financial Group	NNM	B+	111	8425	Bank hldg co/fin'l svc,SC	30.81	5.31	18.12	8.37	19.55	12.18	31258	19.55	17.19	17.70	2.5	33	−22	28.7	−8.2	7.8
33	SJI	✓South Jersey Indus	NY,B,Ch,Ph	B+	90	3828	Hldg co: gas, fuel oil, sand	30.75	4.47	30.12	24.50	32.25	27.80	1797	31.95	30.85	31.30	4.7	14	2	21.4	12.4	15.2
34	PDC	South Texas Drilling & Explor[60]	AS	NR	2	14	Oil&gas drilling,svcs/explor	3.75	0.09	3.25	0.71	7.80	2.37	1220	4.50	3.10	3.50	...	18	...	55.6	62.7	...
35	SRN	Southern Banc(AL)	AS,Ph	NR	5	167	Savings & loan Gadsen, AL	19.37	8.00	11.50	7.25	10.75	8.87	18	10.25	10.20	10.25e	3.4	19	25	14.8	−9.1	−0.7
36	SCE.Q	So Cal Edison 8.375%'QUIDS'	AS	...[61]	1	3.5	Qtly Income Debt Securities	26.87	21.75	25.12	13.00	18.12	7.97	1867	15.15	12.00	15.00	...	..	...	−32.6	−6.5	−1.4
¶37•[7]	SO	✓Southern Co	NY,B,C,Ch,P,Ph	A−	750	223041	Elec util hldg:Southeast	31.56	3.93	35.00	20.37	35.72	20.89	324500	23.86	22.05	23.50	5.7	15	7	...	...	...
38	KTS	South Co Cap Tr I 8.19%[64]'Ex'CorTS'[65]	NY	...[66]	..	...	Corporate-Backed Trust Sec	25.12	24.25	25.31	20.50	26.90	23.50	239	26.90	25.05	25.90	7.9	..	...	24.7	...	...
39	SEHI	Southern Energy Homes	NNM	NR	18	4601	Producer of manufactured homes	18.12	1.87	2.43	0.43	3.29	0.68	5014	3.29	2.25	3.12	...	d	Neg	150	−31.0	−23.6
40•[4]	PCU	✓Southern Peru Copper	NY,P	NR	66	2307	Copper mining,southern Peru	21.12	8.43	16.50	10.62	15.10	11.70	7121	13.57	11.70	11.87	1.6	12	−17	4.0	0.4	−0.8
◇41•[13]	SUG	✓Southern Union	NY,B,Ch,P	B	130	15795	Natural gas dstr: oil & gas	22.22	2.84	27.93	12.61	26.37	17.55	6673	20.54	18.70	20.49	...	32	−8	18.8	17.9	17.4
42	SZB	✓SouthFirst Bancshares	AS	NR	1	88	Savings & loan, Alabama	22.75	9.37	11.37	8.43	11.80	9.68	64	11.59	11.30	11.30e	5.3	12	NM	29.4	−9.7	3.1
¶43•[14]	SOTR	✓SouthTrust Corp	NNM	A+	524	165091	Commercial bkg,Alabama	22.68	0.28	20.53	10.43	26.61	19.25	308662	26.61	24.40	25.67	2.2	16	11	114	11.2	25.7
44	SWTX	✓Southwall Technologies	NNM	C	18	724	Produces thin film coatings	12.00	2.12	14.00	2.56	5.31	2.00	8197	5.31	2.92	5.05	...	d	Neg	−25.2	−2.1	−3.4
¶45•[15]	LUV	✓Southwest Airlines	NY,B,Ch,P,Ph	A+	730	556747	Airline svc mid-so'west U.S.	15.72	0.01	23.32	10.00	23.32	16.00	378582	20.21	18.09	20.01	0.1	25	24	27.2	27.2	32.7
46	OKSB	✓Southwest Bancorp(OK)	NNM	B+	18	747	Commercial banking,Oklahoma	32.75	11.00	21.00	13.31	26.20	16.50	1230	26.20	24.15	26.20	1.8	9	20	69.1	0.9	9.5
◇47	SWX	✓Southwest Gas	NY,B,Ch,P,Ph	B	156	14368	Natural gas,banking,R.E. dvlp	29.50	6.12	23.00	16.87	24.67	19.16	13249	24.24	22.75	23.90	3.4	16	35	38.0	4.7	12.3

Uniform Footnote Explanations-See Page 1. Other: [1]ASE,CBOE,P,Ph:Cycle 1. [2]Ph:Cycle 1. [3]CBOE,P:Cycle 2. [4]ASE:Cycle 3. [5]CBOE,P,Ph:Cycle 2. [6]ASE:Cycle 1. [7]CBOE:Cycle 2. [8]CBOE:Cycle 1. [9]CBOE,P:Cycle 1. [10]ASE,CBOE,P:Cycle 3. [11]ASE,P,Ph:Cycle 1. [12]P:Cycle 2. [13]Ph:Cycle 3. [14]CBOE,P:Cycle 3. [15]ASE,CBOE,P,Ph:Cycle 3. [51]Incl current amts. [52]Ea ADS rep 10 Ord,10 pence. [53]To be determined. [54]Incl $6.4M exchangable shs of subsid. [55]Ea ADS rep 10 Sr'B'shrs,no-par. [56]Ea ADS rep 10 Sr'A'shrs. [57]Ea ADS rep 1 ord shr. [58]Ea ADS rep 1 ord shr,SEK 0.05. [59]ADR equal 1 ord shr, 50y. [60]Plan name chge Pioneer Drilling. [61]Rated A by S&P. [62]Stk dstr of Mirant Corp. [63]Subsid. Pfd in $M. [64]Exch for portion'Deposited Assets're-spec cond. [65]Due 2-1-2037. [66]Rated'BBB+'by S&P. [67]Or earlier upon'Tax Event're-spec cond. [68]Total issue amt. [69]Re-spec cond.

Source: Reprinted by permission of Standard & Poor's, a division of The McGraw-Hill Companies.

closed-end investment funds specializing in worldwide investments, and (c) engaging the services of a private firm specializing in foreign investment portfolio management.

Purchasing Shares of Multinational Corporations Multinational corporations, that is, firms with operations in a number of countries, represent an opportunity for international diversification. For example, the major oil companies have investments and operations throughout the world. The same can be said for large banking firms and mainframe computer manufacturers. When one buys Exxon-Mobil, to some extent one is buying exposure to the world economy (69.4 percent of sales are foreign for this firm). A list of the 20 largest U.S. multinational firms is presented in Table 15-11. Of particular interest is the third column from the left, which represents foreign revenue as a percentage of total revenue, and the fourth column from the right, which represents foreign profit as a percentage of total profit.

Although buying shares in a U.S. multinational firm is an easy route to take to experience worldwide economic effects, some researchers maintain that multinationals do not provide the major *investment* benefits that are desired. Jacquillat and Solnik found that multinationals provide very little risk reduction over and above purely domestic firms (perhaps only 10 percent).[5] The prices of multinational shares tend to move very closely with their own country's financial markets despite their worldwide investments. Thus, U.S. multinationals may not do well in a U.S. bear market even if they have investments in strong markets in other countries. This leaves us to turn to mutual funds and closed-end investment companies as potential international investments.

Mutual Funds and Closed-End Investment Companies As was described in Chapter 2, mutual funds offer the investor an opportunity for diversification as well as professional management. Nowhere is the mutual fund concept more important than in the area of international investments. Those who organize the funds usually have extensive experience in investing overseas and are prepared to deal with the administrative problems. This, of course, does not necessarily lead to superior returns, but the likelihood for inexperienced blunders is reduced.

One may also invest in closed-end investment companies specializing in international equity investments. As described in Chapter 2, a closed-end investment company has a fixed supply of shares outstanding and trades on a national exchange or over-the-counter, much as an individual company does. It may trade at a premium or discount from its net asset value. An example is the Japan Fund.

A listing of internationally oriented funds is presented in Table 2-6. The addresses of these funds can be found in *Forbes* magazine or the *Morningstar Mutual Fund Survey* (also discussed in Chapter 2).

Specialists in International Securities The large investor may consider the option of engaging the services of selected banks and investment counselors with

5. Ibid.

specialized expertise in foreign equities. Major firms include Morgan Guaranty Trust Company, State Street Bank and Trust Company, Batterymarch Financial Management, and Fidelity Trust Company of New York. These firms provide a total range of advisory and management services. However, they often require a minimum investment well in excess of $100,000 and are tailored to the needs of the large institutional investor.

TABLE 15–11 Largest U.S. Multinational Firms (in Millions of U.S. Dollars)

		Revenue			Net Profits[a]			Assets		
2000 Rank	Company	Foreign	Total	Foreign as Percent of Total	Foreign	Total	Foreign as Percent of Total	Foreign	Total	Foreign as Percent of Total
1	Exxon-Mobil	$143,044	$206,083	69.4%	$10,198[b]	$16,948[b]	60.2%	$ 56,742[c]	$ 89,829[c]	63.2%
2	Ford Motor	51,691	170,064	30.4	(599)	5,410	−11.1	19,874[d]	45,804[d]	43.4
3	IBM	51,180	88,396	57.9	3,914	8,093	48.4	14,348[c]	35,797[c]	40.1
4	General Motors	48,233	184,632	26.1	2,893	4,771[e]	60.6[e]	12,578[d]	35,376[d]	35.6
5	Texaco	43,146	60,220	71.6	1,007	2,542	39.6	7,879[c]	15,879[c]	49.6
6	General Electric	42,390	129,853	32.6	5,222	20,686[g]	25.2[g]	159,367	437,006	36.5
7	Citigroup	37,396	111,826	33.4	NA	13,519	NA	269,837[h]	741,114[h]	36.4
8	Wal-Mart Stores	32,100	191,329	16.8	650	6,424[e]	10.1[e]	25,742	78,130	32.9
9	Chevron	31,374	69,058	45.4	2,716	5,185	52.4	27,126	50,832	53.4
10	Hewlett-Packard	27,230	48,732	55.9	2,169	3,561	60.9	2,244[d]	4,500[d]	49.9
11	Compaq Computer	23,417	42,383	55.3	216	595	36.3	1,202[c]	3,431[c]	35.0
12	Enron	22,898	100,789	22.7	500	979	51.1	844[c]	11,743[c]	7.2
13	American Intl Group	22,846	45,972	49.7	NA	5,636	NA	98,105[f]	306,577	32.0
14	JP Morgan Chase	21,338	60,065	35.5	2,963	5,727	51.7	NA	715,348	NA
15	Procter & Gamble	19,913	39,951	49.8	1,492	3,542	42.1	16,967	34,194	49.6
16	Intel	19,814	33,726	58.7	3,571	10,535	33.9	3,905[d]	15,013[d]	26.0
17	Motorola	19,720E	37,580	52.5	1,645	2,231[i]	73.7[i]	16,814	42,343	39.7
18	Philip Morris Cos.	19,280	63,276	30.5	3,105	8,510	36.5	7,425[c]	28,739[c]	25.8
19	Dow Chemical	14,145	23,008	61.5	1,149	1,578[e]	72.8	4,202[c]	9,190[c]	45.7
20	El du Pont de Nemours	13,759	28,268	48.7	1,218	2,375[e]	51.3[e]	5,295[d]	14,182[d]	37.3

[a]From continuing operations.

[b]Net income before corporate and financing activity and merger expense.

[c]Long-lived assets.

[d]Net property, plant and equipment.

[e]Net income before identifiable assets.

Source: *Forbes*, July 23, 2001, p. 136.

[f]Includes proportionate interest in unconsolidated subsidiaries.

[g]Operating profit.

[h]Average assets.

[i]Excludes Canadian operations.

E Estimate

Internet Resources

Website Address	Comments
www.adr.com	Provides screening and research services for American depository receipts
www.global-investor.com	Provides international news and information on foreign markets
cbs.marketwatch.com	Provides news on global markets
www.economist.com	Global magazine providing news on markets and economics
www.wsj.com	Provides information on global markets and economics
www.oecd.org	Provides international economic information and links to related sites
www.rubicon.com/passport/currency/currency.html	Provides currency rates and conversions

Chapter 16

Investments in Real Assets

In this chapter, we turn our attention to real assets; that is, tangible assets that may be seen, felt, held, or collected. Examples of such assets are real estate, gold, silver, diamonds, coins, stamps, and antiques. This is no small area from which to consider investments. For example, the total market value of all real estate holdings in the United States in the early 2000s was in excess of $10 trillion.

As further evidence of value, in the last decade, a Van Gogh painting sold for $40 million, and a 132-carat diamond earring set sold for $6.6 million. In 2000, a Honus Wagner baseball card sold for more than $1 million.

As was pointed out in Chapter 1, in inflationary environments, real assets have at times outperformed financial assets (such as stocks and bonds). With this in mind, the reader is advised to become familiar with these investment outlets—not only to take advantage of the investment opportunities but also to be well aware of the pitfalls. A money manager who is challenged by clients to include real assets in a portfolio (such as real estate or precious metals) must be conversant not only with the opportunities but also with the drawbacks.

ADVANTAGES AND DISADVANTAGES OF REAL ASSETS

As previously mentioned, real assets may offer an opportunity as an inflation hedge because inflation means higher replacement costs for real estate, precious metals, and other physical items. Real assets also serve as an investment hedge against the unknown and feared. When people become concerned about world events, gold and other precious metals may be perceived as the last safe haven for investments. While this has traditionally been the case, it did not prove so in the last decade. Neither the Persian Gulf War of 1991 nor international threats in the mid-1990s and the terrorist attack on September 11, 2001, have moved the price of precious metals to significantly higher levels.

Real assets also may serve as an effective vehicle for portfolio diversification. Since financial and real assets at times move in opposite directions, some efficient diversification may occur. A study by Robichek, Cohn, and Pringle in the *Journal of Business* actually indicates that movements among various types of real and monetary assets are less positively correlated than are those for monetary assets alone.[1] The general findings indicate that enlarging the universe of investment alternatives would benefit the overall portfolio construction in terms of risk-return alternatives.

A final advantage of an investment in real assets is the psychic pleasure that may be provided. One can easily relate to a beautiful painting in the living room, a mint gold coin in a bank lockbox, or an attractive real estate development.

There are many disadvantages to consider as well. Perhaps the largest drawback is the absence of large, liquid, and relatively efficient markets. Whereas stocks or bonds can generally be sold in a few minutes at a value close to the latest quoted trade, such is not likely to be the case for real estate, diamonds, art, and other forms of real assets. It may take many months to get the desired price for a real asset, and even then, there is an air of uncertainty about the impending transaction until it is consummated.

Furthermore, there is the problem of dealer spread or middleman commission. Whereas in the trading of stocks and bonds where spreads or commissions are very small (usually 1 or 2 percent), dealer spreads for real assets can be as large as 20 to 25 percent or more. This is particularly true for small items that do not have great value. On more valuable items, such as rare paintings, valuable jewels, or mint gold coins, the dealer spread tends to be smaller (perhaps 5 to 10 percent) but still more than that on securities.

The investor in real assets generally receives no current income (with the possible exception of real estate) and may incur storage and insurance costs. Furthermore, there may be the problem of high unit cost for investments. You cannot easily acquire multiple art masterpieces.

A final drawback or caveat in real assets is the hysteria or overreaction that tends to come into the marketplace from time to time. Gold, silver, diamonds, and coins may be temporarily bid out of all proportion to previously anticipated value. This happened in the late 1980s. The last buyer, who arrives too late, may end up owning a very unprofitable investment. The trick is to get into the recurring cycle early enough to take advantage of the capital gains opportunities that occur for real assets. Also, you should buy items of high enough quality so that you can ride out the setbacks if your timing is incorrect.

In the remainder of this chapter, we will examine real estate, gold, silver, diamonds, and other collectibles as investment outlets. Because real estate lends itself more directly to analytical techniques familiar to students of finance, it will receive a proportionately larger share of our attention.

---

1. Alexander A. Robichek, Richard A. Cohn, and John J. Pringle, "Return on Alternative Media and Implications for Portfolio Construction," *Journal of Business*, July 1972, pp. 427–43.

REAL ESTATE AS AN INVESTMENT

Approximately half the households in the United States own real estate as a home or investment. Also, many firms in the brokerage and investment community have also moved into real estate. As an example, Merrill Lynch has acquired real estate affiliates to broker property, conduct mortgage banking activities, and package real estate syndications. Pension fund managers are also increasing the real estate component in their portfolio, going from virtually no representation two decades ago to almost 10 percent at present.

Some insight into changing real estate values may be gained from Figure 16-1. We see the gain for a dollar invested in real estate in 1946 as compared with fixed-income investments and common stock.

Real estate investments may include such outlets as your own home, duplexes and apartment buildings, office buildings, shopping centers, industrial buildings, hotels and motels, as well as undeveloped land. The investor may participate as an individual, as part of a limited partnership real estate syndicate, or through a real estate investment trust.

FIGURE 16–1 Growth in Value: 1946–2001 ($1 of Investment)

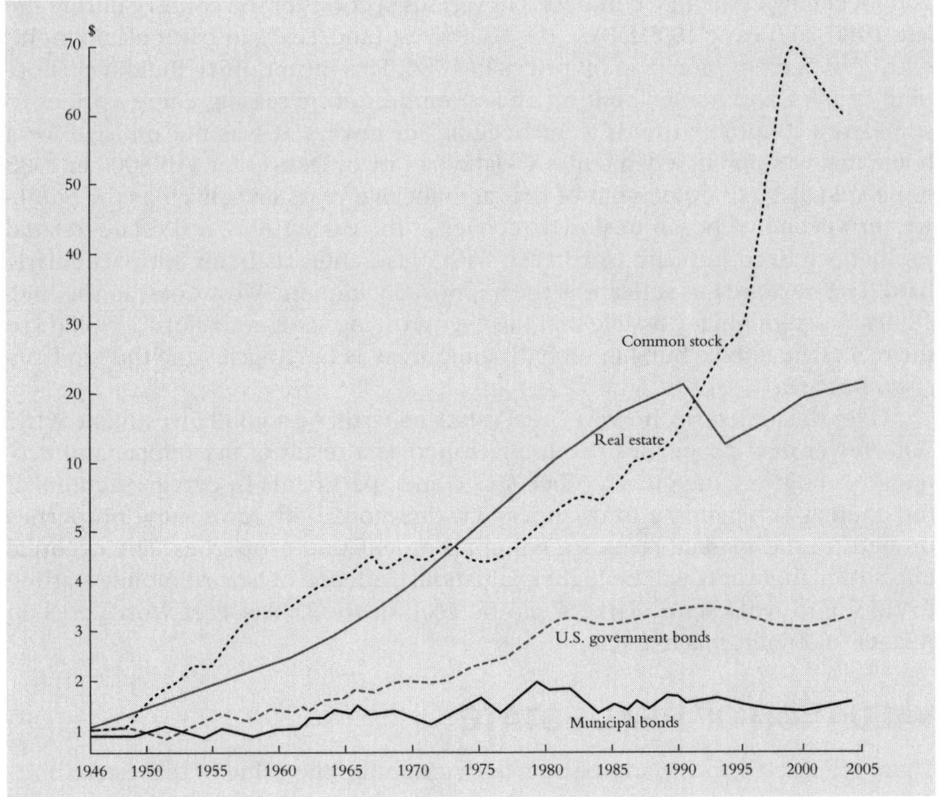

Throughout the rest of the section, we will discuss real estate values in the recent past and relate it to the future outlook. We will also evaluate a typical real estate investment, consider new methods of real estate financing, and examine limited partner syndicates and real estate investment trusts.

Real Estate in the Last Decade and the Future Outlook

The mid-1980s started out as a bad time for real estate with the passage of the Tax Reform Act of 1986. As part of this legislation, the life over which a real estate investor could write off depreciation for tax purposes was extended from 19 years to 27.5 years for residential rental property and to 39 years for commercial property. This meant that an investor had to wait longer to take full advantage of tax deductions related to real estate. Also, real estate investors not actively involved in the management of property were severely restricted in writing off paper losses from real estate against other forms of income.

The effect of tax reform was to make real estate a less attractive investment. Because of the loss of many traditional tax benefits for real estate, some existing properties had less value, and new construction proceeded at a slower pace.

The initial negative impact of tax reform on real estate was also associated with declining economic conditions in various sections of the country during the late 1980s and early 1990s. First, the Southwest (and Texas in particular) was hit with a 70 percent plunge in oil prices in 1986. This meant office buildings, shopping centers, and homes built on an assumption of increasing energy prices to stimulate economic growth went begging for buyers. It was not unusual for a home that was purchased in Dallas, Oklahoma City, or Denver for $300,000 in 1986 to be sold at 50 to 60 percent of that amount five years later. Even as the Southwestern economy began to slowly recover in the early 1990s, real estate-related problems moved into the Northeast, with Massachusetts being hit particularly hard. The next area to suffer was the supposedly immune West Coast in the mid-1990s. Few thought it possible that the ever-growing state of California would see the real estate bubble burst in such dynamic areas as Los Angeles and the San Francisco Bay area.

Over the long term, however, real estate may still be a good investment. Why? With fewer new properties being developed as a result of tax reform and economic conditions, the glut in office space and apartments in certain sections of the country is beginning to disappear. Furthermore, with fewer new properties brought to the market, rents are going up on existing properties. The eventual effect of higher rents will be higher valuation. Evidence of "smart" money starting to flow into real estate markets can be seen in the Dallas–Fort Worth area, in Atlanta, and California markets.

VALUATION OF REAL ESTATE

There are three primary approaches to determining the value of real estate.

The Cost Approach

The first is the cost approach. What better place to start than the cost to replace an asset at current prices? This is fairly easy to determine for relatively new property, where the components that went into the structure are easily identified and priced out. For older buildings, the challenge is somewhat greater because the building materials may no longer be in existence or may be currently prohibited (for example, asbestos). Some would assume a building is at least worth its replacement cost, but that is not always the case. A warehouse or apartment complex that is poorly located may be worth far less than the replacement cost. Also, when a certain part of the country is suffering from an economic setback, there may be no desire to replace the asset. Nevertheless, the cost basis serves as a useful estimate of value when used in conjunction with the other two approaches.

Comparative Sales Value

Many in the real estate industry look to the selling price of comparable real estate to determine value. If you are going to put a four-bedroom, three-bathroom house, with 2,500 square feet on the market, what better way to establish value than to look for recent sales prices for comparable property in the neighborhood? This approach is called the comparative sales value.

Of course, true comparables are difficult to find. While nearby property may appear to be similar, there can be differences in floor plans, landscape, traffic exposure, and so forth. Nevertheless, if a number of comparables can be identified, the differences may be averaged out or a grid established in which a base price is assigned and then modified for each different element.

Although the comparative sales approach is only a helpful guideline, it does have one indisputable value. *Actual sales* did take place at the recorded price.

The Income Approach

For income-producing property, the income approach may be applied. The basic question to be answered is this: "What is the potential annual operating income and at what level should it be valued (capitalized)?"

In its simplest form, this formula may be applied:

$$\frac{\text{Annual net operating income}}{\text{Capitalization rate (Cap rate)}} = \text{Value} \qquad (16\text{–}1)$$

The numerator is determined by an analysis of annual rentals, followed by a subtraction of expenses such as property taxes, insurance, etc. The numbers to be applied are future realistic numbers rather than current or historical values. Perhaps the current gross rentals are \$35,000 per year but could easily be raised to \$40,000 with a minimum of effort. It is this latter number that should be used. The same is true for expenses. If prior tax returns indicate that maintenance and upkeep expenses are too low to maintain the quality of the property, upward adjustments must be made.

The second component in Formula 16-1 is the denominator, the capitalization rate. That is, the rate of return required by investors in similar-type investments. It is normally determined by examining the rate of return on recent transactions. It may be further modified by additional consideration of risk, changes in interest rates, etc.

Assume a property had a projected annual net operating income of $17,500 and a market capitalization rate of 10 percent. The value based on this approach would be $175,000:

$$\frac{\$17{,}500}{0.10} = \$175{,}000$$

While the approach is potentially helpful, it suffers somewhat from oversimplicity. For example, only one number is used for annual net operating income for the foreseeable future when it is quite likely to change over time. Also, different analysts may have difficulty in determining what the capitalization rate should be. At a cap rate of 9 percent, the property is worth $194,444, and at a cap rate of 11 percent, it is only worth $159,091.

Combination of the Three Approaches

In most cases, a final value will be determined by a combination of the three approaches—each imparts significant information, but each also has its shortfalls. While a one-third weighting of the value determined under each approach is appealing, in most cases (particularly those involving litigation), a different weighting approach is likely to be used. Perhaps comparable sales value will receive a 50 percent weighting, the income approach 35 percent, and the cost approach 15 percent.

A MORE COMPREHENSIVE ANALYSIS

In any valuation of an asset, the ultimate worth is based on the present value of future cash flows. This not only applies to stocks, bonds, oil wells, and new business ventures, but to real estate as well.

To determine cash flow variables, we will follow these six steps:

1. Determine the purchase price, the size of the mortgage, and the annual mortgage payment.
2. Compute the net operating income for each year of the anticipated holding period.
3. Translate this to annual cash flow during the holding period.
4. Project the selling price of the property after the holding period.

5. Discount the annual cash flows and the anticipated selling price after the holding period back to the present to determine the present value of the future benefits.
6. Compare the upfront cash commitment to the present value of future benefits to determine if the property provides a positive net present value.

We will now discuss each of these steps.

1. Determine the Purchase Price and Financing Assume the Baily apartment complex (six units) can be purchased for $180,000. Discussion with a mortgage banker (lender) indicates a loan for 80 percent of the value would be available at 12 percent for 20 years. Thus, the loan would be for $144,000:

$$\$180{,}000 \times 80\% = \$144{,}000$$

The balance of the purchase price would be put up in cash ($36,000):

$$\$180{,}000 - \$144{,}000 = \$36{,}000$$

Next, we look up the annual mortgage payment. Examining Table 16–1, we see on the first line that the annual mortgage payment for 20 years at 12 percent is $19,280.

2. Determine the Net Operating Income for Each Year We will assume the buyer intends to hold the property for four years and then sell it. Thus, we determine the value each year in Table 16–2. The values are assumed to slightly increase with the passage of time. Next we translate net operating income into cash flow.

3. Determine Annual Cash Flow Up until now we have only computed income from operations. The real issue is how much cash flow is being generated. Other nonoperating factors that must be considered are interest expense, depreciation, taxable income or losses (and related taxes or tax shield benefits), and repayment of the mortgage.

In Table 16–3, we subtract depreciation and interest expense from net operating income to determine taxable income or loss for each year. But before we

TABLE 16–1 Annual Mortgage Payment for a 20-Year Loan (Principal Amount Equals $144,000)

	8%	10%	12%	14%	16%
Annual mortgage payment	$ 14,667	$ 16,913	($ 19,280)	$ 21,742	$ 24,287
First-year interest expense	11,520	14,400	17,280	20,160	23,040
Total interest over the life of the loan	149,340	194,260	241,600	290,840	341,700

TABLE 16–2 Annual Net Operating Income

	Year 1	Year 2	Year 3	Year 4
Gross annual rental (6 units × $450 × 12 months in first year)	$32,400	$34,100	$36,400	$38,100
Less 5% vacancy rate	1,620	1,705	1,820	1,905
Net rental income	$30,780	$32,395	$34,580	$36,195
Less operating expenses				
Property taxes	$ 5,000	$ 5,100	$ 5,200	$ 5,300
Maintenance	1,500	1,550	1,650	1,710
Utilities	1,960	2,072	2,205	2,310
Insurance	2,200	2,240	2,290	2,340
Total operating expenses	$10,660	$10,962	$11,345	$11,660
Net operating income	$20,120	$21,433	$23,235	$24,535

look at the bottom line in Table 16–3, let's briefly discuss depreciation and interest expense. Straight-line depreciation is based on a straight-line deduction of the value of the depreciable asset over a period for 27.5 years. This time period applies to rental residential property and is mandated under the Tax Reform Act of 1986.

You may recall the purchase price of the property was $180,000. We assume $40,000 of the purchase price represents land (which cannot be depreciated), so the amount of depreciable assets is $140,000. Assuming 27.5-year straight-line depreciation, 3.64 percent (1 ÷ 27.5 years) can be deducted each year. Based on $140,000 in depreciable assets, the annual write-off is $5,096 per year (line 3 in Table 16–3). Depreciation is a particularly valuable deduction because it reduces taxable income but does not represent an actual cash payment.

The deduction for interest expense is also important and changes from year to year as the loan balance becomes smaller. The interest expense is merely given in this case (line 4 of Table 16–3), but it can be easily computed through Internet amortization tables. As an example, in the first year the beginning loan balance is $144,000, and with 12 percent interest, interest owed in the first year is $17,280.

We now look to the bottom line of Table 16–3. The main observation is that there are taxable losses in the first two years and taxable income in the last two years. The losses in the first two years may potentially be used to offset income from other sources. To the extent the investor is actively involved with the property (it is not a passive investment under the terms of the Tax Reform Act of 1986), he or she will be able to use the losses as a tax shield (shelter) for other income.

Assuming the investor is in a 30 percent tax bracket, the taxable losses in Years 1 and 2 translate into the tax shield benefits shown in Table 16–4. Of course, the taxable income in Years 3 and 4 will require that taxes be paid.

We are now in a position to achieve our goal in step 3: determine annual cash flow. We have three forms of cash flow coming in. The first is net operating income (Table 16–2), and the second is annual tax shield benefits or taxes owed (Table

TABLE 16–3 Taxable Income or Loss

	Year 1	Year 2	Year 3	Year 4
Net operating income	$20,120	$21,433	$23,235	$24,535
Less				
Depreciation	5,096	5,096	5,096	5,096
Interest expense	17,280	17,040	16,767	16,405
Taxable income (loss)	$ (2,256)	$ (703)	$ 1,372	$ 3,034

TABLE 16–4 Tax Shield Benefits or Taxes Owed

	Year 1	Year 2	Year 3	Year 4
Taxable income (or loss)	$(2,256)	$(703)	$1,372	$3,034
Tax rate	30%	30%	30%	30%
Tax shield benefits or taxes owed	$ 677	$ 211	$ (412)	$ (910)

TABLE 16–5 Annual Cash Flow

	Year 1	Year 2	Year 3	Year 4
Net operating income	$20,120	$21,433	$23,235	$24,535
Tax shield benefit or taxes owed	677	211	(412)	(910)
Annual mortgage payment	(19,280)	(19,280)	(19,280)	(19,280)
Cash flow	$ 1,517	$ 2,364	$ 3,543	$ 4,345

16-4). The third annual cash flow is the annual mortgage payment.[2] We can turn back to the circled item in Table 16-1 to easily determine this value. It will apply to each of the four years of the holding period.

The three sources of cash flow are brought together in Table 16-5 to determine the total annual value of cash flow.

We now move on to step 4. That is, after determining the annual cash flows during the four-year holding period, it is time to look at the potential sales price for the property after the holding period.

4. Project the Sales Price The investor initially paid $180,000 for the property, and we assume it increases in value by 6 percent per year over the four-year

2. The interest component of the annual mortgage payment was deducted in computing taxable income or loss, but it was not subtracted out as a cash item. Therefore, it is appropriately included as part of the annual mortgage payment to determine cash flow.

holding period. For four periods at 6 percent, the compound sum factor is 1.262. This translates into a sales value of $227,160:

$180,000	Purchase price
× 1.262	Compound sum factor
$227,160	Value after 4 years

The investor, who is now the seller, will likely have to pay a real estate commission and other fees, which we will assume total 7 percent. The amount is $15,901 (7% × $227,160). This leaves the investor with a value of $211,259:

$227,160	Sales price
− 15,901	Commission and fees
$211,259	Net proceeds

To the extent the net proceeds exceed the book value of the property, a capital gains tax will also have to be paid. The book value of the property is equal to the initial purchase price minus depreciation to date. The purchase price was $180,000, and four years of depreciation at $5,096 per year have been taken (third line of Table 16–3). Thus the book value is:

$180,000	Purchase price
− 20,384	4 years of depreciation (4 × $5,096)
$159,616[3]	Book value

The difference between the net proceeds from the sale and the book value is $51,643:

$211,259	Net proceeds
− 159,616	Book value
$ 51,643	Capital gain

The profit is categorized as a capital gain and it is subject to a maximum tax rate of 20 percent. You will recall the investor paid a 30 percent tax on normal operating income, but investments held for over a year normally qualify for preferential capital gains treatment.

The capital gains tax in this case would be $10,329 (20% × $51,643). This would leave the investor with funds from the sale of $200,930:

3. This value is the same as taking depreciable assets of $140,000 minus depreciation to date of $20,384 and adding back $40,000 in original land value:

$140,000	Depreciable assets
− 20,384	Depreciation to date
$119,616	
+ 40,000	Land
$159,616	Book value

$211,259	Net proceeds
– 10,329	Capital gains tax
$200,930	Funds from the sale

From this sum, the investor must pay off the mortgage balance that exists after four years as he or she closes out the ownership position. The mortgage bank informs us this is equal to $134,432.[4]

The cash flows from the sale minus the mortgage balance leaves the investor with net cash flow from the sale of $66,498:

$200,930	Funds from the sale
– 134,432	Payoff of mortgage
$ 66,498	Net cash flow (from sale)

5. Determine the Present Value of All Benefits Because we have computed the annual cash flows from the four years of operations as well as the net cash flow from selling the property, we are now in a position to determine the present value of the benefits. We assume the investor in this particular example has a required return of 12 percent on real estate investments, and we use that as the discount rate in Table 16–6. The present value of the future cash flows is $50,818.

6. Compare the Upfront Cash Payment to the Benefits The upfront cash investment was $36,000, and the present value of all future cash flows is $50,818. This indicates a net present value for the investment of $14,818:

$50,818	Present value of future cash flows
– 36,000	Upfront cash investment
$14,818	Net present value

TABLE 16–6 Present Value of the Cash Flows

Year	Cash Flow (Table 16–5)	Present Value Factor (12%)	Present Value
1	$ 1,517	0.893	$ 1,355
2	2,364	0.797	1,884
3	3,543	0.712	2,523
4	70,843[a]	0.636	45,056
	Total present value of cash flows		$50,818

[a]Fourth-year annual cash flow of $4,345 plus net cash flow from the sale of $66,498.

4. This value is computed by subtracting the repayment of principal each year from the initial mortgage.

Clearly, the project earns well in excess of the required return on the investment of 12 percent and is an acceptable investment. The actual yield or interest rate of return is slightly in excess of 22 percent. But keep in mind that real estate may be a very illiquid investment and almost all the return is based on a 6 percent annual increase in value. The annual operating gains are almost negligible. Nevertheless, this does appear to be an attractive investment.

FINANCING OF REAL ESTATE

One of the essential considerations in any real estate investment analysis is the cost of financing. In the prior example, we said a loan for $144,000 over 20 years at 12 percent interest would have yearly payments of $19,280. Note in Table 16-1 the effects of various interest rates on annual payments.

We see that the difference in annual payments ranges from $14,667 at 8 percent up to $24,287 at 16 percent. Even more dramatic is the increase in total interest paid over the life of the loan; it goes from $149,340 at 8 percent to $341,700 at 16 percent. (Keep in mind that the total loan was only $144,000.)

An investor who has the unlikely opportunity to shift out of the loan at 16 percent into one at 8 percent might be willing to pay as much as $94,446.16 for the privilege (tax effects are not specifically considered here):

16 percent interest − 8 percent interest = Dollar difference in annual payments
$24,287 − $14,667 = $9,620

The present value of $9,620 over 20 years assuming an 8 percent discount rate is:

$9,620 × 9,818 = $94,449.16

Thus, it is easy to appreciate the role of interest rates in a real estate investment decision. No industry is more susceptible to the impact of changing interest rates than real estate. Each time the economy overheats and interest rates skyrocket, the real estate industry comes to a standstill. With the eventual easing of interest-rate pressures, the industry once again enjoys a recovery.

Types of Mortgages

In actuality, a whole set of mortgage arrangements is available as alternatives to the fixed-interest-rate mortgage (particularly for home mortgages). The borrower must now be prepared to consider such alternative lending arrangements as the adjustable rate mortgage, the graduated payment mortgage, and the shared appreciation mortgage.

Adjustable Rate Mortgage (ARM) Under this mortgage arrangement, the interest rate is adjusted regularly. If interest rates go up, borrowers may either increase their normal payments or extend the maturity date of the loan at the same fixed-payment level to fully compensate the lender. Similar downside adjustments can also be made if interest rates fall. Generally, adjustable rate mortgages are initially made at rates 1 to 2 percent below fixed-interest-rate mortgages because the lender enjoys the flexibility of changing interest rates and is willing to share the benefits with the borrower. Adjustable rate mortgages currently account for more than half of the residential mortgage market. Although adjustable rate mortgages usually have an upper boundary (such as 12 or 15 percent or a 6 percent lifetime adjustment over the original borrowing rate), there is a real possibility of default for many borrowers if interest rates reach high levels.

Graduated Payment Mortgage (GPM) Under this type of financial arrangement, the payments start out on a relatively low basis and increase over the life of the loan. This type of mortgage may be well suited to the young borrower who has an increasing repayment capability over the life of the loan. An example would be a 30-year, $60,000 loan at 9 percent that would normally require monthly payments of $583.99 under a standard fixed-payment mortgage. With a graduated payment mortgage, monthly payments might start out as $350 or $400 and eventually progress to more than $700. The GPM plan has been referred to by a few of its critics as the "gyp 'em" plan, in that early payments may not be large enough to cover interest, and therefore, later payments must cover not only the amortization of the loan but also interest on the accumulated, unpaid, early interest. This is not an altogether fair criticism but merely an interpretation of what the graduated payment stream represents.

Shared Appreciation Mortgage (SAM) Perhaps the newest and most innovative of the mortgage payment plans is the shared appreciation mortgage. This provides the lender with a hedge against inflation because he directly participates in any increase in value associated with the property being mortgaged. The lender may enjoy as much as 30 to 40 percent of the appreciation in value over a specified time period, such as 10 years. The lender may take his return from the selling of the property or from the refinancing of the appreciated property value with a new lender. In return for this appreciation-potential privilege, the lender may advance funds at well below current market rates (perhaps at three-fourths of current rates). The shared appreciation mortgage is not yet legal in all states.

Other Forms of Mortgages Somewhat similar to the shared appreciation mortgage is the concept of equity participation that is popular in commercial real estate. Under an equity participation arrangement, the lender not only provides the borrowed capital but part of the equity or ownership funds as well. A major insurance company or savings and loan thus may acquire an equity interest of 10 to 25 percent (or more). This financing arrangement becomes popular each time inflation rears its head. Some lenders are simply unwilling to commit capital for long periods without a participation feature.

Borrowers may also look toward a *second mortgage* for financing. Here, a second lender provides additional financing beyond the first mortgage in return for a secondary claim or lien. The second mortgage is generally for a shorter period of time than the initial mortgage. Primary suppliers of second mortgages in recent times have been sellers of property. Often, to consummate a sale, it is necessary for the seller to supplement the financing provided by a financial institution. Sellers providing second mortgages generally advance the funds at rates below the first mortgage rate to facilitate the sale, whereas other second mortgage lenders (nonsellers) will ask for a few percentage points above the first mortgage rate to compensate for the extra risk of being in a secondary claim position.

In some cases, sellers may actually provide all the financing to the buyer. Usually the terms of the mortgage are for 20 to 30 years, but the seller has the right to call in the loan after three to five years if so desired. The assumption is that the buyer may have an easier time finding his own financing at that point in time. This may or may not be true.

FORMS OF REAL ESTATE OWNERSHIP

Ownership of real estate may take many forms. The investor may participate as an individual, in a regular partnership, through a real estate syndicate (generally a limited partnership), or through a real estate investment trust (REIT).

Individual or Regular Partnership

Investing as an individual or with two or three others in a regular partnership offers the simplest way of getting into real estate from a legal viewpoint. The investors pretty much control their own destinies and can take advantage of personal knowledge of local markets and changing conditions to enhance their returns.

As is true with most smaller and less complicated business arrangements, there is a well-defined center of responsibility that often leads to quick corrective action. However, there may be a related problem of inability to pool adequate capital to engage in large-scale investments as well as the absence of expertise to develop a wide range of investments. Furthermore, there is unlimited liability to the investor(s).

Syndicate or Limited Partnership

To expand the potential for investor participation, a syndicate or limited partnership has traditionally been formed.[5] The limited partnership works as follows: A general partner forms the limited partnership and has unlimited liability for the partnership liabilities. The general partner then sells participation units to the limited partners whose liability is limited to the extent of their initial investment (such as $5,000 or $10,000). Limited liability is particularly important in real estate

5. A syndicate may take the form of a corporation, but this is not common. The term *real estate syndicate* has become virtually synonymous with the limited partnership form of operation.

because mortgage debt obligations may exceed the net worth of the participants. The general partner is normally responsible for managing the property, while the limited partners are merely investors.

Although the restricted liability feature of the limited partnership remains attractive, the Tax Reform Act of 1986 generally restricted the use of limited partnerships as tax shelters. Historically, real estate limited partnerships generated large paper losses through accelerated depreciation (though not cash losses), and these paper losses were used to shelter other forms of income (such as a doctor's salary) from taxation. Under the Tax Reform Act of 1986, a taxpayer is no longer allowed to freely use passive losses to offset other sources of income such as salary or portfolio income. Such losses can only be used to offset income from other passive investments.

Real estate limited partnerships still exist but more for limited liability than for tax reasons. The successful partnerships stress strong cash flow generation and capital appreciation potential. In the earlier cash flow analysis in this chapter, a limited partnership was not involved, and the investor actively participated in managing the property. Some small tax write-offs were allowed, but note that the success of the project was much more dependent on cash flow and potential capital appreciation.

If you decide to invest in a limited partnership, you should follow certain guidelines. You must be particularly sensitive to the front-end fees and commissions the general partner might charge. These can vary anywhere from 5 to 10 percent to as large as 20 to 25 percent. The investor must also be sensitive to any double-dealing the general partner might be doing. An example would be selling property between different partnerships the general partner has formed and taking a commission each time. The inflated paper profits may prove quite deceptive and costly to the uninformed limited partner.

In assessing a general partner and his associated real estate deal, the investor should look at a number of items. First, he should review the prior record of performance of the general partner. Is this the 1st or 10th deal that the general partner has put together? The investor will also wish to be sensitive to any lawsuits against the general partner that might exist. The investor might also wish to ascertain whether he or she is investing in a blind pool arrangement where funds are provided to the general partner to ultimately select properties for investment or if specific projects have already been identified and analyzed.

Finally, the investor may have to decide whether to invest in a limited partnership/syndication that is either *public* or *private* in nature. A public offering generally involves much larger total amounts and has gone through the complex and rigorous process of SEC registration. Of course, SEC registration only attempts to ensure that full disclosure has occurred—it does not judge the prudence of the venture. A private offering of a limited partnership syndication is usually local in scope and restricted to a maximum of 35 investors.

Secondary (resale) markets for both public and private limited partnerships exist, but the dealer spreads and commissions tend to be very high. The spreads on desirable property are perhaps 10 to 15 percent; on less desirable property, 20 to 30 percent or more. Really bad property may approach total illiquidity. As you might anticipate, a public limited partnership has much more resale potential than a private one.

Real Estate Investment Trust

Another form of real estate investment is the real estate investment trust (REIT). REITs are similar to mutual funds or investment companies and trade on organized exchanges or over-the-counter. They pool investor funds, along with borrowed funds, and invest them directly in real estate or use them to make construction or mortgage loans to investors.

The advantage to the investor of a REIT is that he or she can participate in the real estate market for as little as $10 to $20 per share. Furthermore, this is the most liquid type of real estate investment because of the large secondary market for the shares.

REITs were initiated under the Real Estate Investment Trust Act of 1960. Like other investment companies, they enjoy the privilege of single taxation of income (only the stockholder pays and not the trust). To qualify for the tax privilege of a REIT, a firm must receive at least 75 percent of its income from real estate (i.e., rents and interest on mortgage loans) and distribute at least 95 percent of its income as cash dividends.

REITs may take any of three different forms or combinations thereof. Equity trusts buy, operate, and sell real estate as an investment; mortgage trusts make long-term loans to real estate investors; and hybrid trusts engage in the activities of both equity and mortgage trusts. REITs are generally formed and advised by affiliates of commercial banks, insurance companies, mortgage bankers, and other financial institutions. Representative issues include Bank America Realty and Connecticut General Mortgage.

There are more than 400 REITs from which the investor may choose.[6] In Figure 16–2, a *Value Line* data sheet is presented for Washington REIT, a typical industry participant. Many other REITs are also presented in *Value Line.*

GOLD AND SILVER

We now examine a number of other forms of real asset investments. Precious metals represent the most volatile of the investment alternatives. Historically, gold and silver have tended to move up in troubled times and show a decline in value during stable, predictable periods.[7] Observe the movement in the price of gold between 1978 and 2000 in Figure 16–3.

6. Further information on REITs may be acquired from the National Association of Real Estate Investment Trusts, 1101 17th St., N.W., Washington, D.C. 20036.

7. As previously pointed out, this pattern has not been evident in the 1990s but is still thought to carry long-term validity.

FIGURE 16–2 Data Sheet for REIT

WASHINGTON REIT NYSE-WRE | RECENT PRICE 27.47 | P/E RATIO 22.3 (Trailing: 22.3 / Median: NMF) | RELATIVE P/E RATIO 1.45 | DIV'D YLD 5.4% | VALUE LINE 1203

TIMELINESS 3 Raised 3/3/00
SAFETY 2 Raised 7/30/99
TECHNICAL 4 Lowered 4/25/03
BETA .65 (1.00 = Market)

	1992	1993	1994	1995	1996	1997	1998	1999	2000	2001	2002	2003
High:	21.3	24.8	21.1	16.6	17.5	19.6	18.8	18.8	25.0	25.5	30.2	27.7
Low:	14.9	18.6	14.9	13.9	15.3	15.5	15.1	13.8	14.3	20.8	20.4	24.0

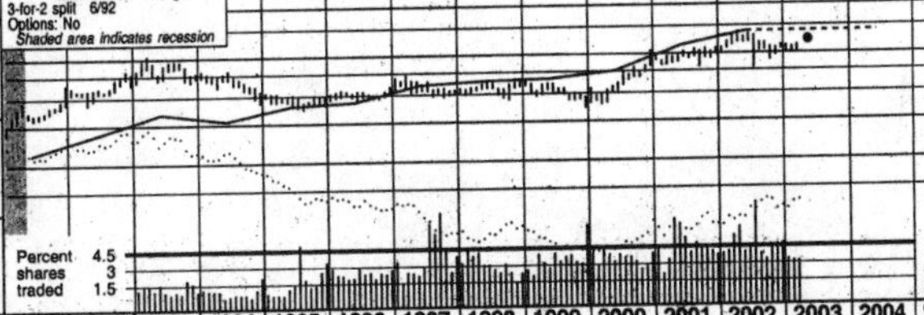

Target Price Range 2006 | 2007 | 2008

LEGENDS
— 1.00 x Dividends p sh divided by Interest Rate
.... Relative Price Strength
3-for-2 split 6/92
Options: No
Shaded area indicates recession

2006-08 PROJECTIONS

	Price	Gain	Ann'l Total Return
High	35	(+25%)	11%
Low	25	(-10%)	4%

Insider Decisions

	J	J	A	S	O	N	D	J	F
to Buy	0	2	0	0	0	0	0	0	0
Options	2	1	1	0	0	0	1	0	1
to Sell	1	0	1	0	0	0	0	0	1

Institutional Decisions

	2Q2002	3Q2002	4Q2002
to Buy	56	53	62
to Sell	44	46	29
Hld's(000)	11482	11646	11672

Percent shares traded 4.5 / 3 / 1.5

% TOT. RETURN 3/03

	THIS STOCK	VL ARITH. INDEX
1 yr.	-4.6	-25.3
3 yr.	104.3	-10.0
5 yr.	106.7	-1.8

1987	1988	1989	1990	1991	1992	1993	1994	1995	1996	1997	1998	1999	2000	2001	2002	2003	2004	© VALUE LINE PUB., INC.	06-08
3.05	2.98	3.94	3.90	4.69	5.64	5.49	5.48	6.29	6.15	7.07	7.11	7.20	7.24	8.33	8.33	*8.15*	*8.33*	Book Value per sh	*9.65*
.63	.69	.78	.83	.88	.89	.93	.96	1.05	1.13	1.23	1.39	1.55	1.79	1.96	1.97	*2.00*	*2.10*	Funds from Ops per sh	*2.65*
.51	.56	.64	.69	.75	.76	.80	.82	.88	.88	.90	.96	1.00	1.16	1.27	1.22	*1.25*	*1.30*	Earnings per sh A	*1.75*
.58	.63	.68	.73	.79	.84	.89	.92	.99	1.03	1.07	1.11	1.16	1.23	1.31	1.39	*1.45*	*1.51*	Div'ds Decl'd per sh B ■	*1.80*
3.27	3.35	3.27	3.83	3.52	4.44	4.78	6.04	7.32	9.65	12.57	14.86	16.19	16.72	16.79	18.04	*19.65*	*20.50*	Loans & Real Est per sh	*25.00*
20.70	20.67	23.22	23.23	25.59	28.21	28.23	28.24	31.75	31.80	35.68	35.69	35.72	35.74	38.83	39.17	*40.00*	*42.00*	Common Shs Outst'g C	*44.00*
258%	287%	236%	188%	195%	215%	287%	238%	144%	160%	142%	139%	126%	146%	181%	214%	*Bold figures are*	*Value Line estimates*	Premium Over Book	*210%*
21.4	20.6	20.6	16.2	18.6	23.4	26.7	22.4	17.5	18.2	19.0	17.7	16.4	15.4	18.4	21.4			Avg Ann'l P/E Ratio	*16.5*
17.4	16.7	17.0	13.6	15.7	20.0	22.9	19.1	14.6	14.2	13.9	12.2	10.6	10.0	12.0	13.3			Avg Ann'l P/FFO Ratio	*11.0*
5.3%	5.5%	5.1%	6.5%	5.7%	4.7%	4.1%	5.0%	6.4%	6.4%	6.3%	6.5%	7.1%	6.9%	5.6%	5.3%			Avg Ann'l Div'd Yield	*6.2%*
						39.4	45.5	52.6	65.5	79.4	103.6	119.0	134.7	148.4	152.9	*160*	*170*	Rental Income ($mill)	*235*
						1.5	d.6	.7	.7	1.0	.9	.7	.9	1.7	.7	*1.0*	*1.0*	Other Income ($mill)	*1.0*
						62.8%	62.1%	62.1%	61.8%	62.6%	63.6%	65.1%	66.0%	67.5%	68.3%	*68.0%*	*68.0%*	Operating Margin	*68.0%*
						22.5	23.1	26.1	28.0	30.1	34.3	39.4	41.6	48.1	48.1	*50.0*	*54.5*	Net Profit($mill)	*77.0*
						55.1%	51.4%	49.0%	42.3%	37.5%	33.1%	33.1%	30.9%	32.4%	31.5%	*31.3%*	*32.0%*	Net Profit Margin	*32.8%*
						.7	--	--	--	--	6.6	7.9	3.6	4.3	3.9	*5.0*	*5.0*	Capital Gains (mill)	*5.0*
						137.2	170.6	232.4	306.7	448.3	530.6	578.3	597.6	652.0	706.8	*785*	*860*	Loans & Real Est ($mill)	*1100*
						--	18.0	35.7	112.6	202.7	282.9	330.0	351.3	359.7	402.7	*450*	*475*	Long-Term Debt ($mill)	*550*
						157.3	154.7	199.7	195.6	252.1	253.7	257.2	258.7	323.6	326.2	*325*	*350*	Shr. Equity ($mill)	*425*
						94.9%	95.8%	94.3%	91.5%	87.1%	79.9%	70.1%	68.4%	66.8%	70.2%	*73%*	*72%*	Div'ds Decl'd to FFO	*68%*
						8.4%	9.7%	8.3%	7.9%	6.3%	6.7%	6.8%	7.3%	6.8%	6.4%	*6.5%*	*5.6%*	Expenses to Assets	*7.0%*
						13.8%	14.4%	13.1%	10.1%	7.7%	6.7%	8.6%	8.9%	9.0%	8.6%	*8.5%*	*8.5%*	Return on Total Cap'l	*8.5%*
						14.5%	14.8%	13.1%	14.3%	12.0%	13.5%	15.3%	16.1%	14.9%	14.7%	*15.5%*	*15.0%*	Return on Shr. Equity	*18.0%*

CAPITAL STRUCTURE as of 12/31/02
ST Debt None **Due in 5 Years** $235 mill.
LT Debt $402.7 mill. **LT Interest** $28.0 mill.
(Total interest coverage: 2.7x) (55% of Cap'l)

No Defined Benefit Pension Plan

Pfd Stock None
Shares of Ben'l Int. 39,168,000

MARKET CAP: $1.1 billion (Mid Cap)

FUNDS FLOW ($mill.)	2000	2001	2002
Net Profit Plus Noncash charges	64.3	74.8	77.2
Investments Repaid	--	--	--
Net New Debt	21.3	8.5	43.0
New Equity	.3	62.2	5.5
Investments Funded	42.9	81.8	83.2
Dividends Declared	44.0	49.7	54.4

FINANCIAL POSITION	12/31/01	12/31/02
Senior Debt	359.7	402.7
Subordinated Debt	None	None
Sr Debt/Cap'l Funds	1.11:1	1.23:1
Total Debt/Equity	1.11:1	1.23:1

PORTFOLIO CONDITION	Year Ago	Latest
Mtges Repaid in Quarter (mill.)	N/A	N/A
Loss Reserve—%/Invests.	N/A	N/A
Non-Earn Assets—%/Invests.	N/A	N/A

Calendar	LOANS & REAL ESTATE ($ mill.) Mar.31	Jun.30	Sep.30	Dec.31
2000	577.7	583.8	581.9	597.6
2001	595.5	636.2	630.4	652.0
2002	651.4	693.0	708.4	706.8
2003	*725*	*740*	*760*	*785*
2004	*800*	*820*	*840*	*860*

Calendar	EARNINGS PER SHARE A Mar.31	Jun.30	Sep.30	Dec.31	Full Year
2000	.26	.28	.30	.32	1.16
2001	.30	.33	.32	.32	1.27
2002	.32	.30	.30	.30	1.22
2003	*.30*	*.31*	*.32*	*.32*	*1.25*
2004	*.31*	*.32*	*.33*	*.34*	*1.30*

Calendar	QUARTERLY DIVIDENDS PAID B ■ Mar.31	Jun.30	Sep.30	Dec.31	Full Year
1999	.28	.2925	.2925	.2925	1.16
2000	.2925	.3125	.3125	.3125	1.23
2001	.3125	.3325	.3325	.3325	1.31
2002	.3325	.3525	.3525	.3525	1.39
2003	.3525				

BUSINESS: Washington Real Estate Investment Trust is a self-administered, regional real estate investment trust that invests in properties in the area between Philadelphia and Richmond; all are in the greater Washington, D.C. metropolitan area. 12/31/01 investment portfolio of 59 properties (9.0 mm sq ft), based on cost and share of 2002 operating income: office buildings, 54% and 50%; shopping centers, 17% and 21%; apartment buildings, 13% and 13%; industrial distribution centers, 16% and 16%. Has about 285 empls, 37,000 stkhldrs. Off./dir. own 2.5% of stock; T. Rowe Price, 7.1% (3/03 Proxy). Org.: MD. Chairman, Pres., & CEO: Edmund B. Cronin, Jr. Address: 6110 Executive Boulevard, Suite 800; Rockville, MD 20852. Tel.: 301-984-9400. Internet: www.writ.com.

Washington REIT is feeling the effects of the national economic slowdown, though the company is doing considerably better than some real estate investment trusts with property concentrated in weaker parts of the country. In the last quarter of 2002, operating income from "core properties" (owned for over a year) decreased 3.2%, compared with a 4.7% gain in the first quarter of 2002. Overall occupancy fell to 90.1%, from 95.7% in the prior-year period, with decreases in all four property types. Still, WRE's diversification protected it somewhat, as decreases in profits from the office and industrial/flexible use segments were partially offset by gains in the retail and apartment divisions.

A major new office lease will help 2003 results. The company has just signed a lease for 116,000 square feet of office space in the depressed Tyson's Corner area of northern Virginia. If this lease had been in effect during the last quarter of 2002, office segment profits would have been down around 3% for the period, versus the actual 6.4% decline. This large lease aside, the outlook for WRE in 2003 is mixed. Office rents will probably continue to be pressured by high vacancies resulting from the failures of dot-com and telecom companies. The industrial/flexible space segment's results should reflect the shaky economy; so far, the region has not seen much new leasing activity as a result of higher defense spending and the new homeland security initiative. The apartment division will likely face continued demands for concessions. But retail segment profits should rise again this year.

The federal government will probably continue to be a strong economic engine for the area. For years, the Washington, DC region has received a growing portion of all federal purchases, and we see no reason why that trend should reverse. And WRE's local focus and property diversification should give it a competitive advantage in profiting from the area's future development.

These shares offer chiefly a reasonable dividend, though the yield is below the industry average. Appreciation potential, however, is minimal, as we expect interest rates to rise by 2006-2008.

Sigourney B. Romaine, CFA April 25, 2003

(A) Based on average shares outstanding through '97, diluted thereafter. Excludes gains on property sales: '98, 19¢; '99, 22¢; '00, 10¢; '01, 11¢; '02, 10¢. Excludes gain from accounting change: '99, 2¢. Next earnings report due mid-May.
(B) Next dividend meeting late May; goes ex mid-June. Dividend payment dates: end of March, June, Sept., and Dec.
■ Dividend reinvestment plan available.
(C) In mill., adj. for stk. split.

Company's Financial Strength	B++
Stock's Price Stability	100
Price Growth Persistence	25
Earnings Predictability	100

Source: Reproduced with the permission of Value Line Publishing, Inc.

FIGURE 16–3 Movement in Gold Prices

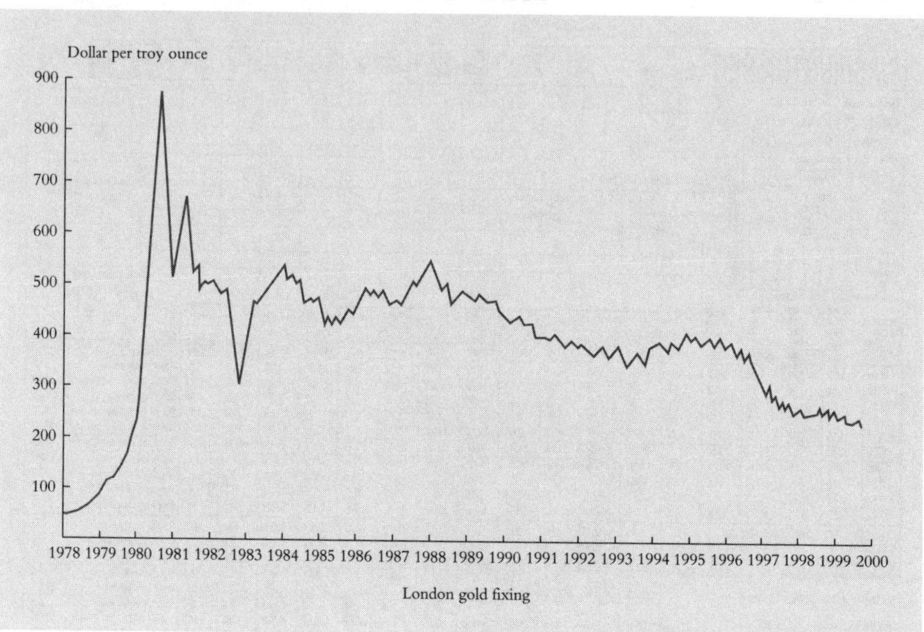

Gold

Major factors that tend to drive up gold prices are fear of war, political instability, and inflation (these were particularly evident in Figure 16–3 after 1979 with the takeover of U.S. embassies in Iran and double-digit inflation). Conversely, moderation in worldwide tensions and lower inflation cause a decline in gold prices.

Gold may be owned in many different forms, and a survey by *Kiplinger's Personal Finance Magazine* indicated that 30 percent of the U.S. population with incomes of more than $40,000 per year owned gold (directly or indirectly) or other forms of precious metals. Let's examine the different forms of gold ownership.

Gold Bullion Gold bullion includes gold bars or wafers. The investor may own anywhere from 1 troy ounce to 10,000 troy ounces (valued at approximately $2.8 million in 2000). Smaller bars generally trade at a 6 to 8 percent premium over pure gold bullion value, with larger bars trading at a 1 to 2 percent premium. Gold bullion may provide storage problems, and unless the gold bars remain in the custody of the bank or dealer who initially sells them, they must be reexamined before being sold.

Gold Coins Many of the storing and assaying costs associated with gold bullion can be avoided by investing directly in gold coins. There are three basic outlets for investing in gold coins. First, there are *gold bullion coins,* such as the South

African Krugerrand, the Mexican 50 peso, and the Canadian Maple Leaf. These coins trade at a small premium of 2 to 3 percent over pure bullion value and afford the investor an excellent outlet for taking a position in the market. A second form is represented by *common date gold coins* that are no longer minted, such as the U.S. double eagle, the British sovereign, or the French Napoleon. These coins may trade at as much as 50 to 100 times their pure gold bullion value because of their value as collectibles. Finally, there are gold coins that are *old* and *rare* and that may trade at a numismatic value into the thousands or hundreds of thousands of dollars.

Gold Stocks In addition to gold bullion and gold coins, the investor may take a position in gold by simply buying common stocks that have heavy gold-mining positions. Examples of companies listed on U.S. exchanges include Battle Mountain (U.S. based), Placer Dome Inc. (Canadian based), and Homestake Mining (U.S. based). Because these securities often move in the opposite direction of the stock market as a whole, they may provide excellent portfolio diversification.

Gold Futures Contracts Finally, the gold investor may consider trading in futures contracts. Gold futures are traded on five different U.S. exchanges and on many foreign exchanges.[8]

Silver

Silver has many of the same investment characteristics as gold in terms of being a hedge against inflation and a potential safe haven for investment during troubled times. Silver moved from $5 a troy ounce in 1976 to more than $50 an ounce in early 1980 and then back to $5 an ounce in 2000.

More so than gold, silver has heavy industrial and commercial applications. Areas of utilization include photography, electronic and electrical manufacturing, electroplating, dentistry, and silverware and jewelry. It is estimated that industrial uses of silver exceed annual production by 150 million ounces per year. Furthermore, the supply of silver does not necessarily increase with price because silver is a by-product of copper, lead, zinc, and gold. Because of the undersupply factor, many consider silver to be appropriate for long-term holding.

Investment in silver can also take many different forms. Some may choose to buy *silver bullion* in the form of silver bars. Because the price of silver generally is 1/25 to 1/75 the price of gold and larger bulk is involved for an equivalent dollar size investment, the storage and carrying costs can be quite high. Second, *silver coins* may be bought in large bags or as rare coins for their numismatic value. Keep in mind that dimes, quarters, and half-dollars minted during and before 1965 were 90 percent pure silver. As a third outlet, the investor may wish to consider *silver futures contracts.* Finally, the investor may purchase *stocks* of firms that have interests in silver mining, such as Hecla Mining or Echo Bay Mines.

8. There are also options on gold futures on the Comex.

PRECIOUS GEMS

Precious gems include diamonds, rubies, sapphires, and emeralds. Diamonds and other precious gems have appeal to investors because of their small size, easy concealment, and great durability. They are particularly popular in Europe because of a long-standing distrust of paper currencies as a store of value.

The reason diamonds are so valuable can be best understood by considering the production process. It is estimated that 50 to 200 *tons* of rock or sand is required to uncover one carat (1⁄142 of an ounce) of quality diamonds.

The distribution of diamonds is under virtual monopolistic control by De Beers Consolidated Mines of South Africa, Ltd. It controls the distribution of approximately 80 percent of the world's supply and has a stated policy of maintaining price control. Diamonds have generally enjoyed a steady, somewhat spectacular movement in price. For example, the price of a "D" color, one-carat, flawless, polished diamond increased more than tenfold between 1974 and 1980.

Of course, not all diamonds have done so well. Furthermore, there have been substantial breaks in the market, such as in 1974 and 1980–82 when diamond prices declined by one-fourth and more. Even with large increases in value, the diamond investor does not automatically come out ahead. Dealer markups may be anywhere from 10 to 100 percent so three to five years of steady gain may be necessary to show a substantial profit.

In no area of investment is product and market knowledge more important. Either you must be an expert yourself or know that you are dealing with an "honest" expert. Diamonds are judged on the basis of the four *c*'s (color, clarity, carat weight, and cut), and the assessment of any stone should be certified by a member of the Gemological Institute of America. As is true of most valuable items, the investor is well advised to purchase the highest quality possible. You are considerably better off using the same amount of money to buy a higher quality, smaller carat diamond than a lesser quality, high-carat diamond.

BASEBALL CARDS AS COLLECTIBLES

Although we most often associate baseball cards with the 10-year-old child who coaxes $2.00 from his parents to buy a pack of cards in the drugstore, there is actually a half-billion dollar a year industry out there. There are 100,000 serious baseball card collectors and millions of child arbitragers doing business on a daily basis.

Other forms of sports memorabilia have value as well. A baseball clearly autographed by Babe Ruth is worth about $7,000. An authentic Lou Gehrig game-worn uniform carries a $310,000 price tag. A truly enterprising collector went so far as to pay $500 for the dental records of Eddie Cicotte, a long-deceased pitcher for the infamous Chicago Black Sox of 1919.

Nevertheless, baseball cards and sports memorabilia have not fared particularly well since the last edition of this book was published. The fabled Mickey Mantle 1952 Topps baseball card has declined in value from $50,000 to $25,000 (it originally cost a penny), and the Nolan Ryan 1968 Topps rookie card has declined from $2,000 to $1,200. Overall, baseball cards have declined in value by 25 percent in the last four years.

Why the decline? Baseball cards, like other forms of collectibles and real assets, are viewed as a hedge against inflation, and there has been very little inflation against which it has been necessary to hedge. Also, the baseball players strike of the mid-1990s turned many fans against the game—not only at the turnstiles but in general enthusiasm for the game. This factor has translated into less devoted collectors of baseball cards as well. Also, the oversupply of baseball cards by an expanding group of card manufacturers is another negative.

There have been ups and downs in the baseball card market before, and the patient, contrarian investor may wish to view the current market as a buying opportunity for old, valuable cards in mint condition that are being sold by distressed owners.

There is an interesting exception to the current downturn in the market. In 2000, a 1910 Honus Wagner tobacco baseball card sold for more than $1 million. The previous high for the Wagner card was $640,000 in 1996. In 1985, it had changed hands at $110,000. Why all the upside momentum? Wagner did not approve of smoking, and when his card appeared in a tobacco-related set around 1910, he forced the American Tobacco Company to pull all but 100 off the market. Now, only 40 Wagner cards are thought to exist, and the law of supply and demand has clearly set in.

Also, other forms of baseball memorabilia (besides cards) have done extremely well in the last few years. It all started with the Sotheby's (www.sothebys.com) auction of the Barry Halper memorabilia collection in 2000. Mr. Halper, a multimillionaire and minority owner of the New York Yankees, had the largest memorabilia collection of items such as autographed baseballs (going back to the 1920s), players' uniforms, and Ty Cobb and Babe Ruth signed documents in existence. The auction brought in two and three times the anticipated value of cherished items and started a renewed interest in memorabilia. As evidence, Mastro Fine Sports (www.mastronet.com) of Oakbrook, Illinois, conducts memorabilia auctions over the Internet four or five times a year and normally grosses $5 to $7 million per auction. A 1927 Yankees autographed baseball, which was worth $5,000 a few years before, went for $70,000. An autographed copy of the 1948 *Babe Ruth Story* purchased by one of the authors for $1,100 in 1999 went for $4,000 in May 2001.

OTHER COLLECTIBLES

A listing of other collectibles for investment might include art, antiques, stamps, Chinese ceramics, rare books, and other items that appeal to various sectors of our society. Each offers psychic pleasure to the investor as well as the opportunity for profit.

Anyone investing in a collectible should have some understanding of current market conditions and of the factors that determine the inherent worth of the item. Otherwise, you may be buying someone else's undesirable holding at a premium price. It is important not to get swept away in a buying euphoria. The best time to buy art, antiques, or stamps is when the bloom is off the market and dealers are overburdened with inventory, not when there is a weekly story in *The Wall Street Journal* or *Business Week* about overnight fortunes being made. There seems to be a pattern or cycle in the collectibles market the same as in other markets (arts, antiques, and stamps actually do move together).

As is true of other markets, the wise investor in the collectibles market must be sensitive to dealer spreads. A price guide that indicates a doubling in value every two or three years may be meaningless if the person with whom you are dealing sells for $100 and buys back for $50. The wise investor/collector can best maintain profits by dealing with other collectors or investors and eliminating the dealer or middleman from the transaction where possible.

Such periodicals as *Money* magazine and the *Collector/Investor* provide excellent articles on the collectibles market. Specialized periodicals, such as *American Arts and Antiques, Coin World, Linn's Stamp News, The Sports Collectors Digest,* and *Antique Monthly,* also are helpful. The interested reader can find books on almost any type of collectible in a public library or large bookstore.

Internet Resources

Website Address	Comments
www.realtor.com	Has property search function, mortgage evaluation function
moneycentral.msn.com	Has property valuation function along with mortgage financing calculator
www.quicken.com	Provides mortgage financing information and payment calculator
www.reit.com	Provides information about real estate investment trusts
www.nareit.com	Website for the industry trade group and provides information and data on REITs
www.hsh.com	Contains database of current residential mortgage rates
www.realestate.com	Provides information on property listings and mortgage financing and reports on property values and analysis
www.gmacrealestate.com	Provides property search, valuation calculation, and mortgage information
www.housevalues.com	Will estimate residential property values and provide report for homes in cities in its database

Index

ABN AMRO Rothschild LLC, 52
Abortive recovery, 201, 202
Account executives, 85, 86
Accounting
  aggressive tactics in, 195–97
  changes in accounting methods, 218–19
  for convertible securities, 321–23
  for warrants, 328–29
Accrual accounting, 172
Acquisitions. *See* Mergers and acquisitions
Adjustable rate mortgages (ARMs), 370–71
Administrative problems, 350
ADRs. *See* American depository receipts
After-hours trading, 68–69
Age of investor, 4
Alcan Aluminum, Ltd., 353
Alternative trading systems (ATSs), 67
Altman, Edward, 176
Amazon.com, 318
AMBAC (American Municipal Bond Assurance Corporation), 250
American Arts and Antiques, 380
American Association of Individual Investors, 28, 92
American Capital, 35
American depository receipts (ADRs), 352–55
American Municipal Bond Assurance Corporation (AMBAC), 250
American Stock Exchange (AMEX), 24, 58, 59, 64, 65, 68, 74, 82, 83, 233
Ameritrade, 69, 71, 92
AMEX. *See* American Stock Exchange
AMEX indexes, 83
AMEX Market Value Index, 65
Amortization, 159
Annual cash flow, 365–67
Annual net operating income, 363–64
Anticipated inflation factor, 11–13
Antique Monthly, 380
Apple Computer, 122, 123, 127, 228
Approximate yield to maturity, 276–77
Arbitrage, 74*n*4
Archipelago, 68
Argentina, 333, 345
Arithmetic mean, 13
ARMs. *See* Adjustable rate mortgages
Art, valued, 4, 15
Asked price, 66, 260
Assets, stock value and, 164
Asset-utilization ratio, 179, 180
ATSs (alternative trading systems), 67
AT&T, 100, 226
Attain, 68
Auctions, Internet, 379
Australia, 132, 348
Automatic Data Processing, 318
Automatic reinvestment, 38
Automobile industry, 103, 114–17, 124–26, 131, 132
Average tax rate, 185
Averages, stock. *See* Indexes and averages

Bache Group, 324
Back-end load provisions, 26
Balance sheets, 169–71
Balanced funds, 31, 35
Banco Bilbao, 318
Bank America Realty, 374
Bankers' acceptances, 266
Banking industry, 47, 52, 54, 138, 253. *See also* Investment banking
Bankruptcy, 73, 176–77, 244, 257, 267
Banz, Rolf W., 220, 233, 234
Bar charts, 203–6
Bargaining power, 131
Barron's, 27, 77, 208, 210–12, 259, 343
Barron's Confidence Index, 211–13, 287
Barry, Christopher B., 228
Base period, 81
Baseball cards, 378–79
Basu, S., 219, 234
Batterymarch Financial Management, 356
Battle Mountain, 377
Bear Stearns, 56
Beaver, William, 176
Bell South Telecommunications, 259
Benchmarks, 41
Beta, 32, 142, 143, 218
Bezos, Jeffrey, 118

Bid price, 66, 260
Bloomberg Tradebook, 68
Blue Bell, 227
Blue-chip stocks, 78, 81
Boesky, Ivan, 74, 222, 224
Bond contracts, 241-43
Bond funds, 32, 35
Bond Guide (Standard & Poor's), 259
Bond market
  composition of, 244, 245
  efficiency of, 262-64
Bond market indicators, 85
Bond price sensitivity, 292, 294-300
Bond prices, 312-16
Bond rating agencies, 255-57
Bond ratings, 250, 254-57, 262-64, 287, 315, 318
Bond reinvestment, 279
  assumptions for, 303-4
  and terminal wealth analysis, 304-6
  with zero-coupons, 207
Bond repayment, 242
Bond swaps, 288-89
Bond tables, 278*n*3, 286
Bond valuation, 271-89, 291-93
  and bond swaps, 288-89
  fundamentals of, 271-74
  and interest rates, 279-88
  Internet resources on, 289
  and rates of return, 274-79
Bond-pricing rules, 285-86
Bonds, 241-65
  capital market theory and efficiency of, 262-64
  contract for, 241-43
  corporate, 250-53
  deep discount vs. par, 287
  distribution procedures for, 254
  federally sponsored credit agency, 247-48
  global market for, 264-65
  Internet resources on, 270
  investors in, 253-54
  junk, 258
  life of, 291-93
  liquidity of, 6
  and moderate inflation, 15
  and power of rating agencies, 257
  quotations for, 259-63
  rate of return for, 13, 14
  ratings for, 254-57
  reinvestment of. *See* Bond reinvestment
  secured vs. unsecured, 243-44
  state and local government, 248-51
  U.S. government, 244-47
  valuation of. *See* Bond valuation
Book value per share (BVPS), 156, 157
Book value to market value effect, 235, 236
Boston, 58
Bottoms, market, 204, 206
Brand names, 131-32
Braniff, 127
Brazil, 333
Breadth of market, 213-15
Breakouts, 203
British Airways, 354
British pound, 65
Brokerage firms, 73
Brokers, 58, 61, 85, 86, 88
Brut/Strike, 68
Bullion, gold, 376
Bush, George H.W., 99, 101
Bush, George W., 100, 154
Business Cycle Indicators, 110
Business cycle(s), 97-117
  and cyclical indicators, 106, 108-13
  and economic activity, 97-108
  expansions and contractions in U.S., 109
  and industry relationships, 114-17
Business Week, 131, 132, 155
Buy orders, 91
Buy-and-hold approach, 6
BVPS. *See* Book value per share

Call options, 64, 65
Call provision, 242, 253, 268, 320
Callable bonds, 315-16
Campbell Resources, Inc., 353
Campeau Corporation, 258
Canada, 242, 257, 339, 340, 342, 348, 353
Canadian Maple Leaf, 377
Capital, 4, 49, 123
Capital appreciation, 5
Capital gains, 368-69
  and municipal bonds, 249*n*5
  and mutual funds, 37, 41, 43
  and stock market, 95-96
Capital goods, 116
Capital market theory, 262-64
Capitalization rate (cap rate), 363, 364
Carter, Jimmy, 99, 154
Cash accounts, 88
Cash dividends, 123
Cash flow per share (CFPS), 156, 157
Cash flows, 364-67, 369
Cash offers, 226-27
Cash position, mutual fund, 215
CBOE. *See* Chicago Board Options Exchange
CDs. *See* Certificates of deposit
Cephalon, 318
Certificates of deposit (CDs), 265, 266
Certified Financial Planners (CFPs), 94
CFPS. *See* Cash flow per share
Charles Schwab, 69, 92, 93
Charts and charting, 200-207
  bar charts, 203-6
  point and figure charts, 204, 206-7
  of support and resistance, 202-3
  of volume, 203
Chase Bank, 54
Chase Manhattan, 227
Check-writing privileges, 31, 39
Chemical Bank, 227
Chemical industry, 134-37
Chevron, 226
Chicago Board of Trade, 65, 74
Chicago Board Options Exchange (CBOE), 65, 81
Chicago Mercantile Exchange, 65
Chicago Stock Exchange, 58, 61
Chicago Tribune, 114
China, 100, 102, 333, 334, 336
Chinese ceramics, 15
Chrysler, 176
Circuit breakers, 75
Cisco Systems, 83, 93, 117
Citicorp, 47
Citigroup, 47, 54
Clinton, Bill, 100, 101, 154
Closed-end funds, 22-25, 355-56
Coca-Cola, 71, 128, 132, 151, 163, 168-75, 178-83, 185-91, 195
Coin World, 380
Coins, 376-77
Colby, Robert W., 207
Colgate Palmolive, 335
Collateral, 243
Collectibles, 3, 377-80
Collector/Investor, 380
Combined earnings and dividend model, 148-50
Comex, 377*n*8

Commercial paper, 266
Commission brokers, 61
Commissions, 6, 26-28, 73, 88, 92, 360
Commodity futures, 3, 65
Common date gold coins, 377
Common stock, 1, 2, 4
  appreciation of, 5
  convertible securities vs., 317-19
  liquidity of, 6
  preferred vs., 267
  risk premium for, 12, 14, 15
Compaq, 123, 195-96
Comparative sales value, 363
Competition
  in capital allocation, 49
  in investment banking, 54-58
Competitive structure of industry, 130-31
Composite indexes, 110, 112
Confirmation, market, 201
Connecticut General Mortgage, 374
Conoco Oil, 135
Conseco Insurance, 225
Consolidated Rutile, 351
Consolidated tape, 59, 60, 68-70
Constant growth dividend model, 144-46
Consumer price index (CPI), 105-7, 152, 153
Continental Airlines, 127
Contracts, bond, 241-43
Contrary opinion rules, 208-11
Conversion premiums, 312-16
Conversion price, 310-20
Conversion ratio, 310-20
Convertible exchangeable preferred stock, 323
Convertible securities, 31, 309-23
  accounting considerations with, 321-23
  common stock purchases vs., 317-19
  corporate advantages and disadvantages of, 320-21
  disadvantages of, 318-19
  innovations in, 323
  Internet resources on, 329
  preferred stock as, 268, 323
  premiums of, 312-16
  price ratio for, 310-20
  and timing, 320
  value of, 311-12
Corporate bond funds, 32
Corporate bonds, 13, 14, 250-53
Correlation coefficient, 339-41
Cost approach to real estate valuation, 363
Cost basis, 38
Costs
  opportunity, 7-8
  of trading, 92-93
Coupon rates, 242, 298-301
Coverage ratios, 255
CPI. *See* Consumer price index
Crash of 1929, 1, 47, 71, 88
Crash of 1987, 1, 58, 69, 74, 99, 338, 339
Credit Suisse First Boston, 52
Creditor claims, 3
Currency fluctuations, 65, 103, 345-49
Current income, 5
Current ratio, 181
Current yield, 274
Cyclical indicators, 106, 108-13
Cyprus, 334
Czech Republic, 100, 333

Daily fluctuations, 200, 204
DaimlerChrysler, 71, 176
Day orders, 92
Day traders, 93
De Beers Consolidated Mines of South Africa, Ltd., 131, 378
Dealer spreads, 37, 360, 380
Dean Witter, 35, 92
Debentures, 243
Debt instruments, 3
Debt security markets, 67
Debt-to-assets ratio, 192
Debt-to-equity ratio, 135-37, 351
Debt-utilization ratio, 181-83
Decline life-cycle stage, 127
Deep discount bonds, 287
Defaults, bond, 252
Deferred call, 242
Deficits, 100-102
Delisting, 61
Dell Computer, 123
DeMark, Thomas R., 207
Depreciation, 172, 368
Deutsche Telekom, 54
Developed markets, 332-34, 339-42
Development life-cycle stage, 122-23
Diamonds, 15, 378
Diffusion index, 110
Direct equity claims, 2
Direct investment, 351-55
Discount basis, 244
Discount brokers, 86, 92, 93
Discount rates, 104
Disney, 78, 163, 226
Distribution, 52-54
  of bonds, 254
  of mutual funds, 37-38
Diversification, 4, 20
  with international securities, 337-41
  with real assets, 360
Dividend valuation models, 143-48
Dividend yield, 183, 184
Dividend-payout ratio, 124, 127, 185
Dividends, 7, 267, 269
  and growth, 123
  from growth-with-income funds, 31
  from mutual funds, 41, 43
  and P/E ratios, 154
  taxes on, 95
Dividends per share (DPS), 156, 157
Dividends to price, 183
DJIA. *See* Dow Jones Industrial Average
DLJ, 55, 56
Dollar-cost averaging, 39-40
Dollar-denominated bonds, 264-65
Dot-com investors, 5
Double-dealing, 373
Dow, Charles, 200
Dow Chemical, 136
Dow Jones averages, 77-80, 83-85
Dow Jones Company, 77, 200
Dow Jones 40 bond averages, 212*n*5
Dow Jones Industrial Average (DJIA), 1, 48, 65, 74, 78-81, 202, 204, 205, 213, 214
Dow Jones Industry Groups, 137, 138
Dow Jones Transportation Average, 202
Dow Jones World Stock Index, 83-85
Dow theory, 200-202
DPS. *See* Dividends per share
Drexel Burnham Lambert, 258
Dreyfus Group, 35
Drug industry. *See* Pharmaceuticals industry
Du Pont, 1, 135-37, 226
Du Pont analysis, 179, 180
Dual listing, 59, 65
Dual trading, 58
Duff & Phelps, 255
Duracell, 227

Duration, 283n7, 293-303
  and coupon rates, 298-301
  influences on, 300-301
  and market rates, 298, 299
  and price sensitivity, 295-300
  uses of, 303
  and zero-coupon bonds, 302

Earnings before interest, taxes, depreciation, and amortization (EBITDA), 159-60
Earnings per share (EPS)
  and companies without earnings, 159-60
  and convertibles, 321-23
  forecasting, 160-63
  and growth, 154-55
  Johnson & Johnson example of, 156-58
  pure short-term model of, 155
  and warrants, 328-29
"Earnings per Share" (Statement of Financial Accounting Standards No. 128), 321
Earnings valuation models, 148-50
Ease of management, 7-8
Eastern Airlines, 127
Eastern Europe, 333
Eastman Kodak, 1
Ebay, 159
EBITDA. *See* Earnings before interest, taxes, depreciation, and amortization
Echo Bay Mines, 377
Eckstein, Otto, 280
ECNs. *See* Electronic communication networks
Economic activity, 97-119
  and business cycle, 97-108
  and cyclical indicators, 106, 108-13
  federal government policy on, 98-101
  and fiscal policy, 101-3
  and growth and inflation, 104-8
  and industry, 129
  and industry relationships, 114-17
  Internet resources on, 119
  and monetary policy, 103-5
  and money supply and stock prices, 113-15
  and the new economy, 117-18
Economic Bureau of Analysis, 104
Economic circumstances of investor, 4-5
Economic indicators, 110-13
Economic policy, 104, 105
Economic structure of industry, 128-30
Economic value added (EVA), 150-51
Economy, U.S., 5
EDGAR, 73
Efficient market hypothesis (EMH), 215-22
  and index funds, 32
  semistrong form of the, 217-20
  strong form of the, 220-22
  weak form of the, 216-17
El Salvador, 334
Electric utilities, 128
Electronic communication networks (ECNs), 47, 58, 67-69
Eli Lilly, 123, 133, 135
Emerging growth companies, 258
Emerging markets, 333-37, 345, 346
Emerging Stock Markets Factbook (International Finance Corporation), 345
EMH. *See* Efficient market hypothesis
Employment Act (1946), 98, 99, 103
The Encyclopedia of Technical Market Indicators (Robert Colby and Thomas Meyers), 207
Energy crisis, 252
Enron, 5
EPS. *See* Earnings per share
Equal-weighted indexes, 82
Equipment trust certificate, 243
Equity participation mortgages, 371
Equity risk premium (ERP), 142-43
ERP. *See* Equity risk premium
Estate planning, 8-9
Estate taxes, 8-9
Estonia, 334
ETFs. *See* Exchange-traded funds
E-Trade, 69, 71, 92
Euro, 100
Eurodollar bonds, 264, 265
European Monetary System, 100
European Monetary Union, 339, 348
EVA. *See* Economic value added
Evaluation, mutual fund, 40-43
Exchange listings, 59-61, 229-31
Exchange privilege, 38
Exchanges
  listing requirements for, 59-61
  organized, 58-59
  seats on, 61
Exchange-traded funds (ETFs), 24-25
Expansion life-cycle stage, 124, 125
Expectations hypothesis, 280-82
Expense ratios, 32, 37
Expenses, management, 36-37
Exports, 102-3
Extraordinary gains and losses, 194
Exxon, 82, 232
Exxon-Mobil, 355

Fabozzi, Frank J., 230
Fallen angel bonds, 258
False signals, 202, 214
Fama, Eugene F., 218, 236
"Family of funds," 35, 38
Fanuc, 351
FASB. *See* Financial Accounting Standards Board
Federal Farm Credit Bank, 247, 248
Federal government policy, 98-101
Federal Home Loan Bank, 247, 248
Federal National Mortgage Association, 67, 247
Federal Open Market Committee (FOMC), 103-4
Federal Reserve, 101, 104, 116
Federal Reserve Board, 72, 88, 98, 99, 104
Federal Reserve System, 88, 351
Federally sponsored credit agency bonds, 247-48
Federated Funds, 35
Fees, management, 36-37
Feldstein, Martin, 280
Fidelity Contrafund, 37
Fidelity Investments, 35, 69, 258
Fidelity Trust Company of New York, 356
FIFO. *See* First-in, first-out
Filo, David, 118
Filter tests, 217
Financial Accounting Standards Board (FASB), 132, 192, 321, 350
Financial assets, 2-4, 13

Financial consultants, 85
Financial statement analysis, 167
Financial statements, 167-97
and aggressive accounting tactics, 195-97
balance sheet as, 169-71
bankruptcy studies of, 176-77
and classification of ratios, 177-78
deficiencies of, 189, 192-95
income statement as, 168-69
Internet resources on, 197
and key ratios, 175-89
and long-term trends, 188-91
ratio analysis of, 175-76
statement of cash flows as, 171-75
Financing, real estate, 365, 370-72
Financing activities, 172-74
First-in, first-out (FIFO), 193-94
Fiscal policy, 101-3
Fisher, Lawrence, 218, 303
Fitch Investors Service, 255
Fixed-charge coverage, 182-83
Fixed-income securities, 241-70
bankers' acceptances as, 266
bonds as. *See* Bonds
CDs as, 265, 266
commercial paper as, 266
Internet resources on, 270
money market accounts as, 267
money market funds as, 266-67
preferred stock as, 267-69
Floating-rate notes, 242
Floor brokers, 61
FOMC. *See* Federal Open Market Committee
Forbes magazine, 28, 155, 356
Forbes Mutual Fund Survey, 31
Forecasting earnings per share, 160-63
Foreign exchange futures, 65
Foreign exchange transactions, 195
Foreign funds, 34, 35
Foreign investors, 254
Foreign stock indexes, 64
Foreign-pay bonds, 265
Form 1099-DIV, 37
Fortune 500, 335
Fortune magazine, 118, 151
France, 24, 57, 58, 342, 350
Frank Russell Company, 83
Frankfurt Stock Exchange, 351
Free cash flow, 160
French, Kenneth R., 236
Friedman, Milton, 113, 114
Front-end load provisions, 26
Full disclosure, 36
Full-service brokerage firms, 92, 93
Fund of funds, 34
Fundamental analysis, 6, 219-20
Futures, commodity, 3
Futures contracts, 377
Futures security markets, 65

Gains, extraordinary, 194
Gateway, 123
GDP. *See* Gross domestic product
GE. *See* General Electric
Gemological Institute of America, 378
Gems. *See* Precious gems
Genentech, 123, 228
General dividend model, 143-44
General Electric (GE), 225, 232, 335
General Motors, 100, 151
General obligation (GO) issues, 249
General partners, 372-73
Generally accepted accounting principles, 350-51
Geometric mean, 13
German mark, 65
Germany, 24, 57, 58, 100, 264, 340, 342
Gerstner, Lou, Jr., 203
Gillette, 227
Glass Steagall Act, 47, 52
Glaxo, 133, 135, 137
Global bond market, 264-65
Global economy, 339
Global funds, 34
GNMA (Government National Mortgage Association), 248
GO (general obligation) issues, 249, 250
Gold, 1-2, 4, 15, 374, 376-77
Gold bullion, 376
Gold coins, 376-77
Gold futures contracts, 377
Gold stocks, 377
Goldman Sachs, 55
Good till canceled (GTC) orders, 92
Goodman, David A., 234, 235
Government National Mortgage Association (GNMA), 248
GPMs (graduated payment mortgages), 371
Graduated payment mortgages (GPMs), 371
Gramm-Leach-Bliley Act, 47, 52, 54
Granville, Joseph, 211
Granville Market Letter, 211
Greenspan, Alan, 104
Gross domestic product (GDP), 99-101, 104-8, 124-26
Gross national product, 104, 105
Growth
and economic activity, 104-8
income vs., 5
in nongrowth industries, 127-28
and P/E ratios, 154
Growth companies, 162-64
Growth funds, 31, 35
Growth life-cycle stage, 123-24
Growth stocks, 162-64
Growth with income funds, 31, 35
GTC (good till canceled) orders, 92
Gulf Oil, 226

Head-and-shoulder pattern, 204
Hecla Mining, 377
Hedge funds, 34, 239
Heineken, 128
Hewlett-Packard, 238
Hidden assets, 164
High yield bonds. *See* Junk bonds
High-tech firms, 83
Hoechst, 351
Homestake Mining, 377
Hong Kong, 24, 64, 67, 339, 342, 344, 345, 350
Housing industry, 116, 247
Hungary, 100, 333
Hysteria, 360

Ibbotson, Roger G., 228
Ibbotson and Associates, 13
IBM, 1, 78, 82, 100, 117, 122, 123, 128, 196-97, 203, 232
Ikenberry, David, 232
Ikenberry, Lakonishok, and Vermaelen (ILV), 232
Immunization, 303
Import taxes, 102-3
Imports, 102-3
Income, 5
Income approach to real estate valuation, 363-64
Income bonds, 244
Income statement method, 161-63
Income statements, 168-69
Independence tests, 216
Index arbitrage, 74*n*4
Index funds, 31-33

Index of Bearish Sentiment, 210
Index-based mutual funds, 24
Indexes and averages, 77-87
- AMEX, 83
- bond, 85, 86
- direction of, 85
- Dow Jones, 77-80, 83-85
- international, 83-85
- mutual fund, 85, 87
- Nasdaq, 83
- NYSE, 82-83
- Russell, 83
- S&P, 78, 80-82
- Value Line, 82
- Wilshire, 83

Indirect equity, 2
Indirect investment, 355-56
"Individual Investor's Guide to Low-Load Mutual Funds" (American Association of Individual Investors), 28
Industrials, 250
Industry, 121-39
- and brand names, 131-32
- and business cycles, 114-17
- competitive structure of, 130-31
- and economic activity, 114-17
- economic factors affecting, 129
- economic structure of, 128-29
- financial statement analysis within an, 185-88
- government regulation of, 129-30
- groupings of, 137-39
- Internet resources on, 139
- life cycles of, 121-28
- mergers and acquisitions within an, 225
- P/E ratios within an, 154
- and rotational investing, 137-39
- structure of, 128-31
- trend analysis of, 132-37

Industry analysis, 121
Inflation, 4
- bonds and moderate, 15
- and capital appreciation, 5
- and economic activity, 104-8
- financial statements affected by, 189, 192-93
- and GDP, 106
- and P/E ratio, 152-53

Inflationary environment, 15
Inflation-indexed Treasury securities, 246-47
Information
- and efficient market hypothesis, 215-22
- international securities, 350-51
- Internet as source of, 93

Initial listing, 60-61
Initial public offerings (IPOs), 55, 227-29, 239
Insider information, 220-22
Insider trading, 72, 74, 258
Instinet, 68
Institutional trading, 69, 70, 253
Insurance industry, 54
Intangible assets, 132, 159
Intel, 66, 83, 93, 117, 203, 238
Interbrand Corp., 131
Interest (mortgage), 367*n*2
Interest rate swaps, 288*n*9
Interest rates, 279-88
- and bonds, 86
- and convertible bonds, 310, 318
- and duration, 295, 298-301
- Internet resources on, 289
- and investment strategy, 283, 285-88
- and monetary policy, 104, 105
- and money supply, 101
- movement of, 279-84
- and mutual fund selection, 35
- and real estate, 370
- term structure of, 280-83
- and UITs, 45
- volatility of, 284

Internal market data, 199
Internal Revenue Service (IRS), 246, 248
International Finance Corporation, 345
International funds, 34, 35
International Monetary Fund, 333
International Paper, 164
International securities, 331-57
- and currency fluctuations and rates of return, 346-49
- direct investment in, 351-55
- diversification benefits with, 337-41
- indirect investment in, 355-56
- Internet resources on, 357
- and market differences, 245-46
- market structures for, 336
- obstacles to, 349-51
- quotations for, 343-45
- return potential of, 342-46
- specialists in, 356

International stock averages, 83-85
Internet, 92-93
Internet auctions, 379
Intrinsic value, 327
Inventory valuation, 193-94
Investing activities, 172, 174
Investment Advisor Act (1940), 73
Investment advisory recommendations, 210-11
Investment banking, 50-58
- competition in, 54-58
- and distribution process, 52-54
- and initial public offerings, 227-28
- performance of, 228-29
- underwriting function of, 50-52

Investment companies, 2-3
Investment Company Act (1940), 36, 73
Investment Company Institute, 19, 24, 44
Investment holdings, 36
Investment quality bonds, 257, 258
Investment(s), 1-17
- and anticipated inflation factor, 11-13
- definition of, 2
- forms of, 2-4
- Internet resources for, 17
- measures of risk and return for, 9-10
- and real rate of return, 11, 12
- and risk premium, 12-16
- setting objectives for, 4-9

Investors Intelligence, 210
IPOs. *See* Initial public offerings
IRAs, 8
IRS. *See* Internal Revenue Service
IShares, 24
Island, 68
Italy, 24, 264, 340

Jacquillat, Bertrand, 355
Jain, Navaan, 118
January effect, 237
Japan, 24, 57, 64, 85, 100, 102, 103, 131, 264, 332, 333, 339, 340, 342, 348, 351
Japan Fund, 356
Japanese yen, 65
Jawboning, 104
Jennings, Robert H., 228

Jensen, Michael G., 218
Jobs, Steve, 122
Johnson & Johnson, 148-49, 151-52, 155-58, 318
J.P. Morgan Overseas Government Bond Index, 347, 348
JPMorgan, 47, 52, 54
Junior debentures, 243
Junk bond funds, 32
Junk bonds, 13, 56, 258, 287*n*8

Kansas City Board of Trade, 65
Kazakhstan, 334
Kemper, 225
Key indicators, 207-15
  Barron's Confidence Index as, 211-13
  breadth of market as, 213-15
  contrary-opinion, 208-11
  mutual fund cash position as, 215
  short sales by specialists as, 213
Kiplinger's Personal Finance Magazine, 376
Korea, 334, 336

Lakonishok, Josef, 232
Language, 351
Last-in, first-out (LIFO), 193-94
LBOs (leveraged buyouts), 227
Lease, Ronald C., 230
Least squares trendline, 160-62
Lebanon, 334
Leslie Fay, 227
Leverage, 182
Leveraged buyouts (LBOs), 227
Levine, Dennis, 74, 224
Lewellen, Wilbur G., 230
Life cycles of industry, 121-28, 163
  decline stage, 127
  development stage, 122-23
  expansion stage, 124, 125
  and growth in nongrowth industries, 127-28
  growth stage, 123-24
  maturity stage, 124-27
LIFO. *See* Last-in, first-out
Limit orders, 91-92
Limited liability, 372-73
Limited partnership, 372-74
Links, electronic, 68
Linn's Stamp News, 380
Lipper Analytical Services, 85
Lipper Mutual Fund Performance Averages, 41, 42, 85, 87
Liquidation, 243
Liquidity, 6, 35
  of bonds, 6
  and international securities, 336
  of market, 49
  and real assets, 360
  and real estate, 6
Liquidity effect, 114
Liquidity preference theory, 282
Liquidity ratio, 180-81
Listing requirements, 59-61, 229-31
L.M. Ericsson, 344-45, 353
Load funds, 26
Local government bonds, 67, 248-51
Lockheed, 176
Lockheed Martin, 176
London, 67, 71, 350
Long positions, 89-91
Long-term debt to equity, 182
Long-term orientation, 6
Long-term trends, 188-91
Los Angeles, California, 58
Losses, 96, 194
Low-load funds, 26

Macaulay, Frederick, 294
Macaulay duration, 294
Malaysia, 334
Management
  ease of, 7-8
  and P/E ratios, 155
Management fees and expenses, 27, 36-37
Mandelker, 226
Manville Corporation, 257
Marathon Oil, 226
Margin accounts, 88-89
Margin calls, 89
Margin requirements, 72
Market
  and individual stocks' P/Es, 156-57
  and international securities, 245-46
  stock repurchases' effect on the, 232-33
Market capitalization, 233-36, 332
Market efficiency, 49, 199, 350. *See also* Technical analysis
Market price limits, 74-75
Market rates of interest, 295, 298-301
Market reversal and confirmation, 201
Market segmentation theory, 282-84
Market value, 235, 236
Market value added (MVA), 151
Marketing expenses, 37
MarketXT, 68
Marshall, William J., 303
Mastro Fine Sports, 379
Maturity, bond, 291-93, 300, 301
Maturity date, 242
Maturity life-cycle stage, 124-27
May Department Stores, 259
MBIA (Municipal Bond Investors Assurance), 250
McCullough v. Maryland, 248
McDonald's, 71, 128, 131, 163
Measures
  of risk and return, 9-10
  of stock market performance, 77, 238-39
Membership, exchange, 61-64
Merck, 5, 123, 135, 232
Mergent, Inc., 259
Mergent Bond Record (Mergent, Inc.), 259
Mergers and acquisitions, 223-27
  in banking industry, 54
  and bond ratings, 257
  cancellation of, 225
  in drug industry, 133
  form of payment for, 226-27
  with leverage buyouts, 227
  and performance of acquired company, 226
  and premiums for acquired company, 223-26
  of Telxon and Symbol, 309-10, 316-17
Merjos, Anna, 230
Merrill Lynch, 35, 52, 55, 61, 62, 71, 85, 92, 93, 258, 361
Mesa Petroleum, 226
Metals, 1-3, 15*n*1, 359, 374, 376-77
Metromedia, 227
Mexican peso, 377
Mexico, 64, 333, 336, 350
Meyers, Thomas A., 207
Micron, 123, 323
Microsoft, 66, 81, 83, 93, 117, 127, 228, 238
Mid-cap funds, 34
Milken, Michael, 74, 222, 224, 258
Miller, Robert E., 228
Minimum maintenance standards, 89, 90
Minneapolis, 65
Mismeasurement, 238-39
Missouri Pacific, 287
Mobil, 226

Monetary policy, 103-5
Money magazine, 380
Money market accounts, 267
Money market funds, 4, 31, 35, 266-67
Money supply, 101, 113-15
Monopolies, 128-29
Monsanto, 136, 232
Moody's, 256-59, 287, 315, 318, 351
Moody's Investors Service, 255
Morgan Guaranty Trust company, 356
Morgan Stanley, 224
Morgan Stanley Capital International (MSCI) Indexes, 24, 84
Morgan Stanley Capital International Perspective, 345
Morgan Stanley Dean Witter, 92
Morningstar, 354
Morningstar Mutual Fund Survey, 28, 32, 40, 356
Morocco, 341
Mortgages, 243, 365, 370-72
  and business cycles, 116
  GNMA, 248
MSCI Europe Index, 40, 41
MSCI Indexes. *See* Morgan Stanley Capital International Indexes
Multinational corporations, 355, 356
Municipal bond funds, 32
Municipal Bond Investors Assurance (MBIA), 250
Municipal bonds, 7, 67, 242, 244, 248-51
Muscarella, Chris, 228
Mutual fund averages, 85
Mutual fund cash position, 215
Mutual funds, 19-45
  advantages and disadvantages of, 21-22
  assets in, 19, 20
  closed-end vs. open-end, 22-25
  distribution and taxation of, 37-38
  diversity of, 28, 31-35
  and dollar-cost averaging, 39-40
  evaluating performance of, 40-43
  exchange-traded, 24-25
  and international markets, 335, 355-56
  with junk-bond emphasis, 258
  open-end, 26-30
  oversight of, 73
  prospectus for, 36-37
  quotations for, 29
  rating system for, 28
  selecting, 35
  and shareholder services, 38-39
  UITs vs., 44-45
MVA (market value added), 151

NASD. *See* National Association of Securities Dealers
Nasdaq. *See* National Association of Securities Dealers Automated Quotations
Nasdaq Composite Index, 48, 83
Nasdaq indexes, 83
Nasdaq 100, 83
Nasdaq Stock Market, 66-67
National Association of Securities Dealers (NASD), 66, 67, 71, 73
National Association of Securities Dealers Automated Quotations (Nasdaq), 64, 66-69, 71, 74, 118, 353
National Bureau of Economic Research (NBER), 106, 108-11
National exchanges, 58
National market issues, 66
National market system, 69-70, 73
Natural resources, 164
NAV. *See* Net asset value
NBER. *See* National Bureau of Economic Research
Net asset value (NAV), 24, 26-28, 41, 43
Net change (NETCHG), 28, 29
Net operating profit after taxes (NOPAT), 150
Net working capital to total assets, 181
Netherlands, 57, 336
Netscape, 228
Net operating income, 363-66
New economy, 117-18
The New Science of Technical Analysis (Thomas DeMark), 207
New stock issues, 227-29
New York, 32, 65
New York Board of Trade, 48
New York Futures Exchanges, 65
New York Stock Exchange (NYSE), 22, 48, 58, 59, 61, 63, 64, 66-71, 73, 74, 78, 81, 82
  ADRs on the, 353-55
  daily short sales for the, 209
  foreign securities trading on the, 352-53
  minimum requirements for, 231
  small caps on, 233
  volume on the, 203
Newly issued bonds, 289
NexGen, 228
NexTrade, 68
Nike, 128
Nikkei 225 Index, 333
No-load funds, 27-30, 31
Nonconstant growth dividend model, 146-48
Nongrowth industries, 127-28
NOPAT (net operating profit after taxes), 150
Nortel Networks Corporation, 353
Norway, 342

OARS (Opening Automated Report Service), 64
Objective(s), investment, 4-9
  current income vs. capital appreciation, 5
  ease-of-management, 7-8
  liquidity, 6
  in mutual fund prospectus, 36
  in retirement and estate-planning, 8-9
  risk and safety in, 4-5
  short-term vs. long-term, 6
  tax, 7
Odd-lot dealers, 62
Odd-lot theory, 208-9
Officers of the company, 72
Old Masters paintings, 15
Olde, 92
Oligopolies, 129
Online brokers, 86, 92-93
Open-end funds, 22, 26-30
Opening Automated Report Service (OARS), 64
Open-market operations, 104
Operating activities, 172, 174
Oppenheimer Special Fund, 37
Opportunity costs, 7-8
Options, 2
Oracle, 66, 83, 117, 159
Order routing systems, 64
Organized exchanges, 58-59
Overreaction, 360
Over-the-counter (OTC) markets, 58, 63-67, 71, 229, 230
Owner-financed mortgages, 372
Ownership, 2, 372-74

Pacific Coast Exchange, 58
PaineWebber, 92

Pakistan, 345
Pan Am, 127
Panama, 334
Par bonds, 287
Par value, 241
Partnership, 372
Pass-through certificates, 248
Patents, 133
Payment (for mergers and acquisitions), 226-27
P/BV. *See* Price-to-book-value ratio
P/E ratio. *See* Price-earnings ratio
Peavy, John W. III, 234, 235
Penn Central, 176
Pension funds, 19, 195, 196, 361
Pepsi, 128, 185, 186, 188
Performance
  of acquiring company, 226
  of investment bankers, 228-29
Perpetual bonds, 242
PFCs. *See* Point and figure charts
Pfizer, 5, 133, 135
Pharmaceuticals industry, 5, 122, 123, 133-37, 154, 195
Philadelphia, Pennsylvania, 58
Philippines, 341, 345
Pink sheets, 66*n*1
Placer Dome Inc., 377
Point and figure charts (PFCs), 204, 206-7
Poland, 100, 333, 336
Policies, mutual fund, 36
Policy statements, 104
Political risk, 349-50
Porter, Michael, 130
Portfolios, mutual fund, 36
Portugal, 334
Preauthorized check plan, 38, 39
Precious gems, 3, 378
Precious metals. *See* Metals
Preferred stock, 3, 267-69, 318, 319, 323
Premiums
  for acquired company, 223-26
  convertible, 312-16
Present value of cash flows, 293, 294, 369
President's Council of Economic Advisors, 99
Price continuity, 63
Price ratios, 183-84
Price sensitivity, bond. *See* Bond price sensitivity
Price stabilization, 63
Price-earnings ratio (P/E), 151-58
  in financial statement analysis, 183, 184
  for individual stocks, 153-55
  and market, 156-57
  pure short-term model of, 155
  small caps and low, 233-36
Price-to-book-value ratio (P/BV), 157, 158, 183, 184, 345-46
Price-to-cash-flow ratio, 158
Price-to-dividend ratio, 158
Price-to-sales ratio, 157, 158
Price-weighted averages, 78
Primary markets
  and bond market investors, 253
  distribution function of, 52-54
  investment banking competition in, 54-58
  organization of, 50-58
  underwriting function of, 50-52
Primary trends, 200-202
Private offerings, 51, 373
Private placements, 254
Privileged information, 224
Profitability ratio, 178-80
Program trading, 74-75
Prospectus, 28, 36-37, 52, 72
Proxy procedures, 72
Prozac, 133, 135
Prudential Securities, 324
Public offerings
  Internet resources on, 239
  of real estate partnerships, 373
Public Service of Indiana, 252
Public utilities, 129, 250-52
Purchase price determination, 365
Purchasing power, 4
Pure bond value, 311-12, 315
Pure pickup yield swaps, 289
Pure short-term earnings model, 155
Put options, 64, 65
Put provision, 242-43
Put-call ratio, 211

Qatar, 333
Quick & Reilly, 92
Quick ratio, 181
Quotations
  for bonds, 259-63
  for international securities, 343-45
  for mutual funds, 29

Rapid-American Corporation, 258
Rates of return, 3, 9-10
  for bonds, 13, 14
  compound annual, 14
  current-yield, 274
  and international securities, 346-49
  real, 11, 12
  and reinvestment assumption, 279
  yield-to-call, 277-79
  yield-to-maturity, 274-77
Ratio analysis, 175-76
Ratios, 175-89
  analysis of, 175-76
  asset-utilization, 179, 180
  and bankruptcy studies, 176-77
  classification of, 177-78
  Coca-Cola example of use of, 185-88
  debt-utilization, 181-83
  dividend-payout, 185
  liquidity, 180-81
  price, 183-84
  profitability, 178-80
  tax, 185
Reagan administration, 101
Reagan, Ronald, 63, 99, 154
Real assets, 2-4, 4, 359-81
  advantages and disadvantages of, 359-60
  collectibles as, 378-80
  gold and silver as, 374, 376-77
  precious gems as, 378
  real estate as. *See* Real estate
  risk premium for, 15
Real estate, 2, 3, 361-75
  comprehensive analysis of, 364-70
  financing of, 370-72
  growth in, 361
  individual vs. partner ownership of, 372
  Internet resources on, 380
  liquidity of, 6
  management of, 7
  ownership forms for, 372-75
  performance of, 362
  and REITs, 374, 375
  syndicate vs. limited partner ownership of, 372-74
  and taxes, 7
  valuation of, 362-64
Real Estate Investment Trust Act (1960), 374
Real estate investment trusts (REITs), 374, 375
Real estate syndicate, 372*n*5
Real rate of return, 11, 12
REDIBook, 68
Regional exchanges, 58
Registered traders, 62

Registration, 54, 71, 73, 254, 373
Regulation
of industry, 129-30
of security markets, 71-75
Reilly, Frank K., 228
Reinganum, Marc R., 220, 233-35
Reinvestment. *See* Bond reinvestment
REITs. *See* Real estate investment trusts
Reporting requirements, 72-73
Repurchases, stock, 231-33
Required rate of return, 142, 143
Resale markets. *See* Secondary markets
Reserve requirements, 104
Resistance levels, 202-3
Resorts International, 258
Retirement, 8-9, 19
Return on equity (ROE), 133, 134
Return potential, 342-46
Returns, mismeasurement vs. superior, 238-39
Reuters, 68
Revco, 258
Revenue bonds, 249, 250
Reversal, market, 201
Rexford, Bradley, 196
Rhoades Corporation, 193-94
Risk, 4-5
measures of, 9-10
political, 349-50
and underwriting, 55
Risk premium, 12-16
Risk-free rate, 11-13, 142
Risk-return characteristics, 14
Ritter, Jay R., 228
Rivalry, 131
RJR Nabisco, 227
ROE. *See* Return on equity
Roll, Richard, 218, 234, 338
Rotational investing, 137-39
Round lots, 20
Royce Value Trust Fund, 22, 23
Rukeyser, Louis, 207
Rule 80A, 74
Rule 390, 68
Runs, 216
Russell indexes, 83
Russia, 100

Safekeeping, 38
Sales per share (SPS), 156, 157
Sales price projection, 367-69
Salomon Brothers, 302
Salomon Smith Barney Inc., 13, 15, 35, 54, 71, 85
SAMs (shared appreciation mortgages), 371
San Francisco, California, 58
Saudi Arabia, 334
Savings rates, 342
Saylor, Michael, 118
Schering-Plough, 135
Schlarbaum, Gary G., 230
Schwartz, Anna, 114
Scotland, 57
SEC. *See* Securities and Exchange Commission
SEC registration, 373
SEC Rule 415, 54, 254
SEC Rule 12b-1, 37
Second mortgages, 371-72
Secondary markets, 49-50, 58-64, 253-54
for CDs, 266
consolidated tape used in, 59, 60
listing requirements for, 59-61
membership in, 61-64
for municipal bonds, 250
organized exchanges in, 58-59
in real estate, 373-74
for UITs, 44
for U.S. government securities, 244, 245
Secondary movements, 200-202
Sector funds, 34
Secured bonds, 243-44
Secured debt, 243
Securities Act (1933), 71-72
Securities Acts Amendments (1975), 69, 71, 73
Securities and Exchange Commission (SEC), 22, 36, 52, 67, 69, 71-75, 88, 167, 221, 254, 350, 373
Securities Exchange Act (1934), 71-74
Securities Investor Protection Act (1970), 73
Securities Investor Protection Corporation (SIPC), 73
Security markets, 47-75
American Stock Exchange as, 64
Chicago Board Options Exchange as, 65
debt, 67
electronic communication networks for, 67-69
environment of, 47-48
functions of, 48-50
the future of, 69-71
futures, 65
institutional trading in, 69, 70
Internet resources on, 75
and investment bankers, 50-58
Nasdaq as, 66-67
over-the-counter, 65-67
primary, 50-58
regulation of, 71-75
secondary, 58-64
Sell orders, 91
Senior debentures, 243
September 11, 2001, terrorist attacks, 48, 58, 100, 102, 316, 339
Serial payment, 242
Service industries, 116, 117
Settlement procedures, 350
SFAS. *See Statement of Financial Accounting Standards*
SFN, 227
Shared appreciation mortgages (SAMs), 371
Shareholder services, 38-39
Shelf registration, 54, 254
Shell Canada, 257
Short positions, 89-91, 209-10
Short sales, 213
Short-term debt instruments, 4
Short-term orientation, 6
Silver, 1, 4, 374, 377
Silver bullion, 377
Silver coins, 377
Silver futures contracts, 377
Silver stocks, 377
Sindelar, J., 228
Singapore, 342
Sinking-fund provision, 242, 295*n*3
SIPC (Securities Investor Protection Corporation), 73
Size of market capitalizations, 34, 233-36
Slovakia, 333
Slovenia, 333
Small cap market, 66, 233-36
Small-cap funds, 34
SmithKline Beecham, 133
Solnik, Bruno, 340, 355
Solomon-Russell World Equity Index, 84
Sony Corporation, 71, 128, 354
Sotheby's, 379
South Africa, 341
South African Krugerrand, 376-77
Southland Corporation, 227
S&P. *See* Standard & Poor's indexes
S&P 100 Index, 81
S&P 400 MidCap Index, 81

S&P 500 Stock Index, 32, 40, 65, 74*n*4, 78, 80-81, 118, 124, 132, 152, 153, 156, 157, 208, 213, 340
S&P 600 SmallCap Index, 81
S&P 1500 Stock Index, 81
S&P Industrials, 124, 125
Specialists, 62-64, 91, 213, 221
Specialty funds, 34
Split ratings, 256
The Sports Collectors Digest, 380
Sports memorabilia, 378-79
Sprint, 52-55
SPS. *See* Sales per share
Stamps, 15
Standard & Poor's, 204, 255-59, 351
Standard & Poor's Security Owners Stock Guide, 269
Standard & Poor's Security Price Index Record, 82
Standard & Poor's (S&P) indexes, 78, 80-82
Standard & Poor's Stock Guide, 354
Standard deviation, 13
Standard Oil of California, 226
Standards, international securities, 351
State bonds, 67, 248-51
State Street Bank and Trust Company, 356
Statement of Financial Accounting Standards (SFAS)
  No. 95, 171
  No. 128, 321
Statements of cash flows, 171-75
Stern Stewart & Co., 150, 151
Stock dividends, 43, 123, 124
Stock issues, new, 227-29
Stock market, 77-96
  buying and selling in the, 85, 86, 88-91
  and capital gains, 95-96
  cash vs. margin accounts for, 88-89
  cost of trading on, 92-93
  indexes and averages of, 77-87
  Internet resources on, 96
  long vs. short positions in, 89-91
  measures of, 77
  orders for, 91-92
  and taxes, 93-96
Stock prices, 113-15
Stock repurchases, 231-33
Stock splits, 78, 82, 124, 176, 218
Stock trades, 227
Stockbrokers, 85
Stocks. *See also* Common stock; Preferred stock
  gold, 377
  P/E for individual, 153-55
Stocks, Bonds, Bills and Inflation 2004 Yearbook, 13-15
Stoll, H. A., 234
Stop orders, 92
Stop-loss orders, 92
Strip-Ts. *See* U.S. Treasury strips
Subindexes, 65
Subordinated debentures, 243
Sun Microsystems, 66, 117
Super Dot, 64
Support levels, 202-3
Support and resistance charts, 202-3
Surpluses, 100-102
Surprise-earnings effect, 238
Swaps, bond, 288-89
Sweden, 344-45, 347, 348
Switzerland, 57, 339, 344-47, 350, 354
Sydney Stock Exchange, 351
Symbol Technologies, Inc., 309-10, 316-17
Syndicates, 52, 372-74
Syngenta, 354
Systematic withdrawal plan, 39

T. Rowe Price European Stock Fund, 28, 30, 40, 41
T. Rowe Price Funds, 35
Taiwan, 333, 334, 335
Tariffs, 102-3
Tax Act (2001), 7-9
Tax Act (2003), 95
Tax ratio, 185
Tax Reform Act (1986), 362, 373
Taxes, 7
  and bond swaps, 289
  and corporate issues, 253
  and economic policy, 99, 100
  and federally sponsored credit agency issues, 248
  and fiscal policy, 101-2
  and international securities, 336, 350
  and mergers and acquisitions, 226-27
  and municipal bond funds, 32
  and municipal bonds, 248-51
  and mutual funds, 37-38
  and preferred stock, 267, 268
  and real estate, 7, 362, 366-69, 373
  and stock market, 93-96
  and UITs, 44
  and U.S. government securities, 245-47
Taxpayer Relief Act (1997), 7
T-bills. *See* U.S. Treasury bills
Technical analysis, 6, 199-222
  basic assumptions of, 200
  charting in, 200-207
  and efficient market hypothesis, 215-22
  Internet resources on, 222
  key indicators series in, 207-15
Technology stocks, 66
Telxon, 309-17
Tender offers, 232
10K statements, 72-73, 167, 192
Terminal wealth analysis, 304-7
Tests of independence, 216
Texas Instruments, 184
Thailand, 334, 341
Third-party guarantees, 250
Three-year return (3-yr % RET), 28, 29
Tick test, 74
Times interest earned, 182
Timing, convertible securities and, 320
TIPS (Treasury Inflation Protection Securities), 246
Tokyo Nikkei 225 Average, 85
Tokyo Stock Exchange, 67, 333, 351
Tombstone advertisement, 52, 53
Top-down valuation process, 97, 98, 121
Tops, market, 204, 206
Toshiba, 351
Total debt to total assets, 182
Total return on investment, 41, 43
Trade deficits, 102-3
Traders, 6, 62
Trading rule tests, 216-17
Transaction costs, 6, 37, 49
Transportation industry, 243
Travelers Insurance, 47, 54
Treasury Inflation Protection Securities (TIPS), 246
Trend analysis, 132-37
Trendline, 204
"Truth in securities" act, 71
TRW, 100
Turkey, 334
Turnover rate, 37
TWA, 127

UBS PaineWebber, 85, 92, 255
UBS Warburg, 52
UITs. *See* Unit investment trusts

Ukraine, 334
Underpricing, 227-28
Underwriting, 50-52, 54-57
Unfriendly takeovers, 226
Union Carbide, 136, 137
Uniroyal, 227
Unisys, 195-96
Unit investment trusts (UITs), 43-45
United Arab Emirates, 333
United Kingdom, 57, 132, 242, 264, 332, 333, 339, 348, 354
U.S. Department of Commerce, 104, 351
U.S. economy, 5, 11
U.S. Food and Drug Administration, 133
U.S. government securities, 67, 104, 142, 244-47, 260-62
U.S. Laboratories, 323, 324
U.S. Steel, 226
U.S. Supreme Court, 248
U.S. Treasury bills (T-bills), 5, 65, 242, 244, 245, 262
  rate of return for, 13, 14
  risk premium for, 12
U.S. Treasury bonds, 65, 245, 260-62
U.S. Treasury notes, 245, 260-62
U.S. Treasury strips (strip-Ts), 245-46, 262, 263
University of Chicago, 233
University of Michigan, 106, 108
Unsecured bonds, 243-44
Upfront cash payment, 369, 370
Utilities, 128, 129, 138, 250-52

Valuation
  of convertible securities, 311-12
  of dividends, 143-48
  of earnings, 148-50
  of real estate, 362-64
  of warrants, 324-27
Valuation of firms, 141-65
  assets in, 164
  average-price-ratio, 157, 158
  basic concepts for, 141
  and dividends, 143-48
  and earnings, 148-50
  and EVA, 150-51
  forecasting earnings per share in, 160-63
  and growth stocks and companies, 162-64
  Internet resources on, 165
  inventory, 193-94
  and price-earnings ratio, 151-57
  risk and return in, 141-43
  10-year average, 157, 158
  without earnings, 159-60
Value Line, 82, 351, 354, 374, 375
Value Line Average, 82
Value Line Index, 65
Value Line ranking effect, 237-39
Value-weighted indexes, 81-83
Van Horne, James, C., 230
Vanguard Group, 35
Vanguard IDX, 32, 33
Variable-rate notes, 242
Venezuela, 345
Vermaelen, Theo, 232
Vetsuypens, Mike, 228
Volume, 58-59, 67, 203

Walker, Jay, 118
Wall Street Journal, 22, 24, 27, 28, 66, 77, 80, 85, 200, 209, 214, 269, 274, 302, 343, 354, 355
"Wall Street Week" (television series), 207
Wal-Mart, 131
Warner Lambert, 133
Warrants, 2, 64, 323-29
  accounting considerations with, 328-29
  corporate use of, 327-28
  valuation of, 324-27
Washington REIT, 374, 375
Washington State Power Authority, 252
Weekend effect, 237
Weighted average life, 292-95
Weil, Roman L., 303
Welcom, 133
Westinghouse Electric, 1
Weyerhaeuser, 164
Whaley, R. E., 234
White knights, 226
Wilshire indexes, 83
World equity markets, 332-37
World Index, 344, 345
World Trade Organization (WTO), 102
WorldCom, 159
Write-offs, 159
WTO (World Trade Organization), 102

Yankee bonds, 264-65
Yawitz, Jess B., 303
Year-to-date return (YTD % RET), 28, 29
Yield curve, 280
Yield spread, 287-88
Yield to call, 277-79
Yield to maturity, 274-77
Ying, Lewellen, Schlarbaum, and Lease (YLSL), 230
Ying, Louis K. W., 230
YLSL (Ying, Lewellen, Schlarbaum, and Lease), 230
YTD % RET. *See* Year-to-date return
Yugoslavia, 334

Z (zeta) score, 176-77
Zero-coupon bonds, 242
  and duration, 302
  and terminal wealth, 307
  U.S. government, 245, 246
Zeta Services Inc., 176
Zurich Insurance, 225